THE BOOK ®

Peugeot 405 (diesel)
Service and Repair Manual

Steve Rendle

(3198-256-1AB2)

Models covered
Saloon and Estate models with diesel engines, including special/limited editions;
1.8 (1769 cc) Turbo and 1.9 (1905 cc) Turbo and normally-aspirated versions

For coverage of petrol engine models, see manual No 1559

© Haynes Publishing 1998

A book in the **Haynes Service and Repair Manual Series**

ISBN **1 85960 198 7**

British Library Cataloguing in Publication Data
A catalogue record for this book is available from the British Library.

ABCDE
FGHIJ

Printed by **J H Haynes & Co Ltd, Sparkford, Nr Yeovil, Somerset BA22 7JJ, England**

Haynes Publishing
Sparkford, Nr Yeovil, Somerset BA22 7JJ, England

Haynes North America, Inc
861 Lawrence Drive, Newbury Park, California 91320, USA

Editions Haynes S.A.
Tour Aurore - La Défense 2, 18 Place des Reflets,
92975 PARIS LA DEFENSE Cedex, France

Haynes Publishing Nordiska AB
Box 1504, 751 45 UPPSALA, Sweden

Contents

LIVING WITH YOUR PEUGEOT 405

Roadside Repairs

Weekly Checks

Lubricants, fluids and tyre pressures

MAINTENANCE

Routine Maintenance and Servicing

Contents

REPAIRS AND OVERHAUL

Engine and Associated Systems

Transmission

Brakes and Suspension

Body equipment

Wiring Diagrams

REFERENCE

Index

The Peugeot 405 diesel model range was introduced into the UK in 1988 in Saloon and Estate forms, with 1.8 litre (1769 cc) Turbo and 1.9 litre (1905 cc) normally-aspirated engines.

All engines are derived from the well-proven XUD series engines, which have appeared in many Peugeot and Citroën vehicles. The engine is of four-cylinder overhead camshaft design, mounted transversely and inclined to the rear, with the transmission mounted on the left-hand side. All models have five-speed manual transmissions.

All models have front-wheel-drive with fully-independent front suspension. The rear suspension is semi-independent with torsion bars and trailing arms.

In 1992, the model range was revised, and the bodywork, suspension and interior were all subtly modified. At the same time, the 1.9 litre (1905 cc) Turbo engine was introduced to replace the ageing 1.7 litre (1769 cc) Turbo version.

Since its introduction, the 405 range has continually been developed. All models have a high trim level, which is very comprehensive in the upper model range. Central locking, electric windows, an electric sunroof and an air bag are all available. Later models are fitted with air conditioning as standard equipment.

For the home mechanic, the Peugeot 405 is a straightforward vehicle to maintain and repair since design features have been incorporated to reduce the actual cost of ownership to a minimum, and most of the items requiring frequent attention are easily accessible.

Your Peugeot 405 Manual

The aim of this manual is to help you get the best value from your vehicle. It can do so in several ways. It can help you decide what work must be done (even should you choose to get it done by a garage), provide information on routine maintenance and servicing, and give a logical course of action and diagnosis when random faults occur. However, it is hoped that you will use the manual by tackling the work yourself. On simpler jobs, it may even be quicker than booking the car into a garage and going there twice, to leave and collect it. Perhaps most important, a lot of money can be saved by avoiding the costs a garage must charge to cover its labour and overheads.

The manual has drawings and descriptions to show the function of the various components, so that their layout can be understood. Then the tasks are described and photographed in a clear step-by-step sequence.

Peugeot 405 GLXd Saloon

Peugeot 405 GTDT Estate

The Peugeot 405 Team

Haynes manuals are produced by dedicated and enthusiastic people working in close co-operation. The team responsible for the creation of this book included:

Author	Steve Rendle
Sub-editor	Carole Turk
Editor & Page Make-up	Bob Jex
Workshop manager	Paul Buckland
Photo Scans	John Martin Paul Tanswell
Cover illustration & Line Art	Roger Healing
Wiring diagrams	Matthew Marke

We hope the book will help you to get the maximum enjoyment from your car. By carrying out routine maintenance as described you will ensure your car's reliability and preserve its resale value.

Acknowledgements

Thanks are due to Champion Spark Plug who supplied the illustrations showing spark plug conditions. Certain other illustrations are the copyright of the Peugeot Talbot Motor Company Limited, and are used with their permission. Special thanks to Gliddons of Taunton who provided several of the project vehicles used in the origination of this manual. Thanks are also due to Sykes-Pickavant Limited, who provided some of the workshop tools, and to all those people at Sparkford who helped in the production of this manual.

We take great pride in the accuracy of information given in this manual, but vehicle manufacturers make alterations and design changes during the production run of a particular vehicle of which they do not inform us. No liability can be accepted by the authors or publishers for loss, damage or injury caused by any errors in, or omissions from, the information given.

Project vehicles

The vehicles used in the preparation of this manual, and which appear in many of the photographic sequences, were a 405 GLX TD Saloon, a 405 GLD Estate, and a 405 GLX TD Estate.

Working on your car can be dangerous. This page shows just some of the potential risks and hazards, with the aim of creating a safety-conscious attitude.

General hazards

Scalding

• Don't remove the radiator or expansion tank cap while the engine is hot.
• Engine oil, automatic transmission fluid or power steering fluid may also be dangerously hot if the engine has recently been running.

Burning

• Beware of burns from the exhaust system and from any part of the engine. Brake discs and drums can also be extremely hot immediately after use.

Crushing

• When working under or near a raised vehicle, always supplement the jack with axle stands, or use drive-on ramps. *Never venture under a car which is only supported by a jack.*
• Take care if loosening or tightening high-torque nuts when the vehicle is on stands. Initial loosening and final tightening should be done with the wheels on the ground.

Fire

• Fuel is highly flammable; fuel vapour is explosive.
• Don't let fuel spill onto a hot engine.
• Do not smoke or allow naked lights (including pilot lights) anywhere near a vehicle being worked on. Also beware of creating sparks (electrically or by use of tools).
• Fuel vapour is heavier than air, so don't work on the fuel system with the vehicle over an inspection pit.
• Another cause of fire is an electrical overload or short-circuit. Take care when repairing or modifying the vehicle wiring.
• Keep a fire extinguisher handy, of a type suitable for use on fuel and electrical fires.

Electric shock

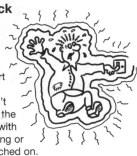

• Ignition HT voltage can be dangerous, especially to people with heart problems or a pacemaker. Don't work on or near the ignition system with the engine running or the ignition switched on.

• Mains voltage is also dangerous. Make sure that any mains-operated equipment is correctly earthed. Mains power points should be protected by a residual current device (RCD) circuit breaker.

Fume or gas intoxication

• Exhaust fumes are poisonous; they often contain carbon monoxide, which is rapidly fatal if inhaled. Never run the engine in a confined space such as a garage with the doors shut.
• Fuel vapour is also poisonous, as are the vapours from some cleaning solvents and paint thinners.

Poisonous or irritant substances

• Avoid skin contact with battery acid and with any fuel, fluid or lubricant, especially antifreeze, brake hydraulic fluid and Diesel fuel. Don't syphon them by mouth. If such a substance is swallowed or gets into the eyes, seek medical advice.
• Prolonged contact with used engine oil can cause skin cancer. Wear gloves or use a barrier cream if necessary. Change out of oil-soaked clothes and do not keep oily rags in your pocket.
• Air conditioning refrigerant forms a poisonous gas if exposed to a naked flame (including a cigarette). It can also cause skin burns on contact.

Asbestos

• Asbestos dust can cause cancer if inhaled or swallowed. Asbestos may be found in gaskets and in brake and clutch linings. When dealing with such components it is safest to assume that they contain asbestos.

Special hazards

Hydrofluoric acid

• This extremely corrosive acid is formed when certain types of synthetic rubber, found in some O-rings, oil seals, fuel hoses etc, are exposed to temperatures above 400°C. The rubber changes into a charred or sticky substance containing the acid. *Once formed, the acid remains dangerous for years. If it gets onto the skin, it may be necessary to amputate the limb concerned.*
• When dealing with a vehicle which has suffered a fire, or with components salvaged from such a vehicle, wear protective gloves and discard them after use.

The battery

• Batteries contain sulphuric acid, which attacks clothing, eyes and skin. Take care when topping-up or carrying the battery.
• The hydrogen gas given off by the battery is highly explosive. Never cause a spark or allow a naked light nearby. Be careful when connecting and disconnecting battery chargers or jump leads.

Air bags

• Air bags can cause injury if they go off accidentally. Take care when removing the steering wheel and/or facia. Special storage instructions may apply.

Diesel injection equipment

• Diesel injection pumps supply fuel at very high pressure. Take care when working on the fuel injectors and fuel pipes.

⚠ *Warning: Never expose the hands, face or any other part of the body to injector spray; the fuel can penetrate the skin with potentially fatal results.*

Remember...

DO

• Do use eye protection when using power tools, and when working under the vehicle.

• Do wear gloves or use barrier cream to protect your hands when necessary.

• Do get someone to check periodically that all is well when working alone on the vehicle.

• Do keep loose clothing and long hair well out of the way of moving mechanical parts.

• Do remove rings, wristwatch etc, before working on the vehicle – especially the electrical system.

• Do ensure that any lifting or jacking equipment has a safe working load rating adequate for the job.

DON'T

• Don't attempt to lift a heavy component which may be beyond your capability – get assistance.

• Don't rush to finish a job, or take unverified short cuts.

• Don't use ill-fitting tools which may slip and cause injury.

• Don't leave tools or parts lying around where someone can trip over them. Mop up oil and fuel spills at once.

• Don't allow children or pets to play in or near a vehicle being worked on.

The following pages are intended to help in dealing with common roadside emergencies and breakdowns. You will find more detailed fault finding information at the back of the manual, and repair information in the main chapters.

If your car won't start and the starter motor doesn't turn

☐ Open the bonnet and make sure that the battery terminals are clean and tight.
☐ Switch on the headlights and try to start the engine. If the headlights go very dim when you're trying to start, the battery is probably flat. Get out of trouble by jump starting (see next page) using a friend's car.

If your car won't start even though the starter motor turns as normal

☐ Is there fuel in the tank?
☐ Does the glow plug warning light come on and then go out when the ignition is switched on? If the light does not come on, check the wiring to the glow plugs and the fuel injection pump stop solenoid. If there is moisture on the wiring, spray a water-repellent aerosol product (such as WD-40 or equivalent) on the wiring terminals shown in the photos.
☐ Is there air in the fuel system? This is only likely if work has recently been done on the fuel system components (such as fitting a new fuel filter). Bleed the fuel system as described in Chapter 4. This will get rid of any air, which may have got into the system.

A Check the condition and security of the battery connections.

B The stop solenoid wiring terminal may cause problems if not connected securely.

C Check the preheating control unit wiring for security.

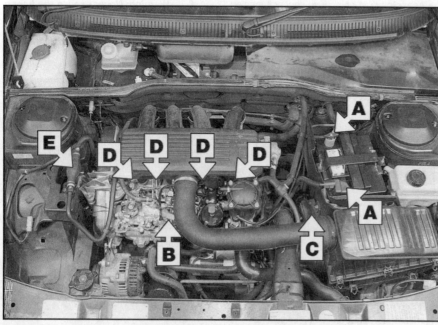

Check that electrical connections are secure (with the ignition switched off) and spray them with a water dispersant spray like WD40 if you suspect a problem due to damp

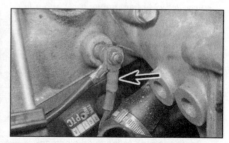

D Check the wiring to the glow plugs.

E If there is air in the fuel system, the system can be bled as described in Chapter 4.

Jump starting

Jump starting will get you out of trouble, but you must correct whatever made the battery go flat in the first place. There are three possibilities:

1 *The battery has been drained by repeated attempts to start, or by leaving the lights on.*

2 *The charging system is not working properly (alternator drivebelt slack or broken, alternator wiring fault or alternator itself faulty).*

3 *The battery itself is at fault (electrolyte low, or battery worn out).*

When jump-starting a car using a booster battery, observe the following precautions:

✔ Before connecting the booster battery, make sure that the ignition is switched off.

✔ Ensure that all electrical equipment (lights, heater, wipers, etc) is switched off.

✔ Make sure that the booster battery is the same voltage as the discharged one in the vehicle.

✔ If the battery is being jump-started from the battery in another vehicle, the two vehcles MUST NOT TOUCH each other.

✔ Make sure that the transmission is in neutral (or PARK, in the case of automatic transmission).

1 Connect one end of the red jump lead to the positive (+) terminal of the flat battery

2 Connect the other end of the red lead to the positive (+) terminal of the booster battery.

3 Connect one end of the black jump lead to the negative (-) terminal of the booster battery

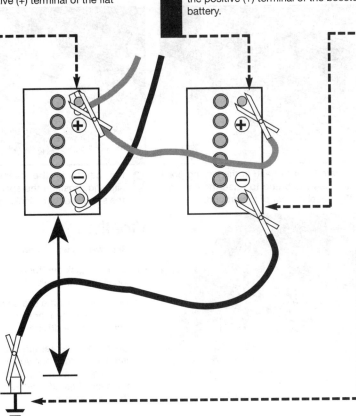

4 Connect the other end of the black jump lead to a bolt or bracket on the engine block, well away from the battery, on the vehicle to be started.

5 Make sure that the jump leads will not come into contact with the fan, drive-belts or other moving parts of the engine.

6 Start the engine using the booster battery, then with the engine running at idle speed, disconnect the jump leads in the reverse order of connection.

Wheel changing

Some of the details shown here will vary according to model. For instance, the location of the spare wheel and jack is not the same on all cars. However, the basic principles apply to all vehicles.

Warning: Do not change a wheel in a situation where you risk being hit by other traffic. On busy roads, try to stop in a lay-by or a gateway. Be wary of passing traffic while changing the wheel – it is easy to become distracted by the job in hand.

Preparation

☐ When a puncture occurs, stop as soon as it is safe to do so.
☐ Park on firm level ground, if possible, and well out of the way of other traffic.
☐ Use hazard warning lights if necessary.

☐ If you have one, use a warning triangle to alert other drivers of your presence.
☐ Apply the handbrake and engage first or reverse gear.
☐ Chock the wheel diagonally opposite the

one being removed – a couple of large stones will do for this.
☐ If the ground is soft, use a flat piece of wood to spread the load under the foot of the jack.

Changing the wheel

1 In the boot, use the wheel brace to loosen the spare wheel cradle bolt.

2 Remove the spare wheel from the cradle.

3 Use the wheel brace to remove the wheel trim.

4 Before raising the car, loosen the wheel bolts slightly using the wheelbrace.

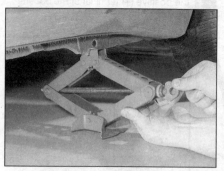

5 Locate the jack head in the jacking point and use the brace to raise the car until the wheel is clear of the ground.

6 For safety in the event of the jack slipping, position the spare wheel under the sill, close to the jacking point.

7 Remove the bolts and lift the wheel clear, then fit the spare wheel. Refit the wheel bolts and tighten moderately with the wheel brace.

8 Lower the car to the ground, then finally tighten the wheel bolts in a diagonal sequence. Fit the wheel trim and secure the damaged wheel in the spare wheel cradle.

Finally...

☐ Remove the wheel chocks.

☐ Stow the jack and tools in the correct locations in the car.

☐ Make sure that the spare wheel cradle is properly secured, or it could drop onto the road while driving.

☐ Check the tyre pressure on the wheel just fitted. If it is low, or if you don't have a pressure gauge with you, drive slowly to the nearest garage and inflate the tyre to the right pressure.

☐ Have the damaged tyre or wheel repaired as soon as possible.

Identifying leaks

Puddles on the garage floor or drive, or obvious wetness under the bonnet or underneath the car, suggest a leak that needs investigating. It can sometimes be difficult to decide where the leak is coming from, especially if the engine bay is very dirty already. Leaking oil or fluid can also be blown rearwards by the passage of air under the car, giving a false impression of where the problem lies.

 Warning: Most automotive oils and fluids are poisonous. Wash them off skin, and change out of contaminated clothing, without delay.

 HAYNES HiNT *The smell of a fluid leaking from the car may provide a clue to what's leaking. Some fluids are distinctively coloured. It may help to clean the car carefully and to park it over some clean paper overnight as an aid to locating the source of the leak.*
Remember that some leaks may only occur while the engine is running.

Sump oil

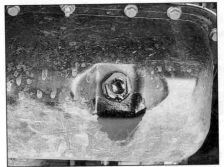

Engine oil may leak from the drain plug...

Oil from filter

...or from the base of the oil filter.

Gearbox oil

Gearbox oil can leak from the seals at the inboard ends of the driveshafts.

Antifreeze

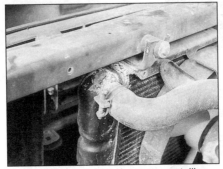

Leaking antifreeze often leaves a crystalline deposit like this.

Brake fluid

A leak occurring at a wheel is almost certainly brake fluid.

Power steering fluid

Power steering fluid may leak from the pipe connectors on the steering rack.

Towing

When all else fails, you may find yourself having to get a tow home – or of course you may be helping somebody else. Long-distance recovery should only be done by a garage or breakdown service. For shorter distances, DIY towing using another car is easy enough, but observe the following points:

☐ Use a proper tow-rope – they are not expensive. The vehicle being towed must display an 'ON TOW' sign in its rear window.
☐ Always turn the ignition key to the 'on' position when the vehicle is being towed, so that the steering lock is released, and that the direction indicator and brake lights will work.
☐ Only attach the tow-rope to the towing eyes provided.
☐ Before being towed, release the handbrake and select neutral on the transmission.
☐ Note that greater-than-usual pedal pressure will be required to operate the brakes, since the vacuum servo unit is only operational with the engine running.
☐ On models with power steering, greater-than-usual steering effort will also be required.

☐ The driver of the car being towed must keep the tow-rope taut at all times to avoid snatching.
☐ Make sure that both drivers know the route before setting off.
☐ Only drive at moderate speeds and keep the distance towed to a minimum. Drive smoothly and allow plenty of time for slowing down at junctions.

Introduction

There are some very simple checks which need only take a few minutes to carry out, but which could save you a lot of inconvenience and expense.

These "Weekly checks" require no great skill or special tools, and the small amount of time they take to perform could prove to be very well spent.

☐ Keeping an eye on tyre condition and pressures, will not only help to stop them wearing out prematurely, but could also save your life.

☐ Many breakdowns are caused by electrical problems. Battery-related faults are particularly common, and a quick check on a regular basis will often prevent the majority of these.

☐ If your car develops a brake fluid leak, the first time you might know about it is when your brakes don't work properly. Checking the level regularly will give advance warning of this kind of problem.

☐ If the oil or coolant levels run low, the cost of repairing any engine damage will be far greater than fixing the leak, for example.

Underbonnet check points

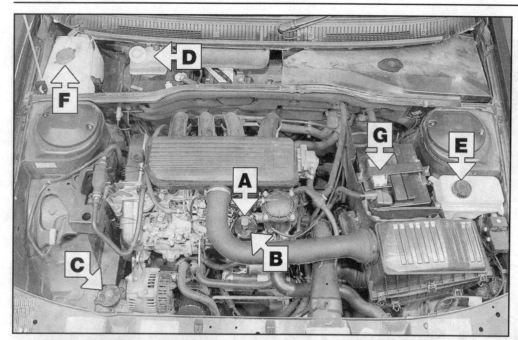

◀ **Non-turbo models**

A *Engine oil level dipstick*
B *Engine oil filler cap*
C *Coolant expansion tank*
D *Brake fluid reservoir*
E *Power steering fluid reservoir*
F *Screen washer fluid reservoir*
G *Battery*

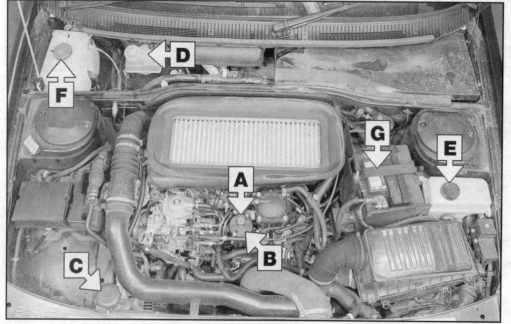

◀ **Turbo models**

A *Engine oil level dipstick*
B *Engine oil filler cap*
C *Coolant expansion tank*
D *Brake fluid reservoir*
E *Power steering fluid reservoir*
F *Screen washer fluid reservoir*
G *Battery*

Engine oil level

Before you start

✔ Make sure your car is on level ground.
✔ Check the oil level before the car is driven, or at least 5 minutes after the engine has been switched off.

HAYNES HiNT *If the oil is checked immediately after driving the vehicle, some of the oil will remain in the upper engine components, resulting in an inaccurate reading on the dipstick!*

The correct oil

Modern engines place great demands on their oil. It is very important that the correct oil for your car is used (See "Lubricants, fluids and tyre pressures").

Car Care

● If you have to add oil frequently, you should check whether you have any oil leaks. Place some clean paper under the car overnight, and check for stains in the morning. If there are no leaks, the engine may be burning oil *(see "Fault Finding")*.

● Always maintain the level between the upper and lower dipstick marks (see photo 3). If the level is too low severe engine damage may occur. Oil seal failure may result if the engine is overfilled by adding too much oil.

1 The dipstick is in a plastic housing at the front of the engine (see "*Underbonnet Check Points*" on page 0•10 for exact location). Withdraw the dipstick.

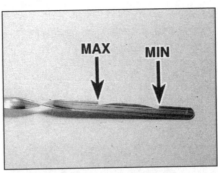
MAX   MIN

3 Note the oil level on the end of the dipstick, which should be between the upper ("MAX") mark and lower ("MIN") mark. Approximately 1.5 litres of oil will raise the level from the lower mark to the upper mark.

2 Using a clean rag or paper towel remove all oil from the dipstick. Insert the clean dipstick into the tube as far as it will go, then withdraw it again.

4 Oil is added through the filler cap. Where applicable, release the clips, then pull out the cap and top-up the level. A funnel may help to reduce spillage. Add the oil slowly, checking the level on the dipstick often. Don't overfill.

Coolant level

⚠ *Warning: DO NOT attempt to remove the expansion tank pressure cap when the engine is hot, as there is a very great risk of scalding. Do not leave open containers of coolant about, as it is poisonous.*

Car Care

● With a sealed-type cooling system, adding coolant should not be necessary on a regular basis. If frequent topping-up is required, it is likely there is a leak. Check the radiator, all hoses and joint faces for signs of staining or wetness, and rectify as necessary.

● It is important that antifreeze is used in the cooling system all year round, not just during the winter months. Don't top-up with water alone, as the antifreeze will become too diluted.

MAX →

1 The coolant level varies with engine temperature. When cold, the coolant level should be on the "MAXI" mark (arrowed). When hot, the level may rise slightly above the "MAXI" mark. A warning light will come on if the level falls dangerously low.

2 To top up the system the expansion tank cap must be removed. **Wait until the engine is cold.** Turn the cap anti-clockwise until it reaches the first stop. Once any pressure is released, push the cap down, turn it to the second stop, and lift off.

3 Add a mixture of water and antifreeze through the expansion tank filler neck, until the coolant is up to the "MAXI" level mark. Refit the cap, turning it clockwise as far as it will go until it is secure.

Brake fluid level

Warning: Brake fluid can harm your eyes and damage painted surfaces, so use extreme caution when handling and pouring it.
Warning: Do not use fluid that has been standing open for some time, as it absorbs moisture from the air, which can cause a dangerous loss of braking effectiveness.

HAYNES HiNT
The fluid level in the reservoir will drop slightly as the brake pads wear down, but the fluid level must never be allowed to drop below the "MIN" mark.

Before you start:
✔ Park the vehicle on level ground.
✔ On models with ABS (anti-lock brakes), switch the ignition off and pump the brake pedal at least 20 times or until the pedal feels hard. Open the bonnet. Switch on the ignition: the hydraulic unit pump will be heard running. Wait until the pump stops, then switch off the ignition.

Safety First!
● If the reservoir requires repeated topping-up this is an indication of a fluid leak somewhere in the system, which should be investigated immediately.
● If a leak is suspected, the car should not be driven until the braking system has been checked. Never take any risks where brakes are concerned.

1 The "MAX" and "DANGER" marks are indicated on the side of the reservoir, which is located in the scuttle at the rear driver's side of the engine compartment. The fluid level must be kept between these two marks.

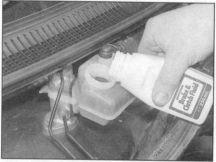

3 Carefully add fluid, avoiding spilling it on surrounding paintwork. Use only the specified hydraulic fluid; mixing different types of fluid can cause damage to the system and/or a loss of braking effectiveness. After filling to the correct level, refit the cap securely. Wipe off any spilt fluid.

2 If topping-up is necessary, first wipe the area around the filler cap with a clean rag before removing the cap. Check the fluid already in the reservoir - the system should be drained and refilled if dirt is seen in the fluid (see Chapter 9 for details).

4 Check the operation of the low fluid level warning light. Chock the roadwheels, release the handbrake, and switch on the ignition. Ask an assistant to press the button on top of the reservoir. The brake fluid level/handbrake warning light should come on. Apply the handbrake and switch off the ignition.

Power steering fluid level

Before you start:
✔ Park the vehicle on level ground.
✔ Set the steering wheel straight-ahead.
✔ The engine should be turned off.

HAYNES HiNT
For the check to be accurate, the steering must not be turned once the engine has been stopped.

Safety First!
● The need for frequent topping-up indicates a leak, which should be investigated immediately.

1 The fluid level is visible through the translucent material of the reservoir, and should be between the maximum (A) and minimum (B) level lines marked on the side of the reservoir.

2 If topping-up is necessary, and before removing the cap, wipe the area so that dirt does not enter the reservoir. Unscrew the cap, allowing the fluid to drain from the bottom of the cap as it is removed.

3 Top-up to the "MAX" mark, using the specified type of fluid. Take great care not to allow dirt to enter the reservoir, and do not overfill the reservoir. When the level is correct, refit the cap.

Screen washer fluid level

Car Care

Screenwash additives not only keep the winscreen clean during foul weather, they also prevent the washer system freezing in cold weather - which is when you are likely to need it most. Don't top up using plain water as the screenwash will become too diluted, and will freeze during cold weather.

Warning: On no account use engine coolant antifreeze in the screen washer system - this may damage the paintwork.

1 The windscreen/headlight washer fluid reservoir is located in the scuttle at the rear right-hand corner of the engine compartment.

2 On Estate models, the tailgate washer fluid reservoir is located behind a hinged cover on the right-hand side of the luggage compartment.

3 When topping-up the reservoir(s) a screenwash additive should be added in the quantities recommended on the bottle.

Wiper blades

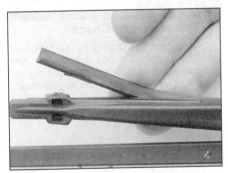

1 Check the condition of the wiper blades; if they are cracked or show any signs of deterioration, or if the glass swept area is smeared, renew them. For maximum clarity of vision, wiper blades should be renewed annually, as a matter of course.

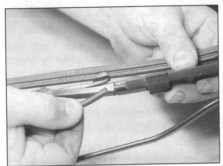

2 To remove a front wiper blade, first prise off the securing clips, and disconnect the washer tube from the arm.

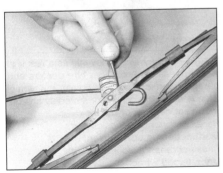

3 Pull the arm fully away from the glass until it locks. Swivel the blade through 90°, then pull up the blade securing clip, and slide the blade out of the arm's hooked end.

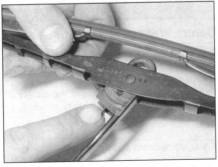

4 On Estate models, to remove a tailgate wiper blade, pull the arm fully away from the glass until it locks. Swivel the blade through 90°, then press the locking tab, and slide the blade out of the arm's hooked end.

Tyre condition and pressure

It is very important that tyres are in good condition, and at the correct pressure - having a tyre failure at any speed is highly dangerous. Tyre wear is influenced by driving style - harsh braking and acceleration, or fast cornering, will all produce more rapid tyre wear. As a general rule, the front tyres wear out faster than the rears. Interchanging the tyres from front to rear ("rotating" the tyres) may result in more even wear. However, if this is completely effective, you may have the expense of replacing all four tyres at once! Remove any nails or stones embedded in the tread before they penetrate the tyre to cause deflation. If removal of a nail does reveal that

the tyre has been punctured, refit the nail so that its point of penetration is marked. Then immediately change the wheel, and have the tyre repaired by a tyre dealer.

Regularly check the tyres for damage in the form of cuts or bulges, especially in the sidewalls. Periodically remove the wheels, and clean any dirt or mud from the inside and outside surfaces. Examine the wheel rims for signs of rusting, corrosion or other damage. Light alloy wheels are easily damaged by "kerbing" whilst parking; steel wheels may also become dented or buckled. A new wheel is very often the only way to overcome severe damage.

New tyres should be balanced when they are fitted, but it may become necessary to re-balance them as they wear, or if the balance weights fitted to the wheel rim should fall off. Unbalanced tyres will wear more quickly, as will the steering and suspension components. Wheel imbalance is normally signified by vibration, particularly at a certain speed (typically around 50 mph). If this vibration is felt only through the steering, then it is likely that just the front wheels need balancing. If, however, the vibration is felt through the whole car, the rear wheels could be out of balance. Wheel balancing should be carried out by a tyre dealer or garage.

1 Tread Depth - visual check

The original tyres have tread wear safety bands (B), which will appear when the tread depth reaches approximately 1.6 mm. The band positions are indicated by a triangular mark on the tyre sidewall (A).

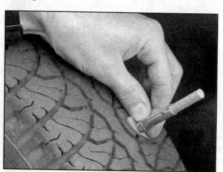

2 Tread Depth - manual check

Alternatively, tread wear can be monitored with a simple, inexpensive device known as a tread depth indicator gauge.

3 Tyre Pressure Check

Check the tyre pressures regularly with the tyres cold. Do not adjust the tyre pressures immediately after the vehicle has been used, or an inaccurate setting will result.

Tyre tread wear patterns

Shoulder Wear

Underinflation (wear on both sides)
Under-inflation will cause overheating of the tyre, because the tyre will flex too much, and the tread will not sit correctly on the road surface. This will cause a loss of grip and excessive wear, not to mention the danger of sudden tyre failure due to heat build-up.
Check and adjust pressures
Incorrect wheel camber (wear on one side)
Repair or renew suspension parts
Hard cornering
Reduce speed!

Centre Wear

Overinflation
Over-inflation will cause rapid wear of the centre part of the tyre tread, coupled with reduced grip, harsher ride, and the danger of shock damage occurring in the tyre casing.
Check and adjust pressures

If you sometimes have to inflate your car's tyres to the higher pressures specified for maximum load or sustained high speed, don't forget to reduce the pressures to normal afterwards.

Uneven Wear

Front tyres may wear unevenly as a result of wheel misalignment. Most tyre dealers and garages can check and adjust the wheel alignment (or "tracking") for a modest charge.
Incorrect camber or castor
Repair or renew suspension parts
Malfunctioning suspension
Repair or renew suspension parts
Unbalanced wheel
Balance tyres
Incorrect toe setting
Adjust front wheel alignment
Note: *The feathered edge of the tread which typifies toe wear is best checked by feel.*

Battery

Caution: *Before carrying out any work on the vehicle battery, read the precautions given in "Safety first" at the start of this manual.*

✔ Make sure that the battery tray is in good condition, and that the clamp is tight. Corrosion on the tray, retaining clamp and the battery itself can be removed with a solution of water and baking soda. Thoroughly rinse all cleaned areas with water. Any metal parts damaged by corrosion should be covered with a zinc-based primer, then painted.

✔ Periodically (approximately every three months), check the charge condition of the battery as described in Chapter 5A.

✔ If the battery is flat, and you need to jump start your vehicle, see *Roadside Repairs*.

1 The battery is located on the left-hand side of the engine compartment. The exterior of the battery should be inspected periodically for damage such as a cracked case or cover.

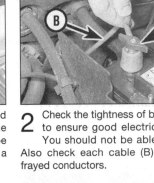

2 Check the tightness of battery clamps (A) to ensure good electrical connections. You should not be able to move them. Also check each cable (B) for cracks and frayed conductors.

Battery corrosion can be kept to a minimum by applying a layer of petroleum jelly to the clamps and terminals after they are reconnected.

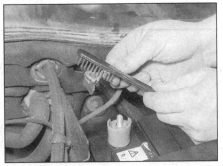

3 If corrosion (white fluffy deposits) is evident, remove the cables from the battery terminals, clean them with a small wire brush, then refit them. Tools for cleaning the battery post and terminals are available.

4 Note that the battery negative terminal stud can be removed for cleaning or renewal. Unscrew the lead clamp, then pull off the plastic insulator, and lever off the stud and cover.

Bulbs and fuses

✔ Check all external lights and the horn. Refer to the appropriate Sections of Chapter 12 for details if any of the circuits are found to be inoperative.

✔ Visually check all accessible wiring connectors, harnesses and retaining clips for security, and for signs of chafing or damage.

If you need to check your brake lights and indicators unaided, back up to a wall or garage door and operate the lights. The reflected light should show if they are working properly.

1 If a single indicator light, stop-light or headlight has failed, it is likely that a bulb has blown and will need to be replaced. Refer to Chapter 12 for details. If both stop-lights have failed, it is possible that the switch has failed (see Chapter 9).

2 If more than one indicator light or tail light has failed it is likely that either a fuse has blown or that there is a fault in the circuit (see Chapter 12). The fuses are located behind a panel on the bottom of the driver's side lower facia panel.

3 To replace a blown fuse, simply pull it out and fit a new fuse of the correct rating (see wiring diagrams in Chapter 12). If the fuse blows again, it is important that you find out why - a complete checking procedure is given in Chapter 12.

Lubricants and fluids

Engine . . . . Multigrade engine oil, viscosity SAE 10W/40 to 20W/50, to API SG/CD or better

Cooling system . . . . Ethylene glycol based antifreeze and soft water

Manual transmission . . . . Gear oil, viscosity 75W/80W, to API GL5

Automatic transmission . . . . Dexron II type ATF (automatic transmission fluid)

Braking system . . . . Hydraulic fluid to SAE J1703F or DOT 4

Power steering . . . . Dexron II type ATF (automatic transmission fluid)

Tyre pressures

Saloon models	Front	Rear
All tyre sizes	2.2 bars (32 psi)	2.2 bars (32 psi)
Estate models		
All tyre sizes:		
Normal load	2.2 bars (32 psi)	2.4 bars (35 psi)
Full load	2.2 bars (30 psi)	2.8 bars (41 psi)

Note: *Refer to the tyre pressure data label at the bottom of the rear edge of the driver's door (visible when the door is open) for the correct tyre pressures for your particular vehicle. Pressures apply only to original-equipment tyres, and may vary if any other make or type is fitted; check with the tyre manufacturer or supplier for correct pressures if necessary.*

Chapter 1
Routine maintenance and servicing

Contents

Degrees of difficulty

Easy, suitable for novice with little experience

Fairly easy, suitable for beginner with some experience

Fairly difficult, suitable for competent DIY mechanic

Difficult, suitable for experienced DIY mechanic

Very difficult, suitable for expert DIY or professional

Lubricants and fluids

Refer to end of "Weekly checks"

Capacities

Engine oil (approximate)

Excluding filter:
Non-turbo models . . . . 4.5 litres
Turbo models . . . . 4.8 litres
Including filter . . . . 5.0 litres
Difference between MAX and MIN dipstick marks (approx.) . . . . 1.5 litres

Cooling system (approximate)

All except 1.9 litre (1905 cc) Turbo engine . . . . 7.8 litres
1.9 litre (1905 cc) Turbo engine . . . . 7.0 litres

Transmission (approximate) . . . . 2.0 litres

Power-assisted steering (approximate) . . . . 2.0 litres

Fuel tank . . . . 70 litres

Engine

Oil filter . . . . Champion F104

Cooling system

Antifreeze mixture:
28% antifreeze . . . . Protection down to -15°C (5°F)
50% antifreeze . . . . Protection down to -30°C (-22°F)

Fuel system

Idle speed:*
A8A and DJZ engines . . . . 775 ± 25 rpm
D8A and DHY engines:
Without air conditioning . . . . 750 +50/-0 rpm
With air conditioning . . . . 800 +50/-0 rpm
D9B engine:
Lucas CAV/Roto-diesel injection pump:
Without air conditioning . . . . 800 +0/-50 rpm
With air conditioning . . . . 850 +0/-50 rpm
Bosch injection pump:
Without air conditioning . . . . 750 +50/-0 rpm
With air conditioning . . . . 800 +50/-0 rpm
Anti-stall speed:
Lucas CAV/Roto-diesel injection pump . . . . 900 ± 50 rpm
Bosch injection pump . . . . 20 to 50 rpm above idle speed
Anti-stall shim thickness:
Lucas CAV/Roto-diesel injection pump . . . . 3.0 mm
Bosch injection pump . . . . 1.0 mm
Fast idle speed . . . . 950± 50 rpm
Air filter . . . . Champion U543
Fuel filter:
Early models with fuel filter mounted on battery tray:
Lucas CAV/Roto-diesel filter . . . . Champion L132
Bosch filter . . . . Champion L135
Later models with integral fuel filter/thermostat housing . . . . Champion L141
Glow plugs . . . . Champion CH68
Refer to Chapter 2A Specifications for details of engine codes

Brakes

Brake pad friction material minimum thickness . . . . 2.0 mm
Brake shoe friction material minimum thickness . . . . 1.5 mm

Tyre pressures

Refer to end of "Weekly Checks"

Wiper blades

Windscreen . . . . Champion X-5503
Tailgate . . . . Champion X-3303

Torque wrench settings

	Nm	lbf ft
Roadwheel bolts	85	63
Transmission oil filler/level plug	20	15

1 The maintenance intervals in this manual are provided with the assumption that you, not the dealer, will be carrying out the work. These are the minimum maintenance intervals recommended by the manufacturer for vehicles driven daily. If you wish to keep your vehicle in peak condition at all times, you may wish to perform some of these procedures more often. We encourage frequent maintenance, because it enhances the efficiency, performance and resale value of your vehicle.

2 If the vehicle is driven in dusty areas, used to tow a trailer, or driven frequently at slow speeds (idling in traffic) or on short journeys, more frequent maintenance intervals are recommended. Peugeot actually recommend that the service intervals are halved for vehicles which are used under these conditions.

3 When the vehicle is new, it should be serviced by a factory-authorised dealer service department, in order to preserve the factory warranty.

Every 250 miles (400 km) or weekly

☐ Refer to "Weekly Checks".

Every 6000 miles (10 000 km) or 12 months - whichever comes sooner

In addition to all the items listed in "Weekly Checks", carry out the following:

☐ Renew the engine oil and filter (Section 3).
☐ Drain any water from the fuel filter (Section 4).
☐ Check all underbonnet components and hoses for fluid leaks (Section 5).

Every 12 000 miles (20 000 km)

In addition to all the items listed above, carry out the following:

☐ Check the condition of the front brake pads (Section 6).
☐ Check the operation of the handbrake (Section 7).
☐ Check the condition of the auxiliary drivebelt (Section 8).
☐ Check the condition of the brake vacuum pump drivebelt - where applicable (Section 8).
☐ Check and if necessary adjust the clutch mechanism (Section 9).
☐ Check the idle speed and anti-stall speed (Section 10).
☐ Check the condition of the driveshaft rubber gaiters (Section 11).
☐ Check the condition of the steering and suspension components (Section 12).
☐ Check the condition of the air conditioning system refrigerant - where applicable (see Section 13).
☐ Check the condition of the emissions control system hoses and components (Section 14).
☐ Where applicable, renew the pollen filter (Section 15).
☐ Carry out a road test (Section 16).

Every 18 000 miles (30 000 km)

In addition to all the items listed above, carry out the following:

☐ Renew the air filter (Section 17).
☐ Renew the fuel filter (Section 18).
☐ Check the condition of the rear drum brake shoes (Section 19).
☐ Check the condition of the rear disc brake pads (Section 20).
☐ Lubricate all hinges and locks (Section 21).

Every 36 000 miles (60 000 km)

In addition to all the items listed above, carry out the following:

☐ Check the manual transmission oil level, and top-up if necessary (Section 22).
☐ Renew the brake fluid (Section 23).
☐ Renew the timing belt (Section 24) - see **Note** below

Note: *Although the normal interval for timing belt renewal is 72 000 miles (120 000 km), it is strongly recommended that the interval is halved to 36 000 miles (60 000 km) on vehicles which are subjected to intensive use, ie, mainly short journeys or a lot of stop-start driving. The actual belt renewal interval is therefore very much up to the individual owner, but bear in mind that severe engine damage will result if the belt breaks.*

Every 72 000 miles (120 000 km)

In addition to all the items listed above, carry out the following:

☐ Renew the timing belt (Section 24) - this is the interval recommended by Peugeot, but we recommend that the belt is changed more frequently, at 36 000 miles (60 000 km) - see above.

Every 2 years (regardless of mileage)

☐ Renew the coolant (Section 25).

1

Maintenance & Servicing

Underbonnet view of a 1994 Peugeot 405 non-Turbo diesel

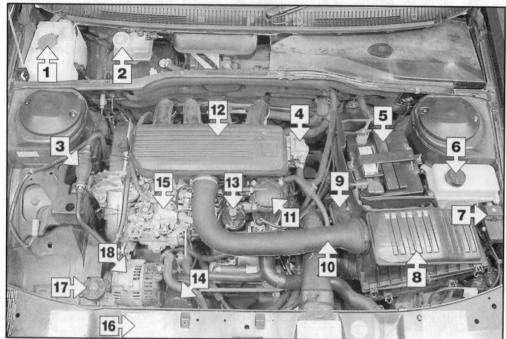

1 Washer fluid reservoir
2 Brake fluid reservoir
3 Fuel system priming bulb
4 Brake vacuum pump
5 Battery
6 Power steering fluid reservoir
7 Fusebox
8 Air cleaner housing
9 Preheating system control unit
10 Air ducting
11 Fuel filter housing
12 Air distribution housing
13 Engine oil level dipstick
   and oil filler cap
14 Oil filter
15 Fuel injection pump
16 Vehicle Identification Number
   (VIN) plate
17 Coolant expansion tank
18 Alternator

Underbonnet view of a 1994 Peugeot 405 Turbo diesel

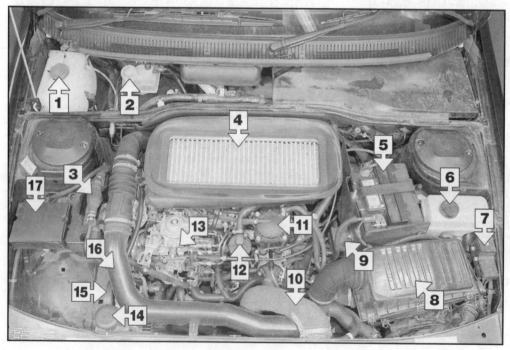

1 Washer fluid reservoir
2 Brake fluid reservoir
3 Fuel system priming bulb
4 Intercooler
5 Battery
6 Power steering fluid reservoir
7 Fusebox
8 Air cleaner housing
9 Preheating system control unit
10 Air intake hose
11 Fuel filter housing
12 Engine oil level dipstick
   and oil filler cap
13 Fuel injection pump
14 Coolant expansion tank
15 Power steering pump
16 Air cleaner-to-intercooler
   tubing
17 Fuse/relay/junction box

Front underbody view of a Peugeot 405 non-Turbo diesel model

1 Power steering pump
2 Engine oil (sump) drain plug
3 Radiator
4 Transmission drain plug
5 Front brake caliper
6 Front suspension lower arm
7 Track-rod
8 Front suspension subframe
9 Exhaust front section
10 Anti-roll bar drop link
11 Rear engine mounting
12 Right-hand driveshaft

Rear underbody view

1 Rear axle assembly front
   mounting
2 Fuel tank
3 Rear axle tube
4 Rear shock absorber
5 Exhaust silencer
6 Spare wheel
7 Handbrake cable adjuster
8 Fuel filler pipe

Maintenance procedures

1 Introduction

1 This Chapter is designed to help the home mechanic maintain his/her vehicle for safety, economy, long life and peak performance.

2 The Chapter contains a master maintenance schedule, followed by Sections dealing specifically with each task in the schedule. Visual checks, adjustments, component renewal and other helpful items are included. Refer to the accompanying illustrations of the engine compartment and the underside of the vehicle for the locations of the various components.

3 Servicing your vehicle in accordance with the mileage/time maintenance schedule and the following Sections will provide a planned maintenance programme, which should result in a long and reliable service life. This is a comprehensive plan, so maintaining some items but not others at the specified service intervals, will not produce the same results.

4 As you service your vehicle, you will discover that many of the procedures can - and should - be grouped together, because of the particular procedure being performed, or because of the close proximity of two otherwise-unrelated components to one another. For example, if the vehicle is raised for any reason, the exhaust can be inspected at the same time as the suspension and steering components.

5 The first step in this maintenance programme is to prepare yourself before the actual work begins. Read through all the Sections relevant to the work to be carried out, then make a list and gather together all the parts and tools required. If a problem is encountered, seek advice from a parts specialist, or a dealer service department.

2 Intensive maintenance

1 If, from the time the vehicle is new, the routine maintenance schedule is followed closely, and frequent checks are made of fluid levels and high-wear items, as suggested throughout this manual, the engine will be kept in relatively good running condition, and the need for additional work will be minimised.

2 It is possible that there will be times when the engine is running poorly due to the lack of regular maintenance. This is even more likely if a used vehicle, which has not received regular and frequent maintenance checks, is purchased. In such cases, additional work may need to be carried out, outside of the regular maintenance intervals.

3 If engine wear is suspected, a compression test or leakdown test (refer to Chapter 2A) will provide valuable information regarding the overall performance of the main internal components. Such a test can be used as a basis to decide on the extent of the work to be carried out. If, for example, a compression or leakdown test indicates serious internal

engine wear, conventional maintenance as described in this Chapter will not greatly improve the performance of the engine, and may prove a waste of time and money, unless extensive overhaul work (Chapter 2B) is carried out first.

4 The following series of operations are those most often required to improve the performance of a generally poor-running engine:

Primary operations

a) Clean, inspect and test the battery (See "Weekly checks").
b) Check all the engine-related fluids (See "Weekly checks").
c) Check the condition and tension of the auxiliary drivebelt (Section 8).
d) Check the condition of the air filter, and renew if necessary (Section 17).
e) Check the fuel filter (Sections 4 and 18).
f) Check the condition of all hoses, and check for fluid leaks (Section 5).
g) Check the idle speed and anti-stall speed (Section 10).

5 If the above operations do not prove fully effective, carry out the following secondary operations:

Secondary operations

All items listed under "Primary operations", plus the following:

a) Check the charging system (Chapter 5A).
b) Check the preheating system (Chapter 5B).
c) Check the fuel system (Chapter 4).

6000 Mile / 12 Month Service

3 Engine oil and filter renewal

Note: *A suitable square-section wrench may be required to undo the sump drain plug on some models. These wrenches can be obtained from most motor factors or your Peugeot dealer.*

1 Frequent oil and filter changes are the most important preventative maintenance procedures which can be undertaken by the DIY owner. As engine oil ages, it becomes diluted and contaminated, which leads to premature engine wear.

2 Before starting this procedure, gather together all the necessary tools and materials. Also make sure that you have plenty of clean rags and newspapers handy, to mop up any spills. Ideally, the engine oil should be warm,

as it will drain better, and more built-up sludge will be removed with it. Take care, however, not to touch the exhaust or any other hot parts of the engine when working under the vehicle. To avoid any possibility of scalding, and to protect yourself from

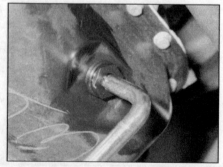

3.3 Slackening the sump drain plug with a square-section wrench

possible skin irritants and other harmful contaminants in used engine oils, it is advisable to wear gloves when carrying out this work. Access to the underside of the vehicle will be greatly improved if it can be raised on a lift, driven onto ramps, or jacked up and supported on axle stands (see "Jacking and Vehicle Support"). Whichever method is chosen, make sure that the vehicle remains level, or if it is at an angle, that the drain plug is at the lowest point. Where necessary remove the splash guard from under the engine.

3 Slacken the drain plug about half a turn; on some models, a square-section wrench may be needed to slacken the plug. Position the draining container under the drain plug, then remove the plug completely **(see illustration)**. If possible, try to keep the plug pressed into the sump while unscrewing it by hand the last couple of turns. Recover the sealing ring from the drain plug **(see Haynes Hint)**.

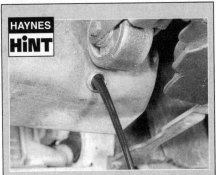

HAYNES HINT

As the engine oil drain plug releases from the threads, move it away sharply so the stream of oil issuing from the sump runs into the container, not up your sleeve!

4 Allow some time for the old oil to drain, noting that it may be necessary to reposition the container as the oil flow slows to a trickle.

5 After all the oil has drained, wipe off the drain plug with a clean rag, and fit a new sealing washer. Clean the area around the drain plug opening, and refit the plug. Tighten the plug securely.

6 To renew the filter, move the container into position under the oil filter, which is located at the front of the cylinder block.

7 Using an oil filter removal tool if necessary, slacken the filter initially, then unscrew it by hand the rest of the way **(see illustration)**. Empty the oil in the old filter into the container.

8 Use a clean rag to remove all oil, dirt and sludge from the filter sealing area on the engine. Check the old filter to make sure that the rubber sealing ring hasn't stuck to the engine. If it has, carefully remove it.

9 Apply a light coating of clean engine oil to the sealing ring on the new filter, then screw it into position on the engine. Tighten the filter firmly by hand only - **do not** use any tools. Where necessary, refit the splash guard under the engine.

10 Remove the old oil and all tools from under the car, then lower the car to the ground (if applicable).

11 Remove the dipstick, then unscrew the oil filler cap. Fill the engine, using the correct

3.7 Using an oil filter removal tool to slacken the oil filter

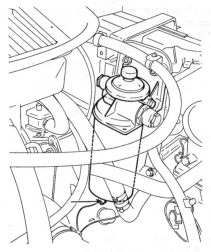

4.3a Fuel filter water drain screw (arrowed) - early Lucas CAV/Roto-diesel filter assembly

grade and type of oil (see *"Weekly checks"*). An oil can spout or funnel may help to reduce spillage. Pour in half the specified quantity of oil first, then wait a few minutes for the oil to fall to the sump. Continue adding oil a small quantity at a time until the level is up to the lower mark on the dipstick. Adding 1.5 litres will bring the level up to the upper mark on the dipstick. Refit the filler cap.

12 Start the engine and run it for a few minutes; check for leaks around the oil filter seal and the sump drain plug. Note that there may be a delay of a few seconds before the oil pressure warning light goes out when the engine is first started, as the oil circulates through the engine oil galleries and the new oil filter (where fitted) before the pressure builds up.

13 Switch off the engine, and wait a few minutes for the oil to settle in the sump once more. With the new oil circulated and the filter completely full, recheck the level on the dipstick, and add more oil as necessary.

14 Dispose of the used engine oil safely, with reference to *"General repair procedures"*

OIL CARE · FOLLOW THE CODE

OIL BANK LINE
0800 66 33 66

Note: It is antisocial and illegal to dump oil down the drain. To find the location of your local oil recycling bank, call this number free.

4 Fuel filter water draining

1 A water drain screw is provided at the base of the fuel filter housing. On later models (with an integral thermostat/fuel filter housing), a plastic tube is attached to the drain screw to aid the draining procedure.

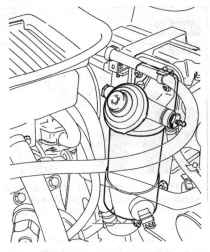

4.3b Fuel filter water drain screw (arrowed) - early Bosch filter assembly

4.3c Opening the fuel filter water drain plug - later models

2 Place a suitable container beneath the drain screw/tube. On later models, cover the clutch bellhousing to prevent water entering the housing.

3 Open the drain screw by turning it anti-clockwise, and allow fuel and water to drain until fuel, free from water, emerges from the end of the screw/tube **(see illustrations)**. Close the drain screw, and tighten it securely.

4 Dispose of the drained fuel safely.

5 Start the engine. If difficulty is experienced, bleed the fuel system (see Chapter 4).

5 Hose and fluid leak check

1 Visually inspect the engine joint faces, gaskets and seals for any signs of water or oil leaks. Pay particular attention to the areas around the cylinder head cover, cylinder head, oil filter and sump joint faces. Bear in mind that, over a period of time, some very slight seepage from these areas is to be expected - what you are really looking for is any indication of a serious leak. Should a leak be found, renew the offending gasket or oil seal by referring to the appropriate Chapters in this manual.

1

HAYNES HiNT

A leak in the cooling system will usually show up as white- or rust-coloured deposits on the area adjoining the leak.

2 Also check the security and condition of all the engine-related pipes and hoses, and all braking system pipes and hoses (**see Haynes Hint**). Ensure that all cable-ties or securing clips are in place, and in good condition. Clips which are broken or missing can lead to

chafing of the hoses, pipes or wiring, which could cause more serious problems in the future.

3 Carefully check the radiator hoses and heater hoses along their entire length. Renew any hose which is cracked, swollen or deteriorated. Cracks will show up better if the hose is squeezed. Pay close attention to the hose clips that secure the hoses to the cooling system components. Hose clips can pinch and puncture hoses, resulting in cooling system leaks. If the original Peugeot crimped-type hose clips are used, it may be a good idea to replace them with standard worm-drive clips.

4 Inspect all the cooling system components (hoses, joint faces, etc) for leaks.

5 Where any problems are found on system components, renew the component or gasket with reference to Chapter 3.

6 With the vehicle raised, inspect the fuel tank and filler neck for punctures, cracks and other damage. The connection between the filler neck and tank is especially critical.

Sometimes a rubber filler neck or connecting hose will leak due to loose retaining clamps or deteriorated rubber.

7 Carefully check all rubber hoses and metal fuel lines leading away from the fuel tank. Check for loose connections, deteriorated hoses, crimped lines, and other damage. Pay particular attention to the vent pipes and hoses, which often loop up around the filler neck and can become blocked or crimped. Follow the lines to the front of the vehicle, carefully inspecting them all the way. Renew damaged sections as necessary. Similarly, whilst the vehicle is raised, take the opportunity to inspect all underbody brake fluid pipes and hoses.

8 From within the engine compartment, check the security of all fuel, vacuum and brake hose attachments and pipe unions, and inspect all hoses for kinks, chafing and deterioration.

9 Where applicable, check the condition of the power steering fluid pipes and hoses.

12 000 Mile Service

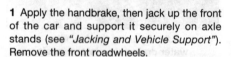

6 Front brake pad check

1 Apply the handbrake, then jack up the front of the car and support it securely on axle stands (see *"Jacking and Vehicle Support"*). Remove the front roadwheels.

2 For a comprehensive check, the brake pads should be removed and cleaned. The operation of the caliper can then also be checked, and the condition of the brake disc itself can be fully examined on both sides. Refer to Chapter 9 for further information.

3 On completion refit the roadwheels and lower the car to the ground.

HAYNES HiNT

For a quick check, the thickness of friction material remaining on each brake pad can be measured through the aperture in the caliper body.

7 Handbrake check and adjustment

Refer to Chapter 9.

8 Auxiliary drivebelt check and renewal

Note: *Peugeot specify the use of a special electronic tool (SEEM C.TRONIC type 105 belt tension measuring tool) to correctly set the auxiliary drivebelt tension. If access to this equipment cannot be obtained, an approximate setting can be achieved using the method described in the following paragraphs. If the method described is used, it is advisable to have the tension checked using the special equipment at the earliest possible opportunity.*

Checking the auxiliary drivebelt tension

1 Apply the handbrake, then jack up the front of the vehicle and support it on axle stands (see *"Jacking and Vehicle Support"*). Remove the right-hand front roadwheel.

2 From underneath the front of the car, prise out the retaining clips, and remove the screws (where applicable), then remove the plastic cover from the wheel arch to gain access to the crankshaft pulley bolt.

3 Using a socket and extension bar fitted over the crankshaft pulley bolt, rotate the crankshaft to that the entire length of the drivebelt can be examined. Examine the

drivebelt for cracks, splitting, fraying or other damage. Check also for signs of glazing (shiny patches) and for separation of the belt plies. Renew the belt if worn or damaged.

4 If the condition of the belt is satisfactory, check the drivebelt tension as described in the following paragraphs, bearing in mind the note at the start of this Section.

Models without power steering or air conditioning

Removal

5 If not already done, proceed as described in paragraphs 1 and 2.

6 Disconnect the battery negative lead.

7 Slacken both the alternator upper and lower mounting nuts/bolts (as applicable).

8 Back off the adjuster bolt to relieve the tension in the drivebelt, then slip the drivebelt from the pulleys (**see illustration**).

Refitting

9 If the belt is being renewed, ensure that the

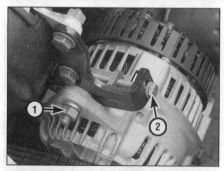

8.8 Alternator upper mounting nut (1) and adjuster bolt (2) - models without power steering or air conditioning

correct type is used. Fit the belt around the pulleys, and take up the slack in the belt by tightening the adjuster bolt.

10 Tension the belt as described in the following paragraphs.

Tensioning

HAYNES HINT *Correct tensioning of the drivebelt will ensure that it has a long life. A belt which is too slack will slip and squeal. Beware, however, of overtightening, as this can cause wear in the alternator bearings.*

11 If not already done, proceed as described in paragraphs 1 and 2.

12 The belt should be tensioned so that, under firm thumb pressure, there is approximately 5.0 mm of free movement at the mid-point between the pulleys (see Note at the beginning of this Section).

13 To adjust, with the upper mounting nut just holding the alternator firm, and the adjuster bolt loosened, turn the adjuster bolt until the correct tension is achieved, then tighten the upper mounting nut.

14 Rotate the crankshaft a couple of times, then re-check the belt tension, and if necessary re-adjust.

15 Reconnect the battery negative lead.

16 Refit the plastic cover to the wheel arch, then refit the roadwheel and lower the vehicle to the ground.

Early models with air conditioning, but not power steering

Removal

17 If not already done, proceed as described in paragraphs 1 and 2.

18 Disconnect the battery negative lead.

19 Slacken the three bolts securing the tensioner pulley bracket, and turn the tensioner pulley until there is sufficient slack for the drivebelt to be removed from the pulleys (see illustration).

Refitting

20 Fit the drivebelt around the pulleys, ensuring that the ribs on the belt are engaged with the gro oves in the pulleys, and that the drivebelt is correctly routed.

21 Tension the belt as follows.

Tensioning

22 If not already done, proceed as described in paragraphs 1 and 2.

23 Correct tensioning of the drivebelt will ensure that it had a long life (see **Haynes Hint**).

24 The belt should be tensioned so that under firm thumb pressure, there is approximately 5.0 mm of free movement at the mid-point between the pulleys on the longest belt run (see Note at the beginning of this Section).

25 To adjust the tension, with the tensioner

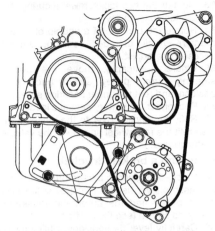

8.19 Tensioner pulley bracket securing bolts (arrowed) - early models with air conditioning, but no power steering

pulley bracket bolts slackened, rotate the tensioner pulley assembly until the correct tension is achieved. Once the belt is correctly tensioned, tighten the pulley bracket securing bolts.

26 Proceed as described in paragraphs 14 to 16.

Early models with power steering, but no air conditioning

Removal

27 If not already done, proceed as described in paragraphs 1 and 2.

28 Disconnect the battery negative lead.

29 Slacken the two lockscrews securing the tensioner roller assembly (see illustration).

30 Turn the tensioner pulley adjuster bolt to move the tensioner pulley away from the drivebelt until there is sufficient slack for the drivebelt to be removed from the pulleys (see illustration).

Refitting

31 Fit the drivebelt around the pulleys in the following order.

a) *Power steering pump/air conditioning compressor.*
b) *Crankshaft.*
c) *Alternator.*
d) *Tensioner pulley.*

8.29 Slacken the two tensioner roller retaining screws (arrowed) . . .

32 Ensure that the ribs on the belt are correctly engaged with the grooves in the pulleys, and that the drivebelt is correctly routed. Take all the slack out of the belt by turning the tensioner pulley adjuster bolt.

33 Tension the belt as follows.

Tensioning

34 If not already done, proceed as described in paragraphs 1 and 2.

35 Correct tensioning of the drivebelt will ensure that it has a long life (see **Haynes Hint**).

36 The belt should be tensioned so that under firm thumb pressure, there is approximately 5.0 mm of free movement at the mid-point between the pulleys on the longest belt run (see Note at the beginning of this Section).

37 To adjust the tension, with the tensioner pulley assembly retaining screws slackened, rotate the adjuster bolt until the correct tension is achieved. Once the belt is correctly tensioned, tighten the pulley assembly retaining screws.

38 Proceed as described in paragraphs 14 to 16.

Later models with power steering or air conditioning

39 Proceed as described in paragraphs 27 to 38 for early models with power steering but no air conditioning.

Later models with power steering and air conditioning

Removal

40 If not already done, proceed as described in paragraphs 1 and 2.

41 Disconnect the battery negative lead.

42 Where applicable, remove the upper securing screw from the power steering pump pulley shield. Push the shield to one side, to allow access to the drivebelt.

43 Slacken the two lockscrews securing the manual tensioner pulley assembly (see illustration).

44 Turn the manual tensioner pulley adjuster bolt to move the tensioner pulley until the holes in the automatic tensioner pulley bracket and the power steering pump bracket are aligned.

1

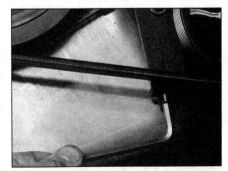

8.30 . . . then turn the tensioner roller adjuster bolt to release the belt tensioner

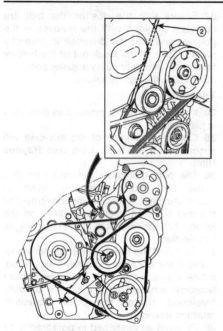

8.43 Auxiliary drivebelt arrangement on models with power steering and air conditioning

A Automatic tensioner pulley
B Manual tensioner pulley
C Adjuster screw
D Lockscrews
1 Holes in tensioner pulley arm and bracket
2 Tensioner pulley locking rod

45 Lock the automatic tensioner pulley in position by inserting a suitable rod (such as a twist drill) through the holes in the automatic tensioner pulley arm and the bracket.
46 Slacken the manual tensioner pulley adjuster screw until the drivebelt can be removed from the pulleys.

Refitting

47 Fit the drivebelt around the pulleys in the following order.
a) Power steering pump.
b) Automatic tensioner pulley.
c) Crankshaft.
d) Air conditioning compressor.
e) Alternator.
f) Manual tensioner pulley.
48 Ensure that the ribs on the belt are correctly engaged with the grooves in the pulleys, and that the drivebelt is correctly routed.
49 Tension the belt as follows.

Tensioning

50 If not already done, proceed as described in paragraphs 1 and 2. Correct tensioning of the drivebelt will ensure that it has a long life (**see Haynes Hint**).
51 Tension the drivebelt by turning the manual tensioner pulley adjuster screw until the rod (see paragraph 45) begins to slide.
52 Remove the rod from the holes in the automatic tensioner pulley arm and the bracket.

53 Tighten the two lockscrews securing the manual tensioner pulley.
54 Rotate the crankshaft a couple of times, then re-check the belt tension, and if necessary re-adjust.
55 Where applicable, move the power steering pump pulley shield back into position, and refit the upper securing screw.
56 Reconnect the battery negative lead.
57 Refit the plastic cover to the wheel arch, then refit the roadwheel and lower the vehicle to the ground.

Renewing a broken drivebelt

58 Proceed as given in paragraphs 40 to 43.
59 Insert a lever between the power steering pump pulley and the automatic tensioner pulley, as shown (**see illustration**).
60 Carefully lever the tensioner pulley away from the power steering pump pulley until a suitable rod can be inserted through the holes in the automatic tensioner pulley arm and the bracket, as described in paragraph 45.
61 Proceed as given in paragraphs 50 to 57.

Brake vacuum pump drivebelt (early models)

Checking the drivebelt tension

62 Examine the drivebelt for cracks, splitting, fraying or other damage. Check also for signs of glazing (shiny patches) and for separation of the belt plies. Renew the belt if worn or damaged. To view the entire length of the belt, the crankshaft can be rotated as described in paragraphs 1 to 3.
63 If the condition of the belt is satisfactory, check the drivebelt tension as described in the following paragraphs, bearing in mind the note at the start of this Section.

⚠️ *Warning: Breakage of the belt in service would lead to a loss of servo assistance, which would greatly reduce the efficiency of the braking system (increasing the required pedal pressure), and could lead to an accident.*

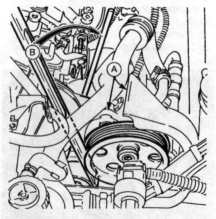

8.59 With power steering pump pulley cover moved aside (A), lever tensioner pulley away from power steering pump pulley (B)

Removal

64 Slacken the pump adjuster bolt, pivot bolt and the adjuster strap lower mounting nut, then unhook the belt from the pump pulley and remove it from the engine.

Refitting and tensioning

65 Locate the new drivebelt over the camshaft drive pulley and the pump pulley.
66 Using a torque wrench, apply a torque of 5 Nm (4 lbf ft) to the adjuster nut (**see illustration**). Maintain this torque, and tighten the bolts in the order shown (1,2,3,4). Re-check the drivebelt tension, and if necessary re-adjust.

9 Clutch adjustment check and control mechanism lubrication

1 Check that the clutch pedal moves smoothly and easily through its full travel.
2 The clutch itself should function correctly, with no trace of slip or drag.
3 Where possible, adjust the clutch cable if necessary, as described in Chapter 6.
4 If excessive effort is required to operate the clutch, check first that the cable is correctly routed and undamaged. Remove the pedal, and make sure that its pivot is properly greased. Refer to Chapter 6 for information.

10 Idle speed and anti-stall speed check and adjustment

1 The usual type of tachometer (rev counter), which works from ignition system pulses, cannot be used on diesel engines. A diagnostic socket is provided for the use of Peugeot test equipment, but this will not normally be available to the home mechanic. If it is not felt that adjusting the idle speed "by ear" is satisfactory, it will be necessary to purchase or hire an appropriate tachometer,

8.66 Tighten the brake vacuum pump pivot and adjuster bolts in the order shown
a Adjuster nut

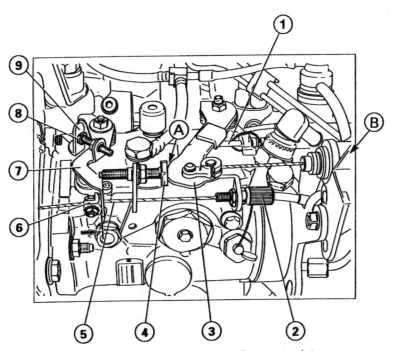

10.3 Lucas fuel injection pump adjustment points

1 *Maximum speed screw*
2 *Fast idle cable screw*
3 *Pump control lever*
4 *Anti-stall screw*
5 *Fast idle cable*
6 *Fast idle cable end fitting*
7 *Fast idle lever*
8 *Idle speed screw*
9 *Manual stop lever*
A *Anti-stall shim location*
B *Accelerator cable screw*

or else leave the task to a Peugeot dealer or other suitably equipped specialist.

2 Before making adjustments, warm up the engine to operating temperature. Make sure that the accelerator cable and fast idle cables are correctly adjusted (see Chapter 4).

Lucas fuel injection pump

3 Place a shim of the correct thickness (see *"Specifications"*), between the pump control lever and the anti-stall adjustment screw **(see illustration)**.
4 Push the manual stop lever back against its

stop, and hold it in position by inserting a 3 mm diameter rod/drill through the hole in the fast idle lever.
5 The engine speed should be as specified for the anti-stall speed (see *"Specifications"*).
6 If adjustment is necessary, loosen the locknut, turn the anti-stall adjustment screw as required, then tighten the locknut.
7 Remove the rod/drill and the shim, and check that the engine is idling at the specified speed (see *"Specifications"*).
8 If adjustment is necessary, loosen the locknut on the idle speed adjustment screw. Turn the screw as required, and retighten the locknut.
9 Move the pump control lever to increase the engine speed to about 3000 rpm, then quickly release the lever. The deceleration period should be between 2.5 and 3.5 seconds, and the engine speed should drop to approximately 50 rpm below idle.
10 If the deceleration is too fast and the engine stalls, unscrew the anti-stall adjustment screw a quarter-turn towards the control lever. If the deceleration is too slow, resulting in poor engine braking, turn the screw a quarter-turn away from the lever.
11 Retighten the locknut after making an adjustment. Recheck the idle speed, and adjust if necessary as described previously.
12 With the engine idling, check the operation of the manual stop control by turning the stop lever clockwise (Chapter 4, Section 1). The engine must stop instantly.
13 Where applicable, disconnect the tachometer on completion.

Bosch fuel injection pump

14 Loosen the locknut, and unscrew the anti-stall adjustment screw until it is clear of the pump control lever **(see illustration)**.
15 Check the idle speed with the figure given in the *"Specifications"*. If adjustment is required, loosen the locknut and turn the idle speed adjustment screw as necessary, then retighten the locknut.
16 Insert a shim or feeler blade of the correct thickness (see *"Specifications"*) between the pump control lever and the anti-stall adjustment screw.

1

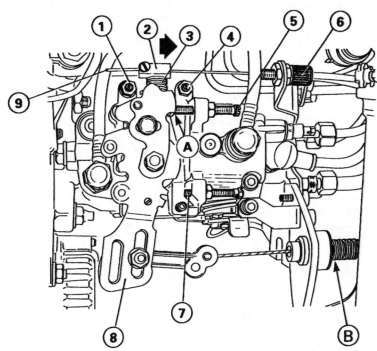

**10.14 Bosch fuel injection pump
adjustment point - non-Turbo engines
(Turbo similar)**

1 *Fast idle lever stop screw*
2 *Fast idle cable end fitting*
3 *Fast idle lever*
4 *Idle speed screw*
5 *Anti-stall speed screw*
6 *Fast idle cable screw*
7 *Maximum speed screw*
8 *Pump control lever*
9 *Fast idle cable*
A *Anti-stall adjustment shim location*
B *Accelerator cable screw*

17 Start the engine and allow it to idle. The engine speed should be as specified for the anti-stall speed (see *"Specifications"*).
18 If adjustment is necessary, loosen the locknut and turn the anti-stall adjustment screw as required. Retighten the locknut.
19 Remove the shim or feeler blade and allow the engine to idle.
20 Move the fast idle lever fully towards the flywheel end of the engine, and check that the engine speed increases to the specified fast idle speed. If necessary, loosen the locknut and turn the fast idle adjusting screw as required, then retighten the locknut.
21 With the engine idling, check the operation of the manual stop control by turning the stop lever (see Chapter 4, Section 1). The engine must stop instantly.
22 Where applicable, disconnect the tachometer on completion.

11 Driveshaft gaiter check

With the vehicle raised and securely supported on stands, turn the steering onto full lock, then slowly rotate the roadwheel. Inspect the condition of the outer constant velocity (CV) joint rubber gaiters, squeezing the gaiters to open out the folds **(see illustration)**. Check for signs of cracking, splits or deterioration of the rubber, which may allow the grease to escape, and lead to water and grit entry into the joint. Also check the security and condition of the retaining clips. Repeat these checks on the inner CV joints. If any damage or deterioration is found, the gaiters should be renewed as described in Chapter 8.

At the same time, check the general condition of the CV joints themselves by first holding the driveshaft and attempting to rotate the wheel. Repeat this check by holding the inner joint and attempting to rotate the driveshaft. Any appreciable movement indicates wear in the joints, wear in the driveshaft splines, or a loose driveshaft retaining nut.

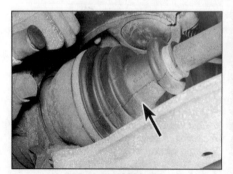

11.1 Check the condition of the driveshaft gaiters (arrowed)

12 Steering and suspension check

Front suspension and steering check

1 Raise the front of the vehicle, and securely support it on axle stands (see *"Jacking and Vehicle Support"*).
2 Visually inspect the balljoint dust covers and the steering rack-and-pinion gaiters for splits, chafing or deterioration. Any wear of these components will cause loss of lubricant, together with dirt and water entry, resulting in rapid deterioration of the balljoints or steering gear.
3 On vehicles with power steering, check the fluid hoses for chafing or deterioration, and the pipe and hose unions for fluid leaks. Also check for signs of fluid leakage under pressure from the steering gear rubber gaiters, which would indicate failed fluid seals within the steering gear.
4 Grasp the roadwheel at the 12 o'clock and 6 o'clock positions, and try to rock it **(see illustration)**. Very slight free play may be felt, but if the movement is appreciable, further investigation is necessary to determine the source. Continue rocking the wheel while an assistant depresses the footbrake. If the movement is now eliminated or significantly reduced, it is likely that the hub bearings are at fault. If the free play is still evident with the footbrake depressed, then there is wear in the suspension joints or mountings.
5 Now grasp the wheel at the 9 o'clock and 3 o'clock positions, and try to rock it as before. Any movement felt now may again be caused by wear in the hub bearings or the steering track-rod balljoints. If the outer balljoint is worn, the visual movement will be obvious. If the inner joint is suspect, it can be felt by placing a hand over the rack-and-pinion rubber gaiter and gripping the track-rod. If the wheel is now rocked, movement will be felt at the inner joint if wear has taken place.
6 Using a large screwdriver or flat bar, check for wear in the suspension mounting bushes by levering between the relevant suspension

12.4 Check for wear in the hub bearings by grasping the wheel and trying to rock it

component and its attachment point. Some movement is to be expected, as the mountings are made of rubber, but excessive wear should be obvious. Also check the condition of any visible rubber bushes, looking for splits, cracks or contamination of the rubber.
7 With the car standing on its wheels, have an assistant turn the steering wheel back and forth, about an eighth of a turn each way. There should be very little, if any, lost movement between the steering wheel and roadwheels. If this is not the case, closely observe the joints and mountings previously described. In addition, check the steering column universal joints for wear, and also check the rack-and-pinion steering gear itself.

Rear suspension check

8 Chock the front wheels, then jack up the rear of the vehicle and support securely on axle stands (see *"Jacking and Vehicle Support"*).
9 Working as described previously for the front suspension, check the rear hub bearings, the suspension bushes and the shock absorber mountings for wear.

Suspension strut/ shock absorber check

10 Check for any signs of fluid leakage around the suspension strut/shock absorber body, or from the rubber gaiter around the piston rod. Should any fluid be noticed, the suspension strut/shock absorber is defective internally, and should be renewed. **Note:** *Suspension struts/shock absorbers should always be renewed in pairs on the same axle.*
11 The efficiency of the suspension strut/shock absorber may be checked by bouncing the vehicle at each corner. Generally speaking, the body will return to its normal position and stop after being depressed. If it rises and returns on a rebound, the suspension strut/shock absorber is probably suspect. Examine also the suspension strut/shock absorber upper and lower mountings for any signs of wear.

13 Air conditioning refrigerant check

⚠ *Warning: Do not attempt to open the refrigerant circuit. Refer to the precautions given in Chapter 3.*

1 In order to check the condition of the refrigerant, a humidity indicator and a sight glass are provided on top of the drier bottle, located in the front, left-hand corner of the engine compartment **(see illustration)**.

Refrigerant humidity check

2 Check the colour of the humidity indicator. Blue indicates that the condition of the

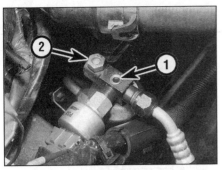

13.1 Air conditioning system drier bottle sight glass (1) and humidity indicator (2)

refrigerant is satisfactory. Pink indicates that the refrigerant is saturated with humidity. If the indicator shows red, the system should be drained and recharged, and a new drier bottle should be fitted. **Note:** *The system should be drained and recharged only by a Peugeot dealer or air conditioning specialist. Do not attempt to carry out the work yourself, as the refrigerant is a highly-dangerous substance (refer to Chapter 3).*

Refrigerant flow check

3 Run the engine, and switch on the air conditioning.
4 After a few minutes, inspect the sight glass, and check the fluid flow. Clear fluid should be visible - if not, the following will help to diagnose the problem:

a) *Clear fluid flow - the system is functioning correctly.*
b) *No fluid flow - have the system checked for leaks by a Peugeot dealer or air conditioning specialist.*
c) *Continuous stream of clear air bubbles in fluid - refrigerant level low - have the system recharged by a Peugeot dealer or air conditioning specialist.*
d) *Milky air bubbles visible - high humidity (see paragraph 2).*

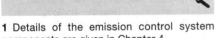

14 Emissions control systems check

1 Details of the emission control system components are given in Chapter 4.
2 Checking consists simply of a visual check for obvious signs of damaged or leaking hoses and joints.

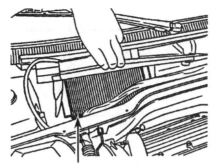

15.4 Removing the pollen filter from the heater air intake duct

3 Detailed checking and testing of the evaporative and/or exhaust emission systems (as applicable) should be entrusted to a Peugeot dealer.

15 Pollen filter renewal

1 On later models, a pollen filter is fitted.
2 Open the bonnet.
3 Release the securing clips, and withdraw the plastic cover from the heater air inlet in the passenger's side of the scuttle at the rear of the engine compartment.
4 Unclip the pollen filter from the heater air inlet duct **(see illustration)**.
5 Refitting is a reversal of removal.

16 Road test

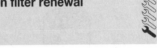

Instruments and electrical equipment

1 Check the operation of all instruments and electrical equipment.
2 Make sure that all instruments read correctly, and switch on all electrical equipment in turn, to check that it functions properly.

Steering and suspension

3 Check for any abnormalities in the steering, suspension, handling or road "feel".
4 Drive the vehicle, and check that there are no unusual vibrations or noises.

5 Check that the steering feels positive, with no excessive "sloppiness", or roughness, and check for any suspension noises when cornering and driving over bumps.

Drivetrain

6 Check the performance of the engine, clutch, transmission and driveshafts.
7 Listen for any unusual noises from the engine, clutch and transmission.
8 Make sure that the engine runs smoothly when idling, and that there is no hesitation when accelerating.
9 Check that, where applicable, the clutch action is smooth and progressive, that the drive is taken up smoothly, and that the pedal travel is not excessive. Also listen for any noises when the clutch pedal is depressed.
10 Check that all gears can be engaged smoothly without noise, and that the gear lever action is not abnormally vague or "notchy".
11 Listen for a metallic clicking sound from the front of the vehicle, as the vehicle is driven slowly in a circle with the steering on full-lock. Carry out this check in both directions. If a clicking noise is heard, this indicates wear in a driveshaft joint (see Chapter 8).

Braking system

12 Make sure that the vehicle does not pull to one side when braking, and that the wheels do not lock prematurely when braking hard.
13 Check that there is no vibration through the steering when braking.
14 Check that the handbrake operates correctly, without excessive movement of the lever, and that it holds the vehicle stationary on a slope.
15 Where applicable, test the operation of the brake servo unit as follows. Depress the footbrake four or five times to exhaust the vacuum, then start the engine. As the engine starts, there should be a noticeable "give" in the brake pedal as vacuum builds up. Allow the engine to run for at least two minutes, and then switch it off. If the brake pedal is now depressed again, it should be possible to detect a hiss from the servo as the pedal is depressed. After about four or five applications, no further hissing should be heard, and the pedal should feel considerably harder.

1

18 000 Mile Service

17 Air filter renewal

1 Release the clips and lift off the air cleaner top cover (see illustration).
2 Withdraw the filter element from the air cleaner body (see illustration).
3 Fit the new element in position in the air cleaner body, making sure that it is the right way round.
4 Refit the top cover and snap the clips in position.

17.1 Air cleaner top cover securing clips

17.2 Withdrawing the air cleaner element

18 Fuel filter renewal

Early models (fuel filter mounted on side of battery tray)

1 The fuel filter is mounted on a bracket bolted to the battery tray on the left-hand side of the engine compartment.
2 Place a suitable container beneath the filter.
3 Loosen the water drain screw on the bottom of the filter, and slacken the air bleed screw (see Chapter 4 for further details). Allow the fuel to drain completely.
Securely tighten the drain screw, then unscrew the through-bolt from the top (Lucas CAV/Roto-diesel) or bottom (Bosch) of the filter (see illustrations).

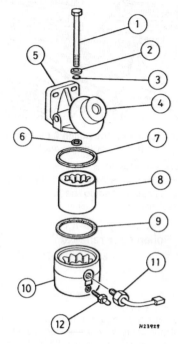

18.3a Early-type Lucas CAV/Roto-diesel fuel filter components

1 Through-bolt
2 Washer
3 Seal
4 Priming pump
5 Filter head
6 Seal
7 Seal
8 Filter cartridge
9 Seal
10 End cap
11 Water sensor (not on all models)
12 Water drain screw

4 On the Lucas CAV/Roto-diesel assembly, this will release the end cap and enable the filter cartage and seals to be removed.
5 On the Bosch assembly, remove the chamber, then the filter element and seals.
6 Clean the filter head, and the end cap or chamber, as applicable.
7 Make sure that the old seals are removed, then locate the new seals in position and fit the new cartridge or element using a reversal of the removal procedure.
8 Prime the fuel system (see Chapter 4).
9 Open the drain screw until clean fuel flows from the hose, then close the drain screw and withdraw the container from under the hose.

Later models (with integral fuel filter/thermostat housing)

10 The fuel filter is located in a plastic housing at the front of the engine (see illustration).
11 Cover the clutch bellhousing with a piece of plastic sheeting, to protect the clutch from fuel spillage.
12 Position a suitable container under the end of the fuel filter drain hose. Open the drain screw on the front of the filter housing, and allow the fuel to drain completely.

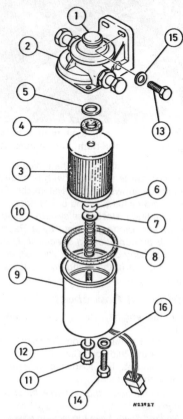

18.3b Early-type Bosch fuel filter components

1 Priming pump
2 Filter head
3 Filter element
4 Seal
5 Washer
6 Seal
7 Washer
8 Spring
9 Chamber
10 Seal
11 Through-bolt
12 Washer
13 Air bleed screw
14 Water drain screw
15 Washer
16 Washer

13 Securely tighten the drain screw, then undo the four retaining screws and lift off the filter housing cover (see illustration).
14 Lift the filter from the housing (see illustration). Ensure that the rubber sealing

18.10 Fuel filter location - later models

18.13 Lift off the fuel filter cover . . .

18.14 . . . then lift the filter from the housing - later models

ring comes away with the filter, and does not stick to the housing/lid.

15 Remove all traces of dirt or debris from inside the filter housing then, making sure its sealing ring is in position, fit the new fuel filter.

16 Coat the threads of the filter cover securing bolts with thread-locking compound, then refit the cover and secure with the bolts.

17 Prime the fuel system (see Chapter 4).

18 Open the drain screw until clean fuel flows from the hose, then close the drain screw and withdraw the container from under the hose.

19 Rear brake shoe check - models with rear drum brakes

Remove the rear brake drums, and check the brake shoes for signs of wear or contamination. At the same time, also inspect the wheel cylinders for signs of leakage, and the brake drum for signs of wear. Refer to the relevant Sections of Chapter 9 for information.

20 Rear disc brake pad check

1 Jack up the rear of the car and support it securely on axle stands (see *"Jacking and Vehicle Support"*). Remove the rear roadwheels.

2 For a comprehensive check, the brake pads should be removed and cleaned. The

HAYNES HiNT *For a quick check, the thickness of friction material remaining on each brake pad can be measured through the aperture in the caliper body.*

operation of the caliper can then also be checked, and the condition of the brake disc itself can be fully examined on both sides. Refer to Chapter 9 for further information.

3 On completion refit the roadwheels and lower the car to the ground.

21 Hinge and lock lubrication

1 Work around the vehicle, and lubricate the hinges of the bonnet, doors and boot lid/tailgate with a light machine oil.

2 Lightly lubricate the bonnet release mechanism and exposed section of inner cable with a smear of grease.

3 Check carefully the security and operation of all hinges, latches and locks, adjusting them where required. Check the operation of the central locking system (if fitted).

4 Where applicable, check the condition and operation of the tailgate struts, renewing them if either is leaking or is no longer able to support the tailgate securely when raised.

1

36 000 Mile Service

22 Manual transmission oil level check

Note: *A square-section wrench may be required to undo the filler/level plug. These wrenches can be obtained from most motor factors or your Peugeot dealer.*

HAYNES HiNT *It may be possible to use the square end fitting on a ratchet handle (as found in a typical socket set) to undo the plug.*

1 Park the car on a level surface. The oil level must be checked before the car is driven, or at least 5 minutes after the engine has been switched off. If the oil level is checked immediately after driving the car, some of the oil will remain distributed around the transmission components, resulting in an inaccurate level reading.

2 Turn the steering wheel on full left-hand lock, then where applicable remove the cover for access to the left-hand side of the transmission.

3 Wipe clean the area around the filler/level plug, which is on the left-hand end of the transmission. Unscrew the plug and clean it; discard the sealing washer **(see illustration)**.

4 The oil level should reach the lower edge of the filler/level hole. A certain amount of oil will have gathered behind the filler/level plug, and will trickle out when it is removed; this does *not* necessarily indicate that the level is correct. To ensure that a true level is established, wait until the initial trickle has stopped, then add oil as necessary until a trickle of new oil can be seen emerging **(see illustrations)**. The level will be correct when the flow ceases; use only good-quality oil of the specified type (see *"Weekly Checks"*).

22.3 Removing the filler/level plug

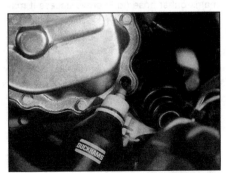

22.4a Topping-up the transmission fluid level

22.4b Oil level is correct when the oil stops flowing out of the filler/level hole

5 Filling the transmission with oil is an extremely awkward operation; above all, allow plenty of time for the oil level to settle properly before checking it. If a large amount had to be added to the transmission, and a large amount flows out on checking the level, refit the filler/level plug and take the vehicle on a short journey so that the new oil is distributed fully around the transmission components, then recheck the level when it has settled again.

6 If the transmission has been overfilled so that oil flows out as soon as the filler/level plug is removed, first check that the car is completely level (front-to-rear and side-to-side), and allow any surplus oil to drain off into a suitable container.

7 When the level is correct, fit a new sealing washer to the filler/level plug. Refit the plug, tightening it to the specified torque wrench setting. Wash off any spilt oil then where applicable refit the access cover.

23 Brake fluid renewal

⚠️ **Warning: Brake hydraulic fluid can harm your eyes and damage painted surfaces, so use extreme caution when handling and pouring it. Do not use fluid that has been standing open for some time, as it absorbs moisture from the air. Excess moisture can cause a dangerous loss of braking effectiveness.**

1 The procedure is similar to that for the bleeding of the hydraulic system as described in Chapter 9, except that the brake fluid reservoir should be emptied by siphoning, using a clean poultry baster or similar before starting, and allowance should be made for the old fluid to be expelled when bleeding a section of the circuit.

2 Working as described in Chapter 9, open the first bleed screw in the sequence, and pump the brake pedal gently until nearly all the old fluid has been emptied from the master cylinder reservoir. Top-up to the "MAX" level with new fluid, and continue pumping until only the new fluid remains in the reservoir, and new fluid can be seen emerging from the bleed screw. Tighten the screw, and top the reservoir level up to the "MAX" level line.

3 Old hydraulic fluid is invariably much darker in colour than the new, making it easy to distinguish the two.

4 Work through all the remaining bleed screws in the sequence until new fluid can be seen at all of them. Be careful to keep the master cylinder reservoir topped-up to above the "MIN" level at all times, or air may enter the system and greatly increase the length of the task.

5 When the operation is complete, check that all bleed screws are securely tightened, and that their dust caps are refitted. Wash off all traces of spilt fluid, and recheck the master cylinder reservoir fluid level.

6 Check the operation of the brakes before taking the car on the road.

24 Timing belt renewal

Refer to Chapter 2A.

25 Coolant renewal

Cooling system draining

⚠️ **Warning: Wait until the engine is cold before starting this procedure. Do not allow antifreeze to come in contact with your skin, or with the painted surfaces of the vehicle. Rinse off spills immediately with plenty of water. Never leave antifreeze lying around in an open container, or in a puddle in the driveway or on the garage floor. Children and pets are attracted by its sweet smell, but antifreeze can be fatal if ingested.**

1 With the engine completely cold, remove the expansion tank filler cap. Turn the cap anti-clockwise until it reaches the first stop. Wait until any pressure remaining in the system is released, then push the cap down, turn it anti-clockwise to the second stop, and lift it off.

2 Position a suitable container beneath the coolant drain outlet at the lower left-hand side of the radiator.

3 Loosen the drain plug (there is no need to remove it completely) and allow the coolant to drain into the container. If desired, a length of tubing can be fitted to the drain outlet to direct the flow of coolant during draining (see illustration).

4 To assist draining, open the cooling system bleed screws. These are located in the heater matrix outlet hose (to improve access it may be located in an extension hose) on the

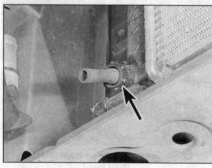

25.3 Radiator drain outlet (arrowed)

25.4 Coolant bleed screw (arrowed) at top of radiator

engine compartment bulkhead, on the top of the thermostat housing or in the coolant hose running to the top of the fuel filter/thermostat housing, and/or in the coolant bypass hose, depending on model. All models also have a bleed screw located at the top left-hand corner of the radiator (see illustration).

5 When the flow of coolant stops, reposition the container below the cylinder block drain plug. It is located at the rear of the cylinder block.

6 Remove the cylinder block drain plug, and allow the coolant to drain into the container.

7 If the coolant has been drained for a reason other than renewal, then provided it is clean and less than two years old, it can be re-used, though this is not recommended.

8 Refit and tighten the radiator and cylinder block drain plugs on completion of draining.

Cooling system flushing

9 If coolant renewal has been neglected, or if the antifreeze mixture has become diluted, then in time, the cooling system may gradually lose efficiency, as the coolant passages become restricted due to rust, scale deposits, and other sediment. The cooling system efficiency can be restored by flushing the system clean.

10 The radiator should be flushed independently of the engine, to avoid unnecessary contamination.

Radiator flushing

11 To flush the radiator, first tighten the radiator drain plug, and the radiator bleed screw.

12 Disconnect the top and bottom hoses and any other relevant hoses from the radiator, with reference to Chapter 3.

13 Insert a garden hose into the radiator top inlet. Direct a flow of clean water through the radiator, and continue flushing until clean water emerges from the radiator bottom outlet.

14 If after a reasonable period, the water still does not run clear, the radiator can be flushed with a good proprietary cleaning agent. It is important that their manufacturer's instructions are followed carefully. If the contamination is particularly bad, insert the hose in the radiator bottom outlet, and reverse-flush the radiator.

Engine flushing

15 To flush the engine, first refit and tighten the cylinder block drain plug, and tighten the cooling system bleed screws.

16 Remove the thermostat (see Chapter 3), then temporarily refit the thermostat cover.

17 With the top and bottom hoses disconnected from the radiator (see Chapter 3 - it may be preferable to disconnect the bottom hose from the engine), insert a garden hose into the radiator top hose. Direct a clean flow of water through the engine, and continue flushing until clean water emerges from the radiator bottom hose.

18 On completion of flushing, refit the thermostat and reconnect the hoses with reference to Chapter 3.

Cooling system filling

19 Before attempting to fill the cooling system, make sure that all hoses and clips are in good condition, and that the clips are tight. Note that an antifreeze mixture must be used all year round, to prevent corrosion of the engine components (see following sub-Section). Also check that the radiator and cylinder block drain plugs, as applicable, are in place and tight.

20 Remove the expansion tank cap.

21 Open all the cooling system bleed screws (see paragraph 4).

22 Some of the cooling system hoses are positioned at a higher level than the top of the radiator expansion tank. It is therefore necessary to use a "header tank" when refilling the cooling system, to reduce the possibility of air being trapped in the system. Although Peugeot dealers use a special header tank, the same effect can be achieved by using a suitable bottle, with a seal between the bottle and the expansion tank **(see illustration and Haynes Hint)**.

23 Fit the "header tank" to the expansion tank and slowly fill the system. Coolant will emerge from each of the bleed screws in turn, starting with the lowest screw. As soon as coolant free from air bubbles emerges from the lowest screw, tighten that screw, and watch the next bleed screw in the system.

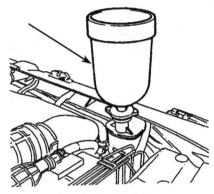

25.22 Peugeot cooling system "header tank" in position

Repeat the procedure until the coolant is emerging from the highest bleed screw in the cooling system and all bleed screws are securely tightened. Keep the "header tank" full during this procedure.

24 Once all the bleed screws are securely tightened, remove the "header tank" and refit the expansion tank cap.

25 Start the engine, and run it at 1500 rpm. Maintain this engine speed until the radiator cooling fan has cut in and out three times.

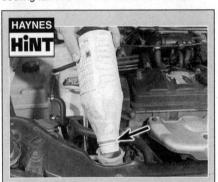

Cut the bottom off an old antifreeze container to make a "header tank" for use when refilling the cooling system. The seal at the point arrowed must be as airtight as possible.

26 Allow the engine to run at idle speed for a few minutes.

27 Stop the engine, and wait for at least ten minutes.

28 Place a large wad of rag around the expansion tank cap, and around your hand, then carefully remove the expansion tank cap. Turn the cap anti-clockwise until it reaches the first stop. Wait until any pressure remaining in the system is released, then push the cap down, turn it anti-clockwise to the second stop, and lift it off.

⚠️ *Warning: Take precautions against scalding, as the cooling system will be hot.*

29 Check the coolant level, and if necessary top-up the expansion tank to just above the "MAXI" level mark (see *"Weekly checks"*).

30 Refit the expansion tank cap.

Antifreeze mixture

31 The antifreeze should always be renewed at the specified intervals. This is necessary not only to maintain the antifreeze properties, but also to prevent corrosion which would otherwise occur as the corrosion inhibitors become progressively less effective.

32 Always use an ethylene-glycol based antifreeze which is suitable for use in mixed-metal cooling systems. The quantity of antifreeze and levels of protection are indicated in the Specifications.

33 Before adding antifreeze, the cooling system should be completely drained, preferably flushed, and all hoses checked for condition and security.

34 After filling with antifreeze, a label should be attached to the expansion tank, stating the type and concentration of antifreeze used, and the date installed. Any subsequent topping-up should be made with the same type and concentration of antifreeze.

35 Do not use engine antifreeze in the windscreen/tailgate washer system, as it will cause damage to the vehicle paintwork. A screenwash additive should be added to the washer system in the quantities stated on the bottle.

1

Chapter 2 Part A:
Engine in-car repair procedures

Contents

Degrees of difficulty

| **Easy,** suitable for novice with little experience | | **Fairly easy,** suitable for beginner with some experience | | **Fairly difficult,** suitable for competent DIY mechanic | | **Difficult,** suitable for experienced DIY mechanic | | **Very difficult,** suitable for expert DIY or professional | |

Specifications

General

Manufacturer's engine codes:*	
1.8 litre (1769 cc) Turbo engine	**A8A** (XUD7TE/L)
1.9 litre (1905 cc) non-turbo, non-catalyst/EGR engine	**D9B** (XUD9A/L)
1.9 litre (1905 cc) non-turbo engine with catalyst/EGR	**DJZ** (XUD9Y)
1.9 litre (1905 cc) Turbo, non-catalyst/EGR engine	**D8A** (XUD9TE/L)
1.9 litre (1905 cc) Turbo engine with catalyst/EGR	**DHY** (XUD9TE/Y)
Bore:	
1.8 litre (1769 cc) engines	80.00 mm
1.9 litre (1905 cc) engines	83.00 mm
Stroke:	
1.8 litre (1769 cc) engine	88.00 mm
1.9 litre (1905 cc) engines	88.00 mm
Direction of crankshaft rotation	Clockwise (viewed from the right-hand side of vehicle/timing belt end of engine)
No 1 cylinder location	At flywheel end of block
Compression ratio (typical):	
1.8 litre (1769 cc) engine	22 : 1
1.9 litre (1905 cc) engine:	
Non-turbo engine	23 : 1
Turbo engine	21.8 : 1

The engine code is stamped on a plate attached to the front of the cylinder block. This is the code most often used by Peugeot. The code given in brackets is the factory identification number, and is not often referred to by Peugeot or this manual.

Compression pressures (engine hot, at cranking speed)

Normal	25 to 30 bars (363 to 435 psi)
Minimum	18 bars (261 psi)
Maximum difference between any two cylinders	5 bars (73 psi)

Camshaft

Drive	Toothed belt
No of bearings	3
Endfloat	0.07 to 0.16 mm

Valve clearances (engine cold)

Inlet	0.15 ± 0.05 mm
Exhaust	0.30 ± 0.05 mm

2A

Lubrication system

Oil pump type	Gear-type, chain-driven off timing belt end of crankshaft

Minimum oil pressure at 90°C (typical):

At idle speed	2.0 bars
At 2000 rpm	3.5 bars
At 4000 rpm	4.5 bars

Torque wrench settings

	Nm	lbf ft
Big-end bearing cap nuts:		
Stage 1	20	15
Stage 2	Tighten through a further 70°	
Camshaft bearing cap nuts	20	15
Camshaft sprocket bolt	45	33
Crankshaft front oil seal housing bolts	16	12
Crankshaft pulley bolt:		
Stage 1	40	30
Stage 2	Tighten through a further 60°	
Cylinder head bolts - refer to Section 13:		
1.8 litre (1769 cc) Turbo (A8A) engines and 1.9 litre (1905 cc) non-Turbo engines:		
Bolts with 16 mm across flats hexagonal heads:		
Stage 1	30	22
Fully slacken all bolts, then:		
Stage 2	70	51
Stage 3	Tighten through a further 120°	
Bolts with Torx heads:		
Stage 1	20	15
Fully slacken all bolts, then:		
Stage 2	60	44
Stage 3	Tighten through a further 180°	
1.9 litre (1905 cc) Turbo engines:		
Stage 1	20	15
Fully slacken all bolts, then:		
Stage 2	60	44
Stage 3	Tighten through a further 220°	
Cylinder head cover bolts	10	7
Engine/transmission left-hand mounting:		
Mounting rubber-to-bracket nuts (all except 1.9 litre Turbo engines) . .	20	15
Mounting bracket-to-body bolts	45	33
Mounting stud	50	36
Centre nut	70	52
Mounting stud bracket bolts (1.9 litre Turbo engines)	60	44
Engine-to-transmission fixing bolts	45	33
Engine/transmission rear mounting:		
Mounting assembly-to-block bolts	45	33
Mounting link-to-mounting bolt	50	37
Mounting link-to-subframe bolt	85	63
Engine/transmission right-hand mounting:		
Engine (tensioner assembly) bracket bolts	18	13
Mounting bracket retaining nuts	45	33
Curved retaining plate bolts	20	15
Flywheel bolts*	50	37
Injection pump sprocket nut	50	37
Injection pump sprocket puller retaining screws	10	7
Belt-driven brake vacuum pump drive pulley bolt	35	26
Main bearing cap bolts:		
All except 1.9 litre (1905 cc) Turbo engines	70	52
1.9 litre (1905 cc) Turbo engines:		
Stage 1	15	11
Stage 2	Tighten through a further 70°	
Oil pump mounting bolts	20	15
Piston oil jet spray tube bolt - Turbo engines	10	7
Sump bolts	20	15
Timing belt cover bolts	8	6
Timing belt tensioner adjustment bolt	18	13
Timing belt tensioner pivot nut	18	13

Apply thread-locking fluid to the bolt threads.

1 General information

How to use this Chapter

This Part of Chapter 2 describes the repair procedures that can reasonably be carried out on the engine while it remains in the vehicle. If the engine has been removed from the vehicle and is being dismantled as described in Part B, any preliminary dismantling procedures can be ignored.

Note that, while it may be possible physically to overhaul items such as the piston/connecting rod assemblies while the engine is in the car, such tasks are not usually carried out as separate operations. Usually, several additional procedures are required (not to mention the cleaning of components and oilways); for this reason, all such tasks are classed as major overhaul procedures, and are described in Part B of this Chapter.

Part B describes the removal of the engine/transmission from the car, and the full overhaul procedures that can then be carried out.

Engine description

The XUD engine is a well-proven modern unit which has appeared in many Peugeot and Citroën vehicles. The engine is of four-cylinder overhead camshaft design, mounted transversely, with the transmission mounted on the left-hand side.

A toothed timing belt drives the camshaft, fuel injection pump and coolant pump. Followers are fitted between the camshaft and valves. Valve clearance adjustment is by means of shims. The camshaft is supported by three bearings machined directly in the cylinder head.

The crankshaft runs in five main bearings of the usual shell type. Endfloat is controlled by thrustwashers either side of No 2 main bearing.

The pistons are selected to be of matching weight, and incorporate fully-floating gudgeon pins retained by circlips.

The oil pump is chain-driven from the front of the crankshaft. An oil cooler is fitted to all engines.

The design of the Turbo engine is the same as the normally-aspirated (non-turbo) version, but components such as the crankshaft, pistons and connecting rods are uprated. It also incorporates oil jets which spray oil onto the undersides of the pistons to keep them cool.

Throughout the manual, it is often necessary to identify the engines not only by their cubic capacity, but also by their engine code. The engine code consists of three letters (eg. D9B). The code is stamped on a plate attached to the front of the cylinder block - see Specifications for further details.

Repair operations possible with the engine in the vehicle

The following operations can be carried out without having to remove the engine from the vehicle:

a) Removal and refitting of the cylinder head.
b) Removal and refitting of the timing belt and sprockets.
c) Removal and refitting of the camshaft.
d) Removal and refitting of the sump.
e) Removal and refitting of the big-end bearings, connecting rods, and pistons*.
f) Removal and refitting of the oil pump.
g) Renewal of the engine/transmission mountings.
h) Removal and refitting of the flywheel.

* Although it is possible to remove these components with the engine in place, for reasons of access and cleanliness it is recommended that the engine is removed.

2 Compression and leakdown tests - description and interpretation

Compression test

Note: *A compression tester specifically designed for diesel engines must be used for this test.*

1 When engine performance is down, or if misfiring occurs which cannot be attributed to the fuel system, a compression test can provide diagnostic clues as to the engine's condition. If the test is performed regularly, it can give warning of trouble before any other symptoms become apparent.

2 A compression tester specifically intended for diesel engines must be used, because of the higher pressures involved. The tester is connected to an adapter which screws into the glow plug or injector hole. On these engines, an adapter suitable for use in the injector holes will be required, due to the limited access to the glow plug holes **(see illustration)**. It is unlikely to be worthwhile buying such a tester for occasional use, but it may be possible to borrow or hire one - if not, have the test performed by a garage.

3 Unless specific instructions to the contrary are supplied with the tester, observe the following points:

a) *The battery must be in a good state of charge, the air filter must be clean, and the engine should be at normal operating temperature.*
b) *All the injectors or glow plugs should be removed before starting the test. If removing the injectors, also remove the flame shield washers, otherwise they may be blown out.*
c) *The stop solenoid must be disconnected, to prevent the engine from running or fuel from being discharged.*

4 There is no need to hold the accelerator

2.2 Performing a compression test

pedal down during the test, because the diesel engine air inlet is not throttled.

5 The actual compression pressures measured are not so important as the balance between cylinders. Values are given in the Specifications.

6 The cause of poor compression is less easy to establish on a diesel engine than on a petrol one. The effect of introducing oil into the cylinders ("wet" testing) is not conclusive, because there is a risk that the oil will sit in the swirl chamber or in the recess on the piston crown instead of passing to the rings. However, the following can be used as a rough guide to diagnosis.

7 All cylinders should produce very similar pressures; any difference greater than that specified indicates the existence of a fault. Note that the compression should build up quickly in a healthy engine; low compression on the first stroke, followed by gradually-increasing pressure on successive strokes, indicates worn piston rings. A low compression reading on the first stroke, which does not build up during successive strokes, indicates leaking valves or a blown head gasket (a cracked head could also be the cause). Deposits on the undersides of the valve heads can also cause low compression.

8 A low reading from two adjacent cylinders is almost certainly due to the head gasket having blown between them; the presence of coolant in the engine oil will confirm this.

9 If the compression reading is unusually high, the cylinder head surfaces, valves and pistons are probably coated with carbon deposits. If this is the case, the cylinder head should be removed and decarbonised (see Part B).

Leakdown test

10 A leakdown test measures the rate at which compressed air fed into the cylinder is lost. It is an alternative to a compression test, and in many ways it is better, since the escaping air provides easy identification of where pressure loss is occurring (piston rings, valves or head gasket).

11 The equipment needed for leakdown testing is unlikely to be available to the home mechanic. If poor compression is suspected, have the test performed by a suitably-equipped garage.

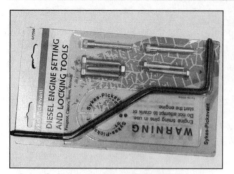

3.4a Suitable tools available for locking engine in position

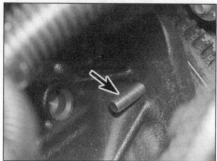

3.4b Rod (arrowed) inserted through cylinder block into timing hole in flywheel

remove the screws (as applicable), then withdraw the plastic cover from the right-hand wing valance (access is easier with the car jacked up and supported on axle stands, with the roadwheel removed - see "*Jacking and Vehicle Support*"). Where necessary, unclip the coolant hoses from the bracket, to improve access further. The crankshaft can then be turned using a suitable socket and extension bar fitted to the pulley bolt. Note that the crankshaft must always be turned in a clockwise direction (viewed from the right-hand side of the vehicle).

4 Insert an 8 mm diameter rod or drill through the hole in the left-hand flange of the cylinder block by the starter motor; if necessary, carefully turn the crankshaft either way until the rod enters the timing hole in the flywheel **(see illustrations)**.

5 Insert three 8 mm bolts through the holes in the camshaft and fuel injection pump sprockets, and screw them into the engine finger-tight **(see illustrations)**.

6 The crankshaft, camshaft and injection pump are now locked in position, preventing unnecessary rotation.

3.5a Bolt (arrowed) inserted through timing hole in camshaft sprocket

3.5b Bolts (arrowed) inserted through timing holes in injection pump sprocket

3 Engine assembly/valve timing holes - general information and usage

Note: *Do not attempt to rotate the engine whilst the crankshaft/camshaft/injection pump are locked in position. If the engine is to be left in this state for a long period of time, it is a good idea to place suitable warning notices inside the vehicle, and in the engine compartment. This will reduce the possibility of the engine being accidentally cranked on the starter motor, which is likely to cause damage with the locking pins in place.*

Note: *Three 8.0 mm diameter bolts and one 8.0 mm diameter rod or drill will be required for this operation.*

1 On all models, timing holes are drilled in the camshaft sprocket, injection pump sprocket and flywheel. The holes are used to align the crankshaft, camshaft and injection pump, and to prevent the possibility of the valves

contacting the pistons when refitting the cylinder head, or when refitting the timing belt. When the holes are aligned with their corresponding holes in the cylinder head and cylinder block (as appropriate), suitable diameter bolts/pins can be inserted to lock both the camshaft, injection pump and crankshaft in position, preventing them from rotating unnecessarily. Proceed as follows.

Note: *With the timing holes aligned, No.4 cylinder is at TDC on its compression stroke.*

2 Remove the upper timing belt covers as described in Section 6.

3 The crankshaft must now be turned until the three bolt holes in the camshaft and injection pump sprockets (one hole in the camshaft sprocket, two holes in the injection pump sprocket) are aligned with the corresponding holes in the engine front plate. The crankshaft can be turned by using a spanner on the pulley bolt. To gain access to the pulley bolt, from underneath the front of the car, prise out the retaining clips and

4 Cylinder head cover - removal and refitting

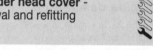

Removal

1 Remove the intercooler (Turbo models) or the air distribution housing (non-turbo models with a D9B engine) as described in Chapter 4.

2 Disconnect the breather hose from the front of the camshaft cover and, where necessary, remove the inlet duct from the inlet manifold.

3 Where applicable, unscrew the securing bolt and remove the fuel hose bracket from the right-hand end of the cylinder head cover **(see illustration)**.

4 Note the locations of any brackets secured by the three cylinder head cover retaining bolts, then unscrew the bolts. Recover the metal and fibre washers under each bolt **(see illustration)**.

5 Carefully move any hoses clear of the cylinder head cover.

6 Lift off the cover, and recover the rubber seal **(see illustration)**. Examine the seal for

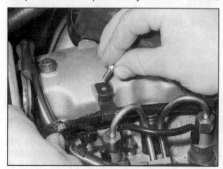

4.3 Removing the fuel hose bracket

4.4 Remove the bolts and washers . . .

4.6 . . . and lift off the cylinder head cover

signs of damage and deterioration, and if necessary, renew it. Similarly, renew the retaining bolt fibre washers if necessary.

Refitting

7 Refitting is a reversal of removal, bearing in mind the following points:

a) *Refit any brackets in their original positions noted before removal.*

b) *Where applicable, refit the intercooler or the air distribution housing, as described in Chapter 4.*

5 Crankshaft pulley - removal and refitting

Note: *It is advisable to use a new pulley retaining bolt on refitting.*

Removal

1 Remove the auxiliary drivebelt as described in Chapter 1.

2 To prevent crankshaft turning whilst the pulley retaining bolt is being slackened, select top gear and have an assistant apply the brakes firmly. If the engine has been removed from the vehicle, lock the flywheel ring gear using the arrangement shown. **Note:** *If the engine is in the car and it proves impossible to hold on the brakes, remove the starter motor and use the locking tool shown to retain the flywheel* **(see illustration).** *Do not* attempt to lock the pulley by inserting a bolt/drill through the timing hole. If the locking pin is in position, temporarily remove it prior to slackening the pulley bolt, then refit it once the bolt has been slackened.

3 Unscrew the retaining bolt and washer, then slide the pulley off the end of the crankshaft. If the pulley locating roll pin or Woodruff key (as applicable) is a loose fit, remove it and store it with the pulley for safe-keeping. If the pulley is a tight fit, it can be drawn off the crankshaft using a suitable puller.

Refitting

4 Ensure that the Woodruff key is correctly located in its crankshaft groove, or that the roll pin is in position (as applicable). Refit the pulley to the end of the crankshaft, aligning its locating groove or hole with the Woodruff key or pin.

5 **Note:** *Although not strictly necessary, it is recommended that the retaining bolt is renewed whenever it is disturbed, due to its tightening sequence (see Specifications at the start of this Chapter).* Thoroughly clean the threads of the pulley retaining bolt, then apply a coat of locking compound to the bolt threads. Peugeot recommend the use of Loctite (available from your Peugeot dealer); in the absence of this, any good-quality locking compound may be used.

6 Refit the crankshaft pulley retaining bolt and washer. Tighten the bolt to the specified

5.2 Notched tool (arrowed) positioned on ring gear teeth to lock flywheel

torque, preventing the crankshaft from turning using the method employed on removal. Once the bolt has been tightened to the Stage 1 setting, angle-tighten it through the specified Stage 2 angle, using a socket and extension bar. It is recommended that an angle-measuring gauge is used during this stage of the tightening, to ensure accuracy. If a gauge is not available, use a dab of white paint to make alignment marks between the bolt and pulley prior to tightening; the marks can then be used to check that the bolt has been rotated sufficiently during tightening.

7 Refit and tension the auxiliary drivebelt as described in Chapter 1.

6 Timing belt covers - removal and refitting

Removal

Upper front cover - early models

1 If procedures are to be carried out which involve removal of the timing belt, remove the right-hand engine mounting-to-body bracket as described in Section 9. This will greatly improve access. Where applicable, remove the air trunking from top of the cover.

2 Release the upper spring clip from the cover.

3 Release the lower securing lug using a screwdriver, then lift the cover upwards from the engine **(see illustration).**

Upper rear cover - early models

4 Remove the upper front cover as described previously.

5 Release the two securing clips, manipulate the cover over the studs on the front of the engine, then withdraw the cover upwards **(see illustration).** Clearance is limited, and if desired, access can be improved by removing the engine mounting bracket (see Section 9).

Upper front cover - later models

6 Where applicable, remove the air trunking from the top of the cover, then slacken and remove the retaining screw and nut, and remove the cover from the engine.

Upper rear cover - later models

7 Remove the front cover as described in

paragraph 6, then undo the retaining bolts and remove the rear cover from the engine.

Lower cover - early models

8 Remove the crankshaft pulley (Section 5).

9 Unscrew the two securing bolts and remove the cover **(see illustration).**

Lower cover - later models

10 Remove the crankshaft pulley (Section 5).

11 Remove both upper covers as described previously.

12 Slacken and remove the retaining nuts and bolts, and remove the lower cover.

Refitting

13 Refitting is a reversal of the relevant removal procedure, ensuring that each cover section is correctly located, and that the cover retaining nuts and/or bolts are tightened to the specified torque.

6.3 Removing the upper front timing belt cover - early models

6.5 Removing the upper rear timing belt cover - early models

6.9 Lower timing belt cover securing bolts (arrowed)

7 Timing belt - removal, inspection, refitting and tensioning

General

1 The timing belt drives the camshaft, injection pump, and coolant pump from a toothed sprocket on the front of the crankshaft. The belt also drives the brake vacuum pump indirectly via the rear ("flywheel") end of the camshaft. If the belt breaks or slips in service, the pistons are likely to hit the valve heads, resulting in expensive damage.

2 The timing belt should be renewed at the specified intervals, or earlier if it is contaminated with oil, or noisy in operation (a "scraping" noise due to uneven wear).

3 If the timing belt is being removed, it is a wise precaution to check the condition of the coolant pump at the same time (check for signs of coolant leakage). This may avoid the need to remove the timing belt again at a later stage, should the coolant pump fail.

Removal

4 Align the engine assembly/valve timing holes as described in Section 3, and lock the camshaft sprocket, injection pump sprocket and flywheel in position. *Do not* attempt to rotate the engine whilst the pins are in position.

5 Remove the crankshaft pulley (Section 5).

6 Remove the right-hand engine mounting-to-body bracket as described in Section 9.

7 Loosen the timing belt tensioner pivot nut and adjustment bolt, then turn the tensioner bracket anti-clockwise to release the tension. Retighten the adjustment bolt to hold the tensioner in the released position. If available, use a 10 mm square drive extension in the hole provided, to turn the tensioner bracket against the spring tension **(see illustration)**.

8 Mark the timing belt with an arrow to indicate its running direction, if it is to be re-used. Remove the belt from the sprockets **(see illustrations)**.

Inspection

9 Check the timing belt carefully for any signs

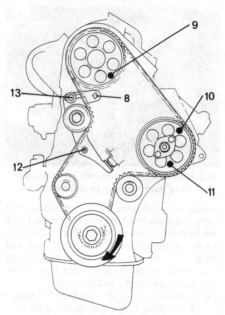

7.7 Removing the timing belt

8 Square hole
9 to 11 Bolts
12 Tensioner pivot nut
13 Adjustment bolt

of uneven wear, split or oil contamination. Pay particular attention to the roots of the teeth. Renew it if there is the slightest doubt about its condition. If the engine is undergoing an overhaul, and has covered more than 36 000 miles (60 000 km) with the existing belt fitted, renew the belt as a matter of course, regardless of its apparent condition. The cost of a new belt is nothing compared with the cost of repairs, should the belt break in service. If signs of oil contamination are found, trace the source of the oil leak and rectify it. Wash down the engine timing belt area and all related components, to remove all traces of oil. Check that the tensioner and idler pulley rotates freely, without any sign of roughness. If necessary, renew as described in Sections 9 and 10 (as applicable).

Refitting and tensioning

10 Commence refitting by ensuring the 8 mm bolts are still fitted to the camshaft and fuel

injection pump sprockets, and that the rod/drill is positioned in the timing hole in the flywheel.

11 Locate the timing belt on the crankshaft sprocket, making sure that, where applicable, the direction of rotation arrow is facing the correct way.

12 Engage the timing belt with the crankshaft sprocket, hold it in position, then feed the belt over the remaining sprockets in the following order:

a) *Idler roller.*
b) *Fuel injection pump.*
c) *Camshaft.*
d) *Tensioner roller.*
e) *Coolant pump.*

13 Be careful not to kink or twist the belt. To ensure correct engagement, locate only a half-width on the injection pump sprocket before feeding the timing belt onto the camshaft sprocket, keeping the belt taut and fully engaged with the crankshaft sprocket. Locate the timing belt fully onto the sprockets **(see illustration)**.

14 Unscrew and remove the bolts from the camshaft and fuel injection pump sprockets, and remove the rod/drill from the timing hole in the flywheel.

15 With the pivot nut loose, slacken the tensioner adjustment bolt while holding the bracket against the spring tension. Slowly release the bracket until the roller presses against the timing belt. Retighten the adjustment bolt and the pivot nut.

16 Rotate the crankshaft through two complete turns in the normal running direction (clockwise). **Do not** rotate the crankshaft backwards, as the timing belt must be kept tight between the crankshaft, fuel injection pump and camshaft sprockets.

17 Loosen the tensioner adjustment bolt and the pivot nut to allow the tensioner spring to push the roller against the timing belt, then tighten both the adjustment bolt and pivot nut to the specified torque.

18 Check that the timing holes are correctly positioned by reinserting the sprocket locking bolts and the rod/drill in the flywheel timing hole - see Section 3. If the timing holes are not correctly positioned, the timing belt has been incorrectly fitted (possibly one tooth out on one of the

7.8a Mark the timing belt with an arrow to indicate its running direction

7.8b Removing the timing belt

7.13 Locate the timing belt on the sprockets as described in text

8.2a Using a home-made tool to prevent the camshaft sprocket from turning

8.2b Holding camshaft using a spanner on the lug between Nos 3 and 4 lobes

8.7 Withdrawing the camshaft sprocket

sprockets) - in this case, repeat the refitting procedure from the beginning.

19 Refit the upper timing belt covers as described in Section 6, but do not lower the vehicle to the ground until the engine mounting-to-body bracket has been refitted.

20 Refit the right-hand engine mounting-to-body bracket, with reference to Section 9.

21 Refit the crankshaft pulley (see Section 5).

8 Timing belt sprockets - removal and refitting

Camshaft sprocket

Removal

1 Remove the upper timing belt covers as described in Section 6.

2 The camshaft sprocket bolt must now be loosened. The camshaft must be prevented from turning as the sprocket bolt is unscrewed; this can be achieved in one of two ways, as follows **(see illustrations)**. Do not remove the camshaft sprocket bolt at this stage.

a) *Make up a tool similar to that shown, and use it to hold the sprocket stationary by means of the holes in the sprocket.*

b) *Remove the cylinder head cover as described in Section 4. Prevent the camshaft from turning by holding it with a suitable spanner on the lug between Nos 3 and 4 camshaft lobes.*

3 Align the engine assembly/valve timing holes (see Section 3), and lock the camshaft sprocket, injection pump sprocket and flywheel in position. *Do not* attempt to rotate the engine whilst the pins are in position.

4 Loosen the timing belt tensioner pivot nut and adjustment bolt, then turn the tensioner bracket anti-clockwise to release the tension, and retighten the adjustment bolt to hold the tensioner in the released position. If available, use a 10 mm square drive extension in the hole provided, to turn the tensioner bracket against the spring tension.

5 Slacken and remove the camshaft sprocket retaining bolt and washer.

6 Unscrew and remove the locking bolt from the camshaft sprocket.

7 With the retaining bolt removed, slide the sprocket off the end of the camshaft **(see illustration)**. Recover the Woodruff key if it is loose. Examine the camshaft oil seal for signs of oil leakage and, if necessary, renew it as described in Section 17.

Refitting

8 Where applicable, refit the Woodruff key to the end of the camshaft, then refit the camshaft sprocket. Note that the sprocket will only fit one way round (with the protruding centre boss against the camshaft), as the end of the camshaft is tapered.

9 Refit the sprocket retaining bolt and washer. Tighten the bolt to the specified torque, preventing the camshaft from turning using one of the methods described in paragraph 2.

10 Where applicable, refit the cylinder head cover as described in Section 4.

11 Align the holes in the camshaft sprocket and the engine front plate, and refit the 8 mm bolt to lock the camshaft in position.

12 Fit the timing belt around the fuel injection pump sprocket (where applicable) and the camshaft sprocket, and tension the timing belt as described in Section 7.

13 Refit the upper timing belt covers as described in Section 6.

Crankshaft sprocket

Removal

14 Remove the crankshaft pulley (Section 5).

15 Proceed as described in paragraphs 1, 3 and 4.

16 Disengage the timing belt from the

crankshaft sprocket, and slide the sprocket off the end of the crankshaft **(see illustration)**.

17 Remove the Woodruff key from the crankshaft, and store it with the sprocket for safe-keeping **(see illustration)**.

18 Examine the crankshaft oil seal for signs of oil leakage and, if necessary, renew it as described in Section 17.

Refitting

19 Refit the Woodruff key to the end of the crankshaft, then refit the crankshaft sprocket (with the flange nearest the cylinder block).

20 Fit the timing belt around the crankshaft sprocket, and tension the timing belt as described in Section 7.

21 Refit the crankshaft pulley (see Section 5).

Fuel injection pump sprocket

Removal

22 Proceed as described in paragraphs 1, 3 and 4.

23 Make alignment marks on the fuel injection pump sprocket and the timing belt, to ensure that the sprocket and timing belt are correctly aligned on refitting.

24 Remove the 8 mm bolts securing the fuel injection pump sprocket in the TDC position.

25 On certain models, the sprocket may be fitted with a built-in puller, which consists of a plate bolted to the sprocket. The plate contains a captive nut (the sprocket securing nut), which is screwed onto the fuel injection pump shaft. On models without the built-in puller, a suitable puller can be made up using a short length of bar, and two M7 bolts screwed into the holes provided in the sprocket.

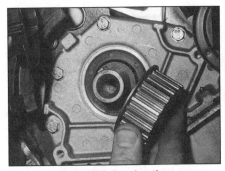

8.16 Withdrawing the crankshaft sprocket

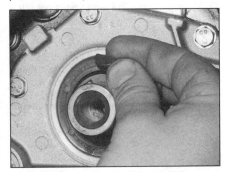

8.17 Removing the Woodruff key from the end of the crankshaft

8.26 Using a home-made tool to prevent fuel injection pump sprocket from turning

26 The fuel injection pump shaft must be prevented from turning as the sprocket nut is unscrewed, and this can be achieved using a tool similar to that shown **(see illustration)**. Use the tool to hold the sprocket stationary by means of the holes in the sprocket.

27 On models with a built-in puller, unscrew the sprocket securing nut until the sprocket is freed from the taper on the pump shaft, then withdraw the sprocket. Recover the Woodruff key from the end of the pump shaft if it is loose. If desired, the puller assembly can be removed from the sprocket by removing the two securing screws and washers.

28 On models not fitted with a built-in puller, partially unscrew the sprocket securing nut, then fit the improvised puller, and tighten the two bolts (forcing the bar against the sprocket nut), until the sprocket is freed from the taper on the pump shaft **(see illustration)**. Withdraw the sprocket, and recover the Woodruff key from the end of the pump shaft if it is loose. Remove the puller from the sprocket.

Refitting

29 Where applicable, refit the Woodruff key to the pump shaft, ensuring that it is correctly located in its groove.

30 Where applicable, if the built-in puller assembly has been removed from the sprocket, refit it, and tighten the two securing screws to the specified torque, ensuring that the washers are in place.

31 Refit the sprocket, then tighten the securing nut to the specified torque, preventing the pump shaft from turning as during removal.

32 Make sure that the 8 mm bolts are fitted to the camshaft and fuel injection pump sprockets, and that the rod/drill is positioned in the flywheel timing hole.

33 Fit the timing belt around the fuel injection pump sprocket, ensuring that the marks made on the belt and sprocket before removal are aligned.

34 Tension the timing belt as described in Section 7.

35 Refit the upper timing belt covers as described in Section 6.

Coolant pump sprocket

36 The coolant pump sprocket is integral with the pump, and cannot be removed.

8.28 Home-made puller fitted to fuel injection pump sprocket

9 Right-hand engine mounting and timing belt tensioner - removal and refitting

General

1 The timing belt tensioner is operated by a spring and plunger housed in the right-hand engine mounting bracket, which is bolted to the end face of the engine. The engine mounting is attached to the mounting on the body via the engine mounting-to-body bracket.

Right-hand engine mounting-to-body bracket

Removal

2 Before removing the bracket, the engine must be supported, preferably using a

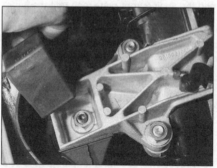

9.5 Lifting a rubber buffer from the engine mounting

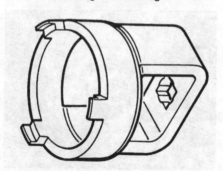

9.7a Peugeot special tool for removing and refitting right-hand engine mounting

suitable hoist and lifting tackle attached to the lifting bracket at the right-hand end of the engine. Alternatively, the engine can be supported using a trolley jack and interposed block of wood beneath the sump, in which case, be prepared for the engine to tilt backwards when the bracket is removed.

3 Release the retaining clips, and position all the relevant hoses and cables clear of the engine mounting assembly and suspension top mounting.

4 Where applicable, unscrew the two retaining bolts, and remove the plate from the top of the mounting damper bolted to the body above the mounting.

5 Where applicable, unscrew the securing nut, then lift out (or unscrew) the rubber buffer to expose the engine mounting bracket-to-body securing nut **(see illustration)**.

6 Unscrew the three nuts securing the bracket to the engine mounting, and the single nut securing the bracket to the body, then lift off the bracket **(see illustration)**.

7 To remove the rubber mounting, first lift off the buffer bracket, where applicable, then unscrew the mounting from the body. **Note:** *On certain models, if the mounting is to be removed, a special tool is needed to unscrew it from the wing panel, and for refitting and tightening to the specified torque* **(see illustrations)**.

Refitting

8 Refitting is a reversal of removal. Tighten the retaining nuts and bolts (and the rubber mounting, where applicable) to the specified torque.

9.6 Removing the engine mounting-to-body bracket

9.7b Improvised special tool for removing engine mounting

9.7c Using the tool . . .

9.7d . . . to unscrew the engine mounting

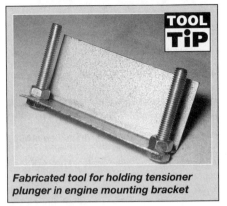

Fabricated tool for holding tensioner plunger in engine mounting bracket

Timing belt tensioner and right-hand engine mounting bracket

Note: *A suitable tool will be required to retain the timing belt tensioner plunger during this operation.*

Removal

9 Remove the engine mounting-to-body bracket as described previously, and remove the auxiliary drivebelt (see Chapter 1).

10 On models where the right-hand engine lifting bracket is attached to the right-hand engine mounting bracket, proceed as follows.

a) *If not already done, support the engine with a trolley jack and interposed block of wood beneath the sump.*

b) *Disconnect the hoist and lifting tackle supporting the engine from the right-hand lifting bracket.*

c) *Unscrew the two retaining bolts and remove the engine lifting bracket.*

11 Align the engine assembly/valve timing holes as described in Section 3, and lock the camshaft sprocket, injection pump sprocket and flywheel in position. *Do not* rotate the engine whilst the pins are in position.

12 Loosen the timing belt tensioner pivot nut and adjustment bolt, then turn the tensioner bracket anti-clockwise until the adjustment bolt is in the middle of the slot, and retighten the adjustment bolt. If available, use a 10 mm square drive extension in the hole provided, to turn the tensioner bracket against the spring tension.

13 Mark the timing belt with an arrow to indicate its running direction, if it is to be re-used. Remove the belt from the sprockets.

14 A tool must now be obtained in order to hold the tensioner plunger in the engine mounting bracket.

15 The Peugeot tool is designed to slide in the two lower bolt holes of the mounting bracket. It should be straightforward to fabricate a similar tool out of sheet metal, and using 10 mm bolts and nuts instead of metal dowel rods **(see Tool Tip)**.

16 Unscrew the two lower engine mounting bracket bolts, then fit the special tool **(see illustrations)**. Grease the inner surface of the tool, to prevent any damage to the end of the tensioner plunger. Unscrew the pivot nut and adjustment bolt, and withdraw the tensioner assembly.

17 Remove the two remaining engine mounting bracket bolts, and withdraw the bracket.

18 Compress the tensioner plunger into the engine mounting bracket, remove the special tool, then withdraw the plunger and spring.

Refitting

19 Refitting is a reversal of removal, bearing in mind the following points:

a) *Tighten all fixings to the specified torque.*

b) *Refit and tension the timing belt as described in Section 7.*

c) *Refit and tighten the auxiliary drivebelt as described in Chapter 1.*

10 Timing belt idler roller - removal and refitting

Removal

1 Remove the auxiliary drivebelt as described in Chapter 1.

2 Align the engine assembly/valve timing holes as described in Section 3, and lock the camshaft sprocket, injection pump sprocket and flywheel in position. *Do not* attempt to rotate the engine whilst the pins are in position.

3 Loosen the timing belt tensioner pivot nut and adjustment bolt, then turn the tensioner bracket anti-clockwise to release the tension, and retighten the adjustment bolt to hold the tensioner in the released position. If available, use a 10 mm square drive extension in the hole provided, to turn the tensioner bracket against the spring tension.

4 Unscrew the two bolts and the stud securing the idler roller assembly to the cylinder block, noting that the upper bolt also secures the engine mounting bracket.

5 Slightly loosen the remaining four engine mounting bolts, noting that the uppermost bolt is on the inside face of the engine front plate, and also secures the engine lifting bracket. Slide out the idler roller assembly.

Refitting

6 Refitting is a reversal of removal, bearing in mind the following points:

a) *Tighten all fixings to the specified torque.*

b) *Tension the timing belt as described in Section 7.*

c) *Refit and tension the auxiliary drivebelt as described in Chapter 1.*

2A

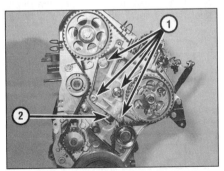

9.16a View of timing belt end of engine

1 *Engine mounting bracket retaining bolts*
2 *Timing belt tensioner plunger*

9.16b Tool in place to hold tensioner plunger in engine mounting bracket - timing belt removed for clarity

11 Camshaft and followers - removal, inspection and refitting

Note: *A new oil seal (or seals) must be used on refitting, and suitable sealing compound will be required for the end bearing caps.*

Removal

1 Remove the cylinder head cover as described in Section 4.

2 Remove the camshaft sprocket as described in Section 8.

3 On models with a brake vacuum pump driven directly from the camshaft, unbolt the pump and move it to one side, with reference to Chapter 9, then proceed to paragraph 5.

4 On models with a belt-driven brake vacuum pump, proceed as follows.

  a) *Remove the drivebelt (see Chapter 1).*
  b) *Prevent the camshaft from turning, as described previously when removing the camshaft sprocket, then unscrew the vacuum pump drive pulley bolt from the end of the camshaft and recover the thrustwasher.*
  c) *Withdraw the pulley, and recover the Woodruff key from the end of the camshaft if it is loose. If the pulley is tight, use a suitable puller to remove it.*

5 The camshaft bearing caps should be numbered from the flywheel end of the engine **(see illustration)**. If the caps are not already numbered, identify them, numbering them from the flywheel end of the engine, and making the marks on the manifold side.

6 Progressively unscrew the nuts, then remove the bearing caps **(see illustrations)**.

7 Lift the camshaft from the cylinder head **(see illustration)**. Remove the oil seal from the timing belt end of the camshaft. Discard the seal; a new one should be used on refitting.

8 Obtain eight small, clean plastic containers, and number them 1 to 8; alternatively, divide a larger container into eight compartments. Using a rubber sucker, withdraw each follower in turn, and place it in its respective container. Do not interchange the cam followers, or the rate of wear will be much increased. If necessary, also remove the shim from the top of the valve stem, and store it with its respective follower. Note that the shim may stick to the inside of the follower as it is withdrawn. If this happens, take care not to allow it to drop out as the follower is removed.

Inspection

9 Examine the camshaft bearing surfaces and cam lobes for signs of wear ridges and scoring. Renew the camshaft if any of these conditions are apparent. Examine the condition of the bearing surfaces, both on the camshaft journals and in the cylinder head/bearing caps. If the head bearing surfaces are worn excessively, the cylinder head will need to be

11.5 Camshaft bearing cap identification mark (arrowed)

11.6b . . . and remove the bearing caps

renewed. If suitable measuring equipment is available, camshaft bearing journal wear can be checked by direct measurement (where the necessary specifications have been quoted by Peugeot), noting that No 1 journal is at the transmission end of the head.

10 Examine the cam follower bearing surfaces which contact the camshaft lobes for wear ridges and scoring. Renew any follower on which these conditions are apparent. If a follower bearing surface is badly scored, also examine the corresponding lobe on the camshaft for wear, as it is likely that both will be worn. Renew worn components as necessary.

Refitting

11 Where removed, refit each shim to the top of its original valve stem. *Do not* interchange the shims, as this will upset the valve clearances (see Section 12).

12 Liberally oil the cylinder head cam follower bores and the followers. Carefully refit the followers to the cylinder head, ensuring that each follower is refitted to its original bore. Some care will be required to enter the followers squarely into their bores.

13 Lubricate the cam lobes and bearing journals with clean engine oil of the specified grade.

14 Temporarily refit the sprocket to the end of the shaft, and position it so that the sprocket timing hole is aligned with the corresponding cut-out in the cylinder head. Also ensure that the crankshaft is still locked in position (see Section 3).

15 Fit the centre bearing cap the correct way

11.6a Unscrew the nuts . . .

11.7 Lifting the camshaft from the cylinder head

round as previously noted, then screw on the nuts and tighten them two or three turns.

16 Apply sealing compound to the end bearing caps on the areas shown **(see illustration)**. Fit them in the correct positions, and tighten the nuts two or three turns.

17 Tighten all the nuts progressively to the specified torque, making sure that the camshaft remains correctly positioned.

18 Check that the camshaft endfloat is as given in the Specifications, using a feeler blade. If not, the camshaft and/or the cylinder head must be renewed. To check the endfloat, push the camshaft fully towards one end of the cylinder head, and insert a feeler blade between the thrust faces of one of the camshaft lobes and a bearing cap **(see illustration)**.

19 If the original camshaft is being refitted, and it is known that the valve clearances are correct, proceed to the next paragraph. Otherwise, check and adjust the valve

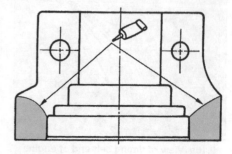

11.16 Apply sealing compound to the end camshaft bearing caps on the areas shown

11.18 Checking the camshaft endfloat using a feeler blade

clearances as described in Section 12. Note that, because the timing belt is still disconnected at this stage, the crankshaft *must* be turned one quarter-turn (either way) from the TDC position, so that all the pistons are halfway down the cylinders. This will prevent the valves striking the pistons when the camshaft is rotated. Remove the rod/drill from the flywheel timing hole, and release the timing belt from the injection pump sprocket while turning the crankshaft.

20 Smear the lips of the new oil seal with clean oil and fit it onto the camshaft end, making sure its sealing lip is facing inwards. Press the oil seal in until it is flush with the end face of the camshaft bearing cap.

21 On models with a belt-driven brake vacuum pump, refit the Woodruff key to the end of the camshaft (where applicable), then refit the pump drive pulley. Refit the thrustwasher and the pulley securing bolt, and tighten the bolt to the specified torque.

22 On models with a brake vacuum pump driven directly from the camshaft, refit the pump and tighten the securing bolts.

23 If the crankshaft has been turned a quarter-turn from TDC to prevent the valves from hitting the pistons, turn it back by the same amount so that pistons 1 and 4 are again at TDC. Do not turn the engine more than a quarter-turn, otherwise pistons 2 and 3 will pass their TDC positions, and will strike the valves.

24 Refit the rod/drill to the flywheel timing hole.

25 Refit the camshaft sprocket (Section 8).

26 Refit the cylinder head cover (Section 4).

12 Valve clearances - checking and adjustment

Checking

1 The importance of having the valve clearances correctly adjusted cannot be overstressed, as they vitally affect engine performance. Checking should not need to be a routine operation, however. It should only be necessary when the valve gear has become noisy, after engine overhaul, or when trying to trace the cause of power loss. The clearances are checked as follows. The engine must be cold for the check to be accurate.

2 Apply the handbrake, then jack up the front of the car and support it on axle stands (see "*Jacking and Vehicle Support*"). Remove the right-hand front roadwheel.

3 From underneath the front of the car, prise out the retaining clips and remove the screws (as applicable), and remove the plastic cover from the wing valance to gain access to the crankshaft sprocket bolt. Where necessary, unclip the coolant hoses from the bracket to improve access further.

4 The engine can now be turned over using a suitable socket and extension bar fitted to the crankshaft pulley bolt.

 HAYNES HINT *The engine will be easier to turn if the fuel injectors or glow plugs are removed.*

5 Remove the cylinder head cover (Section 4).

6 On a piece of paper, draw the outline of the engine with the cylinders numbered from the flywheel end. Show the position of each valve, together with the specified valve clearance. Above each valve, draw two lines for noting (1) the actual clearance and (2) the amount of adjustment required **(see illustration)**.

7 Turn the crankshaft until the inlet valve of No 1 cylinder (nearest the transmission) is fully closed, with the tip of the cam facing directly away from the bucket tappet.

8 Using feeler blades, measure the clearance between the base of the cam and the bucket tappet **(see illustration)**. Record the clearance on line (1).

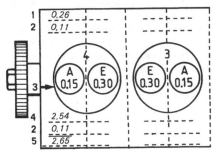

12.6 Example of valve shim thickness calculation

A Inlet
E Exhaust
1 Measured clearance
2 Difference between 1 and 3
3 Specified clearance
4 Thickness of shim fitted
5 Thickness of shim required

9 Repeat the measurement for the other seven valves, turning the crankshaft as necessary so that the cam lobe in question is always facing directly away from the relevant tappet.

10 Calculate the difference between each measured clearance and the desired value, and record it on line (2). Since the clearance is different for inlet and exhaust valves - make sure that you are aware which valve you are dealing with. The valve sequence from either end of the engine is:

In - Ex - Ex - In - In - Ex - Ex - In

11 If all the clearances are within tolerance, refit the cylinder head cover with reference to Section 4, and where applicable, lower the vehicle to the ground. If any clearance measured is outside the specified tolerance, adjustment must be carried out as described in the following paragraphs.

Adjustment

12 Remove the camshaft (see Section 11).

13 Withdraw the first follower and its shim. Be careful that the shim does not fall out of the tappet. Clean the shim, and measure its thickness with a micrometer. The shims carry thickness markings, but wear may have reduced the original thickness, so be sure to check **(see illustrations)**.

2A

12.8 Measuring a valve clearance using a feeler blade

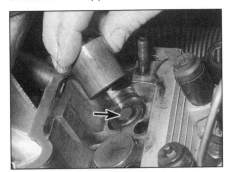

12.13a Withdrawing a cam follower - shim arrowed

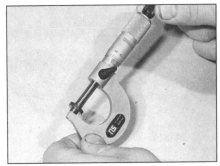

12.13b Measuring a shim thickness using a micrometer

14 Refer to the clearance recorded for the valve concerned. If the clearance was more than that specified, the shim thickness must be increased by the difference recorded (2). If the clearance was less than that specified, the thickness of the shim must be decreased by the difference recorded (2).

15 Draw three more lines beneath each valve on the calculation paper, as shown in illustration 12.6. On line (4) note the measured thickness of the shim, then add or deduct the difference from line (2) to give the final shim thickness required on line (5).

16 Repeat the procedure given in paragraphs 13 to 15 on the remaining valves, keeping each tappet identified for position.

17 When reassembling, oil the shim and fit it into the valve retainer, with the size marking face downwards. Oil the follower, and lower it onto the shim. Do not raise the follower after fitting, as the shim may become dislodged.

18 When all the followers are in position, complete with their shims, refit the camshaft as described in Section 11. Recheck the valve clearances, to make sure they are correct, before refitting the camshaft cover.

13 Cylinder head - removal and refitting

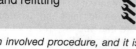

Note: *This is an involved procedure, and it is suggested that the Section is read thoroughly before starting work. To aid refitting, make notes on the locations of all relevant brackets and the routing of hoses and cables before removal. A new cylinder head gasket must be used on refitting, and new cylinder head bolts and washers may be required - see text.*

Removal

1 Disconnect the battery negative lead.

2 Drain the cooling system as described in Chapter 1.

3 Remove the inlet and exhaust manifolds (see Chapter 4). Alternatively (particularly on Turbo models), remove the inlet manifold as described in Chapter 4, then unscrew the exhaust manifold securing nuts, remove the spacers, and remove the manifold studs from the cylinder head (using a stud extractor or two nuts locked together). The exhaust manifold can then be left in place complete with the turbocharger. Ensure that the manifold and turbocharger are adequately supported, taking particular care not to strain the turbocharger oil feed pipe.

4 On models with a belt-driven brake vacuum pump, remove the drivebelt as described in Chapter 1.

5 On models with a direct-drive vacuum pump, disconnect the vacuum hose from the pump **(see illustration)**.

6 Disconnect and remove the fuel injector leak-off hoses **(see illustration)**.

7 Disconnect the fuel pipes from the fuel injectors and the fuel injection pump, and remove the pipes as described in Chapter 4.

8 Unscrew the securing nut and disconnect the feed wire from the relevant glow plug. Recover the washers.

9 Disconnect the coolant hose from the rear, left-hand end of the cylinder head **(see illustration)**.

10 Where applicable, disconnect the small coolant hose from the front timing belt end of the cylinder head **(see illustration)**.

11 Unclip the fuel return hose from the brackets on the cylinder head, and move it to one side **(see illustration)**.

12 Disconnect the accelerator cable from the fuel injection pump (with reference to Chapter 4 if necessary), and move the cable clear of the cylinder head.

13 Remove the fuel filter/thermostat housing as described in Chapter 3.

14 Unscrew the nut or stud securing the coolant hose bracket and the engine lifting bracket to the transmission end of the cylinder head.

15 Remove the camshaft sprocket as described in Section 8.

16 Remove the timing belt tensioner and the right-hand engine mounting bracket as described in Section 9.

17 Remove the timing belt idler roller as described in Section 10.

18 Remove the bolt securing the engine front plate to the fuel injection pump bracket.

19 Remove the nut and bolt securing the engine front plate and the alternator mounting bracket to the fuel injection pump mounting bracket, then remove the engine front plate.

20 Progressively unscrew the cylinder head bolts, in the reverse order to that shown in illustration 13.35 (a T55 Torx bit will be required to loosen the bolts) **(see illustration)**.

13.5 Disconnecting the vacuum hose from the braking system vacuum pump

13.6 Disconnecting a fuel injector leak-off hose

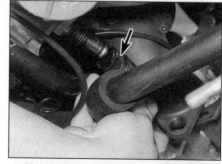

13.9 Disconnecting the coolant hose (arrowed) from the rear of the head

13.10 Disconnecting the coolant hose (arrowed) from the front of the head

13.11 Unclip the fuel return hose from its brackets

13.20 Unscrewing a cylinder head bolt

13.21 Removing a cylinder head bolt and spacer

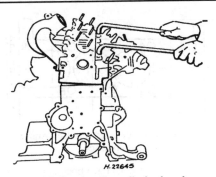

13.22 Freeing the cylinder head using angled rods

13.23 Removing the cylinder head

13.25 Measuring piston protrusion

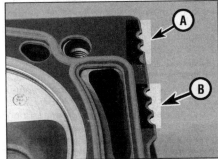

13.27 Cylinder head gasket thickness identification notches (A). Also note engine capacity/type identification notches (B)

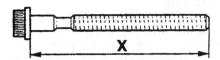

13.29a Measure length (X) of the head bolts, to decide if renewal is required - bolt without shank extension . . .

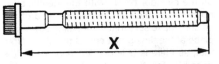

13.29b . . . and bolt with shank extension

2A

21 Lift out the bolts and recover the washers **(see illustration)**.

22 Release the cylinder head from the cylinder block and location dowel by rocking it. The Peugeot tool for doing this consists simply of two metal rods with 90-degree angled ends **(see illustration)**. Do not prise between the mating faces of the cylinder head and block, as this may damage the gasket faces.

23 Lift the cylinder head from the block, and recover the gasket **(see illustration)**.

Gasket selection

24 Check that the timing belt is clear of the fuel injection pump sprocket, then turn the crankshaft until pistons 1 and 4 are at TDC. Position a dial test indicator (dial gauge) on the cylinder block, and zero it on the block face. Transfer the probe to the centre of No 1 piston, then slowly turn the crankshaft back and forth past TDC, noting the highest reading on the indicator. Record this reading.

25 Repeat this measurement procedure on No 4 piston, then turn the crankshaft half a turn (180°) and repeat the procedure on Nos 2 and 3 pistons **(see illustration)**.

26 If a dial test indicator is not available, piston protrusion may be measured using a straight-edge and feeler blades or vernier calipers. However, these methods are inevitably less accurate, and cannot therefore be recommended.

27 Note down the greatest piston protrusion measurement, and use this to determine the correct cylinder head gasket from the

following table. Note that the notches or holes on the centre-line of the gasket identify the engine capacity and type, and have no significance for the gasket thickness **(see illustration)**.

Piston protrusion	Gasket identification
0.54 to 0.77 mm	2 notches
0.77 to 0.82 mm	3 notches

Cylinder head bolt examination

28 The manufacturers recommend that the cylinder head bolts are measured, to determine whether renewal is necessary; however, some owners may wish to renew all the bolts as a matter of course. Note that, if a bolt is modified to locate the gasket (see paragraph 31), a new bolt will be required when finally refitting the cylinder head.

29 Measure the length of each bolt from the base of the head to the end of the shank **(see illustrations)**. Compare the results with the values given in the following table, to determine whether the bolts and washers

should be renewed. **Note:** *Considering the stress which the cylinder head bolts are under, it is highly recommended that they are renewed, regardless of their apparent condition.*

1.8 litre (1769 cc) Turbo (A8A) engines and 1.9 litre (1905 cc) non-Turbo engines - bolts without shank extension

Bolt length	Action required
Up to 121.5 mm	Re-use bolts with new washers
Greater than 121.5 mm	Use new bolts and washers

1.8 litre (1769 cc) Turbo (A8A) engines and 1.9 litre (1905 cc) non-Turbo engines - bolts with shank extension

Bolt length	Action required
Up to 124.5 mm	Re-use bolts with new washers
Greater than 124.5 mm	Use new bolts and washers

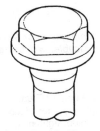

13.29c Head bolt with 16 mm across flats hexagonal head - see Specifications

13.29d Head bolt with Torx head - see Specifications

1.9 litre (1905 cc) Turbo engines - bolts without shank extension

Bolt length	Action required
Up to 146.5 mm	*Re-use bolts with new washers*
Greater than 146.5 mm	*Use new bolts and washers*

1.9 litre (1905 cc) Turbo engines - bolts with shank extension

Bolt length	Action required
Up to 151.5 mm	*Re-use bolts with new washers*
Greater than 151.5 mm	*Use new bolts and washers*

Refitting

30 Turn the crankshaft clockwise (viewed from the timing belt end) until Nos 1 and 4 pistons pass bottom dead centre (BDC) and begin to rise, then position them halfway up their bores. Nos 2 and 3 pistons will also be at their mid-way positions, but descending their bores.

31 Fit the correct gasket the right way round on the cylinder block, with the identification notches or holes at the flywheel end of the engine. Make sure that the locating dowel is in place at the timing belt end of the block. Note that, as there is only one locating dowel, it is possible for the gasket to move as the cylinder head is fitted, particularly when the cylinder head is fitted with the engine in the car (due to the inclination of the engine). In the worst instance, this can allow the pistons and/or the valves to hit the gasket, causing engine damage. To avoid this problem, saw the head off a cylinder head bolt, and file (or cut) a slot in the end of the bolt, to enable it to be turned with a screwdriver. Screw the bolt into one of the bolt holes at the flywheel/driveplate end of the cylinder block, then fit the gasket over the bolt and location dowel. This will ensure that the gasket is held in position as the cylinder head is fitted.

32 Lower the cylinder head onto the block.

33 Apply a smear of grease to the threads, and to the underside of the heads, of the cylinder head bolts. Peugeot recommend the use of Molykote G Rapid Plus (available from your Peugeot dealer); in the absence of the specified grease, any good-quality high-melting-point grease may be used. If washers are fitted under the cylinder head bolts, new ones must be used on refitting.

34 Carefully enter each bolt and washer (where applicable - convex sides uppermost) into its relevant hole (*do not drop it in*) and screw it in finger-tight. Where applicable, after fitting three or four bolts to locate the cylinder head, unscrew the modified bolt fitted in paragraph 31, and fit a new bolt in its place.

35 Working progressively and in the sequence shown, tighten the cylinder head bolts to their Stage 1 torque, using a torque wrench and suitable socket **(see illustration)**. *Note that the torque settings vary depending on the engine type, and the type of bolts used.*

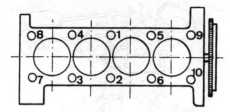

13.35 Cylinder head bolt tightening sequence

36 Once all the bolts have been tightened to the Stage 1 torque setting, fully slacken all the bolts.

37 Again, working progressively in the sequence shown in illustration 13.35, tighten the cylinder head bolts to their Stage 2 torque setting.

38 Once all the bolts have been tightened to the Stage 2 torque setting, working again in the specified sequence, angle-tighten the bolts through the specified Stage 3 angle, using a socket and extension bar. It is recommended that an angle-measuring gauge is used during this stage of tightening, to ensure accuracy. If a gauge is not available, use white paint to make alignment marks between the bolt head and cylinder head prior to tightening; the marks can then be used to check that the bolt has rotated sufficiently.

39 The remainder of the refitting procedure is a reversal of removal, noting the following points:

a) *Ensure that all wiring is correctly routed, and that all connectors are securely reconnected to the correct components.*

b) *Ensure that the coolant hoses are correctly reconnected, and that their retaining clips are securely tightened.*

c) *Ensure that all vacuum/breather hoses are correctly reconnected.*

d) *Reconnect the exhaust system to the manifold, refit the air cleaner housing and ducts, and adjust the accelerator cable, as described in Chapter 4. If the manifolds were removed, refit these as described in Chapter 4.*

e) *Refill the cooling system as described in Chapter 1.*

f) *Reconnect the battery and bleed the fuel system as described in Chapter 4.*

14 Sump - removal and refitting

Note: *A new sump gasket or suitable silicon sealant (as applicable) will be required in refitting.*

Removal

1 Disconnect the battery negative lead.

2 Drain the engine oil, then clean and refit the engine oil drain plug, tightening it securely. If the engine is nearing its service interval when the oil and filter are due for renewal, it is recommended that the filter is also removed, and a new one fitted. After reassembly, the engine can then be refilled with fresh oil. Refer to Chapter 1 for further information.

3 Apply the handbrake, jack up the front of the vehicle and support it on axle stands (see *"Jacking and Vehicle Support"*).

4 Progressively slacken and remove all the sump retaining bolts. Since the sump bolts vary in length, remove each bolt in turn, and store it in its correct fitted order by pushing it through a clearly-marked cardboard template. This will avoid the possibility of installing the bolts in the wrong locations on refitting.

5 Break the joint by striking the sump with the palm of your hand. Lower the sump, and withdraw it from underneath the vehicle. Where applicable, remove the gasket and discard it; a new one must be used on refitting.

6 While the sump is removed, take the opportunity to check the oil pump pick-up/strainer for signs of clogging or splitting. If necessary, remove the pump as described in Section 15, and clean or renew the strainer.

Refitting

7 Clean all traces of sealant/gasket from the mating surfaces of the cylinder block/crankcase and sump, then use a clean rag to wipe out the sump and the engine's interior.

8 On models where the sump is sealed by a gasket, ensure that all traces of the old gasket have been removed, and that the sump mating surfaces are clean and dry. Position the new gasket on the top of the sump, using a dab of grease to hold it in position.

9 On models where the sump is sealed using silicone sealant, apply a continuous bead of sealant to the sump mating face of the cylinder block, taking great care not to allow any sealant to enter the crankcase.

10 Offer up the sump to the cylinder block/crankcase. Refit its retaining bolts, ensuring that each is screwed into its original location. Tighten the bolts evenly and progressively to the specified torque setting. Where applicable, wipe any excess sealant from the cylinder block/sump joint.

11 Lower the vehicle to the ground, then refill the engine with oil as described in Chapter 1.

15 Oil pump and drive chain - removal, inspection and refitting

Removal

1 Remove the sump as described in Section 14.

2 Slacken and remove the three bolts securing the oil pump to the base of the cylinder block/crankcase. Disengage the pump sprocket from the chain, and remove the oil pump **(see illustration)**. Where necessary, also remove the spacer plate which is fitted behind the oil pump.

15.2 Withdrawing the oil pump

15.4a Unscrewing an oil pump cover bolt

15.4b Lift out the relief valve spring . . .

15.4c . . . and the piston

Inspection

3 Examine the oil pump sprocket for signs of damage and wear, such as chipped or missing teeth. If the sprocket is worn, the pump assembly must be renewed, since the sprocket is not available separately. It is also recommended that the chain and drive sprocket, fitted to the crankshaft, be renewed at the same time. To renew the chain and drive sprocket, first remove the crankshaft timing belt sprocket as described in Section 8. Unbolt the oil seal carrier from the cylinder block. The sprocket and chain can then be slid off the end of the crankshaft. Refer to Part B of this Chapter for further information.

4 Slacken and remove the bolts securing the strainer cover to the pump body. Lift off the strainer cover, and take off the relief valve spring and piston, noting which way round they are fitted (see illustrations).

5 Examine the pump rotors and body for signs of wear ridges or scoring. If worn, the complete pump assembly must be renewed.

6 Examine the relief valve piston for signs of wear or damage, and renew if necessary. The condition of the relief valve spring can only be measured by comparing it with a new one; if there is any doubt about its condition, it should also be renewed. Both the piston and spring are available individually.

7 Thoroughly clean the oil pump strainer with a suitable solvent, and check it for clogging or splitting. If the strainer is damaged, the strainer and cover assembly must be renewed.

8 Locate the relief valve spring and piston in the strainer cover. Refit the cover to the pump body, aligning the relief valve piston with its bore in the pump. Refit the cover retaining bolts, and tighten them securely.

Refitting

9 Offer up the spacer plate (where fitted), then locate the pump sprocket with its drive chain. Seat the pump on the base of the cylinder block/crankcase. Refit the pump bolts, and tighten to the specified torque.

10 Refit the sump as described in Section 14.

16 Oil cooler - removal and refitting

Note: A new oil cooler sealing ring will be required on refitting.

Removal

1 To improve access, firmly apply the handbrake, then jack up the front of the vehicle and support it on axle stands (see "Jacking and Vehicle Support").

2 Drain the cooling system (Chapter 1). Alternatively, clamp the oil cooler coolant hoses

16.5 Oil cooler/oil filter mounting bolt (A) and locating notch (B)

directly above the cooler, and be prepared for coolant loss as the hoses are disconnected.

3 Position a suitable container beneath the oil filter. Unscrew the filter using a filter removal tool if necessary, and drain the oil into the container. If the oil filter is damaged during removal, it must be renewed. Given the low cost of a new oil filter relative to the cost of repairing the damage which could result if a re-used filter springs a leak, it is probably a good idea to renew the filter in any case.

4 Release the hose clips, and disconnect the coolant hoses from the oil cooler.

5 Unscrew the oil cooler/oil filter bolt from the cylinder block, and withdraw the cooler. Note the locating notch in the cooler flange, which fits over the lug on the cylinder block (see illustration). Discard the oil cooler sealing ring; a new one must be used on refitting.

Refitting

6 Fit a new sealing ring to the recess in the rear of the cooler, then offer the cooler to the cylinder block.

7 Ensure that the locating notch in the cooler flange is correctly engaged with the lug on the cylinder block, then refit the mounting bolt and tighten it securely.

8 Fit the oil filter, then lower the vehicle to the ground. Top-up the engine oil level as described in "Weekly checks".

9 Refill or top-up the cooling system as described in Chapter 1 (as applicable). Start the engine, and check the oil cooler for leaks.

2A

17 Oil seals - renewal

Crankshaft timing belt end (front) oil seal

1 Remove the timing belt crankshaft sprocket as described in Section 8.

2 Measure and note the fitted depth of the oil seal.

3 Pull the oil seal from the housing using a hooked instrument. Alternatively, drill a small hole in the oil seal, and use a self-tapping screw and a pair of pliers to remove it (see illustration).

17.3 Using a self-tapping screw and pliers to remove the crankshaft front oil seal

4 Clean the oil seal housing and the crankshaft sealing surface.

5 Dip the new oil seal in clean engine oil, and press it into the housing (open end first) to the previously-noted depth, using a suitable tube or socket.

 HAYNES HINT *A piece of thin plastic or tape wound around the front of the crankshaft is useful to prevent damage to the oil seal as it is fitted.*

6 Where applicable, remove the plastic or tape from the end of the crankshaft.

7 Refit the timing belt crankshaft sprocket as described in Section 8.

Crankshaft flywheel end (rear) oil seal

8 Remove the flywheel (see Section 19).

9 Proceed as described in paragraphs 2 to 6, noting that when fitted, the outer lip of the oil seal must point outwards; if it is pointing inwards, use a piece of bent wire to pull it out. Take care not to damage the oil seal.

10 Refit the flywheel (see Section 19).

Camshaft timing belt end (front) oil seal

11 Remove the camshaft sprocket as described in Section 8. In principle there is no need to remove the timing belt completely, but remember that if the belt has been contaminated with oil, it must be renewed.

12 Hook the oil seal out from the housing using a suitable tool **(see illustration)**. Alternatively, drill a small hole in the oil seal and use a self-tapping screw and a pair of pliers to remove it.

13 Clean the oil seal housing and the camshaft sealing surface.

14 Smear the new oil seal with clean engine oil, then fit it over the end of the camshaft, open end first.

 HAYNES HINT *A piece of thin plastic or tape wound around the front of the camshaft is useful to prevent damage to the oil seal as it is fitted.*

15 Press the seal into the housing until it is flush with the end face of the cylinder head.

17.12 Removing the camshaft front oil seal

Use an M10 bolt (screwed into the end of the camshaft), washers and a suitable tube or socket to press the seal into position.

16 Refit the camshaft sprocket as described in Section 8.

17 Where applicable, fit a new timing belt as described in Section 7.

Camshaft flywheel end (rear) oil seal - models with belt-driven brake vacuum pump

18 For improved access, where applicable, remove the intercooler (Turbo models) or the air distribution housing (D9B engine) as described in Chapter 4.

19 Remove the brake vacuum pump drivebelt as described in Chapter 1.

20 The camshaft must now be prevented from turning as the vacuum pump drive pulley bolt is loosened. This can be achieved in one of two ways as follows.

  a) *Make up a tool similar to that shown in illustration 8.2a in Section 8, and use it to hold the sprocket stationary by means of the holes in the sprocket.*

  b) *Remove the camshaft cover as described in Section 4. Prevent the camshaft from turning by holding it with a suitable spanner on the lug between Nos 3 and 4 camshaft lobes (see illustration 8.2b in Section 8).*

21 Remove the vacuum pump drive pulley bolt from the end of the camshaft, then withdraw the pulley. Recover the Woodruff key if it is loose.

22 Proceed as described in paragraphs 12 to 14.

23 Press the seal into the housing until it is flush with the end face of the cylinder head. Use a suitable bolt (screwed into the end of the camshaft), washers and a tube or socket to press the seal into position.

24 Further refitting is a reversal of removal, but tighten the vacuum pump pulley bolt to the specified torque, and refit and tension the pump drivebelt as described in Chapter 1.

Camshaft flywheel end (rear) oil seal - models with direct-drive brake vacuum pump

25 No oil seal is fitted to the left-hand end of the camshaft. The sealing is provided by an O-ring fitted to the vacuum pump flange. The O-ring can be renewed after unbolting the pump from the cylinder head (see Chapter 9). Note the smaller O-ring which seals the oil feed gallery to the pump - this may also cause leakage from the pump/cylinder head mating faces if it deteriorates or fails **(see illustration)**.

18 Oil level and pressure sensors - general

Refer to Chapter 5A for details.

17.25 Camshaft left-hand oil seal (1) and oil feed gallery O-ring (2) on rear of the brake vacuum pump

19 Flywheel - removal, inspection and refitting

Note: *New flywheel securing bolts must be used on refitting.*

Removal

1 Remove the transmission as described in Chapter 7, then remove the clutch assembly as described in Chapter 6.

2 Prevent the flywheel from turning by locking the ring gear teeth with a similar arrangement to that shown in illustration 5.2 (Section 5). Alternatively, bolt a strap between the flywheel and the cylinder block/crankcase. *Do not* attempt to lock the flywheel in position using the crankshaft pulley locking pin described in Section 3.

3 Slacken and remove the flywheel bolts, and remove the flywheel from the end of the crankshaft. Take care not to drop it; it is heavy. If the flywheel locating dowel is loose in the crankshaft end, remove and store it with the flywheel for safe-keeping. Discard the flywheel bolts; new ones must be used on refitting.

Inspection

4 Examine the flywheel for scoring of the clutch face, and for wear or chipping of the ring gear teeth. If the clutch face is scored, the flywheel may be surface-ground, but renewal is preferable. Seek the advice of a Peugeot dealer or engine reconditioning specialist to see if machining is possible. If the ring gear is worn or damaged, the flywheel must be renewed, as it is not possible to renew the ring gear separately.

Refitting

5 Clean the mating surfaces of the flywheel and crankshaft. Remove any locking compound from the threads of the crankshaft holes, using the correct-size tap, if available.

 HAYNES HINT *If a suitable tap is not available, cut two slots along the threads of one of the old flywheel bolts, and use the bolt to remove the locking compound from the threads.*

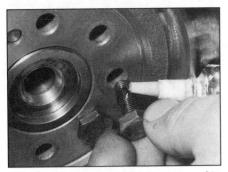

19.6 Applying thread-locking compound to the flywheel bolt threads

19.8 Tighten the flywheel bolts to the specified torque

6 If the new flywheel retaining bolts are not supplied with their threads already pre-coated, apply a suitable thread-locking compound to the threads of each bolt **(see illustration)**.

7 Ensure that the locating dowel is in position. Offer up the flywheel, locating it on the dowel, and fit the new retaining bolts.

8 Lock the flywheel using the method employed on removal, and tighten the retaining bolts to the specified torque **(see illustration)**.

9 Refit the clutch as described in Chapter 6. Remove the flywheel locking tool, and refit the transmission as described in Chapter 7.

---

20 Engine/transmission mountings - inspection and renewal

Inspection

1 If improved access is required, raise the front of the car and support it securely on axle stands (see *"Jacking and Vehicle Support"*).

2 Check the mounting rubber to see if it is cracked, hardened or separated from the metal at any point; renew the mounting if any such damage or deterioration is evident.

3 Check that all the mounting's fasteners are securely tightened; use a torque wrench to check if possible.

4 Using a large screwdriver or a crowbar,

check for wear in the mounting by carefully levering against it to check for free play. Where this is not possible, enlist the aid of an assistant to move the engine/transmission back and forth, or from side to side, while you watch the mounting. While some free play is to be expected even from new components, excessive wear should be obvious. If excessive free play is found, check first that the fasteners are correctly secured, then renew any worn components as described below.

Renewal

Right-hand mounting

5 Refer to Section 9.

Left-hand mounting

6 To improve access, remove the air cleaner (see Chapter 4), and if desired, the battery and battery tray (see Chapter 5A).

7 Place a jack beneath the transmission, with a block of wood on the jack head. Raise the jack until it is supporting the weight of the transmission.

8 Slacken and remove the centre nut and washer from the left-hand mounting, then undo the fixings securing the mounting in position and remove it from the engine compartment.

9 If necessary, slide the spacer (where fitted) off the mounting stud, then unscrew the stud from the top of the transmission housing, and remove it along with its washer. If the

mounting stud is tight, a universal stud extractor can be used to unscrew it.

10 Check all components carefully for signs of wear or damage, and renew as necessary.

11 Clean the threads of the mounting stud, and apply a coat of thread-locking compound to its threads. Refit the stud and washer to the top of the transmission, and tighten it to the specified torque setting.

12 Slide the spacer (where fitted) onto the mounting stud, then refit the rubber mounting. Tighten both the mounting-to-body fixings and the mounting centre nut to their specified torque settings, and remove the jack from underneath the transmission.

13 Where applicable, refit the battery support plate and the battery as described in Chapter 5A, and refit the air cleaner as described in Chapter 4.

Rear mounting

14 If not already done, firmly apply the handbrake, then jack up the front of the vehicle and support it securely on axle stands (see *"Jacking and Vehicle Support"*).

15 Unscrew and remove the bolt securing the rear mounting link to the mounting on the rear of the cylinder block.

16 Remove the bolt securing the rear mounting link to the bracket on the underbody. Withdraw the link.

17 To remove the mounting assembly it will first be necessary to remove the right-hand driveshaft as described in Chapter 8.

18 With the driveshaft removed, undo the retaining bolts and remove the mounting from the rear of the cylinder block.

19 Check carefully for signs of wear or damage on all components, and renew them where necessary.

20 On reassembly, fit the rear mounting assembly to the rear of the cylinder block, and tighten its retaining bolts to the specified torque.

21 Refit the driveshaft as described in Chapter 8.

22 Refit the rear mounting link, and tighten both its bolts to their specified torque settings.

23 Lower the vehicle to the ground.

2A

Chapter 2 Part B:
Engine removal and overhaul procedures

Contents

Degrees of difficulty

Easy, suitable for novice with little experience	**Fairly easy,** suitable for beginner with some experience	**Fairly difficult,** suitable for competent DIY mechanic	**Difficult,** suitable for experienced DIY mechanic	**Very difficult,** suitable for expert DIY or professional

2B

Specifications

Note: *At the time of writing, many specifications for certain engines were not available. Where the relevant specifications are not given here, refer to your Peugeot dealer for further information.*

Cylinder head
Maximum gasket face distortion	0.07 mm (the camshaft must turn freely)
Cylinder head nominal height	157.40 to 157.75 mm
Maximum permissible gasket face refinishing limit	
(in relation to nominal height)	0.4 mm
Swirl chamber protrusion	0 to 0.03 mm

Valves
Valve head diameter:	
Inlet	38.5 mm
Exhaust	33.0 mm
Valve stem diameter:	
Inlet	7.990 to 8.005 mm
Exhaust	7.970 to 7.985 mm

Cylinder block
Cylinder bore diameter:	
1.8 litre (1769 cc) engine:	
Standard	80.000 to 80.018 mm
Production oversize A1	80.030 to 80.048 mm
Oversize R1	80.200 to 80.218 mm
Oversize R2	80.500 to 80.518 mm
Oversize R3	80.800 to 80.818 mm
1.9 litre (1905 cc) engine:	
Standard	83.000 to 83.018 mm
Production oversize A1	83.030 to 83.048 mm
1st oversize R1	83.200 to 83.218 mm
2nd oversize R2	83.500 to 83.518 mm
3rd oversize R3	83.800 to 83.818 mm

Pistons

Piston diameter:

1.8 litre (1769 cc) engine:

Standard	79.930 ± 0.009 mm
Production oversize A1	79.960 ± 0.009 mm
Oversize R1	80.130 ± 0.009 mm
Oversize R2	80.430 ± 0.009 mm
Oversize R3	80.730 ± 0.009 mm

1.9 litre (1905 cc) engine:

Standard	82.930 ± 0.009 mm
Production oversize A1	82.960 ± 0.009 mm
1st oversize R1	83.130 ± 0.009 mm
2nd oversize R2	83.430 ± 0.009 mm
3rd oversize R3	83.730 ± 0.009 mm

Crankshaft

Endfloat	0.07 to 0.32 mm

Main bearing journal diameter:

Standard	59.981 to 60.000 mm
Undersize	59.681 to 59.700 mm

Big-end bearing journal diameter:

Standard	49.984 to 50.000 mm
Undersize	49.681 to 49.700 mm
Maximum bearing journal out-of-round	0.007 mm
Main bearing running clearance *	0.025 to 0.050 mm
Big-end bearing running clearance*	0.025 to 0.050 mm

These are suggested figures, typical for this type of engine - no exact values are stated by Peugeot.

Piston rings

End gaps:

Top and second compression rings	0.20 to 0.40 mm
Oil control ring	0.25 to 0.50 mm

Torque wrench settings

Refer to Chapter 2A Specifications.

1 General information

Included in this Part of Chapter 2 are details of removing the engine/transmission from the car and general overhaul procedures for the cylinder head, cylinder block/crankcase and all other engine internal components.

The information given ranges from advice concerning preparation for an overhaul and the purchase of replacement parts, to detailed step-by-step procedures covering removal, inspection, renovation and refitting of engine internal components.

After Section 6, all instructions are based on the assumption that the engine has been removed from the car. For information concerning in-car engine repair, as well as the removal and refitting of those external components necessary for full overhaul, refer to Part A of this Chapter and to Section 6. Ignore any preliminary dismantling operations described in Part A that are no longer relevant once the engine has been removed from the car.

Apart from torque wrench settings, which are given at the beginning of Part A, all specifications relating to engine overhaul are at the beginning of this Part of Chapter 2.

2 Engine overhaul - general information

1 It is not always easy to determine when, or if, an engine should be completely overhauled, as a number of factors must be considered.

2 High mileage is not necessarily an indication that an overhaul is needed, while low mileage does not preclude the need for an overhaul. Frequency of servicing is probably the most important consideration. An engine which has had regular and frequent oil and filter changes, as well as other required maintenance, should give many thousands of miles of reliable service. Conversely, a neglected engine may require an overhaul very early in its life.

3 Excessive oil consumption is an indication that piston rings, valve seals and/or valve guides are in need of attention. Make sure that oil leaks are not responsible before deciding that the rings and/or guides are worn. Perform a compression or leakdown test, as described in Part A of this Chapter, to determine the likely cause of the problem.

4 Check the oil pressure with a gauge fitted in place of the oil pressure switch, and compare it with that specified. If it is extremely low, the main and big-end bearings, and/or the oil pump, are probably worn out.

5 Loss of power, rough running, knocking or metallic engine noises, excessive valve gear noise, and high fuel consumption may also point to the need for an overhaul, especially if they are all present at the same time. If a complete service does not remedy the situation, major mechanical work is the only solution.

6 A full engine overhaul involves restoring all internal parts to the specification of a new engine. During a complete overhaul, the pistons and the piston rings are renewed, and the cylinder bores are reconditioned. New main and big-end bearings are generally fitted; if necessary, the crankshaft may be reground, to compensate for wear in the journals. The valves are also serviced as well, since they are usually in less-than-perfect condition at this point. Always pay careful attention to the condition of the oil pump when overhauling the engine, and renew it if there is any doubt as to its serviceability. The end result should be an as-new engine that will give many trouble-free miles.

Note: *Critical cooling system components such as the hoses, thermostat and water pump should be renewed when an engine is overhauled. The radiator should be checked carefully, to ensure that it is not clogged or leaking. Also, it is a good idea to renew the oil pump whenever the engine is overhauled.*

7 Before beginning the engine overhaul, read through the entire procedure, to familiarise yourself with the scope and requirements of the job. Overhauling an engine is not difficult if you follow carefully all of the instructions, have the necessary tools and equipment, and pay close attention to all specifications. It can, however, be time-consuming. Plan on the car being off the road for a minimum of two weeks, especially if parts must be taken to an engineering works for repair or reconditioning. Check on the availability of parts and make sure that any necessary special tools and equipment are obtained in advance. Most work can be done with typical hand tools, although a number of precision measuring tools are required for inspecting parts to determine if they must be renewed. Often the engineering works will handle the inspection of parts and offer advice concerning reconditioning and renewal.

Note: *Always wait until the engine has been completely dismantled, and until all components (especially the cylinder block/crankcase and the crankshaft) have been inspected, before deciding what service and repair operations must be performed by an engineering works. The condition of these components will be the major factor to consider when determining whether to overhaul the original engine, or to buy a reconditioned unit. Do not, therefore, purchase parts or have overhaul work done on other components until they have been thoroughly inspected. As a general rule, time is the primary cost of an overhaul, so it does not pay to fit worn or sub-standard parts.*

8 As a final note, to ensure maximum life and minimum trouble from a reconditioned engine, everything must be assembled with care, in a spotlessly-clean environment.

3 Engine/transmission removal - methods and precautions

1 If you have decided that the engine must be removed for overhaul or major repair work, several preliminary steps should be taken.

2 Locating a suitable place to work is extremely important. Adequate work space, along with storage space for the car, will be needed. If a workshop or garage is not available, at the very least, a flat, level, clean work surface is required.

3 Cleaning the engine compartment and engine/transmission before beginning the removal procedure will help keep tools clean and organised.

4 An engine hoist or A-frame will also be necessary. Make sure the equipment is rated in excess of the combined weight of the engine and transmission. Safety is of primary importance, considering the potential hazards involved in lifting the engine/transmission out of the car.

5 If this is the first time you have removed an engine, an assistant should ideally be available. Advice and aid from someone more experienced would also be helpful. There are many instances when one person cannot simultaneously perform all of the operations required when lifting the engine out of the vehicle.

6 Plan the operation ahead of time. Before starting work, arrange for the hire of or obtain all of the tools and equipment you will need. Some of the equipment necessary to perform engine/transmission removal and installation safely and with relative ease (in addition to an engine hoist) is as follows: a heavy duty trolley jack, complete sets of spanners and sockets (see *"Tools and Working Facilities"*), wooden blocks, and plenty of rags and cleaning solvent for mopping up spilled oil, coolant and fuel. If the hoist must be hired, make sure that you arrange for it in advance, and perform all of the operations possible without it beforehand. This will save you money and time.

7 Plan for the car to be out of use for quite a while. An engineering works will be required to perform some of the work which the do-it-yourselfer cannot accomplish without special equipment. These places often have a busy schedule, so it would be a good idea to consult them before removing the engine, in order to accurately estimate the amount of time required to rebuild or repair components that may need work.

8 Always be extremely careful when removing and refitting the engine/transmission. Serious injury can result from careless actions. Plan ahead and take your time, and a job of this nature, although major, can be accomplished successfully.

4 Engine and manual transmission - removal, separation and refitting

Note: *Peugeot recommend that the engine is removed by lowering from the engine compartment, however in practise we found that on models not fitted with air conditioning, there is ample room to lift the engine upwards. Lowering the engine would involve raising the front of the vehicle onto axle stands approximately 500 mm high and also removing the front suspension subframe. On models fitted with air conditioning the engine may be lowered, or alternatively it can be lifted after removing the condenser and the body front panel assembly (the refrigerant must first be evacuated by a qualified engineer if this method is used).*

Removal

Note: *The engine can be removed from the car only as a complete unit with the transmission; the two are then separated for overhaul. An engine hoist and lifting tackle will be required for this operation.*

1 Park the car on firm, level ground. Chock

4.2 Battery tray securing bolts (arrowed)

the rear wheels, then firmly apply the handbrake. Jack up the front of the vehicle, and securely support it on axle stands (see *"Jacking and Vehicle Support"*). Remove both front roadwheels.

2 Set the bonnet in the upright position, and remove the battery and tray (where applicable) as described in Chapter 5A **(see illustration)**.

3 Remove the body front panel assembly with reference to Chapter 11 (see note at the beginning of this Section).

4 Remove the complete air cleaner housing and duct assembly, referring to Chapter 4.

5 If the engine is to be dismantled, working as described in Chapter 1, first drain the oil and remove the oil filter. Clean and refit the drain plug, tightening it securely.

6 Drain the transmission oil as described in Chapter 7. Refit the drain and filler plugs, and tighten them to their specified torque settings.

7 Remove the alternator (see Chapter 5A).

8 Where applicable, remove the power steering pump as described in Chapter 10.

9 On models with air conditioning, unbolt the compressor, and position it clear of the engine. Support the weight of the compressor by tying it to the vehicle body, to prevent any excess strain being placed on the compressor lines whilst the engine is removed. Do not disconnect the refrigerant lines from the compressor (refer to the warnings given in Chapter 3).

10 Drain the cooling system (Chapter 1), then remove the radiator (Chapter 3).

11 Carry out the following operations, using the information given in the relevant Chapters.

a) *Disconnect the fuel supply and return hoses from the fuel injection pump (Chapter 4).*

b) *Where applicable, remove the intercooler or the air distribution housing (Chapter 4).*

c) *Disconnect the accelerator cable from the fuel injection pump, and move it clear of the engine (Chapter 4).*

d) *Disconnect the wiring connector(s) from the fuel injection pump (Chapter 4).*

e) *Disconnect the glow plug feed wire (Chapter 5B).*

f) *Disconnect the brake servo vacuum hose from the vacuum pump (Chapter 9).*

g) *Remove the exhaust system frontpipe (Chapter 4).*

2B

4.13 Disconnecting the clutch cable

4.15 Remove the rear engine/transmission mounting link (arrowed)

12 Referring to Chapter 3, release the retaining clips and disconnect the heater matrix hoses from their connection on the engine compartment bulkhead.

13 Working as described in Chapter 6, disconnect the clutch cable from the transmission, and position it clear of the working area **(see illustration)**.

14 Trace the wiring harness back from the engine to the wiring connector(s) in the engine compartment. Where applicable, release the locking ring(s) by twisting them anti-clockwise and disconnect the connectors. Where applicable, also trace the harness lead(s) back to the relay box, located at the front left-hand corner of the engine compartment, or in the left-hand corner of the scuttle. Unclip the wiring connector plate from the front of the relay box cover then undo the retaining nut and remove the cover. Lift up the engine harness lead cover then undo the nut(s) and release the lead(s) from the relay box. Check that all the relevant connectors have been disconnected, and that the wiring is released from any relevant clips or ties, so that it is free to be removed with the engine/transmission.

15 From underneath the vehicle, slacken and remove the nuts and bolts securing the rear engine/transmission mounting link to the mounting assembly and subframe, and remove the link **(see illustration)**.

16 Disconnect the inboard ends of the driveshafts from the transmission, as described in Chapter 8.

17 Carry out the following operations, using the information given in Chapter 7.

a) *Disconnect the gearchange selector rod/link rods (as applicable) from the transmission.*
b) *Disconnect the speedometer cable from the speedometer drive.*
c) *Disconnect the wiring connector(s) from the reversing light switch and speedometer drive (as applicable).*

18 Manoeuvre the engine hoist into position, and attach the lifting tackle to the lifting brackets bolted onto the cylinder head. Raise the hoist until it is supporting the weight of the engine.

19 Remove the right-hand engine mounting bracket with reference to Part A of this Chapter.

20 On some Turbo models, to give sufficient clearance to enable the engine to be removed from above the engine compartment, it is necessary to remove the turbocharger. Where applicable, remove the turbocharger as described in Chapter 4.

21 Unscrew the nut from the left-hand engine mounting and recover the washer, then unbolt the mounting bracket from the body. Where the bracket is welded in position undo the nuts and washers and remove the rubber mounting

22 Make a final check that any components which would prevent the removal of the engine/transmission from the car have been removed or disconnected. Ensure that components such as the gearchange selector rod are secured so that they cannot be damaged on removal. Ensure that all relevant wiring, hoses and pipes are disconnected and/or released from any brackets attached to the engine/transmission.

23 On models where the battery tray is welded to the body, it is necessary to tilt the engine steeply in order for the transmission to clear the battery tray as the engine/transmission assembly is removed. Where this is the case, support the transmission on a trolley jack. Using the trolley jack, lower the transmission, whilst adjusting the lifting tackle to tilt the engine/transmission assembly.

24 Lift the engine/transmission out of the car, ensuring that nothing is trapped or damaged. Enlist the help of an assistant during this procedure, as it will be necessary to tilt the assembly slightly to clear the body panels. On models equipped with anti-lock brakes, great care must be taken to ensure that the anti-lock braking system unit is not damaged during the removal procedure.

25 Once the engine is high enough, lift it out over the front of the body, and lower the unit to the ground.

Separation

26 With the engine/transmission assembly removed, support the assembly on suitable blocks of wood, on a workbench (or failing that, on a clean area of the workshop floor).

27 Undo the retaining bolts, and remove the flywheel lower cover plate (where fitted) from the transmission.

28 On models with a "pull-type" clutch

release mechanism (see Chapter 6 for further information), tap out the retaining pin or unscrew the retaining bolt (as applicable), and remove the clutch release lever from the top of the release fork shaft. This is necessary to allow the fork shaft to rotate freely, so that it disengages from the release bearing as the transmission is pulled away from the engine. Make an alignment mark across the centre of the clutch release fork shaft, using a scriber, paint or similar, and mark its relative position on the transmission housing (see Chapter 7 for further information).

29 Unscrew the securing bolts, and remove the starter motor from the transmission.

30 Ensure that both engine and transmission are adequately supported, then slacken and remove the remaining bolts securing the transmission to the engine. Note the correct fitted positions of each bolt (and the relevant brackets) as they are removed, to use as a reference on refitting.

31 Carefully withdraw the transmission from the engine, ensuring that the weight of the transmission is not allowed to hang on the input shaft while it is engaged with the clutch friction disc.

32 If they are loose, remove the locating dowels from the engine or transmission, and keep them in a safe place.

33 On models with a "pull-type" clutch, make a second alignment mark on the transmission housing, marking the relative position of the release fork mark after removal. This should indicate the angle at which the release fork is positioned. The mark can then be used to position the release fork prior to installation, to ensure that the fork correctly engages with the clutch release bearing as the transmission is installed.

Refitting

34 If the engine and transmission have been separated, perform the operations described below in paragraphs 35 to 43. If not, proceed to paragraph 44.

35 Apply a smear of high-melting-point grease (Peugeot recommend the use of Molykote BR2 plus - available from your Peugeot dealer) to the splines of the transmission input shaft. Do not apply too much, otherwise there is a possibility of the grease contaminating the clutch friction plate.

36 Ensure that the locating dowels are correctly positioned in the engine or transmission, as applicable.

37 On models with a "pull-type" clutch, before refitting, position the clutch release bearing so that its arrow mark is pointing upwards (bearing fork slots facing towards the front of the engine), and align the release fork shaft mark with the second mark made on the transmission housing (release fork positioned at approximately 60° to clutch housing face). This will ensure that the release fork and bearing will engage correctly as the transmission is refitted to the engine.

38 Carefully offer the transmission to the

engine, until the locating dowels are engaged. Ensure that the weight of the transmission is not allowed to hang on the input shaft as it is engaged with the clutch friction disc.

39 On models with a "pull-type" clutch, with the transmission fully engaged with the engine, check that the release fork and bearing are correctly engaged. If the release fork and bearing are correctly engaged, the mark on the release fork should be aligned with the original mark made on the transmission housing (see Chapter 7 for further information).

40 Refit the transmission-to-engine bolts, ensuring that all the necessary brackets are correctly positioned, and tighten them to the specified torque setting.

41 Refit the starter motor, and securely tighten its retaining bolts.

42 On models with a "pull-type" clutch release mechanism, refit the clutch release lever to the top of the release fork shaft, securing it in position with its retaining pin or bolt (as applicable).

43 Where necessary, refit the lower flywheel cover plate to the transmission, and securely tighten its retaining bolts.

44 Reconnect the hoist and lifting tackle to the engine lifting brackets. With the aid of an assistant, lift the assembly over the engine compartment.

45 The assembly should be tilted as necessary to clear the surrounding components, as during removal; lower the assembly into position in the engine compartment, manipulating the hoist and lifting tackle as necessary. Where necessary, support the transmission using a trolley jack, as during removal.

46 With the engine supported in position in the engine compartment, where applicable, refit the turbocharger, referring to Chapter 4.

47 With the engine/transmission in position, refit the right-hand engine mounting bracket (refer to Part A of this Chapter if necessary). Tighten the mounting nuts/bolts by hand only at this stage.

48 Working on the left-hand mounting, refit the mounting bracket (where removed) to the body and tighten its retaining bolts to the specified torque. Refit the mounting rubber and (where applicable) refit the mounting retaining nuts and washers and the centre nut and washer, tightening them lightly only.

49 From underneath the vehicle, refit the rear engine/transmission mounting link.

50 Rock the engine to settle it on its mountings then go around and tighten all the mounting nuts and bolts to their specified torque settings. Where necessary, once the right-hand mounting bracket nuts have been tightened, refit the rubber damper and curved retaining plate, tightening its retaining bolts to the specified torque. The hoist can then be detached from the engine and removed.

51 The remainder of the refitting procedure is a direct reversal of the removal sequence, noting the following points.

a) Ensure that all wiring is correctly routed and retained by all the relevant retaining clips; all connectors should be correctly and securely reconnected.

b) Prior to reconnecting the driveshafts to the transmission, renew the driveshaft oil seals as described in Chapter 7. Reconnect the driveshafts with reference to Chapter 8.

c) Ensure that all coolant hoses are correctly reconnected, and securely retained by their retaining clips.

d) Adjust the clutch cable as described in Chapter 6.

e) Adjust the accelerator cable as described in Chapter 4.

f) Refill the engine and transmission with correct quantity and type of lubricant, as described in Chapter 7.

g) Refill the cooling system as described in Chapter 1.

h) Bleed the fuel system as described in Chapter 4.

5 Engine overhaul - dismantling sequence

1 It is much easier to dismantle and work on the engine if it is mounted on a portable engine stand. These stands can often be hired from a tool hire shop. Before the engine is mounted on a stand, the flywheel/driveplate should be removed, so that the stand bolts can be tightened into the end of the cylinder block/crankcase.

2 If a stand is not available, it is possible to dismantle the engine with it blocked up on a sturdy workbench, or on the floor. Be extra-careful not to tip or drop the engine when working without a stand.

3 If you are going to obtain a reconditioned engine, all the external components must be removed first, to be transferred to the replacement engine (just as they will if you are doing a complete engine overhaul yourself). These components include the following:

a) Alternator mounting brackets.

b) Power steering pump and air conditioning compressor brackets (where fitted).

c) Thermostat and housing - early models (Chapter 3).

d) Fuel filter/thermostat housing - later models (Chapter 3).

e) Dipstick tube.

f) Fuel injection pump (Chapter 4).

g) All electrical switches and sensors.

h) Inlet and exhaust manifolds (Chapter 4).

i) Oil filter (Chapter 1).

j) Flywheel (Part A of this Chapter).

Note: When removing the external components from the engine, pay close attention to details that may be helpful or important during refitting. Note the fitted position of gaskets, seals, spacers, pins, washers, bolts, and other small items.

4 If you are obtaining a "short" engine (which

consists of the engine cylinder block/crankcase, crankshaft, pistons and connecting rods all assembled), then the cylinder head, sump, oil pump, and timing belt will have to be removed also.

5 If you are planning a complete overhaul, the engine can be dismantled, and the internal components removed, in the order given below, referring to Part A of this Chapter unless otherwise stated.

a) Inlet and exhaust manifolds (Chapter 4).

b) Timing belt, sprockets and tensioner(s).

c) Cylinder head.

d) Flywheel.

e) Sump.

f) Oil pump.

g) Piston/connecting rod assemblies (Section 9).

h) Crankshaft (Section 10).

6 Before beginning the dismantling and overhaul procedures, make sure that you have all of the correct tools necessary. Refer to *"Tools and working facilities"* for further information.

6 Cylinder head - dismantling

Note: *New and reconditioned cylinder heads are available from the manufacturer, and from engine overhaul specialists. Be aware that some specialist tools are required for the dismantling and inspection procedures, and new components may not be readily available. It may therefore be more practical and economical for the home mechanic to purchase a reconditioned head, rather than dismantle, inspect and recondition the original head. A valve spring compressor tool will be required for this operation.*

1 Remove the cylinder head as described in Part A of this Chapter.

2 If not already done, remove the inlet and exhaust manifolds, referring to Chapter 4.

3 Remove the camshaft, followers and shims as described in Part A of this Chapter.

4 Remove the glow plugs (Chapter 5B), and the injectors (Chapter 4).

5 Using a valve spring compressor, compress each valve spring in turn until the split collets can be removed. Release the compressor, and lift off the spring retainer, spring and spring seat (note that some engines have double valve springs). Where applicable, using a pair of pliers, carefully extract the valve stem oil seal from the top of the guide **(see illustrations)**.

6 If, when the valve spring compressor is screwed down, the spring retainer refuses to free and expose the split collets, gently tap the top of the tool, directly over the retainer, with a light hammer. This will free the retainer.

7 Withdraw the valve through the combustion chamber.

8 It is essential that each valve is stored together with its collets, retainer, spring, and

6.5a Compress the valve spring using a spring compressor . . .

6.5b . . . then extract the collets and release the spring compressor

6.5c Remove the spring retainer . . .

6.5d . . . followed by the valve spring . . .

6.5e . . . and the spring seat

6.5f Remove the valve stem oil seal using a pair of pliers

6.8 Place each valve and its associated components in a labelled polythene bag

spring seat. The valves should also be kept in their correct sequence, unless they are so badly worn that they are to be renewed. If they are going to be kept and used again, place each valve assembly in a labelled polythene bag or similar small container (see illustration). Note that No 1 valve is nearest to the transmission (flywheel) end of the engine.

9 If necessary, remove the timing probe balking plug from the timing belt end (injector side) of the cylinder head.

7 Cylinder head and valves - cleaning and inspection

1 Thorough cleaning of the cylinder head and valve components, followed by a detailed inspection, will enable you to decide how much valve service work must be carried out

during the engine overhaul. Note: If the engine has been severely overheated, it is best to assume that the cylinder head is warped - check carefully for signs of this.

Cleaning

2 Scrape away all traces of old gasket material from the cylinder head.
3 Scrape away the carbon from the combustion chambers and ports, then wash the cylinder head thoroughly with paraffin or a suitable solvent.
4 Scrape off any heavy carbon deposits that may have formed on the valves, then use a power-operated wire brush to remove deposits from the valve heads and stems.

Inspection

Note: Be sure to perform all the following inspection procedures before concluding that the services of a machine shop or engine overhaul specialist are required. Make a list of all items that require attention.

Cylinder head

5 Inspect the head very carefully for cracks, evidence of coolant leakage, and other damage. If cracks are found, a new cylinder head should be obtained.
6 Use a straight-edge and feeler blade to check that the cylinder head gasket surface is not distorted (see illustration). If it is, it may be possible to have it machined, provided that the cylinder head is not reduced to less than the specified height. Note: It will be necessary to recut the combustion chambers and valve seats if more than 0.1 mm has been machined

off the cylinder head. This is necessary in order to maintain the correct dimensions between the valve heads, valve guides and cylinder head gasket face.
7 Examine the valve seats in each of the combustion chambers. If they are severely pitted, cracked, or burned, they will need to be renewed or re-cut by an engine overhaul specialist. If they are only slightly pitted, this can be removed by grinding-in the valve heads and seats with fine valve-grinding compound, as described below.
8 Check the valve guides for wear by inserting the relevant valve, and checking for side-to-side motion of the valve. A very small amount of movement is acceptable. If the movement seems excessive, remove the valve. Measure the valve stem diameter (see later in this Section), and renew the valve if it is worn. If the valve stem is not worn, the wear must be in the valve guide, and the guide

7.6 Checking the cylinder head gasket surface for distortion

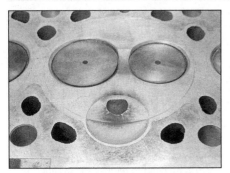

7.10a This swirl chamber shows the initial stages of cracking and burning

7.10b Checking a swirl chamber protrusion

7.12 Measuring a valve stem diameter

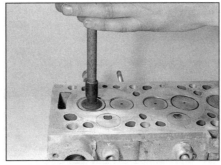

7.15 Grinding-in a valve

a smooth unbroken ring of light grey matt finish is produced on both the valve and seat, the grinding operation is complete. *Do not* grind-in the valves any further than absolutely necessary, or the seat will be prematurely sunk into the cylinder head.

17 When all the valves have been ground-in, carefully wash off *all* traces of grinding compound using paraffin or a suitable solvent, before reassembling the cylinder head.

Valve components

18 Examine the valve springs for signs of damage and discoloration. No minimum free length is specified by Peugeot, so the only way of judging valve spring wear is by comparison with a new component.

19 Stand each spring on a flat surface, and check it for squareness. If any of the springs are damaged, distorted or have lost their tension, obtain a complete new set of springs. It is normal to renew the valve springs as a matter of course if a major overhaul is being carried out.

20 Where applicable, renew the valve stem oil seals regardless of their apparent condition.

Cam followers

21 Examine the surfaces of the cam followers for wear or scoring. If excessive wear is evident, the cam follower should be renewed.

8 Cylinder head - reassembly

2B

Note: *Valve stem oil seals may or may not be fitted, depending on the type of cylinder head. When reassembling the cylinder head, consult a Peugeot dealer as to whether oil seals should be fitted on reassembly, particularly if a new cylinder head is being fitted.*

1 Lubricate the stems of the valves, and insert the valves into their original locations **(see illustration)**. If new valves are being fitted, insert them into the locations to which they have been ground.

2 Refit the spring seat then, where applicable, working on the first valve, dip the new valve stem seal in fresh engine oil. Carefully locate it over the valve and onto the guide. Take care

8.1 Lubricate the valve stems prior to refitting

must be renewed. The renewal of valve guides is best carried out by a Peugeot dealer or engine overhaul specialist, who will have the necessary tools available.

9 If renewing the valve guides, the valve seats should be re-cut or re-ground only *after* the guides have been fitted.

10 Inspect the swirl chambers for burning or damage such as cracking. Small cracks in the chambers are acceptable; renewal of the chambers will only be required if chamber tracts are badly burned and disfigured, or if they are no longer a tight fit in the cylinder head. If there is any doubt as to the swirl chamber condition, seek the advice of a Peugeot dealer or a suitable repairer who specialises in diesel engines. Swirl chamber renewal should be entrusted to a specialist. Using a dial test indicator, check that the swirl chamber protrusion is within the limits given in the Specifications. Zero the dial test indicator on the gasket surface of the cylinder head, then measure the protrusion of the swirl chamber. If the protrusion is not within the specified limits, the advice of a Peugeot dealer or suitable repairer who specialises in diesel engines should be sought **(see illustrations)**.

Valves

11 Examine the head of each valve for pitting, burning, cracks, and general wear. Check the valve stem for scoring and wear ridges. Rotate the valve, and check for any obvious indication that it is bent. Look for pits or excessive wear on the tip of each valve stem. Renew any valve that shows any such signs of wear or damage.

12 If the valve appears satisfactory at this stage, measure the valve stem diameter at several points using a micrometer **(see illustration)**. Any significant difference in the readings obtained indicates wear of the valve stem. Should any of these conditions be apparent, the valve(s) must be renewed.

13 If the valves are in satisfactory condition, they should be ground (lapped) into their respective seats, to ensure a smooth, gas-tight seal. If the seat is only lightly pitted, or if it has been re-cut, fine grinding compound *only* should be used to produce the required finish. Coarse valve-grinding compound should *not* be used, unless a seat is badly burned or deeply pitted. If this is the case, the cylinder head and valves should be inspected by an expert, to decide whether seat re-cutting, or even the renewal of the valve or seat insert (where possible) is required.

14 Valve grinding is carried out as follows. Place the cylinder head upside-down on a bench.

15 Smear a trace of (the appropriate grade of) valve-grinding compound on the seat face, and press a suction grinding tool onto the valve head **(see illustration)**. With a semi-rotary action, grind the valve head to its seat, lifting the valve occasionally to redistribute the grinding compound. A light spring placed under the valve head will greatly ease this operation.

16 If coarse grinding compound is being used, work only until a dull, matt even surface is produced on both the valve seat and the valve, then wipe off the used compound, and repeat the process with fine compound. When

8.2 Fitting a valve stem oil seal using a socket

9.5 Removing a big-end bearing cap and shell

not to damage the seal as it is passed over the valve stem. Use a suitable socket or metal tube to press the seal firmly onto the guide **(see illustration)**.

3 Locate the valve spring(s) on top of the seat, then refit the spring retainer.

4 Compress the valve spring(s), and locate the split collets in the recess in the valve stem. Release the compressor, then repeat the procedure on the remaining valves

Use a dab of grease to hold the collets in position on the valve stem while the spring compressor is released.

5 With all the valves installed, place the cylinder head flat on the bench and, using a hammer and interposed block of wood, tap the end of each valve stem to settle the components.

6 Refit the camshaft, followers and shims as described in Part A of this Chapter.

7 The cylinder head can then be refitted as described in Part A of this Chapter.

9 Piston/connecting rod assembly - removal

1 Remove the cylinder head, sump and oil pump as described in Part A of this Chapter.

2 If there is a pronounced wear ridge at the top of any bore, it may be necessary to remove it with a scraper or ridge reamer, to

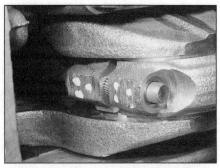

9.3 Connecting rod and big-end bearing cap marked for identification (No 3 shown)

9.6 To protect the journals, tape over the connecting rod stud threads before removal

avoid piston damage during removal. Such a ridge indicates excessive wear of the cylinder bore.

3 Using a hammer and centre-punch, paint or similar, mark each connecting rod and big-end bearing cap with its respective cylinder number on the flat machined surface provided; if the engine has been dismantled before, note carefully any identifying marks made previously **(see illustration)**. Note that No 1 cylinder is at the transmission (flywheel) end of the engine.

4 Turn the crankshaft to bring pistons 1 and 4 to BDC (bottom dead centre).

5 Unscrew the nuts from No 1 piston big-end bearing cap. Take off the cap, and recover the bottom half bearing shell **(see illustration)**. If the bearing shells are to be re-used, tape the cap and the shell together.

6 To prevent the possibility of damage to the crankshaft bearing journals, tape over the connecting rod stud threads **(see illustration)**.

7 Using a hammer handle, push the piston up through the bore, and remove it from the top of the cylinder block. Recover the bearing shell, and tape it to the connecting rod for safe-keeping.

8 Loosely refit the big-end cap to the connecting rod, and secure with the nuts - this will help to keep the components in their correct order.

9 Remove No 4 piston assembly in the same way.

10 Turn the crankshaft through 180° to bring pistons 2 and 3 to BDC (bottom dead centre), and remove them in the same way.

10 Crankshaft - removal

1 Remove the crankshaft sprocket and the oil pump as described in Part A of this Chapter.

2 Remove the flywheel as described in Part A of this Chapter.

3 Remove the pistons and connecting rods, as described in Section 9. If no work is to be done on the pistons and connecting rods, there is no need to remove the cylinder head, or to push the pistons out of the cylinder bores. The pistons should just be pushed far enough up the bores so that they are positioned clear of the crankshaft journals.

4 Check the crankshaft endfloat as described in Section 13, then proceed as follows.

5 Slacken and remove the retaining bolts, and remove the oil seal carrier from the front (timing belt) end of the cylinder block, along with its gasket (where fitted) **(see illustration)**.

6 Remove the oil pump drive chain, and slide the drive sprocket and spacer (where fitted) off the end of the crankshaft. Remove the Woodruff key, and store it with the sprocket for safe-keeping **(see illustrations)**.

7 The main bearing caps should be numbered 1 to 5, starting from the transmission (flywheel) end of the engine **(see illustration)**. If not, mark them accordingly using a centre-punch. Also note the correct fitted depth of the rear crankshaft oil seal in the bearing cap.

8 On all engines, slacken and remove the main bearing cap retaining bolts/nuts, and lift

10.5 Removing the oil seal carrier from the front of the cylinder block

10.6a Remove the oil pump drive chain . . .

10.6b ... then slide off the drive sprocket ...

10.6c ... and remove the Woodruff key from the crankshaft

10.7 Main bearing cap identification markings (arrowed)

10.8 Removing No 2 main bearing cap. Note the thrustwasher (arrowed)

10.9 Lifting out the crankshaft

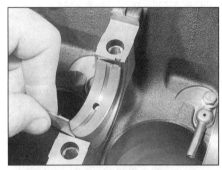

10.10 Remove the upper main bearing shells from the cylinder block/crankcase, and store them with their lower shells

off each bearing cap. Recover the lower bearing shells, and tape them to their respective caps for safe-keeping. Also recover the lower thrustwasher halves from the side of No 2 main bearing cap **(see illustration)**. Remove the rubber sealing strips from the sides of No 1 main bearing cap, and discard them.

9 Lift out the crankshaft **(see illustration)**, and discard the rear oil seal.

10 Recover the upper bearing shells from the cylinder block **(see illustration)**, and tape them to their respective caps for safe-keeping. Remove the upper thrustwasher halves from the side of No 2 main bearing, and store them with the lower halves.

11 Cylinder block/crankcase - cleaning and inspection

Cleaning

1 Remove all external components and electrical switches/sensors from the block. For complete cleaning, the core plugs should ideally be removed **(see illustration)**. Drill a small hole in the plugs, then insert a self-tapping screw into the hole. Pull out the plugs by pulling on the screw with a pair of grips, or by using a slide hammer.

2 On Turbo engines, undo the retaining bolts and remove the piston oil jet spray tubes from inside the cylinder block **(see illustrations)**.

3 Scrape all traces of gasket from the cylinder block/crankcase, taking care not to damage the gasket/sealing surfaces.

4 Remove all oil gallery plugs (where fitted). The plugs are usually very tight - they may

have to be drilled out, and the holes re-tapped. Use new plugs when the engine is reassembled **(see illustration)**.

5 If any of the castings are extremely dirty, all should be steam-cleaned.

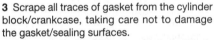

11.1 Cylinder block core plugs (arrowed)

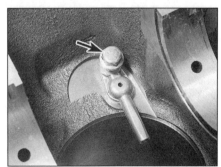

11.2a Unscrew the bolts (arrowed) ...

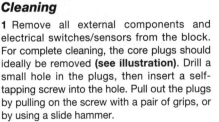

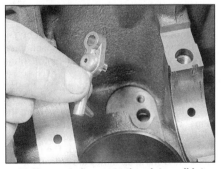

11.2b ... and remove the piston oil jet spray tubes - Turbo engines

11.4 Removing an oil gallery plug

6 After the castings are returned, clean all oil holes and oil galleries one more time. Flush all internal passages with warm water until the water runs clear. Dry thoroughly, and apply a light film of oil to all mating surfaces, to prevent rusting. Also oil the cylinder bores. If you have access to compressed air, use it to speed up the drying process, and to blow out all the oil holes and galleries.

 Warning: Wear eye protection when using compressed air!

7 If the castings are not very dirty, you can do an adequate cleaning job with hot (as hot as you can stand!), soapy water and a stiff brush. Take plenty of time, and do a thorough job. Regardless of the cleaning method used, be sure to clean all oil holes and galleries very thoroughly, and to dry all components well. Protect the cylinder bores as described above, to prevent rusting.

8 All threaded holes must be clean, to ensure accurate torque readings during reassembly. To clean the threads, run the correct-size tap into each of the holes to remove rust, corrosion, thread sealant or sludge, and to restore damaged threads **(see illustration)**. If possible, use compressed air to clear the holes of debris produced by this operation.

 HAYNES HiNT *A good alternative is to inject aerosol-applied water-dispersant lubricant into each hole, using the long spout usually supplied. Wear eye protection when cleaning out these holes in this way!*

9 Ensure that all threaded holes in the cylinder block are dry.

10 After coating the mating surfaces of the new core plugs with suitable sealant, fit them to the cylinder block. Make sure that they are driven in straight and seated correctly, or leakage could result.

 HAYNES HiNT *A large socket with an outside diameter which will just fit into the core plug can be used to drive core plugs into position.*

11.8 Cleaning a cylinder block threaded hole using a suitable tap

11 Apply suitable sealant to the new oil gallery plugs, and insert them into the holes in the block. Tighten them securely.

12 On Turbo engines, clean the threads of the piston oil jet retaining bolts, and apply a drop of thread-locking compound to the bolt threads. Refit the piston oil jet spray tubes to the cylinder block, and tighten the retaining bolts to the specified torque setting.

13 If the engine is not going to be reassembled right away, cover it with a large plastic bag to keep it clean; protect all mating surfaces and the cylinder bores as described above, to prevent rusting.

Inspection

14 Visually check the castings for cracks and corrosion. Look for stripped threads in the threaded holes. If there has been any history of internal water leakage, it may be worthwhile having an engine overhaul specialist check the cylinder block/crankcase with special equipment. If defects are found, have them repaired if possible, or renew the assembly.

15 Check each cylinder bore for scuffing and scoring. Check for signs of a wear ridge at the top of the cylinder, indicating that the bore is excessively worn.

16 If the necessary measuring equipment is available, measure the bore diameter of each cylinder liner at the top (just under the wear ridge), centre, and bottom of the cylinder bore, parallel to the crankshaft axis.

17 Next, measure the bore diameter at the same three locations, at right-angles to the crankshaft axis. Compare the results with the figures given in the Specifications. If there is any doubt about the condition of the cylinder bores, seek the advice of a Peugeot dealer or suitable engine reconditioning specialist.

18 If the cylinder bore wear exceeds the permitted tolerances, or if the cylinder walls are badly scored or scuffed, then the cylinders will have to be rebored by a suitably-qualified specialist, and new oversize pistons will have to be fitted. A Peugeot dealer or engineering workshop will normally be able to supply suitable oversize pistons when carrying out the reboring work.

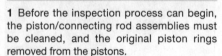

12 Piston/connecting rod assembly - inspection

1 Before the inspection process can begin, the piston/connecting rod assemblies must be cleaned, and the original piston rings removed from the pistons.

2 Carefully expand the old rings over the top of the pistons. The use of two or three old feeler blades will be helpful in preventing the rings dropping into empty grooves **(see illustration)**. Be careful not to scratch the piston with the ends of the ring. The rings are brittle, and will snap if they are spread too far. They are also very sharp - protect your hands and fingers. Note that the third ring

12.2 Removing a piston ring with the aid of a feeler blade

incorporates an expander. Always remove the rings from the top of the piston. Keep each set of rings with its piston if the old rings are to be re-used.

3 Scrape away all traces of carbon from the top of the piston. A hand-held wire brush (or a piece of fine emery cloth) can be used, once the majority of the deposits have been scraped away.

4 Remove the carbon from the ring grooves in the piston, using an old ring. Break the ring in half to do this (be careful not to cut your fingers - piston rings are sharp). Be careful to remove only the carbon deposits - do not remove any metal, and do not nick or scratch the sides of the ring grooves.

5 Once the deposits have been removed, clean the piston/connecting rod assembly with paraffin or a suitable solvent, and dry thoroughly. Make sure that the oil return holes in the ring grooves are clear.

6 If the pistons and cylinder bores are not damaged or worn excessively, and if the cylinder block does not need to be rebored, the original pistons can be refitted. Measure the piston diameters, and check that they are within limits for the corresponding bore diameters **(see illustration)**. If the piston-to-bore clearance is excessive, the block will have to be rebored, and new pistons and rings fitted. Normal piston wear shows up as even vertical wear on the piston thrust surfaces, and slight looseness of the top ring in its groove. New piston rings should always be used when the engine is reassembled.

7 Carefully inspect each piston for cracks around the skirt, around the gudgeon pin

12.6 Measuring a piston diameter using a micrometer

12.14a Prise out the circlip . . .

12.14b . . . withdraw the gudgeon pin . . .

12.14c . . . and separate the piston from the connecting rod

holes, and at the piston ring "lands" (between the ring grooves).

8 Look for scoring and scuffing on the piston skirt, holes in the piston crown, and burned areas at the edge of the crown. If the skirt is scored or scuffed, the engine may have been suffering from overheating, and/or abnormal combustion which caused excessively high operating temperatures. The cooling and lubrication systems should be checked thoroughly. Scorch marks on the sides of the pistons show that blow-by has occurred. A hole in the piston crown, or burned areas at the edge of the piston crown, indicates that abnormal combustion (pre-ignition, knocking, or detonation) has been occurring. If any of the above problems exist, the causes must be investigated and corrected, or the damage will occur again. The causes may include incorrect injection pump timing, or a faulty injector.

9 Corrosion of the piston, in the form of pitting, indicates that coolant has been leaking into the combustion chamber and/or the crankcase. Again, the cause must be corrected, or the problem may persist in the rebuilt engine.

10 New pistons can be purchased from a Peugeot dealer.

11 Examine each connecting rod carefully for signs of damage, such as cracks around the big-end and small-end bearings. Check that

the rod is not bent or distorted. Damage is highly unlikely, unless the engine has been seized or badly overheated. Detailed checking of the connecting rod assembly can only be carried out by a Peugeot dealer or engine repair specialist with the necessary equipment.

12 Due to the tightening procedure for the connecting rod big-end cap nuts, it is highly recommended that the big-end cap nuts and bolts are renewed as a set prior to refitting.

13 The gudgeon pins are of the floating type, secured by two circlips. The pistons and connecting rods can be separated as follows.

14 Using a small flat-bladed screwdriver, prise out the circlips, and push out the gudgeon pin **(see illustrations)**. Hand pressure should be sufficient to remove the pin. Identify the piston and rod to ensure correct reassembly. Discard the circlips - new ones *must* be used on refitting.

15 Examine the gudgeon pin and connecting rod small-end bearing for signs of wear or damage. Wear can be cured by renewing both the pin and bush. Bush renewal, however, is a specialist job - press facilities are required, and the new bush must be reamed accurately.

16 The connecting rods themselves should not need renewal, unless seizure or some other major mechanical failure has occurred. Check the alignment of the connecting rods visually, and if the rods are not straight, take them to an engine specialist.

17 Examine all components, and obtain any new parts from your Peugeot dealer. If new pistons are purchased, they will be supplied complete with gudgeon pins and circlips. Circlips can also be purchased individually.

18 Position the piston so that the cloverleaf recess in the piston crown is positioned as shown in relation to the connecting rod big-end bearing shell cut-out **(see illustration)**. Apply a smear of clean engine oil to the gudgeon pin. Slide it into the piston and through the connecting rod small-end. Check that the piston pivots freely on the rod, then secure the gudgeon pin in position with two new circlips. Ensure that each circlip is correctly located in its groove in the piston.

13 Crankshaft - inspection

Checking crankshaft endfloat

1 If the crankshaft endfloat is to be checked, this must be done when the crankshaft is still installed in the cylinder block/crankcase, but is free to move (see Section 10).

2 Check the endfloat using a dial gauge in contact with the end of the crankshaft. Push the crankshaft fully one way, and then zero the gauge. Push the crankshaft fully the other way, and check the endfloat. The result can be compared with the specified amount, and will give an indication as to whether new thrustwashers are required **(see illustration)**.

3 If a dial gauge is not available, feeler blades can be used. First push the crankshaft fully towards the flywheel end of the engine, then use feeler blades to measure the gap between the web of No 2 crankpin and the thrustwasher **(see illustration)**.

2B

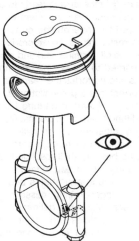

12.18 The cloverleaf recess in the crown must face the same way as the bearing shell cut-out in the connecting rod

13.2 Checking crankshaft endfloat using a dial gauge

13.3 Checking crankshaft endfloat using feeler blades

Inspection

4 Clean the crankshaft using paraffin or a suitable solvent, and dry it, preferably with compressed air if available. Be sure to clean the oil holes with a pipe cleaner or similar probe, to ensure that they are not obstructed.

> ⚠️ **Warning: Wear eye protection when using compressed air!**

5 Check the main and big-end bearing journals for uneven wear, scoring, pitting and cracking.
6 Big-end bearing wear is accompanied by distinct metallic knocking when the engine is running (particularly noticeable when the engine is pulling from low speed) and some loss of oil pressure.
7 Main bearing wear is accompanied by severe engine vibration and rumble - getting progressively worse as engine speed increases - and again by loss of oil pressure.
8 Check the bearing journal for roughness by running a finger lightly over the bearing surface. Any roughness (which will be accompanied by obvious bearing wear) indicates that the crankshaft requires regrinding (where possible) or renewal.
9 If the crankshaft has been reground, check for burrs around the crankshaft oil holes (the holes are usually chamfered, so burrs should not be a problem unless regrinding has been carried out carelessly). Remove any burrs with a fine file or scraper, and thoroughly clean the oil holes as described previously.
10 Using a micrometer, measure the diameter of the main and big-end bearing journals, and compare the results with the Specifications **(see illustration)**. By measuring the diameter at a number of points around each journal's circumference, you will be able to determine whether or not the journal is out-of-round. Take the measurement at each end of the journal, near the webs, to determine if the journal is tapered. Compare the results obtained with those given in the Specifications.
11 Check the oil seal contact surfaces at each end of the crankshaft for wear and damage. If the seal has worn a deep groove in the surface of the crankshaft, consult an engine overhaul specialist; repair may be possible, but otherwise a new crankshaft will be required.

13.10 Measuring a crankshaft big-end journal diameter

12 If the crankshaft journals have not already been reground, it may be possible to have the crankshaft reconditioned, and to fit oversize shells (see Section 17). If no oversize shells are available and the crankshaft has worn beyond the specified limits, it will have to be renewed. Consult your Peugeot dealer or engine specialist for further information on parts availability.

14 Main and big-end bearings - inspection

1 Even though the main and big-end bearings should be renewed during the engine overhaul, the old bearings should be retained for close examination, as they may reveal valuable information about the condition of the engine. The bearing shells are graded by thickness, the grade of each shell being indicated by the colour code marked on it.
2 Bearing failure can occur due to lack of lubrication, the presence of dirt or other foreign particles, overloading the engine, or corrosion **(see illustration)**. Regardless of the cause of bearing failure, the cause must be corrected (where applicable) before the engine is reassembled, to prevent it from happening again.
3 When examining the bearing shells, remove them from the cylinder block/crankcase, the connecting rods and the connecting rod big-end bearing caps. Lay them out on a clean surface in the same general position as their location in the engine. This will enable you to match any bearing problems with the corresponding crankshaft journal. *Do not* touch any shell's bearing surface with your fingers while checking it, or the delicate surface may be scratched.
4 Dirt and other foreign matter gets into the

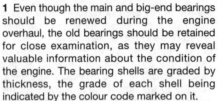

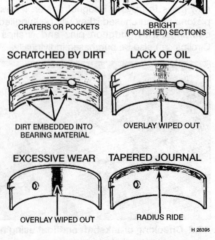

FATIGUE FAILURE	IMPROPER SEATING
CRATERS OR POCKETS	BRIGHT (POLISHED) SECTIONS
SCRATCHED BY DIRT	LACK OF OIL
DIRT EMBEDDED INTO BEARING MATERIAL	OVERLAY WIPED OUT
EXCESSIVE WEAR	TAPERED JOURNAL
OVERLAY WIPED OUT	RADIUS RIDE

H 28395

14.2 Typical bearing failures

engine in a variety of ways. It may be left in the engine during assembly, or it may pass through filters or the crankcase ventilation system. It may get into the oil, and from there into the bearings. Metal chips from machining operations and normal engine wear are often present. Abrasives are sometimes left in engine components after reconditioning, especially when parts are not thoroughly cleaned using the proper cleaning methods. Whatever the source, these foreign objects often end up embedded in the soft bearing material, and are easily recognised. Large particles will not embed in the bearing, and will score or gouge the bearing and journal. The best prevention for this cause of bearing failure is to clean all parts thoroughly, and keep everything spotlessly-clean during engine assembly. Frequent and regular engine oil and filter changes are also recommended.
5 Lack of lubrication (or lubrication breakdown) has a number of interrelated causes. Excessive heat (which thins the oil), overloading (which squeezes the oil from the bearing face) and oil leakage (from excessive bearing clearances, worn oil pump or high engine speeds) all contribute to lubrication breakdown. Blocked oil passages, which usually are the result of misaligned oil holes in a bearing shell, will also oil-starve a bearing, and destroy it. When lack of lubrication is the cause of bearing failure, the bearing material is wiped or extruded from the steel backing of the bearing. Temperatures may increase to the point where the steel backing turns blue from overheating.
6 Driving habits can have a definite effect on bearing life. Full-throttle, low-speed operation (labouring the engine) puts very high loads on bearings, tending to squeeze out the oil film. These loads cause the bearings to flex, which produces fine cracks in the bearing face (fatigue failure). Eventually, the bearing material will loosen in pieces, and tear away from the steel backing.
7 Short-distance driving leads to corrosion of bearings, because insufficient engine heat is produced to drive off the condensed water and corrosive gases. These products collect in the engine oil, forming acid and sludge. As the oil is carried to the engine bearings, the acid attacks and corrodes the bearing material.
8 Incorrect bearing installation during engine assembly will lead to bearing failure as well. Tight-fitting bearings leave insufficient bearing running clearance, and will result in oil starvation. Dirt or foreign particles trapped behind a bearing shell result in high spots on the bearing, which lead to failure.
9 *Do not* touch any shell's bearing surface with your fingers during reassembly; there is a risk of scratching the delicate surface, or of depositing particles of dirt on it.
10 As mentioned at the beginning of this Section, the bearing shells should be renewed as a matter of course during engine overhaul; to do otherwise is false economy. Refer to Section 17 for details of bearing shell selection.

15 Engine overhaul - reassembly sequence

1 Before reassembly begins, ensure that all new parts have been obtained, and that all necessary tools are available. Read through the entire procedure to familiarise yourself with the work involved, and to ensure that all items necessary for reassembly of the engine are at hand. In addition to all normal tools and materials, thread-locking compound will be needed. A suitable tube of liquid sealant will also be required for the joint faces that are fitted without gaskets. It is recommended that Peugeot's own product(s) are used, which are specially formulated for this purpose; the relevant product names are quoted in the text of each Section where they are required.

2 In order to save time and avoid problems, engine reassembly can be carried out in the following order:

a) Crankshaft (Section 17).
b) Piston/connecting rod assemblies (Section 18).
c) Oil pump (See Part A of this Chapter) .
d) Sump (See Part A of this Chapter).
e) Flywheel (See Part A of this Chapter).
f) Cylinder head (See Part A of this Chapter).
g) Timing belt tensioner and sprockets, and timing belt (See Part A of this Chapter).
h) Engine external components.

3 At this stage, all engine components should be absolutely clean and dry, with all faults repaired. The components should be laid out (or in individual containers) on a completely clean work surface.

16 Piston rings - refitting

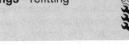

1 Before fitting new piston rings, the ring end gaps must be checked as follows.

2 Lay out the piston/connecting rod assemblies and the new piston ring sets, so that the ring sets will be matched with the same piston and cylinder during the end gap measurement and subsequent engine reassembly.

3 Insert the top ring into the first cylinder, and

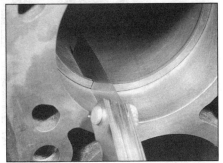

16.5 Measuring a piston ring end gap

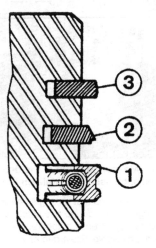

16.10 Piston ring fitting diagram (typical)

1 Oil control ring
2 Second compression ring
3 Top compression ring

push it down the bore using the top of the piston. This will ensure that the ring remains square with the cylinder walls. Position the ring near the bottom of the cylinder bore, at the lower limit of ring travel. Note that the top and second compression rings are different. The second ring is easily identified by the step on its lower surface, and by the fact that its outer face is tapered.

4 Measure the end gap using feeler blades.

5 Repeat the procedure with the ring at the top of the cylinder bore, at the upper limit of its travel **(see illustration)**, and compare the measurements with the figures given in the Specifications.

6 If the gap is too small (unlikely if genuine Peugeot parts are used), it must be enlarged, or the ring ends may contact each other during engine operation, causing serious damage. Ideally, new piston rings providing the correct end gap should be fitted. As a last resort, the end gap can be increased by filing the ring ends very carefully with a fine file. Mount the file in a vice equipped with soft jaws, slip the ring over the file with the ends contacting the file face, and slowly move the ring to remove material from the ends. Take care, as piston rings are sharp, and are easily broken.

7 With new piston rings, it is unlikely that the end gap will be too large. If the gaps are too large, check that you have the correct rings for your engine and for the particular cylinder bore size.

8 Repeat the checking procedure for each ring in the first cylinder, and then for the rings in the remaining cylinders. Remember to keep rings, pistons and cylinders matched up.

9 Once the ring end gaps have been checked and if necessary corrected, the rings can be fitted to the pistons.

10 Fit the piston rings using the same technique as for removal. Fit the bottom (oil

control) ring first, and work up. When fitting the oil control ring, first insert the expander (where fitted), then fit the ring with its gap positioned 180° from the expander gap. Ensure that the second compression ring is fitted the correct way up, with its identification mark (either a dot of paint or the word "TOP" stamped on the ring surface) at the top, and the stepped surface at the bottom **(see illustration)**. Arrange the gaps of the top and second compression rings 120° either side of the oil control ring gap. **Note:** *Always follow any instructions supplied with the new piston ring sets - different manufacturers may specify different procedures. Do not mix up the top and second compression rings, as they have different cross-sections.*

17 Crankshaft - refitting and main bearing running clearance check

Selection of new bearing shells

1 On all engines both the upper and lower bearing shells are of the same thickness. Peugeot produce both a standard set of shells and undersize shells.

Main bearing running clearance check

2 The running clearance check can be carried out using the original bearing shells. However, it is preferable to use a new set, since the results obtained will be more conclusive.

3 Clean the backs of the bearing shells, and the bearing locations in both the cylinder block/crankcase and the main bearing caps.

4 Press the bearing shells into their locations, ensuring that the tab on each shell engages in the notch in the cylinder block/crankcase or bearing cap. Take care not to touch any shell's bearing surface with your fingers. Note that the upper bearing shells all have a grooved bearing surface, whereas the lower shells have a plain bearing surface **(see illustration)**. If the original bearing shells are being used for the check, ensure that they are refitted in their original locations.

5 The clearance can be checked in either of two ways.

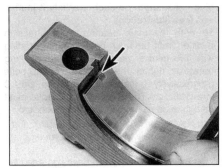

17.4 The lower shells have a plain bearing surface. Ensure that the tab (arrowed) is correctly located in the cap

2B

17.9 Plastigage in place on a crankshaft main bearing journal

17.12 Measuring width of the deformed Plastigage using the scale on the card

6 One method (which will be difficult to achieve without a range of internal micrometers or internal/external expanding calipers) is to refit the main bearing caps to the cylinder block/crankcase, with bearing shells in place. With the cap retaining bolts tightened to the specified torque, measure the internal diameter of each assembled pair of bearing shells. If the diameter of each corresponding crankshaft journal is measured and then subtracted from the bearing internal diameter, the result will be the main bearing running clearance.

7 The second (and more accurate) method is to use an American product known as "Plastigage". This consists of a fine thread of perfectly-round plastic, which is compressed between the bearing shell and the journal. When the shell is removed, the plastic is deformed, and can be measured with a special card gauge supplied with the kit. The running clearance is determined from this gauge. Plastigage should be available from your Peugeot dealer (Part number 9769 42); otherwise, enquiries at one of the larger specialist motor factors should produce the name of a stockist in your area. The procedure for using Plastigage is as follows.

8 With the main bearing upper shells in place, carefully lay the crankshaft in position. Do not use any lubricant; the crankshaft journals and bearing shells must be perfectly clean and dry.

9 Cut several lengths of the appropriate-size Plastigage (they should be slightly shorter than the width of the main bearings), and place one length on each crankshaft journal axis **(see illustration)**.

10 With the main bearing lower shells in position, refit the main bearing caps. Starting with the centre main bearing and working outwards, tighten the main bearing cap bolts progressively to their specified torque. On 1.9 litre (1905 cc) Turbo engines, the bolts must be tightened using the following procedure.

   a) Tighten the bearing cap bolts evenly and progressively to the Stage 1 torque setting.

   b) Once all the bolts have been tightened to the Stage 1 setting, angle-tighten them through the specified Stage 2 angle, using a socket and extension bar. It is

recommended that an angle-measuring gauge is used during this stage of the tightening, to ensure accuracy. If a gauge is not available, use a dab of white paint to make alignment marks between the bolt and bearing cap prior to tightening; the marks can then be used to check that the bolt has been rotated sufficiently during tightening.

Take care not to disturb the Plastigage, and *do not* rotate the crankshaft at any time during this operation.

11 Remove the main bearing cap bolts and carefully lift off the caps, keeping then in order. Again, take great care not to disturb the Plastigage or rotate the crankshaft. If any of the bearing caps are difficult to remove, free them by carefully tapping them with a soft-faced mallet.

12 Compare the width of the crushed Plastigage on each journal to the scale printed on the Plastigage envelope, to obtain the main bearing running clearance **(see illustration)**. Compare the clearance measured with that given in the Specifications at the start of this Chapter.

13 If the clearance is significantly different from that expected, the bearing shells may be the wrong size (or excessively worn, if the original shells are being re-used). Before deciding that different-size shells are required, make sure that no dirt or oil was trapped between the bearing shells and the caps or block when the clearance was measured. If the Plastigage was wider at one end than at the other, the crankshaft journal may be tapered.

14 If the clearance is not as specified, use the reading obtained to calculate the necessary grade of bearing shells required. When calculating the bearing clearance required, bear in mind that it is always better to have the running clearance towards the lower end of the specified range, to allow for wear in use.

15 Where necessary, obtain the required grades of bearing shell, and repeat the running clearance checking procedure as described above.

16 On completion, carefully scrape away all traces of the Plastigage material from the crankshaft and bearing shells. Use your fingernail, or a wooden or plastic scraper which is unlikely to score the bearing surfaces.

Final crankshaft refitting

17 Carefully lift the crankshaft out of the cylinder block once more.

18 Using a little grease, stick the upper thrustwashers to each side of the No 2 main bearing upper location. Ensure that the oilway grooves on each thrustwasher face outwards (away from the cylinder block) **(see illustration)**.

19 Place the bearing shells in their locations as described earlier. If new shells are being fitted, ensure that all traces of protective grease are cleaned off using paraffin. Wipe dry the shells and connecting rods with a lint-free cloth. Liberally lubricate each bearing shell in the cylinder block/crankcase and cap with clean engine oil **(see illustration)**.

20 Lower the crankshaft into position so that Nos 2 and 3 cylinder crankpins are at TDC; Nos 1 and 4 cylinder crankpins will be at BDC, ready for fitting No 1 piston. Check the crankshaft endfloat as described in Section 13.

21 Lubricate the lower bearing shells in the main bearing caps with clean engine oil. Make sure that the locating lugs on the shells engage with the corresponding recesses in the caps.

22 Fit main bearing caps Nos 2 to 5 to their correct locations, ensuring that they are fitted the correct way round (the bearing shell tab recesses in the block and caps must be on the same side). Insert the bolts, tightening them only loosely at this stage.

17.18 Fitting a thrustwasher to No 2 main bearing upper location

17.19 Ensure tab (arrowed) is correctly located in the block, and apply clean oil

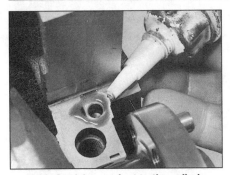

17.23 Applying sealant to the cylinder block No 1 main bearing cap mating face

17.24a Fitting a sealing strip to No 1 main bearing cap

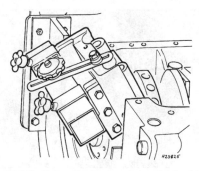

17.24b Using the Peugeot special tool to fit No 1 main bearing cap

17.25a Fitting No 1 main bearing cap, using metal strips to retain the side seals

17.25b Removing a metal strip from No 1 main bearing cap using pliers

17.26 Tightening a main bearing cap bolt

17.27 Trim the bearing cap sealing strips, so that they protrude above the block mating surface by approximately 1 mm

23 Apply a small amount of sealant to the No 1 main bearing cap mating face on the cylinder block, around the sealing strip holes **(see illustration)**.

24 Locate the tab of each sealing strip over the pins on the base of No 1 bearing cap, and press the strips into the bearing cap grooves. It is now necessary to obtain two thin metal strips, of 0.25 mm thickness or less, in order to prevent the strips moving when the cap is being fitted. Peugeot garages use the tool shown, which acts as a clamp. Metal strips (such as old feeler blades) can be used, provided all burrs which may damage the sealing strips are first removed **(see illustrations)**.

25 Where applicable, oil both sides of the metal strips, and hold them on the sealing strips. Fit the No 1 main bearing cap, insert the bolts loosely, then carefully pull out the

metal strips in a horizontal direction, using a pair of pliers **(see illustrations)**.

26 Tighten the main bearing cap bolts to the specified torque, with reference to paragraph 10 **(see illustration)**.

27 Using a sharp knife, trim off the ends of the No 1 bearing cap sealing strips, so that they protrude above the cylinder block/crankcase mating surface by about 1 mm **(see illustration)**.

28 Check that the crankshaft rotates freely.

29 Fit a new crankshaft rear oil seal as described in Part A of this Chapter.

30 Refit the piston/connecting rod assemblies to the crankshaft as described in Section 18.

31 Refit the Woodruff key, then slide on the oil pump drive sprocket and spacer (where fitted), and locate the drive chain on the sprocket.

32 Ensure that the mating surfaces of the front oil seal carrier and cylinder block are clean and dry. Note the correct fitted depth of the oil seal then, using a large flat-bladed screwdriver, lever the old seal out of the housing.

33 Apply a smear of suitable sealant to the oil seal carrier mating surface. Ensure that the locating dowels are in position, then slide the carrier over the end of the crankshaft and into position on the cylinder block. Tighten the carrier retaining bolts to the specified torque.

34 Fit a new crankshaft front oil seal as described in Part A of this Chapter.

35 Ensuring that the drive chain is correctly located on the sprocket, refit the oil pump and sump as described in Part A of this Chapter.

36 Refit the flywheel as described in Part A of this Chapter.

37 Where removed, refit the cylinder head as described in Part A of this Chapter.

2B

---

18 Piston/connecting rod assembly - refitting and big-end bearing clearance check

Selection of bearing shells

1 There are a number of sizes of big-end bearing shell produced by Peugeot; a standard size for use with the standard crankshaft, and oversizes for use once the crankshaft journals have been reground.

2 Consult your Peugeot dealer for the latest information on parts availability. To be safe, always quote the diameter of the crankshaft big-end crankpins when ordering bearing shells.

3 Prior to refitting the piston/connecting rod assemblies, it is recommended that the big-end bearing running clearance is checked as follows.

Big-end bearing running clearance check

4 Clean the backs of the bearing shells, and the bearing locations in both the connecting rod and bearing cap.

5 Press the bearing shells into their locations, ensuring that the tab on each shell engages in the notch in the connecting rod and cap. Take

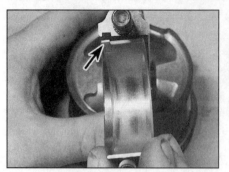

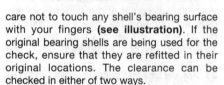

18.5 Fitting a bearing shell to a connecting rod - ensure the tab (arrowed) engages with the recess in the connecting rod

18.19a The cloverleaf-shaped cut-out (arrowed) must be on the oil filter side of the engine

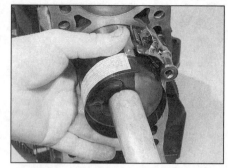

18.19b Tap the piston into the bore using a hammer handle

care not to touch any shell's bearing surface with your fingers **(see illustration)**. If the original bearing shells are being used for the check, ensure that they are refitted in their original locations. The clearance can be checked in either of two ways.

6 One method is to refit the big-end bearing cap to the connecting rod, ensuring that they are fitted the correct way around (see paragraph 20), with the bearing shells in place. With the cap retaining nuts correctly tightened, use an internal micrometer or vernier caliper to measure the internal diameter of each assembled pair of bearing shells. If the diameter of each corresponding crankshaft journal is measured and then subtracted from the bearing internal diameter, the result will be the big-end bearing running clearance.

7 The second, and more accurate method is to use Plastigage (see Section 17).

8 Ensure that the bearing shells are correctly fitted. Place a strand of Plastigage on each (cleaned) crankpin journal.

9 Refit the (clean) piston/connecting rod assemblies to the crankshaft, and refit the big-end bearing caps, using the marks made or noted on removal to ensure that they are fitted the correct way around.

10 Tighten the bearing cap nuts as described later in paragraph 21. Take care not to disturb the Plastigage, nor rotate the connecting rod during the tightening sequence.

11 Dismantle the assemblies without rotating the connecting rods. Use the scale printed on the Plastigage envelope to obtain the big-end bearing running clearance.

12 If the clearance is significantly different from that expected, the bearing shells may be the wrong size (or excessively worn, if the original shells are being re-used). Make sure that no dirt or oil was trapped between the bearing shells and the caps or block when the clearance was measured. If the Plastigage was wider at one end than at the other, the crankshaft journal may be tapered.

13 Note that Peugeot do not specify a recommended big-end bearing running clearance. The figure given in the Specifications is a guide figure, which is typical for this type of engine. Before condemning the

components concerned, refer to your Peugeot dealer or engine reconditioning specialist for further information on the specified running clearance. Their advice on the best course of action to be taken can then also be obtained.

14 On completion, carefully scrape away all traces of the Plastigage material from the crankshaft and bearing shells. Use your fingernail, or some other object which is unlikely to score the bearing surfaces.

Final piston/ connecting rod refitting

Note: *A piston ring compressor tool will be required for this operation.*

15 Note that the following procedure assumes that the main bearing caps are in place (see Section 17).

16 Ensure that the bearing shells are correctly fitted as described earlier. If new shells are being fitted, ensure that all traces of the protective grease are cleaned off using paraffin. Wipe dry the shells and connecting rods with a lint-free cloth.

17 Lubricate the cylinder bores, the pistons, and piston rings, then lay out each piston/connecting rod assembly in its respective position.

18 Start with assembly No 1. Make sure that the piston rings are still spaced as described in Section 16, then clamp them in position with a piston ring compressor.

19 Insert the piston/connecting rod assembly into the top of cylinder No 1. Ensure that the cloverleaf-shaped cut-out on the piston crown

is towards the front (oil filter side) of the cylinder block. Using a block of wood or hammer handle against the piston crown, tap the assembly into the cylinder until the piston crown is flush with the top of the cylinder **(see illustrations)**.

20 Ensure that the bearing shell is still correctly installed. Liberally lubricate the crankpin and both bearing shells. Taking care not to mark the cylinder bore, pull the piston/connecting rod assembly down the bore and onto the crankpin. Refit the big-end bearing cap, tightening its retaining nuts finger-tight at first. Note that the faces with the identification marks must match (which means that the bearing shell locating tabs abut each other).

21 Tighten the bearing cap retaining nuts evenly and progressively to the Stage 1 torque setting. Once both nuts have been tightened to the Stage 1 setting, angle-tighten them through the specified Stage 2 angle, using a socket and extension bar. It is recommended that an angle-measuring gauge is used during this stage of the tightening, to ensure accuracy **(see illustrations)**. If a gauge is not available, use a dab of white paint to make alignment marks between the nut and bearing cap prior to tightening; the marks can then be used to check that the nut has been rotated sufficiently during tightening.

22 Once the bearing cap retaining nuts have been correctly tightened, rotate the crankshaft. Check that it turns freely; some

18.21a Tighten the big-end bearing cap nuts to the stage 1 specified torque . . .

18.21b . . . then through the angle specified for stage 2

stiffness is to be expected if new components have been fitted, but there should be no signs of binding or tight spots.

23 Refit the remaining three piston/connecting rod assemblies in the same way.

24 Refit the cylinder head, oil pump and sump as described in Part A of this Chapter.

19 Engine -
initial start-up after overhaul

1 With the engine refitted in the vehicle, double-check the engine oil and coolant levels. Make a final check that everything has been reconnected, and that there are no tools or rags left in the engine compartment.

2 Disconnect the wiring from the stop solenoid on the injection pump (see Chapter 4), then turn the engine on the starter motor until the oil pressure warning light goes out. On Turbo models, it is vital to ensure that the turbocharger lubrication circuit has been primed - crank the engine on the starter motor in several ten-second bursts, pausing for half a minute or so between each burst. Reconnect the solenoid when satisfied that oil pressure has been established.

3 Prime the fuel system as described in Chapter 4.

4 Fully depress the accelerator pedal, turn the ignition key to position "M", and wait for the preheating warning light to go out.

5 Start the engine, noting that this may take a little longer than usual, due to the fuel system components having been disturbed.

6 While the engine is idling, check for fuel, water and oil leaks. Don't be alarmed if there are some odd smells and smoke from parts getting hot and burning off oil deposits.

7 Assuming all is well, keep the engine idling until hot water is felt circulating through the top hose, then switch off the engine.

8 Check the injection pump timing, and the idle speed setting, then switch the engine off.

9 After a few minutes, recheck the oil and coolant levels as described in *"Weekly Checks"*, and top-up as necessary.

10 If new pistons, rings or crankshaft bearings have been fitted, the engine must be treated as new, and run-in for the first 500 miles (800 km). *Do not* operate the engine at full-throttle, or allow it to labour at low engine speeds in any gear. It is recommended that the oil and filter be changed at the end of this period.

2B

Chapter 3
Cooling, heating and ventilation systems

Contents

Degrees of difficulty

Easy, suitable for novice with little experience	**Fairly easy,** suitable for beginner with some experience	**Fairly difficult,** suitable for competent DIY mechanic	**Difficult,** suitable for experienced DIY mechanic	**Very difficult,** suitable for expert DIY or professional

Specifications

Thermostat

Opening temperatures:
  Starts to open:
    Models up to 1992 . . . . 88°C
    Models from 1993 . . . . 83°C
  Fully open:
    Models up to 1992 . . . . 100°C
    Models from 1993 . . . . 93°C

Torque wrench setting	**Nm**	**lbf ft**
Coolant pump securing bolts	15	11

---

1 General information and precautions

General information

The cooling system is of pressurised type, comprising a coolant pump driven by the timing belt, an aluminium crossflow radiator with integral expansion tank, electric cooling fan(s), a thermostat, heater matrix, and all associated hoses and switches.

The system functions as follows. Cold coolant in the bottom of the radiator passes through the bottom hose to the coolant pump, where it is pumped around the cylinder block and head passages, and through the oil cooler(s) (where fitted). After cooling the cylinder bores, combustion surfaces and valve seats, the coolant reaches the underside of the thermostat, which is initially closed. The coolant passes through the heater, and is returned via the cylinder block to the coolant pump.

When the engine is cold, the coolant circulates only through the cylinder block, cylinder head, and heater. When the coolant reaches a predetermined temperature, the thermostat opens, and the coolant passes through the top hose to the radiator. As the coolant circulates through the radiator, it is cooled by the inrush of air when the car is in forward motion. The airflow is supplemented by the action of the electric cooling fan(s) when necessary. Upon reaching the bottom of the radiator, the coolant has now cooled, and the cycle is repeated.

When the engine is at normal operating temperature, the coolant expands, and some of it is displaced into the expansion tank, incorporated in the side of the radiator. Coolant collects in the tank, and is returned to the radiator when the system cools.

On models fitted with an engine oil cooler, the coolant is also passed through the oil cooler.

The electric cooling fan(s) mounted in front of the radiator are controlled by a thermostatic switch. At a predetermined coolant temperature, the switch/sensor actuates the fan.

Precautions

 Warning: Do not attempt to remove the expansion tank filler cap, or to disturb any part of the cooling system, while the engine is hot, as there is a high risk of scalding. If the expansion tank filler cap must be removed before the engine and radiator have fully cooled (even though this is not recommended), the pressure in the cooling system must first be relieved. Cover the cap with a thick layer of cloth, to avoid scalding, and slowly unscrew the filler cap until a hissing sound is heard. When the hissing has stopped, indicating that the pressure has reduced, slowly unscrew the filler cap until it can be removed; if more hissing sounds are heard, wait until they have stopped before unscrewing the cap completely. At all times, keep well away from the filler cap opening, and protect your hands.

3

Warning: Do not allow antifreeze to come into contact with your skin, or with the painted surfaces of the vehicle. Rinse off spills immediately, with plenty of water. Never leave antifreeze lying around in an open container, or in a puddle in the driveway or on the garage floor. Children and pets are attracted by its sweet smell, but antifreeze can be fatal if ingested.

Warning: If the engine is hot, the electric cooling fan may start rotating even if the engine is not running. Be careful to keep your hands, hair, and any loose clothing well clear when working in the engine compartment.

Warning: Refer to Section 11 for precautions to be observed when working on models equipped with air conditioning.

2 Cooling system hoses - disconnection and renewal

Note: Refer to the warnings given in Section 1 of this Chapter before proceeding. Hoses should only be disconnected once the engine has cooled sufficiently to avoid scalding.

1 If the checks described in Chapter 1 reveal a faulty hose, it must be renewed as follows.

2 First drain the cooling system (see Chapter 1). If the coolant is not due for renewal, it may be re-used, providing it is collected in a clean container.

3 To disconnect a hose, proceed as follows, according to the type of hose connection.

Conventional hose connections - general instructions

4 On conventional connections, the clips used to secure the hoses in position may be either standard worm-drive clips or disposable crimped types. The crimped type of clip is not designed to be re-used and should be replaced with a worm drive type on reassembly.

5 To disconnect a hose, use a screwdriver to slacken or release the clips, then move them along the hose, clear of the relevant inlet/outlet. Carefully work the hose free. The hoses can be removed with relative ease when new - on an older car, they may have stuck.

6 If a hose proves to be difficult to remove, try to release it by rotating its ends before attempting to free it. Gently prise the end of the hose with a blunt instrument (such as a flat-bladed screwdriver), but do not apply too much force, and take care not to damage the pipe stubs or hoses. Note in particular that the radiator inlet stub is fragile; do not use excessive force when attempting to remove the hose. If all else fails, cut the hose with a sharp knife, then slit it so that it can be peeled off in two pieces. Although this may prove expensive if the hose is otherwise

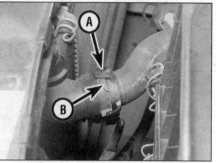

2.12a Twist the connector until the clips (A) are clear of the lugs (B)

undamaged, it is preferable to buying a new radiator. Check first, however, that a new hose is readily available.

7 When fitting a hose, first slide the clips onto the hose, then work the hose into position. If crimped-type clips were originally fitted, use standard worm-drive clips when refitting the hose. If the hose is stiff, use a little soapy water as a lubricant, or soften the hose by soaking it in hot water. Do not use oil or grease, which may attack the rubber.

8 Work the hose into position, checking that it is correctly routed, then slide each clip back along the hose until it passes over the flared end of the relevant inlet/outlet, before tightening the clip securely.

9 Refill the cooling system (see Chapter 1).

10 Check thoroughly for leaks as soon as possible after disturbing any part of the cooling system.

Radiator hose(s) - bayonet-type connection

Note: A new O-ring should be used when reconnecting the hose.

Removal

11 On later models, the radiator hoses are connected to the radiator using a plastic bayonet-type connection. To disconnect this type of connector, proceed as follows.

12 Twist the end of the hose (with the connector) anti-clockwise until the clips on the connector are clear of the retaining lugs on the radiator stub, then pull the end of the hose from the radiator. Recover the O-ring from the end of the hose connector **(see illustrations)**.

3.5a Depress the securing clip . . .

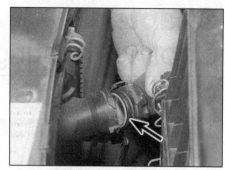

2.12b Recover the O-ring (arrowed) from the end of the hose connector

Refitting

13 Fit a new O-ring to the hose connector, then reconnect the hose using a reversal of the removal procedure. Twist the end of the hose fully clockwise to ensure that the retaining clips are engaged with the lugs on the radiator stub.

3 Radiator - removal, inspection and refitting

Removal

1 Disconnect the battery negative lead.

2 Where applicable, disconnect the wiring from the coolant level sensor, mounted in the right-hand side of the radiator.

3 Similarly, where applicable disconnect the wiring from the cooling fan switch, mounted right-hand side of the radiator.

4 Drain the cooling system (see Chapter 1).

5 Where applicable, depress the securing clip, and release the air inlet tube from the body front panel, above the radiator **(see illustrations)**.

6 Disconnect the upper radiator hose from the left-hand end of the radiator, with reference to Section 2.

7 It is now necessary to disconnect the lower radiator hose(s) from the right-hand side of the radiator. On some models, particularly those where conventional hose clips are used, this is a straightforward task. On other models (where bayonet connectors are used on a large-capacity radiator), it is impossible to

3.5b . . . and withdraw the air intake tube

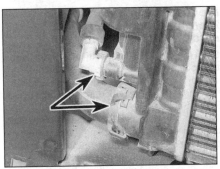

3.7 Lower radiator hose connections viewed with body front panel removed

3.9 Releasing a radiator upper securing clip

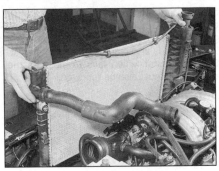

3.10 Lifting out the radiator

gain access to the lower radiator hose connections without removing the body front panel assembly, as described in Chapter 11 **(see illustration)**.

8 Once all the radiator hoses have been disconnected, proceed as follows.

9 If not already done, working at the top of the radiator, release the two securing clips, and tilt the radiator back towards the engine **(see illustration)**.

10 Lift the radiator from the engine compartment **(see illustration)**.

Inspection

11 If the radiator has been removed due to suspected blockage, reverse-flush it as described in Chapter 1. Clean dirt and debris from the radiator fins, using an air line (in which case, wear eye protection) or a soft brush. Be careful, as the fins are sharp, and easily damaged.

12 If necessary, a radiator specialist can perform a "flow test" on the radiator, to establish whether an internal blockage exists.

13 A leaking radiator must be taken to a specialist for permanent repair. Do not try to weld or solder a leaking radiator, as damage to the plastic components may result.

14 In an emergency, minor leaks from the radiator can be cured by using a suitable radiator sealant, in accordance with its manufacturer's instructions, with the radiator *in situ*.

15 If the radiator is to be sent for repair or renewed, remove all hoses, and the cooling fan switch (where fitted).

16 Inspect the radiator mounting rubbers, and renew them if necessary.

Refitting

17 Refitting is a reversal of removal, bearing in mind the following points:

a) *Ensure that the lower lugs on the radiator are correctly engaged with the mounting rubbers in the body panel.*

b) *Reconnect the hoses with reference to Section 2, using new O-rings where applicable.*

c) *Where applicable, refit the body front panel assembly, referring to Chapter 11.*

d) *On completion, refill the cooling system as described in Chapter 1.*

4 Thermostat - removal, testing and refitting

Removal

Note: *A new sealing ring may be required on refitting, and on early models a new thermostat housing cover gasket will be required.*

1 Disconnect the battery negative lead.

2 Drain the cooling system as described in Chapter 1.

3 Where necessary, release any relevant wiring and hoses from the retaining clips, and position clear of the thermostat housing to improve access. On some models, access is also improved if the air cleaner ducting is removed is removed (see Chapter 4).

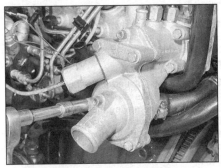

4.4a Unscrewing a thermostat cover securing bolt - early model

4.5 Remove the circlip (arrowed) to release the thermostat from the cover - early models

4 Unscrew the retaining bolts, and carefully withdraw the thermostat housing cover to expose the thermostat. Take care not to strain the coolant hose(s) connected to the cover **(see illustrations)**. Where applicable, recover the gasket.

5 Where applicable, using circlip pliers, remove the thermostat retaining circlip **(see illustration)**.

6 Lift the thermostat from the housing, or cover (as applicable), and recover the sealing ring(s) **(see illustration)**.

Testing

7 A rough test of the thermostat may be made by suspending it with a piece of string in a container full of water. Heat the water to bring it to the boil - the thermostat must open by the time the water boils. If not, renew it.

8 If a thermometer is available, the precise

4.4b Two of the three thermostat cover securing bolts (arrowed) - later models

4.6 Lifting the thermostat from the housing - later models

3

opening temperature of the thermostat may be determined; compare with the figures given in the Specifications. The opening temperature is also marked on the thermostat.
9 A thermostat which fails to close as the water cools must also be renewed.

Refitting

10 Refitting is a reversal of removal, bearing in mind the following points:
  a) *Examine the sealing ring(s) for signs of damage or deterioration, and if necessary, renew.*
  b) *Ensure that the thermostat is fitted the correct way round, with the spring(s) facing into the housing.*
  c) *Where applicable, use a new gasket when fitting the housing cover (thoroughly clean the mating faces of the cover and housing first).*
  d) *On completion, refill the cooling system as described in Chapter 1.*

5 Electric cooling fan(s) - testing, removal and refitting

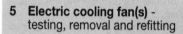

Testing

1 Current supply to the cooling fan(s) is via the ignition switch (see Chapter 10) and a fuse (see Chapter 12). The circuit is completed by the cooling fan thermostatic switch, which (on most models) is mounted in the radiator. On models with air conditioning, the cooling fans are controlled by the "Bitron" sensor - see Section 6.
2 If a fan does not appear to work, run the engine until normal operating temperature is reached, then allow it to idle. The fan should cut in within a few minutes (before the temperature gauge needle enters the red section, or before the coolant temperature warning light comes on). If not, switch off the ignition and disconnect the wiring plug from the cooling fan switch. Bridge the two contacts in the wiring plug using a length of spare wire, and switch on the ignition. If the fan now operates, the switch is probably faulty, and should be renewed.
3 If the fan still fails to operate, check that battery voltage is available at the feed wire to the switch; if not, then there is a fault in the feed wire (possibly due to a fault in the fan motor, or a blown fuse). If there is no problem with the feed, check that there is continuity between the switch earth terminal and a good earth point on the body; if not, then the earth connection is faulty, and must be re-made.
4 If the switch and the wiring are in good condition, the fault must lie in the motor itself. The motor can be checked by disconnecting it from the wiring loom, and connecting a 12-volt supply directly to it.

Removal

5 Remove the radiator (see Section 3).

5.7 Fan motor securing bolts (arrowed) - viewed from rear (grille panel side)

6 Remove the front grille panel (Chapter 11).
7 Working behind the fan blades, unscrew the three motor securing bolts, and withdraw the motor/fan assembly forwards from the shroud **(see illustration)**. The plug on the motor will be released from the wiring connector as the motor is pulled forwards.

Refitting

8 Refitting is a reversal of removal, but refit the radiator with reference to Section 3.

6 Cooling system electrical switches and sensors - testing, removal and refitting

Electric cooling fan thermostatic switch - models without air conditioning

Testing

1 Testing of the switch is described in Section 5, as part of the electric cooling fan test procedure.

Removal

2 The switch is located in the right-hand side of the radiator. The engine and radiator should be cold before removing the switch.
3 Disconnect the battery negative lead.
4 Partially drain the cooling system to just below the level of the switch (as described in Chapter 1). Alternatively, have ready a suitable bung to plug the switch aperture in the radiator when the switch is removed. If this method is used, take care not to damage the radiator, and do not use anything which will allow foreign matter to enter the radiator.
5 Disconnect the wiring plug from the switch.
6 Carefully unscrew the switch from the radiator, and recover the sealing ring. If the system has not been drained, plug the switch aperture to prevent further coolant loss.

Refitting

7 Refitting is a reversal of removal, using a new sealing ring. Tighten the switch, and refill (or top-up) the cooling system (see Chapter 1).
8 On completion, start the engine and run it until it reaches normal operating temperature. Continue to run the engine, and check that the cooling fan cuts in and out correctly.

Electric cooling fan thermostatic switch - models with air conditioning

9 On most models fitted with air conditioning, the cooling fans are controlled by the "Bitron" sensor. This is located in the thermostat housing, and is described in more detail later in this Section.
10 On some later models with air conditioning, the cooling fan(s) is/are controlled by a switch mounted in the radiator, as described previously for models without air conditioning. It will be self-evident which type of switch is used. If no switch is fitted to the radiator, the "Bitron" sensor is used to control the fan(s).

Coolant temperature gauge/ temperature warning light sender

Testing

11 The coolant temperature gauge/warning light sender is screwed into the thermostat housing **(see illustration)**.
12 The temperature gauge (where fitted) is fed with a stabilised voltage from the instrument panel feed (via the ignition switch and a fuse). The gauge earth is controlled by the sender. The sender contains a thermistor - an electronic component whose electrical resistance decreases at a predetermined rate as its temperature rises. When the coolant is cold, the sender resistance is high, current flow through the gauge is reduced, and the gauge needle points towards the blue (cold) end of the scale. As the coolant temperature rises and the sender resistance falls, current flow increases, and the gauge needle moves towards the upper end of the scale. If the sender is faulty, it must be renewed.
13 On models with a temperature warning light, the light is fed with a voltage from the instrument panel. The light earth is controlled by the sender. The sender is effectively a switch, which operates at a predetermined temperature to earth the light and complete the circuit. If the light is fitted in addition to a gauge, the senders for the gauge and light are incorporated in a single unit, with two wires, one each for the light and gauge earths. On models with air conditioning, the light is operated via the "Bitron" sensor - see paragraphs 19 to 21.

6.11 Disconnecting the wiring plug from the temperature gauge/light sender

14 If the gauge develops a fault, first check the other instruments; if they do not work at all, check the instrument panel electrical feed. If the readings are erratic, there may be a fault in the voltage stabiliser, which will necessitate renewal of the stabiliser (the stabiliser is integral with the instrument panel printed circuit board - see Chapter 12). If the fault lies in the temperature gauge alone, check it as follows.

15 If the gauge needle remains at the "cold" end of the scale when the engine is hot, disconnect the sender wiring plug, and earth the relevant wire to the cylinder head. If the needle then deflects when the ignition is switched on, the sender unit is proved faulty, and should be renewed. If the needle still does not move, remove the instrument panel (Chapter 12) and check the continuity of the wire between the sender unit and the gauge, and the feed to the gauge unit. If continuity is shown, and the fault still exists, then the gauge is faulty, and the gauge unit should be renewed.

16 If the gauge needle remains at the "hot" end of the scale when the engine is cold, disconnect the sender wire. If the needle then returns to the "cold" end of the scale when the ignition is switched on, the sender unit is proved faulty, and should be renewed. If the needle still does not move, check the remainder of the circuit as described previously.

17 The same basic principles apply to testing the warning light. The light should illuminate when the relevant sender wire is earthed.

Removal and refitting

18 The procedure is similar to that described previously in this Section for the electric cooling fan thermostatic switch. On some models, access to the switch is very poor, and other components may need to be removed before the sender unit can be reached.

"Bitron" temperature sensor - models with air conditioning

Testing

19 The sensor forms part of the air conditioning "Bitron" control system (see Section 11). Testing of the sensor should be entrusted to a Peugeot dealer.

Removal and refitting

20 The "Bitron" temperature sensor is screwed into the thermostat housing, which is bolted onto the left-hand end of the cylinder head.

21 The procedure is similar to that described previously in this Section for the electric cooling fan thermostatic switch. On some models, access to the switch is very poor, and other components may need to be removed before the sender unit can be reached.

6.23 Disconnecting the wiring plug from the pre-heating system coolant temperature sensor

Pre-heating system coolant temperature sensor - later Turbo models

Testing

22 The sensor forms part of the pre-heating system (see Chapter 4), and testing should be entrusted to a Peugeot dealer.

Removal and refitting

23 The sensor is located at the rear of the fuel filter/thermostat housing **(see illustration)**.

24 The procedure is similar to that described previously in this Section for the electric cooling fan thermostatic switch.

EGR system coolant temperature sensor

Testing

25 The sensor forms part of the EGR system (see Chapter 4), and testing should be entrusted to a Peugeot dealer.

Removal and refitting

26 The sensor is located at the rear of the fuel filter/thermostat housing.

27 The procedure is similar to that described previously in this Section for the electric cooling fan thermostatic switch.

7 Coolant pump - removal and refitting

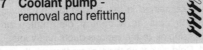

Note: *A new gasket must be used on refitting.*

Removal

1 The coolant pump is driven by the timing belt, and is bolted to the cylinder block at the timing belt end of the engine.

2 Drain the cooling system (see Chapter 1).

3 Remove the timing belt as described in Chapter 2.

4 Where necessary, for access to the coolant pump, remove the timing belt tensioner and/or the rear timing belt cover as described in Chapter 2.

5 Remove the securing bolts, and withdraw the pump from the cylinder block (access is most easily obtained from under the wheel arch). Recover the gasket **(see illustrations)**.

Refitting

6 Ensure that all mating faces are clean.

7 Refit the pump using a new gasket.

8 Where applicable refit the rear timing belt cover and/or the timing belt tensioner with reference to Chapter 2.

9 Refit the timing belt as described in Chapter 2.

10 Refill the cooling system as described in Chapter 1.

8 Thermostat/fuel filter housing - removal and refitting

Removal

Note: *A new gasket must be used when refitting the main housing.*

1 Disconnect the battery negative lead.

2 Drain the cooling system as described in Chapter 1.

3 Place a plastic sheet over the transmission bellhousing and the starter motor, to prevent any fuel spilled during the following procedure from causing damage.

4 Remove the fuel filter as described in Chapter 1.

5 Disconnect the wiring plugs from the coolant sensors mounted in the top of the housing.

6 Disconnect the coolant hoses from the plastic thermostat housing.

7 Disconnect the coolant hose from the stub at the rear of the housing.

8 Unscrew the bolt securing the plastic fuel filter housing to the main housing, then withdraw the plastic housing and move it clear

7.5a Unscrew the securing bolts . . .

7.5b . . . and remove the coolant pump

3

8.8a Unscrew the securing bolt (arrowed) . . .

8.8b . . . withdraw the plastic housing . . .

8.8c . . . and recover the O-ring

8.9a Unscrew the three securing bolts (arrowed) . . .

8.9b . . . and withdraw the main thermostat housing

of the main housing. Recover the O-ring from the base of the plastic housing (see illustrations).

9 Unscrew the three securing bolts, and withdraw the main housing from the cylinder head (see illustrations). Recover the gasket.

10 Disconnect the coolant hose from the base of the housing, and remove the housing.

Refitting

11 Refitting is a reversal of removal, bearing in mind the following points:

a) Examine the condition of the O-ring on the base of the plastic housing, and renew if necessary.

b) Use a new gasket when refitting the main housing.

c) Ensure that all hoses, pipes and wires are correctly reconnected.

d) Refill the cooling system as described in Chapter 1.

e) On completion, prime the fuel system as described in Chapter 4.

9 Heating and ventilation system - general information

1 The heating/ventilation system consists of a blower motor (housed behind the facia), face level vents in the centre and at each end of the facia, and air ducts to the front footwells.

2 Two types of system are fitted to the model range. On basic specification models, the heating/ventilation system is manually-

controlled. On higher specification models, the system is electronically-controlled. The components of both systems are identical, with the exception of the control unit. Additionally, on models with the electronically-controlled system, temperature sensors and a thermostat are fitted to automatically control the temperature of the air inside the vehicle according to the position of the temperature control knob.

3 The control unit is located in the facia, and the controls operate flap valves to deflect and mix the air flowing through the various parts of the heating/ventilation system. The flap valves are contained in the air distribution housing, which acts as a central distribution unit, passing air to the various ducts and vents.

4 Cold air enters the system through the grille at the rear of the engine compartment. If required, the airflow is boosted by the blower, and then flows through the various ducts, according to the settings of the controls. Stale air is expelled through ducts at the rear of the vehicle. If warm air is required, the cold air is passed over the heater matrix, which is heated by the engine coolant.

5 A recirculation switch enables the outside air supply to be closed off, while the air inside the vehicle is recirculated. This can be useful to prevent unpleasant odours entering from outside the vehicle, but should only be used briefly, as the recirculated air inside the vehicle will soon become stale.

10 Heater/ventilation components - removal and refitting

Heater/ventilation control unit - models up to 1992

Removal

1 Disconnect the battery negative lead.

2 Where applicable, remove the radio/cassette player as described in Chapter 12.

3 Move the steering column to its lowest position.

4 Remove the lighting control stalk switch (right-hand-drive models) or the wash/wipe control stalk switch (left-hand-drive models), as described in Chapter 12. Note that there is no need to disconnect the switch wiring, but the switch must be moved to allow clearance for removal of the centre facia panel.

5 Unclip the trim panel from the lower edge of the instrument panel to expose the upper centre facia panel securing screw. Remove the screw (see illustration).

6 Unclip the oddments tray from the front of the facia centre panel.

7 Unclip the ashtray and remove it from the facia.

8 Unscrew the five centre facia panel securing screws exposed by removal of the oddments tray and ashtray (see illustration).

9 Pull the centre facia panel forwards from the facia, then reach behind the panel and disconnect the wiring from the switches,

10.5 Removing the upper centre facia panel securing screw - models up to 1992

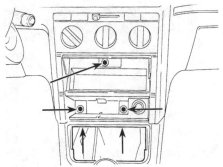

10.8 Centre facia panel securing screws (arrowed) - models up to 1992

10.10 Two of the heater control unit screws (arrowed) - models up to 1992

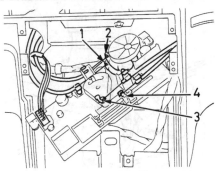

10.11 Heater control cables must be reconnected in the order 1, 2, 3 and 4 - models up to 1992

clock, and cigarette lighter, as applicable. Note the locations of the wiring connectors to ensure correct refitting, and remove the facia panel.

10 Unscrew the four heater control unit securing screws, then manipulate the unit from the facia, and disconnect the control cables and/or wiring plugs **(see illustration)**. The cables can be disconnected after releasing the metal spring clips securing the cable sheaths to the control unit.

Refitting

11 Refitting is a reversal of removal, bearing in mind the following points, but note that the control cables must be reconnected in the order shown **(see illustration)**.

12 Refit the radio/cassette player with reference to Chapter 12.

Heater/ventilation control unit - models from 1993

Note: *Refer to the facia removal procedure in Chapter 11 for relevant illustrations of facia housing removal.*

Removal

13 Disconnect the battery negative lead.

14 Remove the centre console (Chapter 11).

15 Open the ashtray cover, and unscrew the two screws located at the bottom of the ashtray housing.

16 Where applicable, remove the radio/cassette player as described in Chapter 12. On models not fitted with a radio/cassette player, prise out the oddments tray.

17 Remove the two securing screws from the top of the radio/cassette player/oddments tray housing, then withdraw the housing from the facia. Where applicable, disconnect the wiring plug(s) from the rear of the housing.

18 Prise the blanking plate from the top corner of the facia centre ventilation nozzle housing. Remove the now-exposed securing screw.

19 Remove the four housing securing screws located under the heater control panel. Two screws are accessible from the front of the housing, and two screws from underneath.

20 Carefully prise the switches from below the centre facia ventilation nozzles to reveal the remaining housing securing screw. Remove the screw.

21 Pull the housing forwards, and disconnect the wiring from the clock, then withdraw the housing.

22 Remove the two securing screws located at the top of the heater control unit **(see illustration)**.

23 Pull the control unit forwards from the facia.

24 Working at the top of the unit, disconnect the two control cables and the wiring plug. The cables can be disconnected after releasing the metal spring clips securing the cable sheaths to the control unit **(see illustration)**. Note the cable locations to ensure correct refitting.

25 Working under the unit, disconnect the remaining control cable, then withdraw the unit.

Refitting

26 Refitting is a reversal of removal, ensuring that the cables are correctly routed and securely reconnected.

Heater/ventilation control cables

Removal

27 Disconnect the cables from the heater control unit by removing the control unit as described previously in this Section.

28 With the heater control unit removed, access can be gained to the cable connections on the heater unit, behind the facia **(see illustration)**. Access may be improved by removing surrounding panels with reference to Chapter 11.

29 Note the locations and routing of the cables to ensure correct refitting.

Refitting

30 Refitting is a reversal of removal, bearing in mind the following points.

a) *The cables are of a preset length, and no adjustment is required, although small adjustments can be made by repositioning the cable sheaths in the securing clips.*

b) *When reconnecting the air inlet flap cable, the cable must be routed around the air inlet duct, not behind it* **(see illustration)**.

c) *Refit the heater control unit as described previously in this Section.*

3

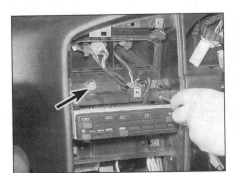

10.22 Remove the heater control unit securing screws - models from 1993

10.24 Disconnect the control cables from the heater control unit - models from 1993

10.28 Heater control cable metal spring clip (arrowed) at heater unit

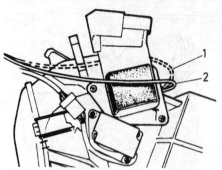

10.30 Correct routing of heater air inlet flap control cable - models up to 1992

1 Incorrect routing   2 Correct routing

10.35 Remove the screw securing the heater pipes to the matrix connector

10.36a Remove the two securing screws . . .

Heater matrix

Removal

31 Remove the complete facia assembly as described in Chapter 11.

32 Drain the cooling system as described in Chapter 1.

 To avoid draining the cooling system, clamp the coolant hoses as close as possible to the heater matrix pipes, in the engine compartment.

33 Place a tray under the heater pipe connections in the passenger compartment, and place absorbent cloths on the carpet, in case of coolant spillage.

34 Where applicable, unscrew the bolt securing the heater pipes.

35 Unscrew the screw(s) securing the heater pipes to the connector on the heater matrix **(see illustration)**.

36 To remove the matrix from the heater assembly, unscrew the two securing screws, then carefully withdraw the matrix from its housing in the heater assembly, moving the heater pipes aside as the matrix is withdrawn. Recover the O-rings from the matrix pipe connections **(see illustrations)**.

Refitting

37 Refitting is a reversal of removal, bearing in mind the following points.

a) *Use new O-rings when reconnecting the heater matrix pipes to the connector on the heater matrix.*

b) *Refit the facia assembly as described in Chapter 11.*

c) *On completion, refill (or top-up) the cooling system as described in Chapter 1.*

Complete heater assembly - models without air conditioning

Removal

38 Remove the complete facia assembly as described in Chapter 11.

39 Drain the cooling system as described in Chapter 1.

10.36b . . . then withdraw the heater matrix . . .

 To avoid draining the cooling system, clamp the coolant hoses as close as possible to the heater matrix pipes, in the engine compartment.

40 Working in the engine compartment, disconnect the coolant hoses from the heater matrix (it may be necessary to remove other components for access on some models).

41 Where applicable, remove the securing screws, and remove the plastic shields from the heater air inlet, and the windscreen wiper motor in the scuttle at the rear of the engine compartment. This will expose the heater securing bolts **(see illustration)**.

42 Working in the scuttle, unscrew the heater securing bolts.

43 Unclip the air ducts connecting the heater assembly to the floor heating.

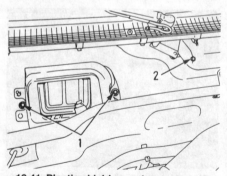

10.41 Plastic shield securing screws (1) and heater securing bolt (2)

10.36c . . . and recover the O-rings from the pipe connections

44 Place a tray under the heater pipe connections in the passenger compartment, and place absorbent cloths on the carpet, in case of coolant spillage.

45 Where applicable, unscrew the bolt securing the heater pipes.

46 Unscrew the screw(s) securing the heater pipes to the connector on the heater matrix.

47 Unscrew the bolt from the lower right-hand corner of the heater unit **(see illustration)**.

48 Disconnect the wiring plugs from the heater assembly, and release the wiring harnesses from any clips. Note the routing of the wiring to ensure correct refitting.

49 Pull the heater assembly back from the bulkhead to disengage the matrix connector from the heater pipes. Withdraw the heater assembly from the vehicle (complete with the control unit), being prepared for coolant spillage. Recover the O-rings from the matrix pipe connections.

10.47 Heater unit lower right-hand securing bolt (arrowed)

Refitting

50 Refitting is a reversal of removal, bearing in mind the following points.

a) *Use new O-rings when reconnecting the heater matrix pipes to the connector on the heater matrix.*

b) *Ensure that the wiring harnesses are routed as noted before removal.*

c) *Refit the facia assembly (Chapter 11).*

d) *On completion, refill (or top-up) the cooling system as described in Chapter 1.*

Complete heater assembly - models with air conditioning

Removal

Warning: Do not remove the heater unit until the air conditioning circuit has been discharged by an expert.

51 Before carrying out any work, have the air conditioning refrigerant circuit discharged by a qualified air conditioning specialist.

52 Working in the engine compartment, unscrew the nuts securing the clamp to the evaporator refrigerant pipes at the engine compartment bulkhead.

53 Slide the clamp back along the pipes, away from the bulkhead.

54 Pull the two refrigerant pipes from the relief valve on the bulkhead.

55 Proceed as described in paragraphs 38 to 49 inclusive, but note that it will be necessary to disconnect the wiring plugs from the air conditioning electrical components mounted on the heater assembly. Note the locations of the connectors, and the routing of the wiring harnesses.

Refitting

56 Refitting is a reversal of removal, noting the following points.

a) *Ensure that all wiring plugs are correctly reconnected, and that the wiring is routed as noted before removal.*

b) *Use new O-rings when reconnecting the heater matrix pipes to the connector on the heater matrix.*

c) *Refit the facia assembly (Chapter 11).*

d) *Use new O-rings when reconnecting the refrigerant pipes to the relief valve at the bulkhead.*

e) *On completion, refill (or top-up) the cooling system as described in Chapter 1, and have the refrigerant circuit recharged by a qualified air conditioning specialist.*

Heater blower motor

Removal

57 Working under the passenger's side of the facia, release the securing clips and withdraw the carpet trim panel from under the facia.

58 If desired, to improve access, remove the glovebox as described in Chapter 11.

59 Reach up under the facia and disconnect the blower motor wiring plug. Where applicable, release the wiring from the clip(s) on the motor casing **(see illustration)**.

60 Unscrew the three securing screws from the bottom of the motor casing, and withdraw the motor assembly **(see illustration)**.

Refitting

61 Refitting is a reversal of removal.

Heater blower control module

Removal

62 The control module assembly is located in the motor casing.

63 Remove the blower motor as described previously in this Section.

64 Where applicable, pull the rubber grommet from the motor casing, and disconnect the wiring from the motor **(see illustration)**. Note the wire locations to ensure correct refitting.

65 Working through the fan blades, remove the screws, and/or release the clips securing the motor assembly to the casing (release the clips using a pair of pliers or a screwdriver, depending on the type of clip encountered) **(see illustrations)**.

66 Withdraw the motor/fan blade assembly from the casing **(see illustration)**.

67 Disconnect the wiring plug from the rear of the control module **(see illustration)**.

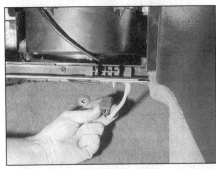

10.59 Disconnect the blower motor wiring plug

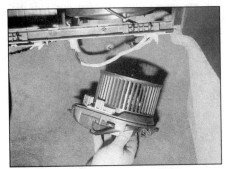

10.60 Withdrawing the heater blower motor

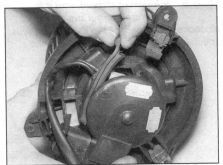

10.64 Pull the rubber grommet from the motor casing for access to the wiring

10.65a Remove the securing screws . . .

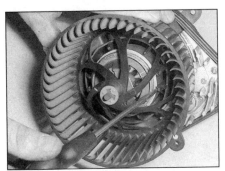

10.65b . . . and release the clips . . .

10.66 . . . then withdraw the motor

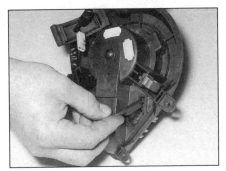

10.67 Disconnect the wiring plug . . .

3

10.68a . . . then remove the securing screws . . .

68 Remove the two screws, and withdraw the control module **(see illustrations)**.

Refitting

69 Refitting is a reversal of removal.

11 Air conditioning system - general information and precautions

General information

1 An air conditioning system is available on certain models up to 1992, and on all models from 1993. It enables the temperature of incoming air to be lowered, and also dehumidifies the air, which makes for rapid demisting and increased comfort.

2 The cooling side of the system works in the same way as a domestic refrigerator. Refrigerant gas is drawn into a belt-driven compressor, and passes into a condenser mounted on the front of the radiator, where it loses heat and becomes liquid. The liquid passes through an expansion valve to an evaporator, where it changes from liquid under high pressure to gas under low

10.68b . . . and withdraw the control module

pressure. This change is accompanied by a drop in temperature, which cools the evaporator. The refrigerant returns to the compressor, and the cycle begins again.

3 Air blown through the evaporator passes to the air distribution unit, where it is mixed with hot air blown through the heater matrix to achieve the desired temperature in the passenger compartment.

4 The heating side of the system works in the same way as on models without air conditioning (see Section 9).

5 The operation of the system is controlled electronically by the "Bitron" control unit, which controls the electric cooling fan(s), the compressor, and the facia-mounted warning light. Any problems with the system should be referred to a Peugeot dealer.

Precautions

Warning: The refrigeration circuit may contain a liquid refrigerant (Freon), and it is therefore dangerous to disconnect any part of the system without specialised knowledge and equipment.

6 When an air conditioning system is fitted, it is necessary to observe special precautions whenever dealing with any part of the system, or its associated components. If for any reason the system must be disconnected, entrust this task to your Peugeot dealer or a refrigeration engineer

7 The refrigerant is potentially dangerous, and should only be handled by qualified persons. If it is splashed onto the skin, it can cause frostbite. It is not itself poisonous, but in the presence of a naked flame (including a cigarette) it forms a poisonous gas. Uncontrolled discharging of the refrigerant is dangerous, and potentially damaging to the environment.

8 Do not operate the air conditioning system if it is known to be short of refrigerant, as this may damage the compressor.

12 Air conditioning system components - removal and refitting

Warning: Do not attempt to open the refrigerant circuit. Refer to the precautions given in Section 11.

1 The only operation which can be carried out easily without discharging the refrigerant is renewal of the compressor drivebelt. This is described in Chapter 1. (The "Bitron" temperature sensor may be renewed using the information in Section 6.) All other operations must be referred to a Peugeot dealer or an air conditioning specialist.

2 If necessary, the compressor can be unbolted and moved aside, without disconnecting its flexible hoses, after removing the drivebelt.

Chapter 4
Fuel, exhaust and emission control systems

Contents

Degrees of difficulty

Easy, suitable for novice with little experience	**Fairly easy,** suitable for beginner with some experience 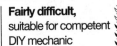	**Fairly difficult,** suitable for competent DIY mechanic 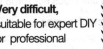	**Difficult,** suitable for experienced DIY mechanic	**Very difficult,** suitable for expert DIY or professional

Specifications

General

System type . . . . Rear-mounted fuel tank, distributor fuel injection pump with integral transfer pump, indirect injection. Turbocharger and intercooler on some engines

Firing order . . . . 1-3-4-2 (No 1 at flywheel end)

Manufacturer's engine codes:*
   1.8 litre (1769 cc) Turbo engine **A8A** (XUD7TE/L)
   1.9 litre (1905 cc) non-turbo, non-catalyst/EGR engine **D9B** (XUD9A/L)
   1.9 litre (1905 cc) non-turbo engine with catalyst/EGR . . . . **DJZ** (XUD9Y)
   1.9 litre (1905 cc) Turbo, non-catalyst/EGR engine **D8A** (XUD9TE/L)
   1.9 litre (1905 cc) Turbo engine with catalyst/EGR . . . . **DHY** (XUD9TE/Y)

*The engine code is stamped on a plate attached to the front of the cylinder block. This is the code most often used by Peugeot. The code given in brackets is the factory identification number, and is not often referred to by Peugeot or this manual.

Maximum speed

1.8 litre (1769 cc) Turbo engines . . . . 4800 rpm
1.9 litre (1905 cc) non-turbo engines . . . . 5150 ± 125 rpm
1.9 litre (1905 cc) Turbo engines . . . . 5100 ± 80 rpm

Injection pump (Lucas)

Direction of rotation . . . . Clockwise, viewed from sprocket end
Static timing:
   Engine position . . . . No 4 piston at TDC
   Pump position . . . . Value shown on pump - see Text
Dynamic timing (at idle speed):
   A8A engine . . . . 9°
   D8A engine . . . . 11° ± 1°
   D9B engine . . . . 15° ± 1°
   DHY engine . . . . 11° ± 1°
   DJZ engine:
      Models up to 1992 . . . . 13.5° ± 1°
      Models from 1993 . . . . 12° ± 1°

4

Injection pump (Bosch)

Direction of rotation .... Clockwise, viewed from sprocket end
Static timing:
  Engine position .... No 4 piston at TDC
  Pump timing measurement:
    1.8 litre (1769 cc) Turbo (A8A) engine .... 0.80 ± 0.02 mm
    1.9 litre (1905 cc) non-turbo engines:
      D9B engine .... 0.90 ± 0.02 mm
      DJZ engine .... 0.77 ± 0.02 mm
    1.9 litre (1905 cc) Turbo engines:
      D8A engine .... 0.66 ± 0.02 mm
      DHY engine .... 0.66 ± 0.02 mm
Dynamic timing (at idle speed):
  1.8 litre (1769 cc) Turbo (A8A) engine .... 14° ± 1°
  1.9 litre (1905 cc) non-turbo engines:
    D9B engine .... 15° ± 1°
    DJZ engine .... 13.5° ± 1°
  1.9 litre (1905 cc) Turbo engines:
    D8A engine .... 11° ± 1°
    DHY engine .... 11° ± 1°

Injectors

Type .... Pintle
Opening pressure:
  1.8 litre (1769 cc) Turbo engines .... 130 bars
  1.9 litre (1905 cc) non-turbo engines:
    Bosch fuel injection pump .... 130 bars
    Lucas CAV/Roto-diesel fuel injection pump .... 125 bars
  1.9 litre (1905 cc) Turbo engines .... 175 bars

Turbocharger

Boost pressure (approximate):
  1.8 litre (1769 cc) engine .... 0.85 bar at 3000 rpm
  1.9 litre (1905 cc) engine .... 1.0 bar at 3000 rpm

Torque wrench settings

	Nm	lbf ft
Exhaust system:		
Manifold/turbocharger joint bolt nuts	10	7
Clamping ring nuts	20	15
Fuel pipe union nuts	20	15
Injection pump mounting nuts/bolts	20	15
Injection pump sprocket nut	50	37
Injection pump sprocket puller bolts	10	7
Injection pump timing hole blanking plug:		
Lucas pump	6	4
Bosch pump	15	11
Injectors to cylinder head	90	66
No 4 cylinder TDC blanking plug	30	22
Stop solenoid:		
Lucas pump	15	11
Bosch pump	20	15
Turbocharger mounting bolts	55	41
Turbocharger oil feed pipe union	25	18
Turbocharger oil return pipe union:		
Models with 5.0 mm thick union nut	25	18
Models with 8.0 mm thick union nut	45	33

---

1 General information and precautions

General information

1 The fuel system consists of a rear-mounted fuel tank, a fuel filter with integral water separator, a fuel injection pump, injectors and associated components. On some early models, the fuel is heated by coolant passing through the coolant housing at the rear of the engine. On later models, before passing through the filter, the fuel is heated by coolant flowing through the base of the fuel filter/thermostat housing. A turbocharger and intercooler are fitted to some engines.

2 Fuel is drawn from the fuel tank to the fuel injection pump by a vane-type transfer pump incorporated in the fuel injection pump. Before reaching the pump, the fuel passes through a fuel filter, where foreign matter and water are removed. Excess fuel lubricates the moving components of the pump, and is then returned to the tank.

3 The fuel injection pump is driven at half-crankshaft speed by the timing belt. The high pressure required to inject the fuel into the compressed air in the swirl chambers is achieved by a cam plate acting on a single piston on the Bosch pump, or by two opposed pistons forced together by rollers

1.9a Hand-operated stop lever (arrowed) - Lucas pump

1.9b Hand-operated stop lever (arrowed) - Bosch pump

running in a cam ring on the Lucas (CAV) pump. The fuel passes through a central rotor with a single outlet drilling which aligns with ports leading to the injector pipes.

4 Fuel metering is controlled by a centrifugal governor, which reacts to accelerator pedal position and engine speed. The governor is linked to a metering valve, which increases or decreases the amount of fuel delivered at each pumping stroke. On turbocharged models, a separate device also increases fuel delivery with increasing boost pressure.

5 Basic injection timing is determined when the pump is fitted. When the engine is running, it is varied automatically to suit the prevailing engine speed by a mechanism which turns the cam plate or ring.

6 The four fuel injectors produce a homogeneous spray of fuel into the swirl chambers located in the cylinder head. The injectors are calibrated to open and close at critical pressures to provide efficient and even combustion. Each injector needle is lubricated by fuel, which accumulates in the spring chamber and is channelled to the injection

pump return hose by leak-off pipes.

7 Bosch or Lucas fuel system components may be fitted, depending on the model. Components from the latter manufacturer are marked either "CAV", "Roto-diesel" or "Con-diesel", depending on their date and place of manufacture. With the exception of the fuel filter assembly, replacement components must be of the same make as those originally fitted.

8 Cold starting is assisted by preheater or "glow" plugs fitted to each swirl chamber. A thermostatic sensor in the cooling system operates a fast idle lever on the injection pump to increase the idling speed when the engine is cold. On turbocharged models, the injection timing is advanced when the engine is cold by a coolant-fed capsule.

9 A stop solenoid cuts the fuel supply to the injection pump rotor when the ignition is switched off, and there is also a hand-operated stop lever for use in an emergency (see illustrations).

10 Provided that the specified maintenance is carried out, the fuel injection equipment will

give long and trouble-free service. The injection pump itself may well outlast the engine. The main potential cause of damage to the injection pump and injectors is dirt or water in the fuel.

11 Servicing of the injection pump and injectors is very limited for the home mechanic, and any dismantling or adjustment other than that described in this Chapter must be entrusted to a Peugeot dealer or fuel injection specialist.

Precautions

 Warning: It is necessary to take certain precautions when working on the fuel system components, particularly the fuel injectors. Before carrying out any operations on the fuel system, refer to the precautions given in "Safety first!" at the beginning of this manual, and to any additional warning notes at the start of the relevant Sections.

2 Fuel system - priming and bleeding

1 After disconnecting part of the fuel supply system or running out of fuel, it is necessary to prime the system and bleed off air which may have entered the system components.

2 All models have a hand-operated priming pump. On early models, where the fuel filter is on the side of the battery tray, the priming pump consists of a push-button mounted on top of the fuel filter head. On later models, the priming pump consists of a rubber bulb, which is located on the right-hand side of the engine compartment (see illustrations).

3 To prime the system, loosen the bleed screw located on the fuel filter head, or in the injection pump inlet pipe union bolt, depending on model.

4 Pump the priming pump until fuel free from air bubbles emerges from the bleed screw. Retighten the bleed screw.

5 Switch on the ignition (to activate the stop solenoid) and continue pumping the priming plunger until firm resistance is felt, then pump a few more times.

4

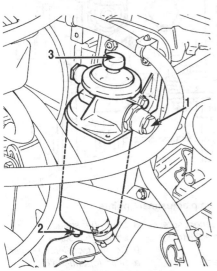

2.2a Hand-operated fuel system priming pump - early models (Bosch filter assembly)

1 *Air bleed screw*
2 *Water drain screw*
3 *Priming push-button*

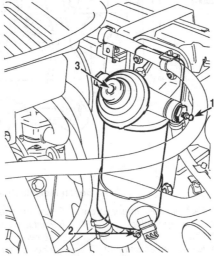

2.2b Hand-operated fuel system priming pump - early models (Lucas CAV/ Roto-diesel filter assembly)

1 *Air bleed screw*
2 *Water drain screw*
3 *Priming push-button*

2.2c Hand-operated fuel system priming pump - later models

6 If a large amount of air has entered the pump, place a wad of rag around the fuel return union on the pump (to absorb spilt fuel), then slacken the union. Operate the priming plunger (with the ignition switched on to activate the stop solenoid), or crank the engine on the starter motor in 10 second bursts, until fuel free from air bubbles emerges from the fuel union. Tighten the union and mop up split fuel.

 Warning: Be prepared to stop the engine if it should fire, to avoid excessive fuel spray and spillage.

7 If air has entered the injector pipes, place wads of rag around the injector pipe unions at the injectors (to absorb spilt fuel), then slacken the unions. Crank the engine on the starter motor until fuel emerges from the unions, then stop cranking the engine and retighten the unions. Mop up spilt fuel. *Refer to the warning in the previous paragraph.*

8 Start the engine with the accelerator pedal fully depressed. Additional cranking may be necessary to finally bleed the system before the engine starts.

3 Maximum speed - checking and adjustment

Caution: The maximum speed adjustment screw is sealed by the manufacturers at the factory, using paint or a locking wire and a lead seal. There is no reason why it should require adjustment. Do not disturb the screw if the vehicle is still within the warranty period, otherwise the warranty will be invalidated. This adjustment requires the use of a tachometer suitable for use on diesel engines.

1 Run the engine to operating temperature.

2 Have an assistant fully depress the accelerator pedal, and check that the maximum engine speed is as given in the Specifications. Do not keep the engine at maximum speed for more than two or three seconds.

3 If adjustment is necessary, stop the engine, then loosen the locknut, turn the maximum speed adjustment screw as necessary, and retighten the locknut **(see illustrations)**.

4 Repeat the procedure in paragraph 2 to check the adjustment.

5 Stop the engine and disconnect the tachometer.

4 Fast idle thermostatic sensor - removal, refitting and adjustment

Removal

Note: *A new sealing washer must be used when refitting the sensor.*

1 The thermostatic sensor is located in the

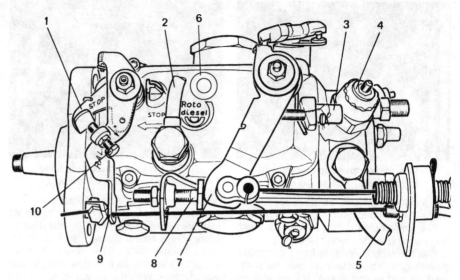

3.3a Lucas fuel injection pump adjustment points

1 Manual stop lever	4 Stop solenoid	8 Anti-stall adjustment screw
2 Fuel return pipe	5 Fuel inlet	9 Fast idle lever
3 Maximum speed adjustment screw	6 Timing access plug	10 Idle speed adjustment screw
	7 Control (accelerator) lever	

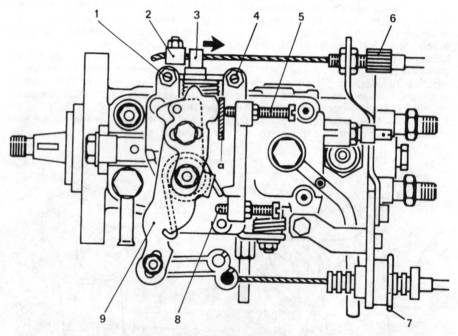

3.3b Bosch fuel injection pump adjustment points

1 Fast idle adjustment screw	5 Anti-stall adjustment screw	8 Maximum speed adjustment screw
2 Cable end fitting	6 Fast idle cable adjustment screw	9 Control (accelerator) lever
3 Fast idle lever	7 Accelerator cable adjustment screw	a Shim for anti-stall adjustment
4 Idle speed adjustment screw		

side of the thermostat housing cover on early models, or in the thermostat/fuel filter housing on later models.

2 For improved access on later models, if desired, on Turbo models remove the intercooler, and on non-turbo models with D9B engine remove the air distribution housing. If necessary, also remove the inlet

4.4a Fast idle cable end fitting clamp nut (arrowed) - Lucas pump

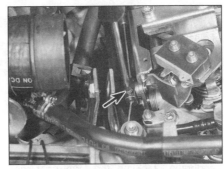

4.4b Loosening fast idle cable end fitting clamp screw (arrowed) - Bosch pump

4.5 Sliding the fast idle cable from the adjustment screw - Bosch pump

4.6 Fast idle thermostatic sensor (arrowed)

duct, and disconnect the breather hose from the engine oil filler tube. Refer to the relevant Sections of this Chapter for further information.

3 Drain the cooling system as described in Chapter 1.

4 Loosen the clamp screw or nut (as applicable), and disconnect the fast idle cable end fitting from the inner cable at the fuel injection pump fast idle lever **(see illustrations)**.

5 Slide the cable from the adjustment screw located in the bracket on the fuel injection pump **(see illustration)**.

6 Using a suitable open-ended spanner, unscrew the thermostatic sensor from the fuel filter/thermostat housing, and withdraw the sensor complete with the cable **(see illustration)**. Recover the sealing washer, where applicable.

Refitting

7 If sealing compound was originally used to fit the sensor in place of a washer, thoroughly clean all traces of old sealing compound from the sensor and housing. Ensure that no traces of sealant are left in the internal coolant passages of the housing.

8 Fit the sensor, using suitable sealing compound or a new washer as applicable, and tighten it.

9 Insert the adjustment screw into the bracket on the fuel injection pump, and screw on the locknut finger-tight.

10 Insert the inner cable through the fast idle lever, and position the end fitting on the cable,

but do not tighten the clamp screw or nut (as applicable).

11 Adjust the cable as described in the following paragraphs.

Adjustment

12 With the engine cold, push the fast idle lever fully towards the flywheel end of the engine. Tighten the clamp screw or nut with the cable end fitting touching the lever.

13 Adjust the screw to ensure that the fast idle lever is touching its stop, then tighten the locknut.

14 Measure the exposed length of the inner cable.

15 Where necessary, refit the intercooler or the air distribution housing, and reconnect the breather hose to the engine oil filler tube.

16 Refill the cooling system as described in Chapter 1, and run the engine to its normal operating temperature.

17 Check that the fast idle cable is slack. If not, it is likely that the sensor is faulty.

18 With the engine hot, check that there is approximately 0.5 to 1 mm of free play in the cable on Lucas injection pumps and 5 to 6 mm of free play in the cable on Bosch injection pumps. This indicates that the thermostatic sensor is functioning correctly.

19 Check that the engine speed increases when the fast idle lever is pushed towards the flywheel end of the engine. With the lever against its stop, the fast idle speed should be as specified (refer to Chapter 1 for details of how to check engine speed accurately).

20 Stop the engine.

5 Stop solenoid - description, removal and refitting

Caution: Be careful not to allow dirt into the injection pump during this procedure.

Description

1 The stop solenoid is located on the end of the fuel injection pump **(see illustrations)**. Its purpose is to cut the fuel supply when the ignition is switched off. If an open-circuit occurs in the solenoid or supply wiring, it will be impossible to start the engine, as the fuel will not reach the injectors. The same applies if the solenoid plunger jams in the "stop" position. If the solenoid jams in the "run" position, the engine will not stop when the ignition is switched off.

2 If the solenoid has failed and the engine will not run, a temporary repair may be made by removing the solenoid as described in the following paragraphs. Refit the solenoid body without the plunger and spring. Tape up the wire so that it cannot touch earth. The engine can now be started as usual, but it will be necessary to use the manual stop lever (see Section 1, paragraph 9) on the fuel injection pump (or to stall the engine in gear) to stop it.

Removal

Note: *A new sealing washer or O-ring (as applicable) will be required on refitting.*

3 Disconnect the battery negative lead.

4 On models fitted with a Bosch fuel injection pump, it may be necessary to unbolt the fast

5.1a Removing the stop solenoid wiring cover (arrowed) - Bosch pump

5.1b Removing the stop solenoid wiring cover - Lucas pump

4

idle cable support bracket from the side of the fuel injection pump, to improve access. Refer to Section 4 if it proves necessary to disconnect the cable from the bracket.

5 Withdraw the rubber boot (where applicable), then unscrew the terminal nut and disconnect the wire from the top of the solenoid.

6 Carefully clean around the solenoid, then unscrew and withdraw the solenoid, and recover the sealing washer or O-ring (as applicable). Recover the solenoid plunger and spring if they remain in the pump. Operate the hand-priming pump as the solenoid is removed, to flush away any dirt.

Refitting

7 Refitting is a reversal of removal, using a new sealing washer or O-ring and tightening the solenoid to the specified torque setting.

8 If the fast idle cable was disconnected, reconnect and adjust it (see Section 4).

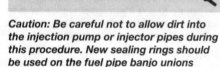

6 Fuel injection pump - removal and refitting

Caution: Be careful not to allow dirt into the injection pump or injector pipes during this procedure. New sealing rings should be used on the fuel pipe banjo unions when refitting.

Removal

1 Disconnect the battery negative lead.

2 Where necessary, cover the alternator with a plastic bag, as a precaution against spillage of diesel fuel.

3 For improved access, on Turbo models remove the intercooler, and on non-turbo models with D9B engine remove the air distribution housing. If necessary, also remove the inlet duct, and disconnect the breather hose from the engine oil filler tube. Refer to the relevant Sections of this Chapter for further information.

4 Chock the rear wheels and release the handbrake. Jack up the front right-hand corner of the vehicle until the wheel is just clear of the ground. Support the vehicle on an axle stand *(see "Jacking and Vehicle Support")* and engage the 4th or 5th gear. This will enable the engine to be turned easily by turning the right-hand wheel. Alternatively, the engine can be turned using a spanner on the crankshaft pulley bolt, but on most models access is limited. It will be easier to turn the engine if the glow plugs are removed (see Chapter 5).

5 Remove the upper timing belt covers with reference to Chapter 2.

6 Where necessary, disconnect the hoses from the vacuum converter on the end of the fuel injection pump.

7 Disconnect the accelerator cable from the fuel injection pump, with reference to Section 11.

8 Disconnect the fast idle cable from the fuel injection pump, with reference to Section 4.

9 Loosen the clip, or undo the banjo union,

and disconnect the fuel supply hose. Recover the sealing washers from the banjo union, where applicable. Cover the open end of the hose, and refit and cover the banjo bolt to keep dirt out **(see illustrations)**.

10 Disconnect the main fuel return pipe and the injector leak-off return pipe banjo union **(see illustration)**. Recover the sealing washers from the banjo union. Again, cover the open end of the hose and the banjo bolt to keep dirt out. Take care not to get the inlet and outlet banjo unions mixed up.

11 Disconnect all relevant wiring from the pump. Note that on certain Bosch pumps, this can be achieved by simply disconnecting the wiring connectors at the brackets on the pump **(see illustration)**. On some pumps, it will be necessary to disconnect the wiring from the individual components (some connections may be protected by rubber covers).

12 Unscrew the union nuts securing the injector pipes to the fuel injection pump and injectors. Counterhold the unions on the pump, while unscrewing the pipe-to-pump union nuts. Remove the pipes as a set. Cover open unions to keep dirt out, using small plastic bags **(see illustrations)**.

> **HAYNES HiNT** *Fingers cut from discarded (but clean!) rubber gloves provide excellent protection for open fuel unions.*

13 Turn the crankshaft until the two bolt holes in the fuel injection pump sprocket are

6.9a Disconnecting the fuel pump fuel supply banjo union. Note sealing washers (arrowed) - Bosch pump

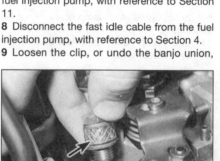

6.9b Refitting the fuel supply banjo bolt with a small section of fuel hose (arrowed) to prevent dirt ingress - Bosch pump

6.10 Injection pump fuel return pipe banjo union (arrowed) - Bosch pump

6.11 Disconnecting a fuel injection pump wiring plug - Bosch pump

6.12a Unscrewing a fuel pipe-to-injector union

6.12b Cover the open end of the injector to prevent dirt ingress

6.12c Unscrewing a fuel pipe-to-pump union - Bosch pump

6.12d Removing a fuel pipe assembly

6.14 Bolts inserted through timing holes in injection pump sprocket

6.15 Mark the injection pump in relation to the mounting bracket (arrowed)

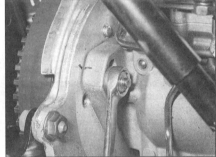

6.16a Unscrewing an injection pump front mounting nut - Bosch pump

6.16b Unscrewing an injection pump rear mounting nut (arrowed) - Bosch pump

aligned with the corresponding holes in the engine front plate.

14 Insert two M8 bolts through the holes, and hand-tighten them. Note that the bolts must retain the sprocket while the fuel injection pump is removed, thereby making it unnecessary to remove the timing belt **(see illustration)**.

15 Mark the fuel injection pump in relation to the mounting bracket, using a scriber or felt tip pen **(see illustration)**. This will ensure that the correct pump timing is retained when refitting.

16 Unscrew the three front mounting nuts, and recover the washers. Unscrew and remove the rear mounting nut and bolt, noting the locations of the washers, and support the injection pump on a block of wood **(see illustrations)**.

17 Release the injection pump sprocket from the pump shaft, as described in Chapter 2A, Section 8. Note that the sprocket can be left engaged with the timing belt as the pump is withdrawn from its mounting bracket. Refit the M8 bolts to retain the sprocket in position while the pump is removed.

18 Carefully withdraw the pump. Recover the Woodruff key from the end of the pump shaft if it is loose, and similarly recover the bush from the rear of the mounting bracket **(see illustrations)**.

Refitting

19 Commence refitting the injection pump by fitting the Woodruff key to the shaft groove (if removed).

20 Offer the pump to the mounting bracket,

6.18a Removing an injection pump - Bosch pump

and support on a block of wood, as during removal.

21 Engage the pump shaft with the sprocket, and refit the sprocket as described in Chapter 2A, Section 8. Ensure that the Woodruff key does not fall out of the shaft as the sprocket is engaged.

22 Align the marks made on the pump and mounting bracket before removal. If a new pump is being fitted, transfer the mark from the old pump to give an approximate setting.

23 Refit and lightly tighten the pump mounting nuts and bolt.

24 Set up the injection timing, as described in Sections 7, 8 and 9 (as applicable).

25 Refit and reconnect the injector fuel pipes.

26 Reconnect all relevant wiring to the pump.

27 Reconnect the fuel supply and return hoses, and tighten the unions, as applicable. Use new sealing washers on the banjo unions.

6.18b Recover the bush from the rear of the pump mounting bracket

28 Reconnect the fast idle cable, and adjust it as described in Section 4.

29 Reconnect and adjust the accelerator cable with reference to Section 11.

30 Where necessary, reconnect the hoses to the vacuum converter.

31 Refit the upper timing belt covers.

32 Lower the vehicle to the ground.

33 Where applicable, refit the intercooler or the air distribution housing.

34 Remove the plastic bag used to cover the alternator.

35 Reconnect the battery negative lead.

36 Bleed the fuel system as described in Section 2.

37 Start the engine, and check the fuel injection pump adjustments as described in Chapter 1.

4

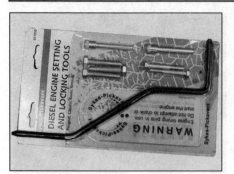

7.3 TDC setting and locking tools for setting injection timing on diesel engines

7 Injection timing - checking methods and adjustment

1 Checking the injection timing is not a routine operation. It is only necessary after the injection pump has been disturbed.
2 Dynamic timing equipment does exist, but it is unlikely to be available to the home mechanic. The equipment works by converting pressure pulses in an injector pipe into electrical signals. If such equipment is available, use it in accordance with its maker's instructions.
3 Static timing as described in this Chapter gives good results if carried out carefully. A dial test indicator will be needed, with probes and adapters appropriate to the type of injection pump **(see illustration)**. Read through the procedures before starting work, to find out what is involved.

8 Injection timing (Lucas fuel injection pump) - checking and adjustment

Caution: The maximum engine speed and transfer pressure settings, together with timing access plugs, are sealed using locking wire and lead seals. Do not disturb the wire if the vehicle is still within the warranty period otherwise the warranty will be invalidated. Also do not attempt the timing procedure unless accurate instru-

mentation is available. Suitable special tools for carrying out pump timing should be available from larger motor factors or your Peugeot dealer. Refer to the precautions given in Section 1 of this Chapter before proceeding.
Note: *To check the injection pump timing a special timing probe and mounting bracket (Peugeot tool No. 0117AM) is required* **(see illustration 8.4)**. *Without access to this piece of equipment, injection pump timing should be entrusted to a Peugeot dealer or other suitably equipped specialist.*
1 If the injection timing is being checked with the pump in position on the engine, rather than as part of the pump refitting procedure, disconnect the battery negative lead and cover the alternator with a clean cloth or plastic bag to prevent the possibility of fuel being spilt onto it. Remove the injector pipes as described in paragraph 12 of Section 6.
2 Referring to Chapter 2A, align the engine assembly/valve timing holes to lock the crankshaft in position. Remove the crankshaft locking tool, then turn the crankshaft **backwards** (anti-clockwise) approximately a quarter of a turn.
3 Unscrew the access plug from the guide on the top of the pump body and recover the sealing washer **(see illustration)**. Insert the special timing probe into the guide, making sure it is correctly seated against the guide sealing washer surface. **Note:** *The timing probe must be seated against the guide sealing washer surface and not the upper lip of the guide for the measurement to be accurate.*
4 Mount the bracket on the pump guide (Peugeot tool No. 0117AM) and securely mount the dial gauge (dial test indicator) in the bracket so that its tip is in contact with the bracket linkage **(see illustration)**. Position the dial gauge so that its plunger is at the mid-point of its travel and zero the gauge.
5 Rotate the crankshaft slowly in the correct direction of rotation (clockwise) until the crankshaft locking tool can be re-inserted.

6 With the crankshaft locked in position read the dial gauge; the reading should correspond to the value marked on the pump (there is a tolerance of ± 0.04 mm). The timing value may be marked on a plastic disc attached to the front of the pump, or alternatively on a tag attached to the pump control lever **(see illustrations)**.
7 If adjustment is necessary, slacken the front pump mounting nuts and the rear mounting bolt, then slowly rotate the pump body until the point is found where the specified reading is obtained on the dial gauge. When the pump is correctly positioned, tighten both its front mounting nuts and the rear bolt to their specified torque settings.
8 Withdraw the timing probe slightly, so that it is positioned clear of the pump rotor dowel, and remove the crankshaft locking pin. Rotate the crankshaft through one and three quarter rotations in the normal direction of rotation.
9 Slide the timing probe back into position ensuring that it is correctly seated against the guide sealing washer surface, not the upper lip, then zero the dial gauge.
10 Rotate the crankshaft slowly in the correct direction of rotation (clockwise) until the crankshaft locking tool can be re-inserted. Recheck the timing measurement.
11 If adjustment is necessary, slacken the pump mounting nuts and bolt and repeat the operations in paragraphs 7 to 10.
12 When the pump timing is correctly set, remove the dial gauge and mounting bracket and withdraw the timing probe.
13 Refit the screw and sealing washer to the guide and tighten it securely.

8.6a Pump timing value (x) marked on plastic disc - Lucas pump

8.3 Removing the injection pump timing inspection plug - Lucas pump

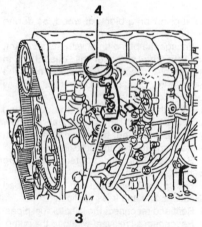

8.4 Peugeot injection pump timing gauge (4) and mounting bracket (3) in position on the injection pump

8.6b Pump timing values marked on label (1) and tag (2) - Lucas pump

14 If the procedure is being carried out as part of the pump refitting sequence, proceed as described in Section 6.

15 If the procedure is being carried out with the pump fitted to the engine, refit the injector pipes tightening their union nuts to the specified torque. Reconnect the battery, then bleed the fuel system (see Section 2). Start the engine and adjust the idle speed and anti-stall speeds as described in Chapter 1.

9 Injection timing (Bosch fuel injection pump) - checking and adjustment

Caution: Some of the injection pump settings and access plugs may be sealed by the manufacturers at the factory, using paint or locking wire and lead seals. Do not disturb the seals if the vehicle is still within the warranty period, otherwise the warranty will be invalidated. Also do not attempt the timing procedure unless accurate instrumentation is available.

1 If the injection timing is being checked with the pump in position on the engine, rather than as part of the pump refitting procedure, disconnect the battery negative lead and cover the alternator with a clean cloth or plastic bag to prevent the possibility of fuel being spilt onto it. Remove the injector pipes as described in paragraph 12 of Section 6.

2 If not already having done so, slacken the clamp screw and/or nut (as applicable) and slide the fast idle cable end fitting arrangement along the cable so that it is no longer in contact with the pump fast idle lever (ie, so the fast idle lever returns to its stop) (see Section 4).

3 Referring to Chapter 2A, align the engine assembly/valve timing holes to lock the crankshaft in position. Remove the crankshaft locking tool, then turn the crankshaft *backwards* (anti-clockwise) approximately a quarter of a turn.

4 Unscrew the access screw, situated in the centre of the four injector pipe unions, from the rear of the injection pump. As the screw is removed, position a suitable container beneath the pump to catch any escaping fuel. Mop up any spilt fuel with a clean cloth.

5 Screw the adapter into the rear of the pump and mount the dial gauge in the adapter **(see illustration)**. If access to the special adapter cannot be gained (Peugeot tool No. 0117F), they can be purchased from most good motor factors. Position the dial gauge so that its plunger is at the mid-point of its travel and securely tighten the adapter locknut.

6 Slowly rotate the crankshaft back and forth whilst observing the dial gauge, to determine when the injection pump piston is at the bottom of its travel (BDC). When the piston is correctly positioned, zero the dial gauge.

7 Rotate the crankshaft slowly in the correct direction until the crankshaft locking tool can be re-inserted.

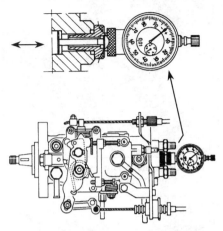

9.5 Dial test indicator and timing probe for use with Bosch pump

8 The reading obtained on the dial gauge should be equal to the specified pump timing measurement given in the Specifications at the start of this Chapter. If adjustment is necessary, slacken the front and rear pump mounting nuts and bolts and slowly rotate the pump body until the point is found where the specified reading is obtained. When the pump is correctly positioned, tighten both its front and rear mounting nuts and bolts securely.

9 Rotate the crankshaft through one and three quarter rotations in the normal direction of rotation. Find the injection pump piston BDC as described in paragraph 6 and zero the dial gauge.

10 Rotate the crankshaft slowly in the correct direction of rotation (clockwise) until the crankshaft locking tool can be re-inserted (bringing the engine back to TDC). Recheck the timing measurement.

11 If adjustment is necessary, slacken the pump mounting nuts and bolts and repeat the operations in paragraphs 8 to 10.

12 When the pump timing is correctly set, unscrew the adapter and remove the dial gauge.

13 Refit the screw and sealing washer to the pump and tighten it securely.

14 If the procedure is being carried out as part of the pump refitting sequence, proceed as described in Section 6.

15 If the procedure is being carried out with the pump fitted to the engine, refit the injector pipes tightening their union nuts to the specified torque setting. Reconnect the battery then bleed the fuel system as described in Section 2. Start the engine and adjust the idle speed and anti-stall speeds as described in Chapter 1. Also adjust the fast idle cable as described in Section 4.

10 Fuel injectors - testing, removal and refitting

> **Warning: Exercise extreme caution when working on the fuel injectors. Never expose the hands or any part of the body to injector spray, as the high working pressure can cause the fuel to penetrate the skin, with possibly fatal results. You are strongly advised to have any work which involves testing the injectors under pressure carried out by a dealer or fuel injection specialist.**

Testing

1 Injectors do deteriorate with prolonged use, and it is reasonable to expect them to need reconditioning or renewal after 60 000 miles (100 000 km) or so. Accurate testing, overhaul and calibration of the injectors must be left to a specialist. A defective injector which is causing knocking or smoking can be located without dismantling as follows.

2 Run the engine at a fast idle. Slacken each injector union in turn, placing rag around the union to catch spilt fuel, and being careful not to expose the skin to any spray. When the union on the defective injector is slackened, the knocking or smoking will stop.

Removal

Note: *New copper washers and fire seal washers must be used on refitting.*

3 For improved access, on Turbo models remove the intercooler, and on non-turbo models with D9B engine remove the air distribution housing. If necessary, also remove the inlet duct, and disconnect the breather hose from the engine oil filler tube. Refer to the relevant Sections of this Chapter for further information.

4 Carefully clean around the injectors and injector pipe union nuts.

5 Pull the leak-off pipes from the injectors **(see illustration)**.

6 Unscrew the union nuts securing the injector pipes to the fuel injection pump. Counterhold the unions on the pump when

10.5 Pulling a leak-off pipe from a fuel injector

4

10.7 Unscrewing an injector pipe union nut

10.8 Unscrew the injectors, and remove them from the cylinder head

10.9a Removing a fuel injector copper washer . . .

unscrewing the nuts. Cover open unions to keep dirt out, using small plastic bags.

 HAYNES HiNT *Fingers cut from discarded (but clean!) rubber gloves provide excellent protection for open fuel unions.*

7 Unscrew the union nuts and disconnect the pipes from the injectors **(see illustration)**. If necessary, the injector pipes may be completely removed. Note carefully the locations of the pipe clamps, for use when refitting. Cover the ends of the injectors, to prevent dirt ingress.
8 Unscrew the injectors using a deep socket or box spanner (27 mm across-flats), and remove them from the cylinder head **(see illustration)**.
9 Recover the copper washers and fire seal washers from the cylinder head. Also recover the sleeves if they are loose **(see illustrations)**.

Refitting

10 Obtain new copper washers and fire seal washers. Also renew the sleeves, if they are damaged.
11 Take care not to drop the injectors, or allow the needles at their tips to become damaged. The injectors are precision-made to fine limits, and must not be handled roughly. In particular, never mount them in a bench vice.
12 Commence refitting by inserting the sleeves (if removed) into the cylinder head, followed by the fire seal washers (convex face uppermost), and copper washers.
13 Insert the injectors and tighten them to the specified torque.
14 Refit the injector pipes and tighten the union nuts. Make sure the pipe clamps are in their previously-noted positions. If the clamps are wrongly positioned or missing, problems may be experienced with pipes breaking or splitting.
15 Reconnect the leak-off pipes.
16 Refit the intercooler or air distribution housing where applicable.
17 Start the engine. If difficulty is experienced, bleed the fuel system as described in Section 2.

10.9b . . . fire seal washer . . .

11 Accelerator cable - removal, refitting and adjustment

Removal

1 Working in the engine compartment, operate the pump control lever on the fuel injection pump, and release the cable inner from the lever **(see illustration)**.
2 Pull the outer cable out from its mounting bracket rubber grommet **(see illustration)**. Where fitted, slide the flat washer off the end of the cable, and remove the spring clip.
3 Working back along the length of the cable, free it from any retaining clips or ties, noting its correct routing.
4 Where necessary remove the lower trim from underneath the driver's side of the facia panel.
5 Working from inside the vehicle, disconnect

11.2 Pulling the accelerator cable outer from the bracket

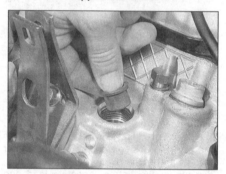

10.9c . . . and sleeve

the cable from the accelerator pedal by depressing the lugs on the plastic end fitting and pushing the fitting from the pedal **(see illustration)**.
6 Release the outer cable from its retainer on the pedal mounting bracket, then tie a length of string to the end of the cable.

11.1 Releasing the accelerator cable inner from the lever on the injection pump

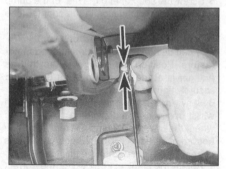

11.5 Depress the lugs (arrowed) to release the accelerator cable from the pedal

11.10 Refitting the spring clip to the accelerator cable groove

7 Return to the engine compartment, release the cable grommet from the bulkhead and withdraw the cable. When the end of the cable appears, untie the string and leave it in position - it can then be used to draw the cable back into position on refitting.

Refitting

8 Tie the string to the end of the cable, then use the string to draw the cable into position through the bulkhead. Once the cable end is visible, untie the string, then clip the outer cable into its pedal bracket retainer, and clip the inner cable into position in the pedal end. The remaining procedure is a reversal of removal, but adjust it as follows.

Adjustment

9 Remove the spring clip from the accelerator outer cable. Ensuring that the pump control lever is fully against its stop, gently pull the cable out of its grommet until all free play is removed from the inner cable.
10 With the cable held in this position, refit the spring clip to the last exposed outer cable groove in front of the rubber grommet and washer. When the clip is refitted and the outer cable is released, there should only be a small amount of free play in the inner cable (see illustration).
11 Have an assistant depress the accelerator pedal, and check that the control lever opens fully and returns smoothly to its stop.

12 Accelerator pedal - removal and refitting

Removal

1 Disconnect the accelerator cable from the pedal as described in Section 11.
2 Remove the screws from the pedal pivot bush and lift out the pedal.
3 Examine the pivot bush and shaft for signs of wear, and renew as necessary.

Refitting

4 Refitting is a reversal of the removal procedure, applying a little multi-purpose grease to the pedal pivot point. On completion, adjust the accelerator cable (see Section 11).

13 Fuel level sender - removal and refitting

Note: *A new rubber sealing ring must be used on refitting.*

Removal

1 Disconnect the battery negative lead.
2 For access to the sender unit, fold the rear seat cushion forwards or remove the rear seats as described in Chapter 11.
3 Using a screwdriver, carefully prise the plastic access cover from the floor to expose the sender unit.
4 Disconnect the wiring connector from the sender unit, and tape the connector to the vehicle body to prevent it from disappearing behind the tank (see illustration).
5 Mark the hoses for identification purposes, then slacken the feed and return hose retaining clips. Where the crimped-type Peugeot hose clips are fitted, cut the clips and discard them; use standard worm-drive hose clips on refitting. Disconnect both hoses from the top of the sender unit, and plug the hose ends.
6 Noting the alignment marks on the tank, sender unit and the locking ring, unscrew the ring and remove it from the tank. This is best accomplished by using a screwdriver on the raised ribs of the locking ring, as follows. Carefully tap the screwdriver to turn the ring anti-clockwise until it can be unscrewed by hand.
7 Carefully lift the sender unit from the top of the fuel tank, taking great care not to bend the sender unit float arm, or to spill fuel onto the interior of the vehicle. Recover the rubber sealing ring and discard it - a new one must be used on refitting. If necessary remove the filter from the bottom of the unit and wash it in clean fuel.

Refitting

8 Refitting is a reversal of the removal procedure, noting the following points:
 a) *Prior to refitting, fit a new rubber sealing ring to the sender unit.*
 b) *Refit the sender unit to the tank, aligning its arrow with the right-hand alignment*

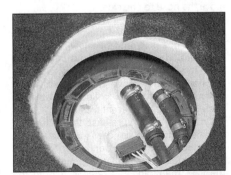

13.4 Fuel level sender unit location (plastic cover removed)

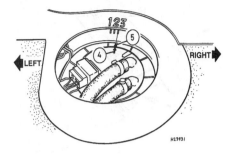

13.8 Fuel level sender unit correctly refitted

1, 2 and 3 Alignment marks on fuel tank
4 Alignment mark on sender unit
5 Alignment mark on locking ring

 mark on the fuel tank. Secure the sender in position with the locking ring, and check that the locking ring, sender unit and fuel tank marks are all correctly aligned (see illustration).
 c) *Ensure the feed and return hoses are correctly reconnected and securely retained by their clips.*

14 Fuel tank - removal and refitting

Removal

1 Before removing the fuel tank, all fuel must be drained from the tank. Since a fuel tank drain plug is not provided, it is preferable to carry out the removal operation when the tank is nearly empty. Before proceeding, disconnect the battery negative lead and syphon or hand-pump the remaining fuel from the tank. Store the fuel in a metal or plastic container which can be sealed.
2 Remove the exhaust system and relevant heat shield(s) as described in Section 21.
3 Disconnect the handbrake cable at the adjuster mechanism, and release the primary cable from any clips on the fuel tank. Position the cable clear of the tank.
4 Disconnect the wiring connector from the fuel level sender unit, as described in Section 13.
5 Working at the right-hand side of the fuel tank, release the retaining clips then disconnect the filler neck vent pipe and main filler neck hose from the fuel tank/filler neck. Where necessary, also disconnect the breather hose(s). Some breather hoses are joined to the tank with quick-release fittings; to disconnect these fittings, slide the cover along the hose then depress the centre ring and pull the hose out of its fitting (see illustration).
6 Trace the fuel feed and return hoses back from the right-hand side of the tank to their union with the fuel pipes. Slacken the retaining clips and disconnect both hoses from the fuel pipes. Where the crimped-type

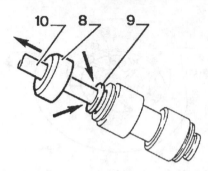

14.5 Fuel tank breather hose quick release connector

8 Cover   9 Centre ring   10 Hose

Peugeot hose clips are fitted, cut the clips and discard them; use standard worm-drive hose clips on refitting. Plug the hose and pipe ends, to prevent the entry of dirt into the system.

7 Place a trolley jack with an interposed block of wood beneath the tank, then raise the jack until it is supporting the weight of the tank.

8 Slacken and remove the retaining nut and bolts, then remove the two support rods from the underside of the tank **(see illustration)**.

9 Slowly lower the fuel tank out of position, disconnecting any other relevant vent pipes as they become accessible (where necessary), and remove the tank from underneath the vehicle.

10 If the tank is contaminated with sediment or water, remove the sender unit (Section 13), and swill the tank out with clean fuel. The tank is injection-moulded from a synthetic material - if seriously damaged, it should be renewed. However, in certain cases, it may be possible to have small leaks or minor damage repaired. Seek the advice of a specialist before attempting to repair the fuel tank.

Refitting

11 Refitting is the reverse of the removal procedure, noting the following points.

a) When lifting the tank back into position, take care to ensure that none of the hoses become trapped between the tank and vehicle body.

b) Ensure all pipes and hoses are correctly routed, and securely held in position with their retaining clips.

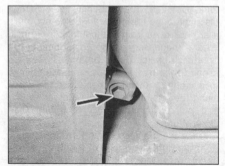

14.8 Fuel tank support rod retaining bolt (arrowed)

c) Reconnect the handbrake cable and adjust the handbrake as described in Chapter 9.

d) On completion, refill the tank with a small amount of fuel, and check for signs of leakage prior to taking the vehicle out on the road.

15 Manifolds - removal and refitting

Note: *On some Turbo models, the inlet and exhaust manifolds may share the same gasket. Where this is the case, it is recommended that both manifolds are removed, whenever one is removed, in order that the gasket can be renewed. It is possible to remove the manifolds individually, in which case the original gasket would be re-used, but this is not recommended.*

Inlet manifold

Note: *Renew the manifold gasket(s) when refitting.*

Removal

1 Disconnect the battery negative lead.

2 For improved access, on Turbo models remove the intercooler, and on non-turbo models with D9B engine remove the air distribution housing. If necessary, also remove the inlet duct, and disconnect the breather hose from the engine oil filler tube. Refer to the relevant Sections of this Chapter for further information. Note that on some models, to give sufficient clearance between the engine and the bulkhead to remove the manifold, it may be necessary to remove the right-hand engine mounting (see Chapter 2A), and tilt the engine forwards; if this is done, ensure that the engine is adequately supported using a jack and block of wood, or a hoist.

3 Disconnect the end of the accelerator cable from the fuel injection pump, with reference to Section 11. Release the cable from its clips, noting their locations, and position the cable to one side, clear of the manifolds.

4 Similarly, disconnect the brake servo vacuum hose from the vacuum pump, and move the hose to one side.

5 On models equipped with an exhaust gas recirculation (EGR) system, disconnect the vacuum hoses from the flow valve and recirculation valve. Slacken and remove the nuts and bolts securing each valve to the manifolds and remove both valves as an assembly. Recover the gasket fitted between each valve and its relevant manifold.

6 On Turbo models, release the hose clips and disconnect the air hoses from the air tube which connects the turbocharger to the air cleaner tubing. Manipulate the air tube from the inlet manifold, and remove it from the engine compartment. Push a wad of (clean!) rag into the open end of the turbocharger air

15.7 Inlet manifold securing bolts (A) and hex bolt (B - loosen but do not remove) on Turbo models - engine removed for clarity

hose (or the turbocharger itself, if the hose has been removed completely), to prevent the possibility of dirt ingress. Also release the securing clip, and remove the intercooler air hose from the turbocharger.

7 Using a suitable hexagon bit or Allen key, remove the six bolts securing the inlet manifold. Loosen, but do not remove, the central hexagon manifold securing bolt - the manifold is slotted **(see illustration)**.

8 Withdraw the manifold from the cylinder head.

Refitting

9 Refitting is a reversal of removal, bearing in mind the following points.

a) Renew the gasket(s) when refitting the manifold.

b) Tighten all fixings to the specified torques, where applicable.

c) Reconnect the accelerator cable to the fuel injection pump. Adjust the cable if necessary, with reference to Section 11.

d) Ensure that all relevant hoses and pipes are correctly reconnected and routed.

e) Where applicable, refit the right-hand engine mounting as described in Chapter 2A.

Exhaust manifold

Note: *Renew the manifold gasket(s) when refitting.*

Removal

10 For improved access, remove the inlet manifold as described previously in this Section. This is essential on Turbo models. If desired, also unbolt the resonator box from the manifold with reference to Section 21.

11 If the inlet manifold is to be left in place, proceed as described in paragraphs 1 to 4, then proceed as follows. On models with an exhaust gas recirculation (EGR) system also carry out the operation described in paragraph 5.

12 On non-turbo models, disconnect the exhaust frontpipe from the manifold, with reference to Section 21.

13 On Turbo models, remove the turbocharger as described in Section 17.

14 On certain models, it may be necessary to unbolt the resonator chamber from the manifold, to allow sufficient clearance for the manifold to be removed.

15.15 Exhaust manifold securing nuts (arrrowed) on Turbo models - viewed with engine removed for clarity

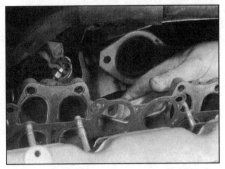

15.16 Lifting the exhaust manifold and gasket from the cylinder head

15 Unscrew the six exhaust manifold securing nuts, and recover the spacers from the studs **(see illustration)**.

16 Lift the exhaust manifold from the cylinder head, and recover the gasket(s) (where fitted) **(see illustration)**.

17 It is possible that some of the manifold studs may be unscrewed from the cylinder head when the manifold securing nuts are unscrewed. In this event, the studs should be screwed back into the cylinder head once the manifolds have been removed, using two manifold nuts locked together.

Refitting

18 Refitting is a reversal of removal, bearing in mind the following points.

a) Renew the manifold gasket(s) on refitting (where fitted). Where no gaskets are fitted, apply a smear of suitable sealant to the manifold mating surface.

b) Where applicable, refit the turbocharger as described in Section 17.

c) Where applicable, reconnect the exhaust frontpipe to the exhaust manifold as described in Section 21.

d) Tighten all fixings to the specified torque, where applicable.

e) Reconnect the accelerator cable to the fuel injection pump. Adjust the cable if necessary, with reference to Section 11.

f) Ensure that all relevant hoses and pipes are correctly reconnected and routed.

16 Turbocharger - description and precautions

Description

1 A turbocharger is fitted to some engines. It increases engine efficiency by raising the pressure in the inlet manifold above atmospheric pressure. Instead of the air simply being sucked into the cylinders, it is forced in. Additional fuel is supplied by the injection pump in proportion to the increased air inlet.

2 Energy for the operation of the turbocharger comes from the exhaust gas. The gas flows through a specially-shaped housing (the turbine housing) and in so doing,

spins the turbine wheel. The turbine wheel is attached to a shaft, at the end of which is another vaned wheel known as the compressor wheel. The compressor wheel spins in its own housing, and compresses the inlet air on the way to the inlet manifold.

3 Between the turbocharger and the inlet manifold, the compressed air passes through an intercooler. This is an air-to-air heat exchanger, mounted over the engine, and supplied with cooling air ducted through the bonnet insulation. The purpose of the intercooler is to remove from the inlet air some of the heat gained in being compressed. Because cooler air is denser, removal of this heat further increases engine efficiency.

4 Boost pressure (the pressure in the inlet manifold) is limited by a wastegate, which diverts the exhaust gas away from the turbine wheel in response to a pressure-sensitive actuator. A pressure-operated switch operates a warning light on the instrument panel in the event of excessive boost pressure developing.

5 The turbo shaft is pressure-lubricated by an oil feed pipe from the main oil gallery. The shaft "floats" on a cushion of oil. A drain pipe returns the oil to the sump.

Precautions

6 The turbocharger operates at extremely high speeds and temperatures. Certain precautions must be observed, to avoid premature failure of the turbo, or injury to the operator.

7 Do not operate the turbo with any of its parts exposed, or with any of its hoses

17.2 Disconnecting the oil feed pipe from the turbocharger

removed. Foreign objects falling onto the rotating vanes could cause excessive damage, and (if ejected) personal injury.

8 Do not race the engine immediately after start-up, especially if it is cold. Give the oil a few seconds to circulate.

9 Always allow the engine to return to idle speed before switching it off - do not blip the throttle and switch off, as this will leave the turbo spinning without lubrication.

10 Allow the engine to idle for several minutes before switching off after a high-speed run.

11 Observe the recommended intervals for oil and filter changing, and use a reputable oil of the specified quality. Neglect of oil changing, or use of inferior oil, can cause carbon formation on the turbo shaft, leading to subsequent failure.

17 Turbocharger - removal and refitting

Removal

1 Remove the inlet manifold as described in Section 15. Note that it will almost certainly be necessary to remove the right-hand engine mounting (see Chapter 2A), and tilt the engine forwards in order to give sufficient clearance to remove the turbocharger.

2 Unscrew the union nut, and disconnect the oil feed pipe from the top of the turbocharger **(see illustration)**.

3 Apply the handbrake, then jack up the front of the vehicle and support securely on axle stands (see "Jacking and Vehicle Support").

4 Disconnect the exhaust frontpipe from the turbocharger, with reference to Section 21.

5 Working under the vehicle, loosen the securing clips, and remove the hose connecting the turbocharger oil return pipe to the pipe on the cylinder block **(see illustration)**.

6 Where applicable, remove the screw securing the oil feed pipe to the support bracket at the rear of the cylinder block.

7 Unscrew the union nut securing the oil feed pipe to the cylinder block, then withdraw the

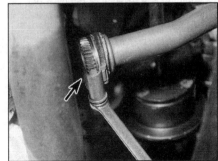

17.5 Remove the hose (arrowed) connecting the turbocharger oil return pipe to the pipe on the cylinder block

17.7a Unscrew the union nut . . .

17.7b . . . and withdraw the oil feed pipe

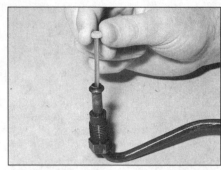

17.8 Removing filter from the oil feed pipe

17.9 Turbocharger lower securing bolts (arrowed) - viewed from underneath

17.10 Unscrewing the turbocharger upper securing bolt

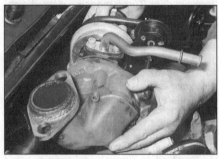

17.11 Withdrawing the turbocharger

oil feed pipe from above the engine (see illustrations).

8 Remove the filter from the cylinder block end of the oil feed pipe (where fitted), and examine it for contamination (see illustration). Clean or renew if necessary.

9 Working under the vehicle, unscrew and remove the two lower turbocharger securing bolts (see illustration).

10 Support the turbocharger, then remove the upper turbocharger securing bolt, and recover the spacer (see illustration).

11 Carefully manipulate the turbocharger out through the top of the engine compartment (see illustration). If necessary, to improve clearance for turbocharger removal, remove the three securing bolts and separate the exhaust elbow from the turbocharger unit. If it is to be refitted, store the turbocharger carefully, and plug its openings to prevent dirt ingress.

Refitting

12 Refitting is a reversal of removal, bearing in mind the following points:

a) If a new turbocharger is being fitted, change the engine oil and filter. Also renew the filter in the oil feed pipe.

b) Do not fully tighten the oil feed pipe unions until both ends of the pipe are in place. When tightening the oil return pipe union, position it so that the return hose is not strained.

c) Refit the inlet manifold as described in Section 15.

d) Before starting the engine, prime the turbo lubrication circuit by disconnecting the stop solenoid lead at the fuel pump, and cranking the engine on the starter for

three ten-second bursts. After starting, wait at least 30 seconds before revving the engine beyond fast-idle speed.

18 Turbocharger - examination and renovation

1 With the turbocharger removed, inspect the housing for cracks or other visible damage.

2 Spin the turbine or the compressor wheel, to verify that the shaft is intact and to feel for excessive shake or roughness. Some play is normal, since in use, the shaft is "floating" on a film of oil. Check that the wheel vanes are undamaged.

3 On the KKK turbo, the wastegate and actuator are integral, and cannot be checked or renewed separately. On the Garrett turbo, the wastegate actuator is a separate unit. Consult a Peugeot dealer or other specialist if it is thought that testing or renewal is necessary.

19.2 Disconnect the air inlet tubing (arrowed)

4 If the exhaust or induction passages are oil-contaminated, the turbo shaft oil seals have probably failed. (On the induction side, this will also have contaminated the intercooler, which should if necessary be flushed with a suitable solvent.)

5 No DIY repair of the turbo is possible. New units may be available on an exchange basis.

19 Intercooler - removal and refitting

Removal

1 Lift the rubber surround/seal from the top of the intercooler.

2 Disconnect the air inlet tubing from the right-hand end of the intercooler (see illustration).

3 Disconnect the small hose from the front edge of the intercooler (see illustration).

19.3 Disconnect the small hose (arrowed) from the front edge of the intercooler

19.4 Disconnect the two hoses from the valve at the left-hand end of the intercooler

19.5 Unscrewing a front intercooler securing bolt

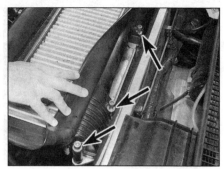

19.6 Rear intercooler securing bolts (arrowed)

4 Where applicable, disconnect the two hoses from the valve clipped to the left-hand end of the intercooler **(see illustration)**.

5 Unscrew the two or three (as applicable) front intercooler bolts **(see illustration)**.

6 Unscrew the two or three (as applicable) rear intercooler bolts **(see illustration)**.

7 Lift the intercooler from the engine, and recover the sealing ring from the manifold joint if it is loose **(see illustrations)**.

Refitting

8 Before refitting, check that the intercooler fins are clear, and if necessary remove any debris using a soft brush. Check the manifold sealing ring, and renew if necessary.

9 Refitting is a reversal of removal.

19.7a Lift the intercooler from the engine . . .

19.7b . . . and recover the sealing ring

---

20 Air cleaner and associated components - removal and refitting

Air cleaner

Removal

1 Loosen the clip on the upper air inlet duct.

2 Release the securing clips, then remove the cover and lift out the air filter.

3 To remove the housing, release the lower clips, disconnect the lower duct and lift out the housing **(see illustration)**.

Refitting

4 Refitting is a reversal of removal, but if necessary wipe out dirt from the housing and cover.

Air distribution housing - non-turbo models with D9B engine

Removal

5 Disconnect the air hose and the crankcase breather hose from the front of the air distribution housing.

6 Unscrew the two bolts securing the housing to the front mounting brackets **(see illustration)**. Recover the spacer plates.

7 Unscrew the four bolts securing the housing to the inlet manifold. Recover the washers **(see illustration)**.

8 Lift the housing from the inlet manifold, and recover the seals.

Refitting

9 Refitting is a reversal of removal, but examine the condition of the seals and renew if necessary.

21 Exhaust system - general information and component renewal

General information

1 The exhaust system consists of three sections: the frontpipe (which incorporates the catalytic converter where fitted), the intermediate pipe, and the tailpipe. The frontpipe-to-manifold/turbocharger elbow joint is of the spring-loaded ball type, to allow for movement in the exhaust system, and the intermediate pipe and tailpipe joints are secured by clamping rings.

2 The system is suspended throughout its entire length by rubber mountings.

3 On some models, a resonator box is bolted directly to the exhaust manifold.

20.3 Removing the air cleaner housing

20.6 Front air distribution housing securing bolt (arrowed)

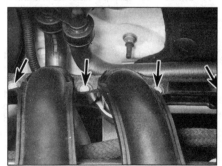

20.7 Air distribution housing-to-inlet manifold bolts (arrowed)

4

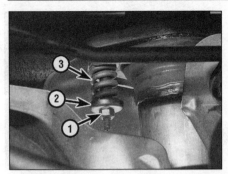

21.6a Exhaust frontpipe-to-turbocharger securing nut (1), spring cup (2) and spring (3) - viewed from underneath the vehicle

21.6b Exhaust frontpipe-to-turbocharger securing bolts (arrowed) - viewed from engine compartment

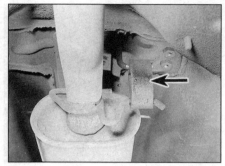

21.10 Tailpipe mounting rubber (arrowed)

Removal

4 Each exhaust section can be removed individually, or alternatively, the complete system can be removed as a unit. Even if only one part of the system needs attention, it is often easier to remove the whole system and separate the sections on the bench.

5 To remove the system or part of the system, first jack up the front or rear of the car and support it on axle stands (see *"Jacking and Vehicle Support"*). Alternatively, position the car over an inspection pit or on car ramps.

Frontpipe (including catalytic converter, where applicable)

6 Undo the nuts/bolts securing the frontpipe flange joint to the manifold/turbocharger elbow and, where applicable the single bolt securing the frontpipe to its mounting bracket. Separate the flange joint and collect the gasket and/or spring cups and springs **(see illustrations)**.

7 Slacken and remove the nuts from the frontpipe rear flange joint, and recover the clamp. Withdraw the front pipe from underneath the vehicle, and recover the gasket.

Intermediate pipe

8 Undo the clamp nuts at each end of the intermediate pipe, then remove the pipe from under the vehicle.

Tailpipe and silencer

9 Slacken the tailpipe clamp nuts and disengage the clamp from the flange joint.

10 Unhook the tailpipe from its mounting rubbers and remove it from the vehicle **(see illustration)**.

Resonator box

11 Working at the top of the exhaust manifold, unscrew loosen the two resonator box securing bolts **(see illustration)**.

12 Working underneath the vehicle, support the resonator box, then remove the two securing bolts, lower the resonator box and recover the gasket.

Complete system

13 Undo the nuts securing the frontpipe flange joint to the manifold/turbocharger elbow, and the single bolt securing the

frontpipe to its mounting bracket. Separate the flange joint and collect the gasket and/or springs and cups. Free the system from all its mounting rubbers and lower it from under the vehicle.

Heat shield(s)

14 The heat shields are secured to the underside of the body (and on some models to the fuel tank) by various nuts and bolts. Each shield can be removed once the relevant exhaust section has been removed. If a shield is being removed to gain access to a component located behind it, it may prove sufficient in some cases to remove the retaining nuts and/or bolts, and simply lower the shield, without disturbing the exhaust system.

Refitting

15 Each section is refitted by reversing the removal sequence, noting the following points.

a) *Ensure that all traces of corrosion have been removed from the flanges and renew all necessary gaskets.*

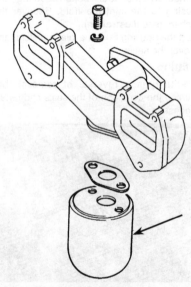

21.11 Resonator box (arrowed) mounted on exhaust manifold

b) *Inspect the rubber mountings for signs of damage or deterioration, and renew as necessary.*

c) *Prior to assembling the spring-loaded joint, a smear of high-temperature grease should be applied to the joint mating surfaces.*

d) *Where joints are secured together by a clamping ring, apply a smear of exhaust system jointing paste to the flange joint, to ensure a gas-tight seal. Tighten the clamping ring nuts evenly and progressively to the specified torque setting, so that the clearance between the clamp halves remains equal on either side.*

e) *Prior to tightening the exhaust system fasteners, ensure that all rubber mountings are correctly located, and that there is adequate clearance between the exhaust system and vehicle underbody.*

22 Emission control systems - general information

1 Certain engines are equipped with systems designed to reduce the emission of harmful by-products of the combustion process into the atmosphere.

2 The following systems may be fitted according to model.

Crankcase emission control system - all models

3 A crankcase ventilation system is fitted to all models.

4 Oil fumes and piston blow-by gases (combustion gases which have passed by the piston rings) are drawn from the crankcase and the camshaft cover through the oil filler tube, into the air inlet tract. The oil filler tube contains an oil separator. The gases are then drawn in to the engine together with fresh air/fuel mixture.

Exhaust emission control system - DJZ and DHY engines

5 To minimise the level of exhaust gas pollutants released into the atmosphere, a catalytic converter is fitted, located in the exhaust system.

6 The catalytic converter consists of a canister containing a fine mesh impregnated with a catalyst material, over which the exhaust gases pass. The catalyst speeds up the oxidation of harmful carbon monoxide, unburnt hydrocarbons and soot, effectively reducing the quantity of harmful products reaching the atmosphere.

Exhaust gas recirculation system - DJZ (XUD9/Y) engine and DHY (XUD9TE/Y) engines

7 This system is designed to recirculate small quantities of exhaust gas into the inlet tract, and therefore into the combustion process. This process reduces the level of oxides of nitrogen present in the final exhaust gas which is released into the atmosphere.

8 The volume of exhaust gas recirculated is controlled by vacuum supplied from the brake servo vacuum pump, via a solenoid valve controlled by the system electronic control unit. Before reaching the solenoid valve, the vacuum from the brake servo passes to a vacuum converter mounted on the fuel injection pump. The purpose of the vacuum converter is to modify the vacuum supplied to the solenoid valve according to engine load. The converter uses the position of the accelerator lever on the pump to operate a cam, springs and valve to vary the amount of vacuum as the load on the engine varies.

9 A vacuum-operated valve is fitted to the exhaust manifold to regulate the quantity of exhaust gas recirculated. The valve is operated by the vacuum supplied by the solenoid valve.

10 Additionally, a butterfly valve mounted on the inlet manifold allows the ratio of air to recycled exhaust gas to be controlled. The butterfly valve also enables the exhaust gases to be drawn into the inlet manifold at idle or under light load, when the valve on the exhaust manifold is fully open. Without the butterfly valve, the inlet manifold would be effectively at atmospheric pressure, and the vacuum created by the opening of the inlet valves would not be sufficient to cause the exhaust gas to circulate.

11 The system is controlled by an electronic control unit which receives information on coolant temperature and engine speed.

Atmospheric pressure correction system - DHY (XUD9TE/Y) engine

12 This system allows the timing advance function of the fuel injection pump to be cancelled, in order to reduce smoke emissions at predetermined combinations of engine temperature and atmospheric pressure. The system operates in conjunction with the preheating system (see Chapter 5), according to information supplied by a coolant temperature sensor and an atmospheric pressure switch.

23 Emission control systems - testing and component renewal

Crankcase emission control system components

Testing

1 If the system is thought to be faulty, firstly, check that the hoses are unobstructed. On high mileage vehicles, particularly when regularly used for short journeys, a jelly-like deposit may be evident inside the crankcase emission control system hoses. If excessive deposits are present, the relevant hose(s) should be removed and cleaned.

2 Periodically inspect the system hoses for security and damage, and renew them as necessary. Note that damaged or loose hoses can cause various engine running problems (erratic idle speed, stalling, etc) which can be difficult to trace.

Component renewal

3 Renewal procedures for the hoses and oil filler tube are self-evident.

Exhaust emission control system

Testing

4 The system can only be tested accurately using a suitable exhaust gas analyser

Component renewal

5 The catalytic converter is fitted in the exhaust system between the manifold and intermediate sections.

6 Removal and refitting are as described for the exhaust front section in Section 21.

Exhaust gas recirculation system

Testing

7 Testing of the system should be entrusted to a Peugeot dealer.

Component renewal

8 At the time of writing, no specific information was available regarding removal and refitting of the system components.

Atmospheric pressure correction system

Testing

9 Testing of the system should be entrusted to a Peugeot dealer.

Component renewal

10 Refer to Chapter 3 for details of the coolant temperature sensor.

11 Refer to Chapter 5 for details of the preheating system relay/timer unit.

12 No details were available for the atmospheric pressure switch at the time of writing.

4

Chapter 5 Part A:
Starting and charging systems

Contents

Degrees of difficulty

Easy, suitable for novice with little experience	**Fairly easy,** suitable for beginner with some experience	**Fairly difficult,** suitable for competent DIY mechanic 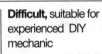	**Difficult,** suitable for experienced DIY mechanic	**Very difficult,** suitable for expert DIY or professional

Specifications

System type . . . .   12-volt, negative earth

Battery
Type . . . .   Fulmen, Delco or Steco
Charge condition:
  Poor . . . .   12.5 volts
  Normal . . . .   12.6 volts
  Good . . . .   12.7 volts

1 General information and precautions

General information

The engine electrical system consists mainly of the charging and starting systems. Because of their engine-related functions, these components are covered separately from the body electrical devices such as the lights, instruments, etc (which are covered in Chapter 12). Refer to Part B for information on the preheating system.

The electrical system is of the 12-volt negative earth type.

The battery is of the low maintenance or "maintenance-free" (sealed for life) type and is charged by the alternator, which is belt-driven from the crankshaft pulley.

The starter motor is of the pre-engaged type incorporating an integral solenoid. On starting, the solenoid moves the drive pinion into engagement with the flywheel ring gear before the starter motor is energised. Once the engine has started, a one-way clutch prevents the motor armature being driven by the engine until the pinion disengages from the flywheel.

Precautions

Further details of the various systems are given in the relevant Sections of this Chapter. While some repair procedures are given, the usual course of action is to renew the component concerned. The owner whose interest extends beyond mere component renewal should obtain a copy of the "Automobile Electrical & Electronic Systems Manual", available from the publishers of this manual.

It is necessary to take extra care when working on the electrical system to avoid damage to semi-conductor devices (diodes and transistors), and to avoid the risk of personal injury. In addition to the precautions given in "Safety first!" at the beginning of this manual, observe the following when working on the system:

Always remove rings, watches, etc before working on the electrical system. Even with the battery disconnected, capacitive discharge could occur if a component's live terminal is earthed through a metal object. This could cause a shock or nasty burn.

Do not reverse the battery connections. Components such as the alternator, electronic control units, or any other components having semi-conductor circuitry could be irreparably damaged.

If the engine is being started using jump leads and a slave battery, connect the batteries positive-to-positive and negative-to-negative (see "Booster battery (jump) starting"). This also applies when connecting a battery charger.

Never disconnect the battery terminals, the alternator, any electrical wiring or any test instruments when the engine is running.

Do not allow the engine to turn the alternator when the alternator is not connected.

Never "test" for alternator output by "flashing" the output lead to earth.

Never use an ohmmeter of the type incorporating a hand-cranked generator for circuit or continuity testing.

Always ensure that the battery negative lead is disconnected when working on the electrical system.

Before using electric-arc welding equipment on the car, disconnect the battery, alternator and components such as electronic control units to protect them from the risk of damage.

The radio/cassette unit fitted as standard equipment by Peugeot may be equipped with a built-in security code to deter thieves. If the power source to the unit is cut, the anti-theft system will activate. Even if the

5A

power source is immediately reconnected, the radio/cassette unit will not function until the correct security code has been entered. Therefore, if you do not know the correct security code for the radio/cassette unit do not disconnect the battery negative terminal of the battery or remove the radio/cassette unit from the vehicle. Refer to "Radio/ cassette unit anti-theft system precaution" in the Reference section of this manual for further information.

2 Electrical fault-finding - general information

Refer to Chapter 12.

3 Battery - testing and charging

Standard and low maintenance battery - testing

1 If the vehicle covers a small annual mileage, it is worthwhile checking the specific gravity of the electrolyte every three months to determine the state of charge of the battery. Use a hydrometer to make the check and compare the results with the following table. The temperatures quoted in the table are ambient (air) temperatures. Note that the specific gravity readings assume an electrolyte temperature of 15°C (60°F); for every 10°C (50°F) below 15°C (60°F) subtract 0.007. For every 10°C (50°F) above 15°C (60°F) add 0.007.

	Above 25°C(77°F)	Below 25°C(77°F)
Fully-charged	1.210 to 1.230	1.270 to 1.290
70% charged	1.170 to 1.190	1.230 to 1.250
Discharged	1.050 to 1.070	1.110 to 1.130

2 If the battery condition is suspect, first check the specific gravity of electrolyte in each cell. A variation of 0.040 or more between any cells indicates loss of electrolyte or deterioration of the internal plates.
3 If the specific gravity variation is 0.040 or more, the battery should be renewed. If the cell variation is satisfactory but the battery is discharged, it should be charged as described later in this Section.

Maintenance-free battery - testing

4 In cases where a "sealed for life" maintenance-free battery is fitted, topping-up and testing of the electrolyte in each cell is not possible. The condition of the battery can therefore only be tested using a battery condition indicator or a voltmeter.
5 Certain models may be fitted with a "Delco" type maintenance-free battery, with a built-in charge condition indicator. The indicator is

located in the top of the battery casing, and indicates the condition of the battery from its colour. If the indicator shows green, then the battery is in a good state of charge. If the indicator turns darker, eventually to black, then the battery requires charging, as described later in this Section. If the indicator shows clear/yellow, then the electrolyte level in the battery is too low to allow further use, and the battery should be renewed. **Do not** attempt to charge, load or jump start a battery when the indicator shows clear/yellow.
6 If testing the battery using a voltmeter, connect the voltmeter across the battery and compare the result with those given in the Specifications under "charge condition". The test is only accurate if the battery has not been subjected to any kind of charge for the previous six hours. If this is not the case, switch on the headlights for 30 seconds, then wait four to five minutes before testing the battery after switching off the headlights. All other electrical circuits must be switched off, so check that the doors and tailgate are fully shut when making the test.
7 If the voltage reading is less than 12.2 volts, then the battery is discharged, whilst a reading of 12.2 to 12.4 volts indicates a partially discharged condition.
8 If the battery is to be charged, remove it from the vehicle (Section 4) and charge it as described later in this Section.

Standard and low maintenance battery - charging

Note: *The following is intended as a guide only. Always refer to the manufacturer's recommendations (often printed on a label attached to the battery) before charging a battery.*
9 Charge the battery at a rate of 3.5 to 4 amps and continue to charge the battery at this rate until no further rise in specific gravity is noted over a four hour period.
10 Alternatively, a trickle charger charging at the rate of 1.5 amps can safely be used overnight.
11 Specially rapid "boost" charges which are claimed to restore the power of the battery in 1 to 2 hours are not recommended, as they can cause serious damage to the battery plates through overheating.
12 While charging the battery, note that the temperature of the electrolyte should never exceed 37.8°C (100°F).

Maintenance-free battery - charging

Note: *The following is intended as a guide only. Always refer to the manufacturer's recommendations (often printed on a label attached to the battery) before charging a battery.*
13 This battery type takes considerably longer to fully recharge than the standard type, the time taken being dependent on the extent of discharge, but it can take anything up to three days.

14 A constant voltage type charger is required, to be set, when connected, to 13.9 to 14.9 volts with a charger current below 25 amps. Using this method, the battery should be usable within three hours, giving a voltage reading of 12.5 volts, but this is for a partially discharged battery and, as mentioned, full charging can take considerably longer.
15 If the battery is to be charged from a fully discharged state (condition reading less than 12.2 volts), have it recharged by your Peugeot dealer or local automotive electrician, as the charge rate is higher and constant supervision during charging is necessary.

4 Battery - removal and refitting

Note: *On models equipped with a Peugeot anti-theft alarm system, where possible, disable the alarm before disconnecting the battery (see Chapter 12). If a Peugeot radio/cassette unit is fitted, refer to "Radio/cassette unit anti-theft system - precaution" in the "Reference" section of this manual.*

Removal

1 The battery is located at the right-hand rear corner of the engine compartment.
2 Disconnect the battery terminals, negative terminal first, by unscrewing the wing nuts or clamp bolts. The negative terminal must always be disconnected first, and reconnected last.
3 Unscrew the nuts and remove the battery clamp **(see illustration)**.
4 Lift the battery from the battery tray.
5 If necessary, release the wiring clips and unbolt the battery tray from the engine compartment. Note that on early models, it will be necessary to unbolt the fuel filter assembly before the battery tray can be removed.

Refitting

6 Refitting is a reversal of removal, but smear petroleum jelly on the terminals when reconnecting the leads, and always reconnect the positive lead first, and the negative lead last.

4.3 Battery clamp securing nuts (arrowed)

5 Charging system - testing

Note: *Refer to the warnings given in "Safety first!" and in Section 1 of this Chapter before starting work.*

1 If the ignition warning light fails to illuminate when the ignition is switched on, first check the alternator wiring connections for security. If satisfactory, check that the warning light bulb has not blown, and that the bulbholder is secure in its location in the instrument panel. If the light still fails to illuminate, check the continuity of the warning light feed wire from the alternator to the bulbholder. If all is satisfactory, the alternator is at fault, and should be renewed or taken to an auto-electrician for testing and repair.

2 If the ignition warning light illuminates when the engine is running, stop the engine and check that the drivebelt is correctly tensioned (see Chapter 1) and that the alternator connections are secure. If all is so far satisfactory, have the alternator checked by an auto-electrician for testing and repair.

3 If the alternator output is suspect even though the warning light functions correctly, the regulated voltage may be checked as follows.

4 Connect a voltmeter across the battery terminals, and start the engine.

5 Increase the engine speed until the voltmeter reading remains steady; the reading should be approximately 12 to 13 volts, and no more than 14 volts.

6 Switch on as many electrical accessories (eg, the headlights, heated rear window and heater blower) as possible, and check that the alternator maintains the regulated voltage at around 13 to 14 volts.

7 If the regulated voltage is not as stated, the fault may be due to worn brushes, weak brush springs, a faulty voltage regulator, a faulty diode, a severed phase winding, or worn or damaged slip rings. The alternator should be renewed or taken to an auto-electrician for testing and repair.

6 Alternator drivebelt - removal, refitting and tensioning

Refer to the procedure given for the auxiliary drivebelt in Chapter 1.

7 Alternator - removal and refitting

Removal

1 Disconnect the battery negative lead.
2 Slacken the auxiliary drivebelt (Chapter 1).
3 Remove the rubber covers, where

7.3a Remove the rubber covers . . .

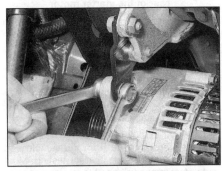

7.4 Unscrew the upper alternator securing nut and bolt

applicable, then unscrew the securing nuts and disconnect the wiring from the rear of the alternator **(see illustrations)**.

4 Unscrew the nut (and bolt, where applicable) securing the alternator to the upper mounting bracket/adjuster bracket, as applicable **(see illustration)**.

5 Unscrew the lower mounting through-bolt (there is no need to remove it completely), and withdraw the alternator from the engine compartment **(see illustration)**.

Refitting

6 Refit in reverse order, tensioning the belt as described in Chapter 1.

8 Alternator - testing and overhaul

If the alternator is thought to be suspect, it should be removed from the vehicle and taken to an auto-electrician for testing. Most auto-electricians will be able to supply and fit brushes at a reasonable cost. However, check on the cost of repairs before proceeding as it may prove more economical to obtain a new or exchange alternator.

9 Starting system - testing

Note: *Refer to the precautions given in "Safety first!" and in Section 1 of this Chapter before starting work.*

7.3b . . . then disconnect the wiring from the rear of the alternator

7.5 Unscrew the lower through-bolt (arrowed) and withdraw the alternator

1 If the starter motor fails to operate when the ignition key is turned to the appropriate position, the following possible causes may be to blame.

a) The battery is faulty.
b) The electrical connections between the switch, solenoid, battery and starter motor are somewhere failing to pass the necessary current from the battery through the starter to earth.
c) The solenoid is faulty.
d) The starter motor is mechanically or electrically defective.

2 To check the battery, switch on the headlights. If they dim after a few seconds, this indicates that the battery is discharged - recharge (see Section 3) or renew the battery. If the headlights glow brightly, operate the ignition switch and observe the lights. If they dim, then this indicates that current is reaching the starter motor - therefore, the fault must lie in the starter motor. If the lights continue to glow brightly (and no clicking sound can be heard from the starter motor solenoid), this indicates that there is a fault in the circuit or solenoid - refer to the following paragraphs. If the starter motor turns slowly when operated, but the battery is in good condition, then this indicates that either the starter motor is faulty, or there is considerable resistance somewhere in the circuit.

3 If a fault in the circuit is suspected, disconnect the battery leads (including the earth connection to the body), the starter/solenoid wiring, and the engine/transmission earth strap. Thoroughly clean the connections, reconnect the leads and wiring, then use a

5A

voltmeter or test light to check that full battery voltage is available at the battery positive lead connection to the solenoid, and that the earth is sound. Smear petroleum jelly around the battery terminals to prevent corrosion - corroded connections are among the most frequent causes of electrical system faults.

4 If the battery and all connections are in good condition, check the circuit by disconnecting the wire from the solenoid blade terminal. Connect a voltmeter or test light between the wire end and a good earth (such as the battery negative terminal), and check that the wire is live when the ignition switch is turned to the "start" position. If it is, then the circuit is sound - if not, the circuit wiring can be checked as described in Chapter 12.

5 The solenoid contacts can be checked by connecting a voltmeter or test light between the battery positive feed connection on the starter side of the solenoid, and earth. When the ignition switch is turned to the "start" position, there should be a reading or lighted bulb, as applicable. If there is no reading or lighted bulb, the solenoid is faulty, and should be renewed.

6 If the circuit and solenoid are proved sound, the fault must lie in the starter motor. In this event, it may be possible to have the starter motor overhauled by a specialist, but check on the cost of spares before proceeding, as it may prove more economical to obtain a new or exchange motor.

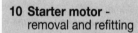

10 Starter motor - removal and refitting

Removal

1 Disconnect the battery negative lead.
2 Where applicable, to improve access remove the air cleaner and/or the air trunking with reference to Chapter 4.
3 Unscrew the two securing nuts, and disconnect the electrical connections at the rear of the starter motor **(see illustration)**.
4 Unscrew the three bolts securing the starter motor to the gearbox housing, supporting the motor as the bolts are withdrawn. Recover the washers under the bolt heads, and note the locations of any wiring or hose brackets secured by the bolts **(see illustration)**. Note that the top securing bolts may foul the clutch release mechanism as it is withdrawn, but there is no need to withdraw it completely to remove the starter motor.
5 Withdraw the starter motor from the engine.

Refitting

6 Refitting is a reversal of the removal

10.3 Unscrew the two nuts (arrowed) and disconnect the wiring from the rear of the starter motor

procedure, ensuring that any brackets are in place under the bolt heads, as noted before removal.

11 Starter motor - testing and overhaul

If the starter motor is thought to be suspect, it should be removed from the vehicle and taken to an auto-electrician for testing. Most auto-electricians will be able to supply and fit brushes at a reasonable cost. However, check on the cost of repairs before proceeding as it may prove more economical to obtain a new or exchange motor.

12 Ignition switch - removal and refitting

The ignition switch is integral with the steering column lock, and can be removed with reference to Chapter 10.

13 Oil pressure warning light switch - removal and refitting

Removal

1 The switch is located at the front of the cylinder block, above the oil filter mounting. Note that on some models access to the switch may be improved if the vehicle is jacked up and supported on axle stands so that the switch can be reached from underneath (see *"Jacking and Vehicle Support"*).
2 Disconnect the battery negative lead.
3 Remove the protective sleeve from the wiring plug (where applicable), then disconnect the wiring from the switch.

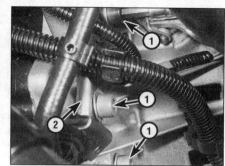

10.4 Unscrew the starter motor securing bolts (1). Note the location of the bracket (2)

4 Unscrew the switch from the cylinder block, and recover the sealing washer. Be prepared for oil spillage, and if the switch is to be left removed from the engine for any length of time, plug the hole in the cylinder block.

Refitting

5 Examine the sealing washer for damage or deterioration and if necessary renew.
6 Refit the switch, complete with washer, and tighten it securely. Reconnect the wiring connector.
7 Lower the vehicle to the ground then check and, if necessary, top-up the engine oil as described in Chapter 1.

14 Oil level sensor - removal and refitting

1 According to model the oil level sensor is located on the front side of the cylinder block above the oil filter, or on the rear left-hand side of the cylinder block.
2 The removal and refitting procedure is as described for the oil pressure switch in Section 13. Access is most easily obtained from underneath the vehicle **(see illustration)**.

14.2 Removing the oil level sensor from the cylinder block - viewed with engine removed

Chapter 5 Part B:
Preheating system

Contents

Degrees of difficulty

Easy, suitable for novice with little experience	**Fairly easy,** suitable for beginner with some experience	**Fairly difficult,** suitable for competent DIY mechanic	**Difficult,** suitable for experienced DIY mechanic	**Very difficult,** suitable for expert DIY or professional 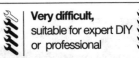

Specifications

Torque wrench setting	Nm	lbf ft
Glow plugs	22	16

---

1 Preheating system - description and testing

Description

1 Each swirl chamber has a heater plug (commonly called a glow plug) screwed into it. The plugs are electrically-operated before and during start-up when the engine is cold. Electrical feed to the glow plugs is controlled by a relay/timer unit.

2 On certain models, the glow plugs provide a "post-heating" function, whereby the glow plugs remain switched on for a period after the engine has started. Once the starter has been switched off, the glow plugs begin a timed 3-minute "post-heating" cycle. The operation of the plugs cannot be cancelled for the first 15 seconds, but after the first 15 seconds, the supply to the plugs will be interrupted by:

a) Operation of the accelerator pedal beyond a travel of 13 mm for a duration of more than 2.5 seconds (see Section 4).

b) A coolant temperature of more than 60°C (see Chapter 3).

3 A warning light in the instrument panel tells the driver that preheating is taking place. When the light goes out, the engine is ready to be started. The voltage supply to the glow plugs continues for several seconds after the light goes out. If no attempt is made to start, the timer then cuts off the supply, in order to avoid draining the battery and overheating the glow plugs.

Testing

4 If the system malfunctions, testing is ultimately by substitution of known good units, but some preliminary checks may be made as follows.

5 Connect a voltmeter or 12-volt test lamp between the glow plug supply cable and earth (engine or vehicle metal). Make sure that the live connection is kept clear of the engine and bodywork.

6 Have an assistant switch on the ignition, and check that voltage is applied to the glow plugs. Note the time for which the warning light is lit, and the total time for which voltage is applied before the system cuts out. Switch off the ignition.

7 At an under-bonnet temperature of 20°C, typical times noted should be 5 or 6 seconds for warning light operation, followed by a further 10 seconds supply after the light goes out. Warning light time will increase with lower temperatures and decrease with higher temperatures.

8 If there is no supply at all, the relay or associated wiring is at fault.

9 To locate a defective glow plug, on Turbo models remove the intercooler, and on non-turbo models with D9B engine remove the air distribution housing. If necessary, also remove the inlet duct, and disconnect the breather hose from the engine oil filler tube. Refer to Chapter 4 for further information. Disconnect the main supply cable and the interconnecting wire or strap from the top of the glow plugs. Be careful not to drop the nuts and washers.

10 Use a continuity tester, or a 12-volt test lamp connected to the battery positive terminal, to check for continuity between each glow plug terminal and earth. The resistance of a glow plug in good condition is very low (less than 1 ohm), so if the test lamp does not light or the continuity tester shows a high resistance, the glow plug is certainly defective.

11 If an ammeter is available, the current draw of each glow plug can be checked. After an initial surge of 15 to 20 amps, each plug should draw 12 amps. Any plug which draws much more or less than this is probably defective.

12 As a final check, the glow plugs can be removed and inspected as described in the following Section.

2 Glow plugs - removal, inspection and refitting

Removal

Caution: If the preheating system has just been energised, or if the engine has been running, the glow plugs will be very hot.

1 Disconnect the battery negative lead. To improve access, if desired, on Turbo models remove the intercooler, and on non-turbo models with the D9B engine remove the air distribution housing. If necessary, also remove the inlet duct, and disconnect the breather hose from the engine oil filler tube. Similarly, where applicable, unclip the fuel hose from the brackets on the cylinder head. Refer to Chapter 4 for further information.

2 Unscrew the nut from the relevant glow plug terminal(s), and recover the washer(s). Note that the main supply cable is connected to Number 1 cylinder glow plug and an interconnecting wire is fitted between the four plugs **(see illustrations)**.

3 Where applicable, carefully move any obstructing pipes or wires to one side to enable access to the relevant glow plug(s).

2.2a Unscrew the nut . . .

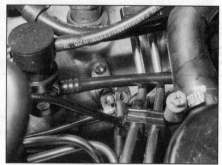

2.2b . . . and disconnect the main supply cable (where necessary) . . .

2.2c . . . and the interconnecting wire from the glow plug

2.4 Unscrew the glow plug and remove it from the cylinder head

4 Unscrew the glow plug(s) and remove from the cylinder head **(see illustration)**.

Inspection

5 Inspect each glow plug for physical damage. Burnt or eroded glow plug tips can be caused by a bad injector spray pattern. Have the injectors checked if this sort of damage is found.

6 If the glow plugs are in good physical condition, check them electrically using a 12 volt test lamp or continuity tester as described in the previous Section.

7 The glow plugs can be energised by applying 12 volts to them to verify that they heat up evenly and in the required time. Observe the following precautions.

a) Support the glow plug by clamping it carefully in a vice or self-locking pliers. Remember it will become red-hot.

b) Make sure that the power supply or test lead incorporates a fuse or overload trip to protect against damage from a short-circuit.

c) After testing, allow the glow plug to cool for several minutes before attempting to handle it.

8 A glow plug in good condition will start to glow red at the tip after drawing current for 5 seconds or so. Any plug which takes much longer to start glowing, or which starts glowing in the middle instead of at the tip, is defective.

Refitting

9 Refit by reversing the removal operations. Apply a smear of copper-based anti-seize

compound to the plug threads and tighten the glow plugs to the specified torque. Do not overtighten, as this can damage the glow plug element.

---

3 Preheating system control unit - removal and refitting

Removal

1 The unit is located on the left-hand side of the engine compartment bulkhead, behind the battery on early models, or on the side of the battery tray on later models **(see illustration)**.
2 Disconnect the battery negative lead.
3 Unscrew the retaining nut securing the unit to the bulkhead. Recover the washer.
4 Where applicable, disconnect the wiring connector(s) from the base of the unit, then

3.1 Preheating system control unit location (arrowed) - later models

unscrew the two retaining nuts and free the main feed and supply wires from the unit (recover the washers). Remove the unit from the engine compartment.

Refitting

5 Refitting is a reversal of removal, ensuring that the wiring is correctly reconnected.

---

4 Post heating cut-off switch - adjustment, removal and refitting

Adjustment

1 The switch is mounted on a bracket on the top of the fuel injection pump.
2 Before proceeding, check that the accelerator cable is correctly adjusted as described in Chapter 4.
3 Make a mark on the inner accelerator cable, 1.0 mm from the point where the cable enters the cable sheath end fitting **(see illustration)**.
4 Move the pump control lever until the mark made on the inner accelerator cable is against the end of the cable sheath end fitting.
5 Loosen the switch securing screws.
6 Carefully move the switch, until the contacts just click open.
7 Tighten the switch securing screws.

Removal

8 Release the switch wiring from any clips, then disconnect the switch wiring connector, and release the connector from the bracket on the fuel injection pump.
9 Unscrew the two securing screws and withdraw the switch.

Refitting

10 Refitting is a reversal of removal, but on completion, adjust the switch as described previously in this Section.

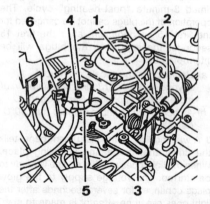

4.3 Post heating cut-off switch adjustment

1 Mark made on inner cable
2 Cable sheath end fitting
3 Pump control lever
4 Switch securing screws
5 Switch
6 Switch contacts

Chapter 6
Clutch

Contents

Degrees of difficulty

Easy, suitable for novice with little experience	Fairly easy, suitable for beginner with some experience	Fairly difficult, suitable for competent DIY mechanic	Difficult, suitable for experienced DIY mechanic	Very difficult, suitable for expert DIY or professional

Specifications

Type	Single dry plate with diaphragm spring, cable-operated

Clutch pedal travel*:

Models up to 1992	145 mm
Models from 1993-on	162.0 ± 12.0 mm

From mid-1994 an automatically adjusted cable was progressively introduced - see text

Friction plate diameter

Non-turbo models	200 mm
Turbo models	215 mm

Torque wrench settings	Nm	lbf ft
Pressure plate retaining bolts	25	18

1 General information

The clutch consists of a friction plate, a pressure plate assembly, a release bearing and the release mechanism; all of these components are contained in the large cast-aluminium alloy bellhousing, sandwiched between the engine and the transmission. The release mechanism is mechanical, being operated by a cable.

The friction plate is fitted between the engine flywheel and the clutch pressure plate, and is allowed to slide on the transmission input shaft splines.

The pressure plate assembly is bolted to the engine flywheel. When the engine is running, drive is transmitted from the crankshaft, via the flywheel, to the friction plate (these components being clamped securely together by the pressure plate assembly) and from the friction plate to the transmission input shaft.

To interrupt the drive, the spring pressure must be relaxed. On the models covered in this manual, two different types of clutch release mechanism are used. The first is a

conventional "push-type" mechanism, where an independent clutch release bearing, fitted concentrically around the transmission input shaft, is pushed onto the pressure plate assembly. The second is a "pull-type" mechanism, where the clutch release bearing is an integral part of the pressure plate assembly, and is lifted away from the friction plate.

On models with the conventional "push-type" mechanism, at the transmission end of the clutch cable, the outer cable is retained by a fixed mounting bracket, and the inner cable is attached to the release fork lever. Depressing the clutch pedal pulls the control cable inner wire, and this rotates the release fork by acting on the lever at the fork's upper end. The release fork then presses the release bearing against the pressure plate spring fingers. This causes the springs to deform and releases the clamping force on the pressure plate. Some early models are fitted with a clutch release mechanism where the release lever pivots on a ball-stud located in the gearbox bellhousing, instead of on a pivot shaft as on later models.

On models with the "pull-type" mechanism, at the transmission end of the clutch cable, the inner cable is attached to a fixed mounting

bracket, and the outer cable acts against the release fork lever. Depressing the clutch pedal rotates the release fork. The release fork then lifts the release bearing, which is attached to the pressure plate springs, away from the friction plate, and releases the clamping force exerted at the pressure plate periphery.

As the friction plate linings wear the clutch pedal height will increase, and it is therefore necessary to adjust the clutch cable at regular intervals to ensure correct operation of the clutch. However from mid 1994 an automatically adjusted clutch cable was progressively introduced, and could be fitted to earlier models - the modification includes removing the clutch pedal return spring and fitting a rubber stop. The automatic adjuster is built into the central part of the cable.

2 Clutch - adjustment

Note: *This Section does not apply to models fitted with an automatically adjusted cable.*

1 The clutch adjustment is checked by measuring the clutch pedal travel. If a new cable has been fitted, settle it in position by

6

2.2 To check the clutch adjustment, measure the clutch pedal travel as described in text

2.5 Adjusting the clutch cable

depressing the clutch pedal at least twenty times.

2 Ensure there are no obstructions beneath the clutch pedal. Depress the clutch pedal fully to the floor, and measure the distance from the centre of the clutch pedal pad to the floor. Now release the pedal and again measure the distance from the pedal to the floor **(see illustration)**.

3 Subtract the first measurement from the second to obtain the clutch pedal travel. If this is not with the range given in the Specifications at the start of this Chapter, adjust the clutch as follows.

4 The clutch cable is adjusted by means of the adjuster nut on the transmission end of the inner cable. On some models, access to the locknut is limited and, if required, the air cleaner duct or housing components can be removed or disconnected to improve access. Refer to Chapter 4 for further information.

5 Working in the engine compartment, slacken the locknut on the end of the clutch cable. Adjust the position of the adjuster nut, then re-measure the clutch pedal travel. Repeat this procedure until the clutch pedal travel is as specified **(see illustration)**.

6 Once the adjuster nut is correctly positioned, and the pedal travel is correctly set, securely tighten the cable locknut. Where necessary, refit any disturbed air cleaner duct/housing components as described in Chapter 4.

3 Clutch cable - removal and refitting

Removal

1 If necessary, to improve access remove the air cleaner duct or housing components as described in Chapter 4. Also remove the battery, battery tray and mounting plate (see Chapter 5A).

2 Working in the engine compartment, release the inner cable and outer cable fittings from the clutch release lever and mounting bracket, and free the cable from the transmission housing - on early models it will be necessary to remove the locking clip from the gearbox bracket **(see illustrations)**.

Where necessary, fully slacken the locknut and adjuster nut from the end of the clutch cable to aid removal.

3 Working inside the vehicle, remove the trim panel as necessary then depress the spring clip on the clutch pedal plastic link assembly to release the inner cable end from the link **(see illustration)**.

4 Return to the engine compartment and pull back the bellows on the cable where it enters the bulkhead. Pull on the cable outer sheath to disengage the cable stop on the pedal bracket. Withdraw the cable through the bulkhead **(see illustration)**.

5 Release the cable from the clips on the subframe. Note its correct routing, and remove the cable from the vehicle.

6 Examine the cable, looking for worn end fittings or a damaged outer casing, and for signs of fraying of the inner cable. Check the cable's operation; the inner cable should move smoothly and easily through the outer casing. Remember that a cable that appears serviceable when tested off the car may well be much heavier in operation when in its working position. Renew the cable if it shows signs of excessive wear or any damage.

Refitting

7 Before refitting the cable turn the bellows inside out to enable the cable to pass fully through the bulkhead. Also make sure that the bush on the cable stop is locked in the special groove.

8 Apply a thin smear of multi-purpose grease to the cable end fittings, then pass the cable

3.2a Slacken the clutch cable locknut and adjuster nut (where necessary), then free the inner cable end fittings . . .

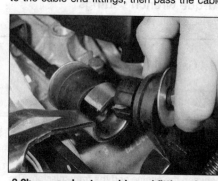

3.2b . . . and outer cable end fittings from the release lever and mounting bracket

3.2c Removing the locking clip from the gearbox bracket

3.3 Showing inner cable spring clip (arrowed) at top of clutch pedal (cable removed)

3.4 Withdrawing the clutch cable from the bulkhead

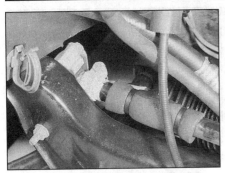

3.13 Foam sleeve on the anti-roll bar

3.15 Clutch cable attached to the release arm

through the engine compartment bulkhead.

9 From inside the vehicle, engage the cable end in the plastic link at the top of the clutch pedal. Make sure the end is fully locked in the link.

10 Push on the outer cable to engage the cable stop in the pedal bracket. The cable end is fully engaged when the spring clip is engaged in the second groove on the cable stop.

11 Engage the bellows in the bulkhead.

12 Route the cable in front of the anti-roll bar, ensuring it is free of the heater hoses and, where fitted, the power-assisted steering hoses.

13 If there has been evidence of contact between the cable and the anti-roll bar and there is no foam sleeve fitted to the anti-roll bar, then a foam sleeve should be obtained from your dealer and stuck to the anti-roll bar **(see illustration)**.

14 Clip the cable to the subframe.

15 Connect the cable to the clutch release arm **(see illustration)**. Ensure that the cable spacers and washers are correctly positioned against the lever/mounting bracket, and where necessary refit the cable locking clip.

16 Where applicable, check and adjust the clutch pedal travel as described in Section 2.

17 Refit the trim panel, battery, and air cleaner duct as necessary.

4 Clutch pedal - removal and refitting

The procedure for removing and refitting the clutch pedal is the same as that described for the brake pedal in Chapter 9.

On completion, adjust the cable as described in Section 2 of this Chapter.

5 Clutch assembly - removal, inspection and refitting

 Warning: Dust created by clutch wear and deposited on the clutch components may contain asbestos, which is a health

hazard. *DO NOT blow it out with compressed air, or inhale any of it. DO NOT use petrol or petroleum-based solvents to clean off the dust. Brake system cleaner or methylated spirit should be used to flush the dust into a suitable receptacle. After the clutch components are wiped clean with rags, dispose of the contaminated rags and cleaner in a sealed, marked container.*

Note: *Although some friction materials may no longer contain asbestos, it is safest to assume that they DO, and to take precautions accordingly.*

Removal

1 Unless the complete engine/transmission is to be removed from the car and separated for major overhaul (see Chapter 2), the clutch can be reached by removing the transmission as described in Chapter 7.

2 Before disturbing the clutch, use chalk or a marker pen to mark the relationship of the pressure plate assembly to the flywheel.

3 Working in a diagonal sequence, slacken the pressure plate bolts by half a turn at a time, until spring pressure is released and the bolts can be unscrewed by hand.

4 Prise the pressure plate assembly off its locating dowels, and collect the friction plate, noting which way round the friction plate is fitted.

Inspection

Note: *Due to the amount of work necessary to remove and refit clutch components, it is usually considered good practice to renew the clutch friction plate, pressure plate assembly and release bearing as a matched set, even if only one of these is actually worn enough to require renewal. It is also worth considering the renewal of the clutch components on a preventive basis if the engine and/or transmission have been removed for some other reason.*

5 When cleaning clutch components, read first the warning at the beginning of this Section; remove dust using a clean, dry cloth, and working in a well-ventilated atmosphere.

6 Check the friction plate linings for signs of wear, damage or oil contamination. If the friction material is cracked, burnt, scored or damaged, or if it is contaminated with oil or grease (shown by shiny black patches), the friction plate must be renewed.

7 If the friction material is still serviceable, check that the centre boss splines are unworn, that the torsion springs are in good condition and securely fastened, and that all the rivets are tight. If any wear or damage is found, the friction plate must be renewed.

8 If the friction material is fouled with oil, this must be due to an oil leak from the crankshaft left-hand oil seal, from the sump-to-cylinder block joint, or from the transmission input shaft. Renew the seal or repair the joint, as appropriate, as described in Chapter 2 or 7, before installing the new friction plate.

9 Check the pressure plate assembly for obvious signs of wear or damage; shake it to check for loose rivets or worn or damaged fulcrum rings, and check that the drive straps securing the pressure plate to the cover do not show signs (such as a deep yellow or blue discoloration) of overheating. If the diaphragm spring is worn or damaged, or if its pressure is in any way suspect, the pressure plate assembly should be renewed.

10 Examine the machined bearing surfaces of the pressure plate and of the flywheel; they should be clean, completely flat, and free from scratches or scoring. If either is discoloured from excessive heat, or shows signs of cracks, it should be renewed - although minor damage of this nature can sometimes be polished away using emery paper.

11 Check that the release bearing rotates smoothly and easily, with no sign of noise or roughness. On "push-type" clutches also check that the surface itself is smooth and unworn, with no signs of cracks, pitting or scoring. If there is any doubt about its condition, the bearing must be renewed. On clutches with a "pull-type" release mechanism, this means that the complete pressure plate assembly must also be renewed.

Refitting

12 On reassembly, ensure that the bearing surfaces of the flywheel and pressure plate are completely clean, smooth, and free from oil or grease. Use solvent to remove any protective grease from new components.

13 Fit the friction plate so that its spring hub assembly faces away from the flywheel; there may be a marking showing which way round the plate is to be refitted **(see illustration)**.

5.13 Ensure the friction plate is fitted the correct way around, then install the pressure plate

6

14 Refit the pressure plate assembly, aligning the marks made on dismantling (if the original pressure plate is re-used), and locating the pressure plate on its three locating dowels. Fit the pressure plate bolts, but tighten them only finger-tight, so that the friction plate can still be moved.

15 The friction plate must now be centralised, so that when the transmission is refitted, its input shaft will pass through the splines at the centre of the friction plate.

16 Centralisation can be achieved by passing a screwdriver or other long bar through the friction plate and into the hole in the crankshaft; the friction plate can then be moved around until it is centred on the crankshaft hole. Alternatively, a clutch-aligning-tool can be used to eliminate the guesswork; these can be obtained from most accessory shops. A home-made aligning tool can be fabricated from a length of metal rod or wooden dowel which fits closely inside the crankshaft hole; if necessary use insulating tape wound around it to match the diameter of the friction plate splined hole.

17 When the friction plate is centralised, tighten the pressure plate bolts evenly and in a diagonal sequence to the specified torque setting.

18 Apply a thin smear of molybdenum disulphide grease (Peugeot recommend the use of Molykote BR2 Plus - available from your Peugeot dealer) to the splines of the friction plate and the transmission input shaft, and also to the release bearing bore and release fork shaft. **Note:** *As from 1993 the friction plate has a nickeled hub and Peugeot recommend that neither the hub nor the input shaft are greased. Since the nickeled hub can be fitted to earlier models, check which type is fitted before greasing the components.*

19 Refit the transmission as described in Chapter 7.

6 Clutch release mechanism - removal, inspection and refitting

Note: *Refer to the warning concerning the dangers of asbestos dust at the beginning of Section 5.*

Removal

1 Unless the complete engine/transmission is to be removed from the car and separated for major overhaul (see Chapter 2), the clutch release mechanism can be reached by removing the transmission only, as described in Chapter 7.

Pivot shaft type

2 On models with a conventional "push-type" release mechanism, unhook the release bearing from the fork, and slide it off the input shaft **(see illustration)**. Drive out the roll pin, and remove the release lever from the top of

6.2 Clutch release bearing (arrowed) and release fork and shaft

6.3b . . . release fork shaft

the release fork shaft. Discard the roll pin - a new one must be used on refitting.

3 On both types of clutch, depress the retaining tabs, then slide the upper bush off the end of the release fork shaft. Disengage the shaft from its lower bush, and manoeuvre it out from the transmission. Depress the retaining tabs, and remove the lower pivot bush from the transmission housing **(see illustrations)**.

Ball-stud type

4 Release the spring clips and slide the bearing from the guide sleeve.

5 Withdraw the release fork from the ball-stud and from the rubber gaiter in the bellhousing.

Inspection

6 Check the release mechanism, renewing any component which is worn or damaged. Carefully check all bearing surfaces and points of contact.

7 On the ball-stud type release mechanism the fork bush may be renewed as follows. First drill out the rivets which secure the old bush. Remove the bush and discard it. Position the new bush on the fork and pass its rivets through the holes. Heat the rivets with a cigarette lighter or a low powered blowlamp, then peen over their heads while they are still hot. If the ball-stud requires renewal, remove it with a slide hammer having a suitable claw. Support the casing and drive in the new stud using a soft metal drift.

8 When checking the release bearing itself, note that it is often considered worthwhile to renew it as a matter of course. Check that it

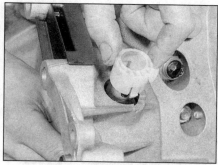

6.3a Removing the upper bush . . .

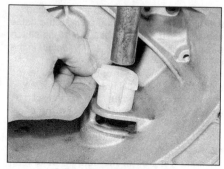

6.3c . . . and lower bush

rotates smoothly and easily, with no sign of noise or roughness, and that the surface itself is smooth and unworn, with no signs of cracks, pitting or scoring. If there is any doubt about its condition, the bearing must be renewed. On models with a "pull-type" release mechanism, this means that the complete pressure plate assembly must be renewed, as described in Section 5.

Refitting

Pivot shaft type

9 Apply a smear of molybdenum disulphide grease to the shaft pivot bushes and the contact surfaces of the release fork.

10 Locate the lower pivot bush in the transmission, ensuring it is securely retained by its locating tangs, and refit the release fork. Slide the upper bush down the shaft, and clip it into position in the transmission housing.

11 On models with a conventional "push-type" release mechanism, refit the release lever to the shaft. Align the lever with the shaft hole, and secure it in position by tapping a new roll pin fully into position. Slide the release bearing onto the input shaft, and engage it with the release fork.

12 Refit the transmission as described in Chapter 7.

Ball-stud type

13 Apply a smear of molybdenum disulphide grease to the bush, then refit the release fork. Press it onto the ball-stud until it snaps home.

14 Slide the bearing onto the guide sleeve and engage the spring clips.

15 Refit the transmission (see Chapter 7).

Chapter 7
Manual transmission

Contents

Degrees of difficulty

Easy, suitable for novice with little experience	**Fairly easy,** suitable for beginner with some experience	**Fairly difficult,** suitable for competent DIY mechanic	**Difficult,** suitable for experienced DIY mechanic	**Very difficult,** suitable for expert DIY or professional

Specifications

General

Type . . . . Manual, five forward speeds and reverse. Synchromesh on all forward speeds

Designation . . . . BE1/5 or BE3/5

Lubrication
Recommended oil . . . . See "Lubricants, fluids and tyre pressures"
Capacity . . . . 2.0 litres

Torque wrench settings

	Nm	lbf ft
Gearchange selector rod to lever pivot bolt	15	11
Gearchange linkage bellcrank pivot bolt	28	21
Oil filler/level plug	22	16
Oil drain plug	35	26
Clutch release bearing guide sleeve bolts	12	9
Reversing light switch	25	18
Left-hand engine/transmission mounting:		
Mounting rubber-to-bracket nuts (all except 1.9 litre Turbo engines) . .	20	15
Mounting bracket-to-body bolts	45	33
Mounting stud	50	36
Centre nut	70	52
Mounting stud bracket bolts (1.9 litre Turbo engines)	60	44
Engine-to-transmission fixing bolts	45	33
Clutch cable bracket retaining bolts ("pull-type" clutch only)	18	13

1 General information

The transmission is contained in a cast-aluminium alloy casing bolted to the engine's left-hand end, and consists of the gearbox and final drive differential - often called a transaxle. Early models are fitted with the BE1 transmission, whilst later models are fitted with the improved BE3. The two types of transmission are essentially identical, all differences being internal.

Drive is transmitted from the crankshaft via the clutch to the input shaft, which has a splined extension to accept the clutch friction plate, and rotates in sealed ball-bearings. From the input shaft, drive is transmitted to the output shaft, which rotates in a roller bearing at its right-hand end, and a sealed ball-bearing at its left-hand end. From the output shaft, the drive is transmitted to the differential crownwheel, which rotates with the differential case and planetary gears, thus driving the sun gears and driveshafts. The rotation of the planetary gears on their shaft allows the inner roadwheel to rotate at a slower speed than the outer roadwheel when the car is cornering.

The input and output shafts are arranged side by side, parallel to the crankshaft and driveshafts, so that their gear pinion teeth are in constant mesh. In the neutral position, the output shaft gear pinions rotate freely, so that drive cannot be transmitted to the crownwheel.

Gear selection is via a floor-mounted lever and selector rod mechanism. The selector rod causes the appropriate selector fork to move its respective synchro-sleeve along the shaft, to lock the gear pinion to the synchro-hub. Since the synchro-hubs are splined to the output shaft, this locks the pinion to the shaft, so that drive can be transmitted. To ensure that gear-changing can be made quickly and quietly, a synchro-mesh system is fitted to all forward gears, consisting of baulk rings and spring-loaded fingers, as well as the gear

7

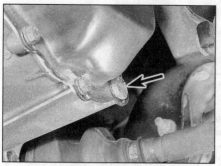

2.4 Gearbox filler/level plug location (arrowed)

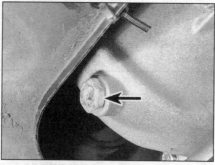

2.5 Gearbox drain plug location (arrowed)

pinions and synchro-hubs. The synchro-mesh cones are formed on the mating faces of the baulk rings and gear pinions.

On early BE1 type transmissions inadvertent selection of reverse gear is prevented by a reverse release plunger, operated by cable from the gear lever.

2 Manual transmission - draining and refilling

Note: *A suitable square section wrench may be required to undo the transmission filler/level and drain plugs on some models. These wrenches can be obtained from most motor factors or your Peugeot dealer.*

1 This operation is much quicker and more efficient if the car is first taken on a journey of sufficient length to warm the engine/transmission up to normal operating temperature.

2 Park the car on level ground, switch off the ignition and apply the handbrake firmly. For improved access, jack up the front of the car and support it securely on axle stands (see *"Jacking and Vehicle Support"*). Note that the car must be lowered to the ground and level, to ensure accuracy, when refilling and checking the oil level.

3 Where applicable, prise out retaining clips and remove the access cover from underneath the left-hand wheelarch liner.

4 Wipe clean the area around the filler/level plug, which is situated on the left-hand end of the transmission, next to the end cover. Unscrew the filler/level plug from the transmission and recover the sealing washer **(see illustration)**.

5 Position a suitable container under the drain plug (situated at the rear of the transmission, on the base of the differential housing) and unscrew the plug **(see illustration)**.

6 Allow the oil to drain completely into the container. If the oil is hot, take precautions against scalding. Clean both the filler/level and the drain plugs, being especially careful to wipe any metallic particles off the magnetic inserts. Discard the original sealing washers; they should be renewed whenever they are disturbed.

7 When the oil has finished draining, clean the drain plug threads and those of the transmission casing, fit a new sealing washer and refit the drain plug, tightening it to the specified torque wrench setting. If the car was raised for the draining operation, now lower it to the ground.

8 Refilling the transmission is an extremely awkward operation. Above all, allow plenty of time for the oil level to settle properly before checking it. Note that the car must be parked on flat level ground when checking the oil level. **Note:** *On early models fitted with a reverse release cable, easier access can be obtained to top-up the gearbox by disconnecting the reverse release cable from the top of the gearbox and adding oil through the reverse plunger orifice.*

9 Refill the transmission with the exact amount of the specified type of oil then check the oil level as described in Chapter 1; if the correct amount was poured into the transmission and a large amount flows out on

checking the level, refit the filler/level plug and take the car on a short journey so that the new oil is distributed fully around the transmission components, then check the level again on your return. Refit the access cover and secure it in position with the retaining clips.

3 Gearchange linkage - general information and adjustment

1 If a stiff, sloppy or imprecise gearchange leads you to suspect that a fault exists within the linkage, first dismantle it completely, and check it for wear or damage as described in Section 4. Reassemble it, applying a smear of the special grease to all bearing surfaces **(see illustration)**.

2 If this does not cure the fault, the car should be examined by an expert, as the fault must lie within the transmission itself. There is no adjustment as such in the linkage.

3 On some early models fitted with the BE1 gearbox, it is possible to adjust the length of the main engagement link rod, however this is for initial setting-up only and is not intended to provide a form of compensation for wear. If the link rod has been renewed, or if the length of the original is incorrect, adjust it as follows.

4 Firmly apply the handbrake, then jack up the front of the vehicle and support it on axle stands (see *"Jacking and Vehicle Support"*). Access to the link rod is poor, but it can be reached both from above and below the vehicle.

5 Measure the length of the main engagement link rod between centres (ie not the total length of the rod). If it is not 246.0 mm, slacken the

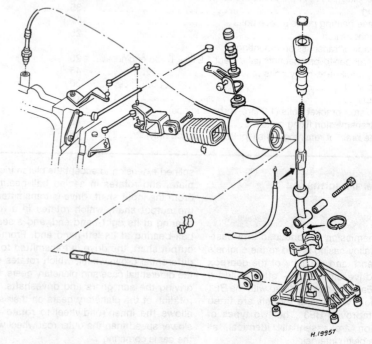

3.1 Gearchange linkage, gear lever and reverse release cable - early BE1-type transmission

locknut then carefully lever the link rod end off its balljoint on the transmission. Turn the end of the rod until the specified distance between the link rod balljoint centres is obtained, then press the disconnected end of the rod firmly back onto its balljoint and securely tighten the link rod locknut.

6 Check that all gears can be selected, and that the gearchange lever returns properly to its correct at-rest (neutral) position.

4 Gear lever, gearchange linkage and reverse release cable - removal and refitting

Gear lever

Removal

1 Remove the centre console as described in Chapter 11.

2 Where applicable, disconnect the reverse release cable from the gear lever as described later in this Section.

3 Undo and withdraw the gear change rod fork bolt at the bottom of the gear lever. This is accessible through the holes in the sides of the plastic gear lever support housing **(see illustration)**.

4 Undo the four nuts securing the gear lever support housing to the floor panel, noting the console support tube and earth lead, where applicable.

5 Withdraw the housing and gear lever.

6 To remove the lever from the housing, extract the circlip, or prise out the retaining clip lugs (as applicable) and withdraw the lever. Where applicable, recover the ball cups.

Refitting

7 Refitting is a reversal of removal, applying a little light grease to the gear lever pivot ball.

Gearchange linkage

Removal

8 First disconnect the main gearchange rod from the bottom of the gear lever as described in paragraph 3.

9 Remove the bolt from the fork on the ball and socket assembly and disconnect the rod from the bellcrank.

10 Pull the rubber bellows from the rod then

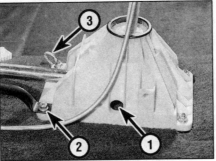

4.3 Gear lever support housing - early BE1-type transmission

1 Gearchange rod fork bolt hole
2 Console support bracket
3 Earth lead

withdraw the rod into the vehicle interior. It may be necessary to remove one of the front seats in order to do this.

11 Firmly apply the handbrake, then jack up the front of the vehicle and support it on axle stands (see *"Jacking and Vehicle Support"*).

12 The bellcrank and ball-and-socket are mounted on the steering rack housing **(see illustration)**. To remove the assembly, disconnect the control rod fork end as previously described and disconnect the link rods from their balljoints.

13 Remove the cap from the bellcrank pivot bolt, unscrew the bolt and withdraw the bellcrank assembly **(see illustration)**.

14 Inspect all the linkage components for

signs of wear or damage, paying particular attention to the pivot bushes, and renew worn components as necessary.

Refitting

15 Refitting is a reversal of this procedure, applying a little grease to the bulkhead grommet to ease the passage of the rod through the grommet. Ensure the grommet is not dislodged during the process.

16 The bellcrank selection and engagement lever link rods are a push-fit on the balljoint end fittings. Note that the fixed link rod is retained at its bracket end by a circlip.

17 Where possible, adjust the main engagement rod as described in Section 3.

Reverse lever cable - early BE1 type transmission

Removal

18 Disconnect the cable at the gearbox end by unscrewing the plastic nut and withdrawing the release plunger **(see illustrations)**.

19 Remove the centre console as described in Chapter 11.

20 Disconnect the cable from the gear lever by unhooking it from its location on the gear lever **(see illustration)**.

21 Withdraw the cable into the engine bay.

Refitting

22 Refitting is a reversal of removal. There is no adjustment possible. In order to feed the cable through the gear lever support housing, it may be easier to remove the support housing from the floor panel as described earlier.

4.12 Bellcrank and ball-and-socket assembly

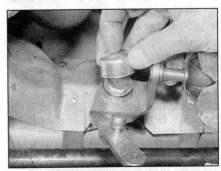

4.13 Removing the cap from the bellcrank pivot bolt

4.18a Reverse release plunger location (arrowed) - early BE1-type transmission

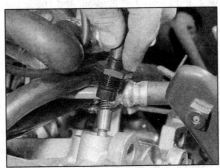

4.18b Withdrawing the reverse release plunger - early BE1-type transmission

4.20 Reverse release cable at gear lever end - early BE1-type transmission

7

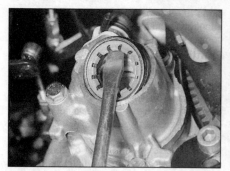

5.7 Use a large flat-bladed screwdriver to prise the driveshaft oil seals out of position

5.8a Fit the new seal to the transmission, noting the plastic seal protector . . .

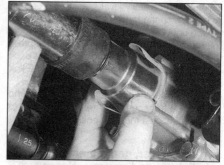

5.8b . . . and tap it into position using a tubular drift

5 Oil seals - renewal

Driveshaft oil seals

Note: *A balljoint separator tool will be required for this operation.*

1 Chock the rear wheels, apply the handbrake, then jack up the front of the car and support it on axle stands (see *"Jacking and Vehicle Support"*). Remove the appropriate front roadwheel.

2 Drain the transmission oil (see Section 2).

3 Slacken and remove the suspension lower balljoint nut and disconnect the hub carrier from the lower arm, using a balljoint separator tool (see Chapter 10). Unscrew and remove the bolt securing the anti-roll bar drop link to the lower arm. Proceed as described under the relevant sub-heading.

Right-hand seal

4 Loosen the two intermediate bearing retaining bolt nuts, then rotate the bolts through 90° so that their offset heads are clear of the bearing outer race.

5 Carefully pull the hub carrier assembly outwards, and pull on the inner end of the driveshaft to free the intermediate bearing from its mounting bracket.

6 Once the driveshaft end is free from the transmission, slide the dust seal off the inner end of the shaft, noting which way around it is fitted, and support the inner end of the driveshaft to avoid damaging the constant velocity joints or gaiters.

7 Carefully prise the oil seal out of the transmission, using a large flat-bladed screwdriver **(see illustration)**.

8 Remove all traces of dirt from the area around the oil seal aperture, then apply a smear of grease to the outer lip of the new oil seal. Fit the new seal into its aperture, and drive it squarely into position using a suitable tubular drift which bears only on the hard outer edge of the seal, until it abuts its locating shoulder. If the seal was supplied with a plastic protector sleeve, leave this in position until the driveshaft has been refitted **(see illustrations)**.

HAYNES HiNT *The seal can be driven into position using a large-diameter socket.*

9 Thoroughly clean the driveshaft splines, then apply a thin film of grease to the oil seal lips and to the driveshaft inner end splines.

10 Slide the dust seal into position on the end of the shaft, ensuring that its flat surface is facing the transmission.

11 Carefully locate the inner driveshaft splines with those of the differential sun gear, taking care not to damage the oil seal, then align the intermediate bearing with its mounting bracket, and push the driveshaft fully into position. If necessary, use a soft-faced mallet to tap the outer race of the bearing into position in the mounting bracket.

12 Ensure the intermediate bearing is correctly seated, then rotate its retaining bolts back through 90° so that their offset heads are resting against the bearing outer race, and tighten the retaining nuts to the specified torque. Remove the plastic seal protector (where supplied), and slide the dust seal tight up against the oil seal.

13 Reconnect the hub carrier to the lower arm, and refit the bolt securing the anti-roll bar drop link to the lower arm, with reference to Chapter 10. Tighten the fixings to the specified torque.

14 Refit the roadwheel, then lower the vehicle to the ground and tighten the roadwheel bolts to the specified torque.

15 Refill the transmission with the specified type and amount of fluid/oil, and check the level using the information given in Chapter 1.

Left-hand seal

16 Pull the hub carrier outwards and withdraw the driveshaft inner constant velocity joint from the transmission, taking care not to damage the driveshaft oil seal. Support the driveshaft, to avoid damaging the constant velocity joints or gaiters.

17 Renew the oil seal as described above in paragraphs 7 to 9.

18 Carefully locate the inner constant velocity joint splines with those of the differential sun gear, taking care not to damage the oil seal, and push the driveshaft

fully into position. Where fitted, remove the plastic protector from the oil seal.

19 Carry out the operations described above in paragraphs 13 to 15.

Input shaft oil seal

20 Remove the transmission as described in Section 8.

21 Undo the three bolts securing the clutch release bearing guide sleeve in position, and slide the guide off the input shaft, along with its O-ring or gasket (as applicable). Recover any shims or thrustwashers which have stuck to the rear of the guide sleeve, and refit them to the input shaft.

22 Carefully lever the oil seal out of the guide using a suitable flat-bladed screwdriver **(see illustration)**.

23 Before fitting a new seal, check the input shaft's seal rubbing surface for signs of burrs, scratches or other damage, which may have caused the seal to fail in the first place. It may be possible to polish away minor faults of this sort using fine abrasive paper; however, more serious defects will require the renewal of the input shaft. Ensure that the input shaft is clean and greased, to protect the seal lips on refitting.

24 Dip the new seal in clean oil, and fit it to the guide sleeve.

25 Fit a new O-ring or gasket (as applicable) to the rear of the guide sleeve, then carefully slide the sleeve into position over the input shaft. Refit the retaining bolts and tighten them to the specified torque setting **(see illustrations)**.

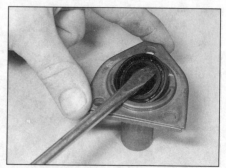

5.22 Levering the input shaft seal from the guide sleeve

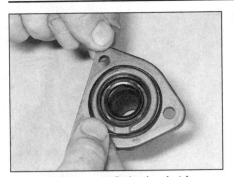

5.25a Fit a new O-ring/gasket (as applicable) . . .

5.25b . . . then refit the guide sleeve over the input shaft . . .

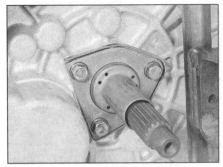

5.25c . . . and secure it in position with its three retaining bolts

26 Take the opportunity to inspect the clutch components if not already done (Chapter 6). Finally, refit the transmission as described in Section 8.

Selector shaft oil seal

27 Park the car on level ground, apply the handbrake, then jack up the front of the vehicle and support it on axle stands (see *"Jacking and Vehicle Support"*). Remove the left-hand front roadwheel, and unclip the access cover from the centre of the wheel arch liner.

28 Using a large flat-bladed screwdriver, lever the link rod balljoint off the transmission selector shaft, and disconnect the link rod.

29 Using a large flat-bladed screwdriver, carefully prise the selector shaft seal out of the housing, and slide it off the end of the shaft **(see illustrations)**.

30 Before fitting a new seal, check the selector shaft's seal rubbing surface for signs of burrs, scratches or other damage, which may have caused the seal to fail in the first place. It may be possible to polish away minor faults of this sort using fine abrasive paper; however, more serious defects will require the renewal of the selector shaft.

31 Apply a smear of grease to the new seal's outer edge and sealing lip, then carefully slide the seal along the selector rod. Press the seal fully into position in the transmission housing.

32 Refit the link rod to the selector shaft, ensuring that its balljoint is pressed firmly onto the shaft. Lower the car to the ground.

6 Reversing light switch - testing, removal and refitting

Testing

1 The reversing light circuit is controlled by a plunger-type switch that is screwed into the top of the transmission casing. If a fault develops in the circuit, first ensure that the circuit fuse has not blown.

2 To test the switch, disconnect the wiring connector, and use a multimeter (set to the resistance function) or a battery-and-bulb test circuit to check that there is continuity

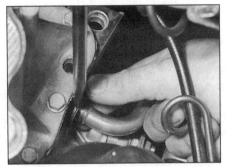

5.29a Use a screwdriver to prise the selector shaft seal out of position . . .

between the switch terminals only when reverse gear is selected. If this is not the case, and there are no obvious breaks or other damage to the wires, the switch is faulty, and must be renewed.

Removal

3 Where necessary, to improve access to the switch, it may be necessary to remove the air inlet duct(s) as described in the relevant Part of Chapter 4. If necessary, also remove the battery and mounting tray (see Chapter 5).

4 Disconnect the wiring connector, then unscrew the switch from the transmission casing along with its sealing washer **(see illustration)**.

Refitting

5 Fit a new sealing washer to the switch, then screw it back into position in the top of the transmission housing and tighten it to the

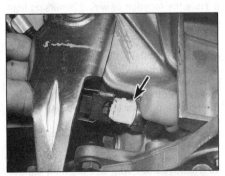

6.4 Disconnect the wiring connector from the reversing light switch (arrowed)

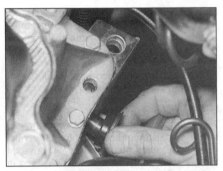

5.29b . . . then slide the seal of the shaft

specified torque setting. Reconnect the wiring connector, and test the operation of the circuit. Refit any components removed for access.

7 Speedometer drive - removal and refitting

Removal

1 Chock the rear wheels, firmly apply the handbrake, then jack up the front of the car and support it on axle stands (see *"Jacking and Vehicle Support"*). The speedometer drive is situated on the rear of the transmission housing, next to the inner end of the right-hand driveshaft.

2 Pull out the speedometer cable retaining pin, and disconnect the cable from the speedometer drive. Where necessary, disconnect the wiring connector from the speedometer drive.

3 Slacken and remove the retaining bolt, along with the heat shield (where fitted), and withdraw the speedometer drive and driven pinion assembly from the transmission housing, along with its O-ring **(see illustrations)**.

4 If necessary, the pinion can be slid out of the housing, and the oil seal can be removed from the top of the housing. Examine the pinion for damage, and renew if necessary. Renew the housing O-ring as a matter of course.

5 If the driven pinion is worn or damaged, also examine the drive pinion in the transmission housing for similar signs.

6 To remove the drive pinion, first disengage

7

7.3a Slacken and remove the retaining bolt . . .

7.3b . . . then withdraw the speedometer drive from the transmission

7.6a Undo the three bolts (arrowed) . . .

the right-hand driveshaft from the transmission, as described in Section 5. Undo the three retaining bolts, and remove the speedometer drive housing from the transmission, along with its O-ring. Remove the drive pinion from the differential gear, and recover any adjustment shims from the gear **(see illustrations)**.

Refitting

7 Where the drive pinion has been removed, refit the adjustment shims to the differential gear, then locate the speedometer drive on the gear, ensuring it is correctly engaged in the gear slots **(see illustration)**. Fit a new O-ring to the rear of the speedometer drive housing, then refit the housing to the transmission and securely tighten its retaining bolts. Inspect the driveshaft oil seal for signs of wear, and renew if necessary. Refit the driveshaft to the transmission, using the information given in Section 5.

8 Apply a little grease to the lips of the seal and to the driven pinion shaft, and slide the pinion into position in the speedometer drive.

9 Fit a new O-ring to the speedometer drive and refit it to the transmission; ensure the drive and driven pinions are correctly engaged.

10 Refit the retaining bolt and the heat shield (where fitted), and tighten the bolt. Where necessary, reconnect the wiring connector to the speedometer drive.

11 Apply a smear of oil to the speedometer cable O-rings, then reconnect the cable to the drive, and secure it in position with the retaining pin. Lower the vehicle to the ground.

---

8 Manual transmission - removal and refitting

Note: *The following procedure is involved, and it is advisable to read through before proceeding. It may prove easier to remove the transmission complete with the engine, as described in Chapter 2.*

Removal

Note: *A hoist and lifting tackle, and a balljoint separator tool will be required for this operation.*

1 Prop the bonnet open in its vertical position.

2 To improve access, remove the battery and

7.6b . . . and remove the housing, O-ring and drive pinion from the transmission

support tray as described in Chapter 5. Where applicable, also remove the air cleaner assembly and associated hoses (Chapter 4).

3 On early models where the fuel filter assembly is mounted on the battery tray, unscrew the two securing bolts, and move the filter assembly to one side, clear of the working area. If necessary, disconnect one of the fuel hoses to allow the filter assembly to be moved sufficiently - in this case, be prepared for fuel spillage, and plug or cover the open ends of the hose and filter head.

4 During this procedure, the engine must be tilted down at the gearbox end. To enable this, where applicable, remove the power-assisted steering pump without disconnecting the hoses, tying it back out of the way. Also remove the pump support bracket.

5 Disconnect the clutch cable from the transmission with reference to Chapter 6.

6 Note the location of wiring (reversing light switch, earth leads, etc), hoses and brackets then detach them from the transmission.

7 Remove the starter motor (Chapter 5). Also (if applicable) remove the air cleaner bracket.

8 On early models disconnect the reverse release cable from the transmission by unscrewing the plastic nut and withdrawing the release plunger (see Section 4). Tie the cable to one side.

9 Apply the handbrake, then jack up the front of the vehicle and support on axle stands (see *"Jacking and Vehicle Support"*).

10 Remove both front wheels, then remove the engine undertray and wheel arch lower mudshield, if fitted.

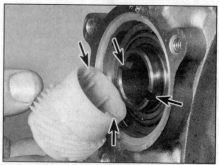

7.7 On refitting, ensure the drive pinion dogs are correctly engaged with the gear slots (arrowed)

11 Drain the transmission oil as described in Section 2. Refit and tighten the drain plug on completion.

12 Where applicable, unbolt the support member located between the subframe and left-hand front valance.

13 Unbolt both anti-roll bar drop links from the front suspension lower arms. Refer to Chapter 10 if necessary.

14 Slacken and remove the suspension lower balljoint nut and disconnect the hub carrier from the lower arm, using a balljoint separator tool (see Chapter 10). Wedge the lower end of the right-hand swivel hub outwards using a block of wood.

15 On models with 1.9 litre Turbo engines, proceed as follows.

a) *Support the subframe on a trolley jack, with an interposed block of wood.*

b) *Release any wiring/cables/hoses from the clip on the subframe, and move them clear to enable the subframe to be removed.*

c) *Unscrew and remove the bolts securing the steering gear to the subframe.*

d) *Unscrew and remove the subframe mounting bolts (see Chapter 10).*

e) *Lower the subframe and remove it from under the front of the car.*

16 Unscrew and remove the through-bolt and nut from the rear engine mounting.

17 Loosen the two driveshaft intermediate bearing retaining bolt nuts, then rotate the bolts through 90°, so that their offset heads are clear of the bearing outer race (see Chapter 8).

18 Carefully pull the hub carrier assembly

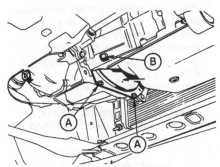

8.29 Transmission bellhousing lower cover bolts (A) and transmission-to-engine lower mounting bolt (B)

8.31a Remove the centre nut and washer from the left-hand mounting . . .

8.31b . . . then undo the two retaining bolts and remove the mounting bracket assembly

8.32a Slide the spacer off the mounting stud . . .

8.32b . . . and unscrew the mounting stud. If the stud is tight, use a stud extractor

outwards, and pull on the inner end of the driveshaft to free the intermediate bearing from its mounting bracket.

19 Once the driveshaft end is free from the transmission, support the inner end of the shaft using wire or string. Do not allow the end of the driveshaft to hang down.

20 Pull the left-hand driveshaft from the transmission and support it using wire or string.

21 Using a flat-bladed screwdriver, carefully lever the gearchange mechanism link rods off their respective balljoints on the transmission. Position the rods clear of the transmission.

22 To avoid placing undue strain on the exhaust system when the engine is lowered, disconnect the exhaust front section from the manifold/turbocharger, with reference to Chapter 4. If necessary, release the exhaust system from the front rubber mountings, and move it clear of the engine and transmission.

23 Later in the removal procedure, the left-hand end of the engine/gearbox unit must be moved forwards. On some models fitted with air conditioning, to enable this it may be necessary to remove the radiator as described in Chapter 3. If the radiator is removed, place a large wad of rag over the air conditioning condenser to protect against damage.

24 Disconnect the speedometer cable from the transmission by extracting the pin and pulling the cable from the extension housing.

25 Unbolt and remove the final drive speedo-meter drive extension housing, recovering the shim and O-ring seal.

26 Unscrew the speedometer drive gear support bolt and the transmission extension

mounting bolts. Separate the drive gear support and remove the final drive extension.

27 Recover the speedometer drive gear and adjustment shim.

28 Unbolt the transmission bellhousing lower cover.

29 Unscrew the transmission-to-engine lower mounting bolt located above the right-hand side of the final drive (see illustration).

30 Attach a suitable hoist and lifting tackle to the engine, and take the weight of the engine and transmission. Alternatively place a jack with a block of wood beneath the engine, to take the weight of the engine.

31 Unscrew the nut from the left-hand engine mounting and recover the washer, then unbolt the mounting bracket from the body. Where the bracket is welded in position undo the nuts and washers and remove the rubber mounting (see illustrations).

32 Slide the spacer (where fitted) off the

mounting stud, then unscrew the stud from the top of the transmission housing and remove it along with its washer. If the mounting stud is tight, a universal stud extractor can be used to unscrew it (see illustrations). On models with 1.9 litre Turbo engines, Unscrew the securing bolts and remove the mounting stud bracket from the top of the transmission.

33 On models with 1.9 litre Turbo engines, with a "pull-type" clutch release mechanism (see Chapter 6), tap out the retaining pin or unscrew the retaining bolt (as applicable) and remove the clutch release lever from the top of the release fork shaft. This is necessary to allow the fork shaft to rotate freely, to disengage from the release bearing as the transmission is pulled away from the engine. Make an alignment mark across the centre of the clutch release fork shaft using a scriber, paint or similar, and mark its position relative to the transmission housing (see illustrations). Undo the retaining bolts,

8.33a On models with a "pull-type" clutch, withdraw the retaining pin . . .

8.33b . . . then remove the clutch release lever . . .

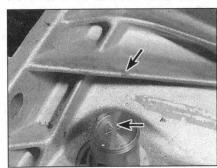

8.33c . . . and make a mark between the release fork shaft and housing (arrowed)

7

and remove the clutch cable bracket from the top of the transmission housing.

34 Using the hoist or jack, as applicable, lower the engine as far as possible without unduly straining the right-hand engine mounting. Move the transmission end forward as far as possible. Take care not to damage surrounding components in the engine compartment.

35 Support the transmission on a trolley jack with a block of wood between the jack and transmission to spread the load.

36 Unscrew the engine-to-transmission mounting bolts. Note the correct fitted positions of each bolt, and note the locations of any brackets secured by the bolts, to ensure correct refitting. Make a final check that all components have been disconnected, and are positioned clear of the transmission so that they will not hinder the removal procedure.

37 With the engine-to-transmission bolts removed, move the trolley jack and transmission to the left, to free the transmission from its locating dowels, then pivot the differential end of the transmission upwards (to enable it to clear the subframe).

38 Once the transmission is free, lower the jack and manoeuvre the unit out from under the car. Remove the locating dowels from the transmission or engine if they are loose, and keep them in a safe place.

39 On models with a "pull-type" clutch, make a second alignment mark on the transmission housing, marking the relative position of the release fork mark after removal, noting the angle at which the release fork is positioned. This mark can then be used to position the release fork before refitting, to ensure that the fork correctly engages with the clutch release bearing as the transmission is installed.

Refitting

40 The transmission is refitted by a reversal of the removal procedure, bearing in mind the following points:

a) *Except on 1993-on models with a nickeled clutch friction plate hub (see Chapter 6), apply a little high-melting-point grease (Peugeot recommend the use of Molykote BR2 plus - available from your Peugeot dealer) to the splines of the transmission input shaft. Do not apply too much, otherwise there is a possibility of the grease contaminating the clutch friction plate.*

b) *Ensure the locating dowels are correctly positioned in the engine transmission and/or engine prior to installation.*

c) *Before refitting, ensure that the clutch friction plate is centralised (Chapter 6).*

d) *On models with a "pull-type" clutch, before refitting, position the clutch release*

8.40a On models with a "pull-type" clutch, prior to refitting the transmission, align the release fork mark with the second mark made on removal

8.40b Apply thread-locking fluid to the mounting stud threads

bearing so that its arrow mark is pointing upwards (bearing fork slots facing towards the front of the engine), and align the release fork shaft mark with the second mark made on the transmission housing (release fork positioned at approximately 60° to the clutch housing face) **(see illustration)**. *This will ensure that the release fork and bearing will engage correctly as the transmission is refitted to the engine. If the bearing and fork are correctly engaged, the mark on the shaft should be aligned with the original mark made on the transmission housing.* **Ensure the release fork and bearing are correctly engaged before bolting the transmission onto the engine.**

e) *Ensure that the engine-to-transmission mounting bolts are fitted to their correct locations, and make sure that any brackets noted during removal are in place on the bolts.*

f) *Apply thread-locking fluid to the left-hand engine/transmission mounting stud threads, prior to refitting it to the transmission* **(see illustration)**. *Tighten the stud to the specified torque.*

g) *Tighten all nuts and bolts to the specified torque (where given), with reference to the appropriate Chapters where necessary.*

h) *Check the condition of the speedometer drive extension housing O-ring, and renew if necessary.*

i) *Renew the driveshaft oil seals then reconnect the driveshafts as described in Chapter 8.*

j) *Adjust the clutch cable as described in Chapter 6.*

k) *Where applicable, refit the radiator, and refill the cooling system as described in Chapter 1.*

l) *On completion, refill the transmission with the specified type and quantity of lubricant, as described in Chapter 1.*

m) *If any fuel lines were disconnected during the removal procedure, bleed the fuel system as described in Chapter 4.*

9 Manual transmission overhaul - general information

Overhauling a manual transmission is a difficult and involved job for the DIY home mechanic. In addition to dismantling and reassembling many small parts, clearances must be precisely measured and, if necessary, changed by selecting shims and spacers. Internal transmission components are also often difficult to obtain, and in many instances, extremely expensive. Because of this, if the transmission develops a fault or becomes noisy, the best course of action is to have the unit overhauled by a specialist repairer, or to obtain an exchange reconditioned unit. Be aware that some transmission repairs can be carried out with the transmission in the car.

Nevertheless, it is not impossible for the more experienced mechanic to overhaul the transmission, provided the special tools are available, and the job is done in a deliberate step-by-step manner, so that nothing is overlooked.

The tools necessary for an overhaul include internal and external circlip pliers, bearing pullers, a slide hammer, a set of pin punches, a dial test indicator, and possibly a hydraulic press. In addition, a large, sturdy workbench and a vice will be required.

During dismantling of the transmission, make careful notes of how each component is fitted, to make reassembly easier and more accurate.

Before dismantling the transmission, it will help if you have some idea what area is malfunctioning. Certain problems can be closely related to specific areas in the transmission, which can make component examination and replacement easier. Refer to the *"Fault finding"* Section at the end of this manual for more information.

Chapter 8
Driveshafts

Contents

Degrees of difficulty

Easy, suitable for novice with little experience	**Fairly easy,** suitable for beginner with some experience	**Fairly difficult,** suitable for competent DIY mechanic	**Difficult,** suitable for experienced DIY mechanic	**Very difficult,** suitable for expert DIY or professional

Specifications

Lubrication (overhaul only - see text)

Lubricant type/specification . . . . Use only special grease supplied in sachets with gaiter kits - joints are otherwise pre-packed with grease and sealed

Torque wrench settings	Nm	lbf ft
Driveshaft nut:		
Models up to November 1992	265	194
Models from November 1992:		
Early (solid) type hub carrier*	320	235
Later (hollow) type hub carrier*	325	240
Right-hand driveshaft intermediate bearing retaining bolt nuts	20	15
Suspension lower arm balljoint nut		
Models with solid hub carrier*	30	22
Models with hollow hub carrier*	45	33
Anti-roll bar drop link-to-lower arm bolt	65	48
Roadwheel bolts	85	63

*See note in Chapter 10, Section 2 for details

---

1 General information

Drive is transmitted from the differential to the front wheels by means of two solid-steel driveshafts of unequal length.

Both driveshafts are splined at their outer ends, to accept the wheel hubs, and are threaded so that each hub can be fastened by a large nut. The inner end of each driveshaft is splined, to accept the differential sun gear.

Constant velocity (CV) joints are fitted to each end of the driveshafts, to ensure that the smooth and efficient transmission of power at all suspension and steering angles.

On the right-hand side, due to the length of the driveshaft, the inner constant velocity joint is situated approximately halfway along the shaft's length, and an intermediate support bearing is mounted in the engine/transmission rear mounting bracket. The inner end of the driveshaft passes through the bearing (which prevents any lateral movement of the driveshaft inner end) and the inner constant velocity joint outer member.

2 Driveshaft - removal and refitting

Removal

Note: *Do not allow the vehicle to rest on its wheels with one or both driveshafts removed, as damage to the wheel bearing(s) may result. If moving the vehicle is unavoidable, temporarily insert the outer end of the driveshaft(s) in the hub(s) and tighten the hub nut(s): in this case, the inner end(s) of the driveshaft(s) must be supported, for example by suspending with string from the vehicle underbody. Do not allow the driveshaft to hang down under its own weight.*

Note: *A balljoint separator tool will be required for this operation. A new suspension lower balljoint nut will be required on refitting.*

1 Chock the rear wheels and firmly apply the handbrake, then jack up the front of the vehicle and support securely on axle stands (see *"Jacking and Vehicle Support"*). Remove the appropriate front roadwheel.

HAYNES HiNT *On models where access to the driveshaft nut can be obtained by removing the wheel trims, before jacking up the vehicle, loosen the driveshaft nut as follows:*

a) *Chock the front wheels, and remove the wheel trim.*

b) *Have an assistant firmly apply the footbrake.*

c) *Withdraw the R-clip and remove the locking cap from the driveshaft nut.*

d) *Loosen the driveshaft nut using a socket and extension.*

2 On models equipped with ABS, remove the ABS wheel sensor as described in Chapter 9.

3 If the driveshaft nut has been loosened, proceed to paragraph 6, otherwise withdraw the R-clip and remove the locking cap from the driveshaft retaining nut **(see illustrations)**.

4 Refit at least two roadwheel bolts to the front hub, and tighten them securely. Have an assistant firmly depress the brake pedal to prevent the front hub from rotating, then using a socket and a long extension bar, slacken

8

2.3a Withdraw the R-clip . . .

2.3b . . . and remove the locking cap from the driveshaft nut

and remove the driveshaft retaining nut. Alternatively, a tool can be fabricated from two lengths of steel strip (one long, one short) and a nut and bolt; the nut and bolt forming the pivot of a forked tool. Bolt the tool to the hub using two wheel bolts, and hold the tool to prevent the hub from rotating as the driveshaft retaining nut is undone **(see Tool Tip)**. This nut is very tight; make sure that there is no risk of pulling the car off the axle stands. (If the roadwheel trim allows access to the driveshaft nut, the initial slackening can be done with the wheels chocked and on the ground.)

5 Slacken and partially unscrew the suspension lower balljoint nut (unscrew the nut as far as the end of the threads on the balljoint to prevent damage to the threads as the joint is released), then release the balljoint using a balljoint separator tool **(see illustration)**. Remove the nut.

6 Unscrew the bolt securing the anti-roll bar drop link to the suspension lower arm **(see illustration)**.

7 Place a container beneath the transmission end of the driveshaft to catch escaping oil/fluid which will be released as the end of the driveshaft is withdrawn.

Left-hand driveshaft

8 Turn the steering to full right-lock, then carefully pull the hub carrier assembly outwards, and withdraw the driveshaft outer constant velocity joint from the hub assembly.

If necessary, the shaft can be tapped out of the hub using a soft-faced mallet.

9 Support the driveshaft, then withdraw the inner constant velocity joint from the transmission, taking care not to damage the driveshaft oil seal. Remove the driveshaft from the vehicle.

Right-hand driveshaft

10 Loosen the two intermediate bearing retaining bolt nuts, then rotate the bolts through 90°, so that their offset heads are clear of the bearing outer race **(see illustrations)**.

11 Turn the steering to full left-lock, then carefully pull the hub carrier assembly outwards, and withdraw the driveshaft outer constant velocity joint from the hub assembly. If necessary, the shaft can be tapped out of the hub using a soft-faced mallet.

12 Support the outer end of the driveshaft, then pull on the inner end of the shaft to free the intermediate bearing from its mounting bracket.

13 Once the driveshaft end is free from the transmission, slide the dust seal off the inner end of the shaft, noting which way around it is fitted, and remove the driveshaft from the vehicle.

Refitting

14 Before installing the driveshaft, examine the driveshaft oil seal in the transmission for signs of damage or deterioration and, if necessary, renew it, referring to the appropriate Part of Chapter 7 for further information. (Having got this far it is worth renewing the seal as a matter of course.)

15 Thoroughly clean the driveshaft splines, and the apertures in the transmission and hub assembly. Apply a thin film of grease to the oil seal lips, and to the driveshaft splines and shoulders. Check that all gaiter clips are securely fastened.

Left-hand driveshaft

16 Offer up the driveshaft, and locate the joint splines with those of the differential sun gear, taking great care not to damage the oil seal. Push the joint fully into position.

17 Locate the outer constant velocity joint splines with those of the hub, and slide the joint back into position in the hub.

18 Align the suspension lower balljoint with the lower arm, then fit and tighten a new retaining nut to the specified torque setting.

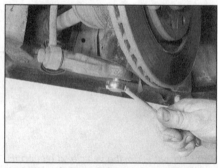

2.5 Slackening the suspension lower balljoint nut

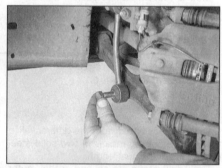

2.6 Unscrew the bolt securing the anti-roll bar drop link to the lower arm

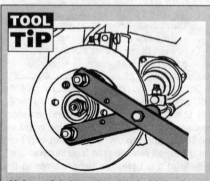

Using a fabricated tool to hold the front hub stationary whilst the driveshaft retaining nut is slackened

2.10a On the right-hand driveshaft, slacken the two intermediate bearing retaining bolt nuts . . .

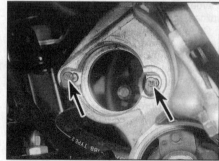

2.10b . . . then turn bolts through 90° to disengage their offset heads (arrowed) from bearing (driveshaft removed for clarity)

2.27 Locate the dust seal on the inner end of the right-hand driveshaft, ensuring that it is fitted the correct way round

19 Reconnect the anti-roll bar drop link to the lower arm, and tighten the securing bolt to the specified torque.

 HAYNES HiNT *On models where access to the driveshaft nut can be obtained by removing the wheel trim, the driveshaft nut can be tightened with the footbrake firmly applied, and the vehicle resting on its wheels.*

20 Lubricate the inner face and threads of the driveshaft retaining nut with clean engine oil, and refit it to the end of the driveshaft. Use the method employed on removal to prevent the hub from rotating, and tighten the driveshaft retaining nut to the specified torque. Check that the hub rotates freely.
21 Engage the locking cap with the driveshaft nut so that one of its cut-outs is aligned with the driveshaft hole. Secure the cap in position with the R-clip.
22 Where necessary, refit the ABS wheel sensor, with reference to Chapter 9.
23 Refit the roadwheel, then lower the vehicle to the ground and tighten the roadwheel bolts to the specified torque.
24 Refill the transmission with the specified type and amount of fluid/oil, and check the level using the information given in Chapter 1.

Right-hand driveshaft

25 Check that the intermediate bearing rotates smoothly, without any sign of roughness or undue free play between its inner and outer races. If necessary, renew the bearing as described in Section 5. Examine the dust seal for signs of damage or deterioration, and renew if necessary.
26 Apply a smear of grease to the outer race of the intermediate bearing, and to the inner lip of the dust seal.
27 Pass the inner end of the shaft through the bearing mounting bracket, then carefully slide the dust seal into position on the driveshaft, ensuring that its flat surface is facing the transmission **(see illustration)**.
28 Carefully locate the inner driveshaft splines with those of the differential sun gear, taking care not to damage the oil seal. Align the intermediate bearing with its mounting

2.30 Secure the intermediate bearing in position, then slide the dust seal up tight against the driveshaft oil seal

bracket, and push the driveshaft fully into position. If necessary, use a soft-faced mallet to tap the outer race of the bearing into position in the mounting bracket.
29 Locate the outer constant velocity joint splines with those of the hub, and slide the joint back into position in the hub.
30 Ensure the intermediate bearing is correctly seated, then rotate its retaining bolts back through 90°, so that their offset heads are resting against the bearing outer race. Tighten the retaining nuts to the specified torque. Ensure that the dust seal is tight against the driveshaft oil seal **(see illustration)**.
31 Carry out the operations described above in paragraphs 19 to 24.

 3 Driveshaft rubber gaiters - renewal

Note: *Check on the availability of suitable spare parts before contemplating gaiter renewal.*

Outer joint

1 Remove the driveshaft from the car as described in Section 2.
2 Secure the driveshaft in a vice equipped with soft jaws, and release the two rubber gaiter retaining clips. If necessary, the gaiter retaining clips can be cut to release them.
3 Slide the rubber gaiter down the shaft, to expose the outer constant velocity joint. Scoop out the excess grease.
4 Using a hammer and suitable soft metal drift, sharply strike the inner member of the outer joint to drive it off the end of the shaft. The joint is retained on the driveshaft by a circlip, and striking the joint in this manner forces the circlip into its groove, so allowing the joint to slide off.
5 Once the joint assembly has been removed, remove the circlip from the groove in the driveshaft splines, and discard it. A new circlip must be fitted on reassembly.
6 Withdraw the rubber gaiter from the driveshaft, and slide off the gaiter inner end plastic bush.
7 With the constant velocity joint removed from the driveshaft, thoroughly clean the joint

using paraffin, or a suitable solvent, and dry it thoroughly. Carry out a visual inspection of the joint.
8 Move the inner splined driving member from side to side, to expose each ball in turn at the top of its track. Examine the balls for cracks, flat spots, or signs of surface pitting.
9 Inspect the ball tracks on the inner and outer members. If the tracks have widened, the balls will no longer be a tight fit. At the same time, check the ball cage windows for wear or cracking between the windows.
10 If on inspection, any of the constant velocity joint components are found to be worn or damaged, it will be necessary to renew the complete joint assembly (where available), or even the complete driveshaft (where no joint components are available separately). Refer to your Peugeot dealer for information on parts availability. If the joint is in good condition, obtain a repair kit consisting of a new gaiter, circlip, retaining clips, and the correct type and quantity of grease.
11 To install the new gaiter, refer to the accompanying illustrations, and perform the operations shown **(see illustrations 3.11a to 3.11k)**. Be sure to stay in order, and follow the captions carefully. Note that the hard plastic rings are not fitted to all gaiters, and the gaiter retaining clips supplied with the repair kit may be different to those shown in the sequence. To secure this other type of clip in position, lock the ends of the clip together, then remove any slack in the clip by carefully compressing the raised section of the clip using a pair of side cutters.

3.11a Fit the hard plastic rings to the outer CV joint gaiter . . .

3.11b . . . then slide on the new plastic bush (arrowed), and seat it in its recess in the shaft. Slide the gaiter onto the shaft . . .

8

3.11c ... and seat the gaiter inner end on top of the plastic bush

3.11d Fit the new circlip to its groove in the driveshaft splines ...

3.11e ... then locate the joint outer member on the splines, and slide over the circlip. Ensure the joint is firmly retained by the circlip before proceeding

3.11f Pack the joint with grease, working it well into the ball tracks while twisting the joint, then locate the gaiter outer lip in its groove on the outer member

3.11g Fit the outer gaiter retaining clip and, using a hook fabricated out of welding rod and a pair of pliers, pull the clip tightly to remove all slack

3.11h Bend the clip end back over the buckle, then cut off the excess clip

3.11i Fold the clip end underneath the buckle ...

3.11j then fold the buckle firmly down onto the clip to secure the clip in position

3.11k Carefully lift the gaiter inner end to equalise air pressure in the gaiter, then secure the inner gaiter retaining clip in position using the same method

12 Check that the constant velocity joint moves freely in all directions, then refit the driveshaft to the car as described in Section 2.

Inner joint

13 Remove the driveshaft from the vehicle as described in Section 2.
14 Remove the outer constant velocity joint as described above in paragraphs 1 to 4.
15 Tape over the splines on the driveshaft, and carefully remove the outer constant velocity joint rubber gaiter, and the gaiter inner end plastic bush. It is recommended that the outer joint gaiter is also renewed, regardless of its apparent condition.
16 Release the retaining clips, then slide the

gaiter off the shaft, and remove its plastic bush. As the gaiter is released, the joint outer member will also be freed from the end of the shaft (see illustrations).
17 Thoroughly clean the joint using paraffin, or a suitable solvent, and dry it thoroughly. Check the tripod joint bearings and joint outer member for signs of wear, pitting or scuffing on their bearing surfaces. Check that the bearing rollers rotate smoothly and easily around the tripod joint, with no traces of roughness.
18 If on inspection, the tripod joint or outer member reveal signs of wear or damage, it will be necessary to renew the complete

driveshaft assembly, since the joint is not available separately. If the joint is in satisfactory condition, obtain a repair kit consisting of a new gaiter, retaining clips, and the correct type and quantity of grease. Although not strictly necessary, it is also recommended that the outer constant velocity joint gaiter is renewed, regardless of its apparent condition.
19 On reassembly, pack the inner joint with the grease supplied in the gaiter kit. Work the grease well into the bearing tracks and rollers, while twisting the joint.
20 Clean the shaft, using emery cloth to remove any rust or sharp edges which may

3.16a Release the inner gaiter retaining clips, and remove the joint outer member

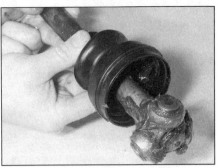

3.16b Slide the gaiter off the end of the driveshaft . . .

3.16c . . . and remove the plastic bush

damage the gaiter, then slide the plastic bush and inner joint gaiter along the driveshaft. Locate the plastic bush in its recess on the shaft, and seat the inner end of the gaiter on top of the bush.

21 Fit the outer member over the end of the shaft, and locate the gaiter in the groove on the joint outer member. Push the outer member onto the joint, so that its spring-loaded plunger is compressed, then lift the outer edge of the gaiter to equalise air pressure in the gaiter. Fit both the inner and outer retaining clips, securing them in position using the information given in paragraph 11. Ensure the gaiter retaining clips are securely tightened, then check that the joint moves freely in all directions.

22 Refit the outer constant velocity joint components using the information given in paragraph 11.

4 Driveshaft overhaul - general information

1 If any of the checks described in Chapter 1 reveal wear in any driveshaft joint, first remove the roadwheel trim or if necessary the roadwheel, for access to the driveshaft nut.

2 If the R-clip is fitted, the driveshaft nut should be correctly tightened; if in doubt, remove the R-clip and locking cap, and use a torque wrench to check that the nut is securely fastened. Once tightened, refit the locking cap and R-clip, then refit the centre

cap or trim. Repeat this check on the remaining driveshaft nut.

3 Road test the vehicle, and listen for a metallic clicking from the front as the vehicle is driven slowly in a circle on full-lock. If a clicking noise is heard, this indicates wear in the outer constant velocity joint. This means that the joint must be renewed; reconditioning is not possible.

4 If vibration, consistent with road speed, is felt through the car when accelerating, there is a possibility of wear in the inner constant velocity joints.

5 To check the joints for wear, remove the driveshafts, then dismantle them as described in Section 3; if any wear or free play is found, the affected joint must be renewed. This means that the complete driveshaft assembly must be renewed, as the joints are not available separately. Consult your Peugeot dealer for information on the availability of exchange/new driveshafts.

5 Right-hand driveshaft intermediate bearing - renewal

Note: *A suitable bearing puller will be required, to draw the bearing and collar off the driveshaft end.*

1 Remove the right-hand driveshaft as described in Section 2.

2 Check that the bearing outer race rotates smoothly and easily, without any signs of

roughness or undue free play between the inner and outer races. If necessary, renew the bearing as follows.

3 Using a long-reach universal bearing puller, carefully draw the collar and intermediate bearing off the driveshaft inner end **(see illustration)**. Apply a smear of grease to the inner race of the new bearing, then fit the bearing over the end of the driveshaft. Using a hammer and suitable piece of tubing which bears only on the bearing inner race, tap the new bearing into position on the driveshaft, until it abuts the constant velocity joint outer member. Once the bearing is correctly positioned, tap the bearing collar onto the shaft until it contacts the bearing inner race.

4 Check that the bearing rotates freely, then refit the driveshaft as described in Section 2.

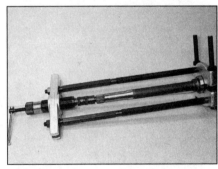

5.3 Using a long-reach bearing puller to remove the intermediate bearing from the right-hand driveshaft

Chapter 9
Braking system

Contents

Degrees of difficulty

Easy, suitable for novice with little experience	Fairly easy, suitable for beginner with some experience	Fairly difficult, suitable for competent DIY mechanic	Difficult, suitable for experienced DIY mechanic	Very difficult, suitable for expert DIY or professional

Specifications

Front brakes

Disc thickness:
  New:
    Solid disc . . . . 10.0 mm
    Ventilated disc . . . . 20.4 mm
  Minimum thickness:
    Solid disc . . . . 9.0 mm
    Ventilated disc . . . . 18.0 mm
Maximum disc run-out . . . . 0.07 mm
Brake pad minimum thickness . . . . Refer to Chapter 1

Rear drum brakes

Drum internal diameter:
  New . . . . 228.6 mm
  Maximum diameter after machining . . . . 229.6 mm
Brake shoe lining minimum thickness . . . . Refer to Chapter 1

Rear disc brakes

Disc thickness:
  New . . . . 8.0 mm
  Minimum thickness . . . . 6.0 mm
Maximum disc run-out . . . . 0.07 mm
Brake pad minimum thickness . . . . Refer to Chapter 1

9

Torque wrench settings

	Nm	lbf ft
Hydraulic pipe unions	15	11
Front brake caliper:		
Guide pin bolts (Girling caliper)**	35	26
Caliper mounting bolts (Bendix caliper):*^:		
Early (solid) type hub carrier	120	89
Later (hollow) type hub carrier	105	77
Caliper mounting bracket bolts (Girling caliper):*^		
Early (solid) type hub carrier	120	89
Later (hollow) type hub carrier	105	77
Rear brake caliper:		
Guide pin bolts*	35	26
Caliper mounting bracket bolts*	55	41
Master cylinder-to-servo unit nuts	15	11
Brake pedal pivot bolt nut	20	15
Vacuum servo unit securing nuts	20	15
ABS wheel sensor securing bolts*	10	7
ABS wheel sensor adjuster bolt (Bendix "integral" ABS)	3	2
ABS hydraulic modulator mounting nuts	20	15
Roadwheel bolts	85	63

*Use thread-locking compound.
**Use new bolts coated with thread-locking compound
^Refer to note in Chapter 10, Section 2.

1 General information

The braking system is of the servo-assisted, dual-circuit hydraulic type. The arrangement of the hydraulic system is such that each circuit operates one front and one rear brake from a tandem master cylinder. Under normal circumstances, both circuits operate in unison. However, in the event of hydraulic failure in one circuit, full braking force will still be available at two wheels.

Some large-capacity engine models have disc brakes all round as standard; other models are fitted with front disc brakes and rear drum brakes. ABS is fitted as standard to certain models, and is offered as an option on most other models (refer to Section 23 for further information on ABS operation).

The front disc brakes are actuated by single-piston sliding type calipers, which ensure that equal pressure is applied to each disc pad.

On models with rear drum brakes, the rear brakes incorporate leading and trailing shoes, which are actuated by twin-piston wheel cylinders. On models not equipped with an underbody-mounted rear brake pressure regulating valve, the wheel cylinders incorporate integral pressure-regulating valves, which control the hydraulic pressure applied to the rear brakes. The regulating valves help to prevent rear wheel lock-up during emergency braking. On some models, an underbody-mounted load-sensitive rear pressure-regulating valve is fitted. A self-adjust mechanism is incorporated, to automatically compensate for brake shoe wear. As the brake shoe linings wear, the footbrake operation automatically operates the adjuster mechanism, which effectively lengthens the shoe strut and repositions the brake shoes, to remove the lining-to-drum clearance.

On models with rear disc brakes, the brakes are actuated by single-piston sliding calipers which incorporate mechanical handbrake mechanisms. A load-sensitive pressure-regulating valve is fitted to regulate the hydraulic pressure applied to the rear brakes. The regulating valve is similar to that fitted to drum brake models with ABS, and helps to prevent rear wheel lock-up during emergency braking.

On all models, the handbrake provides an independent mechanical means of rear brake application.

Note: *When servicing any part of the system, work carefully and methodically; also observe scrupulous cleanliness when overhauling any part of the hydraulic system. Always renew components (in axle sets, where applicable) if in doubt about their condition, and use only genuine Peugeot replacement parts, or at least those of known good quality. Note the warnings given in "Safety first" and at relevant points in this Chapter concerning the dangers of asbestos dust and hydraulic fluid.*

2 Hydraulic system - bleeding

 Warning: Hydraulic fluid is poisonous; wash off immediately and thoroughly in the case of skin contact, and seek immediate medical advice if any fluid is swallowed or gets into the eyes. Certain types of hydraulic fluid are inflammable, and may ignite when allowed into contact with hot components; when servicing any hydraulic system, it is safest to assume that the fluid is inflammable, and to take precautions against the risk of fire as though it is petrol that is being handled. Hydraulic fluid is also an effective paint stripper, and will attack plastics; if any is spilt, it should be washed off immediately, using copious quantities of fresh water. Finally, it is hygroscopic (it absorbs moisture from the air) - old fluid may be contaminated and unfit for further use. When topping-up or renewing the fluid, always use the recommended type, and ensure that it comes from a freshly-opened sealed container.

 Warning: Do not attempt to bleed any part of the hydraulic system on models equipped with the Bendix "integral" ABS. Special equipment is required, and the task must be referred to a Peugeot dealer.

General

1 The correct operation of any hydraulic system is only possible after removing all air from the components and circuit; this is achieved by bleeding the system.

2 During the bleeding procedure, add only clean, unused hydraulic fluid of the recommended type; never re-use fluid that has already been bled from the system. Ensure that sufficient fluid is available before starting work.

3 If there is any possibility of incorrect fluid being already in the system, the brake components and circuit must be flushed completely with uncontaminated, correct fluid, and new seals should be fitted to the various components.

4 If hydraulic fluid has been lost from the system, or air has entered because of a leak, ensure that the fault is cured before proceeding further.

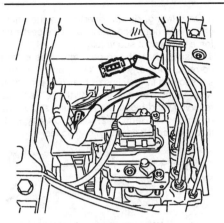

2.10a Disconnect the 3-pin brown wiring connector before bleeding the Bendix "additional" ABS

5 Park the vehicle on level ground, switch off the engine and select first or reverse gear, then chock the wheels and release the handbrake.

6 Check that all pipes and hoses are secure, unions tight and bleed screws closed. Clean any dirt from around the bleed screws.

7 Unscrew the master cylinder reservoir cap, and top the master cylinder reservoir up to the "MAX" level line; refit the cap loosely, and remember to maintain the fluid level at least above the "MIN" level line throughout the procedure, or there is a risk of further air entering the system.

8 There are a number of one-man, do-it-yourself brake bleeding kits currently available from motor accessory shops. It is recommended that one of these kits is used whenever possible, as they greatly simplify the bleeding operation, and also reduce the risk of expelled air and fluid being drawn back into the system. If such a kit is not available, the basic (two-man) method must be used, which is described in detail below.

9 If a kit is to be used, prepare the vehicle as described previously, and follow the kit manufacturer's instructions, as the procedure may vary slightly according to the type being used; generally, they are as outlined below in the relevant sub-section.

10 Whichever method is used, the same sequence must be followed to ensure the removal of all air from the system.

Bleeding sequence

Conventional braking system

a) *Right-hand rear wheel.*
b) *Left-hand front wheel.*
c) *Left-hand rear wheel.*
d) *Right-hand front wheel.*

Bendix "additional" ABS

Note: *Before carrying out any bleeding, switch off the ignition, and disconnect the 3-pin brown wiring connector from the hydraulic modulator assembly* **(see illustration)**.

a) *Rear brake furthest from master cylinder.*
b) *Rear brake nearest master cylinder.*
c) *Front brake furthest from master cylinder.*

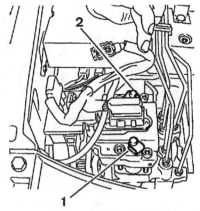

2.10b Bleed the hydraulic modulator using the bleed screws (1) first, and (2) second - Bendix "additional" ABS

d) *Front brake nearest master cylinder.*
e) *Hydraulic modulator* **(see illustration)**.

Bosch "additional" ABS

Note: *Before carrying out any bleeding, switch off the ignition, and disconnect the 4-pin black wiring connector from the hydraulic modulator assembly.*

a) *Left-hand front wheel.*
b) *Right-hand front wheel.*
c) *Left-hand rear wheel.*
d) *Right-hand rear wheel.*

Note: *If difficulty is experienced in bleeding the hydraulic circuit on models with Bosch "additional" ABS, using the above sequence, try bleeding the complete system working in the following order:*

a) *Right-hand rear brake.*
b) *Left-hand rear brake.*
c) *Left-hand front brake.*
d) *Right-hand front brake.*

Bleeding - basic (two-man) method

11 Collect a clean glass jar, a suitable length of plastic or rubber tubing which is a tight fit over the bleed screw, and a ring spanner to fit the screw. The help of an assistant will also be required.

12 Remove the dust cap from the first screw in the sequence **(see illustrations)**. Fit the spanner and tube to the screw, place the

other end of the tube in the jar, and pour in sufficient fluid to cover the end of the tube.

13 Ensure that the master cylinder reservoir fluid level is maintained at least above the "MIN" level line throughout the procedure.

14 Have the assistant fully depress the brake pedal several times to build up pressure, then maintain it on the final downstroke.

15 While pedal pressure is maintained, unscrew the bleed screw (approximately one turn) and allow the compressed fluid and air to flow into the jar. The assistant should maintain pedal pressure, following it down to the floor if necessary, and should not release it until instructed to do so. When the flow stops, tighten the bleed screw again, have the assistant release the pedal slowly, and recheck the reservoir fluid level.

16 Repeat the steps given in paragraphs 14 and 15 until the fluid emerging from the bleed screw is free from air bubbles. If the master cylinder has been drained and refilled, and air is being bled from the first screw in the sequence, allow approximately five seconds between cycles for the master cylinder passages to refill.

17 When no more air bubbles appear, tighten the bleed screw securely, remove the tube and spanner, and refit the dust cap. Do not overtighten the bleed screw.

18 Repeat the procedure on the remaining screws in the sequence, until all air is removed from the system and the brake pedal feels firm again.

Bleeding - using a one-way valve kit

19 As their name implies, these kits consist of a length of tubing with a one-way valve fitted, to prevent expelled air and fluid being drawn back into the system; some kits include a translucent container, which can be positioned so that the air bubbles can be more easily seen flowing from the end of the tube.

20 The kit is connected to the bleed screw, which is then opened. The user returns to the driver's seat, depresses the brake pedal with a smooth, steady stroke, and slowly releases it; this is repeated until the expelled fluid is clear of air bubbles **(see illustration)**.

21 Note that these kits simplify work so

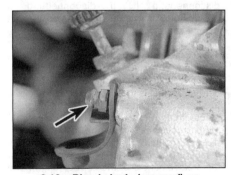

2.12a Bleed nipple (arrowed) on front disc caliper

2.12b Bleed nipple (arrowed) on rear wheel cylinder

9

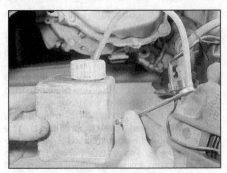

2.20 Using a one-man brake bleeding kit on a front caliper

much that it is easy to forget the master cylinder reservoir fluid level; ensure that this is maintained at least above the "MIN" level line at all times.

Bleeding - using a pressure-bleeding kit

22 These kits are usually operated by the reservoir of pressurised air contained in the spare tyre. However, note that it will probably be necessary to reduce the pressure to a lower level than normal; refer to the instructions supplied with the kit.

23 By connecting a pressurised, fluid-filled container to the master cylinder reservoir, bleeding can be carried out simply by opening each screw in turn (in the specified sequence), and allowing the fluid to flow out until no more air bubbles can be seen in the expelled fluid.

24 This method has the advantage that the large reservoir of fluid provides an additional safeguard against air being drawn into the system during bleeding.

25 Pressure-bleeding is particularly effective when bleeding "difficult" systems, or when bleeding the complete system at the time of routine fluid renewal.

All methods

26 When bleeding is complete, and firm pedal feel is restored, wash off any spilt fluid, tighten the bleed screws securely, and refit their dust caps.

27 Check the hydraulic fluid level in the master cylinder reservoir, and top-up if necessary (see "Weekly Checks").

28 Discard any hydraulic fluid that has been bled from the system; it will not be fit for re-use.

29 Check the feel of the brake pedal. If it feels at all spongy, air must still be present in the system, and further bleeding is required. Failure to bleed satisfactorily after a reasonable repetition of the bleeding procedure may be due to worn master cylinder seals.

30 On models with ABS, reconnect the wiring connector to the hydraulic modulator assembly.

3.2 Flexible hose-to-rigid pipe union at front wheel arch

3 Hydraulic pipes and hoses - renewal

Note: *Before starting work, refer to the note at the beginning of Section 2 concerning the dangers of hydraulic fluid.*

1 If any pipe or hose is to be renewed, minimise fluid loss by first removing the master cylinder reservoir cap, then tightening it down onto a piece of polythene to obtain an airtight seal. Alternatively, flexible hoses can be sealed, if required, using a proprietary brake hose clamp; metal brake pipe unions can be plugged (if care is taken not to allow dirt into the system) or capped immediately they are disconnected. Place a wad of rag under any union that is to be disconnected, to catch any spilt fluid.

2 If a flexible hose is to be disconnected, unscrew the brake pipe union nut before removing the spring clip which secures the hose to its mounting bracket **(see illustration)**.

3 To unscrew the union nuts, it is preferable to obtain a brake pipe spanner of the correct size; these are available from most large motor accessory shops. Failing this, a close-fitting open-ended spanner will be required, though if the nuts are tight or corroded, their flats may be rounded-off if the spanner slips. In such a case, a self-locking wrench is often the only way to unscrew a stubborn union, but it follows that the pipe and the damaged nuts must be renewed on reassembly. Always clean a union and surrounding area before disconnecting it. If disconnecting a component with more than one union, make a careful note of the connections before disturbing any of them.

4 If a brake pipe is to be renewed, it can be obtained, cut to length and with the union nuts and end flares in place, from Peugeot dealers. All that is then necessary is to bend it to shape, following the line of the original, before fitting it to the car. Alternatively, most motor accessory shops can make up brake pipes from kits, but this requires very careful measurement of the original, to ensure that the replacement is of the correct length. The safest answer is usually to take the original to the shop as a pattern.

5 On refitting, do not overtighten the union nuts. It is not necessary to exercise brute force to obtain a sound joint.

6 Ensure that the pipes and hoses are correctly routed, with no kinks, and that they are secured in the clips or brackets provided. After fitting, remove the polythene from the reservoir, and bleed the hydraulic system as described in Section 2. Wash off any spilt fluid, and check carefully for fluid leaks.

4 Front brake pads - renewal

> ⚠ **Warning: Renew both sets of front brake pads at the same time - never renew the pads on only one wheel, as uneven braking may result. Note that the dust created by wear of the pads may contain asbestos, which is a health hazard. Never blow it out with compressed air, and don't inhale any of it. An approved filtering mask should be worn when working on the brakes. DO NOT use petrol or petroleum-based solvents to clean brake parts; use brake cleaner or methylated spirit only.**

1 Apply the handbrake, then jack up the front of the vehicle and support it on axle stands (see "Jacking and Vehicle Support"). Remove the front roadwheels.

2 Trace the brake pad wear sensor wiring back from the pads, and disconnect it from the wiring connector **(see illustration)**. Note the routing of the wiring, and free it from any relevant retaining clips.

3 Push the piston into its bore by pulling the caliper outwards.

4 There are two different types of front brake caliper fitted to the models covered in this manual as follows.

a) *Models with solid front discs - Bendix calipers.*

b) *Models with ventilated front discs - Girling calipers.*

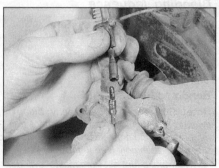

4.2 Disconnecting the pad wear sensor wiring connector

4.5a Extract the spring clip (arrowed) . . .

4.5b . . . then slide the pad retaining plate from the caliper - Bendix caliper

4.6 Withdrawing the outer brake pad - Bendix caliper

4.7 Measuring brake pad friction material thickness

4.12a Correct location of the anti-rattle springs on Bendix brake pads

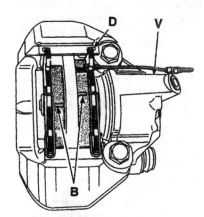

4.12b Correct fitting of brake pads - Bendix caliper

B Grooves
D Pad retaining plate spring clip
V Bleed screw

Bendix caliper

Note: *A new pad retaining plate spring clip should be used on refitting.*

5 Using pliers, extract the small spring clip from the pad retaining plate, and then slide the plate out of the caliper **(see illustrations)**.

6 Withdraw the pads from the caliper, then make a note of the correct fitted position of each anti-rattle spring, and remove the spring from each pad **(see illustration)**.

7 First measure the thickness of each brake pad's friction material **(see illustration)**. If either pad is worn at any point to the specified minimum thickness or less, all four pads must be renewed. Also, the pads should be renewed if any are fouled with oil or grease; as there is no satisfactory way of degreasing friction material, once contaminated. If any of the brake pads are worn unevenly, or are fouled with oil or grease, trace and rectify the cause before reassembly. New brake pads and spring kits are available from Peugeot dealers.

8 If the brake pads are still serviceable, carefully clean them using a clean, fine wire brush or similar, paying particular attention to the sides and back of the metal backing. Clean out the grooves in the friction material, and pick out any large embedded particles of dirt or debris. Carefully clean the pad locations in the caliper body/mounting bracket.

9 Prior to fitting the pads, check that the guide pins are free to slide easily in the caliper body/mounting bracket, and check that the rubber guide pin gaiters are undamaged. Brush the dust and dirt from the caliper and piston, but *do not* inhale it, as it is injurious to

health. Inspect the dust seal around the piston for damage, and the piston for evidence of fluid leaks, corrosion or damage. If attention to any of these components is necessary, refer to Section 10.

10 If new brake pads are to be fitted, the caliper piston must be pushed back into the cylinder to make room for them. Either use a G-clamp or similar tool, or use suitable pieces of wood as levers. Provided that the master cylinder reservoir has not been overfilled with hydraulic fluid, there should be no spillage, but keep a careful watch on the fluid level while retracting the piston. If the fluid level rises above the "MAX" level line at any time, the surplus should be siphoned off or ejected via a plastic tube connected to the bleed screw (see Section 2).

⚠ **Warning: Do not syphon the fluid by mouth, as it is poisonous; use a syringe or an old poultry baster.**

11 Fit the anti-rattle springs to the pads, so that when the pads are installed, the spring end will be located at the opposite end of the pad in relation to the pad retaining plate.

12 Locate the pads in the caliper, ensuring the friction material of each pad is against the brake disc, and check that the anti-rattle spring ends are at the opposite end of the pad to which the retaining plate is to be inserted. Note that if the pads are installed correctly, looking at the pads from the front of the vehicle, the innermost pad groove must be higher than the outer pad groove. Ensure the pads are fitted correctly before proceeding **(see illustrations)**.

13 Slide the retaining plate into place, and install the new small spring clip at its inner end. It may be necessary to file an entry chamfer on the edge of the retaining plate, to enable it to be fitted without difficulty.

14 Reconnect the brake pad wear sensor wiring connectors, ensuring that the outer wire is correctly routed through the anti-rattle spring loops, and that both wires pass through the loop of the bleed screw cap.

15 Depress the brake pedal repeatedly, until the pads are pressed into firm contact with the brake disc, and normal (non-assisted) pedal pressure is restored.

16 Repeat the above procedure on the remaining front brake caliper.

9

4.19 Hold the pin guide pin with an open-ended spanner while slackening the guide pin bolt - Girling caliper

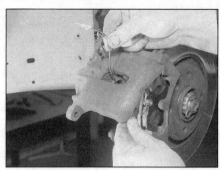

4.20 Pivot the caliper upwards away from the brake pads - Girling caliper

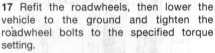

4.22 Ensure that the brake pads are fitted the correct way around, with friction material facing the disc . . .

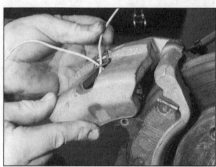

4.23 . . . then refit the caliper, feeding the pad wiring through the caliper aperture

5 Rear brake pads - renewal

Warning: Renew both sets of rear brake pads at the same time - never renew the pads on only one wheel, as uneven braking may result. Note that the dust created by wear of the pads may contain asbestos, which is a health hazard. Never blow it out with compressed air, and don't inhale any of it. An approved filtering mask should be worn when working on the brakes. DO NOT use petrol or petroleum-based solvents to clean brake parts; use brake cleaner or methylated spirit only.

Note: *A new upper caliper guide pin bolt must be used on refitting.*

1 Chock the front wheels, then jack up the rear of the vehicle and support securely on axle stands (*see "Jacking and Vehicle Support"*). Remove the rear roadwheels.

2 Disconnect the handbrake cable end from the operating lever on the caliper.

3 Where applicable, prise off the dust cover, then slacken and remove the upper caliper guide pin bolt, using a slim open-ended spanner to prevent the guide pin itself from rotating. Discard the guide pin bolt - a new bolt must be used on refitting.

4 With the upper guide pin bolt removed, pivot the caliper downwards, away from the brake pads and mounting bracket, taking care not to strain the flexible brake hose.

5 Withdraw the brake pads from the caliper mounting bracket.

6 First measure the thickness of each brake pad's friction material. If either pad is worn at any point to the specified minimum thickness or less, all four pads must be renewed. Also, the pads should be renewed if any are fouled with oil or grease; there is no satisfactory way of degreasing friction material, once contaminated. If any of the brake pads are worn unevenly, or are fouled with oil or grease, trace and rectify the cause before reassembly. New brake pads are available from Peugeot dealers.

7 If the brake pads are still serviceable, carefully clean them using a clean, fine wire brush or similar, paying particular attention to the sides and back of the metal backing. Pick out any large embedded particles of dirt or debris from the friction material. Carefully clean the pad locations in the caliper body/mounting bracket.

8 Prior to fitting the pads, check that the guide pins are free to slide easily in the caliper body/mounting bracket, and check that the rubber guide pin gaiters are undamaged. Brush the dust and dirt from the caliper and piston, but *do not* inhale it, as it is injurious to health. Inspect the dust seal around the piston for damage, and the piston for evidence of

17 Refit the roadwheels, then lower the vehicle to the ground and tighten the roadwheel bolts to the specified torque setting.

18 Check the hydraulic fluid level as described in "Weekly Checks".

Girling caliper

Note: *A new lower guide pin bolt must be used on refitting.*

19 Where applicable, prise off the dust cover, then slacken and remove the lower caliper guide pin bolt, using a slim open-ended spanner to prevent the guide pin itself from rotating **(see illustration)**. Discard the guide pin bolt - a new bolt must be used on refitting.

20 With the lower guide pin bolt removed, pivot the caliper upwards, away from the brake pads and mounting bracket, taking care not to strain the flexible brake hose **(see illustration)**.

21 Withdraw the two brake pads from the caliper mounting bracket, and examine them as described above in paragraphs 7 to 10.

22 Apply a little brake grease to the rear of the pads, then Install the pads in the caliper mounting bracket, ensuring that the friction material of each pad is against the brake disc **(see illustration)**.

23 Position the caliper over the pads, and pass the pad warning sensor wiring through the caliper aperture and underneath the retaining clip **(see illustration)**. If the threads of the new guide pin bolt are not already pre-

coated with locking compound, apply a suitable thread-locking compound to them. Pivot the caliper into position, then install the guide pin bolt, tightening to the specified torque setting while retaining the guide pin with an open-ended spanner. Where applicable, refit the dust cover to the guide pin.

24 Reconnect the brake pad wear sensor wiring connector, ensuring that the wiring is correctly routed through the loop of the caliper bleed screw cap.

25 Depress the brake pedal repeatedly, until the pads are pressed into firm contact with the brake disc, and normal (non-assisted) pedal pressure is restored.

26 Repeat the procedure on the remaining front brake caliper.

27 Refit the roadwheels, then lower the vehicle to the ground and tighten the roadwheel bolts to the specified torque setting.

28 Check the hydraulic fluid level as described in *"Weekly Checks"*.

All calipers

29 New pads will not give full braking efficiency until they have bedded in. Be prepared for this, and avoid hard braking as far as possible for the first hundred miles or so after pad renewal.

fluid leaks, corrosion or damage. If attention is necessary, see Section 11.

9 If new brake pads are to be fitted, the caliper piston must be pushed back into the cylinder to make room for them. Provided that the master cylinder reservoir has not been overfilled with hydraulic fluid, there should be no spillage, but keep a careful watch on the fluid level while retracting the piston. If the fluid level rises above the "MAX" level line at any time, the surplus should be siphoned off or ejected via a plastic tube connected to the bleed screw (see Section 2).

Warning: Do not syphon the fluid by mouth, as it is poisonous; use a syringe or an old poultry baster.

10 Retract the caliper piston by applying pressure, and turning it clockwise. A special tool is available for this purpose but a pair of circlip pliers or any similar tool can be used instead. Take care not to damage the surface of the piston. Turn the piston to position the notches in the piston on the centreline of the slot in the front of the caliper.

11 Fit the pads, sliding them into position in the caliper bracket, with the friction material against the disc.

12 If the threads of the new guide pin bolt are not already pre-coated with thread-locking compound, apply thread-locking compound to them. Pivot the caliper into position, then install the guide pin bolt, tightening to the specified torque while retaining the guide pin with an open-ended spanner. Where applicable, refit the dust cover to the guide pin.

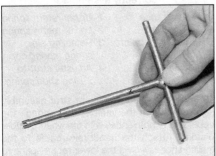

6.6a Forked tool for removing early type Bendix shoe retainer springs

6.7 Removing a later type Bendix shoe retainer spring

13 Reconnect the handbrake cable to the caliper.

14 Depress the brake pedal repeatedly until the pads are pressed against the disc, and normal (non-assisted) pedal pressure is restored.

15 Repeat the procedure on the other rear caliper.

16 Refit the roadwheels, then lower the vehicle to the ground.

17 Check the fluid level ("*Weekly checks*").

18 New pads will not give full braking efficiency until they have bedded in. Be prepared for this, and avoid hard braking as far as possible for the first hundred miles or so after pad renewal.

6 Rear brake shoes - renewal

Warning: Brake shoes must be renewed on both rear wheels at the same time - never renew the shoes on only one wheel, as uneven braking may result. Also, the dust created by wear of the shoes may contain asbestos, which is a health hazard. Never blow it out with compressed air, and don't inhale any of it. An approved filtering mask should be worn when working on the brakes. DO NOT use petrol or petroleum-based solvents to clean brake parts; use brake cleaner or methylated spirit only.

6.6b Removing an early type Bendix shoe retainer spring

6.8 Ease the shoes out of the lower pivot point, and disconnect the lower return spring - Bendix rear brakes

1 Remove the brake drum (see Section 9).

2 Working carefully, and taking the necessary precautions, remove all traces of brake dust from the brake drum, backplate and shoes.

3 Measure the thickness of the friction material of each brake shoe at several points; if either shoe is worn at any point to the specified minimum thickness or less, all four shoes must be renewed as a set. The shoes should also be renewed if any are fouled with oil or grease; there is no satisfactory way of degreasing friction material, once contaminated.

4 If any of the brake shoes are worn unevenly, or fouled with oil or grease, trace and rectify the cause before reassembly.

5 To renew the brake shoes, proceed as described under the relevant sub-heading.

Bendix brake shoes

Note: *The components encountered may vary in detail, but the principles described in the following paragraphs are equally applicable to all models. Make a careful note of the fitted positions of all components before dismantling.*

6 On early models, unhook the shoe retainer springs from the brake backplate using a forked tool similar to that shown. The tool can be improvised using a screwdriver with a notch in the blade. The tool is pushed through the centre of the spring, and the spring hook can then be released from the backplate **(see illustrations)**.

7 On later models, using a pair of pliers, remove the shoe retainer spring cups by depressing and turning them through 90° **(see illustration)**. With the cups removed, lift off the springs and withdraw the retainer pins.

8 Ease the shoes out one at a time from the lower pivot point, to release the tension of the return spring, then disconnect the lower return spring from both shoes **(see illustration)**.

9 Ease the upper end of both shoes out from their wheel cylinder locations, taking care not to damage the wheel cylinder seals, and disconnect the handbrake cable from the trailing shoe **(see Haynes Hint)**. The brake shoe and adjuster strut assembly can then be manoeuvred out of position and away from the backplate. Do not depress the brake pedal until the brakes are reassembled.

Restrain the wheel cylinder piston with a cable-tie or a strong elastic band

9

6.13 Correct fitted position of later type Bendix adjuster strut components

6.17 Apply high-melting-point grease to the shoe contact points on the backplate

6.19a Fitting the brake shoes - early type Bendix brakes

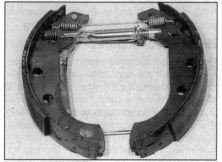

6.19b Rear view of early type Bendix shoe assembly correctly assembled - removed from backplate for clarity

6.19c Front view of early type Bendix shoe assembly correctly assembled - removed from backplate for clarity

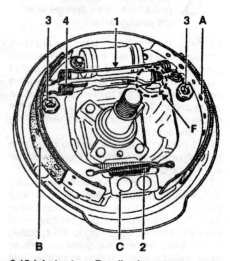

6.19d Later type Bendix shoe components correctly assembled

A Leading shoe
B Trailing shoe
C Lower pivot point
F Adjuster strut mechanism

1 Upper return spring
2 Lower return spring
3 Retaining pin, spring, spring cup
4 Adjuster strut-to-trailing shoe spring

10 With the shoe and adjuster strut assembly on a bench, make a note of the correct fitted positions of the springs and adjuster strut, to use as a guide on reassembly. Release the handbrake lever stop-peg (if not already done), then carefully detach the adjuster strut bolt retaining spring from the leading shoe. Disconnect the upper return spring, then detach the leading shoe and return spring from the trailing shoe and strut assembly. Unhook the spring securing the adjuster strut to the trailing shoe, and separate the two.

11 If genuine Peugeot brake shoes are being installed, it will be necessary to remove the handbrake lever from the original trailing shoe, and install it on the new shoe. Secure the lever in position with a new retaining clip. All return springs should be renewed, regardless of their apparent condition; spring kits are also available from Peugeot dealers.

12 Withdraw the adjuster bolt from the strut, and carefully examine the assembly for signs of wear or damage. Pay particular attention to the threads of the adjuster bolt and the knurled adjuster wheel, and renew if necessary. Note that left-hand and right-hand struts are not interchangeable - they are marked "G" (gauche) and "D" (droit) respectively. Also note that the strut adjuster bolts are not interchangeable; the left-hand strut bolt has a left-handed thread, and the right-hand bolt a right-handed thread.

13 Ensure that the components on the end of the strut are correctly positioned, then apply a little high-melting-point grease to the threads

of the adjuster bolt (see illustration). Screw the adjuster wheel onto the bolt until only a small gap exists between the wheel and the head of the bolt, then install the bolt in the strut.

14 Fit the adjuster strut retaining spring to the trailing shoe, ensuring that the shorter hook of the spring is engaged with the shoe. Attach the adjuster strut to the spring end, then ease the strut into position in its slot in the trailing shoe.

15 Engage the upper return spring with the trailing shoe, then hook the leading shoe onto the other end of the spring, and lever the leading shoe down until the adjuster bolt head is correctly located in its groove. Once the bolt is correctly located, hook its retaining spring into the slot on the leading shoe.

16 Peel back the rubber protective caps, and check the wheel cylinder for fluid leaks or other damage; check that both cylinder pistons are free to move easily. Refer to Section 12, if necessary, for information on wheel cylinder renewal.

17 Prior to installation, clean the backplate, and apply a smear of high-temperature brake grease or anti-seize compound to all those surfaces of the backplate which bear on the shoes, particularly the wheel cylinder pistons and lower pivot point (see illustration). Do not allow the lubricant to foul the friction material.

18 Ensure that the handbrake lever stop-peg is correctly located against the edge of the trailing shoe, and remove the elastic band or cable-tie (as applicable) fitted to the wheel cylinder.

19 Manoeuvre the shoe and strut assembly into position on the vehicle, and engage the upper end of both shoes with the wheel cylinder pistons. Attach the handbrake cable to the trailing shoe lever. Fit the lower return spring to both shoes, and ease the shoes into position on the lower pivot point (see illustrations).

20 Tap the shoes to centralise them with the backplate, then refit the shoe retainer pins and springs, and secure them in position with the spring cups (later models); hook the retainer springs to the brake backplate using the forked tool described in paragraph 6 (early models).

21 Using a screwdriver, turn the strut adjuster wheel to expand the shoes until the brake drum just slides over the shoes.

22 Refit the brake drum (see Section 9).

23 Repeat the above procedure on the remaining rear brake.

24 Once both sets of rear shoes have been renewed, adjust the lining-to-drum clearance by repeatedly depressing the brake pedal. Whilst depressing the pedal, have an assistant listen to the rear drums, to check

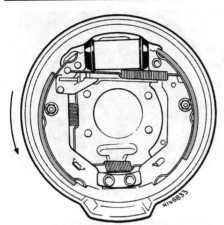

6.27 Correct fitted positions of Girling rear brake components
Arrow indicates direction of wheel rotation

that the adjuster strut is functioning correctly; if so, a clicking sound will be emitted by the strut as the pedal is depressed.

25 Check and, if necessary, adjust the handbrake as described in Section 17.

26 On completion, check the hydraulic fluid level as described in *"Weekly Checks"*.

Girling brake shoes

27 Make a note of the correct fitted positions of the springs and adjuster strut, to use as a guide on reassembly **(see illustration)**.

28 Carefully unhook both the upper and lower return springs, and remove them from the brake shoes.

29 Using a pair of pliers, remove the leading shoe retainer spring cup by depressing it and turning through 90°. With the cup removed, lift off the spring, then withdraw the retainer pin and remove the shoe from the backplate. Unhook the adjusting lever spring, and remove it from the leading shoe.

30 Detach the adjuster strut, and remove it from the trailing shoe.

31 Remove the trailing shoe retainer spring cup, spring and pin as described above, then detach the handbrake cable and remove the shoe from the vehicle. Do not depress the brake pedal until the brakes are reassembled.

Wrap a strong elastic band or a cable-tie around the wheel cylinder pistons to retain them.

32 If genuine Peugeot brake shoes are being installed, it will be necessary to remove the adjusting lever from the original leading shoe, and install it on the new shoe. All return springs should be renewed, regardless of their apparent condition; spring kits are also available from Peugeot dealers.

33 Withdraw the forked end from the adjuster strut, and carefully examine the assembly for signs of wear or damage. Pay particular attention to the threads and the knurled adjuster wheel, and renew if necessary. Note that left-hand and right-hand struts are not

interchangeable; the left-hand fork has a left-handed thread, and the right-hand fork a right-handed thread.

34 Peel back the rubber protective caps, and check the wheel cylinder for fluid leaks or other damage; check that both cylinder pistons are free to move easily. Refer to Section 12, if necessary, for information on wheel cylinder renewal.

35 Prior to installation, clean the backplate, and apply a thin smear of high-temperature brake grease or anti-seize compound to all those surfaces of the backplate which bear on the shoes, particularly the wheel cylinder pistons and lower pivot point. Do not allow the lubricant to foul the friction material.

36 Ensure that the handbrake lever stop-peg is correctly located against the edge of the trailing shoe, and remove the elastic band or cable-tie (as applicable) fitted to the wheel cylinder.

37 Locate the upper end of the trailing shoe in the wheel cylinder piston, then refit the retainer pin and spring, and secure it in position with the spring cup. Connect the handbrake cable to the lever.

38 Screw in the adjuster wheel until the minimum strut length is obtained, then hook the strut into position on the trailing shoe (note that the left and right-hand adjusters are not interchangeable - see paragraph 33). Rotate the adjuster strut forked end, so that the cut-out of the fork will engage with the leading shoe adjusting lever once the shoe is installed **(see illustration)**.

39 Fit the spring to the leading shoe adjusting lever, so that the shorter hook of the spring engages with the lever.

40 Slide the leading shoe assembly into position, ensuring that it is correctly engaged with the adjuster strut fork, and that the fork cut-out is engaged with the adjusting lever. Ensure that the upper end of the shoe is located in the wheel cylinder piston, then secure the shoe in position with the retainer pin, spring and spring cup.

41 Install the upper and lower return springs, then tap the shoes to centralise them with the backplate.

42 Using a screwdriver, turn the strut adjuster wheel to expand the shoes until the brake drum just slides over the shoes.

43 Refit the brake drum as described in Section 9.

44 Repeat the above procedure on the remaining rear brake.

45 Once both sets of rear shoes have been

6.38 On Girling rear brake shoes, adjuster strut fork cut-out (A) must engage with leading shoe adjusting lever on refitting

renewed, adjust the lining-to-drum clearance by repeatedly depressing the brake pedal. Whilst depressing the pedal, have an assistant listen to the rear drums, to check that the adjuster strut is functioning correctly; if so, a clicking sound will be emitted by the strut as the pedal is depressed.

46 Check and, if necessary, adjust the handbrake as described in Section 17.

47 On completion, check the hydraulic fluid level as described in *"Weekly Checks"*.

All shoes

48 New shoes will not give full braking efficiency until they have bedded in. Be prepared for this, and avoid hard braking as far as possible for the first hundred miles or so after shoe renewal.

---

7 Front brake disc - inspection, removal and refitting

Note: *Before starting work, refer to the note at the beginning of Section 4 concerning the dangers of asbestos dust.*

Inspection

Note: *If either disc requires renewal, BOTH should be renewed at the same time, to ensure even and consistent braking. New brake pads should also be fitted.*

1 Apply the handbrake, then jack up the front of the car and support it on axle stands (see *"Jacking and Vehicle Support"*). Remove the appropriate front roadwheel.

2 Slowly rotate the brake disc so that the full area of both sides can be checked; remove the brake pads if better access is required to the inboard surface. Light scoring is normal in the area swept by the brake pads, but if heavy scoring or cracks are found, the disc must be renewed.

3 It is normal to find a lip of rust and brake dust around the disc's perimeter; this can be scraped off if required. If, however, a lip has formed due to excessive wear of the brake pad swept area, then the disc's thickness must be measured using a micrometer **(see illustration)**. Take measurements at several places around the disc, at the inside and outside of the pad swept area; if the disc has

7.3 Using a micrometer to measure disc thickness

7.4 Checking disc run-out using a dial gauge

7.8 Disc securing screws (arrowed)

7.7 Removing a Girling caliper mounting bracket bolt

worn at any point to the specified minimum thickness or less, the disc must be renewed.

4 If the disc is thought to be warped, it can be checked for run-out. Either use a dial gauge mounted on any convenient fixed point, while the disc is slowly rotated, or use feeler blades to measure (at several points all around the disc) the clearance between the disc and a fixed point, such as the caliper mounting bracket **(see illustration)**. If the measurements obtained are at the specified maximum or beyond, the disc is excessively warped, and must be renewed; however, it is worth checking first that the hub bearing is in good condition (Chapters 1 and/or 10). Also try the effect of removing the disc and turning it through 180º, to reposition it on the hub; if the run-out is still excessive, the disc must be renewed.

5 Check the disc for cracks, especially around the wheel bolt holes, and any other wear or damage, and renew if necessary.

Removal

6 On models with Bendix calipers, remove the brake pads as described in Section 4.

7 On models with Girling calipers, unscrew the two bolts securing the caliper mounting bracket to the hub carrier **(see illustration)**. Using a piece of wire or string, tie the caliper to the front suspension coil spring, to avoid placing any strain on the fluid hose.

8 Use chalk or paint to mark the relationship of the disc to the hub, then remove the screw(s) securing the brake disc to the hub, and remove the disc **(see illustration)**. If it is tight, lightly tap its rear face with a hide or plastic mallet.

Refitting

9 Refitting is the reverse of the removal procedure, noting the following points:

a) *Ensure that the mating surfaces of the disc and hub are clean and flat.*

b) *Align (if applicable) the marks made on removal, and securely tighten the disc retaining screws.*

c) *If a new disc has been fitted, use a suitable solvent to wipe any preservative coating from the disc, before refitting the caliper.*

d) *On models with Girling calipers, refit the caliper as described in Section 10.*

e) *On models with Bendix calipers, refit the pads as described in Section 4.*

f) *Refit the roadwheel, then lower the vehicle to the ground and tighten the roadwheel bolts to the specified torque. On completion, repeatedly depress the brake pedal until normal (non-assisted) pedal pressure returns.*

8 Rear brake disc - inspection, removal and refitting

Note: *Before starting work, refer to the note at the beginning of Section 4 concerning the dangers of asbestos dust.*

Inspection

Note: *If either disc requires renewal, BOTH should be renewed at the same time, to ensure even and consistent braking. New brake pads should be fitted also.*

1 Firmly chock the front wheels, then jack up the rear of the car and support it on axle stands (see *"Jacking and Vehicle Support"*). Remove the appropriate rear roadwheel.

2 Inspect the disc as described in Section 7.

Removal

3 Remove the brake pads as described in Section 5.

4 Use chalk or paint to mark the relationship of the disc to the hub, then remove the screw(s) securing the brake disc to the hub, and remove the disc. If it is tight, lightly tap its rear face with a hide or plastic mallet.

Refitting

5 Refitting is the reverse of the removal procedure, noting the following points:

a) *Ensure that the mating surfaces of the disc and hub are clean and flat.*

b) *Align (if applicable) the marks made on removal, and securely tighten the disc retaining screw(s).*

c) *If a new disc has been fitted, use a suitable solvent to wipe any preservative coating from the disc, before refitting the caliper.*

d) *Refit the brake pads as described in Section 5.*

e) *Refit the roadwheel, then lower the vehicle to the ground and tighten the roadwheel bolts to the specified torque.*

9 Rear brake drum - removal, inspection and refitting

Note: *Before starting work, refer to the note at the beginning of Section 4 concerning the dangers of asbestos dust.*

Removal

1 Chock the front wheels, then jack up the rear of the vehicle and support it on axle stands (see *"Jacking and Vehicle Support"*). Remove the appropriate rear roadwheel.

2 Remove the drum retaining screw **(see illustration)**.

3 It should now be possible to withdraw the brake drum by hand. It may be difficult to remove the drum due to the brake shoes binding on the inner circumference of the drum. If the brake shoes are binding, proceed as follows.

a) *First check that the handbrake is fully released, then referring to Section 17 for further information, fully slacken the handbrake cable adjuster nut, to obtain maximum free play in the cable.*

b) *Insert a screwdriver through the access hole in the rear brake drum, so that it*

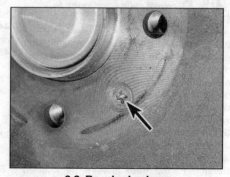

9.2 Rear brake drum retaining screw (arrowed)

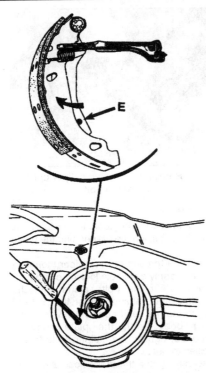

9.3b Releasing the handbrake operating lever

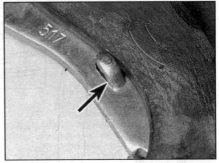

9.9 Check that the handbrake lever stop-peg (arrowed) is against the shoe edge

9.3a Using a screwdriver inserted through the brake drum to release the handbrake operating lever

E Handbrake operating lever stop-peg location

contacts the handbrake operating lever on the trailing brake shoe. Push the lever until the stop-peg slips behind the brake shoe web, allowing the brake shoes to retract fully (see illustrations). The brake drum can now be withdrawn.

Inspection

Note: *If either drum requires renewal, BOTH should be renewed at the same time, to ensure even and consistent braking. New brake shoes should also be fitted.*

4 Working carefully, remove all traces of brake dust from the drum, but avoid inhaling the dust, as it is injurious to health.

5 Clean the outside of the drum, and check it for obvious signs of wear or damage, such as cracks around the roadwheel bolt holes; renew the drum if necessary.

6 Examine carefully the inside of the drum. Light scoring of the friction surface is normal, but if heavy scoring is found, the drum must be renewed. It is usual to find a lip on the drum's inboard edge which consists of a mixture of rust and brake dust; this should be scraped away, to leave a smooth surface which can be polished with fine (120- to 150-grade) emery paper. If, however, the lip is due to the friction surface being recessed by excessive wear, then the drum must be renewed.

7 If the drum is thought to be excessively worn, or oval, its internal diameter must be measured at several points using an internal

micrometer. Take measurements in pairs, the second at right-angles to the first, and compare the two, to check for signs of ovality. Provided that it does not enlarge the drum to beyond the specified maximum diameter, it may be possible to have the drum refinished by skimming or grinding; if this is not possible, the drums on both sides must be renewed. Note that if the drum is to be skimmed, BOTH drums must be refinished, to maintain a consistent internal diameter on both sides.

Refitting

8 If a new brake drum is to be installed, use a suitable solvent to remove any preservative coating that may have been applied to its interior. Note that it may also be necessary to shorten the adjuster strut length, by rotating the strut wheel, to allow the drum to pass over the brake shoes.

9 Ensure that the handbrake lever stop-peg is correctly repositioned against the edge of the brake shoe web **(see illustration)**, and ensure that the mating faces of the hub and brake drum are clean, then slide the brake drum onto the hub.

10 Refit and tighten the drum retaining screw.

11 Depress the footbrake several times to operate the self-adjusting mechanism.

12 Repeat the above procedure on the remaining rear brake assembly (where necessary), then check and, if necessary, adjust the handbrake cable as described in Section 17.

13 On completion, refit the roadwheel(s), then lower the vehicle to the ground and tighten the wheel bolts to the specified torque.

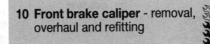

10 Front brake caliper - removal, overhaul and refitting

Note: *Before starting work, refer to the note at the beginning of Section 2 concerning the dangers of hydraulic fluid, and to the warning at the beginning of Section 4 concerning the dangers of asbestos dust.*

Bendix caliper

Removal

1 Apply the handbrake, then jack up the front of the vehicle and support it on axle stands (*see "Jacking and Vehicle Support"*). Remove the appropriate roadwheel.

2 Minimise fluid loss by first removing the master cylinder reservoir cap, and then tightening it down onto a piece of polythene, to obtain an airtight seal. Alternatively, use a brake hose clamp, a G-clamp or a similar tool to clamp the flexible hose **(see illustration)**.

3 Remove the brake pads as described in Section 4.

4 Clean the area around the union, then loosen the fluid hose union nut.

5 Slacken the two bolts securing the caliper assembly to the hub carrier and remove them along with the mounting plate, noting which way around the plate is fitted. Lift the caliper assembly away from the brake disc, and unscrew it from the end of the fluid hose. Plug the open ends of the caliper and hose to prevent dirt ingress and fluid loss.

Overhaul

6 The caliper can be overhauled after obtaining the relevant repair kit from a Peugeot dealer. Ensure that the correct repair kit is obtained for the caliper being worked on. Note the locations of all components to ensure correct refitting, and lubricate the new seals using clean brake fluid. Follow the assembly instructions supplied with the repair kit **(see illustration)**.

10.2 Using a clamp on the caliper hydraulic hose

9

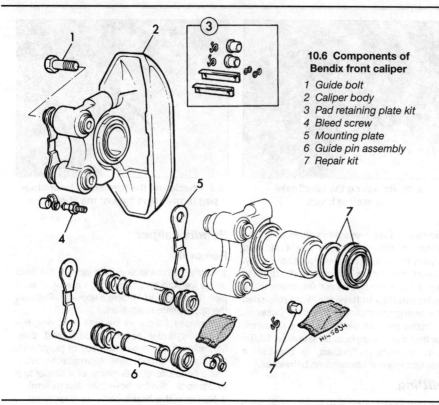

10.6 Components of Bendix front caliper

1 Guide bolt
2 Caliper body
3 Pad retaining plate kit
4 Bleed screw
5 Mounting plate
6 Guide pin assembly
7 Repair kit

10.13 Removing a Girling caliper upper guide pin bolt

Refitting

7 Screw the caliper fully onto the flexible hose union, then position the caliper over the brake disc.

8 Clean the threads of the caliper mounting bolts, and apply a suitable locking compound to them. Refit the bolts along with the mounting plate, ensuring that the plate is fitted so that its bend curves away from the caliper body. With the plate correctly positioned, tighten the caliper bolts to the specified torque.

9 Securely tighten the brake hose union nut, then refit the brake pads as described in Section 4.

10 Remove the brake hose clamp or polythene, as applicable, and bleed the hydraulic system as described in Section 2. Note that, providing the precautions described were taken to minimise brake fluid loss, it should only be necessary to bleed the relevant front brake.

11 Refit the roadwheel, then lower the vehicle to the ground and tighten the roadwheel bolts to the specified torque.

Girling caliper

Removal

Note: New guide pin bolts must be used on refitting.

12 Proceed as described in paragraphs 1 to 4.

13 Where applicable, remove the dust cover, then slacken and remove the upper caliper guide pin bolt, using a slim open-ended spanner to prevent the guide pin itself from rotating **(see illustration)**. Discard the guide pin bolt - a new bolt must be used on refitting. Lift the caliper away from the disc, and unscrew it from the end of the fluid hose. Plug the open ends of the caliper and hose to prevent dirt ingress and fluid loss.

Overhaul

14 Proceed as described in paragraph 6 **(see illustration)**.

Refitting

15 Screw the caliper body fully onto the flexible hose union.

16 If the threads of the new guide pin bolts are not already pre-coated with locking compound, apply a suitable locking compound to them.

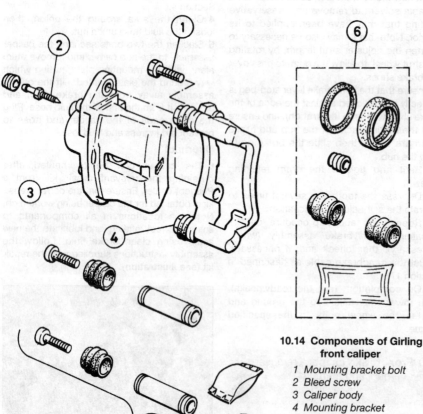

10.14 Components of Girling front caliper

1 Mounting bracket bolt
2 Bleed screw
3 Caliper body
4 Mounting bracket
5 Guide pin assembly
6 Repair kit

H.20680

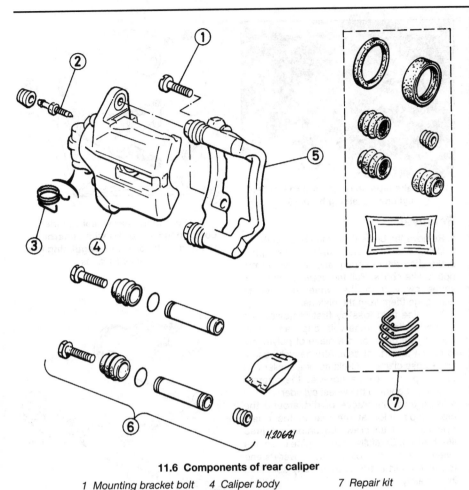

H.20681

11.6 Components of rear caliper

1 Mounting bracket bolt	4 Caliper body	7 Repair kit
2 Bleed screw	5 Mounting bracket	
3 Handbrake lever spring	6 Guide pin assembly	

17 Manoeuvre the caliper into position, and fit the new upper guide pin bolt. Tighten the guide pin bolt to the specified torque, while retaining the guide pin with an open-ended spanner. Where applicable, refit the dust cover to the guide pin bolt.

18 Proceed as described in paragraphs 9 to 11.

---

11 Rear brake caliper - removal, overhaul and refitting

Note: *Before starting work, refer to the note at the beginning of Section 2 concerning the dangers of hydraulic fluid, and to the warning at the beginning of Section 4 concerning the dangers of asbestos dust.*

Note: *New caliper guide pin bolts must be used on refitting.*

Note: *To avoid the requirement to pre-bleed the caliper before refitting, unless the unit is to be overhauled, do not drain the hydraulic fluid from the caliper - plug the fluid port in the caliper to prevent fluid loss. Peugeot parts dealers will supply new calipers filled with brake fluid.*

Removal

1 Chock the front wheels, then jack up the rear of the vehicle and support it on axle stands (see *"Jacking and Vehicle Support"*). Remove the appropriate roadwheel.

2 Minimise fluid loss by first removing the master cylinder reservoir cap, and then tightening it down onto a piece of polythene, to obtain an airtight seal. Alternatively, use a brake hose clamp, a G-clamp or a similar tool to clamp the flexible hose.

3 Remove the brake pads (see Section 5).

4 Clean the area around the union, then loosen the fluid hose union nut.

5 Where applicable, prise off the dust cover, then slacken and remove the lower caliper guide pin bolt, using a slim open-ended spanner to prevent the guide pin itself from rotating. Discard the guide pin bolt - a new bolt must be used on refitting. Lift the caliper away from the disc, and unscrew it from the end of the fluid hose. Plug the open ends of the caliper and hose to prevent dirt ingress and fluid loss.

Overhaul

6 The caliper can be overhauled after obtaining the relevant repair kit from a

Peugeot dealer. Ensure that the correct repair kit is obtained for the caliper being worked on. Note the locations of all components to ensure correct refitting, and lubricate the new seals using clean brake fluid. Follow the assembly instructions supplied with the repair kit **(see illustration)**.

Caliper pre-bleeding

Note: *This operation must be carried out whenever the caliper has been overhauled or drained of its fluid, and the operation must be carried out with the caliper removed.*

7 With the rear of the vehicle supported on axle stands, and the relevant roadwheel removed, proceed as follows.

8 Reconnect the fluid hose to the caliper, and tighten the union nut.

9 Place a trolley jack beneath the right-hand rear suspension trailing arm, and raise the arm to actuate the rear brake pressure regulating valve (see Section 21).

10 Position the caliper vertically, with the bleed screw uppermost, and keep it in this position throughout the following bleeding operation.

> **HAYNES HiNT** *Rest the caliper on a block of wood under the vehicle.*

11 Place a block of wood approximately 20.0 mm thick between the caliper piston and the caliper body (ie, in the position normally occupied by the brake pads) to prevent the piston from being ejected.

12 Remove the brake hose clamp or polythene, as applicable, then connect a hose and bottle to the bleed screw, and bleed the caliper using one of the methods described in Section 2 (note that Peugeot recommend that pressure bleeding equipment is used). When the fluid emerging is free from air bubbles, tighten the bleed screw **(see illustration)**.

13 Continue to pressurise the hydraulic

11.12 Rear caliper ready for pre-bleeding

1 Bleed screw   2 Wooden block

9

system (*eg*, by "pumping" the brake pedal) until the caliper piston contacts the block of wood.

14 Open the caliper bleed screw, and remove the block of wood from the caliper.

15 Push the caliper piston fully into the caliper bore. Retract the caliper piston by applying pressure, and turning it clockwise. A special tool is available for this purpose but a pair of circlip pliers or any similar tool can be used instead. Take care not to damage the surface of the piston. Turn the piston to position the notches in the piston on the centreline of the slot in the front of the caliper.

16 Tighten the bleed screw.

17 Refit the block of wood to the caliper, then repeat the procedure described in paragraphs 12 to 16 inclusive.

18 On completion, ensure that the bleed screw is tightened, then disconnect the bleed hose.

19 Lower the trailing arm and remove the trolley jack, then refit the caliper as follows.

Refitting

Note: *Provided that the caliper has not been drained of its fluid, the unit can be refitted as follows. If the caliper has been overhauled or drained for any reason, the pre-bleeding procedure described in the preceding paragraphs **must** be carried out before refitting.*

20 Screw the caliper body fully onto the flexible hose union (if not already done).

21 If the threads of the new guide pin bolts are not already pre-coated with locking compound, apply a suitable locking compound to them.

22 Manoeuvre the caliper into position, and fit the new lower guide pin bolt. Tighten the guide pin bolt to the specified torque, while retaining the guide pin with an open-ended spanner. Where applicable, refit the dust cover to the guide pin bolt.

23 Securely tighten the brake hose union nut (if not already done), then refit the brake pads as described in Section 5.

24 Remove the brake hose clamp or polythene, as applicable, and bleed the hydraulic system as described in Section 2 (if not already done). Note that, providing the precautions described were taken to minimise brake fluid loss, it should only be necessary to bleed the relevant rear brake.

25 Refit the roadwheel, then lower the vehicle to the ground and tighten the roadwheel bolts to the specified torque.

---

12 Rear wheel cylinder -
removal, overhaul and refitting

Note: *Before starting work, refer to the note at the beginning of Section 2 concerning the dangers of hydraulic fluid, and to the warning at the beginning of Section 4 concerning the dangers of asbestos dust.*

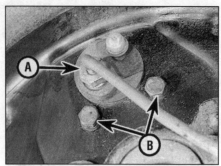

12.4 Brake pipe union (A) and rear wheel cylinder retaining bolts (B)

Removal

1 Remove the brake drum (see Section 9).

2 Using pliers, carefully unhook the upper brake shoe return spring, and remove it from both brake shoes. Pull the upper ends of the shoes away from the wheel cylinder to disengage them from the pistons.

3 Minimise fluid loss by first removing the master cylinder reservoir cap, and then tightening it down onto a piece of polythene, to obtain an airtight seal. Alternatively, use a brake hose clamp, a G-clamp or a similar tool to clamp the flexible hose at the nearest convenient point to the wheel cylinder.

4 Wipe away all traces of dirt around the brake pipe union at the rear of the wheel cylinder, and unscrew the union nut **(see illustration)**. Carefully ease the pipe out of the wheel cylinder, and plug or tape over its end to prevent dirt entry. Wipe off any spilt fluid immediately.

5 Unscrew the two wheel cylinder retaining bolts from the rear of the backplate, and remove the cylinder, taking great care not to allow surplus hydraulic fluid to contaminate the brake shoe linings.

Overhaul

Models without underbody-mounted rear brake pressure-regulating valve (see Section 21)

6 It is not possible to overhaul the cylinder, since no components are available separately. If faulty, the complete wheel cylinder assembly must be renewed.

Models with underbody-mounted rear brake pressure-regulating valve (see Section 21)

7 The wheel cylinder can be overhauled after obtaining the relevant repair kit from a Peugeot dealer. Ensure that the correct repair kit is obtained for the wheel cylinder being worked on. Note the locations of all components to ensure correct refitting, and lubricate the new seals using clean brake fluid. Follow the assembly instructions supplied with the repair kit **(see illustrations)**.

Refitting

8 Ensure that the backplate and wheel cylinder mating surfaces are clean, then

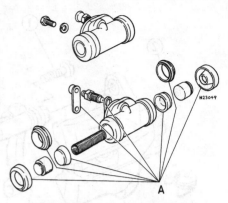

12.7a Girling rear wheel cylinder components - models with underbody-mounted brake pressure-regulating valve
A Repair kit items

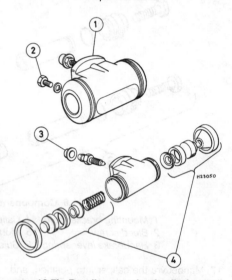

12.7b Bendix rear wheel cylinder components - models with underbody-mounted brake pressure-regulating valve

1 Cylinder	*3 Bleed screw*
2 Securing bolt	*4 Repair kit items*

spread the brake shoes and manoeuvre the wheel cylinder into position.

9 Engage the brake pipe, and screw in the union nut two or three turns to ensure that the thread has started.

10 Insert the two wheel cylinder retaining bolts, and tighten them securely. Now fully tighten the brake pipe union nut.

11 Remove the clamp from the flexible brake hose, or the polythene from the master cylinder reservoir (as applicable).

12 Ensure that the brake shoes are correctly located in the cylinder pistons, then carefully refit the brake shoe upper return spring, using a screwdriver to stretch the spring into position.

13 Refit the brake drum (see Section 9).

14 Bleed the brake hydraulic system (see Section 2). Providing precautions were taken to minimise loss of fluid, it should only be necessary to bleed the relevant rear brake.

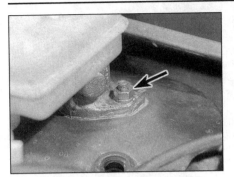

13.5 Master cylinder securing nut (arrowed)

13.7 Removing the master cylinder from the vacuum servo

14.4 Pedal pivot bolt and nut (arrowed)

13 Master cylinder - removal, overhaul and refitting

Removal

1 Disconnect the battery negative lead.
2 Remove the cap from the brake fluid reservoir, place a piece of polythene sheet over the filler neck, and refit the cap tightly. Alternatively, siphon all the fluid from the reservoir using an old teat pipette or poultry baster. This will minimise fluid loss during the following procedure.

 HAYNES HINT *Spread some cloth over the vacuum servo unit and surrounding area to catch fluid drips as the master cylinder is removed.*

3 To improve the clearance available for removal, remove the windscreen wiper arms (see Chapter 12), then remove the scuttle cover panel from the front edge of the windscreen (see Chapter 11).
4 Disconnect the wiring from the low brake fluid level warning sensor.
5 Unscrew the two nuts securing the master cylinder to the brake vacuum servo unit **(see illustration)**.
6 Unscrew the union nuts, and disconnect the brake fluid pipes from the master cylinder.
7 Lift the master cylinder, complete with the fluid reservoir, from the servo unit **(see illustration)**. Hold a cloth under the assembly to catch any fluid spillage. Recover the sealing ring.
8 Unscrew the clamp nut and bolt, release the plastic clamp, and withdraw the fluid reservoir from the master cylinder.

Overhaul

9 No spare parts are available from Peugeot for the master cylinder, and if faulty the complete unit must be renewed.

Refitting

10 Refitting is a reversal of removal, bearing in mind the following points.
 a) *Examine the master cylinder sealing ring and renew if necessary.*

 b) *Ensure that the brake pipe union nuts are securely tightened.*
 c) *Refit the windscreen wiper arms with reference to Chapter 12.*
 d) *On completion, remove the polythene, where applicable, then top-up and bleed the hydraulic system as described in Section 2.*

14 Brake pedal - removal and refitting

Note: *On models fitted with the Bendix "integral" ABS, the hydraulic modulator unit must be removed in order to remove the brake pedal. This task **must** be entrusted to a Peugeot dealer - see Section 23.*

Removal

1 The pedal assembly is removed complete with the vacuum servo, and the procedure is described in Section 15.
2 With the servo/pedal assembly removed, proceed as follows.
3 Remove the securing clip, and withdraw the pin securing the servo pushrod to the pedal.
4 Unscrew the nut from the pedal pivot bolt, and withdraw the pivot bolt to release the pedals **(see illustration)**.

Refitting

5 Refitting is a reversal of removal, but renew the nylon pedal pivot bushes if they are worn, and refit the servo/pedal assembly as described in Section 15.

15 Vacuum servo unit - testing, removal and refitting

Testing

1 To test the operation of the servo unit, depress the footbrake several times to exhaust the vacuum, then start the engine whilst keeping the pedal firmly depressed. As the engine starts, there should be a noticeable "give" in the brake pedal as the vacuum builds up. Allow the engine to run for at least two

minutes, then switch it off. If the brake pedal is now depressed it should feel normal, but further applications should result in the pedal feeling firmer, with the pedal stroke decreasing with each application.
2 If the servo does not operate as described, first inspect the servo unit check valve as described in Section 16.
3 If the servo unit still fails to operate satisfactorily, the fault lies within the unit itself. Repairs to the unit are not possible - if faulty, the servo unit must be renewed.

Removal

4 Disconnect the battery negative lead.
5 Remove the windscreen wiper motor/linkage assembly as described in Chapter 12.
6 Disconnect the wiring from the low brake fluid level warning sensor.
7 Pull the vacuum check valve from the grommet in the top of the servo **(see illustration)**.
8 Unscrew the two nuts securing the master cylinder to the brake vacuum servo unit, then ease the master cylinder up to disengage it from the servo, without disconnecting the fluid pipes. Take care not to strain the fluid pipes. If necessary, release the fluid pipes from their locating clips to enable them to move sufficiently.
9 Working in the driver's footwell, remove the carpet trim panel from under the facia to expose the pedal assemblies.
10 Where applicable, working under the facia, unscrew the bolts securing the relay bracket and the wiring connector bracket(s) to improve access.

15.7 Pulling the vacuum check valve from the servo

9

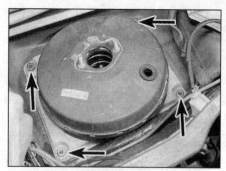

15.14 Unscrew the nuts (arrowed) securing the servo to the scuttle

15.15 Removing the vacuum servo/pedal bracket assembly

15.16 Unscrew the nuts (arrowed) securing the servo to the pedal bracket

11 Where applicable, depress the retaining clip and detach the end of the clutch cable from the pedal (see Chapter 6).

12 Disconnect the wiring plug from the stop light switch.

13 Prise off the brake and clutch pedal rubbers.

14 Working in the scuttle, unscrew and remove the four nuts securing the servo to the scuttle **(see illustration)**.

15 Manoeuvre the complete vacuum servo, pedal bracket and pedal assembly from the scuttle **(see illustration)**.

16 Unscrew the four nuts securing the servo to the pedal bracket, and withdraw the servo **(see illustration)**. Where applicable recover the gasket.

17 The servo is a sealed unit, and if faulty, the complete unit must be renewed.

Refitting

18 Refitting is a reversal of removal, bearing in mind the following points.

a) Use a new gasket when refitting the servo.

b) Refit the wiper motor/linkage assembly with reference to Chapter 12.

c) Check the stop light adjustment with reference to Section 22.

d) Check the clutch cable adjustment as described in Chapter 6.

16 Vacuum servo unit check valve - removal, testing and refitting

Removal

1 For access to the valve, open the bonnet. The valve is a push-fit in the top of the brake vacuum servo unit located in the scuttle at the rear of the engine compartment.

2 Slacken the retaining clip (where fitted), and disconnect the vacuum hose from the servo unit check valve.

3 Withdraw the valve from its rubber sealing grommet, using a pulling and twisting motion. Remove the grommet from the servo.

Testing

4 Examine the check valve for signs of

damage, and renew if necessary. The valve may be tested by blowing through it in both directions. Air should flow through the valve in one direction only - when blown through from the servo unit end of the valve. Renew the valve if this is not the case.

5 Examine the rubber sealing grommet and flexible vacuum hose for signs of damage or deterioration, and renew as necessary.

Refitting

6 Fit the sealing grommet into position in the servo unit.

7 Carefully ease the check valve into position, taking great care not to displace or damage the grommet. Reconnect the vacuum hose to the valve and, where necessary, securely tighten its retaining clip.

17 Handbrake - checking and adjustment

Checking

1 The handbrake is correctly adjusted when the rear wheels are fully locked when the handbrake lever has been pulled up by six to eight notches. This adjustment tolerance will be maintained if the automatic adjuster mechanism is operating correctly to compensate for brake shoe/pad wear.

2 To check the adjustment, proceed as follows.

3 Start the engine and release the handbrake.

4 Depress the brake pedal fully two or three times with the engine running, then stop the engine.

5 Chock the front wheels, then jack up the rear of the vehicle, and support securely on axle stands (see "Jacking and Vehicle Support").

6 Apply the handbrake between six to eight notches, and check that both rear wheels are locked. If the wheels do not lock, or if the wheels lock before the handbrake lever has moved through at least six notches, adjust the mechanism as follows.

Adjustment - rear drum brakes

7 With the vehicle raised and supported at

the rear, where applicable, remove the rear body undershield for access to the handbrake cable adjuster **(see illustration)**.

8 Slacken the locknut on the handbrake adjuster mechanism and turn the adjuster nut until the brake shoes are just beginning to drag on the drums.

9 Pull up the handbrake lever, and check that both rear wheels are locked with the lever pulled up between six and eight notches. If not, readjust using the adjuster nut as necessary.

10 With the mechanism correctly adjusted, tighten the adjuster locknut then, where applicable, refit the rear body undershield, and lower the vehicle to the ground.

11 Check that the "handbrake on" warning light illuminates with the handbrake lever at the first notch of its travel. If necessary, adjust the switch as described in Chapter 12.

Adjustment - rear disc brakes

12 Where applicable, remove the rear body undershield for access to the handbrake cable adjuster, then lower the rear of the vehicle to the ground.

13 Chock the front wheels, and ensure that the handbrake is released.

14 Slacken the locknut on the handbrake adjuster mechanism, then turn the adjuster nut until there is a clearance of approximately 2.0 mm between the end faces of the cable end fittings and the handbrake operating levers on the rear calipers **(see illustration)**.

15 Operate the levers on the calipers manually, and check that the levers return fully to their stops when released.

16 Turn the adjuster nut to give a dimension

17.7 Handbrake cable adjuster (arrowed)

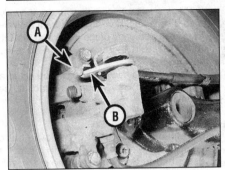

17.14 Adjust the clearance between the cable end fitting (A) and the handbrake operating lever (B) at the caliper

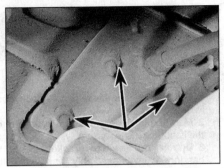

18.5 Three of the handbrake lever securing nuts (arrowed)

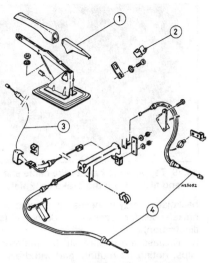

19.4 Handbrake lever and cable components

1 Handbrake lever   3 Primary cable
2 Switch assembly   4 Secondary cables

of approximately 15.0 mm between the rear face of the adjuster nut and the end of the threaded adjuster rod.

17 Proceed as described in paragraphs 9 to 11.

18 Handbrake lever - removal and refitting

Removal

1 Disconnect the rear of the handbrake primary cable from the right-hand secondary cable under the rear of the vehicle, as described in Section 19.

2 On models with a "lowline" centre console, pull the handbrake lever up, then unclip the front edge of the handbrake aperture trim panel from the top of the centre console. Withdraw the trim panel over the handbrake lever.

3 On models with a "highline" centre console, remove the centre console as described in Chapter 11.

4 Working under the vehicle, where applicable, for access to the handbrake lever securing nuts, remove the exhaust intermediate section as described in Chapter 4, then remove the underbody heat shield(s).

5 Unscrew the four handbrake lever securing nuts, noting that on certain models two of the nuts also secure an exhaust mounting bracket **(see illustration)**.

6 Carefully lower the lever assembly from under the vehicle, and disconnect the wiring plug from the "handbrake on" warning light switch. The mounting plate may be stuck to the floor with sealant, in which case cut around the plate with a sharp knife. Where applicable, recover the gasket.

7 Disconnect the end of the cable from the lever, then release the cable sheath from the lever mounting plate.

Refitting

8 Refitting is a reversal of removal, bearing in mind the following points.

a) Use a new gasket or new sealant, as applicable when refitting the lever

mounting plate to the floor (clean the mating faces of the mounting plate and floor).

b) Where applicable, ensure that the exhaust mounting bracket is in position under the handbrake lever securing nuts, and refit the exhaust intermediate section with reference to Chapter 4.

c) On completion, check and if necessary adjust the handbrake mechanism as described in Section 17.

19 Handbrake cables - removal and refitting

Primary cable

Removal

1 Jack up the vehicle and support on axle stands (see "Jacking and Vehicle Support").

2 Where applicable, remove the rear body undershield.

3 To gain access to the cable on certain models, it may be necessary to remove the heat shields from under the fuel tank and the rear underbody. To gain access to remove the heat shields, it may be necessary to remove the clamp securing the exhaust rear section to the intermediate section - this will allow the exhaust sections to move sufficiently to manipulate the heat shields out from under the vehicle.

4 Release the handbrake, then slacken the locknut on the adjuster mechanism and back off the adjuster nut **(see illustration)**.

5 Release the primary cable from the clips on the underbody, then release the cable from the right-hand secondary cable at the connector, and from the adjuster bracket.

6 Working under the handbrake lever, detach the cable sheath from the lever mounting plate.

7 On models with a "lowline" centre console, pull the handbrake lever up, then unclip the front edge of the handbrake aperture trim panel from the top of the centre console. Withdraw the trim panel over the handbrake lever.

8 On models with a "highline" centre console, remove the centre console as described in Chapter 11.

9 Pull the handbrake lever up to the 5th notch of travel, for access to the end of the cable.

10 Pull the end of the cable forwards and down to release it from the lug on the lever.

11 Feed the cable down through the lever mounting plate, and withdraw it from under the vehicle.

Refitting

12 Refitting is a reversal of removal, bearing in mind the following points.

a) Ensure that the cable is routed correctly, and is free from kinks.

b) On completion, check and if necessary adjust the handbrake mechanism as described in Section 17.

Secondary cable - models with rear drum brakes

Removal

13 Proceed as described in paragraphs 1 and 2.

14 Slacken the locknut on the adjuster mechanism and back off the adjuster nut.

15 If the left-hand cable is being removed, remove the adjuster nut from the end of the threaded adjuster rod, then detach the end of the cable from the adjuster bracket.

16 If the right-hand cable is being removed, disconnect the secondary cable from the primary cable at the connector.

17 Remove the relevant brake drum as described in Section 9.

18 Using a pair of pliers, unhook the end of the handbrake cable from the operating lever on the trailing brake shoe.

19 Where applicable, tap the cable sheath end fitting from the aperture in the brake backplate, and feed the cable through the

9

19.19 Tapping the handbrake cable sheath end fitting from the brake backplate

backplate (it may be necessary to remove the brake shoes for access - see Section 6) **(see illustration).**

20 Release the cable from the underbody clips, noting its routing, and withdraw the cable from under the vehicle.

Refitting

21 Refitting is a reversal of removal, bearing in mind the following points.

a) *Ensure that the cable is routed correctly, and is free from kinks.*
b) *Refit the brake drum (see Section 9).*
c) *On completion, check and if necessary adjust the handbrake mechanism as described in Section 17.*

Secondary cable - models with rear disc brakes

Removal

22 Proceed as described in paragraphs 1 and 2.

23 Slacken the locknut on the adjuster mechanism and back off the adjuster nut.

24 If the left-hand cable is being removed, remove the adjuster nut from the end of the threaded adjuster rod, then detach the end of the cable from the adjuster bracket.

25 If the right-hand cable is being removed, disconnect the secondary cable from the primary cable at the connector.

26 Disconnect the end of the cable from the operating lever on the caliper, then release the cable sheath from the caliper bracket.

27 Release the cable from the underbody clips, noting its routing, and withdraw the cable from under the vehicle.

Refitting

28 Refitting is a reversal of removal, bearing in mind the following points.

a) *Ensure that the cable is routed correctly, and is free from kinks.*
b) *On completion, check and if necessary adjust the handbrake mechanism as described in Section 17.*

---

20 Handbrake "on" warning light switch - removal and refitting

Removal

1 Remove the handbrake lever as described in Section 18.

2 Mark the position of the switch bracket on the handbrake lever assembly.

3 Unbolt the switch bracket from the handbrake lever assembly, and unclip the switch.

Refitting

4 Refitting is a reversal of removal. If necessary, the position of the switch bracket can be adjusted (the hole in the bracket is elongated) to ensure that the warning light is off with the handbrake released, and on with the handbrake applied.

---

21 Rear brake pressure-regulating valve (underbody-mounted) - removal and refitting

Note: *On some models equipped with rear drum brakes, the pressure regulating valves are integral with the rear wheel cylinders. If fitted, the underbody-mounted pressure regulating valve is located on the right-hand side of the rear axle assembly.*

 Warning: Do not attempt to remove the pressure-regulating valve on models equipped with the Bendix "integral" ABS system. On these models, the task should be entrusted to a Peugeot dealer - see Section 23.

Note: *On refitting, the valve must be adjusted using specialist test equipment. This task must be entrusted to Peugeot dealer.*

Removal

1 Chock the front wheels, then jack up the rear of the vehicle and support securely on axle stands (see *"Jacking and Vehicle Support"*).

2 Unhook the valve operating spring from the bracket attached to the trailing arm.

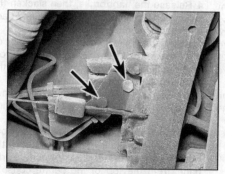

21.4 Rear brake pressure-regulating valve securing bolts (arrowed)

---

3 Place a suitable container under the valve, then disconnect the fluid pipes from the valve. Plug the open ends of the pipes and the valve to prevent dirt ingress and to reduce fluid spillage.

4 Unscrew the securing bolts, and withdraw the valve from its mounting bracket **(see illustration).**

Refitting

5 Refitting is a reversal of removal, but on completion bleed the hydraulic system as described in Section 2, and have the valve adjusted by a Peugeot dealer.

---

22 Stop-light switch - removal, refitting and adjustment

Removal

1 The switch is mounted on the brake pedal bracket **(see illustration).**

2 Disconnect the battery negative lead.

3 If necessary to improve access, remove the carpet trim panel from under the driver's side facia.

4 Disconnect the wiring plug from the switch, then pull the switch from the bracket to remove it.

Refitting

5 Depress the brake pedal fully.

6 Push the switch fully into its bracket as far as the stop.

7 Release the brake pedal, and allow it to contact the switch. The switch should retract, and automatically reset itself.

8 Reconnect the wiring plug, then reconnect the battery negative lead.

9 Check that the stop lights operate when the brake pedal is depressed with the ignition switched on.

10 If the stop lights fail to operate, and the wiring is in good order, renew the switch.

Adjustment

11 The switch is self-adjusting, and can be reset by removing and then refitting it as described previously in this Section.

12 If the switch fails to operate satisfactorily after removal and refitting, renew the switch.

22.1 Stop-light switch (arrowed) on brake pedal bracket

23 Anti-lock braking system (ABS) - general information

General

1 ABS is available as an option on certain models covered by this manual, and is fitted as standard equipment on some models. The purpose of the system is to prevent the wheel(s) locking during heavy braking. This is achieved by automatic release of the brake on the relevant wheel, followed by re-application of the brake. The system comprises an electronic control module, a hydraulic modulator block, the hydraulic solenoid valves and accumulators, the electrically-driven pump, and the roadwheel sensors.

2 The system operates on all four wheels, and vehicles may be fitted with rear disc or rear drum brakes.

3 The system prevents wheel lock-up by regulating the hydraulic pressure to the brakes.

4 Solenoids (which control the fluid pressure to the calipers) are controlled by the electronic control unit, which itself receives signals from the wheel sensors (fitted to all four wheels), which monitor the speed of rotation of each wheel. By comparing these speed signals from the wheels, the control unit can determine the speed at which the vehicle is travelling. It can then use this speed to determine when a wheel is decelerating at an abnormal rate, compared to the speed of the vehicle, and therefore predicts when a wheel is about to lock. During normal operation, the system functions in the same way as a non-ABS braking system.

5 The ABS system is fail-safe, and should a failure occur, a self-monitoring test facility is incorporated in the system which can be used in conjunction with dealer test equipment for fault diagnosis.

6 Three different types of ABS may be fitted, depending on model, as follows.

Bendix "integral" ABS

7 This system is fitted to certain models up to 1993 as standard equipment. The system is fitted instead of a conventional system, and the brake pedal acts directly on the hydraulic control unit, which replaces the master cylinder and vacuum servo in a conventional braking system.

8 The system operates at very high fluid pressure, typically 158 to 183 bar, generated by an electric pump fitted to the modulator assembly.

9 The system is fail-safe and will continue to operate even if one wheel sensor should fail. In the event of total failure, the control unit will revert the system to normal braking.

 Warning: Due to the complexity of the system, the very high fluid pressures involved, and the need for special bleeding

equipment and pressure gauges, any operation requiring removal or disconnection of any hydraulic component, pipe or fitting must only be carried out by a suitably-equipped Peugeot dealer. Failure to heed this warning may result in personal injury, or malfunction of the system at a critical time. Work on vehicles equipped with the Bendix "integral" ABS should therefore be confined to routine maintenance operations.

Bendix "additional" ABS

10 The Bendix "additional" system is fitted as an option to certain models, and the ABS components are fitted in addition to the conventional braking system components.

11 The system uses the pressure provided by the conventional master cylinder and vacuum servo.

12 The system is fail-safe, and conventional braking is maintained through the servo and master cylinder in the event of an ABS failure.

13 The braking system can be safely bled, and the fluid can be renewed as described in Chapter 1, as the system operates using the conventional pressure supplied by the master cylinder and servo.

Bosch 2E "additional" ABS

14 The Bosch 2E additional system is fitted to certain later models from 1993, and is similar to the Bendix "additional" system described previously.

24 Anti-lock braking system (ABS) components - removal and refitting

Front wheel sensor

Removal

1 Disconnect the battery negative lead.

2 To improve access, apply the handbrake, then jack up the front of the vehicle and support securely on axle stands (see *"Jacking and Vehicle Support"*). If desired, remove the roadwheel.

3 Trace the wiring back from the sensor, then

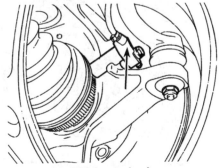

24.5 ABS front wheel sensor (arrowed)

disconnect the sensor wiring connector (on most models, the sensor wiring is routed through the inner wing panel, and the connector is located in the engine compartment).

4 Release the sensor wiring from any securing clips and, where applicable, push the wiring grommet from the inner wing panel and feed the wiring through the panel.

5 Unscrew the securing bolt, and withdraw the sensor from the hub carrier **(see illustration)**.

Refitting

6 Before refitting a sensor, ensure that the tip is clean. Where applicable, on new sensors remove the protective sticker from the tip.

7 Fit the sensor to the hub carrier.

8 Clean the sensor securing bolt, then apply thread-locking compound to the bolt threads. Fit the bolt and tighten to the specified torque.

9 On models fitted with the Bendix "integral" ABS system, proceed as follows **(see illustration)**.

   a) *Loosen the sensor adjuster bolt.*

   b) *Position a 0.5 mm feeler blade between the sensor tip and the sensor ring on the driveshaft.*

   c) *Press the sensor lightly against the feeler blade, and tighten the adjuster bolt to the specified torque.*

   d) *Remove the feeler blade.*

10 On completion, where applicable refit the roadwheel and lower the vehicle to the ground.

Rear wheel sensor

Removal

11 Disconnect the battery negative lead.

12 To improve access, chock the front wheels, then jack up the rear of the vehicle and support securely on axle stands (see *"Jacking and Vehicle Support"*).

13 Trace the wiring back from the sensor, then disconnect the sensor wiring connector (on most models, the sensor wiring is routed through the floor of the vehicle, and the connector is located behind the luggage compartment side trim panel).

14 Release the wiring from the clips underneath the vehicle, and feed the wiring through the floor panel.

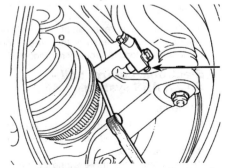

24.9 ABS front wheel sensor adjustment (adjuster arrowed) - Bendix "integral" ABS

9

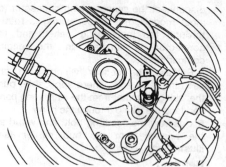

24.15 Rear wheel ABS sensor (arrowed)

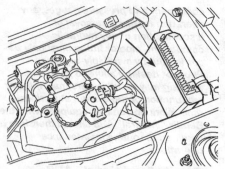

24.20 Electronic control unit location (arrowed) - Bendix "integral" ABS (left-hand-drive models shown)

24.27 Bosch ABS electronic control unit securing screws (arrowed)

15 Unscrew the securing bolt, and remove the sensor from the trailing arm **(see illustration)**.

Refitting

16 Before refitting a sensor, ensure that the tip is clean. Where applicable, on new sensors remove the protective sticker from the tip.
17 Lightly grease the sensor location in the trailing arm, then refit the sensor.
18 Clean the sensor securing bolt, then apply thread-locking compound to the bolt threads. Fit the bolt and tighten to the specified torque.

Electronic control unit - Bendix ABS systems

Removal

19 Disconnect the battery negative lead.
20 The unit is located in the scuttle at the rear of the engine compartment **(see illustration)**.
21 Open the bonnet, and unclip the cover from the top of the scuttle to expose the control unit.
22 Release the securing clip, and disconnect the wiring plug from the top of the control unit.
23 Unscrew the clamp bolts or nuts, as applicable, securing the unit to the housing, then carefully withdraw the unit. Note that on some models, it may be necessary to disconnect the control unit wiring harness earth lead before the unit can be withdrawn.
24 Where applicable, separate the control unit from the mounting bracket.

Refitting

25 Refitting is a reversal of removal, but where applicable ensure that the wiring harness earth lead is securely reconnected.

Electronic control unit - Bosch ABS system

Removal

26 Disconnect the battery negative lead, then unclip the control unit cover from the top of the modulator assembly.
27 Disconnect the three wiring connectors from the control unit, then slacken and remove the six Torx retaining screws, and lift

the control unit away from the modulator assembly **(see illustration)**.

Refitting

28 Refitting is a reversal of the removal procedure. Ensure that the wiring connectors are securely reconnected, and do not overtighten the retaining screws.

Hydraulic control unit and modulator assembly - Bendix "integral" ABS

Note: *Refer to the Warning in Section 23.*
29 No attempt should be made to remove any of the hydraulic system components on models equipped with the Bendix "integral" ABS - refer the operation to a Peugeot dealer.

Modulator assembly - Bendix "additional" ABS

Removal

30 Disconnect the battery negative lead.
31 Where applicable, unclip the plastic cover, then disconnect the wiring connectors from the modulator assembly.
32 Mark the locations of the hydraulic fluid pipes to ensure correct refitting, then unscrew the union nuts, and disconnect the pipes from the modulator assembly. Be prepared for fluid spillage, and plug the open ends of the pipes and the modulator, to prevent dirt ingress and further fluid loss. Note the position of the clip on the brake pipes to ensure correct refitting.

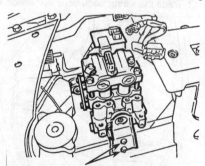

24.33 Modulator assembly vertical mounting bracket-to-main bracket nuts (arrowed) - Bendix "additional" ABS

33 Working under the modulator, unscrew the two nuts securing the vertical mounting plate to the main bracket **(see illustration)**. Withdraw the plate and the mounting rubber assembly.
34 Unscrew the two nuts securing the remaining mounting studs to the main bracket, then manipulate the modulator assembly from the bracket.

Refitting

 Warning: Do not reconnect the wiring connectors to the modulator until the hydraulic circuits have been bled as described in Section 2.

35 Refitting is a reversal of removal, bearing in mind the following.
a) *Before refitting, examine the mounting rubbers, and renew if necessary.*
b) *Reconnect the fluid pipes to the assembly, as noted before removal, ensuring that no dirt enters the system. Ensure that the brake pipe clip is fitted as noted before removal.*
c) *Before reconnecting the wiring connectors, bleed the complete hydraulic system as described in Section 2.*

Modulator assembly - Bosch ABS

36 Refer to paragraphs 30 to 35 of this Section for the Bendix "additional" ABS.

25 Vacuum pump - removal and refitting

Belt-driven pump

Removal

1 Where applicable, to improve access, remove the intercooler or the air inlet box, as described in Chapter 4.
2 Disconnect the hoses from the pump, noting their locations to ensure correct refitting **(see illustration)**.

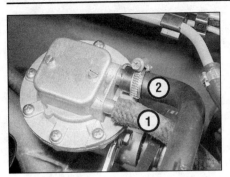

25.2 Belt-driven vacuum pump vacuum hose (1) and discharge hose (2)

25.4 Removing a belt-driven vacuum pump from the inlet manifold

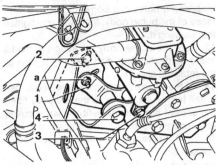

25.6 Belt-driven vacuum pump mounting details - tighten bolts in numerical order
a Adjuster nut

3 Slacken the pump adjuster and mounting bolts, then pivot the pump towards the engine until the drivebelt can be slid from the pump pulley.

4 Remove the pump adjuster and mounting bolts, and withdraw the pump from the bracket on the inlet manifold **(see illustration)**.

Refitting

5 Refitting is a reversal of removal, but ensure that the hoses are correctly reconnected (use new hose clips if necessary), and before tightening the adjuster and mounting bolts, tension the drivebelt as follows.

6 Using a torque wrench, apply a torque of 5 Nm (4 lbf ft) to the adjuster nut **(see illustration)**. Maintain this torque, then tighten the bolts in the order shown (1, 2, 3, 4).

7 On completion, unscrew the oil level plug from the side of the pump, and check that the level is up to the lower edge of the hole. If necessary, top-up the oil level using clean engine oil. Refit and securely tighten the plug.

Direct-drive pump

Removal

Note: *New O-rings must be used on refitting.*

8 If necessary, to improve access remove the intercooler as described in Chapter 4.

9 Release the retaining clip and disconnect the vacuum hose from the pump.

10 Slacken and remove the three bolts and

washers securing the pump to the cylinder head, then remove the pump, along with its two O-rings - new ones must be used on refitting.

Refitting

11 Fit new O-rings to the pump recesses, then align the drive dog with the slot in the end of the camshaft, and refit the pump to the cylinder head, ensuring that the O-rings remain correctly seated **(see illustrations)**.

12 Refit the pump mounting bolts and washers, and tighten them securely.

13 Reconnect the vacuum hose to the pump and tighten its securing clip.

14 Where applicable, refit the intercooler as described in Chapter 4.

26 Vacuum pump - testing and overhaul

Testing

1 The operation of the braking system vacuum pump can be checked using a vacuum gauge.

2 Disconnect the vacuum pipe from the pump, and connect the gauge to the pump union using a suitable length of hose. On the belt-driven pump, ensure that the drivebelt is correctly tensioned.

3 Start the engine and allow it to idle, then measure the vacuum created by the pump. As a guide, after one minute, a minimum of approximately 500 mm Hg should be recorded. If the vacuum registered is significantly less than this, it is likely that the pump is faulty. However, seek the advice of a Peugeot dealer before condemning the pump.

Overhaul

Belt-driven pump

4 Remove the pump with reference to Section 25.

5 Undo the two screws securing the cover to the top of the pump, then lift off the cover **(see illustration)**. Remove the three valves from the top of the pump, along with their seals, making a careful note of which way round the valves are fitted.

6 Make alignment marks between the pump upper body and the main pump body. Undo the retaining screws, then lift off the upper body.

7 Unscrew the retaining nut, and remove the diaphragm and support plates from the pump piston. Remove the O-ring from its recess in the top of the piston.

8 Turn the pulley until the piston is at the top of its stroke, then check the piston-to-bore wear by moving the piston from side to side. If wear is excessive, the complete vacuum pump assembly must be renewed.

9 If the piston wear is acceptable, examine the pump diaphragm and valves for signs of splitting and deterioration, and renew as necessary. It is recommended that the diaphragm and valves are renewed as a matter of course whenever the pump is stripped. Repair kits are available from Peugeot dealers.

10 Ensure that all components are clean, and fit the new O-ring to the top of the piston.

11 Position a support plate on either side of the diaphragm, ensuring that the flat surfaces of each plate are facing the diaphragm, and that the larger of the two support plates is at the bottom. Refit the diaphragm and support plate assembly to the piston, and secure it in position with the retaining nut. Ensure that the

25.11a Fit new O-rings (arrowed) to the pump recess . . .

25.11b . . . then refit the pump; ensure drive dog is correctly engaged with camshaft slot (arrowed) - direct-drive pump

9

diaphragm holes are correctly aligned with those of the pump body, then securely tighten the retaining nut.

12 Refit the upper body, aligning the marks made on dismantling, and securely tighten all the retaining screws.

13 Fit the valve seals to the upper body, then install the valves, ensuring that they are fitted the correct way round. Refit the valve cover, and securely tighten its retaining screws.

14 Refit the vacuum pump as described in Section 25.

Direct-drive pump

15 Overhaul of the direct-drive pump is not possible, since no components are available separately. If faulty, the complete pump assembly must be renewed.

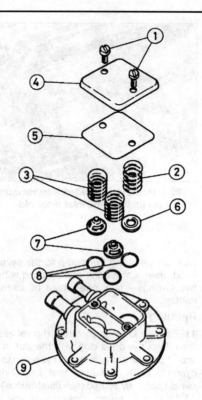

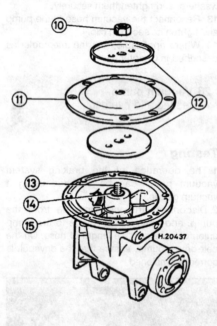

26.5 Exploded view of belt-driven vacuum pump

1 Cover screws
2 Inlet valve spring
3 Outlet valve springs
4 Cover
5 Gasket
6 Inlet valve
7 Outlet valves
8 Seals
9 Upper pump body
10 Nut
11 Diaphragm
12 Support plates
13 Screw
14 O-ring
15 Piston

Chapter 10
Suspension and steering

Contents

Degrees of difficulty

Easy, suitable for novice with little experience	Fairly easy, suitable for beginner with some experience	Fairly difficult, suitable for competent DIY mechanic	Difficult, suitable for experienced DIY mechanic	Very difficult, suitable for expert DIY or professional

Specifications

Wheel alignment and steering angles
Front wheel toe setting . . . . 1.0 ± 0.5 mm toe-in

Roadwheels
Type . . . . Pressed steel or aluminium alloy (depending on model)
Size . . . . 5.5J x 14 or 6J x 15

Torque wrench settings

	Nm	lbf ft
Front suspension		
Hub carrier-to-suspension strut clamp nut/bolt:*		
Early (solid) type hub carrier	55	41
Later (hollow) type hub carrier	45	33
Suspension strut top mounting nuts:		
Models up to 1992	25	18
Models from 1993	20	15
Suspension strut upper mounting retaining nut	55	41
Lower balljoint nut (hub carrier-to-lower arm):*		
Early (solid) type hub carrier	30	22
Later (hollow) type hub carrier	45	33
Lower arm front pivot nut/bolt	75	55
Lower arm rear securing nuts/bolts		
Models up to 1992	45	33
Models from 1993	70	52
Anti-roll bar-to-subframe clamp bolts	25	18
Anti-roll bar metal clamp bolts	20	15
Anti-roll bar drop link-to-anti-roll bar nuts/bolts	65	48
Anti-roll bar drop link-to-lower arm bolts:		
Models up to 1992	75	55
Models from 1993	65	48
Subframe front securing bolts:		
Models up to 1992	60	44
Models from 1993	55	41

10

Torque wrench settings

	Nm	lbf ft
Front suspension (continued)		
Subframe rear securing bolts:		
M12 bolts	90	66
M14 bolts	150	111
Lower balljoint to hub carrier:*		
Early (solid) type hub carrier	260	192
Later (hollow) type hub carrier	250	184
Rear suspension		
Rear hub nut	275	200
Shock absorber securing nuts/ bolts	110	81
Suspension assembly-to-rear mounting bolts	25	18
Suspension assembly-to-front mounting nuts	60	44
Rear suspension mounting-to-body bolts	55	41
Front suspension mounting-to-body bolts	55	41
Steering		
Steering wheel securing nut	35	26
Universal joint clamp bolt	20	15
Steering gear-to-subframe bolts:		
Models up to 1992	40	35
Models from 1993	90	66
Track rod end balljoint nut:*		
Early (solid) type hub carrier	45	33
Later (hollow) type hub carrier	35	26
Track rod end locknut	45	33
Roadwheels		
Wheel bolts	85	63

See note in Section 2.

1 General information

The independent front suspension is of the MacPherson strut type, incorporating coil springs and integral telescopic shock absorbers. The MacPherson struts are located by transverse lower suspension arms, which utilise rubber inner mounting bushes. The front hub carriers, which carry the wheel bearings, brake calipers and the hub/disc assemblies, are bolted to the MacPherson struts. The hub carriers are connected to the lower arms via balljoints attached to the hub carriers. A front anti-roll bar is fitted to all models. The anti-roll bar is rubber-mounted onto the subframe, and is connected to the lower arms via drop links.

The rear suspension is of the semi-independent trailing arm type, which consists of two trailing arms, linked by a tubular crossmember. A torsion bar is fitted transversely between each trailing arm and the opposite suspension side member. An anti-roll bar is fitted between the trailing arms. The complete rear axle assembly is mounted onto the vehicle underbody via four rubber mountings.

The steering column has a universal joint fitted in the centre of its length, which is connected to an intermediate shaft having a second universal joint at its lower end. The lower universal joint is clamped to the steering gear pinion by means of a clamp bolt.

The steering gear is mounted onto the front subframe, and is connected by two track rods, with balljoints at their outer ends, to the steering arms projecting rearwards from the swivel hubs. The track rod ends are threaded, to facilitate adjustment.

Power-assisted steering is fitted as standard on some models, and is available as an option on most others. The hydraulic power steering system is powered by a belt-driven pump, which is driven off the crankshaft pulley.

2 Front hub carrier assembly - removal and refitting

Removal

Note: *All Nyloc nuts disturbed on removal must be renewed as a matter of course. These nuts have threads which are pre-coated with locking compound (this is only effective once). A balljoint separator tool will be required for this operation.*

Note: *Do not allow the vehicle to rest on its wheels with one or both driveshafts disconnected from the swivel hubs, as damage to the wheel bearing(s) may result. If moving the vehicle is unavoidable, temporarily insert the outer end of the driveshaft(s) in the hub(s) and tighten the hub nut(s).*

Note: *It is recommended that a coil spring compressor tool is used during the removal and refitting of the hub carrier. The hub carrier*

can be removed without a spring compressor, but because of the long length of the strut with the spring in a released state, it is difficult to separate the hub carrier from the strut, and unacceptable strain could be exerted on the driveshaft joint. Do not attempt to use a make-shift method of compressing the spring, as there is a risk of component damage and personal injury.

Note: *Two different types of hub carrier assembly may be fitted, depending on model. The earlier hub carriers are solid. The later hub carriers are hollow, and can be identified from the hole at the top of the assembly (see illustration 2.19a). When refitting note that the torque wrench settings differ for the two types of hub carrier (see "Specifications"). Modified lower arms are fitted in conjunction with the later hub carriers, and the early and late type components are not interchangeable - if components are renewed, make sure that the correct new parts are obtained.*

1 Chock the rear wheels, then firmly apply the handbrake. Jack up the front of the vehicle, and support it on axle stands (see "Jacking and Vehicle Support"). Remove the appropriate front roadwheel.

2 On models with ABS, remove the wheel sensor as described in Chapter 9.

3 Remove the R-clip, and withdraw the locking cap from the driveshaft retaining nut **(see illustration)**.

4 Refit at least two roadwheel bolts to the front hub, and tighten them securely. Have an assistant firmly depress the brake pedal, to prevent the front hub from rotating, then using

2.3 Withdraw the R-clip from the driveshaft nut locking cap

2.11 Release the lower balljoint using a balljoint separator tool

2.12 Hub carrier-to-suspension strut clamp nut (arrowed)

a socket and extension bar, slacken and remove the driveshaft retaining nut. Alternatively, a tool can be fabricated from two lengths of steel strip (one long, one short) and a nut and bolt; the nut and bolt forming the pivot of a forked tool. Bolt the tool to the hub using two wheel bolts, and hold the tool to prevent the hub from rotating as the driveshaft nut is undone.

5 Unscrew the two bolts securing the brake caliper/mounting bracket assembly to the swivel hub, and slide the caliper assembly off the disc. Recover the mounting plate, where applicable. Using a piece of wire or string, tie the caliper to the front suspension coil spring, to avoid placing any strain on the hydraulic brake hose.

6 Use chalk or paint to mark the relationship of the disc to the hub, then remove the screw(s) securing the brake disc to the hub, and remove the disc. If it is tight, lightly tap its rear face with a hide or plastic mallet.

7 Where applicable, slacken and remove the bolt securing the wiring/hose retaining bracket to the top of the hub carrier.

8 To ease removal of the hub carrier, fit spring compressor tools to the coil spring on the strut, in accordance with the manufacturer's instructions, and lightly tighten the compressors. Note that the hub carrier can be removed without using spring compressors, but difficulty may be encountered disconnecting hub carrier from the lower end of the strut.

9 Unscrew the bolt securing the anti-roll bar drop link to the lower arm.

10 Slacken and partially unscrew the track rod end nut (unscrew the nut as far as the end of the threads on the balljoint to prevent damage to the threads as the joint is released), then release the balljoint using a balljoint separator tool. Remove the nut.

11 Similarly, slacken the lower balljoint nut (securing the hub carrier to the lower arm), then release the balljoint using a separator tool **(see illustration)**. Remove the nut.

12 Undo the nut and withdraw the hub carrier-to-suspension strut clamp bolt, noting that the bolt fits from the rear of the vehicle **(see illustration)**.

13 Where applicable, tighten the compressor tools, and compress the spring sufficiently to enable the lower end of the strut to be disconnected from the hub carrier.

14 Insert a lever into the slot in the hub carrier, and spread the slot until the hub carrier can be released from the strut.

> **HAYNES HINT** *To spread the slot in the hub carrier, engage an 8.0 mm Allen key or hexagon bit in the slot, then turn the key/bit to spread the slot.*

15 Free the hub carrier assembly from the end of the strut, then release it from the outer constant velocity joint splines, and remove it from the vehicle. If necessary, tap the end of the driveshaft (using a soft-faced mallet) to free it from the hub carrier. Support the free, outboard end of the driveshaft by suspending it using wire or string - do not allow the driveshaft to hang down under its own weight.

Refitting

16 Where applicable, fit the spring compressor tools in position as during removal, ensure that the driveshaft outer constant velocity joint and hub splines are clean, then slide the hub fully onto the driveshaft splines.

17 Slide the hub carrier assembly fully onto the suspension strut, aligning the slot in the hub carrier with the lug on the base of the strut. Also ensure that the stop boss on the strut is in contact with the top surface of the hub carrier **(see illustration)**. Release the tool used to spread the hub carrier slot.

18 Insert the hub carrier-to-suspension strut clamp bolt from the rear side of the strut, then fit a new nut to the clamp bolt, and tighten it to the specified torque.

19 Two types of hub carrier may be fitted. The later type can be identified from the hole at the top of the assembly **(see illustration)**. When refitting a later type hub carrier, proceed as follows.

a) *After tightening the clamp bolt, measure the gap between the hub carrier clamp lugs (see illustration). The gap must not be less than specified. If the gap is less than specified, proceed as follows.*

b) *Check the condition of the lower end of the strut. If the strut cylinder has been crushed, the shock absorber will be damaged, and the strut must be renewed.*

c) *If the strut is not damaged, but the gap between the clamp lugs is still less than specified, renew the hub carrier.*

2.17 Lug (1) and stop boss (2) on lower end of strut

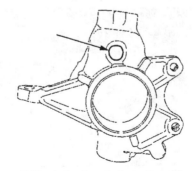

2.19a Later type hub carrier with identification hole (arrowed)

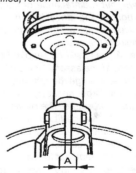

2.19b Gap (A) on later type hub carrier clamp lugs must not be less than 6.5 mm

10

20 Align the balljoint with the lower arm, then fit the balljoint nut, and tighten to the specified torque.
21 Engage the track rod balljoint in the hub carrier, then fit a new retaining nut and tighten it to the specified torque.
22 Refit the bolt securing the anti-roll bar drop link to the lower arm, and tighten to the specified torque.
23 Refit the brake disc to the hub, ensuring that the marks made before removal are aligned, then refit the brake caliper/mounting bracket. Apply suitable locking fluid to the caliper/mounting bracket bolts then, where applicable refit the mounting plate, ensuring that the plate is fitted so that its bend curves away from the caliper body, and refit the bolts. Tighten the bolts to the specified torque.
24 Lubricate the inner face and threads of the driveshaft retaining nut with clean engine oil, and refit it to the end of the driveshaft. Use the method employed on removal to prevent the hub from rotating, and tighten the driveshaft retaining nut to the specified torque (see Chapter 8). Check that the hub rotates freely.
25 Engage the locking cap with the driveshaft nut so that one of its cut-outs is aligned with the driveshaft hole. Secure the cap with the R-clip.
26 Where applicable, slacken and remove the spring compressor tools.
27 Where applicable, refit the ABS wheel sensor as described in Chapter 9.
28 Where applicable, refit the wiring retaining bracket to the top of the hub carrier, and tighten its retaining bolt securely. Ensure that the earth lead is in position beneath the bolt, where applicable.
29 Refit the roadwheel, then lower the vehicle to the ground and tighten the roadwheel bolts to the specified torque.

3 Front hub bearings - renewal

Note: *The bearing is a sealed, pre-adjusted and pre-lubricated, double-row roller type, and is intended to last the car's entire service life without maintenance or attention. Never overtighten the driveshaft nut beyond the specified torque wrench setting in an attempt to "adjust" the bearing.*
Note: *A press will be required to dismantle and rebuild the assembly; if such a tool is not available, a large bench vice and spacers (such as large sockets) will serve as an adequate substitute. The bearing's inner races are an interference fit on the hub; if the inner race remains on the hub when it is pressed out of the hub carrier, a knife-edged bearing puller will be required to remove it.*
1 Remove the hub carrier assembly as described in Section 2.
2 Support the hub carrier securely on blocks

3.3 Front hub bearing retaining circlip (arrowed)

or in a vice. Using a tubular spacer which bears only on the inner end of the hub flange, press the hub flange out of the bearing. If the bearing's outboard inner race remains on the hub, remove it using a bearing puller (see note above).
3 Extract the bearing retaining circlip from the inner end of the hub carrier assembly **(see illustration)**.
4 Where necessary, refit the inner race back in position over the ball cage, and securely support the inner face of the hub carrier. Using a tubular spacer which bears only on the inner race, press the complete bearing assembly out of the hub carrier.
5 Thoroughly clean the hub and hub carrier, removing all traces of dirt and grease, and polish away any burrs or raised edges which might hinder reassembly. Check both for cracks or any other signs of wear or damage, and renew them if necessary. Renew the circlip, regardless of its apparent condition.
6 On reassembly, apply a light film of oil to the bearing outer race and hub flange shaft, to aid installation of the bearing.
7 Securely support the hub carrier, and locate the bearing in the hub. Press the bearing fully into position, ensuring that it enters the hub squarely, using a tubular spacer which bears only on the bearing outer race.
8 Once the bearing is correctly seated, secure the bearing in position with the new circlip, ensuring that it is correctly located in the groove in the hub carrier.
9 Securely support the outer face of the hub flange, and locate the hub carrier bearing inner race over the end of the hub flange.

4.2 Suspension strut top mounting nuts (arrowed)

Press the bearing onto the hub, using a tubular spacer which bears only on the inner race of the hub bearing, until it seats against the hub shoulder. Check that the hub flange rotates freely, and wipe off any excess oil or grease.
10 Refit the hub carrier assembly as described in Section 2.

4 Front suspension strut - removal and refitting

Removal

Note: *All Nyloc nuts disturbed on removal must be renewed as a matter of course. These nuts have threads which are pre-coated with locking compound (this is only effective once).*
Note: *It is recommended that a coil spring compressor tool is used during the removal and refitting of the strut. The strut can be removed without a spring compressor, but because of the long length of the strut with the spring in a released state, it is difficult to separate the hub carrier from the strut, and unacceptable strain could be exerted on the driveshaft joint. Do not attempt to use a make-shift method of compressing the spring, as there is a risk of component damage and personal injury.*
1 Chock the rear wheels, apply the handbrake, then jack up the front of the vehicle and support on axle stands (see *"Jacking and Vehicle Support"*). Remove the appropriate roadwheel.
2 Working in the engine compartment, where applicable remove the plastic cover from the strut top mounting, then slacken but do not remove the two strut top mounting nuts **(see illustration)**.
3 Where applicable, unclip any wiring and/or hoses from the lower arms.
4 Unscrew the bolt securing the anti-roll bar drop link to the lower arm.
5 Undo the nut and withdraw the hub carrier-to-suspension strut clamp bolt, noting that the bolt fits from the rear of the strut **(see illustration)**. Discard the nut - a new one must be used on refitting.
6 To ease removal of the hub carrier, fit spring compressor tools to the coil spring on the strut, in accordance with the manufacturer's

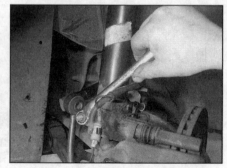
4.5 Unscrewing the hub carrier-to-suspension strut clamp bolt

instructions, and lightly tighten the compressors. Note that the strut can be removed without using spring compressors, but difficulty may be encountered disconnecting hub carrier from the lower end of the strut.

7 Insert a lever into the slot in the hub carrier, and spread the slot until the hub carrier can be released from the strut.

HAYNES HiNT *To spread the slot in the hub carrier, engage an 8.0 mm Allen key or hexagon bit in the slot, then turn the key/bit to spread the slot.*

8 Free the hub carrier from the strut, then remove the two strut top mounting nuts, and withdraw the strut from under the wheel arch.

Refitting

9 Where applicable, fit the coil spring compressors as during removal, then manoeuvre the strut assembly into position. Feed the top mounting studs through the holes in the body, and fit the mounting nuts.

10 Engage the lower end of the strut with the hub carrier. Align the slot in the hub carrier with the lug on the base of the strut. Also ensure that the stop bosses on the strut are in contact with the top surface of the hub carrier. Release the tool used to spread the hub carrier slot.

11 Insert the hub carrier-to-suspension strut clamp bolt from the rear side of the strut, then fit a new nut to the clamp bolt, and tighten it to the specified torque.

12 Refit the bolt securing the anti-roll bar drop link to the lower arm and tighten to the specified torque.

13 Tighten the two strut top mounting nuts to the specified torque.

14 Where applicable, carefully slacken and then remove the spring compressors.

15 Where applicable, clip any wiring/hoses into position on the strut.

16 Refit the roadwheel, then lower the vehicle to the ground and tighten the roadwheel bolts to the specified torque.

5 Front suspension strut - overhaul

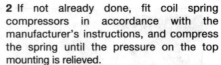

Warning: Before attempting to dismantle the front suspension strut, a suitable tool to hold the coil spring in compression must be obtained. Adjustable coil spring compressors are readily-available, and are recommended for this operation. Any attempt to dismantle the strut without such a tool is likely to result in damage or personal injury.

Note: *The components encountered may vary in detail, but the principles described in the following paragraphs are equally applicable to all models. Make a careful note of the fitted positions of all components before dismantling.*

1 With the strut removed as described in Section 4, clean the exterior of the unit, then mount it in a soft-jawed vice.

2 If not already done, fit coil spring compressors in accordance with the manufacturer's instructions, and compress the spring until the pressure on the top mounting is relieved.

3 Unscrew the top mounting nut. Use a ring spanner to unscrew the nut, and counterhold the piston rod using a 7.0 mm Allen key **(see illustration)**.

4 Remove the nut and recover the washer, then lift off the cupped washer, mounting plate, rubber buffer, and the two dished plates.

5 Lift off the upper spring seat.

6 Withdraw the washer and the rubber gaiter.

7 Remove the bump stop.

8 Remove the coil spring. If the spring is to be renewed, remove the compressors, otherwise leave them in position for reassembly.

9 Inspect the strut for signs of leakage from the piston rod seal. With the strut held vertically, operate the piston over its full range of movement in both directions, checking that the resistance is even and firm. If the resistance is weak or jerky, if there is any fluid seepage, or if there is any damage to the strut or corrosion of the piston rod, then strut must be renewed. Note that struts should always be renewed in pairs. At the same time, check the coil spring for condition, and any signs of distortion or damage. If spring renewal is necessary, again note that both front springs should be renewed as a pair.

10 Reassemble the strut using a reversal of the dismantling procedure, and following the accompanying illustration sequence **(see illustrations 5.10a to 5.10l)**.

5.3 Counterhold the piston rod and unscrew the top mounting nut

5.10a Refit the coil spring, with the compressors in position . . .

5.10b . . . making sure the lower end of the spring locates against the stop (arrowed)

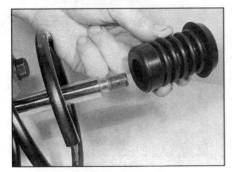

5.10c Refit the bump stop . . .

5.10d . . . followed by the rubber gaiter . . .

5.10e . . . and the washer . . .

10

5.10f . . . fit the upper spring seat, followed by . . .

5.10g . . . the lower . . .

5.10h . . . and upper dished plates . . .

5.10i . . . the rubber buffer . . .

5.10j . . . the mounting plate . . .

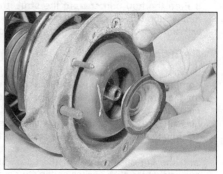

5.10k . . . the cupped washer . . .

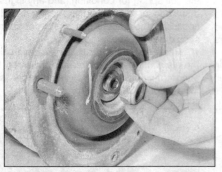

5.10l . . . and the plain washer and nut

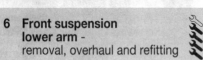

6 Front suspension lower arm -
removal, overhaul and refitting

Removal

Note: *All Nyloc nuts disturbed on removal must be renewed as a matter of course. These nuts have threads which are pre-coated with locking compound (this is only effective once). A balljoint separator tool will be required for this operation.*

Note: *Two different types of hub carrier assembly may be fitted, depending on model. The earlier hub carriers are solid. The later hub carriers are hollow, and can be identified from the hole at the top of the assembly (see illustration 2.19a). When refitting note that the torque wrench settings differ for the two types of hub carrier (see "Specifications"). Modified lower arms are fitted in conjunction with the later hub carriers, and the early and late type components are not interchangeable*

- if components are renewed, make sure that the correct new parts are obtained.

1 Apply the handbrake, then jack up the front of the vehicle and support on axle stands (*see "Jacking and Vehicle Support"*). Remove the relevant roadwheel.

2 Remove the bolt securing the anti-roll bar drop link to the lower arm **(see illustration)**.

3 Slacken and partially unscrew the lower balljoint nut (unscrew the nut as far as the end of the threads on the balljoint to prevent damage to the threads as the joint is released), then release the balljoint using a balljoint separator tool. Remove the nut.

4 Counterhold the nut, and unscrew the lower arm front pivot bolt **(see illustration)**. Withdraw the bolt.

5 Unscrew the two lower arm rear securing nuts **(see illustration)**.

6 Working at the rear of the subframe, loosen the two subframe rear mounting bolts to allow the rear of the subframe to be lowered

sufficiently for the lower arm rear clamp studs to clear the subframe (approximately 10.0 mm). Note that the subframe bolts may be covered by plastic plugs on certain models **(see illustration 6.5)**.

7 Withdraw the lower arm.

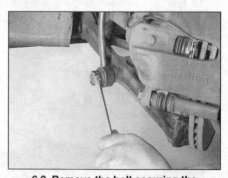

6.2 Remove the bolt securing the anti-roll bar drop link to the lower arm

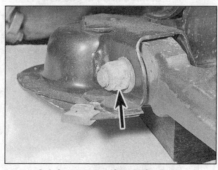

6.4 Lower arm front pivot nut (arrowed)

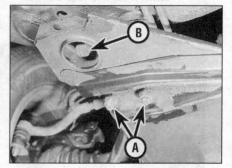

6.5 Lower arm rear securing nuts (A) and subframe rear mounting bolt (B)

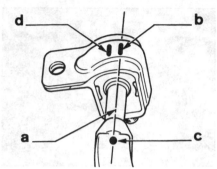

6.11a Lower arm rear mounting bush fitting position

A Bush assembly
B Area to apply lubricant
X = 254.0 mm

Overhaul

8 Thoroughly clean the lower arm and the area around the arm mountings, removing all traces of dirt and underseal if necessary, then check carefully for cracks, distortion or any other signs of wear or damage, paying particular attention to the mounting bushes, and renew components as necessary.
9 Examine the shank of the pivot bolt for signs of wear or scoring, and renew if necessary.
10 Examine the mounting bushes for deterioration or damage.
11 The mounting bushes can be renewed, but a press or suitable alternative tools will be required. If the rear mounting bush is renewed, it must be pressed into the position shown, and the marks on the bush and the lower arm must be aligned. Note that some bushes have two alignment marks, in which case the mark nearest the bolt hole should be ignored. Use a little silicon lubricant to aid fitting of the bushes **(see illustrations)**.

Refitting

12 Refitting is a reversal of removal, bearing in mind the following points.
 a) *Renew all Nyloc nuts.*
 b) *Tighten all fixings to the specified torque.*
 c) *On completion, have the front wheel alignment checked at the earliest opportunity with reference to Section 25.*

6.11b Alignment marks on lower arm rear mounting bush

a Area to apply lubricant
b & c Alignment marks
d Ignore

---

7 Front suspension lower balljoint - removal and refitting

Note: *Peugeot special tool (-).0615.J will be required to unscrew and tighten the balljoint. If this tool is not available, the task should be entrusted to a Peugeot dealer.* **Do not** *attempt the work using an improvised tool.*

Removal

1 Remove the hub carrier as described in Section 2.
2 Tap the dust shield from the balljoint, using a drift **(see illustration)**.
3 Fit the special tool (-).0615.J to the balljoint, engaging the tool with the cut-outs in the balljoint, and secure it by screwing the tool locknut onto the threaded section of the balljoint **(see illustration)**. Engage a swing bar or wrench with the tool, and unscrew the balljoint.

Refitting

4 Refitting is a reversal of removal, bearing in mind the following points.
 a) *Tighten the balljoint as far as possible by hand before finally tightening to the specified torque using the special tool.*
 b) *Take care not to damage the balljoint rubber gaiter during fitting.*
 c) *Lock the balljoint in position by staking into one of the notches in the hub carrier.*

 d) *Lock the dust shield in position by staking it in one of the cut-outs in the balljoint.*
 e) *Refit the hub carrier as described in Section 2.*

---

8 Front anti-roll bar components - removal and refitting

Anti-roll bar

Removal

Note: *All Nyloc nuts disturbed on removal must be renewed as a matter of course. These nuts have threads which are pre-coated with locking compound (this is only effective once).*
Note: *After refitting, the anti-roll bar adjustment should be checked by a Peugeot dealer at the earliest opportunity (the suspension must be compressed using special equipment in order to carry out the check).*

1 Apply the handbrake, then jack up the front of the vehicle and support on axle stands (see "Jacking and Vehicle Support"). Remove the roadwheels.
2 Remove the bolts securing the anti-roll bar drop links to the lower arms.
3 Unscrew the bolts securing the drop links to the ends of the anti-roll bar, and withdraw the drop links **(see illustration)**. If necessary, counterhold the ends of the drop links using a suitable Allen key or hexagon bit.
4 Make (horizontal) alignment marks between the anti-roll bar and the clamps securing the anti-roll bar to the subframe, so that the anti-roll bar can be fitted in exactly the same position.
5 Unscrew the clamp bolts, then withdraw the clamp assemblies. Recover the spacers. Note that there is no need to remove the metal clamps (fitted on the bar, at the inside edges of the main clamps), which prevent the anti-roll bar from moving laterally **(see illustration)**.
6 Manipulate the anti-roll bar out from under the vehicle. Note that it may be necessary to loosen the two subframe rear mounting bolts to allow the rear of the subframe to be lowered sufficiently to allow clearance to remove the anti-roll bar. Note that the

7.2 Tap the dust shield (arrowed) from the balljoint

7.3 Peugeot special tool for removing front suspension lower balljoint

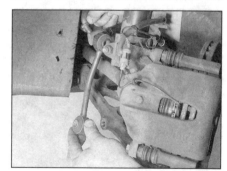

8.3 Removing an anti-roll bar drop link

10

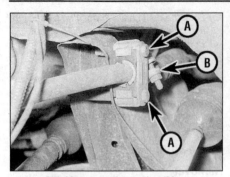

8.5 Unscrew the anti-roll bar clamp bolts (A). There is no need to remove the metal clamp (B)

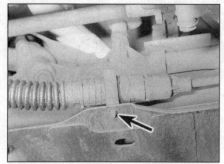

9.5 Release the clip (arrowed) securing the clutch cable to the subframe

9.6 Remove the (arrowed) screws securing the underbody shields to the subframe

subframe bolts may be covered by plastic plugs on certain models. On some models, it may also prove necessary to unbolt the steering gear from the subframe.

7 If the inner metal clamps on the anti-roll bar are to be removed, mark their positions so that they can be refitted in their original positions.

Refitting

8 Refitting is a reversal of removal, bearing in mind the following points.

a) *Ensure that all marks on the anti-roll bar and the clamps are aligned.*

b) *Do not fully tighten the anti-roll bar clamp bolts until the car is resting on its wheels.*

c) *Tighten all fixings to the specified torque.*

d) *On completion, have the anti-roll bar adjustment checked by a Peugeot dealer at the earliest opportunity.*

Drop link

Removal

Note: *All Nyloc nuts disturbed on removal must be renewed as a matter of course. These nuts have threads which are pre-coated with locking compound (this is only effective once.)*

9 Apply the handbrake, then jack up the front of the vehicle and support on axle stands (see *"Jacking and Vehicle Support"*). Remove the roadwheels.

10 Remove the bolt securing the drop link to the lower arm.

11 Unscrew the bolt securing the drop link to the end of the anti-roll bar, and withdraw the

drop link. If necessary, counterhold the end of the drop link using a suitable Allen key or hexagon bit.

Refitting

12 Refitting is a reversal of removal. Tighten the fixings to the specified torque.

9 Front suspension subframe - removal and refitting

Removal

Note: *All Nyloc nuts disturbed on removal must be renewed as a matter of course. These nuts have threads which are pre-coated with locking compound (this is only effective once).*

1 Apply the handbrake, then jack up the front of the vehicle and support securely on axle stands (see *"Jacking and Vehicle Support"*).

2 Remove the suspension lower arms as described in Section 6.

3 Remove the steering gear (see Section 19).

4 Remove the rear engine mounting as described in Chapter 2.

5 Where applicable, release the clip securing the clutch cable to the subframe **(see illustration)**.

6 Where applicable, remove the screws and/or clips securing the underbody shields and wheel arch liners to the subframe **(see illustration)**.

7 Work around the subframe, and release any pipes, hoses and wiring from the clips and brackets on the subframe. Note that it may be

necessary to disconnect certain components on some models. Make a note of the routing of all pipes, hoses and wiring to ensure correct refitting.

8 Support the subframe using a trolley jack and interposed block of wood. Make sure that the jack is positioned to adequately support the subframe without danger of the assembly falling off the jack.

9 Unscrew the four subframe mounting bolts, and carefully lower the subframe from under the vehicle **(see illustration)**. Note that the subframe rear mounting bolts may be covered by plastic plugs on certain models.

Refitting

10 From approximately November 1988, revised subframe rear mounting bolts were introduced. The later bolts incorporate a captive washer in place of the Bellville washer fitted to earlier bolts. If the earlier Bellville washers are found to be cracked, the later bolts with captive washers should be fitted. It is advisable to take the opportunity to fit the later type of bolts as a matter of course, to avoid possible problems in the future.

11 From approximately mid-1992, the subframe rear mountings were modified. The rear mounting bolts were increased in size from M12 to M14, and torque wrench setting was changed accordingly.

12 Subframes with M14 bolts can be identified from the 6.0 mm holes located behind the rear mountings **(see illustration)**.

13 Body shells with fixings provided for the M14 bolts can be identified from the two

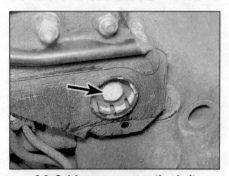

9.9 Subframe rear mounting bolt (arrowed)

9.12 Modified front subframe components
A 6.0 mm diameter holes   B Body shell stiffeners

10.4a Tap the cap from the centre of the hub . . .

10.4b . . . then tap up the staking on the hub nut

10.6a Using a puller to draw the rear hub assembly from the stub axle

10.6b Removing the inner bearing race . . .

10.6c . . . and the oil seal support cup

stiffeners located under the floor (see illustration 9.12).

14 A few vehicles were fitted with the earlier body shells (with M12 bolt holes and no stiffeners), and the later subframe (with M14 bolt holes and 6.0 mm identification holes). On these models, the subframe is secured with special M12 shouldered bolts.

15 If either the subframe or the body shell are renewed, carry out the action given in the table below, according to the type of components fitted. Use only the specified parts, available from a Peugeot dealer.

16 Further refitting is a reversal of removal, bearing in mind the following points.

a) Clean the threads of the subframe mounting bolts, and apply thread-locking compound before refitting.

b) Refit the rear engine mounting with reference to Chapter 2.

c) Refit the steering gear (see Section 19).

d) Refit the lower arms with reference to Section 6.

e) Tighten all fixings to the specified torque.

10 Rear hub assembly - removal and refitting

Removal

Note: Do not remove the hub assembly unless it is absolutely necessary. A puller will be

required to draw the hub assembly off the stub axle, and the hub bearing will almost certainly be damaged by the removal procedure. A new oil seal support cup, and a new hub nut and hub cap will be required on refitting.

1 On models with rear disc brakes, remove the brake disc as described in Chapter 9.

2 On models with rear drum brakes, remove the brake drum as described in Chapter 9. If desired, to improve access for hub removal, also remove the brake shoes.

3 Where applicable, remove the ABS wheel sensor as described in Chapter 9. Note that there is no need to disconnect the wiring connector, but move the sensor to one side, clear of the working area.

4 Using a hammer and a large flat-bladed screwdriver, carefully tap and prise the cap out of the centre of the hub. Discard the cap -

a new one must be used on refitting. Using a hammer and a chisel-nosed tool, tap up the staking securing the hub retaining nut to the groove in the stub axle (see illustrations).

5 Using a socket and long bar, slacken and remove the rear hub nut, and withdraw the thrustwasher. Discard the hub nut - a new nut must used on refitting.

6 Using a puller, draw the hub assembly off the stub axle, along with the outer bearing race. With the hub removed, use the puller to draw the inner bearing race off the stub axle, then remove the oil seal support cup, noting which way around it is fitted (see illustrations).

7 Refit the races to the hub bearing, and check the hub bearing for signs of roughness. It is recommended that the bearing should be renewed as a matter of course, as it is likely to have been damaged during removal. This means that the complete hub assembly must be renewed, since it is not possible to obtain the bearing separately.

8 With the hub removed, examine the stub axle shaft for signs of wear or damage. The stub axle is integral with the trailing arms, and if damaged, the complete assembly must be renewed.

Refitting

9 Lubricate the stub axle shaft with clean engine oil, then slide on the new oil seal support cup, ensuring it is fitted the correct way round.

10 Fit the new bearing inner race, and tap it fully onto the stub axle using a hammer and a tubular drift which bears only on the flat inside edge of the race (see Tool Tip overleaf).

10

Front subframe parts compatibility table - see Section 9

New parts fitted	Parts not renewed	Action to be taken	Bolt dia.
Body shell with M14 subframe fixings	Subframe with M12 mounting bolt holes	Discard M14 cage nuts fitted to body shell (accessible from inside body shell), and fit M12 cage nuts	M12
Subframe with M14 mounting bolt holes	Body shell with M12 subframe fixings	Discard the subframe rear mounting bolts and fit special M12 shouldered bolts	M12
Subframe with M14 mounting bolt holes, and body shell with M14 subframe fixings	None	Fit M14 bolts with plastic protectors	M14

TOOL TIP

Using a socket and the old hub nut to fit the bearing inner race

10.11a Fit the hub assembly . . .

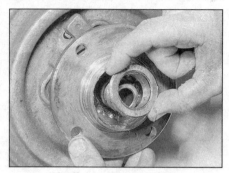

10.11b . . . followed by the outer bearing race . . .

10.12a . . . and the thrustwasher

10.12b Using a hammer and punch . . .

10.12c . . . stake the hub nut firmly into the stub axle groove

11 Ensure that the bearing is packed with grease, then slide the hub assembly onto the stub axle. Fit the new outer bearing race, and tap it into position using a tubular drift until the hub nut can be fitted to finally draw the hub into position (see illustrations).

12 Fit the thrustwasher and new hub nut, and tighten the hub nut to the specified torque. Stake the nut firmly into the groove on the stub axle to secure it in position, then tap the new hub cap into place in the centre of the hub (see illustrations).

13 Refit the rear brake disc, or the brake drum (and shoes, where applicable), as described in Chapter 9.

11 Rear hub bearing - renewal

It is not possible to renew the rear hub bearing separately. If the bearing is worn, the complete rear hub assembly must be renewed. Refer to Section 10 for hub removal and refitting procedures.

12 Rear suspension components - general

1 Although it is possible to remove the rear suspension torsion bars, trailing arms and

anti-roll bar independently of the complete rear axle assembly, it is essential to have special tools available to complete the work successfully (see illustration).

2 Due to the complexity of the tasks, and the requirement for special tools to accurately set the suspension geometry on refitting, the removal and refitting of individual rear suspension components is considered to be beyond the scope of DIY work, and should be entrusted to a Peugeot dealer.

3 Procedures for removal and refitting of the rear shock absorbers, and the complete rear suspension assembly are given in Sections 13 and 14 respectively.

13 Rear shock absorber - removal, testing and refitting

Removal

Note: *New shock absorber mounting nuts must be used on refitting.*

1 Drive the rear of the vehicle onto ramps, then apply the handbrake and chock the front wheels. Do not support the vehicle with the trailing arms hanging unsupported.

2 Where applicable, remove the rear body undershield.

3 Counterhold the bolts, and unscrew the

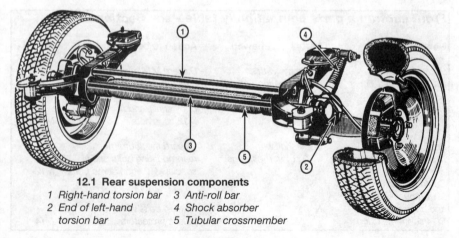

12.1 Rear suspension components
1 Right-hand torsion bar
2 End of left-hand torsion bar
3 Anti-roll bar
4 Shock absorber
5 Tubular crossmember

13.3 Rear shock absorber upper mounting bolt (arrowed)

shock absorber upper and lower securing nuts. Recover the washers **(see illustration)**.

4 Tap the bolts from the mountings to free the shock absorber, then withdraw the unit from under the vehicle.

Testing

5 Examine the shock absorber for signs of fluid leakage or damage. Test the operation of the shock absorber, while holding it in an upright position, by moving the piston through a full stroke and then through short strokes of 50 to 100 mm. In both cases, the resistance felt should be smooth and continuous. If the resistance is jerky, or uneven, or if there is any visible sign of wear or damage, renewal is necessary.

6 Also check the rubber mounting bushes for damage and deterioration. New bushes can be fitted using a long bolt, nut and spacers to draw the bush into position. Lubricate the new bush with soapy water to aid fitting.

7 Inspect the shanks of the mounting bolts for signs of wear or damage, and renew as necessary.

Refitting

8 Prior to refitting the shock absorber, mount it upright in the vice, and operate it fully through several strokes in order to prime it. Apply a smear of multi-purpose grease to both the shock absorber mounting bolts.

9 Manoeuvre the shock absorber into position, and insert its mounting bolts (with washers in place). Note that the bolts fit from the inside of the vehicle, ie the nuts fit on the roadwheel side of the shock absorber.

10 Fit the washers and new nuts to the mounting bolts, but do not tighten the fixings at this stage.

11 Measure the distance between the shock absorber bolt centres, and load the vehicle (by adding weight to the luggage compartment) until a distance of 328.0 mm is obtained between the bolt centres. Tighten the shock absorber mounting nuts and bolts to the specified torque.

12 Drive the vehicle off the ramps.

14 Rear axle assembly - removal and refitting

Removal

Note: *Before carrying out this procedure, it is advisable to run the fuel tank as near empty as possible to minimise the amount of fuel which has to be drained from the tank.*

1 Chock the front wheels, then jack up the rear of the vehicle and support securely on axle stands, until the trailing arms are at maximum extension, with the roadwheels still resting on the ground (see *"Jacking and Vehicle Support"*).

2 Where applicable, remove the rear underbody shield.

3 Remove the rear and intermediate exhaust sections as described in Chapter 4.

4 Empty the fuel tank by either disconnecting the filler pipe and draining, or by siphoning the fuel out through the filler neck. In either case, collect the fuel in a container which can be sealed.

5 Disconnect the fuel filler pipe from the tank (If not already done). Plug the open ends of the tank and the hose to prevent dirt ingress.

6 Remove the rear exhaust heat shield from the underbody.

7 Disconnect the handbrake cables from the adjuster mechanism under the rear underbody, with reference to Chapter 9.

8 Release the handbrake cables from any clips and brackets, and move them clear of the suspension components to facilitate removal.

9 Loosen the fuel tank support rod bolts and nuts as far as possible without removing them, and lower the fuel tank.

10 Disconnect the brake fluid pipes at the unions on the rear suspension assembly, with reference to Chapter 9. Plug the open ends of the unions.

11 On models with a load-sensitive rear brake pressure regulating valve, disconnect the hydraulic pipes at the valve. Again, plug the opens ends of the pipes and the valve.

12 Where applicable, remove the rear ABS wheel sensors. Note that there is no need to

disconnect the wiring connectors, but unclip the wiring harnesses from the rear suspension components, and move the sensors to one side, clear of the working area.

13 Place a trolley jack under the rear suspension tubular crossmember to support the suspension assembly.

14 Make a final check to ensure that all relevant pipes and wires have been disconnected to facilitate removal of the suspension assembly.

15 Using a long-reach splined adapter, unscrew the suspension assembly rear securing bolts, accessible through the holes in the suspension assembly side members **(see illustration)**.

16 Working at the front of the suspension assembly, unscrew the two bolts on each side securing the front mountings to the underbody **(see illustration)**.

17 Lower the trolley jack slightly, and pull the suspension rearwards. If necessary, raise the vehicle body in order for the suspension to clear the fuel tank, then withdraw the suspension assembly from under the vehicle.

Refitting

18 Refitting is a reversal of the removal procedure, bearing in mind the following points.

  a) Tighten all fixings to the specified torque.
  b) Bleed the brake hydraulic system as described in Chapter 9.
  c) Adjust the handbrake mechanism as described in Chapter 9.
  d) On completion, have the rear ride height checked by a Peugeot dealer.

15 Vehicle ride height - checking

Checking of the vehicle ride height requires the use of Peugeot special tools to accurately compress the suspension in a suspension checking bay.

The operation should be entrusted to a Peugeot dealer, as it not possible to carry out checking accurately without the use of the appropriate tools.

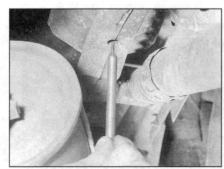

14.15 Using a long-reach splined adapter to unscrew a suspension assembly rear securing bolt

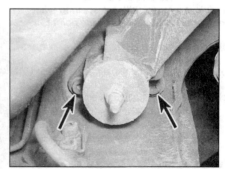

14.16 Unscrew the two bolts (arrowed) on each side securing the suspension mountings to the body

10

16.4 Unscrewing the steering wheel nut

16 Steering wheel -
removal and refitting

Models without air bag

Removal

Note: *A new securing nut and washer must be used on refitting.*

1 Position the front wheel in the straight-ahead position.

2 Prise out the centre trim from the steering wheel.

3 Make alignment marks between the end of the steering column shaft and the steering wheel boss.

4 Using a long-reach socket and extension bar, unscrew the steering wheel securing nut by a few turns **(see illustration)**.

5 Using the palms of the hands, strike the underside of the steering wheel firmly to release the wheel from the column splines.

6 Remove the securing nut, and lift off the steering wheel.

Refitting

7 Refitting is a reversal of removal, but align the marks made before removal, fit a new washer, and tighten the new securing nut to the specified torque.

Models with air bag

Warning: Refer to the precautions given in Chapter 12, Section 24 before proceeding.
Note that the air bag control module is integral with the steering wheel. Additionally, note the following points.

a) *Do not drop the steering wheel, or subject it to impacts.*

b) *Do not attempt to dismantle the steering wheel.*

c) *Do not attempt to fit a steering wheel from another model of vehicle (even a different model of Peugeot 405), as the air bag control module is calibrated for each particular model.*

Removal

Note: *A new securing nut and washer must be used on refitting.*

8 Remove the air bag unit (see Chapter 12).

9 Set the front wheels in the straight-ahead position, and engage the steering lock.

10 Make alignment marks between the end of the steering column shaft and the steering wheel boss.

11 Unscrew the steering wheel retaining nut by several threads.

12 Using the palms of the hands, strike the underside of the steering wheel firmly to release the wheel from the column splines.

13 Separate the two halves of the air bag control unit wiring connector.

14 Remove the steering wheel retaining nut, and recover the washer.

15 Carefully withdraw the steering wheel, feeding the wiring harness (connecting the rotary connector to the air bag control unit) through the wheel as it is withdrawn. Do not disturb the air bag control unit wiring connector (located in the steering wheel).

Refitting

16 Refitting is a reversal of removal, bearing in mind the following points.

a) *Align the marks made before removal.*

b) *Fit a new washer, and tighten the new nut to the specified torque.*

c) *Refit the air bag unit (see Chapter 12).*

17 Steering column - removal, inspection and refitting

Removal

1 Disconnect the battery negative lead.

2 Where applicable, remove the air bag as described in Chapter 12.

3 Remove the steering wheel (see Section 16).

4 Remove the steering column shrouds with reference to Chapter 11.

5 Remove the steering column stalk switches as described in Chapter 12.

6 On models up the 1992, release the securing clips, and lower the fusebox panel from the facia.

7 Working in the footwell, unclip the carpet trim panel from under the facia for access to the steering column pinch-bolt.

8 Working under the steering column, disconnect the three ignition switch wiring connectors **(see illustration)**. Similarly, where applicable disconnect the air bag wiring harness connector.

9 Working in the driver's footwell, make alignment marks on the intermediate shaft and the steering column shaft to aid refitting.

10 Unscrew the clamp bolt securing the steering column shaft to the intermediate shaft **(see illustration)**.

11 Unscrew the two lower steering column securing nuts (models up to 1992) or bolts (models from 1993) **(see illustration)**.

12 Unscrew the upper steering column securing nuts, then withdraw the steering column from the vehicle **(see illustration)**.

13 To remove the intermediate shaft, with the steering column removed, proceed as follows.

a) *Working in the engine compartment, unscrew the shaft-to-steering gear pinion pinch-bolt.*

b) *Withdraw the shaft through the bulkhead grommet into the vehicle interior.*

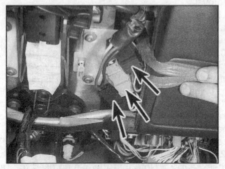

17.8 Ignition switch wiring connectors (arrowed) - models from 1993

17.11 Lower steering column securing nuts (arrowed) - models from 1993

17.10 Unscrewing the steering column shaft-to intermediate shaft clamp bolt

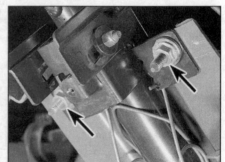

17.12 Steering column upper securing nuts (arrowed) - models up to 1992

Inspection

14 The steering column incorporates a telescopic safety feature. In the event of a front-end crash, the shaft collapses and prevents the steering wheel injuring the driver. Before refitting the steering column, examine the column and mountings for signs of damage and deformation, and renew as necessary.

15 Check the steering column shaft for signs of free play in the column bushes, and check the universal joint for signs of damage or roughness in the joint bearings. If any damage or wear is found on the steering column universal joint or shaft bushes, the column must be renewed as an assembly.

16 Similarly, where applicable, examine the intermediate shaft and renew if the universal joint is worn.

17 If Nyloc-type nuts were used to secure the steering column, these must be renewed as a matter of course.

Refitting

18 Refitting is a reversal of removal, bearing in mind the following points.

19 If the intermediate shaft has been removed, make sure that the bulkhead grommet is not dislodged on refitting.

20 Align the marks made on the intermediate shaft and the steering column shaft before removal.

21 On models fitted with an air bag, do not tighten the column shaft pinch-bolt or refit the trim panel until the procedure given in paragraph 27 has been carried out.

22 Ensure that the column height adjuster lever is in the released position when the column securing nuts/bolts are refitted.

23 Renew any Nyloc nuts.

24 Tighten all fixings to the specified torque.

25 Refit the steering wheel as described in Section 16.

26 Where applicable, refit the air bag as described in Chapter 12.

27 On models with an air bag, on completion, carry out the following procedure.

a) Move the steering column to its fully raised position, then check that the clearance between the rear face of the steering wheel and the front faces of the

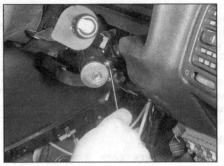

18.5 Unscrewing the lock securing screw

steering column shrouds is 8.0 mm. If the clearance is not as specified, proceed as follows.

b) Loosen the steering column shaft-to-intermediate shaft pinch-bolt, then slide the steering shaft as necessary to give the specified clearance between the steering wheel and the shrouds.

c) Tighten the pinch-bolt, and refit the trim panel.

18 Ignition switch/steering column lock - removal and refitting

Removal

1 Disconnect the battery negative lead.

2 Remove the steering column shrouds as described in Chapter 11.

3 Working under the steering column, locate the three ignition switch wiring connectors, and separate the two halves of each connector. Unclip the connectors from the bracket, and release the wiring harness from any clips.

4 Insert the ignition key and turn it to align with the small arrow on the lock rim.

5 Unscrew the lock securing screw (see illustration).

6 Using a small screwdriver, depress the lock retaining lug, whilst simultaneously pulling the lock from the housing using the key (see illustration).

7 Withdraw the lock assembly, feeding the wiring up through the steering column tube.

18.6 Depress the lock retaining lug, whilst pulling out the lock using the key

8 To separate the ignition switch from the lock, proceed as follows.

a) Remove the two securing screws from the rear of the lock (see illustration).

b) Slide the rear section from the lock body (see illustration).

c) Slide the ignition switch unit from the lock body (see illustration).

Refitting

9 When refitting the ignition switch to the lock, first ensure that the ignition key is removed from the lock, and ensure that the switch wiper is turned anti-clockwise as far as possible. Check that the lugs on the wiper engage with the cut-outs in the lock body.

10 Refit the lock using a reversal of the removal procedure.

19 Steering gear assembly - removal, overhaul and refitting

Removal

Note: All Nyloc nuts disturbed on removal must be renewed as a matter of course. These nuts have threads which are pre-coated with locking compound (this is only effective once).

1 Disconnect the battery negative lead.

2 Apply the handbrake, then jack up the front of the vehicle and support securely on axle stands (see "Jacking and Vehicle Support"). Remove the roadwheels.

3 If desired, to improve access, remove the wheel arch liners, referring to Chapter 11.

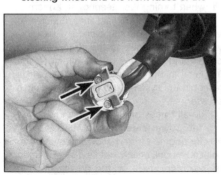

18.8a Remove the two lock securing screws . . .

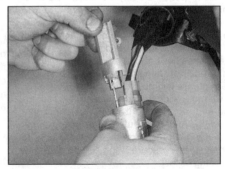

18.8b . . . slide the rear section from the lock body . . .

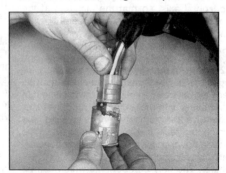

18.8c . . . and slide out the ignition switch

19.8 Using a balljoint separator tool to disconnect the track rod end balljoint

4 On models with power steering, drain the hydraulic fluid as follows.

a) Remove the cap from the fluid reservoir.
b) Place a container under the high pressure fluid pipe union on the steering gear, then unscrew the union.
c) Allow the fluid to drain into the container.
d) Turn the steering from lock-to-lock several times to completely drain the system.
e) Disconnect the low pressure hose from the steering gear.

5 Where applicable, unbolt the heat shield from the steering gear.
6 Prise the cap from the gear linkage pivot, then unscrew the linkage pivot bolt. Move the gear linkage clear of the steering gear, and tie it up out of the way using wire or string.
7 Make alignment marks between the end of the intermediate shaft and the steering gear pinion, then unscrew the clamp bolt securing the intermediate shaft universal joint to the pinion.
8 Working on one side of the vehicle, slacken and partially unscrew the track rod end nut (unscrew the nut as far as the end of the threads on the balljoint to prevent damage to the threads as the joint is released), then release the balljoint using a balljoint separator tool **(see illustration)**. Remove the nut.
9 Repeat the procedure on the remaining side of the vehicle.
10 Unscrew the two bolts securing the steering gear to the subframe. Recover the washers, and spacers, taking careful note of their positions to ensure correct refitting.
11 Rotate the steering gear around its horizontal axis, so that the pinion is at the bottom, then withdraw the assembly from under the right-hand wheel arch.

Overhaul

12 Examine the steering gear assembly for signs of wear or damage, and check that the rack moves freely throughout the full length of its travel, with no signs of roughness or excessive free play between the steering gear pinion and rack. It is possible to overhaul the steering gear assembly housing components, but this task should be entrusted to a Peugeot dealer. The only components which can be renewed easily by the home mechanic are the steering gear gaiters, the track rod balljoints

and the track rods. Track rod, track rod balljoint and steering gear gaiter renewal procedures are covered in Sections 24, 23 and 20 respectively.
13 On models with power steering, inspect all the steering gear fluid unions for signs of leakage, and check that all union nuts are securely tightened. Also examine the steering gear hydraulic ram for signs of fluid leakage or damage, and if necessary renew it.

Refitting

Note: *There have been a number of modifications to the steering gear and the subframe, which alter the dimension of the steering gear-to-subframe mounting points. Different thicknesses of spacer are fitted between the rack and the subframe, and under the mounting bolt heads. Due to the many combinations of different components, and the non-interchangeability of the different components, if either the steering gear or subframe are to be renewed, the advice of a Peugeot dealer should be sought.*

14 Refitting is a reversal of removal, bearing in mind the following points.

a) Use new nuts when reconnecting the track rod ends.
b) Tighten all fixings to the specified torque.
c) On models with power steering, fill and bleed the hydraulic system as described in Section 21.
d) On completion, have the front wheel alignment checked at the earliest opportunity.

20 Steering gear rubber gaiters - renewal

Manual steering gear

1 Remove the track rod balljoint as described in Section 23.
2 Mark the correct fitted position of the gaiter on the track rod, then release the retaining clips and slide the gaiter off the steering gear housing and track rod end.
3 Thoroughly clean the track rod and the steering gear housing, using fine abrasive paper to polish off any corrosion, burrs or sharp edges, which might damage the new gaiter's sealing lips on installation. Scrape off all the grease from the old gaiter, and apply it to the track rod inner balljoint. (This assumes that grease has not been lost or contaminated as a result of damage to the old gaiter. Use fresh grease if in doubt.)
4 Carefully slide the new gaiter onto the track rod end, and locate it on the steering gear housing. Align the outer edge of the gaiter with the mark made on the track rod prior to removal, then secure it in position with new retaining clips.
5 Refit the track rod balljoint as described in Section 23.

Power-assisted steering gear

6 On power-assisted steering gear assemblies, it is only possible to renew the gaiter nearest the drive pinion, ie the right-hand gaiter on right-hand-drive models, and the left-hand gaiter on left-hand-drive models. This can be renewed as described above in paragraphs 1 to 5.
7 The task of renewing the opposite gaiter should be entrusted to a Peugeot dealer. This is necessary since it is not possible to pass the gaiter over the steering rack stud to which the hydraulic ram is fixed. Therefore, the steering gear must be dismantled and the rack removed from the housing to allow the gaiter to be renewed.
8 The only task on this end of the assembly which can be carried out by the home mechanic is the renewal of the track rod inner balljoint dust cover. The dust cover can be renewed once the track rod balljoint has been removed as described in Section 23. On refitting, ensure that the dust cover is correctly located on the track rod and steering rack, then refit the balljoint.

21 Power steering system - bleeding

1 This procedure will only be necessary when any part of the hydraulic system has been disconnected.
2 Referring to *"Weekly Checks"*, remove the fluid reservoir filler cap, and top-up with the specified fluid to the maximum level mark.
3 With the engine stopped, slowly move the steering from lock-to-lock several times to purge out the trapped air, then top-up the level in the fluid reservoir. Repeat this procedure until the fluid level in the reservoir does not drop any further.
4 Start the engine, then slowly move the steering from lock-to-lock several times to purge out any remaining air in the system. Repeat this procedure until bubbles cease to appear in the fluid reservoir.
5 If, when turning the steering, an abnormal noise is heard from the fluid lines, it indicates that there is still air in the system. Check this by turning the wheels to the straight-ahead position and switching off the engine. If the fluid level in the reservoir rises, then air is present in the system, and further bleeding is necessary.
6 Once all traces of air have been removed from the power steering hydraulic system, turn the engine off and allow the system to cool. Once cool, check that fluid level is up to the maximum mark on the power steering fluid reservoir, topping-up if necessary (refer to *"Weekly Checks"* if necessary).

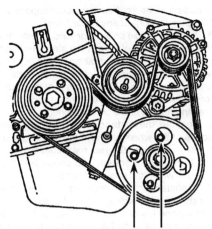

22.8 Unscrew the two front pump mounting bolts (arrowed) - models without air conditioning

22 Power steering pump - removal and refitting

Models without air conditioning

Removal

1 Disconnect the battery negative lead.
2 Drain the fluid from the hydraulic system as follows.

a) Remove the cap from the fluid reservoir.
b) Place a container under the high pressure fluid pipe union on the steering gear, then unscrew the union.
c) Allow the fluid to drain into the container.
d) Turn the steering from lock-to-lock several times to completely drain the system.

3 Apply the handbrake, then jack up the front of the vehicle and support securely on axle stands (see "Jacking and Vehicle Support"). Remove the front right-hand roadwheel.
4 Remove the right-hand wheel arch liner, with reference to Chapter 11 if necessary.
5 Remove the pump drivebelt (see Chapter 1).
6 Unscrew the fluid pipe union, and disconnect the pipe from the pump.
7 Slacken the hose clip, and disconnect the fluid hose from the pump. If the hose clip is of the crimped type, discard it and fit a new worm-drive clip on refitting.
8 Unscrew the two front pump mounting bolts, which can be accessed through the holes in the pump pulley **(see illustration)**.
9 Unscrew the rear pump mounting bolt, and withdraw the pump from the engine **(see illustration)**.

Refitting

10 Refitting is a reversal of removal, bearing in mind the following points.

a) Tighten all fixings to the specified torque.
b) Where applicable, use a new securing clip when reconnecting the fluid hose to the pump.

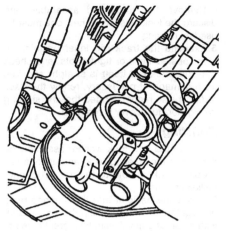

22.9 Pump rear mounting bolt (arrowed) - models without air conditioning

c) Refit and tension the drivebelt as described in Chapter 1.
d) On completion, refill and bleed the system as described in Section 21.

Models with air conditioning

Removal

11 Proceed as described in paragraphs 1 and 2.
12 Remove the pump drivebelt as described in Chapter 1.
13 Unscrew the fluid pipe union, and disconnect the pipe from the pump.
14 Slacken the hose clip, and disconnect the fluid hose from the pump. If the hose clip is of the crimped type, discard it and fit a new worm-drive clip on refitting.
15 Unscrew the three front pump mounting bolts, which can be accessed through the holes in the pump pulley **(see illustration)**.
16 Unscrew the rear pump securing bolt, and withdraw the pump from the engine **(see illustration)**.

Refitting

17 Refer to paragraph 10.

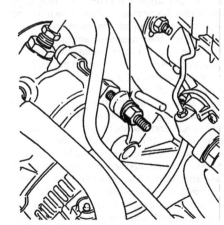

22.16 Unscrew the rear pump securing bolt (arrowed) - models with air conditioning

22.15 Unscrew the three front pump mounting bolts (arrowed) - models with air conditioning

23 Track rod end - removal and refitting

Removal

Note: A new track rod end-to-hub carrier nut must be used on refitting.

1 Apply the handbrake, then jack up the front of the vehicle and support it on axle stands (see "Jacking and Vehicle Support"). Remove the appropriate front roadwheel.
2 If the balljoint is to be re-used, use a straight-edge and a scriber, or similar, to mark its relationship to the track rod.
3 Hold the track rod, and unscrew the track rod end locknut by a quarter of a turn. Do not move the locknut from this position, as it will serve as a handy reference mark on refitting **(see illustration)**.
4 Slacken and partially unscrew the track rod end-to-hub carrier nut (unscrew the nut as far as the end of the threads on the balljoint to prevent damage to the threads as the joint is released), then release the balljoint using a balljoint separator tool **(see illustration)**. Remove the nut.
5 Counting the **exact** number of turns necessary to do so, unscrew the track rod end from the track rod.
6 Count the number of exposed threads between the end of the track rod end and the locknut, and record this figure. If a new track

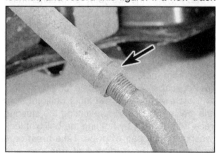

23.3 Track rod end locknut (arrowed)

10

23.4 Disconnecting the track rod end from the hub carrier

rod end is to be fitted, unscrew the locknut from the old track rod end.

7 Carefully clean the balljoint and the threads. Renew the track rod end if its balljoint movement is sloppy or too stiff, if excessively worn, or if damaged in any way; carefully check the stud taper and threads. If the balljoint gaiter is damaged, the complete track rod end assembly must be renewed; it is not possible to obtain the gaiter separately.

Refitting

8 If a new track rod end is to be fitted, screw the locknut onto its threads, and position it so that the same number of exposed threads are visible, as were noted prior to removal.

9 Screw the track rod end onto the track rod by the number of turns noted on removal. This should bring the locknut to within a quarter of a turn of the end face of the track rod, with the alignment marks that were made on removal (if applicable) lined up.

10 Engage the balljoint taper with the hub carrier, then fit a new retaining nut and tighten it to the specified torque.

11 Refit the roadwheel, then lower the vehicle to the ground and tighten the roadwheel bolts to the specified torque.

12 Check and, if necessary, adjust the front wheel toe setting, referring to Section 25, then securely tighten the track rod end locknut.

24 Track rod -
   removal and refitting

Removal

Note: *A new inner balljoint lockwasher must be used on refitting.*

1 Remove the track rod end (see Section 23).

2 Either release the retaining clips and slide the steering gear gaiter off the end of the track rod, or release the track rod balljoint dust cover from rack, and slide it off the track rod (as applicable). See Section 20 for information.

3 Unscrew the track rod inner balljoint from the steering rack end, preventing the steering rack from turning by holding the balljoint lock washer with a pair of grips. Take great care not to mark the surfaces of the rack and balljoint.

4 Remove the track rod assembly, and discard the lock washer - a new one must be used on refitting.

5 Examine the track rod inner balljoint for signs of slackness or tight spots, and check that the track rod itself is straight and free from damage. If necessary, renew the track rod; it is also recommended that the steering gear gaiter/dust cover is renewed.

Refitting

6 Locate the new lock washer assembly on the end of the steering rack, and apply a few drops of locking fluid to the track rod inner balljoint threads.

7 Screw the balljoint into the steering rack, and tighten it whilst retaining the lock washer with a pair of grips. Again, take great care not to damage or mark the track rod balljoint or steering rack.

8 Where a gaiter was removed, carefully slide on the new gaiter, and locate it on the steering gear housing. Turn the steering fully from lock-to-lock, to check that the gaiter is correctly positioned on the track rod, then secure it in position with new retaining clips.

9 Where a dust cover was removed, carefully slide on the new cover, and locate it in its grooves on the steering rack collar and track rod.

25 Wheel alignment and
   steering angles -
   general information

1 Due to the special measuring equipment necessary to accurately check the wheel alignment, and the skill required to use it properly, checking and adjustment is best left to a Peugeot dealer or similar expert. Note that most tyre-fitting shops now possess sophisticated checking equipment. The following is provided as a guide, should the owner decide to carry out a DIY check.

Front wheel toe setting - checking and adjustment

2 The front wheel toe setting is checked by measuring the distance between the front and rear inside edges of the roadwheel rims. Proprietary toe measurement gauges are available from motor accessory shops. Adjustment is made by screwing the balljoints in or out of their track rods, to alter the effective length of the track rod assemblies.

3 For accurate checking, the vehicle must be at the kerb weight, ie unladen and with a full tank of fuel, and the ride height must be correct (see Section 15). Particularly note that the suspension must be compressed to a reference height. Accurate checking and adjustment must be entrusted to a Peugeot dealer. The following information is provided for reference only.

4 Before starting work, check first that the tyre sizes and types are as specified, then check the tyre pressures and tread wear, the roadwheel run-out, the condition of the hub bearings, the steering wheel free play, and the

condition of the front suspension components (Chapter 1). Correct any faults found.

5 Park the vehicle on level ground, check that the front roadwheels are in the straight-ahead position, then rock the rear and front ends to settle the suspension. Release the handbrake, and roll the vehicle backwards 1 metre, then forwards again, to relieve any stresses in the steering and suspension components.

6 Measure the distance between the front edges of the wheel rims and the rear edges of the rims. Subtract the rear measurement from the front measurement, and check that the result is within the specified range.

7 If adjustment is necessary, apply the handbrake, then jack up the front of the vehicle and support it securely on axle stands. Turn the steering wheel onto full-left lock, and record the number of exposed threads on the right-hand track rod end. Now turn the steering onto full-right lock, and record the number of threads on the left-hand side. If there are the same number of threads visible on both sides, then subsequent adjustment should be made equally on both sides. If there are more threads visible on one side than the other, it will be necessary to compensate for this during adjustment. **Note:** *It is most important that after adjustment, the same number of threads are visible on each track rod end.*

8 First clean the track rod end threads; if they are corroded, apply penetrating fluid before starting adjustment. Release the rubber gaiter outboard clips (where necessary), and peel back the gaiters; apply a smear of grease to the inside of the gaiters, so that both are free, and will not be twisted or strained as their respective track rods are rotated.

9 Use a straight-edge and a scriber or similar to mark the relationship of each track rod to its track rod end then, holding each track rod in turn, unscrew its locknut fully.

10 Alter the length of the track rods, bearing in mind the note made in paragraph 8. Screw them into or out of the track rod ends, rotating the track rod using an open-ended spanner fitted to the flats provided. Shortening the track rods (screwing them into their balljoints) will reduce toe-in/increase toe-out.

11 When the setting is correct, hold the track rods and securely tighten the track rod end locknuts. Check that the balljoints are seated correctly in their sockets, and count the exposed threads to check the length of both track rods. If they are not the same, then the adjustment has not been made equally, and problems will be encountered with tyre scrubbing in turns; also, the steering wheel spokes will no longer be horizontal when the wheels are in the straight-ahead position.

12 If the track rod lengths are the same, lower the vehicle to the ground and re-check the toe setting; re-adjust if necessary. When the setting is correct, securely tighten the track rod end locknuts. Ensure that the rubber gaiters are seated correctly, and are not twisted or strained, and secure them in position with new retaining clips (where necessary).

Chapter 11
Bodywork and fittings

Contents

Degrees of difficulty

Easy, suitable for novice with little experience	Fairly easy, suitable for beginner with some experience	Fairly difficult, suitable for competent DIY mechanic	Difficult, suitable for experienced DIY mechanic	Very difficult, suitable for expert DIY or professional

1 General information

The bodyshell is made of pressed steel sections, and is available in 4-door Saloon and 5-door Estate configuration. Most components are welded together, but some use is made of structural adhesives. The front wings are bolted on.

The bonnet, doors and some other vulnerable panels are made of zinc-coated metal, and are further protected by being coated with an anti-chip primer prior to being sprayed.

Extensive use is made of plastic materials, mainly in the interior, but also in exterior components. The front and rear bumpers and the front grille are injection-moulded from a synthetic material which is very strong, and yet light. Plastic components such as wheel arch liners are fitted to the underside of the vehicle, to improve the body's resistance to corrosion.

2 Maintenance - bodywork and underframe

The general condition of a vehicle's bodywork is the one thing that significantly affects its value. Maintenance is easy, but needs to be regular. Neglect, particularly after minor damage, can lead quickly to further deterioration and costly repair bills. It is important also to keep watch on those parts of the vehicle not immediately visible, for instance the underside, inside all the wheel arches, and the lower part of the engine compartment.

The basic maintenance routine for the bodywork is washing - preferably with a lot of water, from a hose. This will remove all the loose solids which may have stuck to the vehicle. It is important to flush these off in such a way as to prevent grit from scratching the finish. The wheel arches and underframe need washing in the same way, to remove any accumulated mud which will retain moisture and tend to encourage rust. Strangely enough, the best time to clean the underframe and wheel arches is in wet weather, when the mud is thoroughly wet and soft. In very wet weather, the underframe is usually cleaned of large accumulations automatically, and this is a good time for inspection.

Periodically, except on vehicles with a wax-based underbody protective coating, it is a good idea to have the whole of the underframe of the vehicle steam-cleaned, engine compartment included, so that a thorough inspection can be carried out to see what minor repairs and renovations are necessary. Steam-cleaning is available at many garages, and is necessary for the removal of the accumulation of oily grime, which sometimes is allowed to become thick in certain areas. If steam-cleaning facilities are not available, there are one or two excellent grease solvents available, which can be brush-applied; the dirt can then be simply hosed off. Note that these methods should not be used on vehicles with wax-based underbody protective coating, or the coating will be removed. Such vehicles should be inspected annually, preferably just prior to Winter, when the underbody should be washed down, and any damage to the wax coating repaired. Ideally, a completely fresh coat should be applied. It would also be worth considering the use of such wax-based protection for injection into door panels, sills, box sections, etc, as an additional safeguard against rust damage, where such protection is not provided by the vehicle manufacturer.

After washing paintwork, wipe off with a chamois leather to give an unspotted clear finish. A coat of clear protective wax polish will give added protection against chemical pollutants in the air. If the paintwork sheen has dulled or oxidised, use a cleaner/polisher combination to restore the brilliance of the shine. This requires a little effort, but such dulling is usually caused because regular washing has been neglected. Care needs to be taken with metallic paintwork, as special non-abrasive cleaner/polisher is required to

11

avoid damage to the finish. Always check that the door and ventilator opening drain holes and pipes are completely clear, so that water can be drained out. Brightwork should be treated in the same way as paintwork. Windscreens and windows can be kept clear of the smeary film which often appears, by the use of proprietary glass cleaner. Never use any form of wax or other body or chromium polish on glass.

3 Maintenance - upholstery and carpets

Mats and carpets should be brushed or vacuum-cleaned regularly, to keep them free of grit. If they are badly stained, remove them from the vehicle for scrubbing or sponging, and make quite sure they are dry before refitting. Seats and interior trim panels can be kept clean by wiping with a damp cloth. If they do become stained (which can be more apparent on light-coloured upholstery), use a little liquid detergent and a soft nail brush to scour the grime out of the grain of the material. Do not forget to keep the headlining clean in the same way as the upholstery. When using liquid cleaners inside the vehicle, do not over-wet the surfaces being cleaned. Excessive damp could get into the seams and padded interior, causing stains, offensive odours or even rot. If the inside of the vehicle gets wet accidentally, it is worthwhile taking some trouble to dry it out properly, particularly where carpets are involved. *Do not leave oil or electric heaters inside the vehicle for this purpose.*

4 Minor body damage - repair

Repairs of minor scratches in bodywork

If the scratch is very superficial, and does not penetrate to the metal of the bodywork, repair is very simple. Lightly rub the area of the scratch with a paintwork renovator, or a very fine cutting paste, to remove loose paint from the scratch, and to clear the surrounding bodywork of wax polish. Rinse the area with clean water.

Apply touch-up paint to the scratch using a fine paint brush; continue to apply fine layers of paint until the surface of the paint in the scratch is level with the surrounding paintwork. Allow the new paint at least two weeks to harden, then blend it into the surrounding paintwork by rubbing the scratch area with a paintwork renovator or a very fine cutting paste. Finally, apply wax polish.

Where the scratch has penetrated right through to the metal of the bodywork, causing the metal to rust, a different repair technique is required. Remove any loose rust from the bottom of the scratch with a penknife, then apply rust-inhibiting paint, to prevent the formation of rust in the future. Using a rubber or nylon applicator, fill the scratch with bodystopper paste. If required, this paste can be mixed with cellulose thinners, to provide a very thin paste which is ideal for filling narrow scratches. Before the stopper-paste in the scratch hardens, wrap a piece of smooth cotton rag around the top of a finger. Dip the finger in cellulose thinners, and quickly sweep it across the surface of the stopper-paste in the scratch; this will ensure that the surface of the stopper-paste is slightly hollowed. The scratch can now be painted over as described earlier in this Section.

Repairs of dents in bodywork

When deep denting of the vehicle's bodywork has taken place, the first task is to pull the dent out, until the affected bodywork almost attains its original shape. There is little point in trying to restore the original shape completely, as the metal in the damaged area will have stretched on impact, and cannot be reshaped fully to its original contour. It is better to bring the level of the dent up to a point which is about 3 mm below the level of the surrounding bodywork. In cases where the dent is very shallow anyway, it is not worth trying to pull it out at all. If the underside of the dent is accessible, it can be hammered out gently from behind, using a mallet with a wooden or plastic head. Whilst doing this, hold a suitable block of wood firmly against the outside of the panel, to absorb the impact from the hammer blows and thus prevent a large area of the bodywork from being "belled-out".

Should the dent be in a section of the bodywork which has a double skin, or some other factor making it inaccessible from behind, a different technique is called for. Drill several small holes through the metal inside the area - particularly in the deeper section. Then screw long self-tapping screws into the holes, just sufficiently for them to gain a good purchase in the metal. Now the dent can be pulled out by pulling on the protruding heads of the screws with a pair of pliers.

The next stage of the repair is the removal of the paint from the damaged area, and from an inch or so of the surrounding "sound" bodywork. This is accomplished most easily by using a wire brush or abrasive pad on a power drill, although it can be done just as effectively by hand, using sheets of abrasive paper. To complete the preparation for filling, score the surface of the bare metal with a screwdriver or the tang of a file, or alternatively, drill small holes in the affected area. This will provide a really good "key" for the filler paste.

To complete the repair, see the Section on filling and respraying.

Repairs of rust holes or gashes in bodywork

Remove all paint from the affected area, and from an inch or so of the surrounding "sound" bodywork, using an abrasive pad or a wire brush on a power drill. If these are not available, a few sheets of abrasive paper will do the job most effectively. With the paint removed, you will be able to judge the severity of the corrosion, and therefore decide whether to renew the whole panel (if this is possible) or to repair the affected area. New body panels are not as expensive as most people think, and it is often quicker and more satisfactory to fit a new panel than to attempt to repair large areas of corrosion.

Remove all fittings from the affected area, except those which will act as a guide to the original shape of the damaged bodywork (eg headlamp shells etc). Then, using tin snips or a hacksaw blade, remove all loose metal and any other metal badly affected by corrosion. Hammer the edges of the hole inwards, in order to create a slight depression for the filler paste.

Wire-brush the affected area to remove the powdery rust from the surface of the remaining metal. Paint the affected area with rust-inhibiting paint; if the back of the rusted area is accessible, treat this also.

Before filling can take place, it will be necessary to block the hole in some way. This can be achieved by the use of aluminium or plastic mesh, or aluminium tape.

Aluminium or plastic mesh, or glass-fibre matting is probably the best material to use for a large hole. Cut a piece to the approximate size and shape of the hole to be filled, then position it in the hole so that its edges are below the level of the surrounding bodywork. It can be retained in position by several blobs of filler paste around its periphery.

Aluminium tape should be used for small or very narrow holes. Pull a piece off the roll, trim it to the approximate size and shape required, then pull off the backing paper (if used) and stick the tape over the hole; it can be overlapped if the thickness of one piece is insufficient. Burnish down the edges of the tape with the handle of a screwdriver or similar, to ensure that the tape is securely attached to the metal underneath.

Bodywork repairs - filling and respraying

Before using this Section, see the Sections on dent, deep scratch, rust holes and gash repairs.

Many types of bodyfiller are available, but generally speaking, those proprietary kits which contain a tin of filler paste and a tube of resin hardener are best for this type of repair. A wide, flexible plastic or nylon applicator will be found invaluable for imparting a smooth and well-contoured finish to the surface of the filler.

Mix up a little filler on a clean piece of card or board - measure the hardener carefully (follow the maker's instructions on the pack), otherwise the filler will set too rapidly or too slowly. Using the applicator, apply the filler paste to the prepared area; draw the applicator across the surface of the filler to achieve the correct contour and to level the surface. As soon as a contour that approximates to the correct one is achieved, stop working the paste - if you carry on too long, the paste will become sticky and begin to "pick-up" on the applicator. Continue to add thin layers of filler paste at 20-minute intervals, until the level of the filler is just proud of the surrounding bodywork.

Once the filler has hardened, the excess can be removed using a metal plane or file. From then on, progressively-finer grades of abrasive paper should be used, starting with a 40-grade production paper, and finishing with a 400-grade wet-and-dry paper. Always wrap the abrasive paper around a flat rubber, cork, or wooden block - otherwise the surface of the filler will not be completely flat. During the smoothing of the filler surface, the wet-and-dry paper should be periodically rinsed in water. This will ensure that a very smooth finish is imparted to the filler at the final stage.

At this stage, the "dent" should be surrounded by a ring of bare metal, which in turn should be encircled by the finely "feathered" edge of the good paintwork. Rinse the repair area with clean water, until all of the dust produced by the rubbing-down operation has gone.

Spray the whole area with a light coat of primer - this will show up any imperfections in the surface of the filler. Repair these imperfections with fresh filler paste or bodystopper, and once more smooth the surface with abrasive paper. If bodystopper is used, it can be mixed with cellulose thinners, to form a really thin paste which is ideal for filling small holes. Repeat this spray-and-repair procedure until you are satisfied that the surface of the filler, and the feathered edge of the paintwork, are perfect. Clean the repair area with clean water, and allow to dry fully.

The repair area is now ready for final spraying. Paint spraying must be carried out in a warm, dry, windless and dust-free atmosphere. This condition can be created artificially if you have access to a large indoor working area, but if you are forced to work in the open, you will have to pick your day very carefully. If you are working indoors, dousing the floor in the work area with water will help to settle the dust which would otherwise be in the atmosphere. If the repair area is confined to one body panel, mask off the surrounding panels; this will help to minimise the effects of a slight mis-match in paint colours. Bodywork fittings (eg chrome strips, door handles etc) will also need to be masked off. Use genuine masking tape, and several thicknesses of newspaper, for the masking operations.

Before commencing to spray, agitate the aerosol can thoroughly, then spray a test area (an old tin, or similar) until the technique is mastered. Cover the repair area with a thick coat of primer; the thickness should be built up using several thin layers of paint, rather than one thick one. Using 400 grade wet-and-dry paper, rub down the surface of the primer until it is really smooth. While doing this, the work area should be thoroughly doused with water, and the wet-and-dry paper periodically rinsed in water. Allow to dry before spraying on more paint.

Spray on the top coat, again building up the thickness by using several thin layers of paint. Start spraying in the centre of the repair area, and then, using a circular motion, work outwards until the whole repair area and about 2 inches of the surrounding original paintwork is covered. Remove all masking material 10 to 15 minutes after spraying on the final coat of paint.

Allow the new paint at least two weeks to harden, then, using a paintwork renovator or a very fine cutting paste, blend the edges of the paint into the existing paintwork. Finally, apply wax polish.

Plastic components

With the use of more and more plastic body components by the vehicle manufacturers (eg bumpers. spoilers, and in some cases major body panels), rectification of more serious damage to such items has become a matter of either entrusting repair work to a specialist in this field, or renewing complete components. Repair of such damage by the DIY owner is not really feasible, owing to the cost of the equipment and materials required for effecting such repairs. The basic technique involves making a groove along the line of the crack in the plastic, using a rotary burr in a power drill. The damaged part is then welded back together, using a hot air gun to heat up and fuse a plastic filler rod into the groove. Any excess plastic is then removed, and the area rubbed down to a smooth finish. It is important that a filler rod of the correct plastic is used, as body components can be made of a variety of different types (eg polycarbonate, ABS, polypropylene).

Damage of a less serious nature (abrasions, minor cracks etc) can be repaired by the DIY owner using a two-part epoxy filler repair. Once mixed in equal parts, this is used in similar fashion to the bodywork filler used on metal panels. The filler is usually cured in twenty to thirty minutes, ready for sanding and painting.

If the owner is renewing a complete component himself, or if he has repaired it with epoxy filler, he will be left with the problem of finding a suitable paint for finishing which is compatible with the type of plastic used. At one time, the use of a universal paint was not possible, owing to the complex range of plastics encountered in body component applications. Standard paints, generally

speaking, will not bond to plastic or rubber satisfactorily, but suitable paints to match any plastic or rubber finish, can be obtained from dealers. However, it is now possible to obtain a plastic body parts finishing kit which consists of a pre-primer treatment, a primer and coloured top coat. Full instructions are normally supplied with a kit, but basically, the method of use is to first apply the pre-primer to the component concerned, and allow it to dry for up to 30 minutes. Then the primer is applied, and left to dry for about an hour before finally applying the special-coloured top coat. The result is a correctly-coloured component, where the paint will flex with the plastic or rubber, a property that standard paint does not normally posses.

---

5 Major body damage - repair

Where serious damage has occurred, or large areas need renewal due to neglect, it means that complete new panels will need welding-in, and this is best left to professionals. If the damage is due to impact, it will also be necessary to check completely the alignment of the bodyshell, and this can only be carried out accurately by a Peugeot dealer using special jigs. If the body is left misaligned, it is primarily dangerous, as the car will not handle properly, and secondly, uneven stresses will be imposed on the steering, suspension and possibly transmission, causing abnormal wear, or complete failure, particularly to such items as the tyres.

---

6 Front bumper -
removal and refitting

Removal

1 Working at the bottom of the bumper, remove the three lower bumper securing screws **(see illustration)**.
2 Working on one side of the vehicle, remove the three screws securing the outer edge of the wheel arch liner, then pull the liner back from the bumper.

6.1 Front bumper lower securing screw

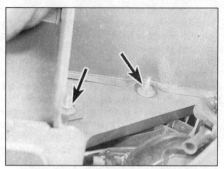

6.3 Front bumper front securing nuts (arrowed)

3 Unscrew the two bumper front securing nuts **(see illustration)**.
4 Unscrew the bolt securing the side of the bumper to the wing panel **(see illustration)**.
5 Repeat the procedure in paragraphs 2 to 4 on the remaining side of the vehicle.
6 Pull the bumper forwards and, where applicable, disconnect the front foglight wiring harness and/or the headlight washer fluid hose. Note the routing of the wiring and/or hose.
7 Remove the bumper.

Refitting

8 Refitting is a reversal of removal but, where applicable, ensure that the foglight wiring and/or washer fluid hose are correctly routed.

7 Rear bumper - removal and refitting

Saloon models

Removal

1 To improve access, chock the front wheels, then jack up the rear of the vehicle and support securely on axle stands (see *"Jacking and Vehicle Support"*).
2 Remove the fixings, and withdraw the rear wheel arch liners (access to the fixings can be improved by removing the rear roadwheels) **(see illustration)**.
3 Unscrew the bumper side securing bolts (one bolt on each side).

7.12 Rear bumper side securing bolt (arrowed) - Estate model

6.4 Front bumper side securing bolt (arrowed)

4 Working under the bottom of the bumper, unscrew the two lower securing bolts.
5 Working in the luggage compartment, locate the number plate light wiring connector, next to the left-hand rear light assembly, and separate the two halves of the connector.
6 Pull the carpet trim panel away from the rear edge of the luggage compartment to expose the two remaining bumper securing bolts.
7 Pull the bumper rearwards, and feed the number plate light wiring harness through the grommet in the rear body panel.

Refitting

8 Refitting is a reversal of removal.

Estate models

Removal

9 Proceed as described in paragraphs 1 and 2.

7.2 Removing a rear wheel arch liner

7.13 Rear bumper side securing bolts (arrowed) - Estate model

10 On models with rear underbody shields fitted under the sides of the bumper, release the exhaust system from its rear mounting (loosen the clamp if necessary), then lower the rear of the system for access to the left-hand rear underbody shield.
11 Where applicable, remove the rear underbody shield(s) to expose the bumper side fixing bolts **(see illustration)**.
12 Unscrew the bumper side securing bolts (one bolt on each side) **(see illustration)**.
13 Unscrew the two bolts on each side, securing the bumper to the underbody brackets, then pull the bumper rearwards from the vehicle **(see illustration)**.

Refitting

14 Refitting is a reversal of removal.

8 Bonnet - removal, refitting and adjustment

Removal

1 Open the bonnet and have an assistant support it, then, using a pencil or felt tip pen, mark the outline position of each bonnet hinge relative to the bonnet, to use as a guide on refitting.
2 Where applicable, unbolt the earth strap from the bonnet.
3 Unscrew the bonnet bolts and, with the help of the assistant, carefully lift the bonnet from the vehicle **(see illustration)**. Store the bonnet out of the way in a safe place.

7.11 Rear underbody shield securing clip (arrowed) - Estate model

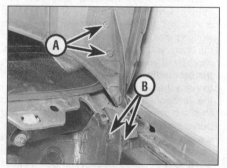

8.3 Hinge-to-bonnet bolts (A) and hinge-to-body bolts (B)

9.3 Bonnet release lever securing bolts (arrowed) - lever mounted on right-hand side

4 Inspect the bonnet hinges for signs of wear and free play at the pivots, and if necessary renew. Each hinge is secured to the body by two bolts. On refitting, apply a smear of multi-purpose grease to the hinges.

Refitting and adjustment

5 With the aid of an assistant, offer up the bonnet and loosely fit the retaining bolts. Align the hinges with the marks made on removal, then tighten the retaining bolts securely.
6 Close the bonnet, and check for alignment with the adjacent panels. If necessary, slacken the hinge bolts and re-align the bonnet to suit. Once the bonnet is correctly aligned, tighten the hinge bolts. Note that the alignment of the bonnet can also be adjusted using the rubber bump stops fitted to the body front panel. To adjust a bump stop, loosen the locknut, then turn the buffer as required, and tighten the locknut.
7 Once the bonnet is correctly aligned, check that the bonnet fastens and releases in a satisfactory manner. If adjustment is necessary, slacken the bonnet striker lock nut and adjust the position of the striker to suit. Once the lock is operating correctly, securely tighten the striker lock nut.

9 Bonnet release cable - removal and refitting

General

1 The cable is in two parts, joined at a connecting plate in the engine compartment. The release lever may be on the left- or right-hand side of the facia, depending on model.

Release lever-to-connecting plate cable - models with release lever on right-hand side of facia

Removal

2 Working inside the vehicle, release the securing clips and drop the fusebox panel down from the facia.
3 Remove the two bolts securing the bonnet release lever to the bracket under the facia (see illustration).

9.5 Disconnecting the bonnet release cable from the connector behind the front body panel

4 Working in the engine compartment, locate the cable connecting plate, positioned behind the body front panel, above the radiator.
5 Where applicable, remove the anti-squeal foam from the cable connector, then disconnect the cable from the connector (see illustration).
6 Work around the engine compartment, and release the cable from any clips and brackets.
7 Tie a length of string to the end of the cable in the engine compartment, then pull the cable through into the vehicle interior, noting its routing.
8 Untie the string from the end of the cable, and leave it in position to aid refitting.

Refitting

9 Commence refitting by tying the end of the new cable to the string in the vehicle interior.
10 Use the string to pull the cable through into the engine compartment, routing it as noted before removal.
11 Make sure that the bulkhead grommet is securely seated in the bulkhead aperture.
12 Further refitting is a reversal of removal.

Release lever-to-connecting plate cable - models with release lever on left-hand side of facia

Removal

13 Working under the facia, remove the release lever securing bolt, and withdraw the lever from the side of the footwell.
14 Proceed as described previously in paragraphs 4 to 8.

Refitting

15 Proceed as described previously in paragraphs 9 to 12.

Connecting plate-to-lock cable

Removal

16 Working in the engine compartment, locate the cable connecting plate, which is at the front of the engine compartment.
17 Where applicable, remove the anti-squeal foam from the cable connector; disconnect the release lever cable from the connector.
18 Disconnect the end of the cable from the lock, then unclip the cable outer from the bracket on the lock, release the cable from any clips on the body, and withdraw the

cable, noting its routing. If desired, access to the lock can be improved by removing the front grille panel (see Section 25).

Refitting

19 Refitting is a reversal of removal.

10 Bonnet lock - removal and refitting

Removal

1 Open the bonnet.
2 Unscrew the two bolts, then withdraw the lock and disconnect the end of the release cable from the lock lever (see illustration).

10.2 Bonnet lock securing bolts (arrowed)

Refitting

3 Refitting is a reversal of removal, but on completion, the operation of the lock.
4 If necessary, adjust the position of the lock striker on the bonnet (loosen the locknut to enable the striker to be moved), until the lock operation is satisfactory.

11 Body front panel assembly - removal and refitting

 Warning: On models with air conditioning, the bolts securing the condenser and the reservoir to the front panel must be removed. Where the front panel is being removed for engine removal, the compressor must also be unbolted from the engine, which will then allow the complete assembly to be moved clear for engine removal. Do not disconnect any refrigerant pipelines unless the system has been recharged - see the precautions in Chapter 3.

Removal

1 Open the bonnet.
2 Disconnect the battery negative lead.
3 To improve access, apply the handbrake, then jack up the front of the vehicle and support securely on axle stands (see "Jacking and Vehicle Support").
4 Remove the front wheel arch liners, with reference to Section 25.

11

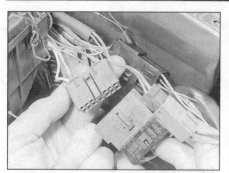

11.7a Disconnecting the front light wiring connectors - models up to 1992

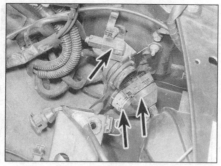

11.7b Disconnect the front light wiring connectors (arrowed) . . .

11.7c . . . and disconnect the plug from the terminal block - models from 1993

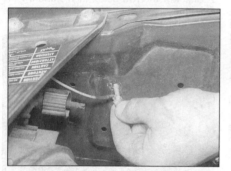

11.8 Unbolt the earth leads from the corners of the engine compartment

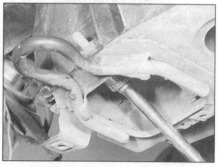

11.12 Removing a body front panel lower securing bolt

11.14 Unscrew the body front panel upper securing bolts

11.16 Withdrawing the body front panel assembly

5 Remove the front bumper, as described in Section 6.

6 Remove the front direction indicator lights, as described in Chapter 12.

7 Disconnect the front light wiring connectors, located at each front corner of the engine compartment on models up to 1992, or in the right-hand corner of the engine compartment on models from 1993 **(see illustrations)**.

8 Unbolt the earth leads from the front corners of the engine compartment **(see illustration)**.

9 Where applicable, remove the headlight adjusters from the brackets on the front panel, with reference to Chapter 12.

10 Where applicable, disconnect the headlight washer tubes.

11 Locate the bonnet release cable connecting plate, which is positioned at the top of the body front panel. Where applicable,

remove the anti-squeal foam from the cable connector, then disconnect the release lever cable from the connector. Unclip the cable from the front panel assembly.

12 Unscrew the bolts securing the bottom of the front panel to the lower crossmember - there may be two or three bolts, depending on model **(see illustration)**.

13 Remove the radiator as described in Chapter 3, but note that provided the radiator is adequately supported in the engine compartment, there is no need to disconnect the coolant hoses (this will avoid the need to drain the cooling system).

14 Remove the two upper securing bolts from each end of the front panel **(see illustration)**.

15 Carefully release the clips securing the lower headlight trim strips to the front wings.

16 Make a final check to ensure that all relevant wiring has been disconnected to enable removal of the front panel assembly, then withdraw the assembly forwards from the front of the vehicle **(see illustration)**.

Refitting

17 Refitting is a reversal of removal.

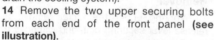

12 Door - removal, refitting and adjustment

Removal

1 The door hinges are welded to the body pillar, and bolted to the door.

2 Where applicable, prise the plastic caps from the hinge pins.

3 Using a pin-punch, drive the roll-pin from the door check strap **(see illustration)**.

4 On models with electrical components inside the door, remove the door trim panel with reference to Section 13. Working inside the door, disconnect all the wiring harness plugs, then feed the wiring through the hole in the front edge of the door. Note the routing of the wiring harness to ensure correct refitting.

5 The door must now be supported in the fully open position.

> **HAYNES HiNT**
> *Support the door by placing blocks of wood, or a jack and block of wood, under its lower edge.*

12.3 Drive the roll-pin (arrowed) from the door check strap

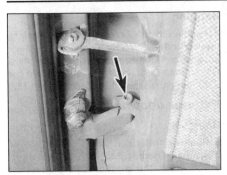

12.6 Door pivot pin (arrowed)

6 Ensure that the door is adequately supported, then unscrew the pivot pins from the hinges **(see illustration)**.
7 Lift the door from the vehicle.

Refitting

8 Refitting is a reversal of removal, noting that the hinge pins fit with their heads towards each other, ie, the upper pin fits from below the hinge, and the lower pin fits from above the hinge.
9 On completion, check the fit of the door with the surrounding body panels. On early models, the fit of the doors can be adjusted as described in paragraph 11.
10 If adjustment of the door lock is required, this can be achieved by altering the position of the lock striker within the elongated bolt holes in the body pillar.

Adjustment - early models only

11 The fit of the door can be adjusted using

shims fitted between the hinge and the door. To add or remove shims, loosen the bolts securing the hinge to the door (the door inner trim panel must be removed for access to the bolts - see Section 13), then fit or remove shims as necessary.

13 Door inner trim panel - removal and refitting

Removal

1 If the trim is being in removed in order to remove the window glass, lower the window to approximately the two-thirds open position.
2 Carefully prise the surround from the door interior handle **(see illustration)**.
3 Remove the loudspeaker cover panel, either by depressing the securing clip at the lower edge of the panel, or by removing the three securing screws from the edge of the panel, as applicable **(see illustration)**.
4 Unscrew the securing screws, withdraw the loudspeaker, and disconnect the wiring.
5 Lift up the inner door lock operating button then, using a small screwdriver, depress the retaining tab, and slide off the button **(see illustration)**.
6 On models with manually-operated windows, carefully pull the window regulator handle from the door.
7 On models with electric windows, disconnect the battery negative lead, then prise the switches from the door, and disconnect the wiring plugs **(see illustration)**.

8 Prise the mirror trim plate from the front corner of the door **(see illustration)**. Where applicable, loosen the clamp screw, and release the mirror adjuster knob from the trim plate.
9 Remove the securing screws and withdraw the armrest (where applicable, prise the trim plate from the armrest to expose the screws) **(see illustration)**.
10 On later models, prise the trim plate from the rear of the door pocket, and unscrew the rear trim panel securing screw **(see illustration)**.
11 Where applicable, using a screwdriver, release the trim panel securing clip located in the loudspeaker aperture.
12 Working around the edge of the door, release the remaining securing clips around the edge of the trim panel, ideally using a forked tool to avoid breaking the clips.
13 Lift the panel to release it from the top of the door, then withdraw the panel. Where applicable, disconnect the wiring plug from

13.2 Removing the door interior handle surround

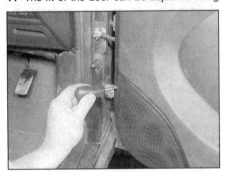

13.3 Removing a loudspeaker cover panel securing screw

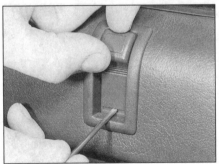

13.5 Depress the retaining tab and slide off the lock operating button

13.7 Removing an electric window switch from the door

13.8 Prise off the mirror trim plate

13.9 Remove the securing screws and withdraw the armrest

13.10 Removing the rear door trim panel securing screw - later model

11

13.14a Position the lock button locating tab in the lower position

13.14b Push the button onto the rod until retaining tab appears in upper hole (arrowed)

the electric windows control unit, which is located on a bracket attached to the rear of the door trim panel.

Refitting

14 Refitting is a reversal of removal, bearing in mind the following points.

a) *Before refitting, check whether any of the trim panel retaining clips were broken on removal, and renew as necessary.*

b) *Ensure that the weatherstrip (with the metal reinforcing strip) is in place on the top of the trim panel before refitting, and check that the weatherstrip engages correctly with the weatherstrip on the door as the trim panel is refitted.*

c) *To refit the inner door lock operating button, first lock the door to ensure that the link rod is in its lowest position. Position the button locating tab in the lower of its two holes, then firmly push*

the button onto the rod until it clips into position and the retaining tab appears in the upper hole (see illustrations).

14 Door handle and lock components - removal and refitting

Interior door handle

Removal

1 Remove the door inner trim panel as described in Section 13.

2 If necessary, peel the plastic sealing sheet from around the handle assembly.

3 Slide the handle assembly towards the front of the door, then pull the assembly from the trim panel and disconnect the link rod **(see illustration)**. If necessary, release the link rod from the clips on the door.

Refitting

4 Refitting is a reversal of removal, ensuring the link rod is correctly reconnected. Where applicable, fit a new sealing sheet if the sheet was damaged during removal, and refit the door trim panel with reference to Section 13.

Exterior door handle

Removal

5 Remove the door inner trim panel as described in Section 13.

6 Peel back the plastic sealing sheet for access to the handle securing nut.

7 Unscrew the handle securing nut then, where applicable, manipulate the plastic shield from the rear of the lock **(see illustrations)**.

8 Withdraw the handle from outside the door, and disconnect the lock operating rod from the handle as it is removed **(see illustration)**.

Refitting

9 Refitting is a reversal of removal, ensuring that the link rod is correctly reconnected. Fit a new sealing sheet if the sheet was damaged during removal, and refit the door trim panel with reference to Section 13.

Front door lock cylinder

10 The lock cylinder can be removed as follows, without the need to remove the door inner trim panel. If no facilities are available to make up the tools, proceed to paragraph 11.

a) *Make up two suitable tools, using a medium-size self-tapping screw brazed to a length of rod for each tool (see illustration).*

14.3 Unhooking the link rod from the interior door handle

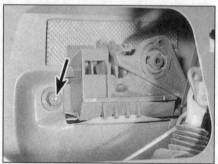

14.7a Exterior door handle securing nut (arrowed) - early model

14.7b Unscrew the securing nut . . .

14.7c . . . and withdraw the plastic shield - later model

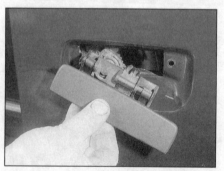

14.8 Withdrawing the exterior door handle

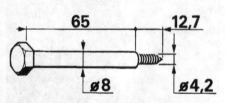

65   12,7

ø8   ø4,2

14.10a Tool for removing door lock cylinder

All dimensions in mm

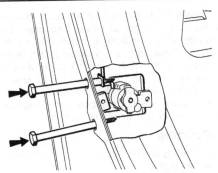

14.10b Using the improvised tools to release the lock cylinder securing clip

14.13b . . . then withdraw the lock cylinder

b) *Open the door, and prise the cover plates from the rear edge of the door.*
c) *Insert the tools through the aperture in the edge of the door, and screw the tools into the lock securing clip as far as the ends of the threads on the self-tapping screws.*
d) *Push the tools to release the securing clip, and withdraw the lock cylinder from outside the door (see illustration). Leave the tools engaged with the clip.*
e) *Refit the lock, and use the tools to pull the securing clip into position.*
f) *Ensure the clip is securely engaged with the lock cylinder, then unscrew the tools from the clip, and refit the cover plates.*

Removal

11 Remove the door inner trim panel as described in Section 13.
12 Peel back the plastic sealing sheet for access to the lock cylinder securing clip.
13 Working inside the door, pull the clip from the rear of the lock cylinder, then remove the lock cylinder from outside the door **(see illustrations)**.

Refitting

14 Refitting is a reversal of removal, but ensure that the lock cylinder clip is securely refitted. Fit a new sealing sheet if the sheet was damaged during removal, and refit the door trim panel with reference to Section 13.

Door lock

Removal

15 Remove the door interior handle and the exterior handle, as described previously in this Section.

14.13a Remove the securing clip . . .

14.16 Remove the door lock securing screws

16 Working at the rear edge of the door, unscrew the three lock securing screws **(see illustration)**.
17 Where applicable, disconnect the wiring plug from the central locking motor on the lock assembly.
18 Lower the lock assembly into the door, and manipulate the lock operating rods until the assembly can be withdrawn through the door aperture. If it proves necessary to disconnect any of the rods, carefully note the routing and location to ensure correct refitting.

Refitting

19 Refitting is a reversal of removal, but ensure that the lock operating rods are correctly located and routed, and refit the door exterior and interior handles as described previously in this Section.

---

15 Door window glass and regulator - removal and refitting

Front door window glass

Removal

1 Remove the door inner trim panel as described in Section 13.
2 Lower the window glass two-thirds of the way.
3 Carefully peel the plastic sealing sheet from the door.
4 Pull the weatherstrip from the lower edge of the window aperture.

5 Partially pull the weatherstrip from the rear and upper edge of the window aperture.
6 Where applicable, disconnect the electric window motor wiring connector, and move the wiring harness to one side.
7 It is now necessary to release the clip securing the window glass to the regulator mechanism.
8 On models up to 1992, this is a difficult operation, as the lugs on the clip must be released from behind the glass. Peugeot tool (-)7.1309 is available for this purpose, but the tool can be improvised by drilling a hole of suitable diameter in a small block of wood or plastic. Push the tool onto the rear of the clip to compress the lugs, whilst at the same time pushing the window glass to release it from the clip **(see illustration)**.
9 On models from 1993, the clip is fitted behind the glass, and can be released by reaching in through the door aperture and turning the clip through a quarter-turn.
10 Lift the glass out through the outside of the window aperture.

Refitting

11 Refitting is a reversal of removal, bearing in mind the following points.
a) *On models up to 1992, ensure that the clip securing the glass to the regulator is securely engaged.*
b) *To ease refitting of the weatherstrips, coat them with soapy water (washing-up liquid is ideal).*
c) *If the plastic sealing sheet was damaged during removal, fit a new sheet.*
d) *Refit the door inner trim panel with reference to Section 13.*

Front door regulator

Removal

12 Remove the window glass as described previously in this Section. Alternatively, release the clip securing the window glass to the regulator mechanism, then lift the glass up and secure it to the top of the door using string adhesive tape - ensure that the glass is secure, and that there is no danger of it dropping back into the door.
13 Where applicable, disconnect the wiring plug(s) from the electric window motor.

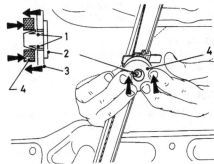

15.8 Using a tool to release the window glass securing clip - models up to 1992

1 Plastic clip lugs   3 Window glass
2 Plastic clip   4 Tool

11

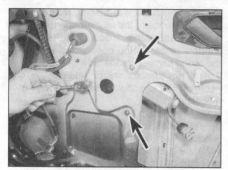

15.14 Unscrew the front door window regulator securing nuts (arrowed)

14 Unscrew the three nuts securing the regulator mechanism to the door (see illustration).
15 Unscrew the two nuts securing the window lift rail to the door.
16 Carefully tilt the assembly and lift it out through the lower aperture in the door (see illustration).

Refitting

17 Refitting is a reversal of removal, but refit the window glass as described previously in this Section.

Rear door sliding window glass

18 Proceed as described for the front door window glass, noting the following points.
a) Fully lower the window glass.
b) The rear glass guide rail must be removed before removing the glass. The guide rail is secured by two bolts (see illustration).

Rear door fixed window glass

Removal

19 Remove the door inner trim panel as described in Section 13.
20 Carefully peel the plastic sealing sheet from the door.
21 Unscrew the two bolts securing the rear window guide rail.
22 Where applicable, prise the trim strip from the fixed window seal.
23 Pull the weatherstrip from the lower edge of the window aperture.
24 Partially pull the weatherstrip from the rear and upper edge of the window aperture.
25 Slide the rear window guide rail downwards into the door.
26 Remove the fixed glass, complete with the seal, by tilting and pulling forwards (see illustration). Note that the rear window guide rail remains attached to the sliding glass.

Refitting

27 Refitting is a reversal of removal, bearing in mind the following points.
a) To ease refitting of the weatherstrips, coat them with soapy water (washing-up liquid is ideal).
b) If the plastic sealing sheet was damaged during removal, fit a new sheet.
c) Refit the door inner trim panel with reference to Section 13.

15.16 Removing the front door window regulator assembly

Rear door regulator

28 The procedure is as described previously in this Section for the front door regulator. Note that there is no need to remove the fixed window glass.

16 Boot lid (Saloon models) - removal, refitting and adjustment

Removal

1 Open the boot lid, and using a pencil or felt tip pen, mark the outline position of each boot lid hinge relative to the boot lid, to use as a guide on refitting.

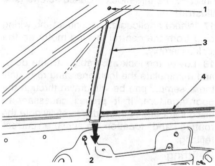

15.18 The rear glass guide rail must be removed before removing the rear door sliding window glass

1 Guide rail upper bolt   3 Guide rail
2 Guide rail lower bolt   4 Weatherstrip

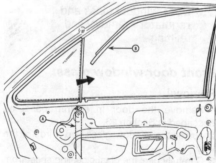

15.26 Removing the rear door fixed window glass

A Guide rail lowered into door   B Weatherstrip

2 Have an assistant hold the boot lid open then, using a pair of pliers, disconnect the spring assisters from the brackets on the body - take care, as the springs are under tension. Note which bracket slots the ends of the springs are positioned in, to ensure correct refitting (see illustration).
3 Unscrew the bolts securing the hinges to the boot lid, and lift off the boot lid.

Refitting

4 Refitting is a reversal of removal, noting the following points.
a) Align the hinges with the marks made on the boot lid before removal.
b) Make sure that the spring assisters are refitted to their original slots in the body brackets.
c) On completion, check the alignment of the boot lid with the surrounding panels, and check the operation of the lock, and if necessary adjust as follows.

Adjustment

5 The alignment of the boot lid can be adjusted by slackening the hinge bolts, and moving the boot lid on the hinges (the holes in the hinges are elongated).
6 There are adjustable rubber stops at each side of the lid to prevent damage to the surrounding panels when closing the lid. There are also rubber stops under each hinge arm, which should be adjusted to prevent the lid from opening too far and causing damage to the front corners of the lid (see illustration).

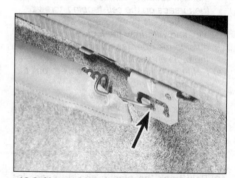

16.2 Note which slots (arrowed) the ends of the boot lid assister springs are positioned in before disconnecting them

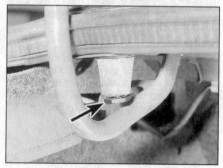

16.6 Rubber stop (arrowed) under boot lid hinge arm

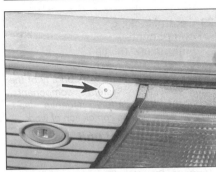

17.3 Drill out the rivets (arrowed) from the body rear trim panel

7 Check that the boot lid lock operation is satisfactory, and if necessary adjust by moving the lock striker (bolted to the boot lid) within its elongated holes.

17 Boot lid lock components (Saloon models) - removal and refitting

Boot lid lock cylinder

Note: *New pop-rivets will be required to refit the body rear trim panel, and on some models the lock cylinder.*

Removal

1 Open the boot lid.
2 Pull the weatherseals from the edge of the rear luggage compartment trim panel, then carefully pull the trim panel from the upper edge of the luggage compartment.
3 Drill out the securing rivets from the top of the body rear trim panel, then unclip the trim panel and withdraw it from the rear of the vehicle **(see illustration)**.
4 Working in the luggage compartment, where applicable unscrew the pinch-bolt, and disconnect the operating rod from the lock cylinder **(see illustration)**. Similarly, disconnect the central locking motor rod, where applicable.
5 Drill out the rivets, or unscrew the securing bolts, as applicable, and withdraw the lock cylinder from the body panel.

Refitting

6 Refitting is a reversal of removal, bearing in mind the following points.
   a) *Refit the body rear trim panel (and the lock cylinder, where applicable) using new pop-rivets.*
   b) *Check the operation of the lock mechanism before refitting the trim panels.*
   c) *If necessary, on models where the operating rod is secured to the lock cylinder with a pinch-bolt, adjust the rod as necessary (by slackening the pinch-bolt) until the lock operation is satisfactory.*

Boot lid lock

Removal

7 Proceed as described in paragraphs 1 and 2.

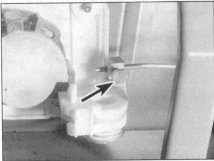
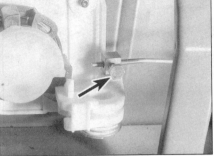

17.4 Unscrew the lock operating rod pinch-bolt (arrowed)

8 Unscrew the two securing bolts, then withdraw the lock and disconnect the operating rod.

Refitting

9 Refitting is a reversal of removal, but check the operation of the lock before refitting the trim panel.

Boot lid lock striker

10 The striker is secured to the boot lid by two bolts, and can be adjusted by moving it within the elongated bolt holes.

18 Tailgate and support struts (Estate models) - removal, refitting and adjustment

Tailgate

Removal

1 Open the tailgate.
2 Remove the securing screws, and withdraw the plastic trim panel from the inside of the tailgate.
3 Working around the edge of the carpeted trim panel, release the securing clips, ideally using a forked tool to avoid breaking the clips. Withdraw the carpeted panel.
4 Disconnect the heated rear window wiring connectors from the contacts on the tailgate.
5 Disconnect the wiring plug from the luggage compartment light switch, and from the alarm sensor switch, where applicable.
6 Where applicable, working through the aperture in the tailgate, disconnect the

tailgate wiper motor and the central locking motor wiring plugs.
7 Disconnect the washer fluid hose from the washer nozzle.
8 Release the wiring harnesses and the washer fluid hose from any clips inside the tailgate.
9 Pull the wiring grommets from the top corners of the tailgate.
10 If the original tailgate is to be refitted, tie string to the ends of all the relevant wiring, then feed the wiring through the top of the tailgate. Untie the string, leaving it in position in the tailgate to assist refitting.
11 Support the tailgate, then prise out the support strut spring clips, and pull the struts from the balljoints on the tailgate.
12 Unscrew the nuts securing the hinges to the top of the tailgate, and carefully lift the tailgate from the vehicle **(see illustration)**.

Refitting

13 Refitting is a reversal of removal, bearing in mind the following points.
   a) *If the original tailgate is being refitted, draw the wiring and washer fluid hose (where applicable) through the tailgate, or through the body panel (as applicable) using the string.*
   b) *If necessary, adjust the rubber buffers to obtain a good fit when the tailgate is shut.*
   c) *Before refitting the tailgate trim panels, check and if necessary adjust the position of the tailgate lock within its elongated holes to achieve satisfactory lock operation.*

Adjustment

14 If necessary, the rubber buffers at the sides of the tailgate can be adjusted to achieve firm closure of the tailgate without slamming. The tailgate lock operation can be adjusted by altering the position of the lock within its elongated holes.

Support struts

Removal

15 Support the tailgate in the open position, with the help of an assistant, or using a stout piece of wood.
16 Using a suitable flat-bladed screwdriver, release the spring clip, and pull the support strut from its balljoint on the tailgate **(see illustration)**.

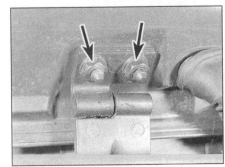

18.12 Hinge-to-tailgate nuts (arrowed)

18.16 Prising the spring clip from a tailgate strut balljoint

11

19.2 Withdraw the plastic trim panel from the tailgate . . .

19.3 . . . then withdraw the carpeted panel

19.4 Tailgate lock cylinder securing rivets (arrowed)

17 Similarly, release the strut from the balljoint on the body, and withdraw the strut from the vehicle.

Refitting

18 Refitting is a reversal of removal, but ensure the spring clips are correctly engaged.

19 Tailgate lock components (Estate models) - removal and refitting

Tailgate lock cylinder

Note: *New pop-rivets will be required to refit the lock cylinder.*

Removal

1 Open the tailgate.
2 Remove the securing screws, and withdraw the plastic trim panel from the inside of the tailgate (see illustration).
3 Working around the edge of the carpeted trim panel, release the securing clips, ideally using a forked tool to avoid breaking the clips. Withdraw the carpeted panel (see illustration).
4 Drill out the rivets securing the lock cylinder assembly to the tailgate (see illustration).
5 Unhook the operating rod(s), and withdraw the assembly from the tailgate.
6 Remove any rivet swarf from the inside of the tailgate.

Refitting

7 Refitting is a reversal of removal, but use new rivets to secure the assembly to the tailgate.

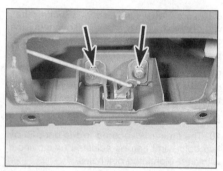

19.9 Tailgate lock securing bolts (arrowed)

Tailgate lock

Removal

8 Proceed as described in paragraphs 1 to 3.
9 Unscrew the two bolts securing the lock to the mounting bracket (see illustration).
10 Unhook the lock operating rod, and withdraw the lock.

Refitting

11 Refitting is a reversal of removal, but before refitting the tailgate trim panels, check the operation of the lock, and if necessary adjust by moving the lock within its elongated bolt holes.

Tailgate lid lock striker

12 The striker is secured to the body by two bolts.

20.1 Central locking electronic control unit (arrowed) viewed with glovebox removed - models up to 1992

20 Central locking components - removal and refitting

Note: *Before attempting work on any of the central locking system components, disconnect the battery negative lead. Reconnect the lead on completion of work.*

Electronic control unit

Removal

1 Remove the glovebox as described in Section 28 to reveal the control unit (see illustration).
2 Where applicable, remove the two securing screws, then unclip the control unit from its location, and disconnect the wiring plug (see illustration).

Refitting

3 Refitting is a reversal of removal.

Door lock motor

4 The motors are fitted to the door lock assemblies. To remove a motor, remove the lock assembly as described in Section 14, then remove the screws securing the motor to the lock assembly.

Tailgate lock motor

Removal

5 Open the tailgate.
6 Remove the securing screws, and withdraw the plastic trim panel from the inside of the tailgate.
7 Working around the edge of the carpeted trim panel, release the securing clips, ideally using a forked tool to avoid breaking the clips. Withdraw the carpeted panel.
8 Unscrew the bolt securing the lock motor to the tailgate (see illustration).
9 Manipulate the motor out from the aperture in the tailgate, then disconnect the lock operating rod and disconnect the wiring plug (see illustration).

Refitting

10 Refitting is a reversal of removal.

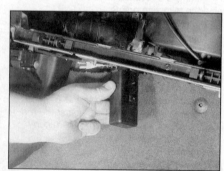

20.2 Removing the central locking electronic control unit - models from 1993

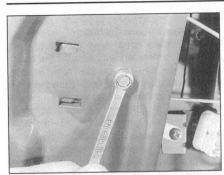

20.8 Unscrewing the tailgate lock motor securing bolt

20.9 Disconnecting the wiring plug from the tailgate lock motor

22 Working inside the luggage compartment, open the cover flap to expose the rear washer fluid reservoir.

23 Remove the two securing screws, then lift out the reservoir to expose the lock motor. Note that there is no need to disconnect the washer fluid tubing.

24 Proceed as described in paragraphs 18 and 19 (**see illustrations**).

Refitting

25 Refitting is a reversal of removal.

Remote control receiver unit

Removal

26 The unit is located in the roof console.

27 Unclip the sunvisors from the roof console.

28 Carefully prise the courtesy light assembly from the console to expose the two roof console front securing screws. Disconnect the wiring plug and remove the light.

29 Similarly, prise the map reading light and the light surround from the console to expose one of the front securing screws. Disconnect the wiring plug and remove the light.

30 Prise the blanking plate from the console then, where applicable, push the sunroof switch from the console.

31 Remove the two console securing screws exposed by removal of the map reading light and sunroof switch, then lower the console from the roof (**see illustration**).

32 Disconnect the wiring plug from the receiver unit.

33 Release the clips, and withdraw the receiver unit from the console (**see illustration**).

Refitting

34 Refitting is a reversal of removal.

20.24a Remove the bolt securing the fuel filler flap lock motor to the body

20.24b Removing the fuel filler flap lock motor - Estate model

Boot lid lock motor

Removal

11 Open the boot lid.

12 Pull the weatherseals from the edge of the rear luggage compartment trim panel, then carefully pull the trim panel from the upper edge of the luggage compartment.

13 Remove the securing screws, then withdraw the lock motor and disconnect the control rod.

14 Disconnect the wiring plug, and withdraw the motor.

Refitting

15 Refitting is a reversal of removal.

Fuel filler flap lock motor - Saloon models

Removal

16 On Saloon models, the motor is located in

the luggage compartment, behind the right-hand side trim panels.

17 Carefully prise the carpeted trim from the side of the luggage compartment, to expose the lock motor.

18 Open the fuel filler flap, and unscrew the bolt securing the motor to the body.

19 Working inside the luggage compartment, unscrew the securing bolt, then withdraw the motor and disconnect the wiring plug.

Refitting

20 Refitting is a reversal of removal. If necessary, glue the trim back into position.

Fuel filler flap lock motor - Estate models

Removal

21 On Estate models, the motor is located in the luggage compartment, behind the rear window washer reservoir.

Remote control transmitter batteries - renewal

Early models

35 Using a small screwdriver, carefully prise the rear cover from the transmitter unit, and remove the three batteries, noting which way round they are fitted (**see illustration**).

36 Fit the new batteries, ensuring that they are fitted the correct way round; the battery and transmitter terminals are marked "+" and "-" to avoid confusion. Clip the transmitter back together.

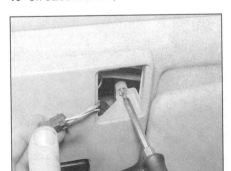

20.31 Removing a roof console securing screw

20.33 Central locking remote control receiver securing clips (arrowed)

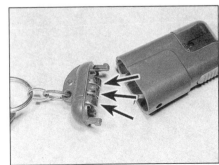

20.35 Rear cover removed from remote transmitter to expose batteries (arrowed)

11

21.2 Disconnecting wiring plug from the electric windows electronic control unit

Later models

37 Remove the small screws securing the two halves of the key/transmitter casing together. Remove the two batteries, noting which way round they are fitted.

38 Fit the new batteries, ensuring that they are fitted the correct way round. Clip the two halves of the casing back together and refit the securing screw.

21 Electric window components - removal and refitting

Electronic control unit

Removal

1 Remove the driver's door inner trim panel as described in Section 13.

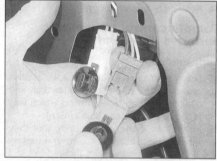

22.3 Disconnecting the door mirror wiring connectors

22.5b . . . and the grommet

2 The control unit is clipped to a bracket on the rear of the door trim panel **(see illustration)**.
3 Unclip the control unit and withdraw it from the panel.

Refitting

4 Refitting is a reversal of removal. Refit the door trim panel as described in Section 13.

Window switches

5 Refer to Chapter 12.

Window regulator motors

6 The regulator motors are integral with the regulator assemblies, and cannot be obtained separately.
7 Removal and refitting details for the regulator assemblies are given in Section 15.

22 Exterior mirrors and associated components - removal and refitting

General

1 A number of different types of rear view mirror may be encountered, according to model, and date of manufacture.
2 The following paragraphs provide a guide to all types.

Mirror

Removal

3 On models with electric mirrors, remove the door inner trim panel (Section 13), then peel back the plastic sealing sheet from the door for access

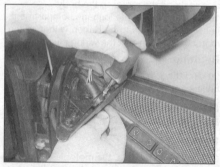

22.4 Loosen the clamp screw and release mirror adjuster knob from the trim plate

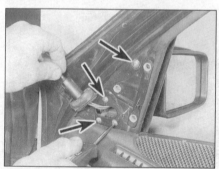

22.6a Remove the four securing screws . . .

to the mirror wiring connector(s). Disconnect the wiring connectors **(see illustration)**.
4 If not already done, prise the mirror trim plate from the inside front corner of the door. Where applicable, loosen the clamp screw, and release the adjuster knob from the trim plate **(see illustration)**.
5 Where applicable, prise the sealing strip and the grommet from the adjuster linkage aperture in the door for access to the lower mirror securing screws **(see illustrations)**.
6 Remove the four securing screws, and withdraw the mirror from the door **(see illustrations)**. Where applicable, feed the wiring up through the door, noting its routing.

Refitting

7 Refitting is a reversal of removal, but where applicable refit the door inner trim panel with reference to Section 13.

Mirror glass

Removal

8 Various methods have been used to retain the glass. On some mirrors, the glass cannot be removed from the housing, and the complete mirror unit must be renewed. The mirror glass may be stuck using adhesive pads; on later types of mirror, the glass may be held by a wire clip, or by a locking ring.
9 To remove a mirror glass secured by a locking ring, tilt the glass fully upwards, then insert a screwdriver at the lower edge of the glass and locate the locking ring. Lever the locking ring towards the door of the vehicle to release the glass **(see illustration)**.

22.5a Prise off the sealing strip . . .

22.6b . . . and withdraw the mirror

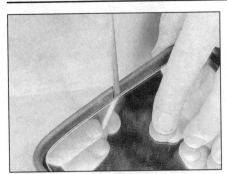

22.9 Releasing a mirror glass locking ring

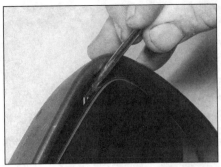

22.10a Prise ends of the clip apart (seen with mirror removed and inverted) . . .

2 Due to the complexity of the sunroof mechanism, considerable skill is required to repair, replace or adjust the sunroof components successfully. Removal of the roof first requires the headlining to be removed, which is a tedious operation, and not a task to be undertaken lightly. Therefore, any problems with this type of sunroof should be referred to a Peugeot dealer.
3 Removal and refitting of the sunroof motor is described in the following paragraphs.
4 Refer to Chapter 12 for details of sunroof switch removal.

Sunroof motor

Removal

5 Disconnect the battery negative lead.
6 Prise out the switch(es) and the light(s) from the roof console to expose the console securing screws. Disconnect the wiring plugs and withdraw the switch(es) and light(s), or move them to one side, as applicable. Where applicable, also prise out the map reading light surround.
7 Unclip the sun visors from the roof console.
8 Remove the screws, and withdraw the roof console. Where applicable, release the wiring connector(s) from the rear of the console.
9 Unscrew the earth lead securing bolt.
10 Unclip the relay bracket from the roof.
11 Unscrew the three screws, and withdraw the motor assembly from the roof **(see illustration)**. Where applicable, disconnect the switch wiring connector.

Refitting

12 Refitting is a reversal of removal.

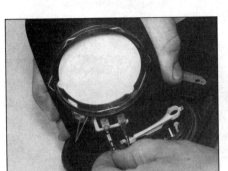

22.10b . . . then withdraw the glass and disconnect the wiring

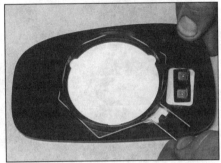

22.10c Recover the spring clip if it is loose

10 To remove a mirror glass secured by a wire clip, working at the bottom edge of the mirror glass, locate the ends of the spring clip which secures the glass. Using a screwdriver, push the ends of the clip together to release the glass. Withdraw the glass, and disconnect the wiring, where applicable. Recover the spring clip if it is loose **(see illustrations)**.

Refitting

11 On models where the glass is secured by a locking ring, where applicable reconnect the wiring to the glass, then locate the glass in the housing, and lever the locking ring away from the door to lock the glass in position.
12 On models where the glass is retained by a wire clip, fit the spring clip to the rear of the mirror glass, ensuring that the clip is correctly located in the slots in the rear of the mirror glass. Push the mirror glass into the mirror until the spring clip locks into position in the mirror adjuster groove. On models where the mirror glass is secured by a wire clip, lightly grease the plastic ring on the adjuster to aid refitting of the spring clip.

Mirror adjustment mechanism

13 The adjustment mechanism is integral with the mirror assembly, and if faulty, the complete mirror must be renewed.

---

23 Windscreen, tailgate and fixed window glass - general information

These areas of glass are secured by the tight fit of the weatherstrip in the body

aperture, and are bonded in position with a special adhesive. Renewal of such fixed glass is a difficult, messy and time-consuming task, which is considered beyond the scope of the home mechanic. It is difficult, unless one has plenty of practice, to obtain a secure, waterproof fit. Furthermore, the task carries a high risk of breakage; this applies especially to the laminated glass windscreen. In view of this, owners are strongly advised to have this sort of work carried out by one of the many specialist windscreen fitters.

---

24 Sunroof - general information

General

1 The factory-fitted sunroof is of the electric tilt/slide type.

24.11 Sunroof motor securing screws (arrowed)

---

25 Body exterior fittings - removal and refitting

Front grille panel

Removal

1 Open the bonnet.
2 Working through the front of the grille, remove the grille front securing screws **(see illustration)**.
3 Working at the top inner corners of the headlights, remove the bolts securing the upper corners of the grille **(see illustration)**.

25.2 Remove the grille front securing screws . . .

11

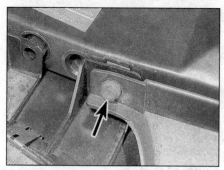

25.3 . . . and the upper securing bolts (arrowed)

25.4 Push out the bonnet release lever securing pin

25.8 Disconnect the washer fluid hose

25.9 Unscrew the grille panel securing screws

25.10 Prise the clip from the end of the panel

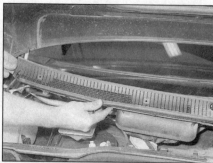

25.11 Removing the scuttle grille panel

4 Where applicable, release the retaining clip, then push out the pin securing the bonnet release lever to the catch **(see illustration)**.
5 Lift the grille panel upwards to disengage the lower locating lugs, and withdraw the panel.

Refitting

6 Refitting is a reversal of removal.

Scuttle grille panel

Removal

7 Remove the wiper arms as described in Chapter 12.
8 Disconnect the washer fluid hose from the T-piece at the right-hand side of the scuttle **(see illustration)**.
9 Unscrew the four scuttle grille panel securing screws **(see illustration)**.
10 Prise off the clip securing the left-hand side of the grille panel to the scuttle **(see illustration)**.
11 Carefully release the weatherstrip from the rear edge of the grille panel, then withdraw the panel from the vehicle **(see illustration)**.

Refitting

12 Refitting is a reversal of removal. Refit the wiper arms with reference to Chapter 12.

Wheel arch liners and mud shields

13 The wheel arch liners are secured by a combination of self-tapping screws, and push-fit clips. Removal is self-evident, and normally the clips can be released by pulling the liner away from the wheel arch.

14 The mud shields are secured in a similar manner, although certain panels may be secured using pop-rivets. Where applicable, drill out the pop-rivets, and use new rivets on refitting.

Body trim strips and badges

15 The various body trim strips and badges are held in position with a special adhesive tape. Removal requires the trim/badge to be heated, to soften the adhesive, and then cut away from the surface. Due to the high risk of damage to the vehicle paintwork during this operation, it is recommended that this task should be entrusted to a Peugeot dealer.

---

26 Seats - removal and refitting

Front seat

⚠️ **Warning: On models with seat belt pre-tensioners, observe the following precautions before attempting to remove the seat.**

a) Remove the ignition key.
b) Disconnect the battery negative lead, and wait for two minutes before carrying out any further work.
c) Disconnect the pre-tensioner wiring plug from the tensioner unit.

Note: Do not tamper with the pre-tensioner unit in any way, and do not attempt to test the unit. Note that the unit is triggered if the

mechanism is supplied with an electrical current (including via an ohmmeter), or if the assembly is subjected to a temperature of greater than 100°C.

Removal

1 Move the seat fully forwards.
2 Tilt the seat backrest forwards.
3 Remove the bolts (one bolt on each side) securing the rear of the seat rails to the floor **(see illustration)**.
4 Move the seat fully rearwards.
5 Remove the bolts (one bolt on each side) securing the front of the seat rails to the floor.
6 Recover the washers, where applicable, then lift the seat from the vehicle.
7 Where applicable, recover the plastic plates from the floor.

Refitting

8 Refitting is a reversal of removal but, where applicable, ensure that the plastic plates are

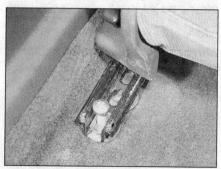

26.3 Front seat rear securing bolt partially removed

26.12a Remove the securing screw . . .

26.18a Rear seat back hinge securing nuts (arrowed) - Estate model

26.18b Split rear seat back inner pivot (arrowed) - Estate model

in position on the floor, and securely tighten the mounting bolts.

Rear seat cushion - Saloon models

Removal

9 Grasp each lower corner of the seat cushion in turn, and push towards the centre of the car, then pull up to release the securing lug.
10 Once both corners have been released, the cushion can be lifted from the vehicle.

Refitting

11 Refitting is a reversal of removal, but take care not to trap the seat belts.

Rear seat back - Saloon models

Removal

12 Where applicable, fold down the rear armrest, and remove the screw securing the armrest trim panel to the body. Withdraw the trim panel **(see illustrations)**.

26.12b . . . and withdraw the armrest trim panel - Saloon model

13 Pull each side of the seat back upwards to disengage it from the securing lugs, then withdraw the assembly from the vehicle.

Refitting

14 Refitting is a reversal of removal, but take care not to trap the seat belts.

Rear seat cushion - Estate models

Removal

15 Pull the rear of the seat cushion upwards, using the strap provided, then unscrew the nuts securing the hinges to the floor **(see illustration)**.

Refitting

16 Refitting is a reversal of removal, but take care not to trap the seat belts.

Rear seat back - Estate models

Removal

17 Release the seat back retaining catches, and tilt the seat back forwards.
18 Unscrew the nuts securing the seat back hinges to the floor, then lift the seat back from the vehicle. On models with split rear seat backs, disengage the inner seat back pivot from the central bracket, and remove each section individually **(see illustrations)**.

Refitting

19 Refitting is a reversal of removal but, where applicable, ensure that the seat belts are not trapped.

27 Seat belt components - removal and refitting

Note: *Note the locations of any spacers and/or washers on the seat belt anchor bolts, to ensure correct refitting.*

Front seat belt

Removal

1 Where applicable, remove the cover, then unscrew the lower seat belt anchor bolt from the edge of the seat.
2 Unclip the roof side trim panels to expose the upper B-pillar trim panel top securing screws. Remove the screws **(see illustration)**.

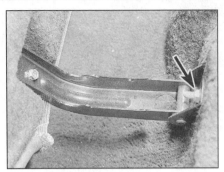

26.15 Rear seat cushion hinge securing nut (arrowed) - Estate model

3 Prise off the trim plate, and unscrew the seat belt upper anchor bolt **(see illustration)**. Recover the spacer.
4 Working at the bottom of the upper B-pillar trim panel, remove the remaining securing screw, then manipulate the panel from the B-pillar **(see illustration)**.

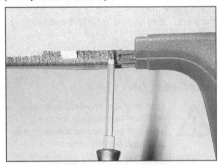

27.2 Removing an upper B-pillar trim panel top securing screw

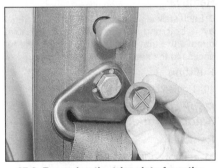

27.3 Removing the trim plate from the front seat belt upper anchor bolt

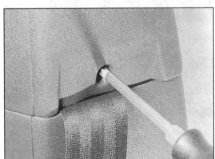

27.4 Removing the upper B-pillar trim panel lower securing screw

11

27.6 Removing a lower B-pillar trim panel bottom securing screw

27.7 Front inertia reel securing bolt (arrowed)

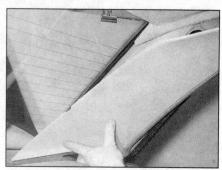

27.13 Pull off the rear quarter trim panel

5 Unscrew the two now-exposed top securing screws from the lower B-pillar trim panel.
6 Unclip the sill trim panels to expose the lower B-pillar trim panel bottom securing screws. Remove the screws, and withdraw the panel from the B-pillar (see illustration).
7 Unscrew the inertia reel bolt, and withdraw the seat belt assembly (see illustration).

Refitting

8 Refitting is a reversal of removal, but securely tighten the seat belt securing bolts.

Front seat belt stalk

 Warning: On models with seat belt pre-tensioners, do not attempt to remove the seat belt stalk assembly, which incorporates the pre-tensioner assembly. Refer the operation to a Peugeot dealer.

Removal

9 Each stalk is secured to the front seat frame by a bolt and washer. Where applicable, remove the trim from the side of the seat for access to the securing bolt.

Refitting

10 Tighten the securing bolt securely.

Rear side seat belts - Saloon models

Removal

11 Remove the seat cushion and back, as described in Section 26.

27.15 Unscrewing the rear side seat belt inertia reel securing bolt - Saloon model

12 Unbolt the lower seat belt anchor.
13 Pull the rear quarter trim panel from the side of the body (see illustration). Take care not to break the clips.
14 Lift up the rear parcel shelf trim panel to expose the inertia reel.
15 Unscrew the securing bolt, and lift out the inertia reel assembly (see illustration).
16 Slide the seat belt webbing through the slot in the parcel shelf trim panel, then withdraw the seat belt assembly.

Refitting

17 Refitting is a reversal of removal, but securely tighten the seat belt anchor bolts.

Rear side seat belts - Estate models

Removal

18 Unbolt the lower seat belt anchor from the body.
19 Fold the rear seat back forwards.
20 Working in the luggage compartment, remove the two parcel shelf support panel front securing screws, and unscrew the seat back catch striker (see illustration).
21 Pull the front end of the parcel shelf support panel away from the body to expose the seat belt inertia reel and the securing bolt (see illustration).
22 Unscrew the inertia reel securing bolt and withdraw the assembly.
23 Feed the seat belt webbing through the slot in the trim panel, then withdraw the assembly from the vehicle.

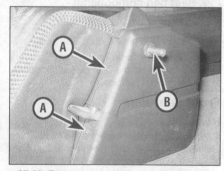

27.20 Remove two front screws (A) and seat back catch striker (B) from the parcel shelf support panel - Estate model

Refitting

24 Refitting is a reversal of removal, but securely tighten the seat belt anchor bolts.

Rear centre belt and buckles

Removal

25 The assemblies can simply be unbolted from the floor panel, after removing the rear seat cushion (Saloon models) or folding the rear seat cushion forwards (Estate models).

Refitting

26 Refitting is a reversal of removal. Tighten all mounting bolts securely.

28 Interior trim - removal and refitting

Door trim panels

1 Refer to Section 13.

Steering column shrouds

Removal

2 Disconnect the battery negative lead.
3 On models with an adjustable steering column, move the column adjuster lever to the released position.
4 Working under the steering column, unscrew the five securing screws, then withdraw the lower column shroud (see illustrations).
5 Disconnect the wiring plug(s) from the

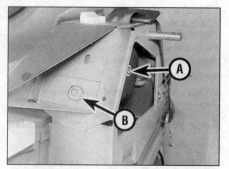

27.21 Rear seat belt inertia reel (A) and securing bolt (B) - Estate model (viewed with parcel shelf support panel removed)

28.4a Remove the securing screws . . .

28.4b . . . and withdraw the lower column shroud

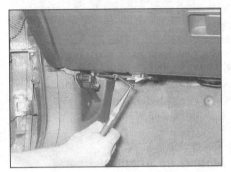

28.13 Remove the hinge pins . . .

28.14 . . . and withdraw the glovebox - models from 1993

instrument panel illumination control, radio/cassette player remote control switch, cruise control switch, and the alarm electronic control unit, as applicable.

6 Unclip the upper shroud from the steering column.

Refitting

7 Refitting is a reversal of removal, but on completion, if it proves necessary to adjust the alignment between the shrouds and the facia, loosen the steering column securing nuts and bolts. The fixings can be accessed through the holes in the lower column shroud (except on models where an electronic control unit is mounted in the lower shroud, in which case the shrouds must be removed again). Adjust the position of the column (and hence shrouds) as necessary, then tighten the column fixings securely.

Glovebox - models up to 1992

Removal

8 Working under the glovebox, push out the two hinge pins, using a suitable punch or thin screwdriver if necessary.

9 Remove the two screws securing the cover to the rear of the lid.

10 Lift off the lid, leaving the cover held by the checkstraps.

11 The checkstraps can be removed by releasing their inner ends.

Refitting

12 Refitting is a reversal of removal, noting that the longer check strap fits on the left.

Glovebox - models from 1993

Removal

13 Working under the glovebox, push out the two hinge pins, using a suitable punch or thin screwdriver if necessary (see illustration).

14 Release the glovebox catch, and withdraw the glovebox from the facia (see illustration).

Refitting

15 Refitting is a reversal of removal.

Carpets

16 The passenger compartment floor carpets are secured at the edges by screws or various types of clips.

17 Carpet removal and refitting is reasonably straightforward, but time-consuming, due to the fact that all adjoining trim panels must be removed first, as must components such as the seats and centre console.

Headlining

18 The headlining is clipped to the roof, and can be withdrawn only once all fittings such as the grab handles, sun visors, sunroof (if fitted), windscreen, centre and rear pillar trim panels, and associated panels have been removed. The door, tailgate and sunroof aperture weatherstrips will also have to be prised clear.

19 Note that headlining removal requires considerable skill and experience if it is to be carried out without damage, and is therefore best entrusted to an expert.

29 Centre console - removal and refitting

"Highline" console - models up to 1992

Removal

1 Disconnect the battery negative lead.

2 Move the seats fully rearwards.

3 Where applicable, remove the securing screws, then prise the side panels from the front of the console. Note that the side panels are retained by clips at their top edges.

4 Prise the cassette box from the front of the console, and remove the two now-exposed screws securing the console to the heater panel.

5 Slide the front seats fully forward.

6 Prise out the blanks from each side at the rear of the console, and remove the rear securing screws.

7 Open the lid of the stowage compartment at the rear of the console, and remove the screw from the compartment floor.

8 Remove the two screws (one on each side) securing the console to the gear lever bracket (see illustration).

9 Pull the handbrake lever dust cover from the console (see illustration).

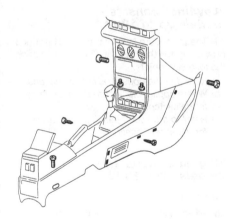

29.8 "Highline" centre console fixings - models up to 1992

29.9 Removing the handbrake lever dust cover - models up to 1992

11

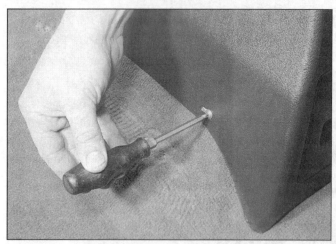

**29.26 Unscrew the console rear screws
("Lowline" console - models from 1993)**

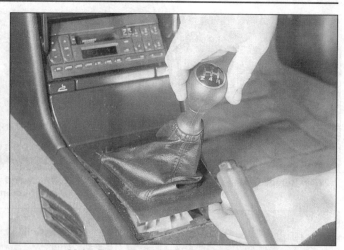

**29.31 Removing gear lever gaiter surround
("Lowline" console - models from 1993)**

10 Prise the gear lever gaiter surround from the top of the console, and pull back the gaiter.
11 Lift the console slightly, then disconnect all relevant wiring, and release the wiring harnesses from any clips under the console.
12 Withdraw the console over the gear lever and the handbrake lever.

Refitting

13 Refitting is a reversal of removal.

"Lowline" console - models up to 1992

14 The procedure is similar to that described previously for the "Highline" console, noting the following points.

a) *Note that the console is in two sections.*
b) *Where applicable, ignore the references to the switches.*
c) *Refer to the accompanying illustrations for the screw locations*

"Highline" console - models from 1993

Removal

15 Where applicable, remove the front armrest.
16 Prise out the trim plate covering the console centre securing screws. Remove the securing screws.
17 Unclip the gear lever gaiter surround from the centre console.
18 Pull up on the gear knob and withdraw the knob/gaiter assembly.
19 Remove the securing screws, and withdraw the side panels from the front of the console to expose the heater air ducts.
20 Remove the screws, and withdraw the air ducts from each side of the console.
21 Working at the front of the console, disconnect the wiring connectors.
22 Fully apply the handbrake, then withdraw the console over the handbrake lever.

Refitting

23 Refitting is a reversal of removal.

"Lowline" console - models from 1993

Removal

24 Disconnect the battery negative lead.
25 Move the front seats as far forward as possible.
26 Unscrew the two centre console rear securing screws, then push the seats back **(see illustration)**.
27 Prise the handbrake lever surround/switch panel from the top of the centre console. Where applicable, disconnect the wiring plugs from the switches in the panel.
28 Pull up the handbrake lever to the "fully on" position.
29 Prise the ashtray from the housing in the facia centre panel.
30 Open the ashtray cover flap, and pull the ashtray from the housing.
31 Proceed as described in paragraphs 17 and 18 **(see illustration)**.
32 Remove the two now-exposed console front securing screws, then lift the console, and withdraw it over the handbrake **(see illustrations)**.

Refitting

33 Refer to paragraph 23.

**29.32a Remove the front
securing screws . . .**

30 Facia assembly - removal and refitting

Models up to 1992

Removal

1 Disconnect the battery negative lead.
2 Remove the steering wheel (Chapter 10).
3 Remove the steering column shrouds as described in Section 28.
4 Remove the instrument panel (Chapter 12).
5 Remove the radio/cassette player as described in Chapter 12.
6 Remove the securing screws, where applicable, and withdraw the side panels from the centre console.
7 Remove the headlight beam adjuster switch as described in Chapter 12.
8 Prise out the ashtray and the oddments tray from the facia centre panel.
9 Remove the two bolts from the ashtray recess, and the single bolt from the radio/cassette player recess **(see illustrations)**.
10 Remove the two screws from the top of the oddments tray recess.
11 Pull the centre facia panel forwards from the facia, then reach behind the panel and disconnect the wiring from the switches, clock,

**29.32b . . . and withdraw the console
("Lowline" console - models from 1993)**

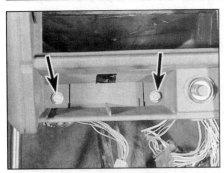

30.9a Remove the two bolts (arrowed) from the ashtray recess . . .

30.9b . . . and the single bolt (arrowed) from the radio/cassette player recess

30.12 Two of the heater control panel securing screws

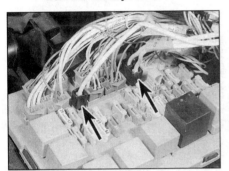

30.16 Disconnect the two main feed connectors (arrowed) from the fusebox

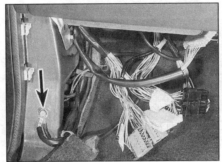

30.18 Unbolt the earth lead (arrowed) from the footwell

30.19 Remove the bolt securing the relay bracket to lower steering column bracket

and cigarette lighter, as applicable. Note the locations of the wiring connectors to ensure correct refitting, and remove the facia panel.

12 Unscrew the four heater control panel-to-facia screws **(see illustration)**.

13 Turn the two securing clips through a quarter-turn, then drop the fusebox panel down from the facia.

14 Unscrew the two bonnet release lever bolts from the bracket under the facia.

15 Disconnect the wiring from the instrument panel lighting rheostat.

HAYNES HINT *Because we found the wiring harnesses to be thoroughly intertwined, we disconnected all the fusebox connectors, marking them to ensure correct refitting. The fusebox can then be removed by releasing the hinge rail.*

16 Disconnect the two main feed connectors from the fusebox **(see illustration)**.

17 Working at each side of the facia, disconnect the facia wiring harness connectors, marking them to ensure correct refitting.

18 Remove the side footwell trim panel (the left-hand side panel for right-hand-drive models, or the right-hand side panel for left-hand-drive models), then unbolt the earth lead from the footwell **(see illustration)**.

19 Where applicable, remove the bolt, and release the relay bracket from the lower steering column bracket **(see illustration)**.

20 Working in the scuttle at the rear of the engine compartment, unscrew the three facia securing nuts **(see illustration)**.

21 Remove the single bolt on each side, securing the lower facia mounting brackets to the footwells **(see illustration)**.

22 Remove the remaining two lower facia bolts, one each side of the centre console.

23 Reach up behind the heater control panel, and remove the upper facia securing bolt **(see illustration)**.

24 Unbolt the bracing bracket between the gear lever bracket and the centre of the facia.

25 Disconnect the remaining steering column stalk switch wiring connectors.

26 Disconnect the wiring from the brake light switch.

27 Disconnect the wiring from the cigarette lighter and the ashtray illumination light.

28 Make a final check around the facia, to ensure that all relevant wiring has been disconnected.

29 Carefully pull the facia panel forwards, feeding the speedometer cable and the wiring harnesses through the apertures in the facia as it is withdrawn. Note the routing of all harnesses and the speedometer cable to ensure correct refitting.

30 With the aid of an assistant, withdraw the

30.20 Facia securing nut (arrowed) in scuttle

30.21 Lower facia mounting bracket-to-footwell bolt (arrowed)

30.23 Upper facia securing bolt (arrowed)

30.34 Unscrew the two screws below the ashtray housing

30.36a Remove screws from top of radio/ cassette player/oddments housing . . .

30.36b . . . then withdraw the housing

30.37 Prise out the blanking plate to expose the ventilation nozzle housing upper securing screw (arrowed)

30.38a Remove the two screws from the front of the ventilation nozzle housing . . .

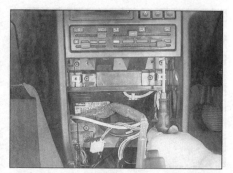

30.38b . . . and the two screws from underneath

facia assembly through one of the door apertures.

Refitting

31 Refitting is a reversal of removal, bearing in mind the following points.

a) *Make sure that the facia locating spigots engage correctly with the holes in the bulkhead.*

b) *Ensure that the wiring harnesses and the speedometer cable are correctly routed through the facia as it is refitted, as noted during removal.*

c) *Ensure that all wiring connectors are correctly reconnected.*

d) *Refit the radio/cassette player and the instrument panel with reference to Chapter 12.*

e) *Refit the steering wheel (see Chapter 10).*

Models from 1993

Removal

32 Disconnect the battery negative lead.
33 Remove the centre console as described in Section 29.
34 Unscrew the two screws located at the bottom of the ashtray housing **(see illustration)**.
35 Where applicable, remove the radio/ cassette player as described in Chapter 12. On models not fitted with a radio/cassette player, prise out the oddments tray.
36 Remove the two securing screws from the top of the radio/cassette player/oddments tray housing, then withdraw the housing from the facia **(see illustrations)**. Where applicable, disconnect the wiring plug(s) from the rear of the panel.

37 Prise the blanking plate from the top corner of the facia centre ventilation nozzle housing. Remove the now-exposed securing screw **(see illustration)**.
38 Remove the four housing securing screws located under the heater control panel. Two screws are accessible from the front of the housing, and two screws from underneath **(see illustrations)**.
39 Carefully prise the switches from below the centre facia ventilation nozzles to reveal the remaining housing securing screw. Remove the screw **(see illustrations)**.
40 Pull the housing forwards, and disconnect the wiring from the clock, then withdraw the housing **(see illustration)**.
41 Working in the driver's footwell, release the securing clips and remove the carpet trim panel from above the pedals. Disconnect the

30.39a Prise the switches from the housing . . .

30.39b . . . then remove the remaining housing securing screw

30.40 Withdrawing the ventilation nozzle housing

30.41a Remove the carpet trim panel . . .

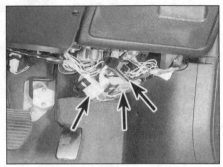

30.41b . . . then disconnect the three wiring connectors (arrowed)

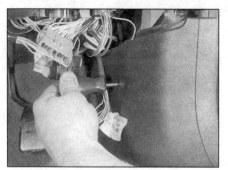

30.42a Remove the securing screw . . .

30.42b . . . then remove the footwell side trim panel

30.43 Pull the connector bracket from the footwell

44 Where applicable (if the earth cable connects to the facia wiring harness), unbolt the earth cable from the footwell, then release the wiring harness from the clips under the facia.

45 Working at the centre of the facia, remove the securing screws, and withdraw the facia centre side trim panels, to expose the heater air ducts (see illustrations).

46 Where applicable remove the screws, and withdraw the air ducts (see illustration).

47 Cut the cable-tie securing the wiring harness to the bracket at the centre of the driver's side facia.

48 Release the plastic clips securing the large connector block to the bracket on the driver's side of the centre facia, then release the connectors from the connector block, and separate the two halves of each connector (see illustration).

49 Similarly, working at the passenger's side of the centre facia, remove the plastic clips securing the connector block to the bracket on the floor and to the heater assembly.

50 Working in the passenger's footwell, release the securing clips, and remove the carpet trim panel from under the facia.

51 Remove the securing screw, then pull up the passenger's footwell side trim panel to release the securing clips. Remove the panel, to expose the wiring connector block. Release the connector block from the footwell, and separate the two halves of each wiring connector.

52 Unbolt the earth lead from the passenger footwell, then release the wiring harnesses from any clips in the footwell (see illustration).

30.45a Remove the securing screws . . .

30.45b . . . and withdraw the facia centre side trim panels

three wiring connectors (see illustrations). Where applicable, release the wiring harnesses from the clips on the facia.

42 Remove the securing screw, then pull up the driver's footwell side trim panel to release the securing clips. Remove the panel, to

expose the wiring connector bracket (see illustrations).

43 Release the two securing clips, and pull the wiring connector bracket from the footwell. Disconnect the connectors from the bracket (see illustration).

30.46 Withdrawing an air duct

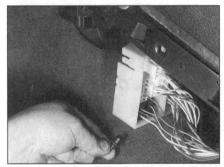

30.48 Release the connector block from the bracket on the driver's side of the facia

30.52 Unbolt the earth lead from the passenger's footwell

11

30.53 Remove the screw and withdraw the bonnet release lever

30.56 Remove the securing screws and withdraw connector/control unit brackets

30.60 Unplug the main wiring harness connectors

30.62a Pull the relay out of its connector . . .

30.62b . . . then pull the connector from the steering column bracket

30.65a Remove the securing clip . . .

53 Remove the securing screw, and withdraw the bonnet release lever from the side of the footwell **(see illustration)**.

54 Remove the steering column shrouds as described in Section 28, but note that, where applicable, there is no need to disconnect the wiring from the radio/cassette player remote control switch - feed the switch wiring up through the facia (the wiring should have been disconnected from the rear of the radio/cassette player), and withdraw the wiring complete with the lower shroud.

55 Remove the steering column as described in Chapter 10.

56 Remove the two securing screws, and withdraw the wiring connector/control unit bracket from the left-hand side of the steering column bracket **(see illustration)**.

57 Where applicable, similarly remove the wiring connector bracket from the right-hand side of the steering column bracket.

58 Remove the instrument panel as described in Chapter 12.

59 Working in the driver's footwell, disconnect the wiring plug from the stop light switch, then release the switch wiring harness from the clips under the facia.

60 Unplug the main wiring harness connectors, from the connector block mounted under the driver's side of the facia **(see illustration)**. To improve access to the wiring connectors, the connector block can be lowered from the facia by removing the two front bolts securing the bracket to the facia, and the rear nut securing the bracket to the stud on the bulkhead.

61 On left-hand-drive models, remove the screw securing the wiring bracket to the driver's side of the bulkhead, next to the clutch pedal.

62 Where applicable, pull the relay out of its connector at the rear of the steering column

bracket, then pull the connector out of the bracket **(see illustrations)**.

63 Remove the heater control unit as described in Chapter 3.

64 Working in the engine compartment, remove the scuttle grille panel (Section 25).

65 Remove the securing clip, and withdraw the plastic shield from the passenger's side of the scuttle **(see illustrations)**.

66 On left-hand-drive models, working in the scuttle, remove the heater inlet duct grille, and move the connector block/electronic control unit housing to one side for access to the facia securing nuts.

67 Working inside the vehicle, unscrew the two bolts securing the facia side brackets to the footwells (one bolt in each footwell) **(see illustration)**.

68 Similarly, unscrew the two centre facia lower securing bolts, one on each side of the facia centre section **(see illustration)**.

30.65b . . . and withdraw the shield from the scuttle

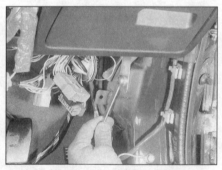

30.67 Unscrew the bolts securing the facia brackets to the footwells

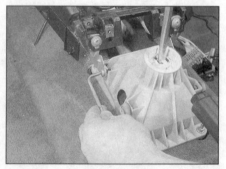

30.68 Unscrew the centre facia lower securing bolts

69 Unscrew the centre facia upper securing bolt, located above the heater control unit **(see illustration)**.

70 Unscrew the two rear centre facia securing bolts, securing the facia brackets to the heater assembly **(see illustration)**.

71 Working in the engine compartment, unscrew the three facia securing nuts located in the scuttle **(see illustration)**.

72 Make a final check to ensure that all relevant wiring harnesses have been unclipped and released from the facia assembly then, with the aid of an assistant, pull the facia back from the bulkhead. Note the location and routing of all wiring harnesses, particularly note the location of the Velcro fixings.

73 Release the speedometer cable sleeve from the instrument panel housing in the facia, then manipulate the facia assembly out through one of the door apertures **(see illustration)**.

Refitting

74 Refitting is a reversal of removal, bearing in mind the following points.

 a) *Reconnect the wiring plugs to the large connector block on the driver's side of the facia before refitting the facia fixings, and bolting the connector block in position.*

 b) *Check that the air ducts are correctly located and engaged with their relevant vents. Access to the passenger's side air duct can be improved by removing the glovebox (see Section 28).*

 c) *Ensure that all wiring harnesses are*

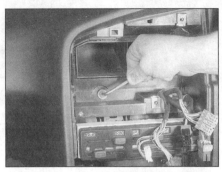

30.69 Unscrew the centre facia upper securing bolt . . .

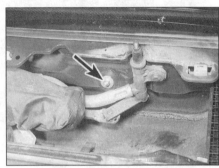

30.71 Facia securing nut (arrowed) in scuttle

correctly located and routed as noted before removal, and ensure that the Velcro fixings are in position, where applicable.

 d) *Refit the heater control unit (Chapter 3).*

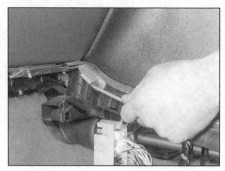

30.70 . . . and the rear centre facia securing bolts

30.73 Release the speedometer cable sleeve from the facia

 e) *Refit the instrument panel with reference to Chapter 12.*

 f) *Refit the steering column (Chapter 10).*

 g) *Refit the centre console with reference to Section 29.*

11

Chapter 12
Body electrical system

Contents

Degrees of difficulty

Easy, suitable for novice with little experience	**Fairly easy,** suitable for beginner with some experience	**Fairly difficult,** suitable for competent DIY mechanic	**Difficult,** suitable for experienced DIY mechanic	**Very difficult,** suitable for expert DIY or professional

Specifications

General

System type . . . . 12-volt negative earth

Fuses . . . . see Wiring Diagrams

Bulbs

	Type	Wattage
Headlights:		
Dip/main beam	H4	60/55
Driving light	H1	55
Front foglight/spoiler-mounted driving light	H3	55
Front sidelights	Push-fit	5
Direction indicator light	Bayonet	21
Direction indicator side repeater	Bayonet	5
Stop/tail light	Bayonet	21/5
Rear tail light	Bayonet	5
Rear foglight	Bayonet	21
Reversing light	Bayonet	21
Number plate light	Push-fit	5

Torque wrench setting

	Nm	lbf ft
Air bag unit securing screws	8	6

---

1 General information and precautions

Warning: Before carrying out any work on the electrical system, read the precautions in "Safety first!" at the beginning of this manual, and in Chapter 5.

The electrical system is of 12-volt negative earth type. Power for the lights and all electrical accessories is supplied by a lead/acid type battery, which is charged by the alternator.

This Chapter covers repair and service procedures for the various electrical components not associated with the engine. Information on the battery, alternator and starter motor can be found in Chapter 5.

It should be noted that, prior to working on any component in the electrical system, the battery negative terminal should first be disconnected, to prevent the possibility of electrical short-circuits and/or fires.

Caution: If the radio/cassette player fitted has an anti-theft security code, (the standard unit has), refer to the precaution in the Reference section of this manual before disconnecting the battery.

12

2 Electrical fault finding - general information

Note: *Refer to the precautions given in "Safety first!" and in Section 1 of this Chapter before starting work. The following tests relate to testing of the main electrical circuits, and should not be used to test delicate electronic circuits (such as anti-lock braking systems), particularly where an electronic control module is used.*

General

1 A typical electrical circuit consists of an electrical component, any switches, relays, motors, fuses, fusible links or circuit breakers related to that component, and the wiring and connectors which link the component to both the battery and the chassis. To help to pinpoint a problem in an electrical circuit, wiring diagrams are included after this chapter.

2 Before attempting to diagnose an electrical fault, first study the appropriate wiring diagram, to obtain a more complete understanding of the components included in the particular circuit concerned. The possible sources of a fault can be narrowed down by noting whether other components related to the circuit are operating properly. If several components or circuits fail at one time, the problem is likely to be related to a shared fuse or earth connection.

3 Electrical problems usually stem from simple causes, such as loose or corroded connections, a faulty earth connection, a blown fuse, a melted fusible link, or a faulty relay (refer to Section 3 for details of testing relays). Visually inspect the condition of all fuses, wires and connections in a problem circuit before testing the components. Use the wiring diagrams to determine which terminal connections will need to be checked, in order to pinpoint the trouble-spot.

4 The basic tools required for electrical fault-finding include a circuit tester or voltmeter (a 12-volt bulb with a set of test leads can also be used for certain tests); a self-powered test light (sometimes known as a continuity tester); an ohmmeter (to measure resistance); a battery and set of test leads; and a jumper wire, preferably with a circuit breaker or fuse incorporated, which can be used to bypass suspect wires or electrical components. Before attempting to locate a problem with test instruments, use the wiring diagram to determine where to make the connections.

5 To find the source of an intermittent wiring fault (usually due to a poor or dirty connection, or damaged wiring insulation), a "wiggle" test can be performed on the wiring. This involves wiggling the wiring by hand, to see if the fault occurs as the wiring is moved. It should be possible to narrow down the source of the fault to a particular section of wiring. This method of testing can be used in conjunction with any of the tests described in the following sub-Sections.

6 Apart from problems due to poor connections, two basic types of fault can occur in an electrical circuit - open-circuit, or short-circuit.

7 Open-circuit faults are caused by a break somewhere in the circuit, which prevents current from flowing. An open-circuit fault will prevent a component from working, but will not cause the relevant circuit fuse to blow.

8 Short-circuit faults are caused by a "short" somewhere in the circuit, which allows the current flowing in the circuit to "escape" along an alternative route, usually to earth. Short-circuit faults are normally caused by a breakdown in wiring insulation, which allows a feed wire to touch either another wire, or an earthed component such as the bodyshell. A short-circuit fault will normally cause the relevant circuit fuse to blow.

Finding an open-circuit

9 To check for an open-circuit, connect one lead of a circuit tester or voltmeter to either the negative battery terminal or a known good earth.

10 Connect the other lead to a connector in the circuit being tested, preferably nearest to the battery or fuse.

11 Switch on the circuit, bearing in mind that some circuits are live only when the ignition switch is moved to a particular position.

12 If voltage is present (indicated either by the tester bulb lighting or a voltmeter reading, as applicable), this means that the section of the circuit between the relevant connector and the battery is problem-free.

13 Continue to check the remainder of the circuit in the same fashion.

14 When a point is reached at which no voltage is present, the problem must lie between that point and the previous test point with voltage. Most problems can be traced to a broken, corroded or loose connection.

Finding a short-circuit

15 To check for a short-circuit, first disconnect the load(s) from the circuit (loads are the components which draw current from a circuit, such as bulbs, motors, heating elements, etc).

16 Remove the relevant fuse from the circuit, and connect a circuit tester or voltmeter to the fuse connections.

17 Switch on the circuit, bearing in mind that some circuits are live only when the ignition switch is moved to a particular position.

18 If voltage is present (indicated either by the tester bulb lighting or a voltmeter reading, as applicable), this means that there is a short-circuit.

19 If no voltage is present, but the fuse still blows with the load(s) connected, this indicates an internal fault in the load(s).

Finding an earth fault

20 The battery negative terminal is connected to "earth" - the metal of the engine/transmission and the car body - and most systems are wired so that they only receive a positive feed, the current returning via the metal of the car body. This means that the component mounting and the body form part of that circuit. Loose or corroded mountings can therefore cause a range of electrical faults, ranging from total failure of a circuit, to a puzzling partial fault. In particular, lights may shine dimly (especially when another circuit sharing the same earth point is in operation), motors (eg wiper motors or the radiator cooling fan motor) may run slowly, and the operation of one circuit may have an apparently-unrelated effect on another. Note that on many vehicles, earth straps are used between certain components, such as the engine/transmission and the body, usually where there is no metal-to-metal contact between components, due to flexible rubber mountings, etc.

21 To check whether a component is properly earthed, disconnect the battery, and connect one lead of an ohmmeter to a known good earth point. Connect the other lead to the wire or earth connection being tested. The resistance reading should be zero; if not, check the connection as follows.

22 If an earth connection is thought to be faulty, dismantle the connection, and clean back to bare metal both the bodyshell and the wire terminal or the component earth connection mating surface. Be careful to remove all traces of dirt and corrosion, then use a knife to trim away any paint, so that a clean metal-to-metal joint is made. On reassembly, tighten the joint fasteners securely; if a wire terminal is being refitted, use serrated washers between the terminal and the bodyshell, to ensure a clean and secure connection. When the connection is remade, prevent the onset of corrosion in the future by applying a coat of petroleum jelly or silicone-based grease, or by spraying on (at regular intervals) a proprietary ignition sealer.

3 Fuses and relays - general information

Fuses

1 Fuses are designed to break a circuit when a predetermined current is reached, in order to protect the components and wiring which could be damaged by excessive current flow. Any excessive current flow will be due to a fault in the circuit, usually a short-circuit (see Section 2).

2 The main fuses are located in the fusebox, below the steering column on the driver's side of the facia.

3 For access to the fuses, on models up to 1992, turn the two securing clips through a quarter-turn, then drop the fusebox panel down from the facia. On models from 1993,

3.3a Release the securing clips
(arrowed) . . .

3.3b . . . and lower the fusebox panel -
early models

3.3c Removing the fusebox cover -
later models

3.4 Fusebox location on right-hand side of
engine compartment

3.7 Removing a fuse using the plastic tool

3.11a Pull out the securing clip . . .

3.11b . . . to release the fusebox -
models from 1993

prise off the cover to expose the fusebox **(see illustrations)**.

4 Additional fuses may be located in the fusebox on the right-hand side of the engine compartment, in front of the suspension strut, and/or at the front left-hand corner of the engine compartment **(see illustration)**.

5 A blown fuse can be recognised from its melted or broken wire.

6 To remove a fuse, first ensure that the relevant circuit is switched off.

7 Using the plastic tool provided in the fusebox, pull the fuse from its location **(see illustration)**.

8 Spare fuses are provided in the blank terminal positions in the fusebox.

9 Before renewing a blown fuse, trace and rectify the cause, and always use a fuse of the correct rating. Never substitute a fuse of a higher rating, or make temporary repairs using

wire or metal foil; more serious damage, or even fire, could result.

10 Note that the fuses are colour-coded as follows. Refer to the wiring diagrams for details of the fuse ratings and the circuits protected.

Colour	Rating
Orange	5A
Red	10A
Blue	15A
Yellow	20A
Clear or white	25A
Green	30A

11 If desired, on models from 1993, the fusebox can be withdrawn from the facia as follows.

a) *Pull off the fusebox cover.*

b) *Locate the red plastic clip at the left-hand side of the fusebox, and pull the clip to release (see illustration).*

c) *Slide the fusebox to the left, and then pull the assembly out from the facia (see illustration).*

12 The following fuses are located in the engine compartment fusebox(es).

a) *Cooling fan.*

b) *ABS.*

c) *Fuel pump (petrol engines).*

d) *Oxygen sensor (petrol engines).*

e) *Engine management electronic control unit (petrol engines).*

Relays

13 A relay is an electrically-operated switch, which is used for the following reasons:

a) *A relay can switch a heavy current remotely from the circuit in which the current is flowing, allowing the use of lighter-gauge wiring and switch contacts.*

b) *A relay can receive more than one control input, unlike a mechanical switch.*

c) *A relay can have a timer function - for example, the intermittent wiper relay.*

14 Most of the relays are located under the facia, behind the main fusebox, and mounted on various brackets around the steering column. The rear wiper motor relay is located in the tailgate, behind the tailgate trim panel. On some models, additional engine-related relays are located in the relay box mounted at the front left-hand corner of the engine compartment, or in the left-hand corner of the scuttle **(see illustrations)**.

15 If a circuit or system controlled by a relay develops a fault, and the relay is suspect, operate the system. If the relay is functioning,

3.14a Removing a relay from the main
fusebox - models up to 1992

12

3.14b Unscrewing a relay bracket securing screw from under the steering column - models from 1993 (viewed with steering column shrouds removed)

3.14c Main relay box located behind fusebox at rear of facia - models from 1993 (viewed with facia removed and inverted)

3.14d Relays in engine compartment relay box - models up to 1992

it should be possible to hear it "click" as it is energised. If this is the case, the fault lies with the components or wiring of the system. If the relay is not being energised, then either the relay is not receiving a main supply or a switching voltage, or the relay itself is faulty. Testing is by the substitution of a known good unit, but be careful - while some relays are identical in appearance and in operation, others look similar but perform different functions.

16 To remove a relay, first ensure that the relevant circuit is switched off. The relay can then simply be pulled out from the socket, and pushed back into position.

---

4 Switches -
removal and refitting

Ignition switch/ steering column lock

1 Refer to Chapter 10.

Steering column combination switches

Models up to 1992

2 Remove the steering column shrouds, as described in Chapter 11.
3 Working under the switch, unscrew the two screws securing the switch to the steering column bracket **(see illustration)**.
4 Withdraw the switch, and disconnect the

wiring connector(s). Note the routing of the wiring to aid refitting.
5 Refitting is a reversal of removal, ensuring the wiring is routed as noted before removal.

Models from 1993

6 Proceed as described previously for models up to 1992, but note that the securing screws are accessed from the front of the switch **(see illustrations)**.

Radio/cassette player remote control and cruise control stalk switches

7 Remove the lower steering column shrouds as described in Chapter 11.
8 Remove the securing screws, and withdraw the switch from the column shroud.
9 Disconnect the wiring plug(s) and remove the switch.

4.3 Steering column combination switch screws (arrowed) - models up to 1992

10 Refitting is a reversal of removal; to refit the steering column shroud, see Chapter 11.

Facia-mounted pushbutton switches

Models up to 1992

11 Use a small flat-bladed screwdriver at the sides of the switch to release the plastic retaining tabs, then carefully prise the switch from the facia **(see illustration)**.
12 Disconnect the wiring plug and withdraw the switch.
13 To refit, reconnect the wiring plug, then push the switch into position in the facia.

Models from 1993

14 Proceed as described previously for models up to 1992, but note that the securing clips are released by prising at the top and bottom of the switch **(see illustration)**.

4.6a Remove the securing screws . . .

4.6b . . . and withdraw the steering column combination switch - models from 1993

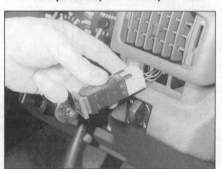

4.11 Removing a driver's side facia-mounted switch - models up to 1992

4.14 Prising out a facia-mounted switch - models from 1993

4.19 Prise the trim panel from the bottom of the oddments tray . . .

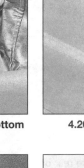

4.20 . . . then prise off the switch trim panel . . .

4.21 . . . and remove the switch

4.24 Prising off a rear centre console switch trim panel . . .

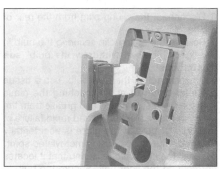

4.25 . . . for access to the switches

Headlight beam adjustment switch

Models up to 1992

15 The switch is integral with the adjustment mechanism. Refer to Section 8 for details of how to remove the mechanism.

Models from 1993

16 Carefully prise the switch from the facia panel using a small screwdriver (take care not to damage the trim), then disconnect the wiring plug and withdraw the switch.
17 Refitting is a reversal of removal.

Heater blower motor switch

18 The switch is integral with the heater control panel, and cannot be renewed separately. Removal and refitting details for the heater control panel are given in Chapter 3.

Centre console-mounted switches

Front switches

19 Prise out the trim panel from the bottom of the oddments tray below the handbrake lever (see illustration).
20 Prise off the switch trim panel (see illustration).
21 Prise the switch from the centre console, and disconnect the wiring plug (see illustration).
22 Refitting is a reversal of removal.

Rear switches

23 Prise the rear ashtray from the centre console.

24 Prise off the switch trim panel (see illustration).
25 Prise the switch from the centre console, and disconnect the wiring plug (see illustration).
26 Refitting is a reversal of removal.

Door-mounted switches

27 Prise the switch from its location in the door, and disconnect the wiring plug.
28 Refitting is a reversal of removal.

Courtesy light switches

Door-pillar-mounted switches

29 Open the door, then prise the rubber gaiter from the switch (see illustration).
30 Remove the securing screw, then carefully withdraw the switch from the door pillar. Disconnect the wiring connector as it becomes accessible, bearing in mind the danger of losing the wiring connector (see Haynes Hint).

4.29 Rubber gaiter pulled back to expose courtesy light securing screw (arrowed)

HAYNES HiNT *Tape the wiring to the door pillar, to prevent it falling back into the door pillar. Alternatively, tie a piece of string to the wiring, to retrieve it.*

31 Refitting is a reversal of removal, but ensure that the rubber gaiter is correctly seated on the switch.

Roof panel-mounted switches

32 The switches are integral with the lights, and cannot be renewed separately.

Luggage compartment light switch

Saloon models

33 Open the boot lid.
34 The switch is located in a bracket at the rear of the boot, and is operated by the boot lid hinge.
35 Release the clips, and pull the switch from the bracket (see illustration).
36 Disconnect the wiring plug and withdraw the switch.
37 Refitting is a reversal of removal.

Estate models

38 The light is operated by a tilt-sensitive switch fitted inside the tailgate.
39 Open the tailgate.
40 Remove the screws, and withdraw the plastic trim panel from inside the tailgate.
41 Working around the edge of the carpeted trim panel, release the securing clips, ideally using a forked tool to avoid breaking the clips. Withdraw the carpeted panel.

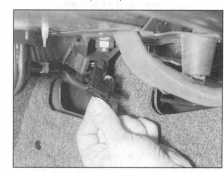

4.35 Removing the luggage compartment courtesy light switch - Saloon model

12

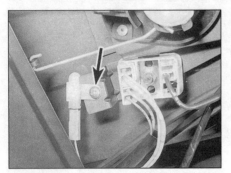

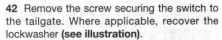

4.42 Luggage compartment courtesy light switch screw (arrowed) - Estate model

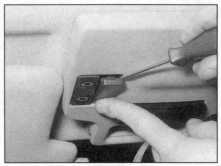

4.46 Prise out the blanking plate . . .

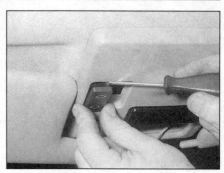

4.47 . . . then prise out the sunroof switch

42 Remove the screw securing the switch to the tailgate. Where applicable, recover the lockwasher **(see illustration)**.
43 Disconnect the wiring plug and withdraw the switch.
44 Refitting is a reversal of removal.

Map reading light switch

45 The switch is integral with the light, and cannot be renewed separately.

Electric sunroof switch

46 Carefully prise the blanking plate (fitted next to the sunroof switch) from the centre console **(see illustration)**.
47 Reach in through the aperture left by removal of the blanking plate, then push out the switch and disconnect the wiring plug **(see illustration)**.
48 Refitting is a reversal of removal.

---

5 Bulbs (exterior lights) - renewal

1 Whenever a bulb is renewed, note the following points.
  a) *Disconnect the battery negative lead before starting work.*
  b) *Remember that, if the light has just been in use, the bulb may be extremely hot.*
  c) *Always check the bulb contacts and holder, ensuring that there is clean metal-to metal contact between the bulb and its live(s) and earth. Clean off any corrosion or dirt before fitting a new bulb.*
  d) *Wherever bayonet-type bulbs are fitted (see Specifications), ensure that the live contact(s) bear firmly against the bulb contact.*
  e) *Always ensure the new bulb is of the correct rating, and that it is completely clean before fitting it; this applies particularly to headlight/foglight bulbs (see below).*

Headlight

2 Working in the engine compartment, release the clip securing the cover to the rear of the headlight unit. Withdraw the cover **(see illustration)**.

3 Disconnect the wiring plug from the rear of the headlight bulb.
4 Release the spring clip securing the bulb in the light unit, then withdraw the bulb **(see illustrations)**.
5 When handling the new bulb, use a tissue or clean cloth, to avoid touching the glass with the fingers; moisture and grease from the skin can cause blackening and rapid failure of this type of bulb. If the glass is accidentally touched, wipe it clean using methylated spirit.
6 Install the new bulb, ensuring that it locates correctly in the light unit. Secure the bulb in position with the spring clip, and reconnect the wiring plug.
7 Refit the cover to the rear of the light unit, and secure with the clip.

Front sidelight

8 The sidelight bulb is located in the rear of the headlight housing.

5.2 Headlight rear cover securing clip (arrowed)

5.4b . . . then withdraw the headlight bulb

9 Working in the engine compartment, release the clip securing the cover to the rear of the headlight unit.
10 On models up to 1992, pull the bulbholder from the rear of the headlight unit. On models from 1993, it will be necessary to twist the bulbholder through a quarter turn before it can be removed **(see illustration)**.
11 The bulb is a push-fit in the bulbholder **(see illustration)**.
12 Refitting is the reverse of the removal procedure, ensuring that the bulbholder seal is in good condition.

Front direction indicator

13 Working in the engine compartment, unhook the indicator light unit retaining spring from the lug behind the light **(see illustration)**.
14 Pull the light forwards from the wing panel.
15 Twist the bulbholder anti-clockwise to release it from the light unit **(see illustration)**.

5.4a Release the spring clip (arrowed) . . .

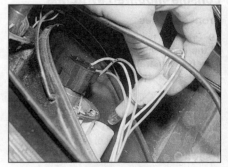

5.10 Pull out the sidelight bulbholder . . .

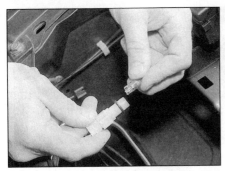

5.11 . . . and withdraw the bulb

5.13 Front direction indicator light retaining spring (arrowed)

5.15 Withdrawing the bulbholder from the front direction indicator light

5.20 Removing the bulbholder from the front direction indicator side repeater light

16 The bulb is a bayonet-fit in the bulbholder.
17 Refitting is a reversal of removal, but ensure that the light unit retaining spring is correctly engaged.

Front direction indicator side repeater

18 Twist the light unit a quarter-turn anti-clockwise, and carefully pull the unit from the wing panel, taking care not to damage the paint.
19 Twist the bulbholder anti-clockwise, and remove it from the light unit.
20 The bulb is a bayonet-fit in the bulbholder **(see illustration)**.
21 Refitting is a reversal of the removal procedure.

Headlight-mounted front driving light

22 On certain models, a driving light is mounted in the headlight unit. The light operates when the headlights are switched to main beam.
23 Proceed as described previously in this Section for the headlight bulb **(see illustrations)**.

Front spoiler-mounted driving light/foglight

Note: *Some models are fitted with front foglights which have no securing screws visible from the front of the lens. At the time of writing, no information was available for this type of foglight.*
24 Two alternative types of light assembly may be fitted, depending on model. On some models, access to the bulb can be obtained

from the behind the spoiler. On other models, the light unit must be removed for access to the bulb.
25 On models where the light unit can be reached from behind the spoiler, reach up

5.23a Headlight-mounted driving light bulb securing clip (arrowed)

5.30 Removing a rear light cluster bulbholder - Saloon model

behind the spoiler and disconnect the wiring from the light. Prise the rubber cover from the light, then release the spring clip and withdraw the bulb.
26 On models where the rear of the light unit is covered by the spoiler, remove the two securing screws from the front of the light unit and withdraw the reflector/lens assembly. Disconnect the wiring from the bulb, then release the spring clip and withdraw the bulb.
27 When handling the new bulb, use a tissue or clean cloth, to avoid touching the glass with the fingers; moisture and grease from the skin can cause blackening and rapid failure of this type of bulb. If the glass is accidentally touched, wipe it clean using methylated spirit.
28 Refitting is the reverse of the removal procedure, ensuring that the bulb locates correctly in its housing.

Rear light cluster

Saloon models

29 Open the boot lid.
30 Squeeze the two retaining clips, and withdraw the bulbholder from the rear of the light unit **(see illustration)**.
31 The bulbs are a bayonet-fit in the bulbholder **(see illustration)**.
32 Fit the new bulb using a reversal of the removal procedure.

Estate models

33 The stop/tail lights and the direction indicator lights are located in the rear wing panels. The remaining rear lights are located in the tailgate.

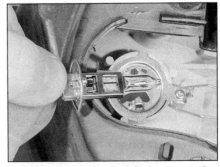

5.23b Removing a headlight-mounted driving light bulb

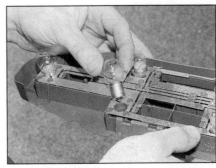

5.31 The bulbs are a bayonet-fit in the bulbholder

12

5.36a Removing a rear wing-mounted light bulbholder - Estate model

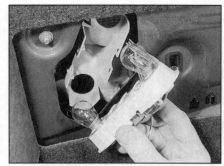

5.36b Removing a tailgate-mounted light bulbholder - Estate model

5.39 Prise the lens from the bumper . . .

5.40 . . . and withdraw the number plate light bulb - Saloon model

5.42 Prise out the number plate light unit . . .

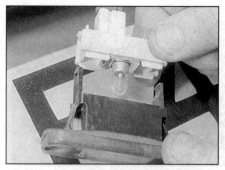

5.43 . . . and unclip the bulbholder from the lens - Estate model

34 Open the tailgate.
35 Turn the retaining clip and open the light unit cover flap.
36 Squeeze the two retaining clips, and withdraw the bulbholder from the rear of the light unit **(see illustrations)**.
37 The bulbs are a bayonet-fit in the bulbholder.
38 Fit the new bulb using a reversal of the removal procedure.

Number plate light

Saloon models

39 Prise the lens from the underside of the bumper for access to the bulb **(see illustration)**.
40 The bulb is a bayonet-fit in the bulbholder **(see illustration)**.
41 Fit the new bulb using a reversal of the removal procedure.

Estate models

42 Carefully prise the light unit from the tailgate **(see illustration)**.
43 Unclip the bulbholder from the lens assembly **(see illustration)**.
44 The bulb is a bayonet-fit in the bulbholder.
45 Fit the new bulb using a reversal of the removal procedure.

6 Bulbs (interior lights) - renewal

General

1 Refer to Section 5, paragraph 1.

Courtesy light, glovebox and luggage compartment lights

2 Carefully prise the lens from the light unit.

Note that in some cases, it may prove necessary to prise out the complete light unit to enable the lens to be removed **(see illustrations)**.
3 The bulb is a push-fit in the holder.
4 Refitting is a reversal of removal.

Map reading light

5 Prise the map reading light from the roof console.
6 The festoon-type bulb is held between the spring contacts **(see illustration)**.
7 Refitting is a reversal of removal.

Heater/ventilation control unit illumination bulbs

Models up to 1992

8 For access to the bulbs, the control unit must be removed as described in Chapter 3, but note that there is no need to disconnect the control cables from the unit. Once the

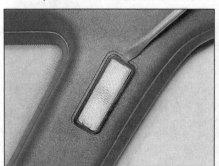

6.2a Prising out a courtesy light

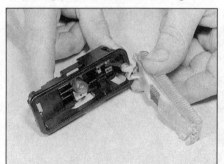

6.2b Prise off the lens for access to the bulb

6.6 Map reading light removed for access to bulb

6.19 Unclip the front panel from the heater control unit

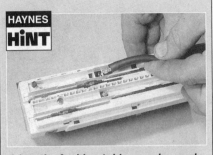

A length of rubber tubing can be used to remove and refit the bulbs

Facia switch illumination bulbs

25 The bulbs are integral with the switches, and cannot be renewed independently.

Instrument panel illumination and warning light bulbs

26 Remove the instrument panel as described in Section 9.
27 Twist the relevant bulbholder anti-clockwise to remove it from the rear of the panel **(see illustration)**.
28 The bulbs are a push-fit in the bulbholders.
29 On completion, refit the instrument panel with reference to Section 9.

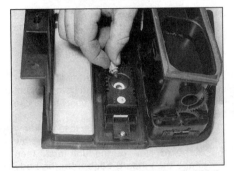

6.23 Removing the clock illumination bulb - models from 1993

6.27 Removing an instrument panel illumination bulb

securing screws have been removed, the control unit can be pulled forwards sufficiently for access to the bulbs without disconnecting the cables.

Models from 1993

9 Disconnect the battery negative lead.
10 Remove the centre console as described in Chapter 11, Section 29.
11 Unscrew the two screws located at the bottom of the ashtray housing.
12 Where applicable, remove the radio/cassette player as described in Section 20. On models not fitted with a radio/cassette player, prise out the oddments tray.
13 Remove the two securing screws from the top of the radio/cassette player/oddments tray housing, then withdraw the housing from the facia. Where applicable, disconnect the wiring plug(s) from the rear of the panel.
14 Prise the blanking plate from the top corner of the facia centre ventilation nozzle housing. Remove the now-exposed securing screw.
15 Remove the four housing securing screws located under the heater control panel. Two screws are accessible from the front of the housing, and two screws from underneath.
16 Carefully prise the switches from below the centre facia ventilation nozzles to reveal the remaining housing securing screw. Remove the screw.
17 Pull the housing forwards, and disconnect the wiring from the clock, then withdraw the housing.
18 Carefully pull the knobs from the heater control levers.

19 Unclip the front panel from the heater control unit to expose the bulbs **(see illustration)**.
20 The bulbs are a push-fit in the bulbholders **(see Haynes Hint)**.
21 Refitting is a reversal of removal.

Clock illumination bulb

22 For access to the clock illumination bulb, remove the clock as described in Section 11. Note that on models from 1993, access to the bulb can be gained once the housing has been removed from the facia - there is no need to remove the clock from the housing.
23 To remove the bulbholder, twist it anti-clockwise **(see illustration)**. The bulb is integral with the bulbholder.
24 Fit the new bulb using a reversal of the removal procedure.

7 Exterior light units - removal and refitting

Note: *Disconnect the battery negative lead before removing any light unit, and reconnect the lead after refitting the unit.*

Headlight

Removal

1 Working in the engine compartment, release the clip securing the cover to the rear of the headlight unit.
2 Disconnect the wiring plugs from the bulbs located in the headlight unit.
3 Remove the direction indicator light as described during the bulb renewal procedure in Section 5.
4 On models with cable-operated headlight adjusters, disconnect the adjuster from the headlight as follows.
  a) *Tun the adjuster and pull it from the bracket on the body front panel.*
  b) *Carefully pull the balljoint from the socket in the rear of the headlight (see illustration).*
5 On models with electrically-operated headlight adjusters, disconnect the wiring plug from the adjuster in the rear of the headlight.
6 Remove the radiator grille panel as described in Chapter 11.
7 Carefully prise the lower trim plate from the bottom of the headlight **(see illustration)**.

7.4 Removing a cable-operated headlight adjuster

7.7 Removing the trim plate from the bottom of the headlight

12

7.8 Outer headlight securing bolts (arrowed)

7.9 Removing a headlight lens securing clip

7.16 Remove the front driving light/foglight cowl securing screws

8 Unscrew the two outer headlight securing bolts, and pull the unit forwards from the body panel **(see illustration)**.

9 If desired, the headlight lens can be renewed by prising off the metal securing clips and withdrawing the lens from the front of the light unit **(see illustration)**.

10 Before fitting a new lens, ensure that the seal located in the groove around the front of the headlight is in good condition, and renew if necessary.

Refitting

11 Refitting is a reversal of removal, but on completion have the headlight beam alignment checked at the earliest opportunity.

Front direction indicator

12 The procedure is described as part of the bulb renewal procedure in Section 5.

Front direction indicator side repeater

13 The procedure is described as part of the bulb renewal procedure in Section 5.

Front spoiler-mounted driving light/foglight

14 Two alternative types of light assembly may be fitted, depending on model. The light may be mounted either directly in the front spoiler, or in a cowl screwed to the front spoiler.

Cowl-mounted light

15 Reach up behind the spoiler, and disconnect the wiring from the light.

16 Remove the two screws securing the light cowl to the spoiler, then withdraw the cowl/light assembly rearwards from the bumper **(see illustration)**.

17 The light unit can be removed from the cowl after unscrewing the knurled securing nut at the rear of the unit **(see illustration)**.

18 Refitting is a reversal of removal, but on completion, check and if necessary adjust the light beam alignment. Adjustment can be made using the knurled nuts at the rear of the unit.

Light mounted directly in spoiler

Note: *Some models are fitted with front foglights which have no securing screws visible from the front of the lens. At the time of writing, no information was available for this type of foglight.*

19 To improve access, jack up the front of the vehicle and support securely on axle stands (see *"Jacking and Vehicle Support"*).

20 Trace the wiring back from the rear of the foglight, and disconnect the wiring connector.

21 Slacken and remove the foglight securing nut, and withdraw the light unit from the spoiler. Recover any washers and spacers, noting their locations to ensure correct refitting.

22 Refitting is a reversal of removal, ensuring that any washers and spacers on the securing stud are positioned as noted before removal.

Rear light cluster

Saloon models

23 Open the boot lid.

24 Squeeze the two retaining clips, and withdraw the bulbholder from the rear of the light unit.

25 Disconnect the wiring plug from the bulbholder.

26 Pull up the luggage compartment weather-strip, and release the luggage compartment inner trim panel from the rear panel to expose the light unit securing nuts.

27 Unscrew the securing nuts, then withdraw the unit from outside the vehicle. Withdraw the outboard side of the unit first, then disengage the inboard edge from the body **(see illustrations)**.

28 Refitting is a reversal of removal

Estate models

29 The stop/tail lights and the direction indicator lights are located in the rear wing panels. The remaining rear lights are located in the tailgate.

30 Open the tailgate.

31 Turn the retaining clip and open the light unit cover flap.

32 Squeeze the two retaining clips, and withdraw the bulbholder from the rear of the light unit.

33 Disconnect the wiring plug from the bulbholder.

34 Unscrew the securing nuts and withdraw the light unit from outside the vehicle **(see illustrations)**.

35 Refitting is a reversal of removal.

Number plate light

Saloon models

36 Remove the two securing screws, then

7.17 Unscrew the nut (arrowed) to separate the light from the cowl

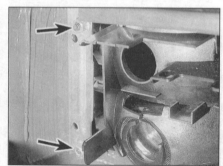

7.27a Unscrew the securing nuts (arrowed) . . .

7.27b . . . then withdraw the rear light unit - Saloon model

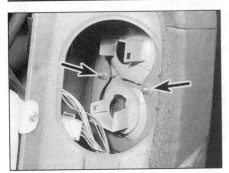

7.34a Rear wing-mounted light cluster securing nuts (arrowed) - Estate model

7.34b Withdrawing a rear wing-mounted light cluster - Estate model

Headlight-mounted adjusters - models up to 1992

Position 1   No load
Position 2   Medium load
Position 3   Maximum load

Headlight-mounted adjusters - models from 1993

Position 1   Front seat occupied
Position 2   All seats occupied and
              luggage compartment full
Position 3   Driver's seat occupied and
              luggage compartment full

Facia-mounted adjuster

Position 0   Front seats occupied
Position 1   All seats occupied
Position 2   All seats occupied and
              luggage compartment full
Position 3   Driver's seat occupied and
              luggage compartment full

4 Where applicable, ensure both adjusters are set to the same position, and be sure to reset if the vehicle load is altered.

Component renewal

Mechanical remote adjuster mechanism

5 Working beneath the facia ventilation nozzles, prise out the three blanking plates covering the instrument panel visor screws.
6 Remove the screws, and lift off the instrument panel visor.
7 Move the steering column to its lowest position.
8 Carefully prise off the headlight adjuster switch knob.
9 Remove the securing screws, and withdraw the driver's side upper facia panel. Disconnect the wiring from the switches in the panel as the panel is removed.
10 Remove the two screws securing the adjuster switch to the facia (see illustration).
11 Working in the engine compartment, turn and pull the adjusters from the brackets behind the headlights. The ends of the adjusters are a push-fit (balljoints) in the rear of the headlights.
12 Unclip the adjuster cables from the brackets and clips in the engine bay. Feed the switch cable through the bulkhead into the engine bay (see Haynes Hint overleaf).

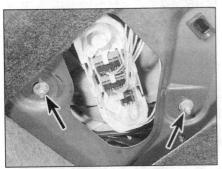

7.34c Tailgate-mounted rear light cluster securing nuts (arrowed) - Estate model

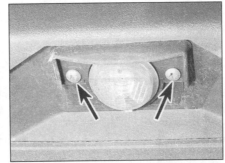

7.36 Number plate light securing screws (arrowed) - Saloon model

withdraw the light unit from the bumper and disconnect the wiring plug (see illustration).
37 Refitting is a reversal of removal.

Estate models

38 Carefully prise the unit from the tailgate and disconnect the wiring plug.
39 Refitting is a reversal of removal.

8 Headlight beam alignment - general information and component renewal

1 Accurate adjustment of the headlight beam is only possible using optical beam-setting equipment, and this work should therefore be carried out by a Peugeot dealer or suitably-equipped workshop.
2 For reference, the headlights can be finely adjusted using a suitable-sized Allen key to rotate the adjuster assemblies fitted to the

rear of each light unit. The outer adjuster alters the vertical height of the beam, whilst the inner adjuster alters the horizontal position of the beam (see illustrations). Prior to adjustment, ensure the vehicle is unladen, and that the adjuster units (see below) are both set to position "0", or "1", as applicable.
3 Each headlight unit is equipped with a three- or four-position vertical beam adjuster unit (depending on model) - this can be used to adjust the headlight beam, to compensate for the relevant load which the vehicle is carrying. The adjuster units may be incorporated into the vertical beam adjuster on the back of the headlight, or on certain models, an adjuster switch is provided on the facia. On models with adjusters mounted on the headlights, access to them can be gained with the bonnet open. The adjusters should be positioned as follows according type, and the load being carried in the vehicle.

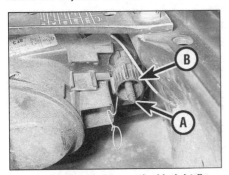

8.2a Headlight beam vertical height fine adjuster (A) and adjuster unit knob (B)

8.2b Headlight beam horizontal fine adjuster (arrowed)

8.10 Headlight adjuster switch securing screws (arrowed)

HAYNES HINT *Tie a length of string to the end of the adjuster cable before pulling it through the bulkhead. Untie the string and leave it in position to aid refitting.*

13 Refitting is a reversal of removal. Where applicable, use the string to pull the cable into position through the bulkhead into the passenger compartment.

Electric adjuster switch

14 Refer to Section 4.

Electric adjuster unit

15 Disconnect the battery negative lead.
16 Working at the rear of the headlight, disconnect the wiring plug from the adjuster unit (mounted in the rear of the headlight).
17 Twist the adjuster unit (or the locking collar, as applicable) to release the adjuster from the aperture in the headlight unit.

---

9 Instrument panel -
removal and refitting

Models up to 1992

Removal

1 Disconnect the battery negative lead.
2 Working beneath the facia ventilation nozzles, prise out the three blanking plates covering the instrument panel visor securing screws **(see illustration)**.
3 Remove the screws, and lift off the instrument panel visor **(see illustrations)**.
4 Move the steering column to its lowest position.
5 Where applicable, carefully prise off the headlight adjuster switch knob **(see illustration)**.
6 Remove the securing screws, and withdraw the driver's side upper facia panel **(see illustration)**. Disconnect the wiring from the switches in the panel as the panel is removed.
7 Unclip the trim panel from the lower edge of the instrument panel to expose the upper centre facia panel securing screw. Remove the screw **(see illustration)**.
8 Remove the instrument panel screws from the top corners of the panel **(see illustration)**.

9 Tilt the instrument panel forwards, and disconnect the speedometer cable from the rear of the panel. Give the cable end fitting a sharp tug to free it from the speedometer.
10 Disconnect the wiring plugs from the rear of the instrument panel, noting their locations to ensure correct refitting.
11 Lift the instrument panel from the facia.

Refitting

12 Refitting is a reversal of removal, but ensure that the wiring plugs are correctly reconnected, and make sure that the cable is securely reconnected to the speedometer, before securing the instrument panel in position in the facia.

Models from 1993

Removal

13 Disconnect the battery negative lead.
14 Release the securing clips, and remove

the lower trim panel from the driver's footwell.
15 Where applicable, move the steering column adjuster lever to the released position.
16 Working under the steering column loosen, but do not remove, the lower steering column securing bolts (note that on some models, it will be necessary to remove the steering column shrouds for access to the steering column securing bolts - see Chapter 11).
17 Similarly, unscrew and remove the two upper steering column securing nuts.
18 Cover the upper steering column shroud with cloth to protect it during the following procedure.
19 Working under the instrument panel, prise the ends of the trim panel upwards to release it from the facia, and withdraw the panel **(see illustration)**. If necessary, unscrew the lower steering column fixings further to enable the column to be lowered sufficiently for access.

9.2 Prise out the blanking plates . . .

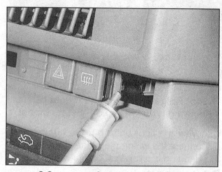

9.3a . . . and remove the visor securing screws

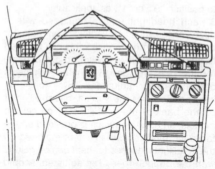

9.3b Instrument panel visor securing screw locations (arrowed)

9.5 Prise off the headlight adjuster switch knob

9.6 Withdrawing the driver's side upper facia panel

9.7 Remove the upper centre facia panel securing screw

9.8 Instrument panel securing screw (arrowed)

9.19 Prise the trim panel from the facia

9.21 Unscrew the lower instrument panel securing screws

9.22 Lever the upper securing clip down . . .

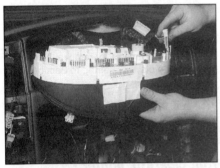

9.23 . . . until the instrument panel can be withdrawn

20 Working in the engine compartment, locate the speedometer cable ball, which rests in a grommet in the engine compartment bulkhead, then pull the ball sharply to release the cable from the speedometer.
21 Unscrew the two lower and single upper instrument panel securing screws **(see illustration)**.
22 Insert a soft plastic or wooden lever between the top instrument panel securing clip (the upper securing screw location) and the facia, and carefully lever the clip down until the instrument panel can be withdrawn forwards **(see illustration)**.
23 Disconnect the wiring plugs from the rear of the panel, and withdraw the panel from the facia **(see illustration)**.

Refitting

24 Refitting is a reversal of removal, bearing in mind the following points.

a) *Before refitting, ensure that the Velcro strip, which retains the wiring looms, is in position at the top of the instrument panel aperture.*
b) *Reconnect the speedometer cable by pushing the cable ball into position in the bulkhead grommet.*
c) *Tighten the steering column securing nuts.*

> **HAYNES HiNT** *Coat the ball with soapy water to aid refitting.*

---

10 Instrument panel components - removal and refitting

General

1 Remove the instrument panel as described in Section 9, then proceed as described under the relevant sub-heading.

Gauges - models up to 1992

2 Release the securing clips, and unscrew the three securing screws, then remove the panel surround/lens assembly from the instrument panel.
3 Unscrew the relevant securing screws or nuts, then withdraw the gauge from the front of the panel.
4 Refitting is a reversal of removal.

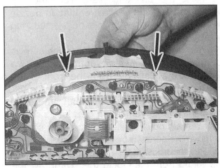

10.5 Two of the instrument panel lens securing screws (arrowed)

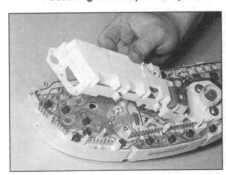

10.8 Removing the cover from the rear of the instrument panel

Gauges - models from 1993

5 Working at the rear of the panel, remove the lens securing screws from around the edge of the panel **(see illustration)**.
6 Remove the two recessed lens securing screws from the rear of the panel **(see illustration)**.
7 Release the securing clips by carefully prising with a screwdriver, then withdraw the lens assembly.
8 Where necessary, for access to the gauge fixings at the rear of the gauge, remove the screws and withdraw the cover from the rear of the instrument panel **(see illustration)**.
9 Unscrew the nuts from the gauge contact studs, or remove the gauge securing screws, as applicable **(see illustration)**.
10 Where applicable, working at the front of the gauge, remove the gauge securing screws **(see illustration)**.

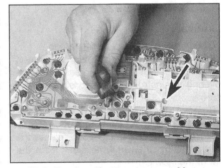

10.6 Remove the two recessed lens securing screws

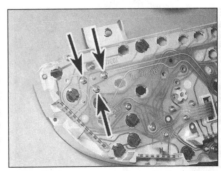

10.9 Fuel gauge securing nuts (arrowed)

12

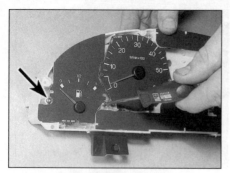

10.10 Remove the gauge
securing screws . . .

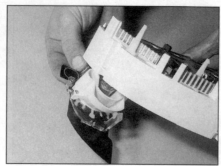

10.11a . . . then withdraw the gauge . . .

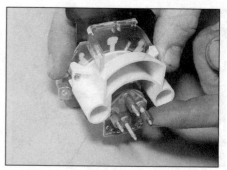

10.11b . . . and recover the spacers from
the studs

11 Carefully withdraw the gauge from the front of the instrument panel, taking care not to damage the circuit board. Where applicable, recover the spacers from the gauge studs **(see illustrations)**.
12 Refitting is a reversal of removal. Make sure that the spacers are in position on the gauge studs, where applicable.

Illumination and warning light bulbs

13 Twist the relevant bulbholder anti-clockwise to release it from the rear of the panel. The bulbs are integral with the bulbholders.

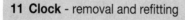

11 Clock - removal and refitting

Models up to 1992

Removal

1 Disconnect the battery negative lead.
2 Working beneath the facia ventilation nozzles, prise out the three blanking plates covering the instrument panel visor securing screws.
3 Remove the screws, and lift off the instrument panel visor **(see illustration 9.3b)**.
4 Working at the rear of the clock, release the securing clips, then pull the clock from the rear of the facia panel.
5 Disconnect the wiring plug and withdraw the clock **(see illustration)**.

Refitting

6 Refitting is a reversal of removal.

Models from 1993

Removal

7 Disconnect the battery negative lead.
8 Remove the centre console as described in Chapter 11, Section 29.
9 Open the ashtray cover, and unscrew the two screws located at the bottom of the ashtray housing.
10 Where applicable, remove the radio/cassette player as described in Section 20. On models not fitted with a radio/cassette player, prise out the oddments tray.
11 Remove the two securing screws from the top of the radio/cassette player/oddments tray housing, then withdraw the housing from the facia. Where applicable, disconnect the wiring plug(s) from the rear of the housing.
12 Prise the blanking plate from the top corner of the facia centre ventilation nozzle housing. Remove the now-exposed securing screw.
13 Remove the four housing securing screws located under the heater control panel. Two screws are accessible from the front of the housing, and a two screws from underneath.
14 Carefully prise the switches from below the centre facia ventilation nozzles to reveal the remaining housing securing screw. Remove the screw **(see illustration)**.
15 Pull the housing forwards, and disconnect the wiring from the clock, then withdraw the housing **(see illustration)**.
16 Working at the rear of the clock, remove

the two securing screws, then withdraw the clock from the housing.

Refitting

17 Refitting is a reversal of removal. Refit the radio/cassette player, referring to Section 20.

12 Cigarette lighter - removal and refitting

Front cigarette lighter - models up to 1992

Removal

1 Disconnect the battery negative lead.
2 Prise the lower stowage tray from the centre console.
3 Prise the side panels from the front of the console.
4 Working behind the ashtray housing, disconnect the wiring from the cigarette lighter and the illumination bulb.
5 Again working behind the housing, depress the cigarette lighter securing clips, and push the unit forwards from the housing.

Refitting

6 Refitting is a reversal of removal.

Front cigarette lighter - models from 1993

7 Disconnect the battery negative lead.
8 Remove the centre console as described in Chapter 11, Section 29.
9 Open the ashtray cover, and unscrew the

11.5 Removing the clock -
models up to 1992

11.14 Remove the centre facia ventilation
nozzle housing lower securing screw . . .

11.15 . . . then withdraw the housing

13.2 "Lights on" warning buzzer (arrowed) - models up to 1992

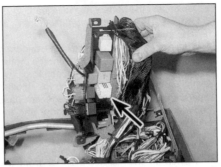

13.3 "Lights on" warning buzzer (arrowed) - models from 1993 (viewed with facia removed and inverted)

two screws located at the bottom of the ashtray housing.

10 Where applicable, remove the radio/cassette player as described in Section 20. On models not fitted with a radio/cassette player, prise out the oddments tray.

11 Remove the two securing screws from the top of the radio/cassette player/oddments tray housing, then withdraw the housing from the facia. Disconnect the wiring plug(s) from the rear of the housing.

12 Working behind the housing, depress the cigarette lighter securing clips, and push the unit forwards from the housing.

Rear cigarette lighter

13 The procedure is similar to that described previously for the front lighter, except that access is obtained by removing the rear ashtray from the centre console.

13 "Lights-on" warning system - general information

1 The purpose of this system is to inform the driver that the lights have been left on once the ignition has been switched off; the buzzer will sound when a door is opened. The system consists of a buzzer unit which is linked to the driver's door courtesy light switch.

2 On models up to 1992, the buzzer unit is located behind the fuses in the facia fusebox, and access can be obtained once the fusebox cover has been removed. The unit is a push-fit in the panel, and can be identified by the slots in its cover **(see illustration)**.

3 On models from 1993, the buzzer unit is located in the relay block, behind the fusebox **(see illustration)**.

4 Refer to Section 4 for information on courtesy light switch removal.

14 Horn - removal and refitting

Removal

1 There may be a single horn or double horns mounted behind the front bumper (on some

models, one horn is mounted on each side of the vehicle).

2 Disconnect the battery negative lead.

3 Where applicable, remove the wheel arch liner(s) to improve access.

4 Reach up behind the bumper, and disconnect the wiring from the horn.

5 Unscrew the nut securing the horn to the mounting bracket, and withdraw the horn **(see illustration)**.

Refitting

6 Refitting is a reversal of removal.

15 Speedometer cable - removal and refitting

Removal

1 Working in the engine compartment, locate the speedometer cable ball, which rests in a grommet in the engine compartment bulkhead, then pull the ball sharply to release the cable from the speedometer.

2 Remove the instrument panel (Section 9).

3 Tie a length of string to the end of the speedometer cable at the speedometer end.

4 Working at the gearbox/transmission end of the cable, remove the pin securing the cable end fitting to the gearbox/transmission housing.

5 Pull the cable through the bulkhead grommet into the engine compartment, then withdraw the cable from the vehicle. If desired, access to the bulkhead grommet can

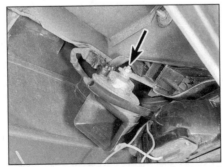

14.5 Horn securing nut (arrowed) - viewed from underneath vehicle

be obtained from the driver's footwell after unclipping the carpet trim panel from the lower facia.

6 Untie the string from the end of the cable, and leave the string in position to aid refitting.

Refitting

7 Refitting is a reversal of removal, but use the string to pull the cable into position, and make sure that the cable ball is correctly located in the bulkhead grommet. Coat the ball with soapy water to aid refitting. If it proves difficult to engage the speedometer cable with the rear of the speedometer, proceed as follows.

  a) Cut the two clips securing the ball/sleeve assembly to the speedometer cable, and slide the ball/sleeve down the cable.
  b) Push the cable until it engages with the speedometer, then slide the ball sleeve into position, and engage it with the bulkhead grommet.
  c) Fit a hose clip or cable-tie to the lower end of the ball/sleeve to secure it in position on the cable.
  d) If it still proves difficult to engage the cable with the speedometer, remove the instrument panel, then carry out the above procedure, engaging the end of the cable with the speedometer directly by hand, before refitting the instrument panel.

16 Wiper arm - removal and refitting

Removal

1 Operate the wiper motor, then switch it off so that the wiper arm returns to the at-rest position.

> **HAYNES HINT** *Stick a piece of masking tape along the edge of the wiper blade, to use as an alignment aid on refitting.*

2 Where applicable, disconnect the washer fluid hose from the end of the connector on the scuttle grille panel **(see illustration)**.

3 Lift up the wiper arm spindle nut cover, then

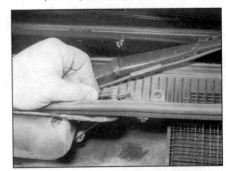

16.2 Disconnect the washer fluid hose from the connector

12

16.3 Slackening the wiper arm nut

slacken and remove the spindle nut **(see illustration)**. Lift the blade off the glass, and pull the wiper arm off its spindle. If necessary, the arm can be levered off the spindle using a suitable flat-bladed screwdriver.

Refitting

4 With the wiper arm and spindle splines clean, refit the arm to the spindle. Align the wiper blade with the tape used on removal.
5 Refit the spindle nut, tightening it securely, and clip the nut cover back into position.
6 Reconnect the washer fluid hose.

17 Windscreen wiper motor and linkage - removal and refitting

Removal

1 The assembly is located in the scuttle at the rear of the engine compartment.

17.8a Windscreen wiper motor securing nut (arrowed)

17.8c Withdrawing the windscreen wiper motor and linkage assembly

2 Disconnect the battery negative lead.
3 Remove the scuttle grille panel as described in Chapter 11.
4 Where applicable, unscrew the securing bolts, and withdraw the cover from the motor.
5 Disconnect the motor wiring connector.
6 On models where there is insufficient clearance for the wiper linkage to pass between the brake master cylinder and the scuttle, move the master cylinder to one side as follows. Remove the nuts securing the brake master cylinder to the vacuum servo unit, then lift the master cylinder from the studs, and pull it back slightly. Do not disconnect any brake pipes.
7 On models with an electronic control module housing located in the rear corner of the engine compartment, which obscures the end wiper linkage securing bolt, the housing must be removed as follows. Lift off the housing cover, then detach the control modules, and remove the housing. Take great care not to damage the control modules - ideally, they should be removed from the vehicle and stored in a safe place (alternatively, temporarily refit the housing and the control modules, once the wiper mechanism has been removed.
8 Unscrew the nuts securing the motor and linkage to the scuttle, then manipulate the assembly out from the engine compartment **(see illustrations)**.
9 If desired, the motor can be separated from the linkage after unscrewing the nuts securing the linkage to the motor spindle, and the three bolts securing the motor to the mounting bracket **(see illustration)**.

17.8b Windscreen wiper linkage securing nut (arrowed)

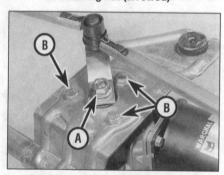

17.9 Wiper motor spindle-to-linkage nut (A) and motor securing bolts (B)

Refitting

10 Refitting is a reversal of removal.

18 Tailgate wiper motor - removal and refitting

Removal

1 Disconnect the battery negative lead.
2 Remove the wiper arm (see Section 16).
3 Unscrew the large spindle nut, and recover the washer and seal.
4 Open the tailgate.
5 Remove the screws, and withdraw the plastic trim panel from inside the tailgate.
6 Working around the edge of the carpeted trim panel, release the securing clips, ideally using a forked tool to avoid breaking the clips. Withdraw the carpeted panel.
7 Unscrew the motor bracket securing bolts, then withdraw the motor assembly from the tailgate, and disconnect the wiring plug **(see illustration)**.

Refitting

8 Refitting is a reversal of removal.

19 Washer system components - removal and refitting

Windscreen/headlight washer fluid reservoir

Removal

1 The reservoir is located in the right-hand corner of the scuttle at the rear of the engine compartment.
2 Disconnect the battery negative lead, then disconnect the wiring from the fluid pump(s).
3 Unscrew the two securing bolts, and lift the reservoir from the scuttle.
4 If the reservoir still contains fluid, empty out the contents into a container, then disconnect the fluid hose from the pump, and withdraw the reservoir.

Refitting

5 Refitting is a reversal of removal.

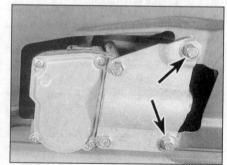

18.7 Tailgate wiper motor securing bolts (arrowed)

19.8a Remove the two securing screws (arrowed) . . .

19.8b . . . and lift out the tailgate washer fluid reservoir

Tailgate washer fluid reservoir

6 Disconnect the battery negative lead.
7 Open the tailgate, then turn the securing clip and open the access panel at the right-hand corner of the luggage compartment for access to the reservoir.
8 Remove the two securing screws, then lift out the reservoir (see illustrations).
9 If the reservoir still contains fluid, empty out the contents into a container, then disconnect the wiring plug and the fluid hose from the pump, and withdraw the reservoir.
10 Refitting is a reversal of removal.

Windscreen/headlight washer pump

Note: Prior to removing the pump, empty the contents of the reservoir, or be prepared for fluid spillage.
11 Disconnect the battery negative lead.
12 Disconnect the wiring connector and the fluid hose from the pump, then carefully ease the pump out of its sealing grommet in the reservoir.
13 Refitting is a reversal of removal.

Tailgate washer pump

14 Disconnect the battery negative lead.
15 Remove the reservoir as described previously in this Section.
16 Disconnect the wiring connector and the fluid hose from the pump, then carefully ease the pump out of its sealing grommet in the reservoir.
17 Refitting is a reversal of removal.

Tailgate washer jet

18 Pull the washer jet from the rear of the tailgate and disconnect the fluid hose.

 Tie a length of string to the end of the fluid hose to prevent it from falling back into the tailgate.

19 Refitting is a reversal of removal.

20 Radio/cassette player - removal and refitting

Radio/cassette player with DIN fittings

Removal

1 Disconnect the battery negative lead.
2 Carefully prise out and remove the small plastic trim panels at each side of the radio/cassette player (see illustration).
3 Insert the removal tools into the holes provided at each side of the unit, until they lock into position. This will release the securing clips (see illustration).
4 Using the tools, pull the unit forwards from the housing, and disconnect the wiring connectors and the aerial lead (see illustration).

20.2 Remove the plastic trim panels from the sides of the radio/cassette player . . .

20.4 . . . and withdraw the unit

5 Withdraw the unit from the facia.
6 Note that some units may have a bracket and rubber buffer fitted to the rear panel. If a new unit is being fitted, transfer these components to the new unit. The buffer sets the depth of the unit in the housing, and prevents the security cover fouling the cassette during insertion and ejection. These parts are available from dealers if they are not fitted.

Refitting

7 To refit the unit, reconnect the wiring plugs and the aerial lead, and push the unit into position until the securing clips lock. Ensure that the wiring harness and aerial lead are routed so that they cannot rub against the unit casing.
8 Refit the plastic covers to each side of the unit, and reconnect the battery negative lead.
9 Where applicable, to activate the unit, enter the security code in accordance with the manufacturer's instructions.

Radio/cassette player with "Peugeot" fixings

Removal

10 Disconnect the battery negative lead.
11 Open the radio/cassette player cover panel.
12 Working at the top of the unit, carefully prise off the trim panel to expose the two holes provided for the removal tools (see illustration).
13 Two removal tools will now be required. These tools can be made by cutting a standard DIN radio/cassette player removal

20.3 . . . then insert the removal tools . . .

20.12 Prise the trim panel from the top of the radio/cassette player

12

20.13 Make up two removal tools - note slot (arrowed) in end of tool

20.14 Insert the removal tools in the holes at the top of the radio/cassette player

tool in half. Alternatively, use two pieces of thin metal rod, with grooves cut in the ends to engage with the retaining clips **(see illustration)**.

14 Insert the removal tools into the holes provided above the unit, until they lock into position. This will release the securing clips **(see illustration)**.

15 Using the tools, pull the unit forwards from the housing, and disconnect the wiring connectors and the aerial lead.

16 Withdraw the unit from the facia.

Refitting

17 Proceed as described in paragraph 7, then refit the trim panel to the top of the unit, and reconnect the battery negative lead.

18 Where applicable, to activate the unit, enter the security code in accordance with the manufacturer's instructions.

21 Loudspeakers - removal and refitting

Door-mounted loudspeakers

1 Disconnect the battery negative lead.

2 Remove the loudspeaker cover panel, either by depressing the securing clip at the lower edge of the panel, or by removing the three securing screws from the edge of the panel, as applicable **(see illustrations)**.

3 Unscrew the securing screws, then withdraw the loudspeaker from the door, and disconnect the wiring plug **(see illustration)**.

4 Refitting is a reversal of removal.

Facia-mounted loudspeakers - models up to 1992

5 Disconnect the battery negative lead.

6 Carefully prise the loudspeaker cover panel from the top of the facia **(see illustration)**.

7 Remove the two securing screws, then withdraw the loudspeaker from the facia, and disconnect the wiring **(see illustration)**.

Facia-mounted loudspeakers - models from 1993

8 Disconnect the battery negative lead.

9 Carefully prise the loudspeaker from the top of the facia, and disconnect the wiring plug **(see illustrations)**. The loudspeaker is integral with the cover panel.

10 Refitting is a reversal of removal.

Rear parcel shelf-mounted loudspeakers - Saloon models

11 Disconnect the battery negative lead.

12 Working in the luggage compartment, on the underside of the parcel shelf, disconnect the wiring from the loudspeaker.

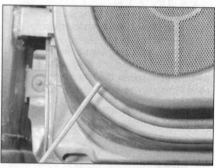

21.2a Release the securing clip . . .

21.2b . . . and remove loudspeaker cover panel from the door - models up to 1992

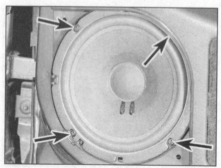

21.3 Door-mounted loudspeaker securing screws (arrowed)

21.6 Remove the loudspeaker cover panel from the top of the facia . . .

21.7 . . . for access to the loudspeaker screws (arrowed) - models up to 1992

21.9a Prise the loudspeaker from the facia . . .

21.9b . . . and disconnect the wiring plug - models from 1993

21.13 Removing the rear loudspeaker - Saloon models

13 Release the plastic securing clips, and push the speaker up through the parcel shelf into the vehicle interior. Remove the unit **(see illustration)**.

14 Refitting is a reversal of removal, but ensure that the locating lug on the loudspeaker engages with the hole in the parcel shelf.

22 Radio aerial - removal and refitting

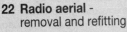

Roof-mounted aerial

1 Note that the aerial mast can simply be unscrewed from the base. To remove the complete aerial assembly, proceed as follows.
2 Disconnect the battery negative lead.
3 Unclip the sun visors from the roof console.

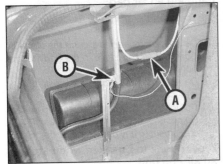

22.13 Aerial lead (A) and earth wire (B) - Saloon (rear wing-mounted manual aerial)

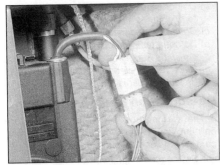

22.18a Disconnecting aerial motor wiring plug - Estate (rear wing-mounted aerial)

4 Carefully prise the courtesy light assembly from the console to expose the two roof console front securing screws. Disconnect the wiring plug and remove the light.
5 Similarly, prise the map reading light an the light surround from the console to expose one of the front securing screws. Disconnect the wiring plug and remove the light.
6 Prise the blanking plate from the console then, where applicable, push the sunroof switch from the console.
7 Remove the two console screws exposed by removal of the map reading light and sunroof switch, then lower the console from the roof, and disconnect the wiring plugs.
8 Prise the metal insulator from the base of the aerial **(see illustration)**.
9 Unscrew the securing nut and disconnect the aerial lead, then withdraw the aerial from the top of the roof.
10 Refitting is a reversal of removal.

Rear wing-mounted aerial

Saloon models

11 Fully retract the aerial.
12 Working in the luggage compartment, remove the trim panels from the left-hand side of the wing panel.
13 Disconnect the aerial lead connector and the earth wire from the bottom of the aerial **(see illustration)**. On models with an electric aerial, disconnect the motor wiring plug.
14 Unscrew the aerial mounting bracket lower fixing bolt.
15 Working at the top of the aerial, unscrew the ring nut securing the assembly to the top

22.15a Unscrew the ring nut . . .

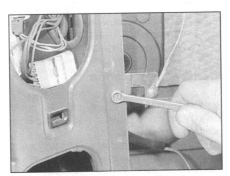

22.18b Unscrew the aerial motor securing bolt . . .

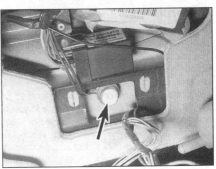

22.8 Roof-mounted radio aerial metal insulator (arrowed)

of the rear wing. Recover the sealing grommet **(see illustrations)**.
16 Withdraw the aerial assembly down into the luggage compartment.
17 Refitting is a reversal of removal.

Estate models

18 The procedure is as described previously for Saloon models, but the upper end of the aerial is retained by a grommet arrangement instead of a ring nut. When removing the aerial, simply pull the top of the aerial down through the grommet **(see illustrations)**.

23 Anti-theft alarm system - general information

Note: This information is applicable only to the anti-theft alarm system fitted by Peugeot as standard equipment.

22.15b . . . and recover sealing grommet - Saloon (rear wing-mounted manual aerial)

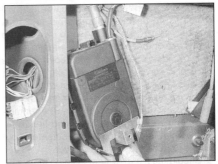

22.18c . . . and withdraw aerial assembly - Estate (rear wing-mounted aerial)

12

General

1 Some models in the range are fitted with an anti-theft alarm system as standard equipment. The alarm is automatically armed and disarmed using the remote central locking transmitter (where applicable). When the system is activated, the alarm indicator light, located on the fascia, will flash continuously. In addition to the alarm function, the system also incorporates an engine immobiliser.

2 Additionally, certain petrol engine models are fitted with a coded engine immobiliser device, operated by a key pad in the centre console.

Anti-theft alarm system

Early models

3 Note that if the doors are operated using the key, the alarm will not be armed or disarmed (as applicable). Locking the doors with the central locking remote transmitter is the only means of activating the alarm system.

4 The alarm system protects the doors and boot or tailgate, as applicable.

5 Should the alarm system become faulty, the vehicle should be taken to a Peugeot dealer for examination.

Later models

6 Note that if the doors are operated using the key, the alarm will not be armed or disarmed (as applicable). If for some reason the remote central locking transmitter fails whilst the alarm is armed, the vehicle must be unlocked using the key. In this case, the alarm system will activate, and must be disarmed using the master switch (see paragraph 8).

7 The alarm system has switches on the bonnet, tailgate and each of the doors. It also has ultrasonic sensing, which detects movement inside the vehicle, via sensors mounted on either side of the vehicle interior. If required, the ultrasonic sensing facility can be switched off, whilst retaining the switched side of the system. To switch off the ultrasonic sensing, with the ignition switch off, depress the alarm switch (mounted on the right of the steering column) until the alarm indicator light on the fascia is continuously lit. Now, when the doors are locked using the remote central locking transmitter, and the alarm is armed, only the switched side of the alarm system is operational (and the alarm indicator light will revert to its flashing mode). This facility is useful, as it allows you to leave the windows/sunroof open, and still arm the alarm. If the windows/sunroof are left open with the ultrasonic sensing not switched off, the alarm may be falsely triggered by a gust of wind.

8 To deactivate the complete alarm system, a master switch is provided in the engine compartment, behind the left-hand headlight. The switch is operated by a dedicated key, and is protected by a plastic cover.

9 Should the alarm system become faulty, the vehicle should be taken to a Peugeot dealer for examination.

Coded engine immobiliser

 Warning: Do not forget the immobiliser code - if the correct code cannot be entered, the engine management electronic control unit must be renewed.

10 This device cuts out the engine management system, and prevents the engine from being started unless a confidential code is keyed into the pad located in the centre console.

11 The code can be chosen by the owner, and full details are given in the vehicle handbook.

12 When the ignition is turned on, if the green light on the key pad is illuminated, the system is not working, and the engine can be started normally. If the red light is illuminated, the system is working (the engine cannot be started, and the alarm will sound if starting is attempted).

13 To de-activate the system, enter the correct code, which should be confirmed by four flashes from the green light, and four beeps. The red light should go out, and the engine can them be started.

14 If the wrong code is entered, the red light will stay on, and the engine cannot be started.

Disconnecting the battery

Early models

15 If the battery has been disconnected, when it is reconnected, the alarm will be activated.

16 The alarm must be de-activated using the remote central locking transmitter.

Later models

17 The following precautions should be observed when disconnecting and reconnecting the battery leads on a vehicle equipped with an alarm system.

18 Before disconnecting the battery, de-activate the alarm siren, using the dedicated key.

19 When reconnecting the battery, as soon as the battery is connected, the alarm is automatically activated. Use the remote transmitter to turn off the alarm, then activate the alarm siren using the dedicated key.

---

24 Air bag system - general information, precautions and system de-activation

---

General information

1 A driver's side air bag is fitted as standard equipment on later models, and is an option on all other models. The air bag is fitted in the steering wheel centre pad.

2 The system is armed only when the ignition is switched on, however, a reserve power source maintains a power supply to the system in the event of a break in the main electrical supply. The system is activated by a "g" sensor (deceleration sensor), and is controlled by an electronic control unit which is integral with the steering wheel.

3 The air bag is inflated by a gas generator, which forces the bag out from its location in the steering wheel.

Precautions

 Warning: The following precautions must be observed when working on vehicles equipped with an air bag system, to prevent the possibility of personal injury.

General precautions

4 The following precautions **must** be observed when carrying out work on a vehicle equipped with an air bag.

a) *Do not disconnect the battery with the engine running.*

b) *Before carrying out any work in the vacinity of the air bag, removal of any of the air bag components, or any welding work on the vehicle, de-activate the system as described in the following sub-Section.*

c) *Do not attempt to test any of the air bag system circuits using test meters or any other test equipment.*

d) *If the air bag warning light comes on, or any fault in the system is suspected, consult a Peugeot dealer without delay. **Do not** attempt to carry out fault diagnosis, or any dismantling of the components.*

Precautions to be taken when handling an air bag

a) *Transport the air bag by itself, bag upward.*

b) *Do not put your arms around the air bag.*

c) *Carry the air bag close to the body, bag outward.*

d) *Do not drop the air bag or expose it to impacts.*

e) *Do not try to dismantle the air bag unit.*

f) *Do not connect any form of electrical equipment to any part of the air bag circuit.*

Precautions to be taken when storing an air bag unit

a) *Store the unit in a cupboard with the air bag upward.*

b) *Do not expose the air bag to temperatures above 80°C.*

c) *Do not expose the air bag to flames.*

d) *Do not attempt to dispose of the air bag - consult a Peugeot dealer.*

e) *Never refit an air bag which is known to be faulty or damaged.*

De-activation of air bag system

5 The system must be de-activated before carrying out any work on the air bag components or surrounding area.

a) *Switch off the ignition.*

b) *Remove the ignition key.*

c) *Switch off all electrical equipment.*

d) *Disconnect the battery negative lead.*

e) *Insulate the battery negative terminal and the end of the battery negative lead to prevent any possibility of contact.*

f) *Wait for at least ten minutes before carrying out any further work.*

Activation of air bag system

6 To activate the system on completion of any work, proceed as follows.

a) *Ensure that there are no occupants in the vehicle, and that there are no loose objects around the vacinity of the steering wheel. Close the vehicle doors and windows.*

b) *Insert the ignition key, and switch on the ignition.*

c) *Reconnect the battery negative lead.*

d) *Switch off the ignition.*

e) *Switch on the ignition once more, and check that the air bag warning light in the steering wheel illuminates for approximately 3 seconds and then extinguishes.*

f) *Switch off the ignition.*

g) *If the air bag warning light does not operate as described in paragraph e), consult a Peugeot dealer before driving the vehicle.*

25 Air bag system components - removal and refitting

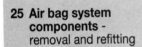

> ⚠ **Warning: Refer to the precautions given in Section 24 before attempting to carry out work on any of the air bag components.**

General

1 The air bag sensors are integral with the electronic control unit, which is itself integral with the steering wheel. The air bag warning light is integral with the air bag unit.

2 Any suspected faults with the air bag system should be referred to a Peugeot dealer - under no circumstances attempt to carry out any work other than removal and refitting of the air bag unit and/or the rotary connector, as described in the following paragraphs.

Air bag electronic control unit

3 The unit is integral with the steering wheel, and cannot be removed independently. Refer to Chapter 10 for steering wheel removal.

Air bag unit

Removal

4 The air bag unit is an integral part of the steering wheel centre boss.

25.7 Turn the steering wheel for access to the two air bag unit screws (arrowed)

5 De-activate the air bag system as described in Section 24.

6 Move the steering wheel as necessary for access to the two air bag unit securing screws. The screws are located at the rear of the steering wheel boss.

7 Remove the two air bag unit securing screws **(see illustration).**

8 Gently pull the air bag unit from the centre of the steering wheel.

9 Carefully unclip the wiring connector from the air bag unit (use the fingers only, and pull the connector upward from the air bag unit).

10 If the air bag unit is to be stored for any length of time, refer to the storage precautions given in Section 24.

Refitting

11 Refitting is a reversal of removal, bearing in mind the following points.

a) *Do not strike the air bag unit, or expose it to impacts during refitting.*

b) *Tighten the air bag unit securing screws to the specified torque.*

c) *On completion of refitting, activate the air bag system as described in Section 24.*

Air bag rotary connector

Removal

12 Remove the air bag unit, as described previously in this Section.

13 Remove the steering wheel as described in Chapter 10.

14 Remove the securing screws, and withdraw the lower steering column shroud. Allow the shroud to hang down, there is not need to disconnect the wiring from the components mounted inside the shroud.

15 Lift off the upper column shroud.

16 Disconnect the electrical supply connector from the rotary connector **(see illustration).**

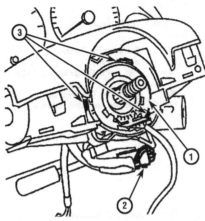

25.16 Air bag rotary connector details

1 *Rotary connector*
2 *Electrical supply connector*
3 *Rotary connector securing clips*

17 Carefully release the three securing clips using a screwdriver, then withdraw the rotary connector.

> ⚠ **Warning: Do not pull out the electrical supply connector when removing the rotary connector.**

Refitting

18 Refitting is a reversal of removal, bearing in mind the following points.

19 Before refitting the steering column shrouds and the air bag unit, check that the wiring harness is routed correctly by moving the steering wheel to check that the wiring is not trapped.

20 Refit the steering wheel (see Chapter 10).

21 Refit the air bag as described previously in this Section, but do not activate the air bag at this stage.

22 On completion, move the steering column to its fully raised position, then check that the clearance between the rear face of the steering wheel and the front faces of the steering column shrouds is 8.0 mm. If the clearance is not as specified, proceed as follows.

a) *Working in the driver's footwell, unclip the carpet trim panel from under the facia for access to the steering column pinch-bolt.*

b) *Loosen the pinch-bolt, then slide the steering shaft as necessary to give the specified clearance between the steering wheel and the shrouds.*

c) *Tighten the pinch-bolt, and refit the trim panel.*

23 Activate the air bag system as described in Section 24.

ITEM	DESCRIPTION	DIAGRAM/ GRID REF.
10	Accessory Relay	3/G2
12	Air Horn	3/A7
13	Air Horn Compressor Relay	3/B6
15	Ashtray Illumination	2b/E3
16	Audible Warning Device	2b/B1
19	Auto. Trans. Switch Stage Illumination	2b/K5
20	Battery	2/D7, 2a/E7, 2b/E7, 3/E8, 3a/B7, 3b/C6,
25	Central Locking Actuator Filler Cap	3a/M1
26	Central Locking Actuator LH Front	3a/K8
27	Central Locking Actuator LH Rear	3a/L8
28	Central Locking Actuator RH Front	3a/K1
29	Central Locking Actuator RH Rear	3a/L1
30	Central Locking Actuator Tailgate	3a/M5
31	Central Locking Control Unit	3a/E7
32	Central Locking Infra-red – Signal Receiver	3a/F5
34	Cigar Lighter	2b/F4
35	Clock	2b/F5
36	Combination Switch – Lighting, Direction Indicators And Horn	2/L4, 2a/J4, 2b/J4, 3/K4
37	Combination Switch – Wash/Wipe	3/K3
46	Dim/Dip Relay	2/F7
47	Dim/Dip Resistor	2/E8
48	Direction Indicator Flasher Relay	2a/D2
49	Direction Indicator LH Front	2a/A8
50	Direction Indicator RH Front	2a/A1
52	Driving Lamp LH	2/A7
53	Driving Lamp Relay	2/F7
54	Driving Lamp RH	2/A2
55	Electric Mirror Control Switch LH	3a/J5
56	Electric Mirror Control Switch RH	3a/J3
57	Electric Mirror LH	3a/G8
58	Electric Mirror RH	3a/G1
59	Electric Window Child Cut-out – (Rear Windows)	3b/L3
60	Electric Window Instantaneous – Lift Unit (One Touch)	3b/F1
61	Electric Window Motor LH Front	3b/K8
62	Electric Window Motor LH Rear	3b/M8
63	Electric Window Motor RH Front	3b/K1
64	Electric Window Motor RH Rear	3b/M1
65	Electric Window Rear Control – Switch (LH Front)	3b/L5
66	Electric Window Rear Control – Switch (LH Rear)	3b/L5
67	Electric Window Rear Control – Switch (RH Front)	3b/L4
68	Electric Window Rear Control – Switch (RH Rear)	3b/L4
69	Electric Window Relay Front	3b/B2
70	Electric Window Relay Rear	3b/C2
71	Electric Window/Sunroof Relay	3b/E3
72	Electric Window Switch LH	3b/J8
73	Electric Window Switch RH (Drivers)	3b/J1
74	Electric Window Switch RH (Drivers – One Touch)	3b/G1
75	Electric Window Switch RH (Passengers)	3b/H1
77	Foglamp Front	2/A3, 2/A6

ITEM	DESCRIPTION	DIAGRAM/ GRID REF.
78	Foglamp Relay	2/F1
79	Foglamp Switch Front	2/H1
80	Foglamp Switch Rear	2/J2
90	Glove Box Lamp	2b/G7
91	Glove Box Lamp Switch	2b/G7
93	Hazard Warning Lamp Switch	2a/J5
94	Headlamp Unit LH	2/A7
95	Headlamp Unit RH	2/A2
96	Heated Rear Window	3/L4
97	Heated Rear Window Relay	3/E2
98	Heated Rear Window Switch	3/H5
99	Heater Blower Motor	3/F5
100	Heater Blower Motor Speed Controller	3/G5
101	Horn	3/A2, 3/A7
106	Ignition Switch	2/K2, 2a/H2, 2b/J3, 3/K2, 3a/G2, 3b/E1,
110	Instrument Cluster	2/H4, 2a/G4, 2b/G3,
111	Instrument Illumination Control	2b/J1, 3/J2
112	Interior Lamp Door Switch LH Front	2b/F8
113	Interior Lamp Door Switch LH Rear	2b/L8
114	Interior Lamp Door Switch RH Front	2b/F1
115	Interior Lamp Door Switch RH Rear	2b/L1
116	Interior Lamp Front	2b/G5
117	Interior Lamp Rear	2b/L5
118	Interior Lamp Timer Relay	2b/A2
121	Lamp Cluster LH Rear	2/M7, 2a/M7
122	Lamp Cluster RH Rear	2/M2, 2a/M2
124	Luggage Comp. Lamp	2b/M5
125	Luggage Comp. Lamp Switch	2b/M5
126	Map Reading Lamp	2b/H5
128	Number Plate Lamp	2/M4, 2/M5
132	Radio/Cassette Unit	3a/G5
133	Reversing Lamp Switch	2/E5
135	Speaker LH Front (Dashboard)	3a/D8
136	Speaker LH Front (Door)	3a/D8
137	Speaker LH Rear	3a/M8
138	Speaker RH Front (Dashboard)	3a/D1
139	Speaker RH Front (Door)	3a/D1
140	Speaker RH Rear	3a/M1
142	Stop-Lamp Switch	2a/D4
143	Sunroof Motor	3b/H5
144	Sunroof Position Switch	3b/G6
145	Sunroof Relay	3b/F5
146	Sunroof Switch	3b/H4
152	Vanity Mirror Illumination	2b/J7
153	Washer Pump Front	3/C3
154	Washer Pump Rear	3/L1
159	Wiper Motor Front	3/B5
160	Wiper Motor Rear	3/M4
161	Wiper Relay Front	3/E3
162	Wiper Relay Rear	3/M6

H24331

T.M.MARKE

Key to wiring diagrams - early models

NOTES:

1. All diagrams are divided into numbered circuits depending on function e.g. Diagram 2: Exterior lighting.
2. Items are arranged in relation to a plan view of the vehicle.
3. Items may appear on more than one diagram so are found using a grid reference e.g. 2/A1 denotes an item on diagram 2 grid location A1.
4. Complex items appear on the diagrams as blocks and are expanded on the internal connections page.
5. Brackets show how the circuit may be connected in more than one way.
6. Not all items are fitted to all models.
7. Wire identification is not by colour, but by letters or numbers appearing on the wire at each end.

INTERNAL CONNECTION DETAILS

KEY TO INSTRUMENT CLUSTER (ITEM 110)

a = +VE Supply
b = Earth
c = Tachometer
d = Tachometer
e = Oil Level Gauge
f = Oil Level Gauge
g = +VE Supply
h = +VE Supply
i = Diagnosis Warning Lamp
j = Coolant Level Warning Lamp
k = Coolant Temperature Gauge
l = High Temp. Warning Lamp
m = +VE Supply
n = Brake Pad Wear Warning Lamp
o = +VE Supply
p = ABS Warning Lamp
q = Direction Indicator Warning Lamp
r = Sidelamp Warning Lamp
s = Dipped Beam Warning Lamp
t = Main Beam Warning Lamp
u = Clock
v = +VE Supply
w = Direction Indicator Warning Lamp
x = Earth
y = Fuel Gauge
z = Low Fuel Warning Lamp
a1 = No Charge Warning Lamp
a2 = Oil Pressure Warning Lamp
a3 = +VE Supply
a4 = Low Brake Fluid Warning Lamp
a5 = Handbrake Warning Lamp
a6 = Instrument Illumination
a7 = Earth
a8 = Oil Temperature Gauge
a9 = Choke Warning Lamp

FUSE	RATING	CIRCUIT
1	15A PRE '89	Heated rear window and heated mirrors
	20A POST '89	
2	5A	Tail lamp LH
3	5A	Rear Foglamp
4	10A	Side, number plate, instrument panel, clock lighting and illumination control
5	10A	Ignition positive, courtesy lamp delay, oil level, tachometer, brake warning lamp, reversing lamps, cooling fan relay
6	15A	Accessories positive, wash/wipe, brake lamps, interior illumination
7	15A PRE '89	Hazard warning lamps
	20A POST '89	
8	20A	Electric windows, sunroof, boot/clock lamps, central locking, front/rear interior lamps, radio memory
9	5A	Radio, battery or accessories positivw
10	15A	Accessories positive, heated rear window, front/rear electric windows, sunroof, clock lamp
11	5A	Tail lamp RH
12	10A	Accessories positive, ABS
13	20A	Electric windows rear
14	25A	Electric windows front, sunroof
15	15A	Electric horn, cigar lighter
	20A	Air horn, cigar lighter
16	5A	Driving lamp LH
17	5A	Driving lamp RH
18	25A	Heater

KEY TO SYMBOLS

PLUG-IN CONNECTOR	
EARTH	
BULB	⊗
DIODE	
LINE CONNECTOR	
FUSE/ FUSIBLE LINK	

H24330
T.M.MARKE

Diagram 1 : Notes, fuses, internal connection details and key to symbols - early models

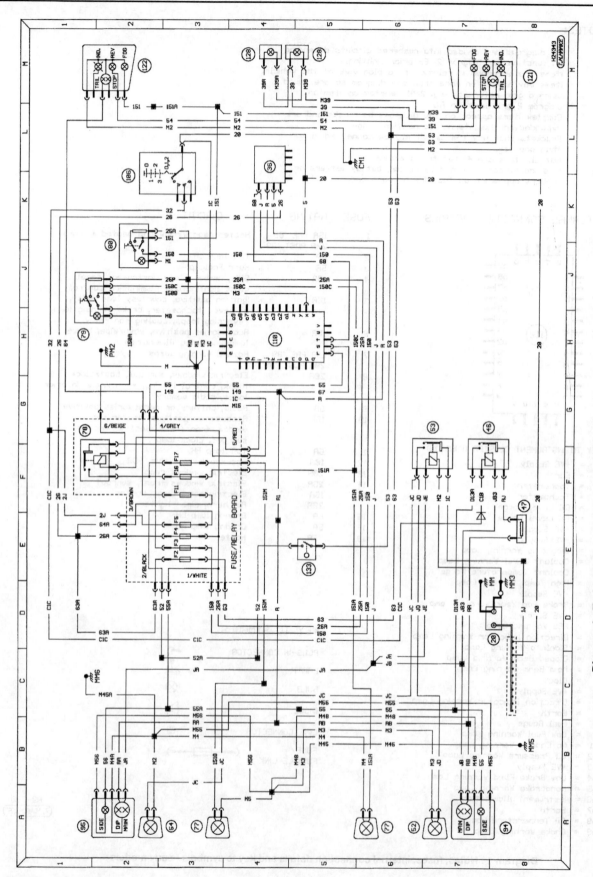

Diagram 2 : Typical exterior lighting (reversing, fog, side and headlights) - early models

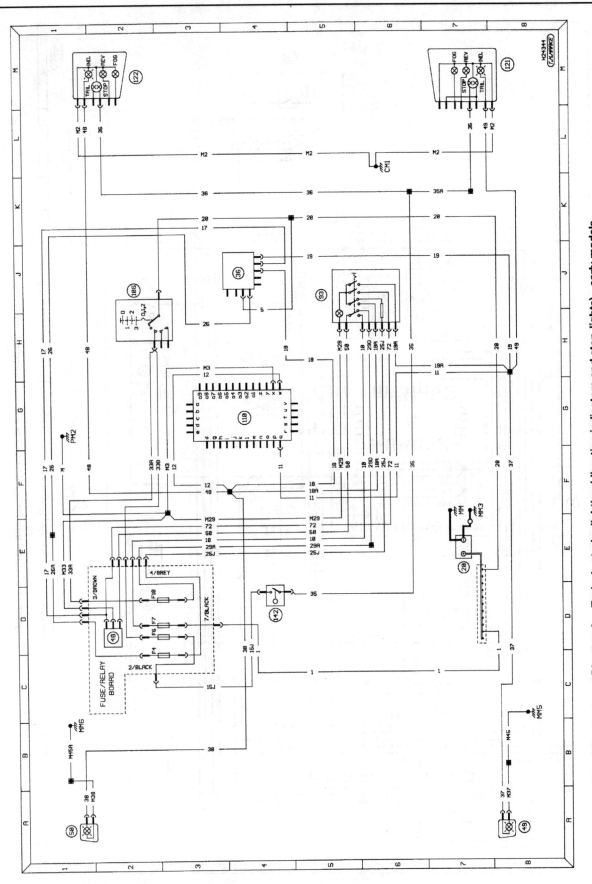

Diagram 2a : Typical exterior lighting (direction indicators and stop-lights) - early models

12

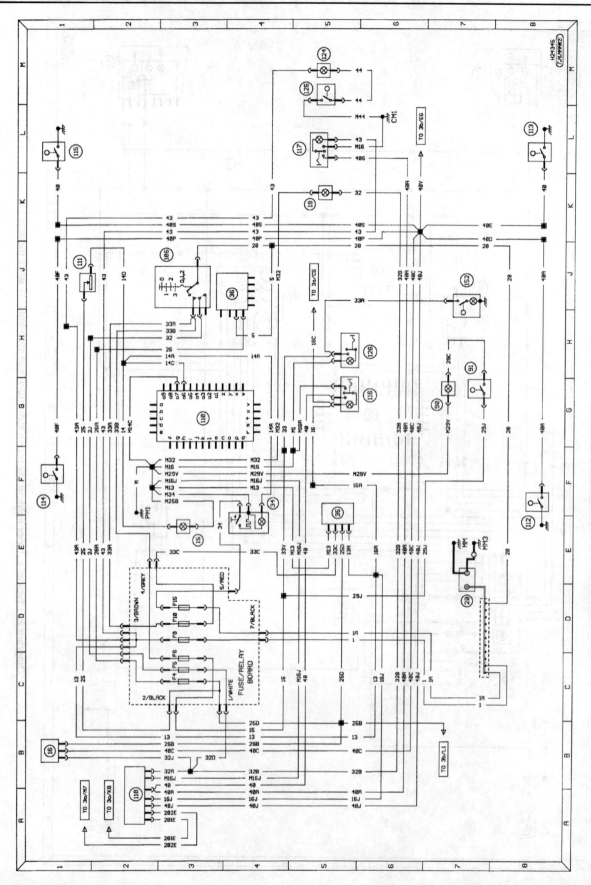

Diagram 2b : Typical interior lighting and associated circuits - early models

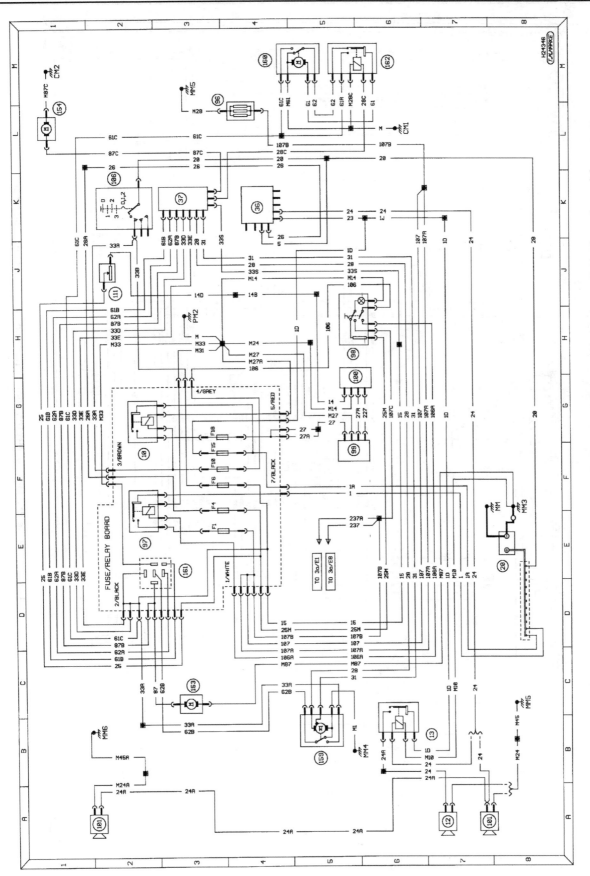

Diagram 3 : Typical ancillary circuits (wash/wipe, horn, heater blower and heated rear window) - early models

12

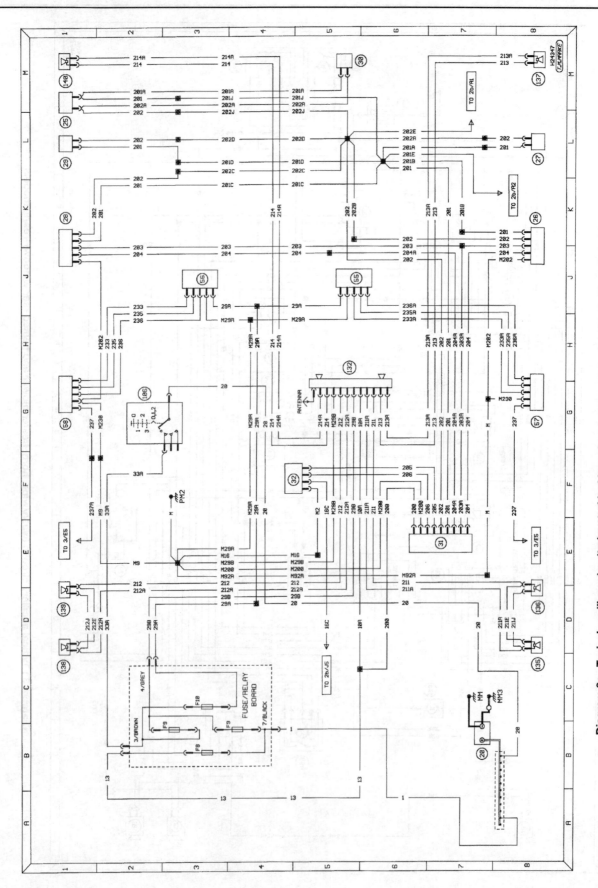

Diagram 3a : Typical ancillary circuits (central locking, electric door mirrors and radio/cassette) - early models

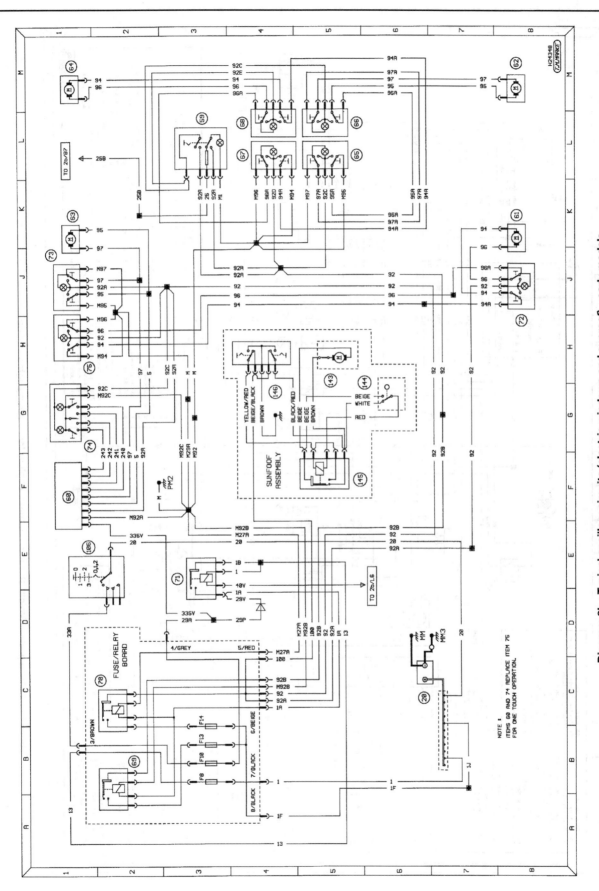

Diagram 3b : Typical ancillary circuits (electric windows and sunroof) - early models

NOTE :
ITEMS 60 AND 74 REPLACE ITEM 75
FOR ONE TOUCH OPERATION.

12

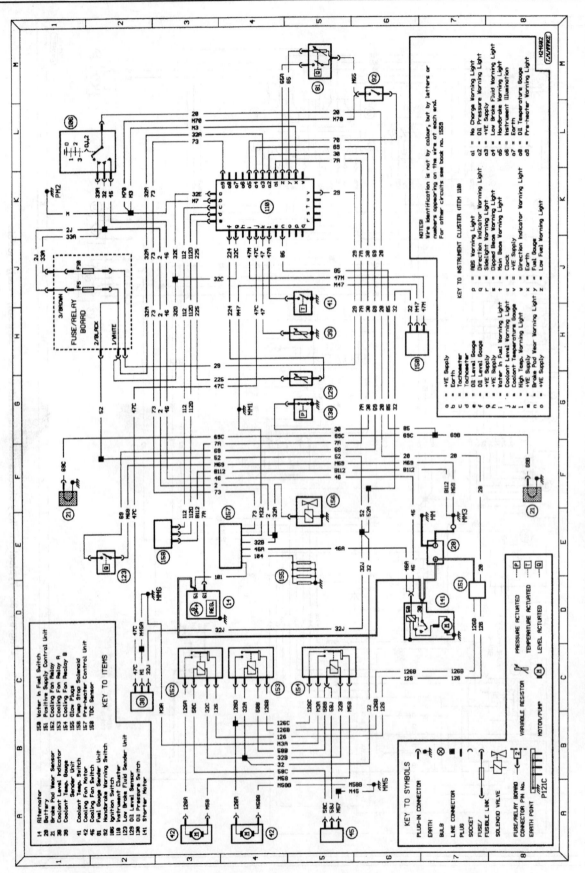

Supplementary diagram : Typical starting, charging, cooling fan, warning lights and gauges - early models

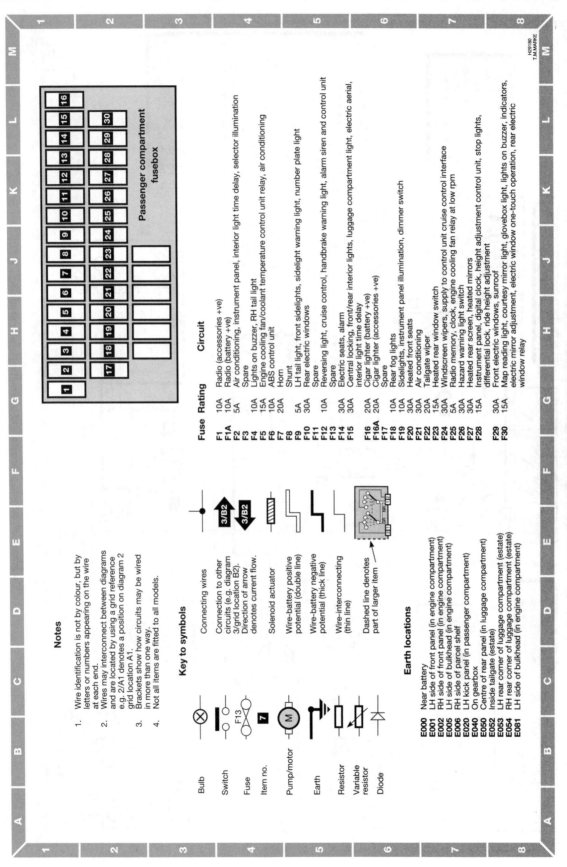

Passenger compartment fusebox

Notes

1. Wire identification is not by colour, but by letters or numbers appearing on the wire at each end.
2. Wires may interconnect between diagrams and are located by using a grid reference e.g. 2/A1 denotes a position on diagram 2 grid location A1.
3. Brackets show how circuits may be wired in more than one way.
4. Not all items are fitted to all models.

Key to symbols

Bulb
Switch
Fuse
Item no.
Pump/motor
Earth
Resistor
Variable resistor
Diode

Connecting wires
Connection to other circuits (e.g. diagram 3/grid location B2).
Direction of arrow denotes current flow.
Solenoid actuator
Wire-battery positive potential (double line)
Wire-battery negative potential (thick line)
Wire-interconnecting (thin line)
Dashed line denotes part of larger item

Fuse	Rating	Circuit
F1	10A	Radio (accessories +ve)
F1A	10A	Radio (battery +ve)
F2	5A	Air conditioning, instrument panel, interior light time delay, selector illumination
F3		Spare
F4	10A	Lights on buzzer, RH tail light
F5	15A	Engine cooling fan/coolant temperature control unit relay, air conditioning
F6	10A	ABS control unit
F7	20A	Horn
F8		Shunt
F9	5A	LH tail light, front sidelights, sidelight warning light, number plate light
F10	30A	Rear electric windows
F11		Spare
F12	10A	Reversing light, cruise control, handbrake warning light, alarm siren and control unit
F13		Spare
F14	30A	Electric seats, alarm
F15	30A	Central locking, front/rear interior lights, luggage compartment light, electric aerial, interior light time delay
F16	20A	Cigar lighter (battery +ve)
F16A	20A	Cigar lighter (accessories +ve)
F17		Spare
F18	10A	Rear fog lights
F19	20A	Sidelights, instrument panel illumination, dimmer switch
F20	30A	Heated front seats
F21	30A	Air conditioning
F22	20A	Tailgate wiper
F23	15A	Heated rear window switch
F24	30A	Windscreen wipers, supply to control unit cruise control interface
F25	5A	Radio memory, clock, engine cooling fan relay at low rpm
F26	30A	Hazard warning light switch
F27	30A	Heated rear screen, heated mirrors
F28	15A	Instrument panel, digital clock, height adjustment control unit, stop lights, differential lock, ride height adjustment
F29	30A	Front electric windows, sunroof
F30	15A	Map reading light, courtesy mirror light, glovebox light, lights on buzzer, indicators, electric mirror adjustment, electric window one-touch operation, rear electric window relay

Earth locations

E000	Near battery
E001	LH side of front panel (in engine compartment)
E002	RH side of front panel (in engine compartment)
E005	LH side of bulkhead (in engine compartment)
E006	RH side of parcel shelf
E020	LH kick panel (in passenger compartment)
E040	On gearbox
E050	Centre of rear panel (in luggage compartment)
E052	Inside tailgate (estate)
E053	LH rear corner of luggage compartment (estate)
E054	RH rear corner of luggage compartment (estate)
E081	LH side of bulkhead (in engine compartment)

H29180
T.M.MARKE

Diagram 1 : Notes, fuses, key to symbols and earth locations - later models

12

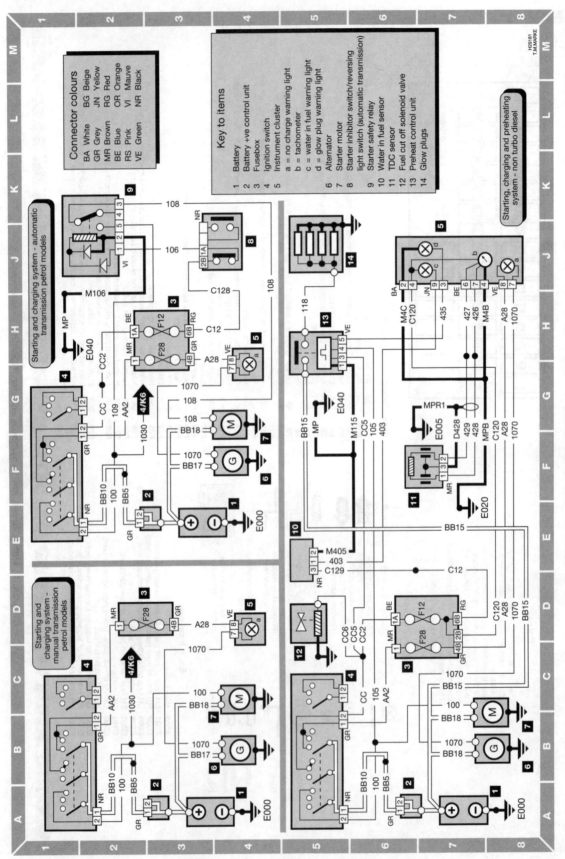

Connector colours

BA	White	BG	Beige
GR	Grey	JN	Yellow
MR	Brown	RG	Red
BE	Blue	OR	Orange
RS	Pink	VI	Mauve
VE	Green	NR	Black

Key to items

1 Battery
2 Battery +ve control unit
3 Fusebox
4 Ignition switch
5 Instrument cluster
   a = no charge warning light
   b = tachometer
   c = water in fuel warning light
   d = glow plug warning light
6 Alternator
7 Starter motor
8 Starter inhibitor switch/reversing
   light switch (automatic transmission)
9 Starter safety relay
10 Water in fuel sensor
11 TDC sensor
12 Fuel cut off solenoid valve
13 Preheat control unit
14 Glow plugs

Starting and charging system - automatic transmission petrol models

Starting and charging system - manual transmission petrol models

Starting, charging and preheating system - non turbo diesel

Diagram 2 : Starting, charging and preheating - later models

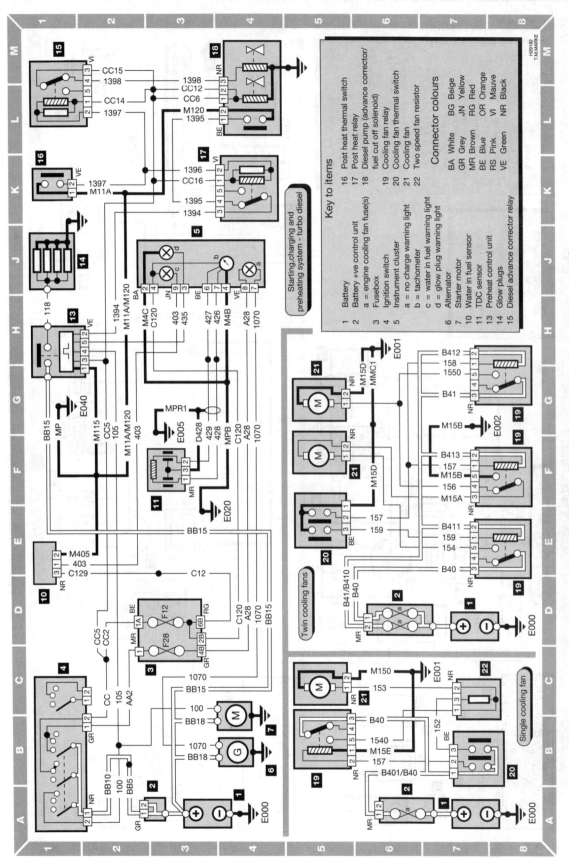

Key to items

1 Battery
2 Battery +ve control unit
 a = engine cooling fan fuse(s)
3 Fusebox
4 Ignition switch
5 Instrument cluster
 a = no charge warning light
 b = tachometer
 c = water in fuel warning light
 d = glow plug warning light
6 Alternator
7 Starter motor
10 Water in fuel sensor
11 TDC sensor
13 Preheat control unit
14 Glow plugs
15 Diesel advance corrector relay

16 Post heat thermal switch
17 Post heat relay
18 Diesel pump (advance corrector/
 fuel cut off solenoid)
19 Cooling fan relay
20 Cooling fan thermal switch
21 Cooling fan
22 Two speed fan resistor

Connector colours

BA	White	BG	Beige
GR	Grey	JN	Yellow
MR	Brown	RG	Red
BE	Blue	OR	Orange
RS	Pink	VI	Mauve
VE	Green	NR	Black

Starting, charging and
preheating system - turbo diesel

Twin cooling fans

Single cooling fan

Diagram 3 : Preheating (turbo diesel) and engine cooling fans - later models

12

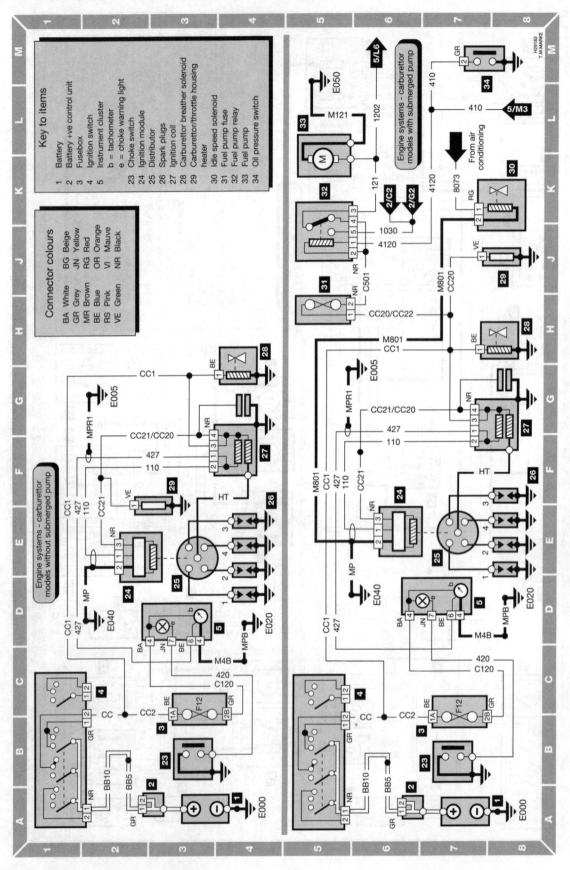

Key to items

1 Battery
2 Battery +ve control unit
3 Fusebox
4 Ignition switch
5 Instrument cluster
   b = tachometer
   e = choke warning light
23 Choke switch
24 Ignition module
25 Distributor
26 Spark plugs
27 Ignition coil
28 Carburettor breather solenoid
29 Carburettor/throttle housing heater
30 Idle speed solenoid
31 Fuel pump fuse
32 Fuel pump relay
33 Fuel pump
34 Oil pressure switch

Connector colours

BA White   BG Beige
GR Grey   JN Yellow
MR Brown   RG Red
BE Blue   OR Orange
RS Pink   VI Mauve
VE Green   NR Black

Diagram 4 : Engine systems (carburettor models) - later models

Engine systems - carburettor models without submerged pump

Engine systems - carburettor models with submerged pump

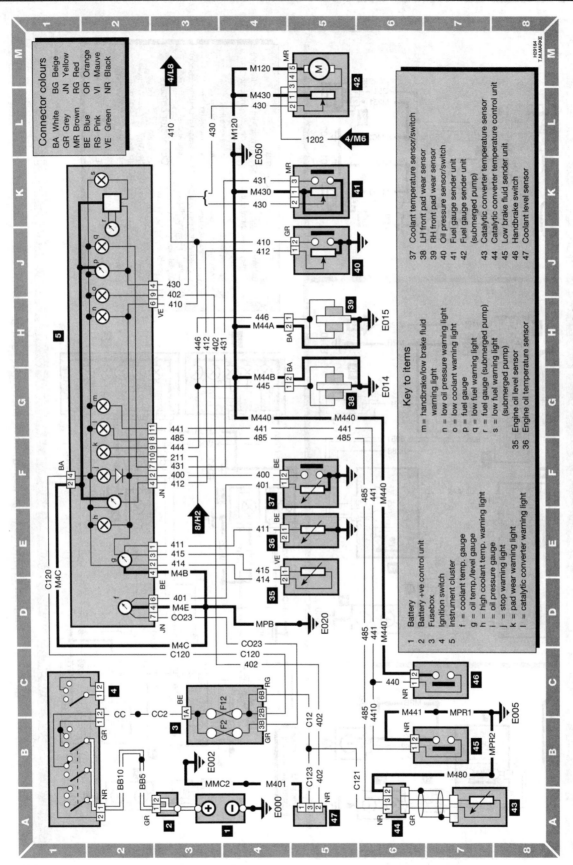

Connector colours

BA	White	BG	Beige
GR	Grey	JN	Yellow
MR	Brown	RG	Red
BE	Blue	OR	Orange
RS	Pink	VI	Mauve
VE	Green	NR	Black

Key to items

1 Battery
2 Battery +ve control unit
3 Fusebox
4 Ignition switch
5 Instrument cluster
  f = coolant temp. gauge
  g = oil temp./level gauge
  h = high coolant temp. warning light
  i = oil pressure gauge
  j = stop warning light
  k = pad wear warning light
  l = catalytic converter warning light
  m = handbrake/low brake fluid
     warning light
  n = low oil pressure warning light
  o = low coolant warning light
  p = fuel gauge
  q = low fuel warning light
  r = fuel gauge (submerged pump)
  s = low fuel warning light
     (submerged pump)
35 Engine oil level sensor
36 Engine oil temperature sensor
37 Coolant temperature sensor/switch
38 LH front pad wear sensor
39 RH front pad wear sensor
40 Oil pressure sensor/switch
41 Fuel gauge sender unit
42 Fuel gauge sender unit
    (submerged pump)
43 Catalytic converter temperature sensor
44 Catalytic converter temperature control unit
45 Low brake fluid sender unit
46 Handbrake switch
47 Coolant level sensor

Diagram 5 : Warning lights and gauges – later models

H29184
T.M.MARKE

12

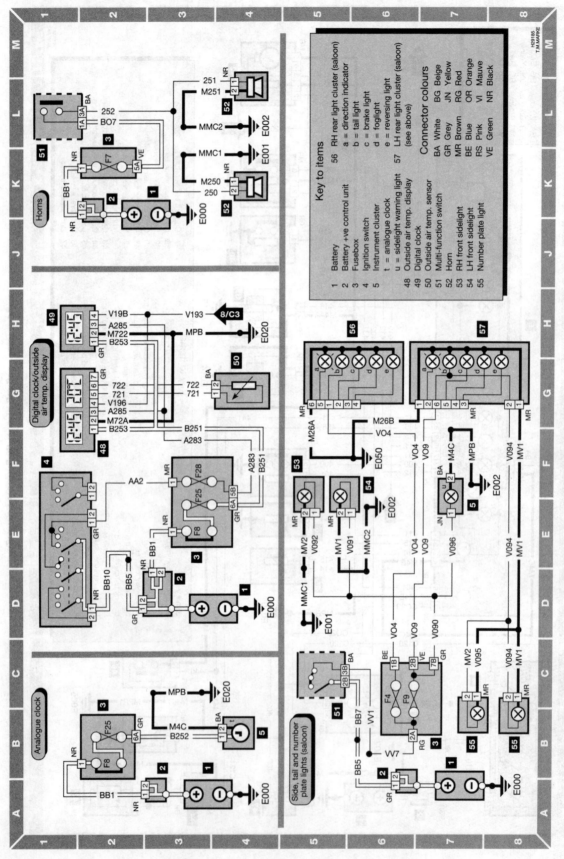

Key to items

1 Battery
2 Battery +ve control unit
3 Fusebox
4 Ignition switch
5 Instrument cluster
  t = analogue clock
  u = sidelight warning light
48 Outside air temp. display
49 Digital clock
50 Outside air temp. sensor
51 Multi-function switch
52 Horn
53 RH front sidelight
54 LH front sidelight
55 Number plate light
56 RH rear light cluster (saloon)
  a = direction indicator
  b = tail light
  c = brake light
  d = foglight
  e = reversing light
57 LH rear light cluster (saloon)
  (see above)

Connector colours

BA White   BG Beige
GR Grey   JN Yellow
MR Brown   RG Red
BE Blue   OR Orange
RS Pink   VI Mauve
VE Green   NR Black

Diagram 6 : External temp. display, clock and exterior lighting – later models

H09185
T.M.MARKE

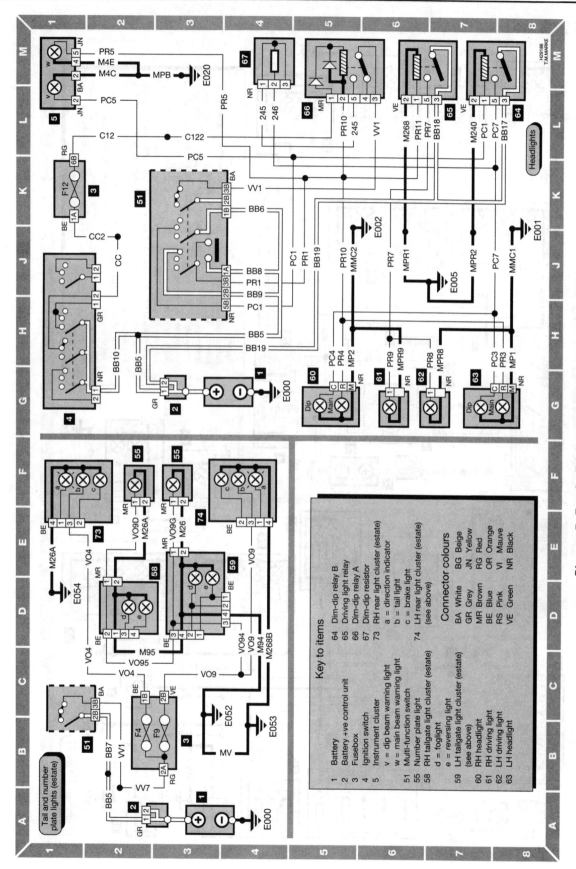

Diagram 7 : Exterior lighting continued - later models

Key to items

1 Battery
2 Battery +ve control unit
3 Fusebox
4 Ignition switch
5 Instrument cluster
   v = dip beam warning light
   w = main beam warning light
51 Multi-function switch
55 Number plate light
58 RH tailgate light cluster (estate)
59 LH tailgate light cluster (estate)
   (see above)
60 RH headlight
61 RH driving light
62 LH driving light
63 LH headlight

64 Dim-dip relay B
65 Driving light relay
66 Dim-dip relay A
67 Dim-dip resistor
73 RH rear light cluster (estate)
   a = direction indicator
   b = tail light
   c = brake light
74 LH rear light cluster (estate)
   (see above)

Connector colours

BA	White	BG	Beige
GR	Grey	JN	Yellow
MR	Brown	RG	Red
BE	Blue	OR	Orange
RS	Pink	VI	Mauve
VE	Green	NR	Black

12

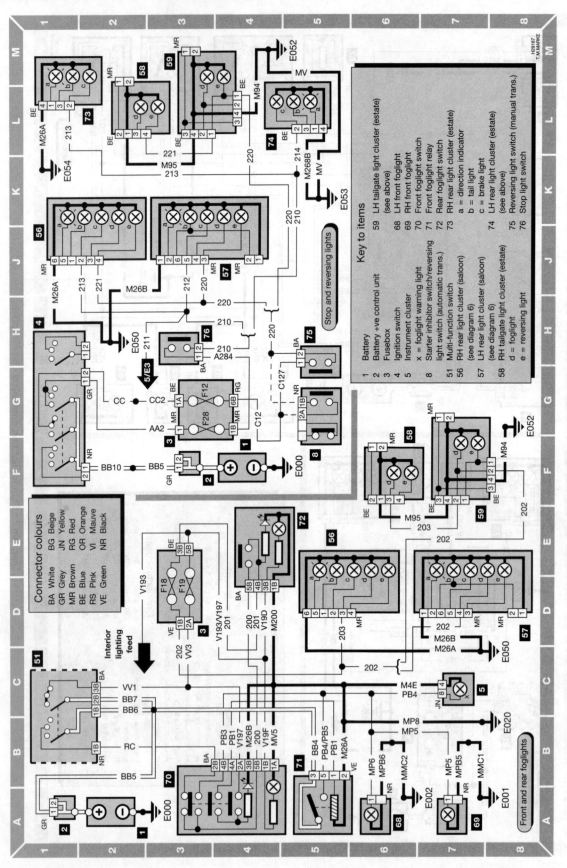

Diagram 8 : Exterior lighting continued - later models

Key to items

1	Battery
2	Battery +ve control unit
3	Fusebox
4	Ignition switch
5	Instrument cluster
	x = foglight warning light
8	Starter inhibitor switch/reversing light switch (automatic trans.)
51	Multi-function switch
56	RH rear light cluster (saloon) (see diagram 6)
57	LH rear light cluster (saloon) (see diagram 6)
58	RH tailgate light cluster (estate)
	d = foglight
	e = reversing light
59	LH tailgate light cluster (estate) (see above)
68	LH front foglight
69	RH front foglight
70	Front foglight switch
71	Front foglight relay
72	Rear foglight switch
73	RH rear light cluster (estate)
	a = direction indicator
	b = tail light
	c = brake light
74	LH rear light cluster (estate) (see above)
75	Reversing light switch (manual trans.)
76	Stop light switch

Stop and reversing lights

Front and rear foglights

Interior lighting feed

Connector colours

BA	White	BG	Beige
GR	Grey	JN	Yellow
MR	Brown	RG	Red
BE	Blue	OR	Orange
RS	Pink	VI	Mauve
VE	Green	NR	Black

H29187
T.M.MARKE

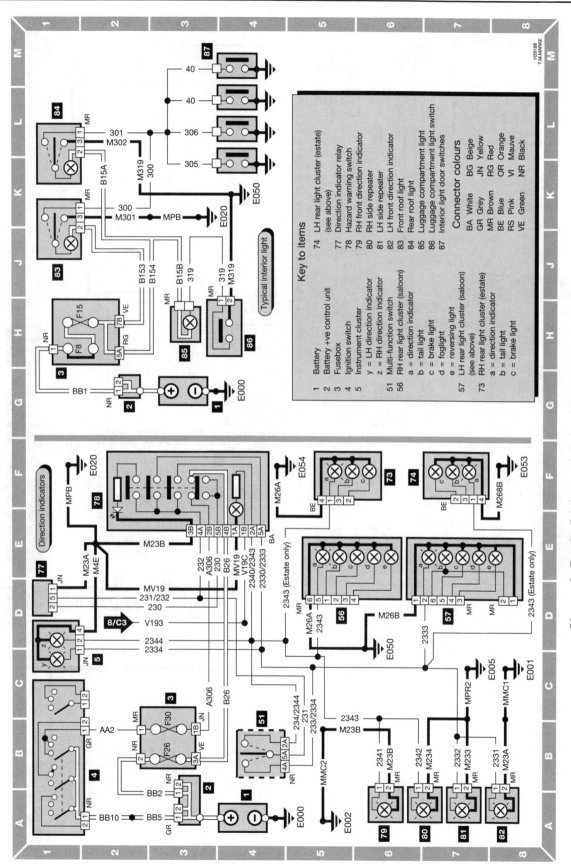

Key to items

1 Battery
2 Battery +ve control unit
3 Fusebox
4 Ignition switch
5 Instrument cluster
   y = LH direction indicator
   z = RH direction indicator
51 Multi-function switch
56 RH rear light cluster (saloon)
    a = direction indicator
    b = tail light
    c = brake light
    d = foglight
    e = reversing light
57 LH rear light cluster (saloon)
    (see above)
73 RH rear light cluster (estate)
    a = tail light
    b = brake light
    c = brake light

74 LH rear light cluster (estate)
    (see above)
77 Direction indicator relay
78 Hazard warning switch
79 RH front direction indicator
80 RH side repeater
81 LH side repeater
82 LH front direction indicator
83 Front roof light
84 Rear roof light
85 Luggage compartment light
86 Luggage compartment light switch
87 Interior light door switches

Connector colours
BA White   BG Beige
GR Grey   JN Yellow
MR Brown   RG Red
BE Blue   OR Orange
RS Pink   VI Mauve
VE Green   NR Black

Diagram 9 : Exterior lighting continued and interior lighting - later models

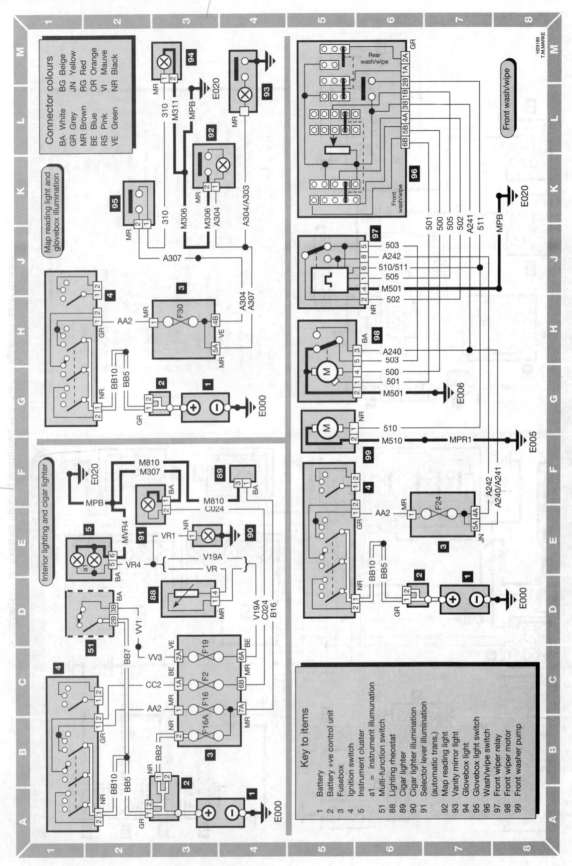

Diagram 10 : Interior lighting continued and front wash/wipe - later models

Connector colours

BA White BG Beige
GR Grey JN Yellow
MR Brown RG Red
BE Blue OR Orange
RS Pink VI Mauve
VE Green NR Black

Map reading light and glovebox illumination

Interior lighting and cigar lighter

Front wash/wipe

Key to items

1 Battery
2 Battery +ve control unit
3 Fusebox
4 Ignition switch
5 Instrument cluster
  a1 = instrument illumunation
51 Multi-function switch
88 Lighting rheostat
89 Cigar lighter
90 Cigar lighter illumination
91 Selector lever illumination
   (automatic trans.)
92 Map reading light
93 Vanity mirror light
94 Glovebox light
95 Glovebox light switch
96 Wash/wipe switch
97 Front wiper relay
98 Front wiper motor
99 Front washer pump

H29189
T.M.MARIE

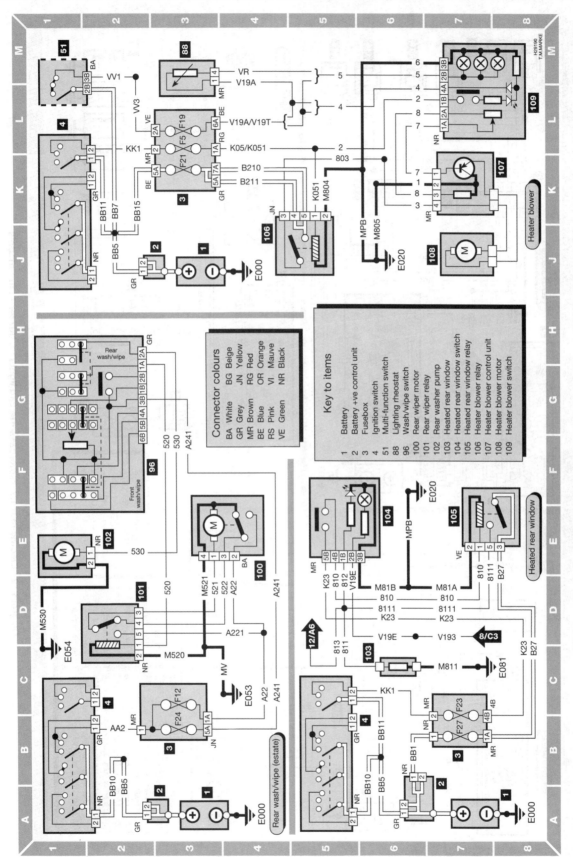

Key to items

1   Battery
2   Battery +ve control unit
3   Fusebox
51 Ignition switch
88 Multi-function switch
96 Lighting rheostat
100 Wash/wipe switch
101 Rear wiper motor
102 Rear wiper relay
103 Rear washer pump
104 Heated rear window
105 Heated rear window switch
106 Heated rear window relay
107 Heater blower relay
108 Heater blower control unit
109 Heater blower motor
    Heater blower switch

Connector colours

BA White   BG Beige
GR Grey   JN Yellow
MR Brown   RG Red
BE Blue   OR Orange
RS Pink   VI Mauve
VE Green   NR Black

Diagram 11 : Rear wash/wipe, heater blower and heated rear window - later models

12

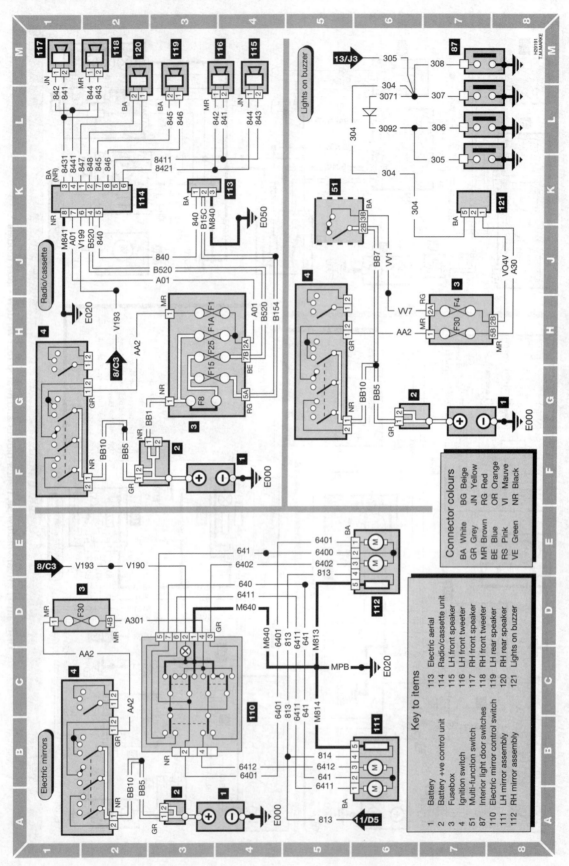

Diagram 12 : Electric mirrors, radio/cassette and lights on buzzer - later models

Connector colours

BA	White	BG	Beige
GR	Grey	JN	Yellow
MR	Brown	RG	Red
BE	Blue	OR	Orange
RS	Pink	VI	Mauve
VE	Green	NR	Black

Key to items

1	Battery	113	Electric aerial
2	Battery +ve control unit	114	Radio/cassette unit
3	Fusebox	115	LH front speaker
4	Ignition switch	116	LH front tweeter
51	Multi-function switch	117	RH front speaker
87	Interior light door switches	118	RH front tweeter
110	Electric mirror control switch	119	LH rear speaker
111	LH mirror assembly	120	RH rear speaker
112	RH mirror assembly	121	Lights on buzzer

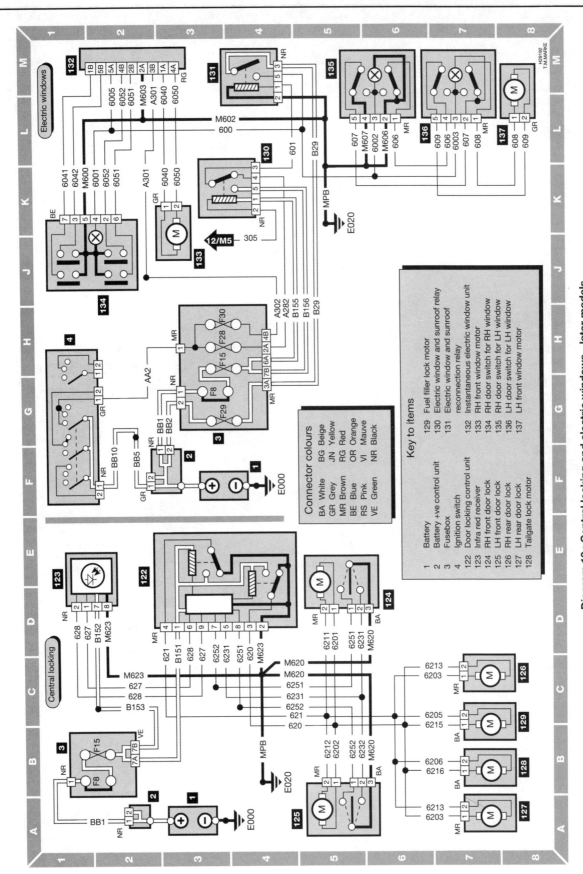

Diagram 13 : Central locking and electric windows - later models

Connector colours

BA	White	BG	Beige
GR	Grey	JN	Yellow
MR	Brown	RG	Red
BE	Blue	OR	Orange
RS	Pink	VI	Mauve
VE	Green	NR	Black

Key to items

1 Battery
2 Battery +ve control unit
3 Fusebox
4 Ignition switch
122 Door locking control unit
123 Infra red receiver
124 RH front door lock
125 LH front door lock
126 RH rear door lock
127 LH rear door lock
128 Tailgate lock motor

129 Fuel filler lock motor
130 Electric window and sunroof relay
131 Electric window and sunroof reconnection relay
132 Instantaneous electric window unit
133 RH front window motor
134 RH door switch for RH window
135 RH door switch for LH window
136 LH door switch for LH window
137 LH front window motor

Electric windows

Central locking

12

Notes

Dimensions and weights

Note: *All figures are approximate, and may vary according to model. Refer to manufacturer's data for exact figures.*

Dimensions

Overall length:
    Saloon models . . . . 4408 mm
    Estate models . . . . 4398 mm
Overall width . . . . 1694 mm
Overall height (unladen):
    Saloon models . . . . 1406 mm
    Estate models . . . . 1445 mm
Wheelbase . . . . 2669 mm

Weights

Kerb weight . . . . 1125 to 1210 kg*
Maximum gross vehicle weight . . . . 1605 to 1690 kg*
Maximum roof rack load . . . . 75 kg
Maximum towing weight (braked trailer) . . . . 1200 kg
Maximum trailer nose weight . . . . 65 kg
Depending on model and specification.

Conversion Factors

Length (distance)

Inches (in)	25.4	= Millimetres (mm)	x 0.0394	= Inches (in)
Feet (ft)	0.305	= Metres (m)	x 3.281	= Feet (ft)
Miles	1.609	= Kilometres (km)	x 0.621	= Miles

Volume (capacity)

Cubic inches (cu in; in³)	x 16.387	= Cubic centimetres (cc; cm³)	x 0.061	= Cubic inches (cu in; in³)
Imperial pints (Imp pt)	x 0.568	= Litres (l)	x 1.76	= Imperial pints (Imp pt)
Imperial quarts (Imp qt)	x 1.137	= Litres (l)	x 0.88	= Imperial quarts (Imp qt)
Imperial quarts (Imp qt)	x 1.201	= US quarts (US qt)	x 0.833	= Imperial quarts (Imp qt)
US quarts (US qt)	x 0.946	= Litres (l)	x 1.057	= US quarts (US qt)
Imperial gallons (Imp gal)	x 4.546	= Litres (l)	x 0.22	= Imperial gallons (Imp gal)
Imperial gallons (Imp gal)	x 1.201	= US gallons (US gal)	x 0.833	= Imperial gallons (Imp gal)
US gallons (US gal)	x 3.785	= Litres (l)	x 0.264	= US gallons (US gal)

Mass (weight)

Ounces (oz)	x 28.35	= Grams (g)	x 0.035	= Ounces (oz)
Pounds (lb)	x 0.454	= Kilograms (kg)	x 2.205	= Pounds (lb)

Force

Ounces-force (ozf; oz)	x 0.278	= Newtons (N)	x 3.6	= Ounces-force (ozf; oz)
Pounds-force (lbf; lb)	x 4.448	= Newtons (N)	x 0.225	= Pounds-force (lbf; lb)
Newtons (N)	x 0.1	= Kilograms-force (kgf; kg)	x 9.81	= Newtons (N)

Pressure

Pounds-force per square inch (psi; lbf/in²; lb/in²)	x 0.070	= Kilograms-force per square centimetre (kgf/cm²; kg/cm²)	x 14.223	= Pounds-force per square inch (psi; lbf/in²; lb/in²)
Pounds-force per square inch (psi; lbf/in²; lb/in²)	x 0.068	= Atmospheres (atm)	x 14.696	= Pounds-force per square inch (psi; lbf/in²; lb/in²)
Pounds-force per square inch (psi; lbf/in²; lb/in²)	x 0.069	= Bars	x 14.5	= Pounds-force per square inch (psi; lbf/in²; lb/in²)
Pounds-force per square inch (psi; lbf/in²; lb/in²)	x 6.895	= Kilopascals (kPa)	x 0.145	= Pounds-force per square inch (psi; lbf/in²; lb/in²)
Kilopascals (kPa)	x 0.01	= Kilograms-force per square centimetre (kgf/cm²; kg/cm²)	x 98.1	= Kilopascals (kPa)
Millibar (mbar)	x 100	= Pascals (Pa)	x 0.01	= Millibar (mbar)
Millibar (mbar)	x 0.0145	= Pounds-force per square inch (psi; lbf/in²; lb/in²)	x 68.947	= Millibar (mbar)
Millibar (mbar)	x 0.75	= Millimetres of mercury (mmHg)	x 1.333	= Millibar (mbar)
Millibar (mbar)	x 0.401	= Inches of water (inH₂O)	x 2.491	= Millibar (mbar)
Millimetres of mercury (mmHg)	x 0.535	= Inches of water (inH₂O)	x 1.868	= Millimetres of mercury (mmHg)
Inches of water (inH₂O)	x 0.036	= Pounds-force per square inch (psi; lbf/in²; lb/in²)	x 27.68	= Inches of water (inH₂O)

Torque (moment of force)

Pounds-force inches (lbf in; lb in)	x 1.152	= Kilograms-force centimetre (kgf cm; kg cm)	x 0.868	= Pounds-force inches (lbf in; lb in)
Pounds-force inches (lbf in; lb in)	x 0.113	= Newton metres (Nm)	x 8.85	= Pounds-force inches (lbf in; lb in)
Pounds-force inches (lbf in; lb in)	x 0.083	= Pounds-force feet (lbf ft; lb ft)	x 12	= Pounds-force inches (lbf in; lb in)
Pounds-force feet (lbf ft; lb ft)	x 0.138	= Kilograms-force metres (kgf m; kg m)	x 7.233	= Pounds-force feet (lbf ft; lb ft)
Pounds-force feet (lbf ft; lb ft)	x 1.356	= Newton metres (Nm)	x 0.738	= Pounds-force feet (lbf ft; lb ft)
Newton metres (Nm)	x 0.102	= Kilograms-force metres (kgf m; kg m)	x 9.804	= Newton metres (Nm)

Power

Horsepower (hp)	x 745.7	= Watts (W)	x 0.0013	= Horsepower (hp)

Velocity (speed)

Miles per hour (miles/hr; mph)	x 1.609	= Kilometres per hour (km/hr; kph)	x 0.621	= Miles per hour (miles/hr; mph)

Fuel consumption*

Miles per gallon (mpg)	x 0.354	= Kilometres per litre (km/l)	x 2.825	= Miles per gallon (mpg)

It is common practice to convert from miles per gallon (mpg) to litres/100 kilometres (l/100km), where mpg x l/100 km = 282

Temperature

Degrees Fahrenheit = (°C x 1.8) + 32   Degrees Celsius (Degrees Centigrade; °C) = (°F - 32) x 0.56

Spare parts are available from many sources, including maker's appointed garages, accessory shops, and motor factors. To be sure of obtaining the correct parts, it may sometimes be necessary to quote the vehicle identification number. If possible, it can also be useful to take the old parts along for positive identification. Items such as starter motors and alternators may be available under a service exchange scheme - any parts returned should be clean.

Our advice regarding spare part sources is as follows.

Officially-appointed garages

This is the best source of parts which are peculiar to your car, and are not otherwise generally available (eg badges, interior trim, certain body panels, etc). It is also the only place at which you should buy parts if the vehicle is still under warranty.

Accessory shops

These are good places to buy materials and components needed for the maintenance of your car (oil, air and fuel filters, spark plugs, light bulbs, drivebelts, oils and greases, brake pads, touch-up paint, etc). Parts like this sold by a reputable shop are of the same standard as those used by the car manufacturer.

Motor factors

Good factors will stock all the components which wear out comparatively quickly and can supply individual components needed for the overhaul of a larger assembly. They may also handle work such as cylinder block reboring, crankshaft regrinding and balancing, etc.

Tyre and exhaust specialists

These outlets may be independent or members of a local or national chain. They frequently offer competitive prices when compared with a main dealer or local garage, but it will pay to obtain several quotes before making a decision. Also ask what 'extras' may be added to the quote - for instance, fitting a new valve and balancing the wheel are both often charged on top of the price of a new tyre.

Other sources

Beware of parts or materials obtained from market stalls, car boot sales or similar outlets. Such items are not invariably sub-standard, but there is little chance of compensation if they do prove unsatisfactory. In the case of safety-critical components such as brake pads there is the risk not only of financial loss but also of an accident causing injury or death.

Second-hand components from a car breaker can be a good buy, but this sort of purchase is best made by the experienced DIY mechanic.

Vehicle identification numbers

Modifications are a continuing and unpublicised process in vehicle manufacture, quite apart from major model changes. Spare parts manuals and lists are compiled upon a numerical basis, the individual vehicle identification numbers being essential to correct identification of the component concerned.

When ordering spare parts, always give as much information as possible. Quote the car model, year of manufacture, body and engine numbers as appropriate.

The *Vehicle Identification Number (VIN)* plate is riveted to the front of the body front panel under the bonnet. The vehicle identification number is also stamped into the engine bulkhead cross panel **(see illustration)**.

The *engine number* is situated on the front face of the cylinder block, and is stamped on a plate which is riveted to the front of the block.

Note: *The first part of the engine number gives the engine code - eg, "D8A".*

The *vehicle paint code* is stamped into the left-hand inner wing panel.

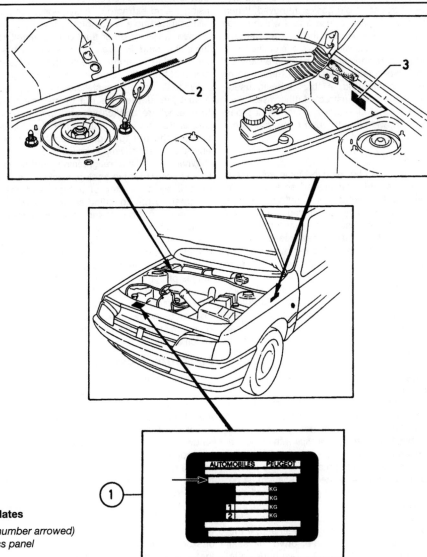

Location of Vehicle Identification Plates

1 *Vehicle Identification Number (VIN) plate (VIN number arrowed)*
2 *Vehicle identification number on bulkhead cross panel*
3 *Vehicle paint code*

Whenever servicing, repair or overhaul work is carried out on the car or its components, it is necessary to observe the following procedures and instructions. This will assist in carrying out the operation efficiently and to a professional standard of workmanship.

Joint mating faces and gaskets

When separating components at their mating faces, never insert screwdrivers or similar implements into the joint between the faces in order to prise them apart. This can cause severe damage which results in oil leaks, coolant leaks, etc upon reassembly. Separation is usually achieved by tapping along the joint with a soft-faced hammer in order to break the seal. However, note that this method may not be suitable where dowels are used for component location.

Where a gasket is used between the mating faces of two components, ensure that it is renewed on reassembly, and fit it dry unless otherwise stated in the repair procedure. Make sure that the mating faces are clean and dry, with all traces of old gasket removed. When cleaning a joint face, use a tool which is not likely to score or damage the face, and remove any burrs or nicks with an oilstone or fine file.

Make sure that tapped holes are cleaned with a pipe cleaner, and keep them free of jointing compound, if this is being used, unless specifically instructed otherwise.

Ensure that all orifices, channels or pipes are clear, and blow through them, preferably using compressed air.

Oil seals

Oil seals can be removed by levering them out with a wide flat-bladed screwdriver or similar tool. Alternatively, a number of self-tapping screws may be screwed into the seal, and these used as a purchase for pliers or similar in order to pull the seal free.

Whenever an oil seal is removed from its working location, either individually or as part of an assembly, it should be renewed.

The very fine sealing lip of the seal is easily damaged, and will not seal if the surface it contacts is not completely clean and free from scratches, nicks or grooves. If the original sealing surface of the component cannot be restored, and the manufacturer has not made provision for slight relocation of the seal relative to the sealing surface, the component should be renewed.

Protect the lips of the seal from any surface which may damage them in the course of fitting. Use tape or a conical sleeve where possible. Lubricate the seal lips with oil before fitting and, on dual-lipped seals, fill the space between the lips with grease.

Unless otherwise stated, oil seals must be fitted with their sealing lips toward the lubricant to be sealed.

Use a tubular drift or block of wood of the appropriate size to install the seal and, if the seal housing is shouldered, drive the seal down to the shoulder. If the seal housing is unshouldered, the seal should be fitted with its face flush with the housing top face (unless otherwise instructed).

Screw threads and fastenings

Seized nuts, bolts and screws are quite a common occurrence where corrosion has set in, and the use of penetrating oil or releasing fluid will often overcome this problem if the offending item is soaked for a while before attempting to release it. The use of an impact driver may also provide a means of releasing such stubborn fastening devices, when used in conjunction with the appropriate screwdriver bit or socket. If none of these methods works, it may be necessary to resort to the careful application of heat, or the use of a hacksaw or nut splitter device.

Studs are usually removed by locking two nuts together on the threaded part, and then using a spanner on the lower nut to unscrew the stud. Studs or bolts which have broken off below the surface of the component in which they are mounted can sometimes be removed using a stud extractor. Always ensure that a blind tapped hole is completely free from oil, grease, water or other fluid before installing the bolt or stud. Failure to do this could cause the housing to crack due to the hydraulic action of the bolt or stud as it is screwed in.

When tightening a castellated nut to accept a split pin, tighten the nut to the specified torque, where applicable, and then tighten further to the next split pin hole. Never slacken the nut to align the split pin hole, unless stated in the repair procedure.

When checking or retightening a nut or bolt to a specified torque setting, slacken the nut or bolt by a quarter of a turn, and then retighten to the specified setting. However, this should not be attempted where angular tightening has been used.

For some screw fastenings, notably cylinder head bolts or nuts, torque wrench settings are no longer specified for the latter stages of tightening, "angle-tightening" being called up instead. Typically, a fairly low torque wrench setting will be applied to the bolts/nuts in the correct sequence, followed by one or more stages of tightening through specified angles.

Locknuts, locktabs and washers

Any fastening which will rotate against a component or housing during tightening should always have a washer between it and the relevant component or housing.

Spring or split washers should always be renewed when they are used to lock a critical component such as a big-end bearing retaining bolt or nut. Locktabs which are folded over to retain a nut or bolt should always be renewed.

Self-locking nuts can be re-used in non-critical areas, providing resistance can be felt when the locking portion passes over the bolt or stud thread. However, it should be noted that self-locking stiffnuts tend to lose their effectiveness after long periods of use, and should be renewed as a matter of course.

Split pins must always be replaced with new ones of the correct size for the hole.

When thread-locking compound is found on the threads of a fastener which is to be re-used, it should be cleaned off with a wire brush and solvent, and fresh compound applied on reassembly.

Special tools

Some repair procedures in this manual entail the use of special tools such as a press, two or three-legged pullers, spring compressors, etc. Wherever possible, suitable readily-available alternatives to the manufacturer's special tools are described, and are shown in use. In some instances, where no alternative is possible, it has been necessary to resort to the use of a manufacturer's tool, and this has been done for reasons of safety as well as the efficient completion of the repair operation. Unless you are highly-skilled and have a thorough understanding of the procedures described, never attempt to bypass the use of any special tool when the procedure described specifies its use. Not only is there a very great risk of personal injury, but expensive damage could be caused to the components involved.

Environmental considerations

When disposing of used engine oil, brake fluid, antifreeze, etc, give due consideration to any detrimental environmental effects. Do not, for instance, pour any of the above liquids down drains into the general sewage system, or onto the ground to soak away. Many local council refuse tips provide a facility for waste oil disposal, as do some garages. If none of these facilities are available, consult your local Environmental Health Department, or the National Rivers Authority, for further advice.

With the universal tightening-up of legislation regarding the emission of environ-mentally-harmful substances from motor vehicles, most current vehicles have tamperproof devices fitted to the main adjustment points of the fuel system. These devices are primarily designed to prevent unqualified persons from adjusting the fuel/air mixture, with the chance of a consequent increase in toxic emissions. If such devices are encountered during servicing or overhaul, they should, wherever possible, be renewed or refitted in accordance with the vehicle manufacturer's requirements or current legislation.

Note: It is antisocial and illegal to dump oil down the drain. To find the location of your local oil recycling bank, call this number free.

OIL CARE · FOLLOW THE CODE

OIL BANK LINE
0800 66 33 66

The jack supplied with the vehicle tool kit should only be used for changing the roadwheels - see *"Wheel changing"* at the front of this manual. When carrying out any other kind of work, raise the vehicle using a hydraulic (or "trolley") jack, and always supplement the jack with axle stands positioned under the vehicle jacking points.

When using a hydraulic jack or axle stands, always position the jack head or axle stand head under, or adjacent to one of the relevant wheel changing jacking points **(see illustration)**.

To raise the front of the vehicle, position the jack with an interposed block of wood underneath the centre of the front subframe. Alternatively, the vehicle can be jacked under the front crossmember, but a block of wood 100 x 100 x 780 mm will be required between the jack and the crossmember. **Do not** jack the vehicle under the sump, or any of the steering or suspension components.

The procedure for raising the rear of the vehicle is as described for the front, but place the jack under either the rear axle tube, for which a shaped block of wood approximately 100 mm long will be required, or under the rear panel using a 150 x 150 x 1200 mm block of wood. **Do not** attempt to raise the vehicle with the jack positioned under the spare wheel, as the vehicle floor will almost certainly be damaged.

The jack supplied with the vehicle located in the jacking points in the ridges on the underside of the sills. Ensure that the jack head is correctly engaged before attempting to raise the vehicle.

Never work under, around, or near a raised vehicle, unless it is adequately supported in at least two places.

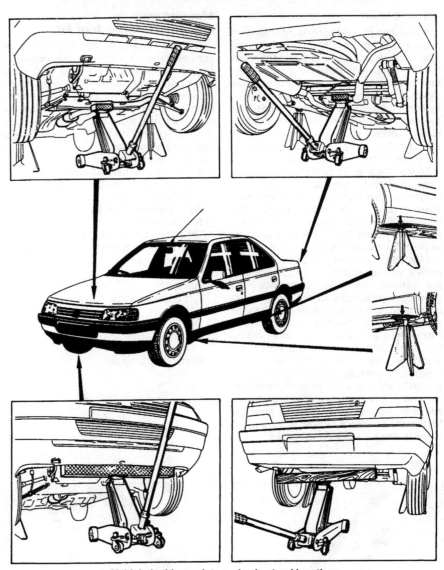

Vehicle jacking points and axle stand locations

Radio/cassette unit Anti-theft System - Precaution

The radio/cassette unit fitted to later models as standard equipment by Peugeot is equipped with a built-in security code, to deter thieves. If the power source to the unit is cut, the anti-theft system will activate. Even if the power source is immediately reconnected, the radio/cassette unit will not function until the correct security code has been entered. Therefore if you do not know the correct security code for the unit, **do not** disconnect the battery negative lead, or remove the radio/cassette unit from the vehicle.

To enter the security code, press the "on/off" button; the unit display will show "CODE".The security code can then be entered using the buttons 1 to 6 on the unit. The unit will be activated automatically if the correct code is entered.

If the incorrect code is entered, the unit will lock, and the word "SECURITY" will be displayed for 2 minutes. After 2 minutes, it will be possible to enter a code again. If 3 wrong codes are entered, the unit will lock for 2 hours. To clear the locking function, leave the unit and the ignition switched on during this period.

If the security code is lost or forgotten, seek the advice of your Peugeot dealer. On presentation of proof of ownership, a Peugeot dealer will be able to provide you with a new security code.

Introduction

A selection of good tools is a fundamental requirement for anyone contemplating the maintenance and repair of a motor vehicle. For the owner who does not possess any, their purchase will prove a considerable expense, offsetting some of the savings made by doing-it-yourself. However, provided that the tools purchased meet the relevant national safety standards and are of good quality, they will last for many years and prove an extremely worthwhile investment.

To help the average owner to decide which tools are needed to carry out the various tasks detailed in this manual, we have compiled three lists of tools under the following headings: *Maintenance and minor repair, Repair and overhaul*, and *Special*. Newcomers to practical mechanics should start off with the *Maintenance and minor repair* tool kit, and confine themselves to the simpler jobs around the vehicle. Then, as confidence and experience grow, more difficult tasks can be undertaken, with extra tools being purchased as, and when, they are needed. In this way, a *Maintenance and minor repair* tool kit can be built up into a *Repair and overhaul* tool kit over a considerable period of time, without any major cash outlays. The experienced do-it-yourselfer will have a tool kit good enough for most repair and overhaul procedures, and will add tools from the *Special* category when it is felt that the expense is justified by the amount of use to which these tools will be put.

Maintenance and minor repair tool kit

The tools given in this list should be considered as a minimum requirement if routine maintenance, servicing and minor repair operations are to be undertaken. We recommend the purchase of combination spanners (ring one end, open-ended the other); although more expensive than open-ended ones, they do give the advantages of both types of spanner.

- [ ] *Combination spanners:*
  Metric - 8 to 19 mm inclusive
- [ ] *Adjustable spanner - 35 mm jaw (approx.)*
- [ ] *Set of feeler blades*
- [ ] *Brake bleed nipple spanner*
- [ ] *Screwdrivers:*
  Flat blade - 100 mm long x 6 mm dia
  Cross blade - 100 mm long x 6 mm dia
- [ ] *Combination pliers*
- [ ] *Hacksaw (junior)*
- [ ] *Tyre pump*
- [ ] *Tyre pressure gauge*
- [ ] *Oil can*
- [ ] *Oil filter removal tool*
- [ ] *Fine emery cloth*
- [ ] *Wire brush (small)*
- [ ] *Funnel (medium size)*

Repair and overhaul tool kit

These tools are virtually essential for anyone undertaking any major repairs to a motor vehicle, and are additional to those given in the *Maintenance and minor repair* list. Included in this list is a comprehensive set of sockets. Although these are expensive, they will be found invaluable as they are so versatile - particularly if various drives are included in the set. We recommend the half-inch square-drive type, as this can be used with most proprietary torque wrenches.

The tools in this list will sometimes need to be supplemented by tools from the *Special* list:

- [ ] *Sockets (or box spanners) to cover range in previous list (including Torx sockets)*
- [ ] *Reversible ratchet drive (for use with sockets)*
- [ ] *Extension piece, 250 mm (for use with sockets)*
- [ ] *Universal joint (for use with sockets)*
- [ ] *Torque wrench (for use with sockets)*
- [ ] *Self-locking grips*
- [ ] *Ball pein hammer*
- [ ] *Soft-faced mallet (plastic/aluminium or rubber)*
- [ ] *Screwdrivers:*
  Flat blade - long & sturdy, short (chubby), and narrow (electrician's) types
  Cross blade – Long & sturdy, and short (chubby) types
- [ ] *Pliers:*
  Long-nosed
  Side cutters (electrician's)
  Circlip (internal and external)
- [ ] *Cold chisel - 25 mm*
- [ ] *Scriber*
- [ ] *Scraper*
- [ ] *Centre-punch*
- [ ] *Pin punch*
- [ ] *Hacksaw*
- [ ] *Brake hose clamp*
- [ ] *Brake/clutch bleeding kit*
- [ ] *Selection of twist drills*
- [ ] *Steel rule/straight-edge*
- [ ] *Allen keys (inc. splined/Torx type)*
- [ ] *Selection of files*
- [ ] *Wire brush*
- [ ] *Axle stands*
- [ ] *Jack (strong trolley or hydraulic type)*
- [ ] *Light with extension lead*

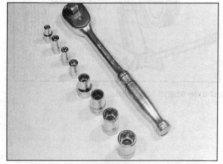

Sockets and reversible ratchet drive

Valve spring compressor

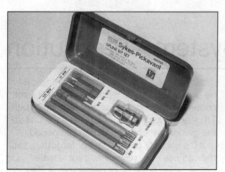

Spline bit set

Piston ring compressor

Clutch plate alignment set

Special tools

The tools in this list are those which are not used regularly, are expensive to buy, or which need to be used in accordance with their manufacturers' instructions. Unless relatively difficult mechanical jobs are undertaken frequently, it will not be economic to buy many of these tools. Where this is the case, you could consider clubbing together with friends (or joining a motorists' club) to make a joint purchase, or borrowing the tools against a deposit from a local garage or tool hire specialist. It is worth noting that many of the larger DIY superstores now carry a large range of special tools for hire at modest rates.

The following list contains only those tools and instruments freely available to the public, and not those special tools produced by the vehicle manufacturer specifically for its dealer network. You will find occasional references to these manufacturers' special tools in the text of this manual. Generally, an alternative method of doing the job without the vehicle manufacturers' special tool is given. However, sometimes there is no alternative to using them. Where this is the case and the relevant tool cannot be bought or borrowed, you will have to entrust the work to a dealer.

☐ Valve spring compressor
☐ Valve grinding tool
☐ Piston ring compressor
☐ Piston ring removal/installation tool
☐ Cylinder bore hone
☐ Balljoint separator
☐ Coil spring compressors (where applicable)
☐ Two/three-legged hub and bearing puller
☐ Impact screwdriver
☐ Micrometer and/or vernier calipers
☐ Dial gauge
☐ Dwell angle meter/tachometer
☐ Universal electrical multi-meter
☐ Cylinder compression gauge (must be suitable for use with a diesel engine)
☐ Clutch plate alignment set
☐ Brake shoe steady spring cup removal tool
☐ Bush and bearing removal/installation set
☐ Stud extractors
☐ Tap and die set
☐ Lifting tackle
☐ Trolley jack

Buying tools

Reputable motor accessory shops and superstores often offer excellent quality tools at discount prices, so it pays to shop around.

Remember, you don't have to buy the most expensive items on the shelf, but it is always advisable to steer clear of the very cheap tools. Beware of 'bargains' offered on market stalls or at car boot sales. There are plenty of good tools around at reasonable prices, but always aim to purchase items which meet the relevant national safety standards. If in doubt, ask the proprietor or manager of the shop for advice before making a purchase.

Care and maintenance of tools

Having purchased a reasonable tool kit, it is necessary to keep the tools in a clean and serviceable condition. After use, always wipe off any dirt, grease and metal particles using a clean, dry cloth, before putting the tools away. Never leave them lying around after they have been used. A simple tool rack on the garage or workshop wall for items such as screwdrivers and pliers is a good idea. Store all normal spanners and sockets in a metal box. Any measuring instruments, gauges, meters, etc, must be carefully stored where they cannot be damaged or become rusty.

Take a little care when tools are used. Hammer heads inevitably become marked, and screwdrivers lose the keen edge on their blades from time to time. A little timely attention with emery cloth or a file will soon restore items like this to a good finish.

Working facilities

Not to be forgotten when discussing tools is the workshop itself. If anything more than routine maintenance is to be carried out, a suitable working area becomes essential.

It is appreciated that many an owner-mechanic is forced by circumstances to remove an engine or similar item without the benefit of a garage or workshop. Having done this, any repairs should always be done under the cover of a roof.

Wherever possible, any dismantling should be done on a clean, flat workbench or table at a suitable working height.

Any workbench needs a vice; one with a jaw opening of 100 mm is suitable for most jobs. As mentioned previously, some clean dry storage space is also required for tools, as well as for any lubricants, cleaning fluids, touch-up paints etc, which become necessary.

Another item which may be required, and which has a much more general usage, is an electric drill with a chuck capacity of at least 8 mm. This, together with a good range of twist drills, is virtually essential for fitting accessories.

Last, but not least, always keep a supply of old newspapers and clean, lint-free rags available, and try to keep any working area as clean as possible.

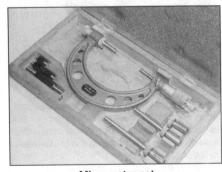

Micrometer set

Dial test indicator ("dial gauge")

Three-legged puller

Compression tester

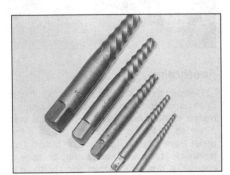

Stud extractor set

This is a guide to getting your vehicle through the MOT test. Obviously it will not be possible to examine the vehicle to the same standard as the professional MOT tester. However, working through the following checks will enable you to identify any problem areas before submitting the vehicle for the test.

Where a testable component is in borderline condition, the tester has discretion in deciding whether to pass or fail it. The basis of such discretion is whether the tester would be happy for a close relative or friend to use the vehicle with the component in that condition. If the vehicle presented is clean and evidently well cared for, the tester may be more inclined to pass a borderline component than if the vehicle is scruffy and apparently neglected.

It has only been possible to summarise the test requirements here, based on the regulations in force at the time of printing. Test standards are becoming increasingly stringent, although there are some exemptions for older vehicles. For full details obtain a copy of the Haynes publication Pass the MOT! (available from stockists of Haynes manuals).

An assistant will be needed to help carry out some of these checks.

The checks have been sub-divided into four categories, as follows:

1 Checks carried out **FROM THE DRIVER'S SEAT**

2 Checks carried out **WITH THE VEHICLE ON THE GROUND**

3 Checks carried out **WITH THE VEHICLE RAISED AND THE WHEELS FREE TO TURN**

4 Checks carried out on **YOUR VEHICLE'S EXHAUST EMISSION SYSTEM**

---

1 Checks carried out **FROM THE DRIVER'S SEAT**

Handbrake

☐ Test the operation of the handbrake. Excessive travel (too many clicks) indicates incorrect brake or cable adjustment.

☐ Check that the handbrake cannot be released by tapping the lever sideways. Check the security of the lever mountings.

Footbrake

☐ Depress the brake pedal and check that it does not creep down to the floor, indicating a master cylinder fault. Release the pedal, wait a few seconds, then depress it again. If the pedal travels nearly to the floor before firm resistance is felt, brake adjustment or repair is necessary. If the pedal feels spongy, there is air in the hydraulic system which must be removed by bleeding.

☐ Check that the brake pedal is secure and in good condition. Check also for signs of fluid leaks on the pedal, floor or carpets, which would indicate failed seals in the brake master cylinder.

☐ Check the servo unit (when applicable) by operating the brake pedal several times, then keeping the pedal depressed and starting the engine. As the engine starts, the pedal will move down slightly. If not, the vacuum hose or the servo itself may be faulty.

Steering wheel and column

☐ Examine the steering wheel for fractures or looseness of the hub, spokes or rim.

☐ Move the steering wheel from side to side and then up and down. Check that the steering wheel is not loose on the column, indicating wear or a loose retaining nut. Continue moving the steering wheel as before, but also turn it slightly from left to right.

☐ Check that the steering wheel is not loose on the column, and that there is no abnormal

movement of the steering wheel, indicating wear in the column support bearings or couplings.

Windscreen and mirrors

☐ The windscreen must be free of cracks or other significant damage within the driver's field of view. (Small stone chips are acceptable.) Rear view mirrors must be secure, intact, and capable of being adjusted.

290mm

Seat belts and seats

Note: *The following checks are applicable to all seat belts, front and rear.*

☐ Examine the webbing of all the belts (including rear belts if fitted) for cuts, serious fraying or deterioration. Fasten and unfasten each belt to check the buckles. If applicable, check the retracting mechanism. Check the security of all seat belt mountings accessible from inside the vehicle.

☐ The front seats themselves must be securely attached and the backrests must lock in the upright position.

Doors

☐ Both front doors must be able to be opened and closed from outside and inside, and must latch securely when closed.

2 Checks carried out WITH THE VEHICLE ON THE GROUND

Vehicle identification

☐ Number plates must be in good condition, secure and legible, with letters and numbers correctly spaced – spacing at (A) should be twice that at (B).

☐ The VIN plate and/or homologation plate must be legible.

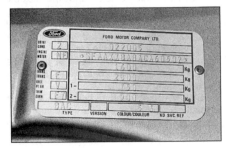

Electrical equipment

☐ Switch on the ignition and check the operation of the horn.

☐ Check the windscreen washers and wipers, examining the wiper blades; renew damaged or perished blades. Also check the operation of the stop-lights.

☐ Check the operation of the sidelights and number plate lights. The lenses and reflectors must be secure, clean and undamaged.

☐ Check the operation and alignment of the headlights. The headlight reflectors must not be tarnished and the lenses must be undamaged.

☐ Switch on the ignition and check the operation of the direction indicators (including the instrument panel tell-tale) and the hazard warning lights. Operation of the sidelights and stop-lights must not affect the indicators - if it does, the cause is usually a bad earth at the rear light cluster.

☐ Check the operation of the rear foglight(s), including the warning light on the instrument panel or in the switch.

Footbrake

☐ Examine the master cylinder, brake pipes and servo unit for leaks, loose mountings, corrosion or other damage.

☐ The fluid reservoir must be secure and the fluid level must be between the upper (**A**) and lower (**B**) markings.

☐ Inspect both front brake flexible hoses for cracks or deterioration of the rubber. Turn the steering from lock to lock, and ensure that the hoses do not contact the wheel, tyre, or any part of the steering or suspension mechanism. With the brake pedal firmly depressed, check the hoses for bulges or leaks under pressure.

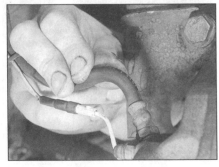

Steering and suspension

☐ Have your assistant turn the steering wheel from side to side slightly, up to the point where the steering gear just begins to transmit this movement to the roadwheels. Check for excessive free play between the steering wheel and the steering gear, indicating wear or insecurity of the steering column joints, the column-to-steering gear coupling, or the steering gear itself.

☐ Have your assistant turn the steering wheel more vigorously in each direction, so that the roadwheels just begin to turn. As this is done, examine all the steering joints, linkages, fittings and attachments. Renew any component that shows signs of wear or damage. On vehicles with power steering, check the security and condition of the steering pump, drivebelt and hoses.

☐ Check that the vehicle is standing level, and at approximately the correct ride height.

Shock absorbers

☐ Depress each corner of the vehicle in turn, then release it. The vehicle should rise and then settle in its normal position. If the vehicle continues to rise and fall, the shock absorber is defective. A shock absorber which has seized will also cause the vehicle to fail.

Exhaust system

☐ Start the engine. With your assistant holding a rag over the tailpipe, check the entire system for leaks. Repair or renew leaking sections.

3 Checks carried out **WITH THE VEHICLE RAISED AND THE WHEELS FREE TO TURN**

Jack up the front and rear of the vehicle, and securely support it on axle stands. Position the stands clear of the suspension assemblies. Ensure that the wheels are clear of the ground and that the steering can be turned from lock to lock.

Steering mechanism

☐ Have your assistant turn the steering from lock to lock. Check that the steering turns smoothly, and that no part of the steering mechanism, including a wheel or tyre, fouls any brake hose or pipe or any part of the body structure.

☐ Examine the steering rack rubber gaiters for damage or insecurity of the retaining clips. If power steering is fitted, check for signs of damage or leakage of the fluid hoses, pipes or connections. Also check for excessive stiffness or binding of the steering, a missing split pin or locking device, or severe corrosion of the body structure within 30 cm of any steering component attachment point.

Front and rear suspension and wheel bearings

☐ Starting at the front right-hand side, grasp the roadwheel at the 3 o'clock and 9 o'clock positions and shake it vigorously. Check for free play or insecurity at the wheel bearings, suspension balljoints, or suspension mountings, pivots and attachments.

☐ Now grasp the wheel at the 12 o'clock and 6 o'clock positions and repeat the previous inspection. Spin the wheel, and check for roughness or tightness of the front wheel bearing.

☐ If excess free play is suspected at a component pivot point, this can be confirmed by using a large screwdriver or similar tool and levering between the mounting and the component attachment. This will confirm whether the wear is in the pivot bush, its retaining bolt, or in the mounting itself (the bolt holes can often become elongated).

☐ Carry out all the above checks at the other front wheel, and then at both rear wheels.

Springs and shock absorbers

☐ Examine the suspension struts (when applicable) for serious fluid leakage, corrosion, or damage to the casing. Also check the security of the mounting points.

☐ If coil springs are fitted, check that the spring ends locate in their seats, and that the spring is not corroded, cracked or broken.

☐ If leaf springs are fitted, check that all leaves are intact, that the axle is securely attached to each spring, and that there is no deterioration of the spring eye mountings, bushes, and shackles.

☐ The same general checks apply to vehicles fitted with other suspension types, such as torsion bars, hydraulic displacer units, etc. Ensure that all mountings and attachments are secure, that there are no signs of excessive wear, corrosion or damage, and (on hydraulic types) that there are no fluid leaks or damaged pipes.

☐ Inspect the shock absorbers for signs of serious fluid leakage. Check for wear of the mounting bushes or attachments, or damage to the body of the unit.

Driveshafts (fwd vehicles only)

☐ Rotate each front wheel in turn and inspect the constant velocity joint gaiters for splits or damage. Also check that each driveshaft is straight and undamaged.

Braking system

☐ If possible without dismantling, check brake pad wear and disc condition. Ensure that the friction lining material has not worn excessively, (A) and that the discs are not fractured, pitted, scored or badly worn (B).

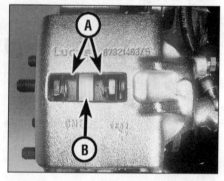

☐ Examine all the rigid brake pipes underneath the vehicle, and the flexible hose(s) at the rear. Look for corrosion, chafing or insecurity of the pipes, and for signs of bulging under pressure, chafing, splits or deterioration of the flexible hoses.

☐ Look for signs of fluid leaks at the brake calipers or on the brake backplates. Repair or renew leaking components.

☐ Slowly spin each wheel, while your assistant depresses and releases the footbrake. Ensure that each brake is operating and does not bind when the pedal is released.

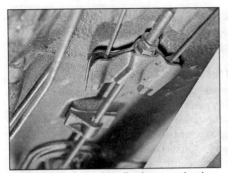

□ Examine the handbrake mechanism, checking for frayed or broken cables, excessive corrosion, or wear or insecurity of the linkage. Check that the mechanism works on each relevant wheel, and releases fully, without binding.

□ It is not possible to test brake efficiency without special equipment, but a road test can be carried out later to check that the vehicle pulls up in a straight line.

Fuel and exhaust systems

□ Inspect the fuel tank (including the filler cap), fuel pipes, hoses and unions. All components must be secure and free from leaks.

□ Examine the exhaust system over its entire length, checking for any damaged, broken or missing mountings, security of the retaining clamps and rust or corrosion.

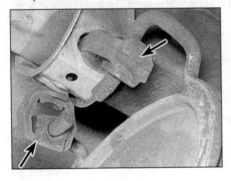

Wheels and tyres

□ Examine the sidewalls and tread area of each tyre in turn. Check for cuts, tears, lumps, bulges, separation of the tread, and exposure of the ply or cord due to wear or damage. Check that the tyre bead is correctly seated on the wheel rim, that the valve is sound and

properly seated, and that the wheel is not distorted or damaged.

□ Check that the tyres are of the correct size for the vehicle, that they are of the same size and type on each axle, and that the pressures are correct.

□ Check the tyre tread depth. The legal minimum at the time of writing is 1.6 mm over at least three-quarters of the tread width. Abnormal tread wear may indicate incorrect front wheel alignment.

Body corrosion

□ Check the condition of the entire vehicle structure for signs of corrosion in load-bearing areas. (These include chassis box sections, side sills, cross-members, pillars, and all suspension, steering, braking system and seat belt mountings and anchorages.) Any corrosion which has seriously reduced the thickness of a load-bearing area is likely to cause the vehicle to fail. In this case professional repairs are likely to be needed.

□ Damage or corrosion which causes sharp or otherwise dangerous edges to be exposed will also cause the vehicle to fail.

4 Checks carried out on YOUR VEHICLE'S EXHAUST EMISSION SYSTEM

Petrol models

□ Have the engine at normal operating temperature, and make sure that it is in good tune (ignition system in good order, air filter element clean, etc).

□ Before any measurements are carried out, raise the engine speed to around 2500 rpm, and hold it at this speed for 20 seconds. Allow

the engine speed to return to idle, and watch for smoke emissions from the exhaust tailpipe. If the idle speed is obviously much too high, or if dense blue or clearly-visible black smoke comes from the tailpipe for more than 5 seconds, the vehicle will fail. As a rule of thumb, blue smoke signifies oil being burnt (engine wear) while black smoke signifies unburnt fuel (dirty air cleaner element, or other carburettor or fuel system fault).

□ An exhaust gas analyser capable of measuring carbon monoxide (CO) and hydrocarbons (HC) is now needed. If such an instrument cannot be hired or borrowed, a local garage may agree to perform the check for a small fee.

CO emissions (mixture)

□ At the time of writing, the maximum CO level at idle is 3.5% for vehicles first used after August 1986 and 4.5% for older vehicles. From January 1996 a much tighter limit (around 0.5%) applies to catalyst-equipped vehicles first used from August 1992. If the CO level cannot be reduced far enough to pass the test (and the fuel and ignition systems are otherwise in good condition) then the carburettor is badly worn, or there is some problem in the fuel injection system or catalytic converter (as applicable).

HC emissions

□ With the CO emissions within limits, HC emissions must be no more than 1200 ppm (parts per million). If the vehicle fails this test at idle, it can be re-tested at around 2000 rpm; if the HC level is then 1200 ppm or less, this counts as a pass.

□ Excessive HC emissions can be caused by oil being burnt, but they are more likely to be due to unburnt fuel.

Diesel models

□ The only emission test applicable to Diesel engines is the measuring of exhaust smoke density. The test involves accelerating the engine several times to its maximum unloaded speed.

Note: *It is of the utmost importance that the engine timing belt is in good condition before the test is carried out.*

□ Excessive smoke can be caused by a dirty air cleaner element. Otherwise, professional advice may be needed to find the cause.

Engine 1
- [ ] Engine fails to rotate when attempting to start
- [ ] Engine rotates, but will not start
- [ ] Engine difficult to start when cold
- [ ] Engine difficult to start when hot
- [ ] Starter motor noisy or excessively-rough in engagement
- [ ] Starter motor turns engine slowly
- [ ] Engine starts, but stops immediately
- [ ] Engine idles erratically
- [ ] Engine misfires at idle speed
- [ ] Engine misfires throughout the driving speed range
- [ ] Engine stalls
- [ ] Engine lacks power
- [ ] Engine backfires
- [ ] Oil pressure warning light illuminated with engine running
- [ ] Engine runs-on after switching off
- [ ] Engine noises

Cooling system 2
- [ ] Overheating
- [ ] Overcooling
- [ ] External coolant leakage
- [ ] Internal coolant leakage
- [ ] Corrosion

Fuel and exhaust systems 3
- [ ] Excessive fuel consumption
- [ ] Fuel leakage and/or fuel odour
- [ ] Excessive noise or fumes from exhaust system

Clutch 4
- [ ] Pedal travels to floor - no pressure or very little resistance
- [ ] Clutch fails to disengage (unable to select gears)
- [ ] Clutch slips (engine speed increases, with no increase in vehicle speed)
- [ ] Judder as clutch is engaged
- [ ] Noise when depressing or releasing clutch pedal

Manual transmission 5
- [ ] Noisy in neutral with engine running
- [ ] Noisy in one particular gear
- [ ] Difficulty engaging gears
- [ ] Jumps out of gear
- [ ] Vibration
- [ ] Lubricant leaks

Driveshafts 6
- [ ] Clicking or knocking noise on turns (at slow speed on full-lock)
- [ ] Vibration when accelerating or decelerating

Braking system 7
- [ ] Vehicle pulls to one side under braking
- [ ] Noise (grinding or high-pitched squeal) when brakes applied
- [ ] Excessive brake pedal travel
- [ ] Brake pedal feels spongy when depressed
- [ ] Excessive brake pedal effort required to stop vehicle
- [ ] Judder felt through brake pedal or steering wheel when braking
- [ ] Pedal pulsates when braking hard
- [ ] Brakes binding
- [ ] Rear wheels locking under normal braking

Suspension and steering systems 8
- [ ] Vehicle pulls to one side
- [ ] Wheel wobble and vibration
- [ ] Excessive pitching and/or rolling around corners, or during braking
- [ ] Wandering or general instability
- [ ] Excessively-stiff steering
- [ ] Excessive play in steering
- [ ] Lack of power assistance
- [ ] Tyre wear excessive

Electrical system 9
- [ ] Battery will not hold a charge for more than a few days
- [ ] Ignition/no-charge warning light remains illuminated with engine running
- [ ] Ignition/no-charge warning light fails to come on
- [ ] Lights inoperative
- [ ] Instrument readings inaccurate or erratic
- [ ] Horn inoperative, or unsatisfactory in operation
- [ ] Windscreen/tailgate wipers inoperative, or unsatisfactory in operation
- [ ] Windscreen/tailgate washers inoperative, or unsatisfactory in operation
- [ ] Electric windows inoperative, or unsatisfactory in operation
- [ ] Central locking system inoperative, or unsatisfactory in operation

Introduction

The vehicle owner who does his or her own maintenance according to the recommended service schedules should not have to use this section of the manual very often. Modern component reliability is such that, provided those items subject to wear or deterioration are inspected or renewed at the specified intervals, sudden failure is comparatively rare. Faults do not usually just happen as a result of sudden failure, but develop over a period of time. Major mechanical failures in particular are usually preceded by characteristic symptoms over hundreds or even thousands of miles. Those components which do occasionally fail without warning are often small and easily carried in the vehicle.

With any fault-finding, the first step is to decide where to begin investigations. Sometimes this is obvious, but on other occasions, a little detective work will be necessary. The owner who makes half a dozen haphazard adjustments or replacements may be successful in curing a fault (or its symptoms), but will be none the wiser if the fault recurs, and ultimately may have spent more time and money than was necessary. A calm and logical approach will be found to be more satisfactory in the long run. Always take into account any warning signs or abnormalities that may have been noticed in the period preceding the fault - power loss, high or low gauge readings, unusual smells, etc - and remember that failure of components such as fuses or spark plugs may only be pointers to some underlying fault.

The pages which follow provide an easy-reference guide to the more common problems which may occur during the operation of the vehicle. These problems and their possible causes are grouped under headings denoting various components or systems, such as Engine, Cooling system, etc. The Chapter and/or Section which deals with the problem is also shown in brackets. Whatever the fault, certain basic principles apply. These are as follows:

Verify the fault. This is simply a matter of being sure that you know what the symptoms are before starting work. This is particularly important if you are investigating a fault for someone else, who may not have described it very accurately.

Don't overlook the obvious. For example, if the vehicle won't start, is there fuel in the tank? (Don't take anyone else's word on this particular point, and don't trust the fuel gauge either!) If an electrical fault is indicated, look for loose or broken wires before digging out the test gear.

Cure the disease, not the symptom. Substituting a flat battery with a fully-charged one will get you off the hard shoulder, but if the underlying cause is not attended to, the new battery will go the same way. Similarly, changing oil-fouled spark plugs for a new set will get you moving again, but remember that the reason for the fouling (if it wasn't simply an incorrect grade of plug) will have to be established and corrected.

Don't take anything for granted. Particularly, don't forget that a "new" component may itself be defective (especially if it's been rattling around in the boot for months), and don't leave components out of a fault diagnosis sequence just because they are new or recently-fitted. When you do finally diagnose a difficult fault, you'll probably realise that all the evidence was there from the start.

1 Engine

Engine fails to rotate when attempting to start

☐ Battery terminal connections loose or corroded ("*Weekly Checks*").
☐ Battery discharged or faulty (Chapter 5A).
☐ Broken, loose or disconnected wiring in the starting circuit (Chapter 5A).
☐ Defective starter solenoid or switch (Chapter 5A).
☐ Defective starter motor (Chapter 5A).
☐ Starter pinion or flywheel ring gear teeth loose or broken (Chapters 2A or 5A).
☐ Engine earth strap broken or disconnected (Chapter 5A).

Engine rotates, but will not start

☐ Fuel tank empty.
☐ Battery discharged (engine rotates slowly) (Chapter 5A).
☐ Battery terminal connections loose or corroded ("*Weekly Checks*").
☐ Air filter element dirty or clogged (Chapter 1).
☐ Preheating system fault (Chapter 5B).
☐ Stop solenoid faulty (Chapter 4).
☐ Air in fuel system (Chapter 4).
☐ Injection pump timing incorrect (Chapter 4).
☐ Low cylinder compressions (Chapter 2A).
☐ Major mechanical failure (eg broken timing belt) (Chapter 2A).
☐ Wax formed in fuel (in very cold weather).

Engine difficult to start when cold

☐ Battery discharged (Chapter 5A).
☐ Battery terminal connections loose or corroded ("*Weekly Checks*").
☐ Air filter element dirty or clogged (Chapter 1).
☐ Preheating system fault (Chapter 5B).
☐ Fast idle valve incorrectly adjusted (Chapter 4).
☐ Low cylinder compressions (Chapter 2A).
☐ Air in fuel system (Chapter 4).
☐ Wax formed in fuel (in very cold weather).
☐ Injection pump timing incorrect (Chapter 4).

Engine difficult to start when hot

☐ Battery discharged (Chapter 5A).
☐ Battery terminal connections loose or corroded ("*Weekly Checks*").
☐ Air filter element dirty or clogged (Chapter 1).
☐ Air in fuel system (Chapter 4).
☐ Low cylinder compressions (Chapter 2A).
☐ Injection pump timing incorrect (Chapter 4).

Starter motor noisy or excessively-rough in engagement

☐ Starter pinion or flywheel ring gear teeth loose or broken (Chapter 2A or 5A).
☐ Starter motor mounting bolts loose or missing (Chapter 5A).
☐ Starter motor internal components worn or damaged (Chapter 5A).

Starter motor turns engine slowly

☐ Battery discharged (Chapter 5A).
☐ Battery terminal connections loose or corroded ("*Weekly Checks*").
☐ Earth strap broken or disconnected (Chapter 5A).
☐ Starter motor wiring loose (Chapter 5A).
☐ Starter motor internal fault (Chapter 5A).

Engine starts, but stops immediately

☐ Air in fuel system (Chapter 4).
☐ Dirt in fuel system (Chapter 4).
☐ Fuel injector fault (Chapter 4).
☐ Incorrectly adjusted idle speed (Chapter 1).

Engine idles erratically

☐ Incorrectly-adjusted idle speed (Chapter 1).
☐ Air filter element clogged (Chapter 1).
☐ Air in fuel system (Chapter 4).
☐ Incorrectly adjusted valve clearances (Chapter 2A).
☐ Uneven or low cylinder compressions (Chapter 2A).
☐ Timing belt incorrectly fitted (Chapter 2A).
☐ Injection pump timing incorrect (Chapter 4).
☐ Camshaft lobes worn (Chapter 2A).
☐ Faulty fuel injector(s) (Chapter 4).

Engine misfires at idle speed

☐ Air in fuel system (Chapter 4).
☐ Faulty fuel injector(s) (Chapter 4).
☐ Incorrectly adjusted valve clearances (Chapter 2A).
☐ Uneven or low cylinder compressions (Chapter 2A).
☐ Disconnected, leaking, or perished crankcase ventilation hoses (Chapter 4).
☐ Injection pump timing incorrect (Chapter 4).

Engine misfires throughout the driving speed range

☐ Fuel filter choked (Chapter 1).
☐ Fuel injection pump fault (Chapter 4).
☐ Fuel tank vent blocked, or fuel pipes restricted (Chapter 4).
☐ Uneven or low cylinder compressions (Chapter 2A).
☐ Faulty fuel injector(s) (Chapter 4).
☐ Injection pump timing incorrect (Chapter 4).

1 Engine (continued)

Engine stalls

☐ Incorrectly adjusted idle speed (Chapter 1).
☐ Fuel filter choked (Chapter 1).
☐ Faulty fuel injector(s) (Chapter 4).
☐ Fuel injection pump fault (Chapter 4).
☐ Fuel tank vent blocked, or fuel pipes restricted (Chapter 4).

Engine lacks power

☐ Fuel filter choked (Chapter 1).
☐ Air in fuel system (Chapter 4).
☐ Fuel injection pump fault (Chapter 4).
☐ Faulty fuel injector(s) (Chapter 4).
☐ Injection pump timing incorrect (Chapter 4).
☐ Uneven or low cylinder compressions (Chapter 2).
☐ Brakes binding (Chapters 1 and 10).
☐ Clutch slipping (Chapter 6).

Engine backfires

☐ Timing belt incorrectly fitted (Chapter 2A).
☐ Fuel injection pump fault (Chapter 4).

Oil pressure warning light illuminated with engine running

☐ Low oil level, or incorrect oil grade ("Weekly Checks").
☐ Faulty oil pressure sensor (Chapter 5A).
☐ Worn engine bearings and/or oil pump (Chapter 2B).
☐ Excessively high engine operating temperature (Chapter 3).
☐ Oil pressure relief valve defective (Chapter 2A).
☐ Oil pick-up strainer clogged (Chapter 2A).
Note: Low oil pressure in a high-mileage engine at tickover is not necessarily a cause for concern. Sudden pressure loss at speed is far more significant. In any event, check the gauge or warning light sender before condemning the engine.

Engine runs-on after switching off

☐ Excessive carbon build-up in engine (Chapter 2B).
☐ Excessively high engine operating temperature (Chapter 3).
☐ Faulty stop solenoid (Chapter 4).

Engine noises

Pre-ignition (pinking) or knocking during acceleration or under load

☐ Excessive carbon build-up in engine (Chapter 2B).
☐ Fuel injection pump fault (Chapter 4).
☐ Faulty fuel injector(s) (Chapter 4).

Whistling or wheezing noises

☐ Leaking exhaust manifold gasket (Chapter 4).
☐ Leaking vacuum hose (Chapter 4 or 9).
☐ Blowing cylinder head gasket (Chapter 2A).

Tapping or rattling noises

☐ Worn valve gear or camshaft (Chapter 2A).
☐ Ancillary component fault (coolant pump, alternator, etc) (Chapters 3, 5A, etc).

Knocking or thumping noises

☐ Worn big-end bearings (regular heavy knocking, perhaps less under load) (Chapter 2B).
☐ Worn main bearings (rumbling and knocking, perhaps worsening under load) (Chapter 2B).
☐ Piston slap (most noticeable when cold) (Chapter 2B).
☐ Ancillary component fault (coolant pump, alternator, etc) (Chapters 3, 5A, etc).

2 Cooling system

Overheating

☐ Insufficient coolant in system ("Weekly Checks").
☐ Thermostat faulty (Chapter 3).
☐ Radiator core blocked, or grille restricted (Chapter 3).
☐ Electric cooling fan or thermostatic switch faulty (Chapter 3).
☐ Inaccurate temperature gauge sender unit (Chapter 3).
☐ Airlock in cooling system (Chapter 3).
☐ Expansion tank pressure cap faulty (Chapter 3).

Overcooling

☐ Thermostat faulty (Chapter 3).
☐ Inaccurate temperature gauge sender unit (Chapter 3).

External coolant leakage

☐ Deteriorated or damaged hoses or hose clips (Chapter 1).
☐ Radiator core or heater matrix leaking (Chapter 3).
☐ Pressure cap faulty (Chapter 3).
☐ Coolant pump internal seal leaking (Chapter 3).
☐ Coolant pump-to-block seal leaking (Chapter 3).
☐ Boiling due to overheating (Chapter 3).
☐ Core plug leaking (Chapter 2B).

Internal coolant leakage

☐ Leaking cylinder head gasket (Chapter 2A).
☐ Cracked cylinder head or cylinder block (Chapter 2A or 2B).

Corrosion

☐ Infrequent draining and flushing (Chapter 1).
☐ Incorrect coolant mixture or inappropriate coolant type (Chapter 1).

3 Fuel and exhaust systems

Excessive fuel consumption

- [ ] Air filter element dirty or clogged (Chapter 1).
- [ ] Preheating system fault (Chapter 4).
- [ ] Incorrectly adjusted idle speed (Chapter 1).
- [ ] Incorrect fuel injection pump timing (Chapter 4).
- [ ] Brakes binding (Chapter 10).
- [ ] Tyres under-inflated (Chapter 1).

Fuel leakage and/or fuel odour

- [ ] Damaged fuel tank, pipes or connections (Chapters 1 and 4).

Excessive noise or fumes from exhaust system

- [ ] Leaking exhaust system or manifold joints (Chapters 1 and 4).
- [ ] Leaking, corroded or damaged silencers or pipe (Chapters 1 and 4).
- [ ] Broken mountings causing body or suspension contact (Chapter 4).

4 Clutch

Pedal travels to floor - no pressure or very little resistance

- [ ] Badly stretched or broken cable (Chapter 6).
- [ ] Incorrect clutch adjustment (Chapter 6).
- [ ] Broken clutch release bearing or arm (Chapter 6).
- [ ] Broken diaphragm spring in clutch pressure plate (Chapter 6).

Clutch fails to disengage (unable to select gears)

- [ ] Incorrect clutch adjustment (Chapter 6).
- [ ] Clutch friction plate sticking on gearbox input shaft splines (Chapter 6).
- [ ] Clutch friction plate sticking to flywheel or pressure plate (Chapter 6).
- [ ] Faulty pressure plate assembly (Chapter 6).
- [ ] Clutch release mechanism worn or incorrectly assembled (Chapter 6).

Clutch slips (engine speed increases, with no increase in vehicle speed)

- [ ] Clutch friction plate linings excessively worn (Chapter 6).
- [ ] Clutch friction plate linings contaminated with oil or grease (Chapter 6).
- [ ] Faulty pressure plate or weak diaphragm spring (Chapter 6).

Judder as clutch is engaged

- [ ] Clutch friction plate linings contaminated with oil or grease (Chapter 6).
- [ ] Clutch friction plate linings excessively worn (Chapter 6).
- [ ] Faulty or distorted pressure plate or diaphragm spring (Chapter 6).
- [ ] Worn or loose engine or gearbox mountings (Chapter 2A).
- [ ] Clutch friction plate hub or gearbox input shaft splines worn (Chapter 6).

Noise when depressing or releasing clutch pedal

- [ ] Worn clutch release bearing (Chapter 6).
- [ ] Worn or dry clutch pedal pivot (Chapter 6).
- [ ] Faulty pressure plate assembly (Chapter 6).
- [ ] Pressure plate diaphragm spring broken (Chapter 6).
- [ ] Broken clutch friction plate cushioning springs (Chapter 6).

5 Manual transmission

Noisy in neutral with engine running

- [ ] Input shaft bearings worn (noise apparent with clutch pedal released, but not when depressed) (Chapter 7).*
- [ ] Clutch release bearing worn (noise apparent with clutch pedal depressed, possibly less when released) (Chapter 6).

Noisy in one particular gear

- [ ] Worn, damaged or chipped gear teeth (Chapter 7).*

Difficulty engaging gears

- [ ] Clutch fault (Chapter 6).
- [ ] Worn or damaged gear linkage (Chapter 7).
- [ ] Worn synchroniser units (Chapter 7).*

Jumps out of gear

- [ ] Worn or damaged gear linkage (Chapter 7).
- [ ] Worn synchroniser units (Chapter 7).*
- [ ] Worn selector forks (Chapter 7).*

Vibration

- [ ] Lack of oil (Chapter 1).
- [ ] Worn bearings (Chapter 7).*

Lubricant leaks

- [ ] Leaking oil seal (Chapter 7).
- [ ] Leaking housing joint (Chapter 7).*

Although the corrective action necessary to remedy the symptoms described is beyond the scope of the home mechanic, the above information should be helpful in isolating the cause of the condition, so that the owner can communicate clearly with a professional mechanic.

6 Driveshafts

Clicking or knocking noise on turns (at slow speed on full-lock)

- [ ] Lack of constant velocity joint lubricant, possibly due to damaged gaiter (Chapter 8).
- [ ] Worn outer constant velocity joint (Chapter 8).

Vibration when accelerating or decelerating

- [ ] Worn inner constant velocity joint (Chapter 8).
- [ ] Bent or distorted driveshaft (Chapter 8).
- [ ] Worn right-hand driveshaft intermediate bearing (Chapter 8).

7 Braking system

Note: *Before assuming that a brake problem exists, make sure that the tyres are in good condition and correctly inflated, that the front wheel alignment is correct, and that the vehicle is not loaded with weight in an unequal manner. Apart from checking the condition of all pipe and hose connections, any faults occurring on the anti-lock braking system should be referred to a Peugeot dealer for diagnosis.*

Vehicle pulls to one side under braking

☐ Worn, defective, damaged or contaminated front or rear brake pads/shoes on one side (Chapters 1 and 9).
☐ Seized or partially-seized front or rear brake caliper/wheel cylinder piston (Chapter 9).
☐ A mixture of brake pad/shoe lining materials fitted between sides (Chapter 9).
☐ Brake caliper or rear brake backplate mounting bolts loose (Chapter 9).
☐ Worn or damaged steering or suspension components (Chapters 1 and 10).

Noise (grinding or high-pitched squeal) when brakes applied

☐ Brake pad or shoe friction lining material worn down to metal backing (Chapters 1 and 9).
☐ Excessive corrosion of brake disc or drum - may be apparent if the vehicle has not been used for some time (Chapters 1 and 9).

Excessive brake pedal travel

☐ Faulty rear drum brake self-adjust mechanism (Chapter 9).
☐ Faulty master cylinder (Chapter 9).
☐ Air in hydraulic system (Chapter 9).
☐ Faulty vacuum servo unit (Chapter 9).
☐ Faulty vacuum pump (Chapter 9).

Brake pedal feels spongy when depressed

☐ Air in hydraulic system (Chapter 9).
☐ Deteriorated flexible rubber brake hoses (Chapters 1 and 9).
☐ Master cylinder mountings loose (Chapter 9).
☐ Faulty master cylinder (Chapter 9).

Excessive brake pedal effort required to stop vehicle

☐ Faulty vacuum servo unit (Chapter 9).
☐ Disconnected, damaged or insecure brake servo vacuum hose (Chapters 1 and 9).
☐ Faulty vacuum pump (Chapter 9).
☐ Primary or secondary hydraulic circuit failure (Chapter 9).
☐ Seized brake caliper or wheel cylinder piston(s) (Chapter 9).
☐ Brake pads or brake shoes incorrectly fitted (Chapter 9).
☐ Incorrect grade of brake pads or brake shoes fitted (Chapter 9).
☐ Brake pads or brake shoe linings contaminated (Chapter 9).

Judder felt through brake pedal or steering wheel when braking

☐ Excessive run-out or distortion of brake disc(s) or drum(s) (Chapter 9).
☐ Brake pad or brake shoe linings worn (Chapters 1 and 9).
☐ Brake caliper or rear brake backplate mounting bolts loose (Chapter 9).
☐ Wear in suspension or steering components or mountings (Chapters 1 and 10).

Pedal pulsates when braking hard

☐ Normal feature of ABS - no fault

Brakes binding

☐ Seized brake caliper piston(s) or wheel cylinder piston(s) (Chapter 9).
☐ Incorrectly-adjusted handbrake mechanism or linkage (Chapter 9).
☐ Faulty master cylinder (Chapter 9).

Rear wheels locking under normal braking

☐ Seized brake caliper piston(s) or wheel cylinder piston(s) (Chapter 9).
☐ Faulty brake pressure regulator (Chapter 9).

8 Steering and suspension

Note: *Before diagnosing suspension or steering faults, be sure that the trouble is not due to incorrect tyre pressures, mixtures of tyre types, or binding brakes.*

Vehicle pulls to one side

☐ Defective tyre (Chapter 1).
☐ Excessive wear in suspension or steering components (Chapters 1 and 10).
☐ Incorrect front wheel alignment (Chapter 10).
☐ Accident damage to steering or suspension components (Chapters 1 and 10).

Wheel wobble and vibration

☐ Front roadwheels out of balance (vibration felt mainly through the steering wheel) (Chapter 10).
☐ Rear roadwheels out of balance (vibration felt throughout the vehicle) (Chapter 10).
☐ Roadwheels damaged or distorted (Chapter 10).
☐ Faulty or damaged tyre (*"Weekly Checks"*).
☐ Worn steering or suspension joints, bushes or components (Chapters 1 and 10).
☐ Wheel bolts loose (Chapter 10).

Excessive pitching and/or rolling around corners, or during braking

☐ Defective shock absorbers (Chapters 1 and 10).
☐ Broken or weak coil spring and/or suspension component (Chapters 1 and 10).
☐ Worn or damaged anti-roll bar or mountings (Chapter 10).

Wandering or general instability

☐ Incorrect front wheel alignment (Chapter 10).
☐ Worn steering or suspension joints, bushes or components (Chapters 1 and 10).
☐ Roadwheels out of balance (Chapter 10).
☐ Faulty or damaged tyre (*"Weekly Checks"*).
☐ Wheel bolts loose (Chapter 10).
☐ Defective shock absorbers (Chapters 1 and 10).

Excessively-stiff steering

☐ Lack of steering gear lubricant (Chapter 10).
☐ Seized track rod end balljoint or suspension balljoint (Chapters 1 and 10).
☐ Broken or incorrectly adjusted auxiliary drivebelt (Chapter 1).
☐ Incorrect front wheel alignment (Chapter 10).
☐ Steering rack or column bent or damaged (Chapter 10).

8 Steering and suspension (continued)

Excessive play in steering

- ☐ Worn steering column universal joint(s) (Chapter 10).
- ☐ Worn steering track rod end balljoints (Chapters 1 and 10).
- ☐ Worn rack-and-pinion steering gear (Chapter 10).
- ☐ Worn steering or suspension joints, bushes or components (Chapters 1 and 10).

Lack of power assistance

- ☐ Broken or incorrectly-adjusted auxiliary drivebelt (Chapter 1).
- ☐ Incorrect power steering fluid level (*"Weekly Checks"*).
- ☐ Restriction in power steering fluid hoses (Chapter 10).
- ☐ Faulty power steering pump (Chapter 10).
- ☐ Faulty rack-and-pinion steering gear (Chapter 10).

Tyre wear excessive

Tyres worn on inside or outside edges

- ☐ Tyres under-inflated (wear on both edges) (*"Weekly Checks"*).
- ☐ Incorrect camber or castor angles (wear on one edge only) (Chapter 10).
- ☐ Worn steering or suspension joints, bushes or components (Chapters 1 and 10).
- ☐ Excessively-hard cornering.
- ☐ Accident damage.

Tyre treads exhibit feathered edges

- ☐ Incorrect toe setting (Chapter 10).

Tyres worn in centre of tread

- ☐ Tyres over-inflated (*"Weekly Checks"*).

Tyres worn on inside and outside edges

- ☐ Tyres under-inflated (*"Weekly Checks"*).
- ☐ Worn shock absorbers (Chapters 1 and 10).

Tyres worn unevenly

- ☐ Tyres out of balance (*"Weekly Checks"*).
- ☐ Excessive wheel or tyre run-out (Chapter 1).
- ☐ Worn shock absorbers (Chapters 1 and 10).
- ☐ Faulty tyre (*"Weekly Checks"*).

9 Electrical system

Note: *For problems associated with the starting system, refer to the faults listed under "Engine" earlier in this Section.*

Battery will not hold a charge for more than a few days

- ☐ Battery defective internally (Chapter 5A).
- ☐ Battery electrolyte level low - where applicable (*"Weekly Checks"*).
- ☐ Battery terminal connections loose or corroded (*"Weekly Checks"*).
- ☐ Auxiliary drivebelt worn - or incorrectly adjusted, where applicable (Chapter 1).
- ☐ Alternator not charging at correct output (Chapter 5A).
- ☐ Alternator or voltage regulator faulty (Chapter 5A).
- ☐ Short-circuit causing continual battery drain (Chapters 5A and 12).

Ignition/no-charge warning light remains illuminated with engine running

- ☐ Auxiliary drivebelt broken, worn, or incorrectly adjusted (Chapter 1).
- ☐ Alternator brushes worn, sticking, or dirty (Chapter 5A).
- ☐ Alternator brush springs weak or broken (Chapter 5A).
- ☐ Internal fault in alternator or voltage regulator (Chapter 5A).
- ☐ Broken, disconnected, or loose wiring in charging circuit (Chapter 5A).

Ignition/no-charge warning light fails to come on

- ☐ Warning light bulb blown (Chapter 12).
- ☐ Broken, disconnected, or loose wiring in warning light circuit (Chapter 12).
- ☐ Alternator faulty (Chapter 5A).

Lights inoperative

- ☐ Bulb blown (Chapter 12).
- ☐ Corrosion of bulb or bulbholder contacts (Chapter 12).
- ☐ Blown fuse (Chapter 12).
- ☐ Faulty relay (Chapter 12).
- ☐ Broken, loose, or disconnected wiring (Chapter 12).
- ☐ Faulty switch (Chapter 12).

Instrument readings inaccurate or erratic

Instrument readings increase with engine speed

- ☐ Faulty voltage regulator (Chapter 12).

Fuel or temperature gauges give no reading

- ☐ Faulty gauge sender unit (Chapters 3 and 4).
- ☐ Wiring open-circuit (Chapter 12).
- ☐ Faulty gauge (Chapter 12).

Fuel or temperature gauges give continuous maximum reading

- ☐ Faulty gauge sender unit (Chapters 3 and 4).
- ☐ Wiring short-circuit (Chapter 12).
- ☐ Faulty gauge (Chapter 12).

Horn inoperative, or unsatisfactory in operation

Horn operates all the time

- ☐ Horn contacts bridged or horn push stuck down (Chapter 12).

Horn fails to operate

- ☐ Blown fuse (Chapter 12).
- ☐ Cable or cable connections loose, broken or disconnected (Chapter 12).
- ☐ Faulty horn (Chapter 12).

Horn emits intermittent or unsatisfactory sound

- ☐ Cable connections loose (Chapter 12).
- ☐ Horn mountings loose (Chapter 12).
- ☐ Faulty horn (Chapter 12).

9 Electrical system (continued)

Windscreen/tailgate wipers inoperative, or unsatisfactory in operation

Wipers fail to operate, or operate very slowly

- ☐ Wiper blades stuck to screen, or linkage seized or binding (*"Weekly Checks"* and Chapter 12).
- ☐ Blown fuse (Chapter 12).
- ☐ Cable or cable connections loose, broken or disconnected (Chapter 12).
- ☐ Faulty relay (Chapter 12).
- ☐ Faulty wiper motor (Chapter 12).

Wiper blades sweep over too large or too small an area of the glass

- ☐ Wiper arms incorrectly positioned on spindles (Chapter 12).
- ☐ Excessive wear of wiper linkage (Chapter 12).
- ☐ Wiper motor or linkage mountings loose or insecure (Chapter 12).

Wiper blades fail to clean the glass effectively

- ☐ Wiper blade rubbers worn or perished (*"Weekly Checks"*).
- ☐ Wiper arm tension springs broken, or arm pivots seized (Chapter 12).
- ☐ Insufficient windscreen washer additive to adequately remove road film (*"Weekly Checks"*).

Windscreen/tailgate washers inoperative, or unsatisfactory in operation

One or more washer jets inoperative

- ☐ Blocked washer jet (Chapter 1).
- ☐ Disconnected, kinked or restricted fluid hose (Chapter 12).
- ☐ Insufficient fluid in washer reservoir (*"Weekly Checks"*).

Washer pump fails to operate

- ☐ Broken or disconnected wiring or connections (Chapter 12).
- ☐ Blown fuse (Chapter 12).
- ☐ Faulty washer switch (Chapter 12).
- ☐ Faulty washer pump (Chapter 12).

Washer pump runs for some time before fluid is emitted from jets

- ☐ Faulty one-way valve in fluid supply hose (Chapter 12).

Electric windows inoperative, or unsatisfactory in operation

Window glass will only move in one direction

- ☐ Faulty switch (Chapter 12).

Window glass slow to move

- ☐ Regulator seized or damaged, or in need of lubrication (Chapter 11).
- ☐ Door internal components or trim fouling regulator (Chapter 11).
- ☐ Faulty motor (Chapter 11).

Window glass fails to move

- ☐ Blown fuse (Chapter 12).
- ☐ Faulty relay (Chapter 12).
- ☐ Broken or disconnected wiring or connections (Chapter 12).
- ☐ Faulty motor (Chapter 12).

Central locking system inoperative, or unsatisfactory in operation

Complete system failure

- ☐ Blown fuse (Chapter 12).
- ☐ Faulty relay (Chapter 12).
- ☐ Broken or disconnected wiring or connections (Chapter 12).

Latch locks but will not unlock, or unlocks but will not lock

- ☐ Faulty switch (Chapter 12).
- ☐ Broken or disconnected latch operating rods or levers (Chapter 11).
- ☐ Faulty relay (Chapter 12).

One motor fails to operate

- ☐ Broken or disconnected wiring or connections (Chapter 12).
- ☐ Faulty motor (Chapter 12).
- ☐ Broken, binding or disconnected latch operating rods or levers (Chapter 11).
- ☐ Fault in door latch (Chapter 11).

A

ABS (Anti-lock brake system) A system, usually electronically controlled, that senses incipient wheel lockup during braking and relieves hydraulic pressure at wheels that are about to skid.

Air bag An inflatable bag hidden in the steering wheel (driver's side) or the dash or glovebox (passenger side). In a head-on collision, the bags inflate, preventing the driver and front passenger from being thrown forward into the steering wheel or windscreen.

Air cleaner A metal or plastic housing, containing a filter element, which removes dust and dirt from the air being drawn into the engine.

Air filter element The actual filter in an air cleaner system, usually manufactured from pleated paper and requiring renewal at regular intervals.

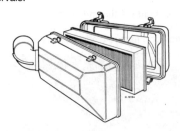

Air filter

Allen key A hexagonal wrench which fits into a recessed hexagonal hole.

Alligator clip A long-nosed spring-loaded metal clip with meshing teeth. Used to make temporary electrical connections.

Alternator A component in the electrical system which converts mechanical energy from a drivebelt into electrical energy to charge the battery and to operate the starting system, ignition system and electrical accessories.

Ampere (amp) A unit of measurement for the flow of electric current. One amp is the amount of current produced by one volt acting through a resistance of one ohm.

Anaerobic sealer A substance used to prevent bolts and screws from loosening. Anaerobic means that it does not require oxygen for activation. The Loctite brand is widely used.

Antifreeze A substance (usually ethylene glycol) mixed with water, and added to a vehicle's cooling system, to prevent freezing of the coolant in winter. Antifreeze also contains chemicals to inhibit corrosion and the formation of rust and other deposits that would tend to clog the radiator and coolant passages and reduce cooling efficiency.

Anti-seize compound A coating that reduces the risk of seizing on fasteners that are subjected to high temperatures, such as exhaust manifold bolts and nuts.

Asbestos A natural fibrous mineral with great heat resistance, commonly used in the composition of brake friction materials.

Asbestos is a health hazard and the dust created by brake systems should never be inhaled or ingested.

Axle A shaft on which a wheel revolves, or which revolves with a wheel. Also, a solid beam that connects the two wheels at one end of the vehicle. An axle which also transmits power to the wheels is known as a live axle.

Axleshaft A single rotating shaft, on either side of the differential, which delivers power from the final drive assembly to the drive wheels. Also called a driveshaft or a halfshaft.

B

Ball bearing An anti-friction bearing consisting of a hardened inner and outer race with hardened steel balls between two races.

Bearing The curved surface on a shaft or in a bore, or the part assembled into either, that permits relative motion between them with minimum wear and friction.

Bearing

Big-end bearing The bearing in the end of the connecting rod that's attached to the crankshaft.

Bleed nipple A valve on a brake wheel cylinder, caliper or other hydraulic component that is opened to purge the hydraulic system of air. Also called a bleed screw.

Brake bleeding Procedure for removing air from lines of a hydraulic brake system.

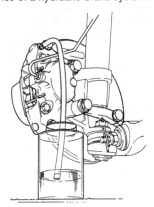

Brake bleeding

Brake disc The component of a disc brake that rotates with the wheels.

Brake drum The component of a drum brake that rotates with the wheels.

Brake linings The friction material which contacts the brake disc or drum to retard the vehicle's speed. The linings are bonded or riveted to the brake pads or shoes.

Brake pads The replaceable friction pads that pinch the brake disc when the brakes are applied. Brake pads consist of a friction material bonded or riveted to a rigid backing plate.

Brake shoe The crescent-shaped carrier to which the brake linings are mounted and which forces the lining against the rotating drum during braking.

Braking systems For more information on braking systems, consult the *Haynes Automotive Brake Manual*.

Breaker bar A long socket wrench handle providing greater leverage.

Bulkhead The insulated partition between the engine and the passenger compartment.

C

Caliper The non-rotating part of a disc-brake assembly that straddles the disc and carries the brake pads. The caliper also contains the hydraulic components that cause the pads to pinch the disc when the brakes are applied. A caliper is also a measuring tool that can be set to measure inside or outside dimensions of an object.

Camshaft A rotating shaft on which a series of cam lobes operate the valve mechanisms. The camshaft may be driven by gears, by sprockets and chain or by sprockets and a belt.

Canister A container in an evaporative emission control system; contains activated charcoal granules to trap vapours from the fuel system.

Canister

Carburettor A device which mixes fuel with air in the proper proportions to provide a desired power output from a spark ignition internal combustion engine.

Castellated Resembling the parapets along the top of a castle wall. For example, a castellated balljoint stud nut.

Castor In wheel alignment, the backward or forward tilt of the steering axis. Castor is positive when the steering axis is inclined rearward at the top.

Catalytic converter A silencer-like device in the exhaust system which converts certain pollutants in the exhaust gases into less harmful substances.

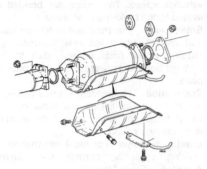

Catalytic converter

Circlip A ring-shaped clip used to prevent endwise movement of cylindrical parts and shafts. An internal circlip is installed in a groove in a housing; an external circlip fits into a groove on the outside of a cylindrical piece such as a shaft.

Clearance The amount of space between two parts. For example, between a piston and a cylinder, between a bearing and a journal, etc.

Coil spring A spiral of elastic steel found in various sizes throughout a vehicle, for example as a springing medium in the suspension and in the valve train.

Compression Reduction in volume, and increase in pressure and temperature, of a gas, caused by squeezing it into a smaller space.

Compression ratio The relationship between cylinder volume when the piston is at top dead centre and cylinder volume when the piston is at bottom dead centre.

Constant velocity (CV) joint A type of universal joint that cancels out vibrations caused by driving power being transmitted through an angle.

Core plug A disc or cup-shaped metal device inserted in a hole in a casting through which core was removed when the casting was formed. Also known as a freeze plug or expansion plug.

Crankcase The lower part of the engine block in which the crankshaft rotates.

Crankshaft The main rotating member, or shaft, running the length of the crankcase, with offset "throws" to which the connecting rods are attached.

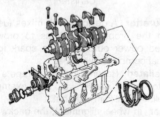

Crankshaft assembly

Crocodile clip See Alligator clip

D

Diagnostic code Code numbers obtained by accessing the diagnostic mode of an engine management computer. This code can be used to determine the area in the system where a malfunction may be located.

Disc brake A brake design incorporating a rotating disc onto which brake pads are squeezed. The resulting friction converts the energy of a moving vehicle into heat.

Double-overhead cam (DOHC) An engine that uses two overhead camshafts, usually one for the intake valves and one for the exhaust valves.

Drivebelt(s) The belt(s) used to drive accessories such as the alternator, water pump, power steering pump, air conditioning compressor, etc. off the crankshaft pulley.

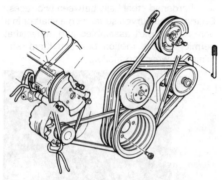

Accessory drivebelts

Driveshaft Any shaft used to transmit motion. Commonly used when referring to the axleshafts on a front wheel drive vehicle.

Drum brake A type of brake using a drum-shaped metal cylinder attached to the inner surface of the wheel. When the brake pedal is pressed, curved brake shoes with friction linings press against the inside of the drum to slow or stop the vehicle.

E

EGR valve A valve used to introduce exhaust gases into the intake air stream.

Electronic control unit (ECU) A computer which controls (for instance) ignition and fuel injection systems, or an anti-lock braking system. For more information refer to the *Haynes Automotive Electrical and Electronic Systems Manual*.

Electronic Fuel Injection (EFI) A computer controlled fuel system that distributes fuel through an injector located in each intake port of the engine.

Emergency brake A braking system, independent of the main hydraulic system, that can be used to slow or stop the vehicle if the primary brakes fail, or to hold the vehicle stationary even though the brake pedal isn't depressed. It usually consists of a hand lever that actuates either front or rear brakes mechanically through a series of cables and linkages. Also known as a handbrake or parking brake.

Endfloat The amount of lengthwise movement between two parts. As applied to a crankshaft, the distance that the crankshaft can move forward and back in the cylinder block.

Engine management system (EMS) A computer controlled system which manages the fuel injection and the ignition systems in an integrated fashion.

Exhaust manifold A part with several passages through which exhaust gases leave the engine combustion chambers and enter the exhaust pipe.

F

Fan clutch A viscous (fluid) drive coupling device which permits variable engine fan speeds in relation to engine speeds.

Feeler blade A thin strip or blade of hardened steel, ground to an exact thickness, used to check or measure clearances between parts.

Feeler blade

Firing order The order in which the engine cylinders fire, or deliver their power strokes, beginning with the number one cylinder.

Flywheel A heavy spinning wheel in which energy is absorbed and stored by means of momentum. On cars, the flywheel is attached to the crankshaft to smooth out firing impulses.

Free play The amount of travel before any action takes place. The "looseness" in a linkage, or an assembly of parts, between the initial application of force and actual movement. For example, the distance the brake pedal moves before the pistons in the master cylinder are actuated.

Fuse An electrical device which protects a circuit against accidental overload. The typical fuse contains a soft piece of metal which is calibrated to melt at a predetermined current flow (expressed as amps) and break the circuit.

Fusible link A circuit protection device consisting of a conductor surrounded by heat-resistant insulation. The conductor is smaller than the wire it protects, so it acts as the weakest link in the circuit. Unlike a blown fuse, a failed fusible link must frequently be cut from the wire for replacement.

G

Gap The distance the spark must travel in jumping from the centre electrode to the side electrode in a spark plug. Also refers to the spacing between the points in a contact breaker assembly in a conventional points-type ignition, or to the distance between the reluctor or rotor and the pickup coil in an electronic ignition.

Adjusting spark plug gap

Gasket Any thin, soft material - usually cork, cardboard, asbestos or soft metal - installed between two metal surfaces to ensure a good seal. For instance, the cylinder head gasket seals the joint between the block and the cylinder head.

Gasket

Gauge An instrument panel display used to monitor engine conditions. A gauge with a movable pointer on a dial or a fixed scale is an analogue gauge. A gauge with a numerical readout is called a digital gauge.

H

Halfshaft A rotating shaft that transmits power from the final drive unit to a drive wheel, usually when referring to a live rear axle.

Harmonic balancer A device designed to reduce torsion or twisting vibration in the crankshaft. May be incorporated in the crankshaft pulley. Also known as a vibration damper.

Hone An abrasive tool for correcting small irregularities or differences in diameter in an engine cylinder, brake cylinder, etc.

Hydraulic tappet A tappet that utilises hydraulic pressure from the engine's lubrication system to maintain zero clearance (constant contact with both camshaft and valve stem). Automatically adjusts to variation in valve stem length. Hydraulic tappets also reduce valve noise.

I

Ignition timing The moment at which the spark plug fires, usually expressed in the number of crankshaft degrees before the piston reaches the top of its stroke.

Inlet manifold A tube or housing with passages through which flows the air-fuel mixture (carburettor vehicles and vehicles with throttle body injection) or air only (port fuel-injected vehicles) to the port openings in the cylinder head.

J

Jump start Starting the engine of a vehicle with a discharged or weak battery by attaching jump leads from the weak battery to a charged or helper battery.

L

Load Sensing Proportioning Valve (LSPV) A brake hydraulic system control valve that works like a proportioning valve, but also takes into consideration the amount of weight carried by the rear axle.

Locknut A nut used to lock an adjustment nut, or other threaded component, in place. For example, a locknut is employed to keep the adjusting nut on the rocker arm in position.

Lockwasher A form of washer designed to prevent an attaching nut from working loose.

M

MacPherson strut A type of front suspension system devised by Earle MacPherson at Ford of England. In its original form, a simple lateral link with the anti-roll bar creates the lower control arm. A long strut - an integral coil spring and shock absorber - is mounted between the body and the steering knuckle. Many modern so-called MacPherson strut systems use a conventional lower A-arm and don't rely on the anti-roll bar for location.

Multimeter An electrical test instrument with the capability to measure voltage, current and resistance.

N

NOx Oxides of Nitrogen. A common toxic pollutant emitted by petrol and diesel engines at higher temperatures.

O

Ohm The unit of electrical resistance. One volt applied to a resistance of one ohm will produce a current of one amp.

Ohmmeter An instrument for measuring electrical resistance.

O-ring A type of sealing ring made of a special rubber-like material; in use, the O-ring is compressed into a groove to provide the sealing action.

Overhead cam (ohc) engine An engine with the camshaft(s) located on top of the cylinder head(s).

Overhead valve (ohv) engine An engine with the valves located in the cylinder head, but with the camshaft located in the engine block.

Oxygen sensor A device installed in the engine exhaust manifold, which senses the oxygen content in the exhaust and converts this information into an electric current. Also called a Lambda sensor.

P

Phillips screw A type of screw head having a cross instead of a slot for a corresponding type of screwdriver.

Plastigage A thin strip of plastic thread, available in different sizes, used for measuring clearances. For example, a strip of Plastigage is laid across a bearing journal. The parts are assembled and dismantled; the width of the crushed strip indicates the clearance between journal and bearing.

Plastigage

Propeller shaft The long hollow tube with universal joints at both ends that carries power from the transmission to the differential on front-engined rear wheel drive vehicles.

Proportioning valve A hydraulic control valve which limits the amount of pressure to the rear brakes during panic stops to prevent wheel lock-up.

R

Rack-and-pinion steering A steering system with a pinion gear on the end of the steering shaft that mates with a rack (think of a geared wheel opened up and laid flat). When the steering wheel is turned, the pinion turns, moving the rack to the left or right. This movement is transmitted through the track rods to the steering arms at the wheels.

Radiator A liquid-to-air heat transfer device designed to reduce the temperature of the coolant in an internal combustion engine cooling system.

Refrigerant Any substance used as a heat transfer agent in an air-conditioning system. R-12 has been the principle refrigerant for many years; recently, however, manufacturers have begun using R-134a, a non-CFC substance that is considered less harmful to the ozone in the upper atmosphere.

Rocker arm A lever arm that rocks on a shaft or pivots on a stud. In an overhead valve engine, the rocker arm converts the upward movement of the pushrod into a downward movement to open a valve.

Rotor In a distributor, the rotating device inside the cap that connects the centre electrode and the outer terminals as it turns, distributing the high voltage from the coil secondary winding to the proper spark plug. Also, that part of an alternator which rotates inside the stator. Also, the rotating assembly of a turbocharger, including the compressor wheel, shaft and turbine wheel.

Runout The amount of wobble (in-and-out movement) of a gear or wheel as it's rotated. The amount a shaft rotates "out-of-true." The out-of-round condition of a rotating part.

S

Sealant A liquid or paste used to prevent leakage at a joint. Sometimes used in conjunction with a gasket.

Sealed beam lamp An older headlight design which integrates the reflector, lens and filaments into a hermetically-sealed one-piece unit. When a filament burns out or the lens cracks, the entire unit is simply replaced.

Serpentine drivebelt A single, long, wide accessory drivebelt that's used on some newer vehicles to drive all the accessories, instead of a series of smaller, shorter belts. Serpentine drivebelts are usually tensioned by an automatic tensioner.

Serpentine drivebelt

Shim Thin spacer, commonly used to adjust the clearance or relative positions between two parts. For example, shims inserted into or under bucket tappets control valve clearances. Clearance is adjusted by changing the thickness of the shim.

Slide hammer A special puller that screws into or hooks onto a component such as a shaft or bearing; a heavy sliding handle on the shaft bottoms against the end of the shaft to knock the component free.

Sprocket A tooth or projection on the periphery of a wheel, shaped to engage with a chain or drivebelt. Commonly used to refer to the sprocket wheel itself.

Starter inhibitor switch On vehicles with an automatic transmission, a switch that prevents starting if the vehicle is not in Neutral or Park.

Strut See MacPherson strut.

T

Tappet A cylindrical component which transmits motion from the cam to the valve stem, either directly or via a pushrod and rocker arm. Also called a cam follower.

Thermostat A heat-controlled valve that regulates the flow of coolant between the cylinder block and the radiator, so maintaining optimum engine operating temperature. A thermostat is also used in some air cleaners in which the temperature is regulated.

Thrust bearing The bearing in the clutch assembly that is moved in to the release levers by clutch pedal action to disengage the clutch. Also referred to as a release bearing.

Timing belt A toothed belt which drives the camshaft. Serious engine damage may result if it breaks in service.

Timing chain A chain which drives the camshaft.

Toe-in The amount the front wheels are closer together at the front than at the rear. On rear wheel drive vehicles, a slight amount of toe-in is usually specified to keep the front wheels running parallel on the road by offsetting other forces that tend to spread the wheels apart.

Toe-out The amount the front wheels are closer together at the rear than at the front. On front wheel drive vehicles, a slight amount of toe-out is usually specified.

Tools For full information on choosing and using tools, refer to the *Haynes Automotive Tools Manual*.

Tracer A stripe of a second colour applied to a wire insulator to distinguish that wire from another one with the same colour insulator.

Tune-up A process of accurate and careful adjustments and parts replacement to obtain the best possible engine performance.

Turbocharger A centrifugal device, driven by exhaust gases, that pressurises the intake air. Normally used to increase the power output from a given engine displacement, but can also be used primarily to reduce exhaust emissions (as on VW's "Umwelt" Diesel engine).

U

Universal joint or U-joint A double-pivoted connection for transmitting power from a driving to a driven shaft through an angle. A U-joint consists of two Y-shaped yokes and a cross-shaped member called the spider.

V

Valve A device through which the flow of liquid, gas, vacuum, or loose material in bulk may be started, stopped, or regulated by a movable part that opens, shuts, or partially obstructs one or more ports or passageways. A valve is also the movable part of such a device.

Valve clearance The clearance between the valve tip (the end of the valve stem) and the rocker arm or tappet. The valve clearance is measured when the valve is closed.

Vernier caliper A precision measuring instrument that measures inside and outside dimensions. Not quite as accurate as a micrometer, but more convenient.

Viscosity The thickness of a liquid or its resistance to flow.

Volt A unit for expressing electrical "pressure" in a circuit. One volt that will produce a current of one ampere through a resistance of one ohm.

W

Welding Various processes used to join metal items by heating the areas to be joined to a molten state and fusing them together. For more information refer to the *Haynes Automotive Welding Manual*.

Wiring diagram A drawing portraying the components and wires in a vehicle's electrical system, using standardised symbols. For more information refer to the *Haynes Automotive Electrical and Electronic Systems Manual*.

Note: *References throughout this index are in the form - "Chapter number" • "page number"*

THE RAF
IN CAMERA

ALSO BY ROY CONYERS NESBIT

Woe to the Unwary
Torpedo Airmen
The Strike Wings
Target: Hitler's Oil (with Ron C. Cooke)
Arctic Airmen (with Ernest Schofield)
Failed to Return
An Illustrated History of the RAF
RAF Records in the PRO (with Simon Fowler, Peter Elliott and Christina Goulter)
The Armed Rovers
The RAF in Camera 1903–1939
The RAF in Camera 1939–1945
Eyes of the RAF

THE RAF

IN CAMERA

ARCHIVE PHOTOGRAPHS FROM THE PUBLIC RECORD OFFICE
AND THE MINISTRY OF DEFENCE

1946–1995

ROY CONYERS NESBIT

Assisted by Oliver Hoare

SUTTON PUBLISHING
IN ASSOCIATION WITH THE PUBLIC RECORD OFFICE

First published in the United Kingdom in 1996 by
Sutton Publishing Limited · Phoenix Mill · Thrupp · Stroud · Gloucestershire
in association with the Public Record Office

Reprinted 1997

British Library Cataloguing in Publication Data

A catalogue record for this book is available from the British Library.

ISBN 0-7509-1056-9 (hardback)

ISBN 0-7509-1522-6 (paperback)

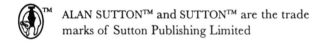 ALAN SUTTON™ and SUTTON™ are the trade
marks of Sutton Publishing Limited

Typeset in 11/15pt Baskerville.
Typesetting and origination by
Sutton Publishing Limited.
Printed in Great Britain by
WBC Limited, Bridgend.

CONTENTS

The historic church of St Clement Danes in the Strand, dating from the ninth century but rebuilt in its present form in 1681 by Sir Christopher Wren, was reduced to a shell by a bombing raid on 10 May 1941. Rebuilt once more, it was reconsecrated on 19 October 1958 as a centre of RAF worship in the presence of the Queen, Prince Philip, and other members of the Royal Family, as shown in this photograph. The electrically-operated bells rang out 'Oranges and Lemons' in celebration. Nowadays, Books of Remembrance in window recesses record the names of more than 125,000 men and women who died during the two world wars while serving in the RAF, the WRAF and associated women's services, the Commonwealth Air Forces, the RFC and the RNAS.

PRO ref: AIR 2/14501

INTRODUCTION

For many years, numerous photographs relating to the activities of the RAF have remained unrecorded in hundreds of documents in the Public Record Office (PRO) at Kew. Another large collection is housed in the Ministry of Defence in London. This series of three volumes is intended to bring representative photographs of both collections to the notice of the general public. The volumes are not intended to provide a comprehensive history of the RAF and its predecessors, but aim to give some indication of the huge numbers of photographs which are available.

In all cases the reference numbers of the photographs appear underneath the captions. The photographs at the PRO are not housed separately but the originals of each may be seen within their relevant documents by visitors who obtain readers' tickets and then request the numbers on computer terminals in the Reference Room. However, it should be noted that documents at the PRO are not normally available for public scrutiny until they are thirty years old, and the same stipulation applies to photographs. For this reason, the majority of the photographs in this third

volume originate from the Ministry of Defence.

A catalogue of the many photographs kept at the PRO is available in the Reference Room, but at the time of writing this is by no means complete. A description of the contents of this catalogue is contained in PRO Records Information leaflet 90. Copies of RAF photographs, or any others found by readers, may be purchased via the Reprographic Ordering Section. Details such as choice of process and scale of charges are set out in PRO General Information leaflet 19. Copies of photographs are available for commercial reproduction from the PRO Image Library, telephone 0181-392-5255. Prices will be given on request.

The photographic prints relating to the RAF housed at the Ministry of Defence are not available for public inspection. The main purpose of this collection is to provide information to the RAF and various Government departments, and not to the general public. However, readers may write to the central library where negatives are held if they wish to purchase copies of photographs contained in these volumes or enquire about others. This is

CS(Photography)P, Ministry of Defence, Court 9 Basement, King Charles Street, London SW1A 2AH, with whom any purchasing arrangements may be made. At present this enormous collection covers the period from the very early days of the RAF and its predecessors up to the Gulf War of 1991. Some photographs in this book from the period after the Gulf War were obtained from RAF Publicity of the Ministry of Defence.

All the photographs in these three volumes are Crown Copyright. Guidelines for those who propose to reproduce photographs are set out in PRO General Information leaflet 15, and the same guidelines also apply to any photographs purchased from the Ministry of Defence.

This volume is the last of the series of three and covers the period after the Second World War up to the end of 1995. The photographs represent the Berlin Airlift, the Mau Mau rebellion in Kenya, anti-terrorist operations in Malaya, the Korean War, the atom bomb tests in Australia, the hydrogen bomb tests in the Pacific, operations in Cyprus, the Suez crisis, the Indonesian confrontation, the Falklands War and the Gulf War. Most post-war aircraft are included in the selection, as are some of the RAF's other activities such as air-sea rescue.

The captions underneath the photographs originate from the documents in which they were located in the PRO or the brief details available in the Ministry of Defence. This information was supplemented by a considerable amount of research in other documents in the PRO or reliable books of reference. Readers who wish to carry out similar research for the period up to 1965 are recommended to purchase a copy of PRO Readers' Guide No.8, *RAF Records in the PRO* by Simon Fowler, Peter Elliott, Roy Conyers Nesbit and Christina Goulter (PRO Publications 1994), available from the PRO Shop, Public Record Office, Ruskin Avenue, Kew, Richmond, Surrey TW9 4DU. This guide also includes an appendix which lists other sources of RAF photographs within Great Britain.

ACKNOWLEDGEMENTS

I should like to express my gratitude to Simon Fowler and Oliver Hoare of the PRO for their painstaking help in hunting for suitable photographs. Similarly, I am most grateful to Group Captain Ian Madelin RAF (Ret'd) and Squadron Leader Peter Singleton RAF (Ret'd) of the Air Historical Branch (RAF), the Ministry of Defence, for permission to include many official photographs housed in the MoD, as well as to Bill Hunt of the Whitehall Library for reproducing the MoD prints and Brian Carter for reproducing the PRO prints. My thanks are also due to Sergeant Rick Brewell of RAF Publicity who kindly provided some of his superb aerial photographs for the final section of the book and helped with their captions. I am extremely grateful to Squadron Leader Dudley Cowderoy RAFVR, Warrant Officer Jack Eggleston RAF (Ret'd) and Roger Hayward for their work in checking and correcting the captions. Any errors which remain after all this expertise are my own responsibility.

Cold War:
The Berlin Airlift

After surface communication between the West and Berlin ceased with the imposition of a Russian blockade from 24 June 1948, the RAF and the USAF began a massive airlift to the city. Within a week the whole of RAF Transport Command's fleet of Avro Yorks and Douglas Dakotas had moved to Wunstorf, about twenty miles north-west of Hanover. The morning shift began at 02.00 hours. In this photograph, Sergeant John Parham is indicating to Aircraftman David Swain the dispersal point where a York needed servicing.

MoD ref: R1087

(*Opposite, top*) The aircrew of a York at Wunstorf planning their sortie to Gatow, the airfield in the British sector of Berlin used by the RAF. The USAF carried supplies to the airfield in the American sector, Tempelhof.

PRO ref: AIR 10/5067

(*Opposite, bottom*) The Flying Control at Wunstorf had to cope with a far greater flow of traffic than ever before. In this photograph, Aircraftman Charles Curran is using an Aldis lamp to flash a green light to the first Dakota in a wave of aircraft, giving the pilot permission to taxi along the perimeter track.

MoD ref: R1774

Enormous floats of supplies were stored in the hangars of airfields operating on the Berlin airlift. It was estimated that 4,500 short tons of food, coal and other essentials would have to be flown into the city each day by the RAF and USAF to supply the two-and-a-half million Berliners.

MoD ref: R1795

The aircraft were normally loaded from trains running into the airfields, but emergency dumps in the hangars were used if these failed to keep pace with demand. The Berlin airlift necessitated an immense and complex organization, with ground staff frequently working a sixteen-hour day.

MoD ref: R1796

The RAF staff in the control tower at Gatow were the first in the world to handle 800 aircraft movements a day. No mistakes were permitted and the work was extremely hard. In this photograph a controller is looking through a hatch into the R/T Monitoring Office to enquire about an aircraft which had called up.

MoD ref: R1833

A WAAF rigger, Corporal Kitty Wood, replacing the stabilizing fin and fitting a fairing on to an Avro York at Gatow on 16 September 1948, assisted by Aircraftman Fred Hames.

MoD ref: R1841

A special load of spares being loaded into York serial MW232.

PRO ref: AIR 55/118

A line of Avro Yorks of the RAF's Transport Command lined up at Gatow airfield in Berlin during the airlift, with serial MW287 of 242 Squadron in the foreground. The aircraft were marshalled in front of the hangars, where a German labour force unloaded them; unloading time averaged out at about ten minutes.

MoD ref: R1818

The Sunderlands of two flying boat squadrons and one operational conversion unit joined in the Berlin Airlift from July 1948, operating between Hamburg and Havel Lake, about five minutes by road from Berlin. These ground crews were photographed on 16 September 1948, sitting in the sun by the boathouse on Havel Lake while waiting for the next Sunderland to call up and give them its expected time of arrival.

MoD ref: R1832

A Sunderland V, serial VB389, of 201 Squadron after landing on Havel Lake on 16 September 1948, with its contents being loaded on to barges. The tonnage carried by the flying boats was quite small but the Berliners were impressed with their contribution. The Sunderlands continued to

operate until December 1948, by which time the lift by land-based aircraft into Berlin's airfields had increased considerably.

MoD ref: R1831

Lübeck in the British zone of Germany was one of three new despatching bases prepared for RAF aircraft. Pierced steel planking was laid down by German workers for the runway. Work continued at a very rapid pace and RAF Dakotas began to use the airfield in August 1948.

PRO ref: AIR 55/118

Civilian aircraft were also chartered to help in the airlift, such as this Dakota of Kearnley Airways being refuelled at Lübeck.

PRO ref: AIR 55/118

The Royal Army Service Corps handled much of the loading at Lübeck. From 27 August 1948 to 22 April 1949, 50,000 short tons were despatched from the airfield.

PRO ref: AIR 55/118

The airfield of Celle in the British zone of West Germany was made available to some of the Douglas C-54 Skymasters of the USAF, partly to help relieve congestion in the American bases of Rhein/Main and Weisbaden, and partly because Celle was nearer Berlin. The Skymaster carried about 10 tons and was a newer aircraft than the York, which could carry up to 9 tons. The rail sidings in this photograph, taken in November 1948, had been extended to bring up stone for forming the sub-base of the runway.

PRO ref: AIR 10/5067

RAF and USAF flyers looking at the target board on 16 September 1948 to check the progress of the airlift.

MoD ref: R1852

Facilities at Schleswigland airfield in the British zone of West Germany were improved to handle the new Handley Page Hastings of the RAF's 47 and 297 Squadrons, which began to replace Avro Yorks in September 1948. Two main loading areas were built, one to handle liquid fuel and the other for dry goods, while the runway was overlaid with asphalt. The Hastings began to operate from this airfield in November 1948, mainly carrying coal for Berlin's industries.

PRO ref: AIR 10/5067

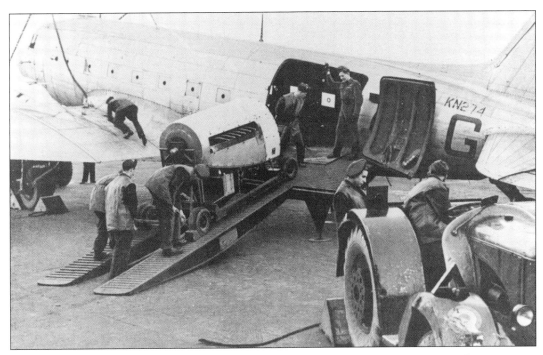

When RAF aircraft engaged on the Berlin airlift, such as this Dakota, serial KN274, they were sent back to the UK for periodic inspection and loaded with parts which needed repair. They returned with spares which were urgently needed.

PRO ref: AIR 10/5067

The RAF flew many children and elderly people out of Berlin to West Germany during the airlift, to reduce pressure on supplies when starvation was a possibility during the winter of 1948–9. The Russians lifted their blockade on 12 May 1949, but the RAF and the USAF continued to fly in supplies for several more months, to build up a stockpile in case of another emergency.

PRO ref: AIR 55/118

The Boeing B-29 Superfortress was known as the Washington by the RAF's Bomber Command when it was acquired at the beginning of the Cold War. Cocooned aircraft were taken out of storage and modernized, the first entering RAF service in August 1950. This photograph of Washingtons from 115 Squadron, based at Marham in Norfolk, was taken on 27 February 1951 during a training flight to Heligoland. The RAF began returning the machines to the USA in 1953 but a few continued in service until 1958.

MoD ref: PRB 1660

INTO THE JET AGE

The Gloster Meteor F8, such as serial WH320 in this photograph, was one of the series which began with the Meteor I supplied to 616 Squadron in July 1944. It entered squadron service in December 1949 and became the major type of single-seat day interceptor employed by the RAF for the next five years. It equipped twenty fighter squadrons as well as ten of the RAuxAF.

PRO ref: DSIR 23/22638

The de Havilland Vampire, which entered squadron service in April 1946, was the second jet fighter in the RAF. The Vampire FB5 was a fighter-bomber variant which followed in 1949. It became the most common type of jet fighter-bomber employed by the RAF until the de Havilland Venom began to appear in 1952. Subsequently, Vampires continued to serve overseas and in Flying Training Command. This photograph of Vampire FB5s of 603 Squadron, based at Turnhouse near Edinburgh, was taken shortly before the RAuxAF squadron disbanded in March 1957.

PRO ref: AIR 27/2712

The North American Sabre equipped RAF squadrons from May 1953 as a stopgap until the arrival of British swept-wing jets. It was a single-seat fighter capable of a maximum speed of 670 mph, primarily employed on defensive duties in West Germany. The machines were replaced by Hawker Hunters from the spring of 1955. These Sabres of 234 Squadron, serials XB885 and XB867, were photographed while in a vertical dive before entering cloud. The squadron was based in West Germany as part of the RAF's 2nd Tactical Air Force.

MoD ref: PRB9232

De Havilland Venoms of 23 Squadron landing at RAF Coltishall in Norfolk in 1955. This squadron was equipped with NF2s and NF3s, the two-seat night fighter version of the single-seat fighter-bomber.

PRO ref: AIR 28/1344

The English Electric Canberra was the first of Britain's jet bombers, entering RAF squadron service in May 1951. It succeeded the Avro Lincoln but was a light bomber with a crew of three. It was unarmed but fast and could carry a bomb load of 6,000 lb. The Canberra B6, with more powerful engines, was introduced in June 1954. This example of a B6, serial WH958 of 12 Squadron based at Binbrook in Lincolnshire, was photographed in September 1958. Some Canberra bombers were phased out when the V-Force of nuclear bombers was built up from 1955, but the reconnaissance versions continued in service.

MoD ref: PRB15899

Another version of the graceful English Electric Canberra was the B(1)8, such as serial XM245 photographed in September 1958 at the Farnborough Air Show. This was a night intruder, armed with four 20 mm guns in a pack beneath the fuselage and capable of carrying up to 5,000 lb of bombs. Four squadrons in Germany were equipped with Canberra B(1)8s from January 1958, and the machine continued in service until June 1971.

MoD ref: PRB15652

While based at Wunstorf in Germany during June 1956, 79 Squadron received Supermarine Swift FR5s to replace its Meteor FR9s. The earlier interceptor version of the Swift, the first swept-wing jet fighter to enter service in the RAF, had proved accident-prone when it was introduced into Fighter Command in February 1954, but it was hoped that a fighter/photo-reconnaissance version would be more successful in tactical work. Nevertheless, there was a high accident rate during the five years that the Swift FR5 remained in service with RAF Germany.

PRO ref: AIR 27/2794

Only twelve Supermarine Swift F7s were built, entering service in April 1957 with No. 1 Guided Weapons Development Squadron at RAF Valley in Anglesey. It was powered by a Rolls-Royce Avon 716 engine and fitted with Fireflash air-to-air missiles.

MoD ref: PRB15794

The Fairey Fireflash air-to-air missile was introduced into the Guided Weapons Development Squadron at RAF Valley in 1957 but did not see service with operational squadrons. It was guided to its target by a radar beam projected from the aircraft. This photograph showing Fireflash missiles being wheeled to Swift F7s was taken on 16 October 1958.

MoD ref: PRB15838

The Hawker Hunter first entered squadron service in July 1954 as a single-seat day interceptor, becoming the RAF's standard fighter at home and in Germany until the arrival of the English Electric Lightning in June 1960. There were several variants of the machine, which could achieve Mach 0.95 at 36,000 feet. It possessed elegant lines and, with its responsive controls and excellent manoeuvrability, delighted pilots and spectators alike in aerobatic displays. This Hunter F6 was photographed while carrying rockets at the Farnborough Air Show in September 1958.

MoD ref: PRB15656

Hunter F6s of 63 Squadron lined up with the pilots and ground crews at Waterbeach in Cambridgeshire on 17 April 1957.

PRO ref: AIR 27/2791

HM The Queen and HRH Prince Philip visiting the Leuchars Wing, consisting of Venom and Hunter aircraft, at Fife on 4 June 1957.

PRO ref: AIR 28/1390

This Fairey Delta 2, serial WG774, powered by a Rolls-Royce Avon RA28 gas-turbine engine, was designed to achieve a world speed record of over 1,000 mph. It made its initial flight from Boscombe Down in Wiltshire on 6 October 1956, flown by Lieutenant-Commander L.P. Twiss. A second machine, serial WG777, flew for the first time on 15 February 1956. The attempt at the speed record was made on 10 March 1956 in serial WG774, flown by Twiss at 38,000 ft between Ford and Chichester in Sussex. He made two runs averaging 1,132 mph and became the first pilot in the world to exceed 1,000 mph. This photograph was taken in September 1958 at the Farnborough Air Show.

MoD ref: PRB15644

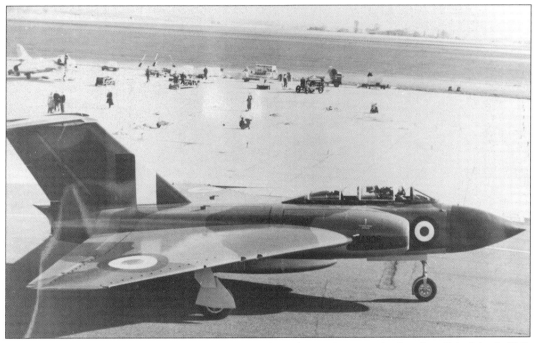

This Gloster Javelin FAW6, serial XA836, of 89 Squadron, photographed at Stradishall in Suffolk on 30 September 1957, was the first of this variant received by the squadron. The Javelin FAW1 entered service in February 1956 as the first twin-jet fighter in the world capable of high performance in all weathers.

PRO ref: AIR 28/1424

Vickers Valiant B1, serial XD816, converted to the tanker role, of 214 Squadron based at Marham in Norfolk, refuelling Gloster Javelin FAW7, serial XH887. This photograph accompanied the Air Estimates file of 1960–61.

PRO ref: AIR 19/1004

The English Electric Lightning F1 was the first of the RAF's supersonic fighters, entering squadron service in June 1960. F1s were followed five months later by these FIAs (with a T4 trainer version in the foreground), fitted with refuelling probes, which were supplied to 56 Squadron at Wattisham in Suffolk. Powered by two Rolls-Royce Avon engines, the Lightning could achieve 1,500 mph at 36,000 feet, twice the speed of the Hawker Hunter it replaced. In addition to two 30 mm Aden guns, it carried two Firestreak air-to-air missiles.

MoD ref: PRB26377

This Lightning F1 of 74 Squadron was photographed at RAF Coltishall in Norfolk on 26 October 1963. The letters beneath the cockpit show that the machine was flown by Flight Lieutenant J.E. Brown while the ground mechanic was Chief Technician Rye.

MoD ref: PRB26227

This photograph of Hawker Hunter F6s, the variant of the famous single-seat interceptor which first entered RAF service in July 1954, appeared in an illustrated programme which accompanied a display held on 20 September 1958 at RAF Norton near Sheffield. This was the headquarters of No. 90 (Signals) Group.

PRO ref: AIR 28/1405

In June 1962 this Hunter T7, serial WV383, was photographed over Kai Tak in Hong Kong, at a time when 20 Squadron was converting from Venom FB4s to Hunter FGA9s. The T7 was the two-seat trainer version of the single-seat Hunter F4. The squadron remained equipped with Hunter FGA9s at Kai Tak until disbanding in January 1967.

MoD ref: CFP1056

Javelin FAW9, serial XH886, of 23 Squadron, based at Leuchars in Fife, photographed on 13 May 1963 while carrying a Firestreak air-to-air missile. The FAW9, the last of the Javelins, was fitted with an in-flight refuelling probe. The Firestreak missile, introduced into squadron service in 1958, was guided to its target by an infrared seeker cell in its nose.

MoD ref: PRB25293

Three Javelin FAW9s, serials XH887, XH708 and XH871, from 64 Squadron at Binbrook in Lincolnshire, fitted with their refuelling probes. They were photographed in October 1963 before the squadron flew out to Calcutta on an exercise. The squadron later provided defence for Singapore. It was disbanded in June 1967.

MoD ref: PRB26130

A Javelin carrying Firestreak air-to-air missiles, photographed with its crew in April 1963 at RAF Geilenkirchen in Germany. It was probably an FAW9 (without its refuelling probe) of 11 Squadron, which was based there at the time.

MoD ref: PRB25359

HOT WAR: KOREA, CYPRUS AND SUEZ

When the Korean War broke out in June 1950, the RAF at home had been drastically reduced after the Second World War, while the Far East Air Force was fully stretched dealing with the Malayan Emergency. Nevertheless, Britain was committed to help the USA resist the communist invasion, as a member of the United Nations. Apart from advice and guidance, with some officers serving with the US 5th Tactical Air Force, the RAF contributed Sunderlands of the Far East Flying Boat Wing. Detachments of 88, 205 and 209 Squadrons flew to Iwakuni on the southern tip of Honshu, Japan, where they came under American command. This photograph was taken on 14 November 1950.

MoD ref: CFP876

The Sunderland Vs of the three RAF squadrons carried out over 1,100 lengthy sorties from their base in Japan, flying on anti-submarine and maritime patrols around North Korea. The results of their reconnaissance work enabled the Americans and British to blockade Korean ports and plan their carrier-borne strikes.

MoD ref: CFP297

Soldiers of the Middlesex Regiment after disembarking from the Hastings troop carrier. All British and Commonwealth brigades were formed into the 1st Commonwealth Division on 28 July 1951.

MoD ref: CFP258

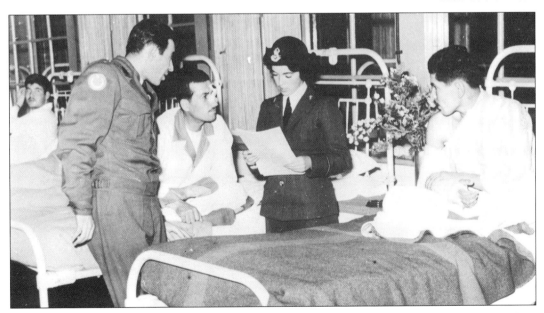

Nursing Sister Flying Officer G. Williams checking Turkish wounded on 5 September 1951 in a ward of Sick Quarters, No. 91 Wing RAAF, Iwakuni. This was to ensure that the men were fit to fly under her medical charge to Singapore.

MoD ref: CFP438

British brigades were formed to participate in the Korean War, mainly from Commonwealth regiments. Some of these soldiers were flown from Japan to Pusan in Korea by Handley Page Hastings of 48 Squadron, normally based at Changi in Singapore. The Hastings troop carrier in this photograph was being guided into position by an American controlman on 10 October 1950.

MoD ref: CFP257

Hastings, serial TG520, of 48 Squadron taxiing out on 5 September 1951 before take-off from Iwakuni airfield for a two-day flight to Singapore, via Clark Field in Manila, with twenty-eight wounded. This was the eighth flight since the squadron began casualty evacuation from Japan during the previous February.

MoD ref: CFP433

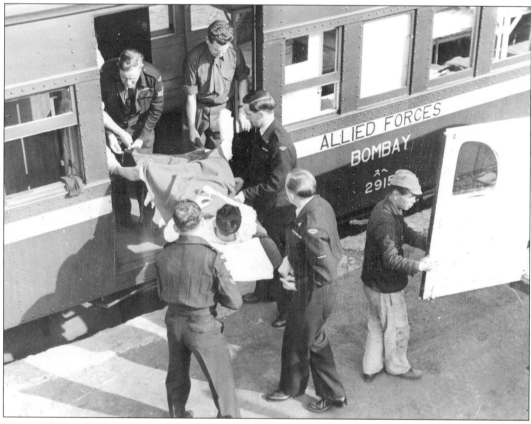

Wounded men being evacuated from Korea on 15 July 1953, twelve days before the armistice was signed at Panmunjon. By this time, approximately 350,000 men of the United Nations had been killed or wounded, while enemy casualties were estimated as not less than 1,500,000.

MoD ref: CFP752

Guerrilla operations began in Cyprus on 1 April 1955, when EOKA (Ethniks Organosis Kypriou Agonistou) exploded a series of bombs in an attempt to ensure that the island was ruled by Greece, against the wishes of the Turkish minority. The first RAF counter-guerrilla operations took the form of searching the sea approaches, to prevent the landing of illegal weapons, and reconnaissance over land by light aircraft and helicopters. On 15 October 1956, 284 Squadron was re-formed in Nicosia with Sycamore HAR14s for general purpose activities and casualty evacuation. This photograph is of a stream take-off with a contingent of the King's Own Yorkshire Light Infantry.

MoD ref: CMP876

A soldier of the King's Own Yorkshire Light Infantry abseiling down a rope from a Sycamore helicopter of 284 Squadron. The method of landing small bodies of troops gave the security forces the advantage of surprise over EOKA bands in the Troodos mountains. Operations continued until Cyprus became an independent republic on 21 September 1960, with Britain retaining sovereignty over certain military bases.

MoD ref: CMP877

When diplomacy failed after Egypt nationalized the Universal Suez Canal Company on 26 July 1956 in defiance of the treaty of 1888, the British and French decided to recover their rights by force. One of the main airfields available for a preliminary air attack on the Egyptian Air Force was RAF Nicosia in Cyprus. On 31 October 1956, Wing Commander Peter Dobson was photographed in the briefing tent while giving crews of the Bomber Wing their instructions for an attack on Kabrit airfield, north of the town of Suez. Thirty-one MiG-15s had been identified here from photo-reconnaissance carried out by Canberra PR 7s of the RAF and Republic F-84s of the French Air Force.

PRO ref: AIR 28/1474

A weapons briefing given on 31 October 1956 to the Bomber Wing by Flight Lieutenant G. Webster in the briefings tent at Nicosia, preparatory to an attack against Almaza airfield, near Cairo, where photo-reconnaissance had revealed twenty-four MiG-15s.

PRO ref: AIR 28/1474

This photograph was taken on 24 July 1956 at Upwood in Huntingdonshire when 61 Squadron took part in the Air Officer Commanding's parade and inspection. The squadron was equipped with Canberra B2s and on 22 and 23 October of that year, flew out to Nicosia as part of the Suez operation, which was code-named 'Musketeer'.

PRO ref: AIR 27/2756

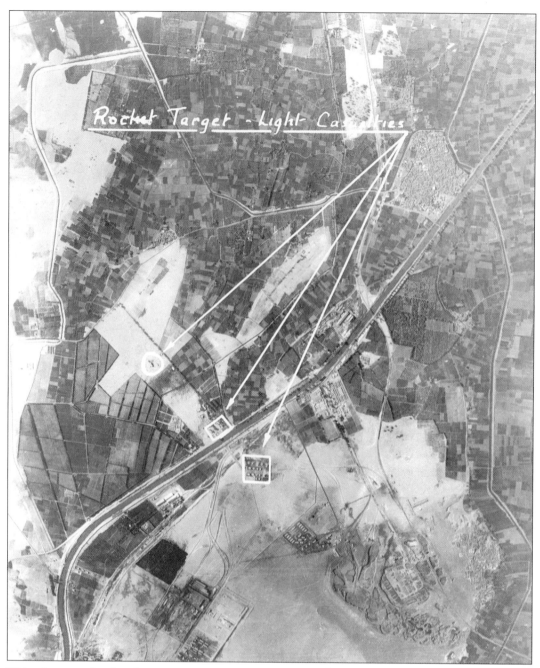

Rocket Target - Light Casualties

This photograph of radio transmission stations at Abu Zabac in Cairo was taken on 18 March 1955 by a Meteor PR 10 of 13 Squadron based at Abu Sueir, at a time when there was still an RAF presence in Egypt. It was used as a target map by the RAF during the Suez crisis. The main radio station was bombed on 2 November 1956 by twenty Canberras of the Cyprus Wing, escorted by twelve Republic F-84s of the French Air Force. It went off the air but soon came back on a different frequency.

PRO ref: AIR 20/10215

This photograph of Mustapha Barracks in Alexandria was also used as a target map by the RAF. It was taken from 30,000 feet on 13 October 1955 by a Meteor PR 10 of 13 Squadron based at Abu Sueir.

PRO ref: AIR 20/10215

Another target map used during the Suez operation was this photograph of oil installations in Cairo, taken on 19 January 1956 by a Meteor PR 10 of 13 Squadron based at Abu Sueir. The last RAF units left Egypt on 17 May 1956.

PRO ref: AIR 20/10215

The RAF's Bomber Wing at Nicosia consisted of six squadrons of Canberra B2s, comprising fifty aircraft, and one squadron of twelve Canberra B6s, all sent out from England. In this photograph taken from the Control Tower, the Canberras were taking off to attack Luxor airfield, further south beside the Nile, on the evening of 2 November 1956. Photo-reconnaissance had revealed twenty-two Ilyushin Il-28 light bombers on this airfield. A Canberra B2 of 27 Squadron is in the foreground, with Meteor NF13s of 39 Squadron and Hunter F4s of 1 Squadron on the right of the runway.

PRO ref: AIR 28/1474

There was so much congestion at Nicosia and Akrotiri in Cyprus that a second bomber force was established at Luqa in Malta for the attack on Egypt, although this island was further from the targets. This force included four squadrons of the new Vickers Valiant B1, the first of the four-jet strategic V-Class bombers which had entered RAF service in February 1955. Twenty-four Valiants had arrived at Luqa by 30 September 1956, although they did not carry the nuclear bombs for which they had been designed.

MoD ref: CMP829

In addition to the Valiants at Luqa, four squadrons of Canberra B2s and B6s arrived at Halfar in Malta from England, comprising twenty-nine aircraft. They joined in the high-level attacks against Egyptian airfields which began in the afternoon of 31 October 1956. This photograph was taken when armourers were bombing up Canberra B2, serial WH951, with 1,000 lb medium-capacity bombs.

MoD ref: CMP853

A Canberra taking off from Halfar for an attack on Egyptian airfields. The Allied aircraft taking part in the operation were painted with 'invasion stripes', consisting of two black and three yellow.

MoD ref: CMP841

A Valiant taking off from Luqa for an attack on Egyptian airfields.

MoD ref: CMP825

Valiant crews being debriefed at Luqa after a bombing raid on Egyptian airfields. After three days, it was estimated that 158 enemy aircraft had been destroyed from the total of 195 originally photographed on the airfields. No aircraft of the RAF or French Air Force were lost from enemy action in these attacks, although a Venom of 8 Squadron, which was among those making low-level attacks from Akrotiri, hit the ground and the pilot was killed.

MoD ref: CMP821

In the early hours of 5 November 1956 a force of eighteen Valettas and fourteen Hastings, led by a Hastings of 114 Squadron, took off from Nicosia for a dropping zone alongside Port Said's Gamil airfield, as shown in this photograph. Each aircraft carried about twenty men of 3 Battalion Parachute Regiment as well as heavy equipment. At the same time, the French Air Force carried French paratroops from Tymbou in Cyprus. Meanwhile, Venoms from Akrotiri strafed the defences of the airfield and Hunters from Nicosia provided top cover, supported by carrier-borne squadrons from the Royal Navy's task force. The paratroops captured the airfield after stiff fighting and all aircraft returned, although nine transports were hit by anti-aircraft fire. Further drops took place in the afternoon.

PRO ref: AIR 27/2758

In the early morning of 6 November 1956, Royal Marine commandos and units of the Royal Tank Regiment stormed the beaches of Port Said, as shown in this photograph of landing craft approaching the shore while covered by helicopters. At the same time, French paratroops and commandos landed nearby at Port Fuad. These assaults were preceded by a naval bombardment and supported by air attacks.

MoD ref: X65958

Fierce fighting with casualties took place at Port Said. There was also damage to property during street clearance, as shown in this photograph taken after the conflict. The British forces were able to link up with the French and start moving down the Suez Canal, but the Security Council of the United Nations insisted on a cease-fire, which took place on the day of the seaborne assaults. Although a military success, the Anglo-French intervention in Egypt was a political failure.

PRO ref: WO 32/16686

THE NUCLEAR AGE

By 1951 Britain had decided to catch up with the United States and Russia with the explosion of an atomic bomb. The site chosen for the first experiment was a lagoon off Hermite Island, in the uninhabited Monte Bello Islands off the coast of Western Australia, as shown in this photograph.

PRO ref: AIR 8/2308

(*Opposite*) This dramatic photograph was taken on 8 November 1957 when Britain exploded her fourth H-bomb. It was dropped from Valiant XD825 flown by Squadron Leader Barney T. Millett, off South East Point, Christmas Island. Each of these H-bombs contained the equivalent of a million tons of TNT and created a mushroom shape up to 60,000 feet high, with ice caps forming on top.

MoD ref: PRB14263

A Lancaster tailplane, placed at 6,707 feet, broadside to the blast, photographed before the explosion.

PRO ref: AIR 8/2309

The elevator was torn off by the force of the blast.

PRO ref: AIR 8/2309

(*Opposite, top left*) The first British atomic bomb was exploded on 3 October 1952 in the frigate HMS *Plym* moored in the lagoon off Hermite Island. The top photograph was taken thirty seconds later, while the bottom one was taken one minute after the explosion, showing a water column and cloud.

PRO ref: AIR 8/2309

(*Opposite, top right*) Two-and-a-half minutes after the explosion.

PRO ref: AIR 8/2309

(*Opposite, bottom*) Seven-and-a-half minutes after the explosion.

PRO ref: AIR 8/2309

After the first explosion in the Monte Bello Islands, alternative sites were sought on land. The next explosions took place on 14 and 16 October 1953 from towers erected on the Emu Field of South Australia. The camp site in this photograph was close to the centre line of the Long Range Weapons Establishment at Woomera.

PRO ref: AVIA 65/1118

The Monte Bello Islands were chosen again for the next nuclear explosions. The RAF collaborated, with photo-reconnaissance Canberras of 542 Squadron sent from Weston Zoyland in Somerset to RAAF Laverton in Western Australia to provide high-level monitoring of radiation and other results. The first experiment took place on Trimouville Island on 16 May 1956 and the second on Alpha Island on 19 June 1956. Observers had to turn their backs for several seconds. Although the bombs were considered small, eerie orange flashes could be seen from hundreds of miles away.

PRO ref: AIR 20/10812

A whole series of A-bomb tests followed in the remote area of Maralinga, or 'Loud Thunder' in the Aborigine language, north of the Nullarbor Plain in South Australia. Explosions took place on 27 September, 1956; 4, 11 and 21 October 1956; 14 and 25 September 1957, and 9 October 1957. Five of these seven tests took place from towers or at ground level. Of the others, the explosion of 11 October 1956 is especially noteworthy since it was the first nuclear bomb dropped by the RAF, from a Vickers Valiant B1 detached from 49 Squadron at Wittering in Northamptonshire and flown by Squadron Leader E.J.G. 'Ted' Flavell. The test of 9 October 1957 took place from an assembly of barrage balloons and the bomb exploded at 300 feet. Meanwhile, the RAF was beginning a series of tests with hydrogen bombs in the Pacific.

PRO ref: AVIA 65/1118

A Centurion Mark II tank after the explosion of an A-bomb at Maralinga.

PRO ref: WO 320/1

A Daimler Scout Car Mark II and dummy soldier, subjected to the blast of an A-bomb at Maralinga.

PRO ref: WO 320/1

In 1956 Vickers Valiant B1s of 49 Squadron at Wittering were being prepared to carry Britain's new hydrogen bomb, which weighed 10,000 lb. The crews trained with the object of testing the H-bomb at Christmas Island, a British possession in the central Pacific slightly north of the Equator. This photograph was taken at Wittering before three aircraft set off to fly westwards across North America and Hawaii to the remote island.

MoD ref: PRB13079

Wing Commander Ken G. Hubbard (on ladder) about to enter Valiant serial XD818 at Wittering, followed by his crew, before taking off on the flight to Christmas Island. On 15 May 1957 he and his crew dropped Britain's first H-bomb near the southern tip of Malden Island, south-east of Christmas Island. It was released from 45,000 feet and set to explode at 8,000 feet. Three more H-bombs were dropped on Malden Island, on 31 May, 19 June and 8 November 1957. Then five more bombs were exploded off Christmas Island, in 1958. These were dropped from a Valiant on 28 April, from a balloon assembly on 22 August, from Valiants on 2 and 11 September, and from a balloon assembly on 22 September.

MoD ref: PRB13075

The men on Christmas Island took part in sports and amused themselves with competitions such as the greasy pole. This photograph was taken on 29 December 1958, over two months after the last British hydrogen bomb was exploded from a balloon assembly.

PRO ref: AIR 28/1700

The Duke of Edinburgh visited Christmas Island on 3–5 April 1959, after the end of the British hydrogen bomb tests. He was photographed while inspecting a detachment of Hastings C1 transports of 36 Squadron, with serial TG557 in the foreground. 217 Squadron was also based at Christmas Island from 14 February 1958 to 13 November 1959, equipped with Whirlwind HAR 2s. The squadron was then disbanded.

PRO ref: AIR 28/1700

The Duke of Edinburgh on his tour of inspection of Christmas Island on 3–5 April 1959. The United States carried out a further series of tests on the same sites during the following year. In 1979, Christmas Island became part of the Republic of Kiribati, an independent member of the British Commonwealth. The islands of Malden and Jarvis, where the explosions took place, remain uninhabited.

PRO ref: AIR 28/1700

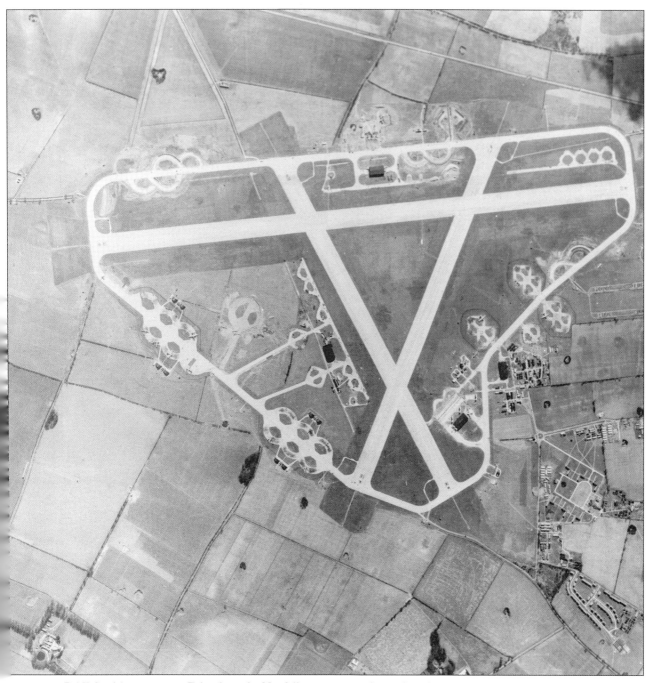

RAF Sculthorpe, near Fakenham in Norfolk, was opened as a bomber station in 1943. It became one of the main bases for reconnaissance aircraft of the USAF's Strategic Air Command during the Cold War. For several years, from 1951, aircraft flew from this station on spy flights over Russia to photograph Soviet nuclear bases. This photograph, taken on 15 March 1951, shows the three runways, one of 3,000 yards length and two of 2,000.

PRO ref: AIR 14/3702

The Avro Vulcan B1 was the second of Britain's V-Class bombers, entering RAF service in July 1956 as part of the nuclear strike force. This Vulcan B1, serial XH497, of 617 Squadron at Scampton in Lincolnshire was photographed on 10 November 1958. In June 1961 a Vulcan of this

famous 'dam-buster' squadron flew non-stop from Scampton to Sydney in Australia, refuelled in the air by Valiant tankers. The flight of 11,000 miles was achieved in 20 hours 3 minutes.

MoD ref: PRB15986

A Blue Steel, the strategic air-to-surface missile with a thermonuclear warhead, developed by Hawker Siddeley Dynamics, being loaded in Vulcan B1, serial XA903, for early trials. The photograph accompanied the Air Estimates papers of 1960–61. The Blue Steel missile finally became operational in February 1963.

PRO ref: AIR 19/1004

This Handley Page Victor B1, serial XA923, of No. 232 Operational Conversion Unit at Gaydon in Warwickshire, flown by Flight Lieutenant A.J.A. Heyns, was photographed in April 1958 while landing at Wyton in Cambridgeshire to join the RAF's Radar Reconnaissance Flight. The Victor was the last of the RAF's three V-bombers, entering service in November 1957 and continuing in this role until 1968. Some were converted to tankers and continued working for many more years.

PRO ref: AIR 29/2999

The Bristol-Ferranti Bloodhound 1 was a surface-to-air missile with a nuclear warhead. From 1958, it was deployed in units of sixteen by Fighter Command in defence of RAF V-bomber bases. This Bloodhound 1 was photographed on 19 November 1958 at RAF North Coates in Lincolnshire, while HRH The Duke of Edinburgh watched it traversing and following a target aircraft.

MoD ref: PRB16001

Vickers Valiant B1, serial XD859, of 214 Squadron based at Marham in Norfolk, converted to the tanker role, refuelling Avro Vulcan serial XA910 of 101 Squadron based at Finningley in Yorkshire. This photograph, taken on 4 November 1959, accompanied the Air Estimates file of 1960–61.

PRO ref: AIR 19/1004

An Avro Vulcan flying over RAF Gan, a remote staging post built on Addu Atoll in the Maldive Islands. The station became operational in August 1957 and was used mainly by RAF aircraft flying over the Indian Ocean to and from Singapore. This photograph accompanied the Air Estimates documents of 1960–61.

PRO ref: AIR 19/1004

One of the visitors to the Far East Air Force was this Victor B1, serial XA926, of 10 Squadron from Cottesmore in Rutland. The machine was taking part in a mobility exercise when photographed on 27 November 1960 while flying at low-level over the coast of Malaya and providing an impressive spectacle to the local people.

MoD ref: CFP1006

THE FAR EAST BUSH WARS

Avro Lincoln *Excalibur*, serial RF484, of a Special Flight at Blackbushe in Hampshire, photographed before departure at 05.00 hours on 9 September 1946 for New Zealand. Lincolns arrived too late to succeed Lancasters in the Second World War but twenty squadrons of Bomber

Command were equipped with these machines. They saw service during the Mau Mau uprising in Kenya and the Malayan Emergency. They were withdrawn in 1963.

PRO ref: AIR 29/476

After the vicious Mau Mau rebellion broke out in Kenya in 1952, the RAF allocated aircraft to support the police and the security forces. Vampire FR9s from 8 Squadron based at Khormaksar in Aden were detached in late 1953 to Eastleigh near Nairobi to help in attacks against terrorist

gangs. These Vampire FR9s were photographed at 16,000 feet while returning from an anti-bandit strike with rockets. Mount Kenya is in the background.

MoD ref: PRB8146

Avro Lincoln B2s of 49 Squadron arrived at Eastleigh in November 1953 from Wittering in Northamptonshire. They were succeeded in January 1954 by Lincolns of 100 Squadron and then by Lincolns of 61 Squadron, all from the same base. Aided by photographic reconnaissance and intelligence reports, the Lincolns carried out a bombing campaign against terrorists hiding in the Aberdare mountains. The Lincoln could carry up to 14,000 lb of bombs and the dismayed terrorists began to come out of the bush to surrender. By early 1955 most of the Mau Mau gangs had been broken up. The RAF's participation in the state of emergency ended in December 1956.

MoD ref: PRB8154

This Westland Dragonfly HC 2, serial WF311, was photographed in February 1950 while being used for trials. The machine was of American design but built in Britain. It carried a pilot with provision for three additional passengers or two stretchers. The first Dragonflies were sent to Malaya and formed the Far East Casualty Evacuation Flight at Seletar in Singapore on 1 April 1950, which became 194 Squadron at Sembawang in Singapore on 1 February 1953. Dragonflies carried out some remarkable work in the Malayan Emergency but they were tiring to fly and serviceability was low in jungle conditions.

PRO ref: PRO 58/54

When emergency powers were invoked in June 1948 against Communist terrorists in the newly-created Federation of Malaya, ageing but reliable C-47 Dakotas were available for service from the RAF. One of their duties was supply dropping to ground forces, employing the successful techniques developed in the Burma campaign of the Second World War. This photograph was taken on 2 July 1951.

MoD ref: CFP427

A training unit was set up in Singapore during June 1950, equipped with Tiger Moths and Harvards, as one of the four squadrons forming the re-created Malayan Auxiliary Air Force. The squadrons, with locally recruited pilots and ground staff, served on short-range transport and visual reconnaissance duties, including anti-terrorist operations, until entering the Royal Malayan Air Force which was established in 1958.

PRO ref: INF 10/316

(*Opposite, top*) In August 1948 three Beaufighter TFXs of 45 Squadron were detached from Negombo in Ceylon to Kuala Lumpur in the fight against Communist terrorists. They proved so successful with their striking power of four 20 mm cannons in the nose and eight rockets under the wings that Beaufighters of 84 Squadron were sent up from Singapore to join them. The remainder of 45 Squadron arrived at Kuala Lumpur on 16 May 1949, when it began to convert to Bristol Brigands. This photograph of a Beaufighter of 45 Squadron being serviced was taken on 10 August 1948.

MoD ref: CFP90

(*Opposite, bottom*) In April 1951 de Havilland Hornet F3s entered service with 33 Squadron at Butterworth near Penang in Malaya, replacing ageing Hawker Tempest F2s. This photograph, taken on 23 April 1952, shows aircraft both parked and taxiing on the airfield.

MoD ref: CFP538

These five Vampire FB5s were photographed on 2 December 1950 at the RAF Maintenance Base at Seletar in Singapore after six had arrived from the UK. Their flight of 8,500 miles was completed in 27¾ flying hours. With its excellent performance and fire power, strong construction and ease of maintenance, the Vampire proved ideal for conditions in Malaya. No. 60 Squadron at Kuala Lumpur received Vampire FB5s in December 1950, replacing Spitfire PR9s, and the squadron continued to operate with these machines until Vampire FB9s arrived two years later.

MoD ref: CFP353

A formation of de Havilland Vampire FB9s of 60 Squadron, based at Tengah in Singapore, photographed on 26 August 1952 when *en route* to bomb Communist camps in the Malayan jungle.

MoD ref: CFP620

The de Havilland Hornet was a long-range fighter with two Rolls-Royce Merlin engines, which first entered RAF squadron service in May 1946. These Hornet F3s of 45 Squadron, based at Tengah, were photographed on 26 August 1952 while en route to attack Communist positions in south Malaya, armed with cannons and rockets.

MoD ref: CFP606

Avro Lincolns of 1 (RAAF) Squadron arrived at Tengah on 16 July 1950 and remained on the station for almost eight years, operating against Communist terrorists. This photograph was taken on 26 August 1952.

MoD ref: CFP642

This series of photographs was taken on
26 April 1950 and constructed as a mosaic.
It shows bombs being dropped by Avro
Lincolns of 57 Squadron from Tengah, with
others exploding on Communist camps in
the Segamat district of Johore.

MoD ref: CFP285

500 lb bombs being dropped on Communist positions by a Lincoln of 1 (RAAF) Squadron on 26 August 1952. The maximum bomb load of the Lincoln was 14,000 lb.

MoD ref: CFP644

Lincolns of 1 (RAAF) Squadron taxiing back to their dispersal points at Tengah after attacking Communist positions on 26 August 1952.

MoD ref: CFP640

Recruitment to the new RAF Regiment (Malaya) from local volunteers began on 1 April 1948 when 91 Rifle Squadron was formed at Kuala Lumpur. Four other Rifle Squadrons were formed later, their original duties being the protection of RAF bases. In June 1948, 91 Squadron also began duties alongside the Army in anti-terrorist work. This photograph was taken in Selangor on 18 August 1952 when A Flight was moving through an oil palm grove in search of a wounded bandit.

MoD ref: CFP582

Airmen of A Flight, 91 Rifle Squadron, RAF Regiment (Malaya) on stand-to with a scout car at a post in Selangor, photographed on 15 August 1952. They were facing an area of rubber trees outside an estate manager's house which had been requisitioned and occupied by the Flight.

MoD ref: CFP577

Airmen of the RAF Regiment (Malaya) preparing to fire a mortar. This photograph was taken on 26 August 1952.

MoD ref: CFP649

The Scottish Aviation Pioneer first entered RAF service in February 1954 with 267 Squadron at Kuala Lumpur. With remarkably short take off and landing runs, it was used for internal security work and for supplying jungle forts. This example was serial XJ465 of 267 Squadron.

MoD ref: CFP978

Spitfire PR 19, serial PS836, of 81 Squadron based at Seletar in Singapore, photographed on 10 March 1954 while on a photo-reconnaissance sortie over a coastal region of Malaya. The last operational flight of any Spitfire was made on 1 April 1954 by 81 Squadron's Spitfire PR 19, serial PS888.

MoD ref: CFP845

Airmen of the RAF Regiment (Malaya), led by Warrant Officer J.J.H. Nichols, circling through a mangrove swamp on 17 July 1954, on the hunt for any boats carrying food to terrorists.

MoD ref: CFP850

The Bristol Sycamore was the first helicopter designed in Britain to enter RAF service, the prototype making its first flight on 24 July 1947. In October 1954, Sycamores began to supplement the Westland Dragonfly HC 2s of 194 Squadron for search and rescue missions in Malaya. The machine carried a crew of two, with three passengers or two stretcher cases and the cruising speed was about 20 mph faster than the Dragonfly. This Sycamore HAR 14, serial XF266, of 194 Squadron was photographed while alighting in a jungle clearing to pick up a casualty.

MoD ref: CFP937

Ground staff of 33 Squadron photographed at Butterworth on 23 March 1955 while loading up a Hornet F3, serial PX328, with two 500 lb bombs. The aircraft had already been armed with four rockets fitted with 60 lb high explosive warheads under the wings and four 20 mm cannons in the nose. It was one of three preparing to make the 5,000th sortie against Communist terrorists in Malaya.

MoD ref: CFP856

Squadron Leader N.P.W. Hancock, the Officer Commanding 33 Squadron, taxiing out to lead the three Hornet F3s on their operation. The squadron lost its identity eight days later when it was merged with 45 Squadron on the same station.

MoD ref: CFP854

This photograph was taken in November 1955 during a radar-siting expedition into the Malayan jungle, headed by Squadron Leader H.E. Bennett. The equipment was a portable radio station employing HF/DF or Morse code. From June 1956 research resulted in the mobile 'Target Director Post' which provided a narrow beam, down which aircraft flew towards the target until receiving a signal telling them to release the bombs. This equipment was the AA GL Radar No. 3 Mk 7, and an average error of 175 yards was achieved at a range of 40,000 yards. Of course, its effectiveness depended on the accurate location of terrorist positions, which was often achieved by aerial photo-reconnaissance.

MoD ref: CFP907

The Hunting Percival Pembroke was a communications aircraft, with a crew of two and accommodation for eight passengers, which entered service with RAF squadrons in September 1954. It was also used for training pilots, navigators and signallers. In January 1956, six of these machines were converted into Pembroke PR 1s and supplied to 81 Squadron at Seletar in Singapore, where they joined in the process of surveying Malaya, an operation which had begun with the squadron's Mosquito PR 34s in July 1949 and was continuing with Meteor PR 10s. From these surveys, updated maps on scales of one inch to a mile and a quarter inch to a mile were continually provided for the ground forces. This photograph is of serial WV746 of 152 Squadron, which began to receive Pembrokes in October 1958, while based at Muharraq in Bahrain. Pembrokes continued in RAF service until 1988.

MoD ref: PRB1260/22

This de Havilland Mosquito PR 34A, serial RG314, of 81 Squadron, based at Seletar in Singapore, was the last operational Mosquito in service with the RAF. The photograph was taken on 5 January 1956 but the aircraft made its final sortie on 16 December 1956, photographing Communist positions in the Malayan jungle. By that time, 81 Squadron had converted to Gloster Meteor PR 10s.

MoD ref: CFP921

Venom FB4s of 8 Squadron being refuelled at Kormaksar in Aden in 1957. In August of that year, a detachment formed part of a small RAF force sent to Sharjah and Bahrain in the Persian Gulf to assist the Sultan of Muscat and Oman in suppressing a Communist insurrection in the interior. Operations continued with the SAS and other regiments until successfully concluded in February 1959.

MoD ref: CMP911

(*Opposite, top*) Men of the RAF Regiment (Malaya) going into action from a Westland Whirlwind HAR 4 helicopter of 155 Squadron, photographed on 13 April 1957 when the squadron was based at Kuala Lumpur. With a crew of three, the machine could achieve rapid deployment of up to five fully-armed troops but it suffered from poor serviceability in jungle conditions, exacerbated by the difficulty of obtaining sufficient spare parts.

MoD ref: CFP966

(*Opposite, bottom*) This photograph was taken when Bristol Sycamore HAR 14, serial XJ918, of 14 Squadron, based at Changi in Singapore, paid one of its regular visits to a landing pad made from bamboo and leaves alongside a jungle fort in north Malaya. The men standing are, left to right: Chief Technician Wilfred Lloyd, Flight Lieutenant Albert Cann (pilot), Dr Malcolm Bolton (employed by the Malayan Government) and a medical orderly. Those seated were members of the Sakai aborigines living in the locality. The time was near the end of the Malayan Emergency, and regulations were finally lifted on 31 July 1960.

MoD ref: CFP1162

Sunderland V, serial DP198, of 205 Squadron, based at Seletar, flying over the waterfront at Singapore. This was the last RAF operational squadron equipped with Sunderlands, which were fully withdrawn by May 1959. Serial DP198 was 'struck off charge' on 1 June 1959.

MoD ref: CFP985

This Bristol Type 192 helicopter, serial XG451, was photographed in November 1959 during tests with various take-off weights. The helicopter division of Bristol was absorbed by Westland during the following March. The machine entered RAF service in December 1961 as the Westland Belvedere, fitted with two twin-rotor engines of 1,600 shaft horse power. Employed on carrying freight and troops, casualty evacuation and supply dropping, it saw operational service in Tanganyika, South Arabia and Borneo before being retired in March 1969.

PRO ref: AIR 2/15354

On 12 May 1960 the last Beaufighter in RAF service, serial RD761 employed as a target-tower, made its final flight from RAF Seletar in Singapore.

MoD ref: CFP1003

In December 1960 a detachment of Beverleys of 47 Squadron was sent from Abingdon in Berkshire to Eastleigh in Kenya, to reinforce British Forces Arabian Peninsula (BFAB) which had a base there and to help with famine relief after severe flooding and crop failure. There was also a threat of violence while negotiations for independence were in progress. This photograph was taken in March 1961 at Nanyuki in Kenya, showing troops of the King's African Rifles disembarking from Beverley serial XB286. Kenya achieved independence on 12 December 1963, although the British presence continued for another year to help suppress dissension in the north of the country.

PRO ref: AIR 27/2866

On 21 August 1962 Sycamore HR14, serial XE310, of 110 Squadron, based at Butterworth in Malaya, dropped a member of the SAS Regiment into the jungle near the Thai border, where a few Communist terrorists were still in hiding in the hope that they could foster another insurrection. The purpose was to rescue an injured pilot of a crashed Auster aircraft of the Army Air Corps. Meanwhile, a party from the SAS Regiment worked its way through the thick jungle.

MoD ref: CFP1052

At the end of 1962, a confrontation with the Indonesian Republic developed, following the objection of the latter to the proposition that the British Crown Colonies of Sarawak and Sabah and the British Protectorate of Brunei, be incorporated with Malaya and Singapore into a new Federation of Malaysia. Insurrections were fomented in Brunei and to help deal with these, troops were airlifted from Singapore to RAF Labuan, an island off the coast of Sabah. Among these were men of the 1st Battalion, The Queen's Own Cameron Highlanders, who were flown out from Seletar on the night 9/10 December 1962 in Beverleys of 34 Squadron. They were photographed while unloading stores at RAF Labuan.

MoD ref: CFP1065

On 10 December 1962, British and Gurkha troops were flown out of RAF Labuan to airstrips near the towns of Seria and Anduki, which were under siege by the rebels. Five Scottish Aviation Twin Pioneers took off for Seria, while one Beverley of 34 Squadron left for Anduki. The soldiers quickly subdued the insurgents at both places but armed rebellion continued elsewhere in North Borneo.

MoD ref: CFP1064

The Twin Pioneers of 209 Squadron continued to take men into and out of small jungle-enclosed airstrips, as shown in this photograph of British troops emplaning on serial XL970 from an airstrip in the Fifth Division of Sarawak, after the formation of the Federation of Malaysia on 16 September 1963. Twin Pioneers were also used for carrying equipment, supply-dropping to small jungle outposts and broadcasting messages by voice to the civil population.

MoD ref: CFP1148

The single-engined Pioneers of 209 Squadron, with their landing runs of 66 yards and take-off runs of 75 yards, proved invaluable for getting in and out of the very small airstrips in Borneo. This light communications aircraft could carry a pilot and four passengers, and was sometimes used for casualty evacuation.

MoD ref: CFP1174

British troops moving into action from Twin Pioneers of 209 Squadron.

MoD ref: CFP1066

Hunter FGA9, serial XJ683, of 20 Squadron, carrying twelve 3-inch rockets, photographed while flying past the twin peaks (known as the Ass's Ears) on the jungle-covered island of Pulau Tioman off the east coast of the Malayan Peninsula. The Hunter FGA9 was converted from the home-based F6 for tropical work. The machines began to fly out to Tengah in Singapore during July 1961, where 20 Squadron was re-formed the following September. This became one of the principal defence squadrons of the Far East Air Force. The squadron was also engaged on patrols from RAF Labuan and RAF Kuching during the confrontation with Indonesia.

MoD ref: CFP1182

Handley Page Hastings also brought troops from RAF Changi in Singapore to RAF Labuan at the beginning of the confrontation with Indonesia. These transports were also engaged on dropping supplies to ground forces, as shown in this photograph of a Hastings fitted with long-range tanks flying over Belaga in Sarawak.

MoD ref: CFP1078

Sycamore HAR14 after touching down at Bongau in Sarawak, having come through a narrow gap between the trees in the background. These light helicopters were ideal for work in the small clearings of the North Borneo jungles.

MoD ref: CFP1156

A Whirlwind HAR10 taking off from a dusty forward airstrip in the far east of Sarawak. This mark of helicopter, which was fitted with a turbine engine instead of the piston engine of the Whirlwind HAR4, first entered RAF service in November 1961. Two squadrons based at Seletar were equipped with these machines, which could carry a crew of three and eight passengers. These were 110 Squadron from July 1963 and 103 Squadron from August 1963, both of which served in North Borneo. They were joined there by 225 Squadron in December 1963 and 230 Squadron in March 1965, both arriving from the UK.

MoD ref: CFP1161

A Whirlwind HAR10 helicopter of 225 Squadron picking up a Gurkha patrol to ferry them to a jungle outpost in Sarawak. This photograph was taken in 1964.

PRO ref: CFP1187

The first RAF squadron to be equipped with the new Westland Belvedere helicopter was 66 Squadron at Odiham in Hampshire. In May 1962 the squadron moved to Seletar, where this photograph was taken. The twin-rotor Belvedere could carry eighteen fully-armed troops in addition to its crew of two; twelve stretcher cases, or a load weighing up to 6,000 lb.

MoD ref: CFP1048

A Belvedere of 66 Squadron lifting an Army truck from RAF Kuching in Sarawak. It was bound for a forward outpost where troops were guarding a potential entry point against infiltration by Indonesian soldiers.

MoD ref: CFP1150

The Hawker Siddeley Argosy C1 was a medium-range tactical transport, capable of carrying a crew of four and about seventy troops, which entered RAF squadron service in February 1962. In August 1963, 215 Squadron arrived at Seletar with these machines and began operating over North Borneo, primarily on transport and supply-dropping duties. This photograph was taken in January 1964 during an exercise in Malaya, when troops and equipment were being loaded into an Argosy at RAF Changi in Singapore.

MoD ref: CFP1081

This photograph, taken in January 1964 from an Argosy of 215 Squadron, illustrates the almost impenetrable terrain of North Borneo, with winding rivers and jungle-clad mountains. The frontier with Indonesia was 800 miles long but fortunately there were only a few feasible points of entry for incursions from Indonesia, which were guarded by British and Commonwealth troops. The whole area was surveyed by Canberra PR 7s of 81 Squadron from Singapore, assisted by Canberra PR 7s of 13 Squadron detached from Malta. Maps were made from the resulting photographs and used by the ground forces.

MoD ref: CFP1080

Anti-aircraft Bofors guns of 40 mm calibre on the airfields at Singapore were manned by the RAF Regiment, in case the Indonesian Air Force decided to mount air attacks during the confrontation. A number of 20 mm Bofors guns were also transferred from naval reserve to boost the air defences.

MoD ref: CFP1191

These men of 15 (Field) Squadron of the RAF regiment were among those detached from Singapore to guard airfields in North Borneo. In fact, the Indonesian Air Force was reluctant to make incursions into the territory, which was patrolled by Hunter FGA9s and Javelin F9s of the RAF.

MoD ref: CFP1173

An airfield in North Borneo guarded by an aircraftman of the RAF Regiment. There was little problem with internal security after the initial riots had been put down, for the great majority of the population supported the security forces. Incursions into North Borneo became so costly for the intruders that they began to peter out. A peace treaty was signed between Malaysia and Indonesia on 11 August 1966.

MoD ref: CFP1175

THE LEARNING CURVE

The Vickers Valetta first entered RAF squadron service in May 1949 as a medium-range transport capable of carrying thirty-four troops or freight, in addition to its crew of four. It continued in this capacity until April 1966 but meanwhile, in 1950, the Valetta T3 entered service as a navigation trainer. This photograph of Valetta T3, serial WG259, showing six astrodomes used by trainee navigators, was taken on 22 March 1954.

MoD ref: PRB7578

The trainee navigators busy at work inside Valetta T3, serial WG259.

MoD ref: PRB7574

The Bristol Brigand was designed to replace the Beaufighter TFX as Coastal Command's torpedo bomber, but, when torpedoes were replaced by rockets, its role was switched to that of ground attack carrying up to 2,000 lb of bombs. It first entered service at RAF Habbaniya in 1949 and subsequently saw service against terrorists in Malaya, employing guns, bombs and rockets. From July 1951 some Brigands were converted to trainers for radar night-fighting duties such as this T5, serial VS837, of the Air Interception Course at RAF Colerne in Wiltshire, photographed on 3 March 1955. These trainers were finally withdrawn from RAF service in March 1958.

MoD ref: PRB9411

The Vickers Varsity T1 was an advanced crew trainer for pilots, navigators and bomb aimers which first entered RAF service in October 1951 and continued until finally withdrawn in May 1976. This prototype, serial VX828, made its maiden flight on 17 July 1949.

MoD ref: PRB817

The Percival Prentice began to replace the long-serving Tiger Moth in November 1947 as the RAF's *ab initio* two-seat trainer. It continued as a trainer for pilots until 1953, although within this period the Chipmunk was introduced as a replacement. It was also employed for training signallers and carrying out communications duties.

MoD ref: PRB3008

The de Havilland Chipmunk became the main replacement for the Tiger Moth and the Prentice as the RAF's basic trainer after its introduction in February 1950. It was gradually withdrawn from 1973 after the introduction of the Scottish Aviation Bulldog, although some continued in service until the late 1980s. These Chipmunks of No. 18 Reserve Flying Training School at Fairoaks in Surrey were photographed in 1951.

MoD ref: PRB2301

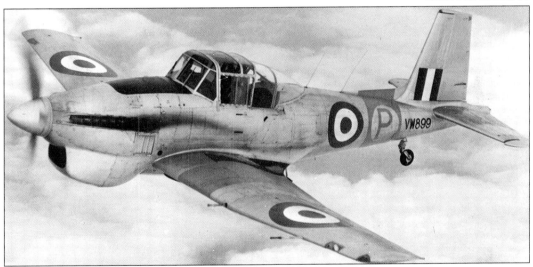

The Boulton Paul Balliol T2 was a two-seat advanced trainer with a piston engine, which first entered the RAF's Flying Training Schools in 1952. It continued in service for about four years, when it was superseded by jet aircraft. This example, serial VW899, photographed 6 September 1950, was one of four prototypes.

MoD ref: PRB814

The Handley Page Marathon was originally built as a short-haul airliner but in December 1953 an adapted version was supplied to the RAF as a navigation trainer. This version, known as the Marathon T11, carried a pilot, wireless operator, an instructor and two trainee navigators. It was fitted with astrodomes and teardrop windows. This Marathon T11, serial XA274, served with No. 1 Air Navigation School at RAF Topcliffe in Yorkshire. Twenty-eight of these machines were supplied, finally being withdrawn in June 1958.

MoD ref: PRB6923

The Hunting Percival Jet Provost T1 was introduced as an experiment during 1955 for primary jet training. Only ten were delivered, to 2 Flying Training School at Hullavington in Wiltshire. Instructors formed a Jet Provost Team named the *Red Pelicans*, painted red and white, for display purposes. This photograph was taken at the Central Flying School at Little Rissington in Gloucestershire in 1964, showing the team in delta formation.

MoD ref: PRB27275

Cadets of the Air Training Corps, photographed on 21 October 1958 during a week's gliding instruction course at RAF Hawkinge in Kent.

MoD ref: PRB15867

A statue of Lord Trenchard, first Marshal of the Royal Air Force and first Chief of the Air Staff, was unveiled on 19 July 1961 in the Victoria Embankment Gardens opposite the Air Ministry by the Prime Minister, the Rt. Hon. Harold Macmillan.

PRO ref: AIR 2/16130

The Hawker Siddeley Gnat was a two-seat jet trainer which entered service with No. 4 Flying Training School at RAF Valley in Anglesey during November 1962. The machine was designed for high performance flying and could exceed the speed of sound in a slight dive. This photograph was taken on 29 April 1963. Two years later, RAF Valley formed its own aerobatic team of Gnats, painted yellow and known as the *Yellowjacks*. This advanced trainer remained in RAF service until November 1978.

MoD ref: PRB24960

Aircraft apprentices at the School of Technical Training, RAF Halton in Buckinghamshire, photographed in March 1963 while removing a gun pack from a Hunter which had previously served with 74 Squadron.

MoD ref: PRB24919

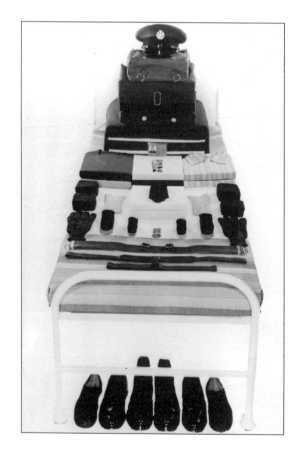

A poster printed in April 1964 which may have struck terror into the hearts of many RAF recruits. It showed thirty-seven articles of an airman's kit laid out for inspection on his bed. However, the official RAF nomenclature had become somewhat less formal by that date. For instance, 'Brush, shoe, polishing' had become simply 'Shoe Brush'.

PRO ref: AIR 2/15168

The Hawker Siddeley Dominie T1 was the first jet aircraft specially designed as an advanced navigation trainer when it entered RAF service in December 1965. This machine, serial XS730, was in service with No. 1 Air Navigation School at RAF Stradishall in Suffolk when photographed in 1966. The machine carries two pilots, a navigation instructor and two trainee navigators, with accommodation for one other crew member. In 1995, Dominies remained in service with No. 6 Flying Training School at RAF Finningley in Yorkshire.

MoD ref: PRB33187

The Scottish Aviation Bulldog T1 is a piston-engined aircraft with the seats side-by-side, employed by the RAF and University Air Squadrons as a primary trainer. It first entered service in April 1973 and is still a standard trainer. The three nearest Bulldogs in this photograph, serials XX659, XX658 and XX657, are currently with Cambridge University Air Squadron at RAF Cambridge, while the furthest aircraft, serial XX644, is with Bristol University Air Squadron at RAF Colerne in Wiltshire.

MoD ref: TN7311/2

The Scottish Aviation Jetstream was introduced into the RAF from June 1973 as a multi-engined trainer for pilots in the transport fleet, but soon afterwards the machines were placed in storage as a result of defence cuts. Some were reintroduced during 1977. This Jetstream serial XX497, with two turbo-prop engines, is on the strength of No. 5 Flying Training School at RAF Finningley in Yorkshire.

MoD ref: TN7636/17

The Shorts Tucano, designed in Brazil, was selected in 1985 as the RAF's basic trainer and began to enter service three years later with Flying Training Schools. It has a single turbo-prop engine and the two seats for instructor and trainee pilot are arranged in tandem.

MoD ref: TN9990/3

MARITIME RECONNAISSANCE AND SEARCH & RESCUE

The Lockheed Neptune MR1 was supplied to the RAF's Coastal Command from January 1952 as a stopgap while Avro Shackletons were coming into service. A long-range maritime reconnaissance aircraft with a crew of seven, it could carry a bomb load of up to 8,000 lb. Four home-based squadrons were equipped with the Neptune, but the machines were returned to the USA from 1956. This photograph was taken on 9 June 1953 when Neptunes were returning from a patrol.

MoD ref: PRB6474

Avro Shackleton MR2, serial WL751, of 224 Squadron over Gibraltar, where the squadron was based from May 1953 to October 1966 while equipped with these machines. The Shackleton was developed from the Lincoln, the MR1 entering service in April 1951, with the MR2 following late in the following year. Known affectionately as '10,000 rivets flying in close formation', variants of the reliable Shackleton formed the mainstay of the RAF's maritime reconnaissance force until 1970. After this, an airborne early warning version continued until the early 1990s.

MoD ref: CMP898

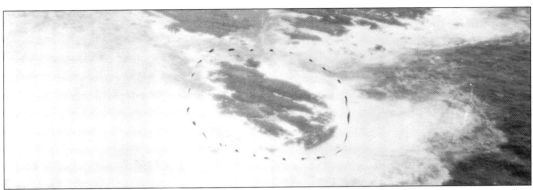

On 1 March 1956 the 550-ton motor vessel *Greenhaven* developed engine trouble in heavy seas off Eire and was driven on to the Roaninish rock, two miles from the coast of Donegal. She began to break up and her crew of ten abandoned the vessel and huddled together in bitter cold on the highest reef of the rock. During the night, the anti-submarine frigate HMS *Wizard* from Londonderry directed her searchlights on the scene to help a lifeboat from Arranmore, but the heavy seas prevented a landing. An air-sea rescue Shackleton MR1A, serial WB828 letter C, flown by Pilot Officer K.H. Wilson, from 120 Squadron at Aldergrove in County Antrim, was called out to assist in the early hours of the next day. The aircraft dropped flares to guide the lifeboat but no rescue was possible. Blankets and food were dropped from the port window as soon as it was light. At 08.00 hours two naval helicopters arrived from Eglinton, near Londonderry, and lifted off the ten marooned men. They were landed at Portnoo, on the coast nearby, and survived their experience.

PRO ref: AIR 27/2761

On 23 May 1953, thirteen pilots from RAF Church Fenton in Yorkshire participated in a demonstration of air-sea rescue. Each in turn was lifted from a dinghy in Bridlington Bay by a Sycamore of 275 Squadron from RAF Thornaby and then landed on the Ground Control Interception station at Bempton, on the shore nearby. Smoke floats were dropped to indicate wind direction and strength to the helicopter pilots.

PRO ref: AIR 27/2718

Air-sea rescue launch 2758, from the RAF's Marine Craft Unit at Newhaven in Sussex, photographed while travelling at high speed on 24 September 1958.

MoD ref: PRB15766

On 31 December 1961 a distress message was received at RAF Changi in Singapore from the Italian vessel SS *Galatea*, which had run aground at night on Pearsons Reef in the South China Sea. A Shackleton MR1A of 205 Squadron, based at Changi, was sent out on a search-and-rescue mission. The vessel was located on the northern and weather side of the reef. Heavy seas were breaking over her, but she did not seem in any immediate danger of sinking.

PRO ref: AIR 27/2985

The destroyer HMS *Caprice* was diverted to the scene to effect a rescue. Three further sorties were flown by Shackletons of 205 Squadron in co-operation with the Royal Navy. On 2 January 1962, the weather moderated sufficiently for the destroyer to rescue all twenty-two Italian seamen on board SS *Galatea*.

PRO ref: AIR 27/2985

Flight Sergeant Eric C. Smith, a winchman in the crew of a Whirlwind HAR10 of 22 Squadron at RAF Chivenor in Devon, was awarded a George Medal for his part in the rescue of French fishermen from the 273 ton trawler *Jeanne Gougy* on 4 November 1962. The trawler from Dieppe had been driven onto rocks at Land's End during the previous night. She was swept by twenty foot breakers while people watched helplessly from the cliffs. Rocket lines fired from the shore proved unsuccessful. A lifeboat from Sennen in Cornwall picked up bodies from the sea but was unable to reach the trawler. One seaman was rescued by a wire lowered by a Whirlwind from Chivenor. At about 11.30 hours another Whirlwind, serial XJ428 flown by Flight Lieutenant J.T. Eggington, arrived. Four more survivors were picked up in turn by the wire lowered from the helicopter. The others were too weak to get into the strop so Flight Sergeant Smith was lowered and went into the wheelhouse. The trawler was lying on her side and the situation was extremely dangerous. Nevertheless, he came out with one semi-conscious man and was winched up. He then returned and came back out of the wheelhouse with the cabin boy, to the cheers of amazed onlookers. He made one more descent to look for other survivors but the danger became so acute that he was ordered to return to the helicopter.

MoD ref: PRB24731

On 13 August 1963 the winchman of a Westland Whirlwind HAR10 of 228 Squadron, based at Leconfield in Yorkshire but detached to Leuchars in Fife, was lowered to pick up the skipper of the Peterhead drifter *Sustain*, who was suffering from suspected appendicitis. The skipper was then flown to Aberdeen for hospital treatment.

MoD ref: PRB25948

The Westland Wessex HC2 first entered RAF squadron service in January 1964 as a short-range helicopter for tactical transport and ground assault, capable of carrying up to sixteen troops as well as its crew of three. It served in Germany, the Arabian Gulf, Cyprus, Hong Kong, Singapore and Malaysia as well as at home. From May 1976, it found an important niche as an RAF search-and-rescue helicopter around the coasts of Britain. This Wessex HC2, serial XR502, of the Wessex Intensive Trials Unit at RAF Odiham in Hampshire was photographed in 1963.

MoD ref: PRB25906

The Hawker Siddeley Nimrod was evolved from the Comet airliner to supply the RAF with a marine reconnaissance aircraft as a replacement for the long-serving Shackleton. The first Nimrod MR1s entered RAF service in October 1969. The MR2s, with more advanced electronic equipment, followed in 1975. This Nimrod MR2, serial XV228, of 206 Squadron from RAF Kinloss in Morayshire, was photographed in July 1981 by Sergeant Jerry Chance of RAF Public Relations while flying over an oil rig in the Moray Firth. The aircraft remained in service in 1995, with the Kinloss Marine Reconnaissance Wing.

MoD ref: 080/5G

Sergeant Mark Redmond of 42
Squadron at RAF St Mawgan in
Cornwall, demonstrating the use of the
Nikon FA camera from the open beam
window of a Nimrod MR2 in 1992.
This is the latest camera to be used by
Nimrod squadrons. It contains a 35 mm
film which takes 36 exposures and gives
superb definition.

MoD ref: 491/92G

The RAF Mountain Rescue Service originated on an *ad hoc* basis in 1942 when airmen who survived crashes in mountainous areas within the UK were losing their lives from injuries and exposure. It developed into a formal organization during the following year. This photograph of a Mountain Rescue Training Course in the Ben Nevis area, with Aonach Berg in the background, was taken in February 1963. The teams work in coordination with RAF search-and-rescue helicopters, which frequently transport them to the area of a crash. They deal with the search and rescue of civilians as well as RAF personnel.

MoD ref: PRB24749

Sea King HAR3, serial XZ593, of 202 Squadron from RAF Leconfield in Yorkshire, photographed in July 1991 by Sergeant Rick Brewell of RAF Public Relations while flying over Flamborough Head.

MoD ref: 654/29

Nimrod MR2, serial XV235, of the Marine Reconnaissance Wing at Kinloss in Morayshire, photographed on 7 May 1992 by Sergeant Rick Brewell of RAF Public Relations while flying over the nuclear submarines HMS *Trenchant* and USS *Spadefish* when they broke through the ice at the North Pole. The ice was too thin on this occasion for the British and American crews to play their usual game of football at the annual rendezvous.

MoD ref: 689/7

SPANNING THE GLOBE

The military version of the Bristol Britannia civil airliner provided RAF Transport Command with a turbo-prop aircraft for strategic operations. This example, serial XL635, named *Bellatrix*, was the first handed over, to 99 Squadron at Lyneham in Wiltshire on 9 June 1959. All Britannias were given the names of stars. They remained in service until January 1976.

MoD ref: PRB16804

A military version of the de Havilland Comet airliner, the first turbo-jet to operate commercial services, entered the RAF's Transport Command in July 1956. Known as the Comet 2, it was employed on long-distance transport duties, with a crew of five and accommodation for forty-four passengers. A version with a longer fuselage and seats for ninety-four passengers entered service in February 1962. It was named the Comet 4, such as serial XR397 in this photograph. Comets remained in RAF service until June 1975.

MoD ref: PRB25033

The Beagle Basset CC1 was an adaptation of a civil executive aircraft, first entering RAF squadron service in 1965. It was intended for the transport of V-bomber crews but its range and performance proved insufficient for this purpose and it was transferred to other light communications until it was withdrawn in 1974. The Basset in this photograph, serial XS743, was one of two used for performance trials at RAF Boscombe Down in Wiltshire before twenty production aircraft were ordered for the RAF.

MoD ref: PRB29016

British Aircraft Company VC10s began to arrive with 10 Squadron at Fairford in Gloucestershire in July 1966. These machines improved the RAF's 'rapid reaction' capacity, each being able to transport 150 troops for over 3,500 miles without refuelling, or double the range with in-flight refuelling. Thirteen VC10s were supplied to 10 Squadron, all named after RAF personnel who had been awarded the Victoria Cross. This machine, serial XV102 named after Guy Gibson VC, was photographed while flying over the Scilly Isles. Other VC10s were converted from civil airliners to the tanker role. In 1995, 10 Squadron at Brize Norton in Oxfordshire still operated ten VC10s in the transport or dual tanker role while 101 Squadron at the same station was equipped with nine machines in the tanker role.

MoD ref: PRB37465

The Short Belfast, a near-relative of the Britannia airliner, was introduced into RAF squadron service in January 1966 as a long-range military transport with turbo-prop engines. It was the first British aircraft designed solely for that purpose, and could carry up to 150 troops or 80,000 lb of freight. Only ten were built, allocated to 53 Squadron, which was disbanded in September 1976. They were all given names, such as serial XR366 *Atlas* in this photograph, which was taken on the Belfast Proving Flight at RAF Boscombe Down in Wiltshire.

MoD ref: PRB31844

The turbo-prop Lockheed Hercules C1 became the mainstay of the RAF's tactical transport fleet after its introduction into squadron service in August 1967. This Hercules serial XV177, the first to be camouflaged in RAF markings, was photographed in 1967 at RAF Boscombe Down in Wiltshire. In 1995 the machine was still in service with the RAF Lyneham Transport Wing but, as with several others of the Hercules fleet, it has been 'stretched' by lengthening the fuselage by fifteen feet. It is designated a Hercules C3 and can carry up to 128 troops, in addition to the crew of five.

MoD ref: T6985

Lockheed TriStar K1 tanker, serial ZD951, of 216 Squadron refuelling a Tornado in flight.

MoD ref: 0095/6

THE FALKLANDS AND GULF WARS

When Argentine forces invaded the Falkland Islands on 2 April 1982, followed by the dependency of South Georgia the following day, Britain was drawn into a conflict on behalf of territories which had been under her protection for over 200 years. The resulting war was fought by combined forces, in which the RAF and the Fleet Air Arm played a prominent part. The American staging airfield of Wideawake on the British island of Ascension, situated in the Atlantic about halfway along the 8,000 miles between the Falklands and London, proved indispensable in these operations. Two Hercules, three Victors and one VC10 of the RAF can be seen in this photograph, as well as a C-141 Starlifter of the USAF.

MoD ref: H3287/1

A stream of supplies was carried to Wideawake airfield by Hercules of the RAF's Transport Wing based at Lyneham in Wiltshire. The aircraft were refuelled in flight by Victor K2 tankers from Marham in Norfolk.

MoD ref: H3286/1

A Hercules of the RAF's Lyneham Transport Wing, showing its refuelling probe, at Wideawake airfield.

MoD ref: H3281

The first elements of the South Atlantic Task Force sailed from Portsmouth on 5 April 1982 bound for Ascension Island and then the Falklands. They were led by the aircraft carriers HMS *Hermes* (photographed here) and HMS *Invincible*.

MoD ref: H3300/1

The liner SS *Canberra*, 43,975 grt, disgorged 1,600 passengers when she arrived at Southampton on 7 April 1982 at the end of a world cruise. She was rapidly fitted up for the South Atlantic Task Force and soon became capable of carrying up to 5,000 troops such as Royal Marines and Commandos. Two helicopter flight decks were lifted into position. This photograph was taken when the liner was moored at Ascension Island.

MoD ref: H3285/1

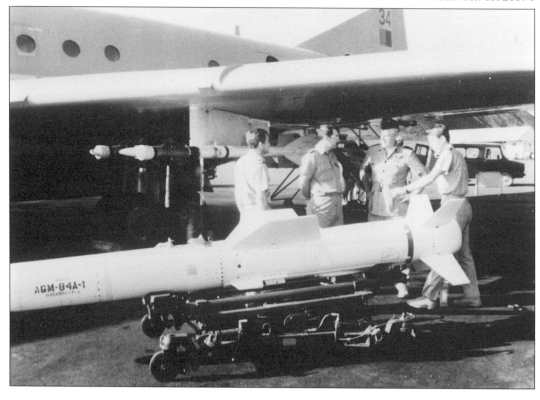

The Nimrod MR2s were then modified with refuelling probes so that from 9 May they were able to fly on maritime sorties of up to nineteen hours when refuelled by Victor K2 tankers. Their role was to hunt for Argentine vessels and submarines and then attack any which entered the 200-mile exclusion zone declared by the British around the Falklands. Meanwhile, some of the Victors were converted to the reconnaissance role and employed on very long-distance work. From 20 April, they reconnoitred South Georgia, which was re-taken five days later by a small task force of the Royal Navy from Gibraltar.

MoD ref: H3284/1

(*Opposite, bottom*) Nimrod MR1s of 42 Squadron from St Mawgan in Cornwall flew out to Wideawake. They were followed on 12 April by Nimrod MR2s of 120, 201 and 206 Squadrons from Kinloss in Morayshire, which were equipped with more effective Searchwater radar. The Nimrods were armed with McDonnell Douglas Harpoon anti-shipping missiles, as shown on the trolley in this photograph. This weapon is radar-guided and has a range of 75 miles at a speed of Mach 0.85. The aircraft were additionally fitted with pylons which enabled them to carry four Sidewinder air-to-air missiles, as can also be seen in this photograph.

MoD ref: H3303/3

Stanley Airport on the Falklands was attacked in the early hours of 1 May by a Vulcan B2 of 44 Squadron, with a crew from 101 Squadron. The aircraft flew from Wideawake, refuelled *en route* by a succession of Victor tankers, and dropped a stick of twenty-one 1,000 lb bombs across the runway. The purpose was primarily to deny the use of the airfield to the Mirages and Super Etendards of the Argentine Air Force from the mainland, which might have been able to operate from there with the aid of arrester gear. More attacks followed at dawn against the airport and a grass airfield at Goose Green by Sea Harriers of the Task Force, the aircraft carriers and other vessels having sailed from Ascension Island on 16 April.

MoD ref: H3288/1

Between 3 and 5 May, nine Harrier GR3s of the RAF's 1 Squadron flew from Wittering in Northamptonshire to Wideawake, refuelled en route by Victor tankers.

MoD ref: H3283/1

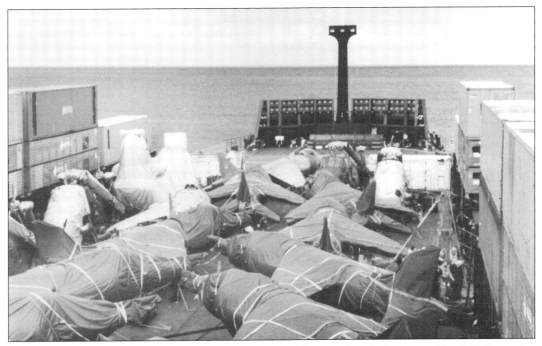

Six of the Harrier GR3s embarked on the container ship MV *Atlantic Conveyor*, which left Ascension for the Falklands on 8 May. Four Chinook HC1 helicopters from the RAF's 18 Squadron at Odiham in Hampshire were also carried on this vessel. All the aircraft were cocooned against the elements and lashed firmly to the deck. Three Harriers remained at Wideawake for defensive purposes, but they embarked later, together with five more, after being replaced by Phantom FGR2s of 29 Squadron from Coningsby in Lincolnshire.

MoD ref: H3292/1

On 18 May the six Harrier GR3s began flying from the container ship MV *Atlantic Conveyor* to the aircraft carrier HMS *Hermes*. Eight more flew to the carrier from Wideawake by means of in-flight refuelling. The role of these RAF Harriers was to relieve the FAA Sea Harriers from air-to-ground duties, enabling these to concentrate on combat with Argentine aircraft flying from the mainland on anti-shipping attacks.

MoD ref: H3205/1

The decks of HMS *Hermes*, 28,700 tons displacement, were covered with aircraft. This photograph shows an RAF Harrier GR3 armed with Paveway 1,000 lb laser-guided bombs, together with two more RAF GR3s, in front of FAA Sea Harriers fitted with fuel tanks and armed with 30 mm cannons and Sidewinder missiles, with an FAA Sea King in the background. The FAA Sea Harriers and helicopters of the two aircraft carriers formed the largest part of the air strike force, although some of the Sea Harriers were flown by RAF pilots on attachment to the Royal Navy. Light helicopters of the Royal Marines and the Army Air Corps also made an essential contribution.

MoD ref: H3280/1

The pilots of the Argentine Air Force attacked the vessels of the South Atlantic Task Force with great courage, flying Dassault-Breguet Mirages, Douglas A-4P Skyhawks, Israel Aircraft Industries Daggers and Dassault Super-Etendards from bases on their mainland. In spite of very heavy losses, some succeeded in firing Aérospatiale AM.39 Exocet sea-skimming missiles. The container ship MV *Atlantic Conveyor* was hit on 25 May, as shown in this photograph. She sank three days later. In the course of the campaign, the Argentines also sank two destroyers, two frigates, a Royal Fleet auxiliary, and badly damaged another auxiliary.

MoD ref: H3275

Three of 18 Squadron's Chinook helicopters were destroyed when the container ship MV *Atlantic Conveyor* was hit by the Exocet missile. On the night of 20/21 May, men of the British amphibious force began landing at San Carlos. On 9 June, an airstrip with 800 feet of aluminium planking was opened nearby in order to enable the Harrier GR3s (which were not able to align their inertial system sufficiently accurately to return to the aircraft carriers without assistance) to operate from the mainland. The remaining Chinook carried out prodigious work after the landings, ferrying troops and supplies from vessels to the mainland. It was disgorging fuel drums when this photograph was taken.

This solitary Chinook was photographed while transporting a truck inland. However, the greatest part of the work of ferrying and casualty evacuation was carried out by helicopters of the Fleet Air Arm, such as Sea Kings, Lynxes and Wessexes. Army and Royal Marine helicopters also played an important part in these operations.

MoD ref: H3290/1

On 28 May, British amphibious forces landed at Goose Green in East Falkland and captured the town after a stiff battle. This IA.58A Pucarà of III Brigada Aerea was photographed after the re-occupation. A turbo-prop aircraft of the Argentine Air Force, it was capable of operating from small airstrips as well as from Stanley Airport.

MoD ref: H3297/1

The RAF lost four Harrier GR3s, three by ground fire and one in an accident. This crashed GR3 was photographed while a British Commando was looking at a rocket launcher used on air-to-ground attacks. The Royal Navy lost six Sea Harriers, two by enemy fire and four in accidents. In addition, the British lost twenty-three helicopters, nineteen of which were in accidents or sunk in vessels.

MoD ref: H3291/1

While the British advanced on Port Stanley from San Carlos, other amphibious landings were made between 6 and 8 June at Bluff Cove. Bitter fighting followed, but the Argentine forces surrendered on 14 June. Those killed in the Task Force numbered 255 servicemen and civilians, with 777 injured. Of

the injured, more than 700 were back in full employment within a few months. Argentine losses were much higher, and over 14,500 became prisoners of war before being repatriated.

MoD ref: H3282/1

The British enlarged the airfield at Port Stanley with about 7,000 feet of runway and a parallel taxiway. Arrester gear and a parking apron were also installed. Steel matting was obtained from the US Marines to help in this process. The airfield was littered with wrecked aircraft. It was estimated that the Argentine Air Force lost 117 aircraft, of which over half were helicopters. In addition, the Task Force captured about thirty other aircraft.

MoD ref: 3298/1

The RAF remained on the Falklands for defensive purposes, as demonstrated in this photograph of armed airmen filing into their Mess for a meal.

MoD ref: H3276/1

With the seasons reversed in the southern hemisphere, the RAF arrived in the Falklands at the onset of winter but only tented accommodation was available at first. The men commented that they had been told to expect a 'temperate climate'.

MoD H3298/1

The Panavia Tornado GR1, a two-seat aircraft with variable wing geometry and an unrivalled capacity for supersonic tactical strikes, earned a place in RAF history when it entered squadron service in January 1982. It was followed by the supersonic interceptor version, the Tornado F2, in April 1987. This Tornado GR1, serial ZA560 of 617 Squadron at RAF Marham in Norfolk, was photographed with Hawk T1 serial XX288 of 2 Tactical Weapons Unit at RAF Chivenor in Devon. In 1995, this Tornado was on the strength of the Tri-National Tornado Training Establishment at RAF Cottesmore in Rutland, while the Hawk was on the strength of 4 Flying Training School at RAF Valley in Anglesey.

MoD ref: PRB7107

The Lockheed TriStar K1 civil airliner entered RAF service in 1983 with 216 Squadron at Brize Norton in Oxfordshire, in order to fulfil a requirement for a long-range tanker following experience in the Falklands War. It is the heaviest aircraft in RAF service. This photograph is of serial ZD949, one of six purchased for the tanker role.

MoD ref: TN9884/3

The BAe Nimrod AEW proved a great disappointment. After many years of work and the expenditure of vast amounts of public money, the project for providing the RAF with an Airborne Early Warning aircraft built in Britain was cancelled in December 1986, in favour of the Boeing AEW Sentry. This Nimrod AEW, serial XZ285, is now stored at RAF Abingdon in Berkshire.

MoD ref: K14/4/309

When Iraqi troops invaded Kuwait in the early hours of 2 August 1990, one of the casualties was this Boeing 747 of British Airways which landed with 367 passengers en route from Heathrow to Madras and Kuala Lumpur. Some of the passengers were held as hostages and the airliner was later blown up by the Iraqis. Four days after this invasion, King Fahd of Saudi Arabia invited foreign governments to send armed forces to protect his country from Iraq. President Bush ordered US forces to prepare operation Desert Shield, in which Britain and many other countries participated under the authority of the Security Council of the United Nations. Under pressure, President Saddam Hussein of Iraq accepted on 6 December 1990 that foreign nationals could leave Kuwait and Iraq, thus abandoning his previous policy of using some of them as 'human shields' at targets which might be attacked by the Coalition Forces.

MoD ref: G92/1/1

On 8 August, the British government announced that it intended to send forces to the Gulf area. Twenty-five Hercules of the Lyneham Transport Wing were committed to the lift of equipment and personnel, with aircraft drawn from 24, 30, 47 and 70 Squadrons as well as from 242 Operational Conversion Unit. The operation began three days later, using Akrotiri in Cyprus as a staging post to and from King Khalid International Airport near Riyadh in Saudi Arabia. Some aircrews flew in excess of nineteen hours a day on this urgent task.

MoD ref: G88/24/1

Hangars at King Khalid International Airport were used to store the immense quantity of supplies brought over by the Lyneham Transport Wing and other transport aircraft. From 1 November, the RAF set up an Air Transport Detachment at this airport for internal distribution of freight and personnel.

MoD ref: G28/4/1

From the beginning of October, British troops were airlifted in the Hercules, mostly from Germany but routed through Lyneham. Puma and other helicopters were also carried. In addition to King Khalid International Airport, the Hercules flew to Dhahran in Saudi Arabia and Thumrait in Oman, with operations continuing by day and night.

MoD ref: G26/1/1

In addition to airports in the Gulf area, the Hercules flew to landing zones in the forward areas of the desert, after these had been prepared by the Royal Engineers. The sharp stones caused wear and tear to the tyres while the landing strips soon became rutted and needed repair. This Hercules

C1, serial XV192, retained its standard camouflage at the time the photograph was taken. None of these aircraft were lost in the war.

MoD ref: G86/8/1

Twelve Jaguar GR1As from 6, 41 and 54 Squadrons of the Coltishall Wing left Britain on 11 August for Thumrait in Oman, with personnel from Coltishall and 226 Operational Conversion Unit at Lossiemouth. In early October this composite squadron moved to Muharraq in Bahrain, were it was integrated into the command structure of the Coalition Air Forces. These Jaguars were replaced later in October by twelve which had been fitted up at Coltishall with more sophisticated equipment and pylons for Sidewinder air-to-air missiles. Replacement personnel also arrived during November and early December. This Jaguar, serial XZ119, of 41 Squadron was photographed while taking off from Muharraq.

MoD ref: G31/16/1

The Jaguar GR1As at Muharraq began operations in daylight on 17 January 1991, when the Desert Storm air war started. They flew initially against targets such as missile sites on the coast of Kuwait and naval vessels. From 11 February some also flew on photo-reconnaissance sorties with camera pods. When the ground war began on 24 February they attacked troop concentrations, artillery, barracks and storage areas. They carried weapons such as 1,000 lb free-fall bombs, cluster-bombs, electronic counter-measure pods, rocket-launcher pods and Sidewinder missiles. The 1,000 lb general-purpose bomb awaiting loading in this photograph is labelled 'SHARON & SOPHIE'S SADDAM SKULLCRUSHER'. The aircraft was already fitted with an overwing AIM-9L Sidewinder missile and was being loaded with a BL755 cluster-bomb. Although they completed over 600 missions and frequently came under fire, all twelve Jaguars survived the conflict.

MoD ref: G27/5/1

Tornado GR1s arrived at Muharraq in Bahrain from 29 August 1990, at Tabuk in Saudi Arabia from 8 October, and at Dhahran in Saudi Arabia from 3 January 1991. About twenty-four aircrews and other personnel were drawn from 9, 14, 15, 16, 17, 20, 27, 31 and 617 Squadrons, while aircraft were provided from RAF Brüggen and RAF Laarbruch. The GR1s commenced operations on 16/17 January, the first night of Desert Storm. Attacks on the first three nights were at low level against Iraqi airfields, employing huge JP233 dispensers being loaded as shown in this photograph. These weapons ejected runway-cratering bombs from the rear section and anti-personnel mines from the front section. After these initial attacks, the Tornados began dropping free-fall bombs from higher level on bridges and other targets. From 2 February they carried Paveway laser-guided bombs, with Buccaneers 'marking' the targets with Pavespike designator pods. On 6 February five more Tornado GR1s arrived, equipped with Thermal Imaging and Airborne Laser Designator (TIALD) pods, which enabled the bombs to be delivered with even more accuracy and without the assistance of the Buccaneers. About forty GR1s flew in the Gulf War and their rate of loss was the highest of all the Coalition Air Forces, six on operations and one in an accident.

In addition, about thirty Tornado F1s served in the conflict, arriving from 11 August 1990, with aircraft and personnel drawn from 5, 11, 23, 25, 29 and 43 Squadrons. These carried out combat air patrols and there were no losses.

Lastly, six Tornado GR1As from 2 and 13 Squadrons arrived at Dhahran on 14 January 1991, equipped with highly sophisticated reconnaissance equipment to hunt for the mobile and elusive Scud missile launchers. These also carried out excellent work and there were no losses.

MoD ref: G19/12/1

The personnel for the twelve Buccaneers were drawn from 12 and 208 Squadrons and 237 Operational Conversion Unit, forming a composite squadron. Buccaneers had served in RAF squadrons since October 1969, and in the FAA for several years beforehand. However, they were to give a remarkably good account of themselves in operations during early 1991.

MoD ref: G56/17/1

Twelve Buccaneer S2Bs from the Lossiemouth Wing flew out to Muharraq in Bahrain between 26 January and 8 February 1991, their main task being laser designation for the Tornado GR1s operating from that base and from Dhahran in Saudi Arabia. This Buccaneer was armed with a Sidewinder air-to-air missile.

MoD ref: G50/27/1

(*Opposite, bottom*) Iraq's most feared weapon was the ground-launched Scud missile, which had a 330 lb conventional warhead and a range of about 375 miles. Although inaccurate, it also had the capability of carrying a chemical or nuclear warhead. Scuds were fired from mobile launchers which were widely dispersed and could be quickly moved from one site to another, thus making their detection and destruction extremely difficult. The first were fired against Israel before dawn on 18 January 1991, causing some casualties in Haifa and Tel Aviv. They posed a serious political and psychological threat, for if Israel entered the war, the Arab countries in the Coalition might break away. The problem was resolved by deploying US Patriot anti-missile missiles in Israel, which destroyed a number of incoming Scuds and assuaged Israeli anger. Other Scuds were destroyed by British SAS mobile units operating in Iraq, calling in air strikes on occasions.

MoD ref: G91/7/1

Men of the RAF Regiment on guard around Tornado dispersals. The Regiment deployed twelve units for the operation, mainly employed on ground defence and guard duties. Its contribution was significant, for the men made up 20 per cent of the RAF's strength in the Gulf War, from a force which comprised less than 3 per cent of the RAF's manpower.

MoD ref: G37/22

The Buccaneers began operating in daylight on 2 February 1991, each carrying a Pavespike laser designator pod, a Sidewinder missile for defence and an electronic counter-measures pod. Two Buccaneers accompanied four Tornados carrying 1,000 lb Paveway laser-guided bombs, all refuelled en route by Victor K2 tankers. Near the target they split into units of two Tornados and one Buccaneer. When a Tornado released its bombs from high level, the Buccaneer designated the target with the laser and continued to track it until the impact of the bombs. From 24 February, the Buccaneers also dropped laser-guided bombs and 'self-designated' the target with their Pavespikes. None of these aircraft were lost in the conflict.

MoD ref: G54/4/1

Eight Victor K2 tankers of 55 Squadron were deployed in the Gulf War, the first flying out from RAF Marham to Muharraq in Bahrain on 14 December 1990. Their duty was air-to-air refuelling of RAF Tornados and Jaguars throughout operation Desert Storm, and they also carried out the same task with carrier-based aircraft of the US Navy.

MoD ref: G33/15/1

This airman was photographed while taking a nap on a bomb trolley bearing four Tactical Munitions Dispensers (TMDs) which were carried by USAF aircraft such as the Lockheed F-16 Fighting Falcon in the Gulf War. The weapon dispensed a mixture of anti-personnel and anti-armour mines.

MoD ref: G55/33/1

Nineteen Puma HC1s formed part of Britain's Support Helicopter Force, drawn from 230 Squadron at RAF Gütersloh and 33 Squadron at RAF Odiham. They were air-freighted from RAF Brize Norton from 1 November 1990 onwards. The Support Helicopter Force was based initially at Al Jubail in Saudi Arabia, but on 21 January 1991 it moved to Riyadh and then up to King Khalid Military City near the border with Kuwait. When the ground war began on 24 February, named operation Desert Sabre, the Pumas flew in close support of the fast-moving British Army, carrying troops and supplies while operating from improvised airstrips in Kuwait and Iraq. All the RAF's helicopters survived the conflict. This photograph is of Puma serial XW224 of 230 Squadron.

MoD ref: G82/5/1

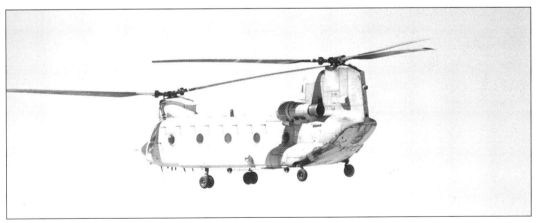

Fifteen Chinook HC1s joined Britain's Support Helicopter Force, drawn from 7 Squadron at Odiham and 18 Squadron at Gütersloh. Three were air-freighted on 24 November 1990, eight arrived by sea on 6 January 1991 and four were air-freighted in the same month. They transported troops and equipment before and during the ground war and some occasionally operated at night. Sea Kings and Lynxes of the Royal Navy formed part of the Support Helicopter Force, arriving from warships. This photograph shows Chinook serial ZA684 of the RAF's 7 Squadron.

MoD ref: G64/36/1

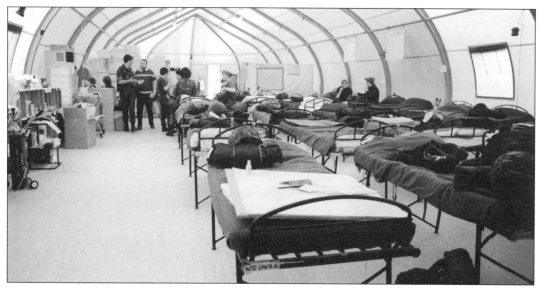

The old RAF hospital at Muharraq in Bahrain was reopened during the Gulf War and staffed with RAF doctors and orderlies, together with flight nursing officers and flight nurses of the Princess Mary's Royal Air Force Nursing Service. These essential personnel also served with mobile field hospitals and No. 1 Aeromedical Evacuation Squadron in Saudi Arabia, while similar staff stood by at RAF Akrotiri and RAF Brize Norton. Fortunately RAF casualties were not numerous.

MoD ref: G32/13/1

The Iraqi forces began to withdraw from Kuwait on 26 February 1991, using every vehicle available, but they were cut off by American and British armoured units before they could reach Basra. The road was soon littered with vehicles wrecked by shelling and air attacks.

MoD ref: G69/23/1

By 27 February, it was claimed that 3,000 of an estimated total of 4,300 Iraqi tanks had been destroyed, as well as 1,850 of 2,900 armoured personnel carriers and 2,140 of 3,100 artillery weapons. Iraqi personnel were surrendering everywhere, terrified in case they received the brutal treatment they had meted out to the Kuwaiti nationals and Coalition prisoners.

MoD ref: G59/20/1

At the end of February 1991, Iraq agreed to implement all the resolutions of the Security Council and President Bush ordered a cease-fire to take effect at 08.00 hours Baghdad time on 1 March 1991. By this time, it was estimated that 100,000 Iraqis had been killed with the same number captured, in contrast to less than 500 killed among the Coalition forces. Fortunately for the Iraqi prisoners, they received humane treatment from the front-line forces, being given medical attention as well as food and water.

MoD ref: G85/35/1

TOWARDS THE
MILLENNIUM

The Hawker Siddeley Buccaneer entered RAF squadron service in October 1969, several years after it had been introduced into the Fleet Air Arm. A two-seater with a speed of Mach 0.92 at sea level, it fulfilled the role of a low-level strike and reconnaissance aircraft. However, it was also found suitable for low-level penetration work in RAF Germany. During the Gulf War, Buccaneers with laser designator pods directed bombs dropped by Tornados onto their targets. The highly successful Buccaneer remained in service with Strike Command until 1994. This photograph of Buccaneers of 208 Squadron flying over the Severn Bridge was taken on 21 July 1975. Squadron Leader Peter Jones (OC B Flight) and Flight Lieutenant Peter Hill were in one aircraft, with Flight Lieutenant Dave Symonds and Squadron Leader Graham Pitchfork (OC A Flight) in the other.

MoD ref: TN7326/29

When it was supplied to the RAF's 1 Squadron in July 1969, the remarkable British Aerospace Harrier GR1 became the first 'vertical take-off and landing' aircraft to enter squadron service with any air force. It is a single-seater capable of a maximum speed of Mach 0.95, employed mainly for ground attack, as was demonstrated during the Falklands War. This Harrier, serial XV279, was one of the development aircraft, photographed at RAF Upavon in Wiltshire on 24 May 1967. In 1995, this machine was used for Weapons Loading Training at RAF Wittering in Northamptonshire.

MoD ref: PRB36900

The Westland/Aérospatiale Puma HC1 entered RAF squadron service in June 1971, replacing the Whirlwind helicopter for ground assault and troop transport. Pumas have served in Germany, Belize, Cyprus, Northern Ireland and the Arabian Gulf. Several of these helicopters remained operational in 1995. This photograph of the Pumas of 230 Operational Conversion Unit at Odiham in Hampshire was taken when flying over the Needles off the Isle of Wight.

MoD ref: TN6368/35

The Sepecat Jaguar GR1 single-seat fighter first entered RAF operational service in March 1974. Eight squadrons in Germany were eventually equipped with Jaguars, which can achieve Mach 1.6 and also carry out the role of ground attack. Jaguar GR1, serial XZ374 (in the foreground) of 20 Squadron at Brüggen in Germany was photographed with a Harrier GR3 when the squadron converted to Jaguars in 1977. In 1995, this machine was still in service with the School of Technical Training at RAF Cosford in Shropshire. Jaguar GR1As, the reconnaissance version, remain in service at RAF Coltishall in Norfolk.

MoD ref: 1830–1

The Boeing Vertol Chinook, with twin rotors, entered RAF squadron service in August 1981. It is a medium-lift helicopter with a crew of four and the capacity for transporting thirty troops or up to 28,000 lb of freight. This Chinook of 18 Squadron was photographed when based at Gütersloh in Germany. The detachment moved there from Odiham in Hampshire in August 1983, after a detachment had served in the Falklands War.

MoD ref: RAFG/107/83/PR

The British Aerospace Hawk T1 is an advanced jet trainer which first entered RAF service in November 1976. As with the Shorts Tucano, the two seats of this aircraft are arranged in tandem. This Hawk T1A, serial XX258, was photographed while carrying a Sea Eagle, an air-to-surface missile with a range of about 60 miles made by British Aerospace Dynamics. In 1995 the aircraft was on the strength of the Central Flying School at RAF Valley in Anglesey.

MoD ref: C3172/B

The Boeing AEW Sentry began operational service with 8 Squadron at RAF Waddington in Lincolnshire during 1991, after a working-up and training period. Adapted from the Boeing 707 airliner and fitted with an enormous rotodome radar antenna for airborne early warning, this aircraft had already seen many years of service with the USAF and NATO. The squadron is equipped with seven Sentries, such as serial ZA104 in this photograph taken by Sergeant Rick Brewell. This aircraft commemorates 80 years of the squadron's continuous service in the RFC and RAF from 1 January 1915.

MoD ref: 836/12

The McDonnell Douglas Phantom was ordered from the USA to fill a gap in RAF requirements, the FG1 as an interceptor and the FG2 for ground attack and reconnaissance. It was a two-seater with a maximum speed of Mach 2.1 and the first machines entered operational service in May 1969. The F3 interceptor, with an improved performance and more sophisticated weapons system, equipped 74 Squadron from March 1984. This Phantom F3, with 56 Squadron markings on the

front and 74 Squadron markings on the tail, was the final year display machine. Flown by Squadron Leader Archie Liggatt with Flight Lieutenant Mark Mainwaring as navigator, it was photographed over the north coast of Norfolk on 8 July 1992 by Sergeant Rick Brewell.

MoD ref: 694/7

A Tornado GR1A of 13 Squadron from Marham in Norfolk, photographed by Sergeant Rick Brewell while flying over Scarborough in Yorkshire. At the same base 2 Squadron is also equipped with this highly sophisticated aircraft, employed on tactical reconnaissance.

MoD ref: 623/95

The EH101 multi-role helicopter is produced by EH Industries, formed by the companies Westland and Augusta. This photograph taken by Petty Officer Fez Parker is of the Royal Navy variant, named the Merlin. A variant is under order for the RAF but has not yet been delivered.

MoD ref: 95/132/6

INDEX